TLV Bible Pathways - 100 Guided Scripture Readings From Genesis to Revelation

The Tree of Life Bible Society, founded in 2008, is a nonprofit ministry that has been commissioned by our greater community to produce and safeguard the creation of a brand-new Biblical text of the Holy Scriptures: from Genesis to Revelation, entitled the Tree of Life Version. The Tree of Life Bible Society exists to fulfill the ancient calling of the Jewish people "to make Name of Adonai known" while carrying out the great commission of His Messiah, *Yeshua* "to make disciples of the world." We safeguard the unique miracle that is the Tree of Life Biblical translation, create tools and resources for growing in the knowledge of Adonai, and promote Biblically-aligned family values.

To learn more: Visit us at www.TLVBibleSociety.org.

Donations towards the Tree of Life Bible Society's mission are received at:

P.O. Box 121328 | Arlington, TX USA

To invite us to share, call: 1 (800) 757-3945

TLV Bible Pathways

100 Guided Scripture Readings

Through Genesis to Revelation

Table of Contents

Introduction

By Daniah Greenberg, TLVBS Founder

Greetings in Messiah *Yeshua*, Jesus, our Savior!

As lifelong Bible readers ourselves, who live according to Jewish lifestyle and practice WHILE acknowledging that Jesus is the promised Messiah, we thought this specific resource might help. We decided to take the 100 illustrations in the Tree of Life Bible and curate the associated Scriptures that will magnify them for you. True covenant love for the God of Israel can only be lived out in our abiding love for one another, across culture and across generations.

Reading the Holy Bible, from Genesis to Revelation, is the cornerstone of our religious freedom and we trust this TLV Pathways Bible can help you understand His plan for you personally. These 100 passages, which include about 25% of the total volume of Biblical text, will help elevate the plot points of Biblical comprehension with a more Hebraic route. We created this pathway for to help you grasp the BIG PICTURE of God's faithfulness to His people - including all those grafted into the covenant through faith in Messiah *Yeshua* (Jesus).

We are using only Biblical text, no commentary, just imagery and primacy. Primacy? Yes, primacy. In providing these selections, to **prime** the pump, we invite you to discover the wisdom of God as your Bible knowledge and vocabulary grows with time. This is not just about which selections we chose, but learning to read them sequentially - again and again - to see the patterns in God's character that are truly magnificent. That's right!

Of course, we are spotlighting stories you probably already recognize, and some you may not. But even with known stories, you may not read them as often as necessary to get the most helpful revelation available. For example: Noah's Ark is pretty recognizable as a story about obedience, but did you know the Biblical moral of that story is that human bloodshed is forbidden and that water cycles are for cleansing?

The Biblical narrative is filled with stories that are meant for fathers and mothers to teach to their children across their lifetime - for their good. Every selection, read in order, over and over, will create a scaffolding of faith you can TRUST to build your life around.

The overarching goal of this resource is to provide you an accessible Bible Literacy tool that helps YOU develop repetitive reading patterns.

More TIME reading, less dissecting and commentary, can lead to a better relationship between YOU and your Creator.

The more TIMES you read, the more you will remember.

The more HALF TIMES you remember His semi-annual feasts, the more you revolve into His unfailing love. His covenant love is relational, so invest the time in learning from Him to become His very own child!

So the heavens and the earth were completed along with their entire array. God completed – on the seventh day – His work that He made, and He ceased – on the seventh day – from all His work that He made.

Genesis 2:1-2 (TLV)

1. God Breathes Life

In the beginning God created the heavens and the earth. Now the earth was chaos and waste, darkness was on the surface of the deep, and the Spirit of God was hovering upon the surface of the water.

Then God said, **"Let there be light!"** and there was light. God saw that the light was good. So God distinguished the light from the darkness. God called the light "day," and the darkness He called "night." So there was evening and there was morning—one day.

Then God said, **"Let there be an expanse in the midst of the water! Let it be for separating water from water."** So God made the expanse and it separated the water that was below the expanse from the water that was over the expanse. And it happened so. God called the expanse "sky."

So there was evening and there was morning—a second day.

Then God said, **"Let the water below the sky be gathered to one place. Let the dry ground appear."** And it happened so. God called the dry ground "land," and the collection of the water He called "seas." And God saw that it was good.

Then God said, **"Let the land sprout grass, green plants yielding seed, fruit trees making fruit, each according to its species with seed in it, upon the land."** And it happened so. The land brought forth grass, green plants yielding seed, each according to its species, and trees making fruit with the seed in it, each according to its species. And God saw that it was good.

So there was evening and there was morning—a third day.

Then God said, **"Let lights in the expanse of the sky be for separating the day from the night. They will be for signs and for seasons and for days and years. They will be for lights in the expanse of the sky to shine upon the land."** And it happened so.

Then God made the two great lights—the greater light for dominion over the day, and the lesser light as well as the stars for dominion over the night.

God set them in the expanse of the sky to shine on the land and to have dominion over the day and over the night and to separate the light from the darkness. And God saw that it was good. So there was evening and there was morning—a fourth day.

Then God said, **"Let the waters swarm with swarms of living creatures! Let flying creatures fly above the land across the expanse of the sky."**

Then God created the large sea creatures and every living creature that crawls, with which the water swarms, according to their species, as well as every winged flying creature, according to their species. And God saw that it was good.

Then God blessed them by saying, **"Be fruitful and multiply and fill the water in the seas. Let the flying creatures multiply on the land."**

So there was evening and there was morning—a fifth day.

Then God said, **"Let the land bring forth living creatures according to their species — livestock, crawling creatures and wild animals, according to their species."** And it happened so.

God made the wild animals according to their species, the livestock according to their species, and everything that crawls on the ground, each according to its species. And God saw that it was good.

Then God said, **"Let Us make man in Our image, after Our likeness! Let them rule over the fish of the sea, over the flying creatures of the sky, over the livestock, over the whole earth, and over every crawling creature that crawls on the land."**

God created humankind in His image,
in the image of God He created him,
male and female He created them.

God blessed them and God said to them, **"Be fruitful and multiply, fill the land, and conquer it. Rule over the fish of the sea, the flying creatures of the sky, and over every animal that crawls on the land."**

Then God said, **"I have just given you every green plant yielding seed that is on the surface of the whole land, and every tree, which has the fruit of a tree yielding seed. They are to be food for you. Also for every wild animal, every flying creature of the sky and every creature that crawls on the land which has life, every green plant is to be food."** And it happened so. So God saw everything that He made, and behold it was very good.

So there was evening and there was morning—the sixth day.

Genesis, chapter 1

2. God Makes a Well-Matched Helper

So the heavens and the earth were completed along with their entire array. God completed – on the seventh day – His work that He made, and He ceased – on the seventh day – from all His work that He made.

Then God blessed the seventh day and sanctified it, for on it He ceased from all His work that God created for the purpose of preparing.

These are the genealogical records of the heavens and the earth when they were created, at the time when *ADONAI Elohim* made land and sky.

Now no shrub of the field was in the land yet, and no green plants of the field had sprouted yet. For *ADONAI Elohim* had not caused it to rain upon the land, and there was no one to work the ground. But a mist came up from the land and watered the whole surface of the ground.

Then *ADONAI Elohim* formed the man out of the dust from the ground and He breathed into his nostrils a breath of life – so the man became a living being.

Then *ADONAI Elohim* planted a garden in Eden in the east, and there He put the man whom He had formed.

Then *ADONAI Elohim* caused to sprout from the ground every tree that was desirable to look at and good for food.

Now the Tree of Life was in the middle of the garden, and also the Tree of Knowledge of Good and Evil.

A river flowed out of Eden to water the garden. From there it divided and became four riverheads. The name of the first is Pishon, the one that winds around the whole land of the Havilah, where there is gold. The gold of that land is good - bdellium and lapis lazuli stones are also there.

The name of the second river is Gihon - it winds around the whole land of Cush. The name of the third river is Tigris - it runs east of Assyria. And the fourth river is Euphrates.

Then *ADONAI Elohim* took the man and gave him rest in the Garden of Eden in order to cultivate and watch over it.

Then *ADONAI Elohim* commanded the man saying, **"From all the trees of the garden you are most welcome to eat. But of the Tree of the Knowledge of Good and Evil you must not eat. For when you eat from it, you most assuredly will die!"**

Then *ADONAI Elohim* said, **"It is not good for the man to be alone. Let Me make a well-matched helper for him."**

ADONAI Elohim had formed from the ground every animal of the field and every flying creature of the sky, so He brought them to the man to see what he would call them. Whatever the man called them - each living creature - that was its name.

So the man gave names to all of the livestock, and to the flying creatures of the sky, and to all the animals of the field; but for the man He did not

Now both of them were naked, the man and his wife,
and they were not ashamed.

Genesis 2:25 (TLV)

find a well-matched helper for him. *ADONAI Elohim* caused a deep sleep to fall on the man and he slept; and He took one of his ribs and closed up the flesh in its place. *ADONAI Elohim* built the rib, which He had taken from the man, into a woman. Then He brought her to the man.

Then the man said, "This one, at last, is bone of my bones and flesh from my flesh. This one is called woman, for from man was taken this one."

This is why a man leaves his father and his mother and clings to his wife; and they become one flesh.

Now both of them were naked, the man and his wife, and they were not ashamed.

Genesis, chapter 2

3. God Covers Adam and Eve

But the serpent was shrewder than any animal of the field that *Adonai Elohim* made. So it said to the woman, "Did God really say, 'You must not eat from all the trees of the garden'?"

The woman said to the serpent, "Of the fruit of the trees, we may eat. But of the fruit of the tree which is in the middle of the garden, God said, 'You must not eat of it and you must not touch it, or you will die.'"

The serpent said to the woman, "You most assuredly won't die! For God knows that when you eat of it, your eyes will be opened and you will be like God, knowing good and evil."

Now the woman saw that the tree was good for food, and that it was a thing of lust for the eyes, and that the tree was desirable for imparting wisdom. So she took of its fruit and she ate. She also gave to her husband who was with her and he ate.

Then the eyes of both of them were opened and they knew that they were naked; so they sewed fig leaves together and made for themselves loin-coverings.

And they heard the sound of *Adonai Elohim* going to and fro in the garden in the wind of the day. So the man and his wife hid themselves from the presence of *Adonai Elohim* in the midst of the Tree of the garden.

Then *Adonai Elohim* called to the man and He said to him, **"Where are you?"**

Then he said, "Your sound—I heard it in the garden and I was afraid. Because I am naked, I hid myself."

Then He said, **"Who told you that you are naked? Have you eaten from the Tree from which I commanded you not to eat?"**

Then the man said, "The woman whom You gave to be with me—she gave me of the Tree, and I ate."

Adonai Elohim said to the woman, **"What did you do?"**

The woman said, "The serpent deceived me and I ate."

Adonai Elohim said to the serpent, **"Cursed are you above all the livestock and above every animal of the field. On your belly will you go, and dust will you eat all the days of your life.**

I will put animosity between you and the woman— between your seed and her seed. He will crush your head, and you will crush his heel."

To the woman He said, **"I will greatly increase your pain from conception to labor. In pain will you give birth to children. Your desire will be toward your husband, yet he must rule over you."**

Then to the man He said, **"Because you listened to your wife's voice and ate of the tree which I commanded you, saying, 'You must not eat of it':**

Cursed is the ground
because of you—
with pain will you eat of it
all the days of your life.

Thorns and thistles
will sprout for you.
You will eat the plants of the field,
By the sweat of your brow
will you eat food,
until you return to the ground,
since from it were you taken.

For you are dust,
and to dust will you return."

Now Adam named his wife Eve because she was the mother of all the living.

ADONAI Elohim made Adam and his wife tunics of skin and He clothed them.

Then *ADONAI Elohim* said, **"Behold, the man has become like one of Us, knowing good and evil. So now, in case he stretches out his hand and takes also from the Tree of Life and eats and lives forever,"** *ADONAI Elohim* sent him away from the Garden of Eden, to work the ground from which he had been taken.

And He expelled the man; and at the east of the Garden of Eden He had *cheruvim* dwell along, with the whirling sword of flame, to guard the way to the Tree of Life.

Genesis, chapter 3

Adonai Elohim made Adam and his wife tunics of skin and He clothed them. Then *Adonai Elohim* said, "Behold, the man has become like one of Us, knowing good and evil. So now, in case he stretches out his hand and takes also from the Tree of Life and eats and lives forever," *Adonai Elohim* sent him away from the Garden of Eden, to work the ground from which he had been taken. And He expelled the man; and at the east of the Garden of Eden He had *cheruvim* dwell along, with the whirling sword of flame, to guard the way to the Tree of Life.

Genesis 3:21-24 TLV

4. God Warns their Son

Now the man had relations with Eve his wife and she became pregnant and gave birth to Cain. She said, "I produced a man with *ADONAI*." Then she gave birth again, to his brother Abel.

Abel became a shepherd of flocks while Cain became a worker of the ground. So it happened after some time that Cain brought an offering of the fruit of the ground to *ADONAI*, while Abel—he also brought of the firstborn of his flock and their fat portions.

Now *ADONAI* looked favorably upon Abel and his offering, but upon Cain and his offering He did not look favorably. Cain became very angry, and his countenance fell.

Then *ADONAI* said to Cain, **"Why are you angry? And why has your countenance fallen? If you do well, it will lift. But if you do not do well, sin is crouching at the doorway. Its desire is for you, but you must master it."**

Cain spoke to Abel his brother. While they were in the field, Cain rose up against Abel his brother and killed him.

Then *ADONAI* said to Cain, **"Where is Abel, your brother?"**

"I don't know," he said. "Am I my brother's keeper?"

Then He said, **"What have you done? The voice of your brother's blood is crying out to Me from the ground. So now, cursed are you from the ground which opened its mouth to receive your brother's blood from your hand. As often as you work the ground, it will not yield its crops to you again. You will be a restless wanderer on the earth."**

Cain said to *ADONAI*, "My iniquity is too great to bear! Since You expelled me today from the face of the ground and I must be hidden from Your presence, then I will be a restless wanderer on the earth—anyone who finds me will kill me!"

But *ADONAI* said to him, **"In that case, anyone who kills Cain is to be avenged seven times over."**

So *ADONAI* put a mark on Cain, so that anyone who found him would not strike him down. Then Cain left *ADONAI*'s presence and dwelled in the Land of Wandering, east of Eden.

Cain was intimate with his wife and she became pregnant and gave birth to Enoch. And he was building a city, and he named the city after the name of his son, Enoch.

And to Enoch was born Irad. Irad fathered Mehujael, and Mehujael fathered Methushael, and Methushael fathered Lamech.

Now Lamech took for himself two wives. The name of the first one was Adah, and the name of the second one was Zillah.

Now the man had relations with Eve his wife and she became pregnant and gave birth to Cain. She said, "I produced a man with *Adonai*." Then she gave birth again, to his brother Abel...

Genesis 4:1-2 TLV

Adah gave birth to Jabal—he was the pioneer of tent dwellers with livestock.

His brother's name was Jubal—he was the pioneer of all who skillfully handle stringed instruments and wind instruments.

Now Zillah also gave birth to Tubal-Cain, the forger of every kind of bronze and iron tools; Tubal-Cain's sister was Naamah.

Lamech said to his wives,
"Adah and Zillah: Hear my voice!
Lamech's wives: Listen to my speech!
For I have killed a man for wounding me, and a boy for bruising me.
If Cain is to be avenged seven times, then Lamech — 77 times!"

Adam was intimate with his wife again, and she gave birth to a son and she named him Seth, "For God has appointed me another seed in place of Abel — since Cain killed him."

To Seth, also was born a son. He named him Enosh.

Then people began to call on *ADONAI*'s Name.

Genesis, chapter 4

5. God Saves a Family

When God created Adam, in the likeness of God He made him. Male and female He created them, and He blessed them and called their name "Adam" when He created them.

Adam lived 130 years, then fathered a son in his likeness, after his image, and named him Seth. Then the days of Adam after he fathered Seth were 800 years, and He fathered other sons and daughters. So all Adam's days that he lived were 930 years, and then he died.

Seth lived 105 years, then fathered Enosh. Seth lived 807 years after he fathered Enosh, and he fathered sons and daughters. So all Seth's days were 912 years, and then he died.

Enosh lived 90 years, then fathered Kenan. Enosh lived 815 years after he fathered Kenan, and he fathered sons and daughters. So all of Enosh's days were 905 years, and then he died.

Kenan lived 70 years, then fathered Mahalalel. Kenan lived 840 years after he fathered Mahalalel, he fathered sons and daughters. So all of Kenan's days were 910 years, and then he died.

Mahalalel lived 65 years, then fathered Jared. Mahalalel lived 830

years after he fathered Jared, and he fathered sons and daughters. So all of Mahalalel's days were 895 years, and then he died.

Jared lived 162 years, then fathered Enoch. Jared lived 800 years after he fathered Enoch, and he fathered sons and daughters. So all of Jared's days were 962 years, and then he died.

Enoch lived 65 years, then fathered Methuselah.

Now Enoch walked with God continually for 300 years after he fathered Methuselah, and he fathered sons and daughters. So all of Enoch's days were 365 years.

And Enoch continually walked with God—then he was not there, because God took him.

Methuselah lived 187 years and fathered Lamech. And Methuselah lived 782 years after he fathered Lamech, and he fathered other sons and daughters. So all of Methuselah's days were 969 years, and then he died.

Lamech lived 182 years and he fathered a son. And he named him Noah saying, "This one will comfort us from our work and from the pain of our hands because of the ground which *ADONAI* cursed."

Lamech lived 595 years after he fathered Noah, and he fathered sons and daughters. So all of Lamech's days were 777 years, and then he died. And Noah was 500 years old when he fathered Shem, Ham and Japheth.

Genesis, chapter 5

Now when humankind began to multiply on the face of the ground and daughters were born to them, then the sons of God saw that the daughters of men were good and they took for themselves wives, any they chose. Then *ADONAI* said, **"My Spirit will not remain with humankind forever, since they are flesh. So their days will be 120 years.**

The Nephilim were on the earth in those days, and also afterward, whenever the sons of God came to the daughters of men, and gave birth to them. Those were the mighty men of old, men of renown.

Then *ADONAI* saw that the wickedness of humankind was great on the earth, and that every inclination of the thoughts of their heart was only evil all the time.

So *ADONAI* regretted that He made humankind on the earth, and His heart was deeply pained.

So *ADONAI* said, **"I will wipe out humankind, whom I have created, from the face of the ground, from humankind to livestock, crawling things and the flying creatures of the sky, because I regret that I made them."** But Noah found favor in *ADONAI*'s eyes.

These are the genealogies of Noah. Noah was a righteous man. He was blameless among his generation.

Noah continually walked with God. Noah fathered three sons: Shem, Ham and Japheth.

Now the earth was ruined before God, and the earth was filled with violence. God saw the earth, and behold it was ruined because all flesh had corrupted their way upon the earth.

Then God said to Noah, **"The end of all flesh is coming before Me, for the earth is filled with violence because of them. Behold, I am about to bring ruin upon them along with the land.**

Make for yourself an ark of gopher wood. You shall make the ark with compartments and smear pitch on it, both inside and out. Now this is how you shall make it: the length of the ark 300 cubits, its breadth 50 cubits, and its height 30 cubits.

You shall make a roof for the ark, and you shall finish it to within a cubit from the top. You shall put the door of the ark in its side. You shall make it with lower, second, and third stories.

Now I am about to bring the flood—water upon the land—to destroy all flesh in which is the spirit of life from under the sky. Everything that is on the land will perish. But I will establish My covenant with you. So you shall come into the ark—you, your sons, your wife, and your sons' wives with you.

Also of every living thing, of all flesh, you shall bring two of everything—male and female—into the ark to keep alive with you. Of the flying creatures according to their kind, of the livestock according to their kind, of all the crawling creatures of the ground according to their kind—two of everything will come to you to keep them alive. As for you: take for yourself every kind of edible food and gather it to yourself. It will be

food for you and for them." So Noah did according to all that God commanded him; he did so exactly.

Genesis, chapter 6

Then *ADONAI* said to Noah, **"Come—you and all your household—into the ark. For you only do I perceive as righteous before Me in this generation.**

Of every clean animal you shall take with you seven of each kind, male and female; and of the animals which themselves are not clean two, male and female; also of the flying creatures of the sky seven of every kind, male and female, to keep offspring alive on the face of the whole land. For in seven more days, I am going to make it rain upon the land forty days and forty nights, and I will wipe out all existence that I made from the face of the ground." So Noah did all just as *ADONAI* commanded him.

Now Noah was 600 years old when the flood came—water upon the land. So Noah, his sons, his wife, and his sons' wives, entered the ark because of the floodwaters.

Of the clean animals and unclean animals, the flying creatures and everything that crawls on the ground, two by two they came to Noah, into the ark, male and female, just as God commanded Noah.

After the seven days, the floodwaters were upon the land. In the six-hundredth year of Noah's life, in the second month, on the seventeenth day of the month, on this day, all the water sources of the great deep burst open, and the windows of the sky were opened. Then there was rain upon the land 40 days and 40 nights.

On that same day Noah, along with Noah's sons Shem, Ham and Japheth, Noah's wife and the three wives of Noah's sons with them, entered the ark, they and every animal according to its kind, and all the livestock according to its kind, and every crawling creature that crawls on the land according to its kind, and every flying creature according to its kind, every bird, every winged creature.

So to Noah and into the ark they went by twos—all flesh in which was the spirit of life. Those that came, male and female of all flesh, came just as God commanded him.

Then *ADONAI* shut him in.

The flood was forty days upon the land, and the waters increased and lifted the ark, so that it rose above the land. The waters overpowered and became very mighty over the land, and the ark drifted on the surface of the water. The waters completely overpowered the land so that all the high mountains beneath the entire sky were covered. The waters rose 15 cubits higher, as the mountains were covered. All flesh perished—those that crawl on the land, the flying creatures, livestock, wild animals, all creatures that swarm upon the land, and all humankind. Everything that had the breath of the spirit of life in its nostrils—everything on dry land—died.

So He wiped out all existence that

was upon the surface of the ground, everything from people to livestock, to crawling creatures, and to flying creatures of the sky. They were wiped out off the land. Only Noah and those with him in the ark survived. The waters overpowered the land for 150 days.

Genesis, chapter 7

Then God remembered Noah and all the wild animals and all the livestock that were with him in the ark.

So God caused a wind to pass over the land and the water subsided. Also the sources of the deep and the windows of the skies were closed up, and the rain from the sky was held back. The waters kept receding gradually from upon the land and the waters decreased by the end of 150 days.

The ark came to rest in the seventh month, on the seventeenth day of the month, upon the mountains of Ararat. The waters went on decreasing until the tenth month. In the tenth month, on the first day of the month, the tops of the mountains appeared.

It was at the end of forty days that Noah opened the window of the ark that he had made. Then he sent out a raven and it kept going back and forth until the waters were drying up from the land.

Then he sent out a dove to see whether the waters had receded from the surface of the ground. But the dove did not find a resting place for the sole of her foot. She returned to him in the ark because water covered the surface of the whole land. He stretched out his hand and he took her, and brought her to him into the ark.

So he waited yet another seven days and again he sent the dove out from the ark. The dove came to him at evening, and surprisingly—a freshly plucked olive leaf was in its mouth. So Noah knew that the waters had receded from the land. After he waited seven more days, he sent out the dove, but she did not return to him again.

It was in his six-hundred-and first year—in the first month, on the first day of the month—that the waters had dried up from the land. Then Noah removed the cover of the ark and he looked, and behold, the surface of the ground had dried up. By the second month, on the twenty-seventh day of the month, the land was dry.

Then God spoke to Noah, saying, **"Come out of the ark, you and your wife, your sons and your sons' wives with you.**

Every animal that is with you of all flesh, including the flying creatures, livestock and every crawling creature that crawls on the land, bring out with you, and let them swarm in the land and be fruitful and multiply upon the land."

So Noah came out, with his sons, his wife, and his sons' wives. Every animal—every crawling creature, every flying creature, everything that crawls upon the land—came out from the ark in their families. Then Noah built an altar to *Adonai* and he took of every clean domestic animal and of every clean flying creature and he offered burnt offerings on the altar.

When *Adonai* smelled the soothing aroma, *Adonai* said in His heart, **"I will never again curse the ground on account of man, even though the inclination of the heart of humankind is evil from youth. Nor will I ever again smite all living creatures, as I have done. While all the days of the land remain, seedtime and harvest, cold and heat, summer and winter, day and night will not cease."**

Genesis, chapter 8

God blessed Noah and his sons, and He said to them, **"Be fruitful and multiply and fill the land. The fear and terror of you will be on every wild animal, and on every flying creature of the sky, with everything that crawls on the ground and with all the fish of the sea—into your hand they are given.**

Every crawling thing that is alive will be food for you, as are the green plants—I have now given you everything. Only flesh with its life—that is, its blood—you must not eat!

Surely your lifeblood will I avenge. From every animal and from every person will I avenge it. From every person's brother will I avenge that person's life. The one who sheds human blood, by a human will his blood be shed, for in God's image He made humanity. But as for you, be fruitful and multiply! Flourish in the land and multiply in it."

Then God said to Noah and to his sons with him, saying, **"Now I, behold, I am about to establish My covenant with you, and with your seed after you, and with every living creature that is with you, including the flying creatures, the livestock, and every wild animal with you, of all that is coming out of the ark—every animal of the earth.**

I will confirm My covenant with you—never again will all flesh be cut off by the waters of the flood, and never again will there be a flood to ruin the land."

Then God said, **"This is the sign of the covenant that I am making between Me and you, and every living creature that is with you for all future generations. My rainbow do I place in the cloud, and it will be a sign of the covenant between Me and the land.**

Whenever I bring clouds over the land and the rainbow appears in the clouds, I will remember My covenant that is between Me and you and every living creature of all flesh. Never again will the waters become a flood to destroy all flesh. When the rainbow is in the cloud, I will look at it, to remember the perpetual covenant between God and every living creature of all flesh that is on the land."

Then God said to Noah, **"This is the sign of the covenant that I have confirmed between Me and all flesh that is on the land."**

Genesis 9:1-17

Then Noah built an altar to *Adonai* and he took of every clean domestic animal and of every clean flying creature and he offered burnt offerings on the altar. When *Adonai* smelled the soothing aroma, *Adonai* said in His heart, "I will never again curse the ground on account of man, even though the inclination of the heart of humankind is evil from youth. Nor will I ever again smite all living creatures, as I have done.

Genesis 8:20-21 TLV

6. God Humbles Pride

Noah's sons who came out from the ark were Shem, Ham and Japheth, and Ham was the father of Canaan. These three were Noah's sons, and from these the whole earth dispersed.

Then Noah, a man of the soil, was first to plant a vineyard. He drank some of the wine, got drunk, and was uncovered in his tent.

Then Ham, Canaan's father, saw his father's private parts and told his two brothers outside. So Shem and Japheth took the cloak and laid it over both their shoulders and walked backwards and with it covered their father's private parts. But their faces were turned away, so they did not see their father's private parts.

When Noah woke up from his wine, he learned what his youngest son had done to him. So he said,
"Cursed is Canaan: the lowest slave will he be to his brothers."

He also said,

"Blessed be *ADONAI*, God of Shem,
and let Canaan be his servant.
May God enlarge Japheth,
may he dwell in the tents of Shem,
and may Canaan be his slave."

Now Noah lived 350 years after the flood. So all Noah's days were 950 years. Then he died.

Genesis 9:18-29

And these are the genealogical records of Noah's sons, Shem, Ham, and Japheth. Sons were born to them after the flood.

Japheth's sons were Gomer, Magog, Madai, Javan, Tubal, Meshech and Tiras. Gomer's sons were Ashkenaz, Riphath and Togarmah. Javan's sons were Elishah and Tarshish, Kittites and Dodanites.

From these the coastlands of the nations spread out in their lands, each one according to his language, according to their families, into their nations.

Ham's sons were Cush, Mizraim, Put and Canaan. Cush's sons were Seba, Havilah, Sabtah, Raamah, and Sabteca. And Raamah's sons were Sheba, and Dedan. Now Cush fathered Nimrod. He started to become mighty in the land.

He was a mighty hunter before *ADONAI*. This is why it is said, "Like Nimrod, a mighty hunter before *ADONAI*."

The beginning of his kingdom included Babel, Erech, Accad and Calneh, in the land of Shinar. From that land he went out to Assyria and built Nineveh, Rechovot-ir, Calah and Resen, between Nineveh and Calah—it is the great city.

Mizraim fathered the Ludites, the Anamites, the Lehabites, the Naphtuhites, the Pathrusites, the Casluhites—from whom came the Philistines—and the Caphtorites.

Canaan fathered Sidon his firstborn, Heth, the Jebusite, the Amorite, the Girgashite, the Hivite, the Arkite, the Sinite, the Arvadite, the Zemarite and

So *ADONAI* scattered them from there over the face of the entire land, and they stopped building the city. This is why it is named Babel, because *ADONAI* confused the languages of the entire world there, and from there *ADONAI* scattered them over the face of the entire world.

Genesis 11:8-9 TLV

the Hamathite—and afterwards, the Canaanite families were scattered.

Now the Canaanite border was from Zidon, as you go toward Gerar, as far as Gaza; as you go toward Sodom and Gomorrah, Admah and Zeboiim, as far as Lasha.

These are Ham's sons according to their families, according to their languages, in their lands, in their nations.

Sons were also born to Shem, who was Japheth's older brother and the father of all the sons of Eber. Shem's sons were Elam, Asshur, Arpachshad, Lud and Aram.

Aram's sons were Uz, Hul, Gether and Mash. Arpachshad fathered Shelah, and Shelah fathered Eber.

Two sons were born to Eber. The name of the first was Peleg—because in his days the land was divided—and his brother's name was Joktan.

Joktan fathered Elmodad, Sheleph, Hazarmaveth, Jerah, Hadoram, Uzal, Diklah, Obal, Abimael, Sheba, Ophir, Havilah and Jobab. All of these are Joktan's sons. Their dwelling place was from Mesha till you come toward Sephar, the eastern hill country.

These are Shem's sons, according to their families, according to their languages, in their lands, according to their nations.

These are the families of the sons of Noah according to their genealogies in their nations, and from these the nations were dispersed on the earth after the flood.

Genesis, chapter 10

Now the entire earth had the same language with the same vocabulary. When they traveled eastward, they found a valley-plain in the land of Shinar and settled there.

They said to one another, "Come! Let's make bricks and bake them until they're hard." So they used bricks for stone, and tar for mortar.

Then they said, "Come! Let's build ourselves a city, with a tower whose top reaches into heaven. So let's make a name for ourselves, or else we will be scattered over the face of the whole land."

Then *Adonai* came down to see the city and the tower that the sons of man had built.

Adonai said, **"Look, the people are one and all of them have the same language. So this is what they have begun to do. Now, nothing they plan to do will be impossible.**

Come! Let Us go down and confuse their language there, so that they will not understand each other's language." So *Adonai* scattered them from there over the face of the entire land, and they stopped building the city.

This is why it is named Babel, because *Adonai* confused the languages of the entire world there, and from there *Adonai* scattered them over the face of the entire world.

Genesis 11:1-9

7. God Speaks to Abram

These are the genealogical records of Shem: Shem was 100 years old when he fathered Arpachshad—two years after the flood. Shem lived 500 years after he fathered Arpachshad, and he fathered sons and daughters.

Arpachshad lived 35 years when he fathered Shelah. Arpachshad lived 403 years after he fathered Shelah, and fathered sons and daughters.

Shelah lived 30 years and he fathered Eber. Shelah lived 403 years after he fathered Eber, and fathered sons and daughters.

Eber lived 34 years and he fathered Peleg. Eber lived 430 years after he fathered Peleg, and he fathered sons and daughters.

Peleg lived 30 years and he fathered Reu. Peleg lived 209 years after he fathered Reu, and he fathered sons and daughters.

Reu lived 32 years and he fathered Serug. Reu lived 207 years after he fathered Serug, and he fathered sons and daughters.

Serug lived 30 years and fathered Nahor. Serug lived 200 years after he fathered Nahor, and he fathered sons and daughters.

Nahor lived 27 years and he fathered Terah. Nahor lived 119 years after he fathered Terah, and he fathered sons and daughters.

Terah lived 70 years when he fathered Abram, Nahor and Haran.

These are Terah's genealogies: Terah fathered Abram, Nahor and Haran.

Haran fathered Lot. Haran died before Terah his father, in the land of his birth, in Ur of the Chaldeans.

Abram and Nahor took wives for themselves. The name of Abram's wife was Sarai, and the name of Nahor's wife was Milcah—the daughter of Haran, father of Milcah and Iscah. Sarai was barren; she did not have a child.

Terah took Abram his son and Lot, Haran's son, his grandson, and Sarai his daughter-in-law, his son Abram's wife, and he took them out of Ur of the Chaldeans to go to the land of Canaan. But when they came to Haran, they settled there.

Terah's days were 205 years, and Terah died in Haran.

Genesis 11:10-32

Then *ADONAI* said to Abram,
"Get going out from your land,
and from your relatives,
and from your father's house,
to the land that I will show you.

My heart's desire is to make you
into a great nation, to bless you,
to make your name great
so that you may be a blessing.

My desire is to bless
those who bless you,
but whoever curses you I will curse,
and in you all the families of the
earth will be blessed."

So Abram went, just as *ADONAI* had spoken to him. Also Lot went with him. (Now Abram was 75 years old when he departed from Haran.) Abram took Sarai his wife, and Lot his nephew, and all their possessions that they had acquired, and the people that they acquired in Haran, and they left to go to the land of Canaan, and they entered the land of Canaan.

Abram passed through the land as far as the place of Shechem, as far as Moreh's big tree. (The Canaanites were in the land then.)

Then *ADONAI* appeared to Abram, and said, **"I will give this land to your seed."** So there he built an altar to *ADONAI*, who had appeared to him. From there he moved to the mountain to the east of Beth-El and erected his tent (with Beth-El to the west and Ai to the east). There he built an altar to *ADONAI* and called on the Name of *ADONAI*. So Abram kept on journeying southward.

Now there was a famine in the land. So Abram went down to Egypt to live as an outsider there, because the famine was severe in the land. Just as he was about to enter Egypt he said to Sarai his wife, "Look, please, I know that you are an attractive woman. So when the Egyptians see you they'll say, 'This is his wife.' And they'll kill me; but you, they'll let live. Please say that you are my sister, so that I'll be treated well for your sake, and my life will be spared because of you."

When Abram came to Egypt, the Egyptians did see that the woman was very beautiful. Indeed, Pharaoh's officials saw her and they raved about her to Pharaoh. Then the woman was taken into Pharaoh's house. But Abram was treated well for her sake, and he got sheep, cattle, male donkeys, male and female slaves, female donkeys and camels.

But *ADONAI* struck Pharaoh and his household with great plagues because of Sarai, Abram's wife. So Pharaoh called Abram and said, "What's this that you did to me? Why didn't you tell me that she is your wife? Why did you say, 'She is my sister,' so that I took her to be my wife? Now, here is your wife. Take—and go!" Then Pharaoh instructed men concerning him, and they expelled him, with his wife, and everything that belonged to him.

Genesis, chapter 12

So Abram went up from Egypt—he and his wife and everything that belonged to him, and Lot with him—to the Negev. Now Abram was very rich in livestock, silver and gold. He proceeded by stages from the Negev as far as Beth-El—to the place where his tent had been at the beginning, between Beth-El and Ai, to the place of the altar that he had made there at first, and there Abram called on the Name of *ADONAI*.

Now Lot, who was going with Abram, also had sheep and cattle and tents, so that the land could not support them living together, because their possessions were many, and they were not able to stay together. So there was a quarrel between the shepherds of Abram's livestock and the shepherds of Lot's livestock. (Now the Canaanites and the Perizzites were living in the land then.)

So Abram said to Lot, "Please, let there be no strife between me and you, or between my shepherds and yours, since we are relatives. Isn't the whole land before you? Please separate yourself from me. If to the left, then I'll go to the right, and if to the right, then I'll go to the left."

Lot lifted up his eyes and saw that the whole area surrounding the Jordan was well watered in its entirety (before *ADONAI* destroyed Sodom and Gomorrah)—like *ADONAI*'s garden, like the land of Egypt—till you come to Zoar. So Lot chose for himself the whole area surrounding the Jordan. Lot journeyed to the east, and they separated from each other.

Abram dwelled in the land of Canaan, and Lot dwelled in the cities of the valley. And he moved his tent from place to place near Sodom. But the people of Sodom were evil—very great sinners against *ADONAI*.

After Lot separated himself from him, *ADONAI* had said to Abram, **"Lift up your eyes, now, and look from the place where you are, to the north, south, east and west. For all the land that you are looking at, I will give to you and to your seed forever.**

I will make your seed like the dust of the earth so that if one could count the dust of the earth, then your seed could also be counted. Get up! Walk about the land through its length and width—for I will give it to you."

So Abram moved his tent from place to place, and came and dwelt by Mamre's large trees, which are in Hebron, and there built an altar to *ADONAI*.

Genesis, chapter 13

Now after he returned from defeating Chedorlaomer and the kings who were with him, the king of Sodom went out to meet him in the Valley of Shaveh (this is the King's Valley). Then Melchizedek, king of Salem, brought out bread and wine—he was a priest of *El Elyon*.

He blessed him and said, "Blessed be Abram by *El Elyon*, Creator of heaven and earth, and blessed be *El Elyon*, Who gave over your enemies into your hand."

Then Abram gave him a tenth of everything.

Then the king of Sodom said to Abram, "Give me the people—the possessions take for yourself."

But Abram said to the king of Sodom, "I raise my hand in oath to *ADONAI*, *El Elyon*, Creator of heaven and earth. Not a thread or even a sandal strap of all that is yours will I take, so you will not say, 'I've made Abram rich!' I claim nothing but what the young men have eaten, and the share of the men who went with me—Aner, Eschol, and Mamre—let them take their share."

Genesis 14:17-24

After these things the word of *ADONAI* came to Abram in a vision saying,

"Do not fear, Abram.

He took him outside and said, "Look up now, at the sky, and count the stars—if you are able to count them." Then He said to him, "So shall your seed be."

Genesis 15:5 TLV

I am your shield,
your very great reward."

But Abram said, "My Lord *ADONAI*, what will You give me, since I am living without children, and the heir of my household is Eliezer of Damascus?"

Then Abram said, "Look! You have given me no seed, so a house-born servant is my heir."

Then behold, the word of *ADONAI* came to him saying, **"This one will not be your heir, but in fact, one who will come from your own body will be your heir."**

He took him outside and said, **"Look up now, at the sky, and count the stars—if you are able to count them."** Then He said to him, **"So shall your seed be."**

Then he believed in *ADONAI* and He reckoned it to him as righteousness.

Then He said to him, **"I am *ADONAI* who brought you out from Ur of the Chaldeans, in order to give you this land to inherit it."**

So he said, "My Lord *ADONAI*, how will I know that I will inherit it?"

Then He said to him, **"Bring Me a three year old young cow, a three year old she-goat, a three year old ram, a turtle-dove and a young bird."**

So he brought all these to Him and cut them in half, and put each piece opposite the other; but he did not cut the birds. Then birds of prey came down upon the carcasses, but Abram drove them away.

When the sun was about to set and a deep sleep fell on Abram, behold, terror of great darkness was falling upon him!

Then He said to Abram, **"Know for certain that your seed will be strangers in a land that is not theirs, and they will be enslaved and oppressed 400 years. But I am going to judge the nation that they will serve. Afterward they will go out with many possessions. But you, you will come to your fathers in peace. You will be buried at a good old age. Then in the fourth generation they will return here—for the iniquity of the Amorites is not yet complete."**

When the sun set and it became dark, behold, there was a smoking oven and a fiery torch that passed between these pieces.

On that day *ADONAI* cut a covenant with Abram, saying, **"I give this land to your seed, from the river of Egypt to the great river, the Euphrates River: the Kenite, the Kenizzites, the Kadmonites, the Hittites, the Perizzites, the Raphaites, the Amorites, the Canaanites, the Girgashites, and the Jebusites."**

Genesis, chapter 15

8. God Tests Abraham and Isaac

Now Sarai, Abram's wife, had not borne him children. But she had an Egyptian slave-girl—her name was Hagar. So Sarai said to Abram, "Look now, *Adonai* has prevented me from having children. Go, please, to my slave-girl. Perhaps I'll get a son by her."

Abram listened to Sarai's voice. So Sarai, Abram's wife, took her slave-girl Hagar the Egyptian—after Abram had lived ten years in the land of Canaan—and gave her to Abram her husband to be his wife.

Then he went to Hagar and she became pregnant. When she saw that she was pregnant, in her eyes her mistress was belittled.

So Sarai said to Abram, "The wrong done to me is because of you! I myself placed my slave-girl in your embrace. Now that she saw that she became pregnant, so in her eyes I am belittled. May *Adonai* judge between you and me!"

Abram said to Sarai, "Look! Your slave -girl is in your hand. Do to her what is good in your eyes."

So Sarai afflicted her, and she fled from her presence. Then the angel of *Adonai* found her by the spring of water in the wilderness, next to the spring on the way to Shur.

He said, **"Hagar, Sarai's slave-girl, where have you come from and where are you going?"**

She said, "I am fleeing from the presence of my mistress Sarai."

The angel of *Adonai* said, **"Return to your mistress and humble yourself under her hand."**

Then the angel of *Adonai* said to her, **"I will bountifully multiply your seed, and they will be too many to count."**

Then the angel of *Adonai* said to her,

> **"Behold, you are pregnant**
> **and about to bear a son,**
> **and you shall name him Ishmael—**
> **for *Adonai* has**
> **heard your affliction.**

He will be a wild donkey of a man. His hand will be against everyone, and everyone's hand against him, and away from all his brothers will he dwell."

So she called *Adonai* who was speaking to her, "You are the God who sees me."

For she said, "Would I have gone here indeed looking for Him who looks after me?" That is why the well is named, the Well of the Living One Who Sees Me. (Behold, it is between Kadesh and Bered.) Then Hagar gave birth to a son for Abram, and Abram named his son, whom Hagar bore, Ishmael. Abram was 86 years old when Hagar gave birth to Ishmael for Abram.

Genesis, chapter 16

When Abram was 99 years old, *Adonai* appeared to Abram, and He said to him, **"I am *El Shaddai*.**

Continually walk before Me and you will be blameless. My heart's desire is to make My covenant between Me and you, and then I will multiply you exceedingly much."

Abram fell on his face, and God spoke with him, saying, **"For My part, because My covenant is with you, you will be the father of a multitude of nations. No longer will your name be Abram, but your name will be Abraham, because I make you the father of a multitude of nations.**

Yes, I will make you exceedingly fruitful, and I will make you into nations, and kings will come forth from you.

Yes, I will establish My covenant between Me and you and your seed after you throughout their generations for an everlasting covenant, in order to be your God and your seed's God after you. I will give to you and to your seed after you the land where you are an outsider—the whole land of Canaan—as an everlasting possession, and I will be their God."

God also said to Abraham, **"As for you, My covenant you must keep, you and your seed after you throughout their generations. This is My covenant that you must keep between Me and you and your seed after you: all your males must be circumcised.**

You must be circumcised in the flesh of your foreskin, and this will become a sign of the covenant between Me and you.

Also your eight-day-olds must be circumcised, every male, throughout your generations, including a house-born slave or a slave bought with money from any foreigner who is not of your seed. Your house-born slave and your purchased slave must surely be circumcised.

So My covenant will be in your flesh for an everlasting covenant. But the uncircumcised male who is not circumcised in the flesh of his foreskin—that person will be cut off from his people; he has broken My covenant."

God also said to Abraham, **"As for Sarai your wife, you shall not call her by the name Sarai. Rather, Sarah is her name. And I will bless her, and moreover, I will give you a son from her. I will bless her and she will give rise to nations. Kings of the peoples will come from her."**

Then Abraham fell on his face and laughed, and said to his heart, "Will a son be born to a 100-year-old man? Or will Sarah—who is 90 years old—give birth?"

So Abraham said to God, "If only Ishmael might live before You!"

But God said, **"On the contrary, Sarah your wife will bear you a son and you must name him Isaac. So I will confirm My covenant with him as an everlasting covenant for his seed after him.**

As for Ishmael, I have heard you. See, I have blessed him and I will make him fruitful, and I will multiply him very, very much. He will father

twelve princes and I will make him a great nation. But My covenant will I establish with Isaac whom Sarah will bear to you at this set time next year."

When He finished speaking with him, God went up from Abraham.

Then Abraham took Ishmael his son and all of his house-born slaves and all his purchased slaves — every male among the men of Abraham's house — and he circumcised the flesh of their foreskin on this very same day, just as God had spoken with him.

Abraham was 99 years old when he was circumcised in the flesh of his foreskin, and his son Ishmael was 13 years old when he was circumcised in the flesh of his foreskin.

On this very same day Abraham and Ishmael his son were circumcised. Also all the men of his house, house-born slaves and slaves purchased from a foreigner, were circumcised with him.

Genesis, chapter 17

Then *Adonai* visited Sarah just as He had said, and *Adonai* did for Sarah just as He had spoken. So Sarah became pregnant and gave birth to a son for Abraham in his old age, at the appointed time that God had told him.

Abraham named his son who was born to him—whom Sarah bore for him—Isaac. Then Abraham circumcised Isaac, his eight-day-old son, just as God had commanded him. Abraham was 100 years old when Isaac his son was born to him.

So Sarah said, "God has made laughter for me! Everyone who hears will laugh with me."

She also said, "Who would have said to Abraham, 'Sarah has nursed children'? For I have given birth to a son in his old age!"

The child grew and was weaned—Abraham made a big feast on the day Isaac was weaned.

But Sarah saw the son of Hagar the Egyptian whom she had born to Abraham—making fun. So she said to Abraham, "Drive out this female slave and her son, for the son of this female slave will not be an heir with my son—with Isaac."

Now the matter was very displeasing in Abraham's eyes on account of his son. But God said to Abraham, **"Do not be displeased about the boy and your slave woman. Whatever Sarah says to you, listen to her voice. For through Isaac shall your seed be called.**

Yet I will also make the son of the slave woman into a nation, because he is your seed."

So Abraham got up early in the morning and took bread and a skin of water and gave them to Hagar, putting them on her shoulder, and the child, and sent her away.

She went and wandered about in the wilderness of Beer-sheba. When the water from the skin was finished, she abandoned the child under one of the bushes. Then she went and sat herself down opposite, about a bowshot away, for she had said, "I can't bear to see the child dying!" So she sat down opposite and lifted up her voice and wept.

Then God heard the boy's voice and the angel of God called to Hagar from heaven, and He said to her, **"What troubles you, Hagar? Do not be afraid, because God has heard the boy's voice where he is. Get up! Lift the boy up, and hold on to him with your hand, for I will make him a great nation."**

Then God opened her eyes and she saw a well of water, and she went and filled the water skin, and gave the boy a drink.

God was with the boy and he grew. He dwelled in the wilderness and became an archer. He dwelled in the wilderness of Paran, and his mother took a wife for him from the land of Egypt.

Genesis 21:1-21

Now it was after these things that God tested Abraham.

He said to him, **"Abraham."**

"*Hineni*," he said.

Then He said, **"Take your son, your only son whom you love—Isaac—and go to the land of Moriah, and offer him there as a burnt offering on one of the mountains about which I will tell you."**

So Abraham got up early in the morning, saddled his donkey and took two of his young men with him, and Isaac his son. He split wood for the burnt offering, and got up and went to the place about which God had told him.

On the third day, Abraham lifted up his eyes and saw the place from a distance. Abraham said to his young men, "Sit yourselves down here with the donkey. As for me and the young man, we'll go over there, worship and return to you."

Then Abraham took the wood for the burnt offering and put it on Isaac his son. In his hand he took
the fire and the knife.

So the two of them walked on together.

Then Isaac said to Abraham his father, "My father?"

Then he said, "Here I am, my son."

He said, "Look. Here's the fire and the wood. But where's the lamb for a burnt offering?"

Abraham said, "God will provide for Himself a lamb for a burnt offering, my son."

The two of them walked on together. Then they came to the place about which God had told him, and Abraham built the altar there, laid out the wood, bound up Isaac his son, and laid him on the altar, on top of the wood.

Then Abraham reached out his hand and took the knife to slaughter his son.

Then Abraham reached out his hand and took the knife to slaughter his son. But the angel of *Adonai* called to him from heaven and said, "Abraham! Abraham!" He said, "*Hineni!*" Then He said, "Do not reach out your hand against the young man—do nothing to him at all. For now I know that you are one who fears God—you did not withhold your son, your only son, from Me."

Genesis 22:10-12 TLV

But the angel of *ADONAI* called to him from heaven and said, "Abraham! Abraham!"

He said, "*Hineni!*"

Then He said, **"Do not reach out your hand against the young man—do nothing to him at all. For now I know that you are one who fears God—you did not withhold your son, your only son, from Me."**

Then Abraham lifted up his eyes and behold, there was a ram, just caught in the thick bushes by its horns. So Abraham went and took the ram, and offered it up as a burnt offering instead of his son.

Abraham named that place, *ADONAI Yireh*,—as it is said today, "On the mountain, *ADONAI* will provide."

The angel of *ADONAI* called to Abraham a second time from heaven and said, **"By Myself I swear—it is a declaration of *ADONAI*—because you have done this thing, and you did not withhold your son, your only son, I will richly bless you and bountifully multiply your seed like the stars of heaven, and like the sand that is on the seashore, and your seed will possess the gate of his enemies. In your seed all the nations of the earth will be blessed—because you obeyed My voice."**

Then Abraham returned to his young men and they got up and went together to Beer-sheba. Then Abraham dwelled in Beer-sheba. Now it was after these things that it was told to Abraham, "Look, Milcah has also borne sons to Nahor your brother: Uz his firstborn, Buz his brother, Kemuel the father of Aram, Chesed, Hazo, Pildash, Yidlaph and Bethuel." Then Bethuel fathered Rebekah. These eight Milcah bore to Nahor, Abraham's brother. His concubine, whose name was Reumah, also bore Tebah, Gaham, Tahash and Maacah.

Genesis, chapter 22

9. God Keeps His Promise

Now Abraham took another wife—her name was Keturah. She bore him Zimran, Jokshan, Medan, Midian, Ishbak and Shuah. Jokshan fathered Sheba and Dedan. Dedan's sons were Asshurim, Letushim and Leummim. Midian's sons were Ephah, Epher, Hanoch, Abida and Eldaah. All of these were Keturah's sons.

Now Abraham gave everything that he had to Isaac, but to the sons of Abraham's concubines, Abraham had given gifts and sent them away from his son Isaac while he was still living, eastward to the land of the east.

Now these are the days of the years of Abraham's life that he lived: 175 years. So Abraham breathed his last and died at a good old age, old and satisfied. Then he was gathered to his peoples.

Then Isaac and Ishmael his sons buried him in the cave of Machpelah in the field of Ephron son of Zohar the Hittite, next to Mamre, the field that Abraham bought from the sons of Heth. There Abraham is buried along with Sarah his wife.

After Abraham's death, God blessed Isaac his son, and Isaac lived near Beer-lahai-roi. Now these are the genealogies of Ishmael, Abraham's son, whom Hagar, Sarah's Egyptian slave-girl, bore to Abraham.

These are the names of the sons of Ishmael, by their names according to their descendants: Ishmael's firstborn, Nebaioth, then Kedar, Adbeel, Mibsam, Mishma, Dumah, Massa, Hadad, Tema, Jetur, Naphish and Kedem. These are Ishmael's sons and these are their names, by their unwalled and walled settlements, twelve princes according to their clans.

These are the years of Ishmael's life: 137 years. He breathed his last, died and was gathered to his peoples. Then they dwelled from Havilah to Shur, which is east of Egypt as you go toward Assyria. Over against all his brothers he fell.

Now these are the genealogies of Isaac, Abraham's son. Abraham fathered Isaac.

Isaac was 40 years old when he took for himself Rebekah, the daughter of Bethuel the Aramean from Paddan-aram, the sister of Laban the Aramean, to be his wife.

Isaac prayed to *ADONAI* on behalf of his wife because she was barren. *ADONAI* answered his plea and his wife Rebekah became pregnant.

But the children struggled with one another inside her, and she said, "If it's like this, why is this happening to me?" So she went to inquire of *ADONAI*.

ADONAI said to her:

"Two nations are in your womb,
and two peoples from your
body will be separated.
One people will be stronger
than the other people,
but the older will serve the
younger."

When her time came to give birth, indeed there were twins in her womb. Now the first came out reddish, all of him was like a fur coat, and they named him Esau.

Afterward his brother came out with his hand holding onto Esau's heel—so he was named Jacob. Isaac was 60 years old when he fathered them.

When the boys grew up, Esau became a man knowledgeable in hunting, an outdoorsman, while Jacob was a mild man, remaining in tents.

Now Isaac loved Esau because he had a taste for wild game, but Rebekah loved Jacob.

Now Jacob cooked a stew. When Esau came in from the field, he was exhausted, so Esau said to Jacob, "Please feed me some of this really red stuff, because I'm exhausted"—that is why he is called Edom.

So Jacob said, "Sell your birthright to me today."

Esau said, "Look, I'm about to die. Of whatever use is this to me—a birthright?"

Jacob said, "Make a pledge to me now." So he made a pledge to him, and sold his birthright to Jacob. Then Jacob gave Esau bread and lentil stew, and he ate and drank, then got up and left. So Esau despised his birthright.

Genesis, chapter 25

Now there was a famine in the land—aside from the previous famine that happened in Abraham's days. So Isaac went to King Abimelech of the Philistines, to Gerar.

Then *ADONAI* appeared to him and said, **"Do not go down to Egypt. Dwell in the land about which I tell you. Live as an outsider in this land and I will be with you and bless you—for to you and to your seed I give all these lands—and I will confirm my pledge that I swore to Abraham your father.**

I will multiply your seed like the stars of the sky and I will give your seed all these lands. And in your seed all the nations of the earth will continually be blessed, because Abraham listened to My voice and kept My charge, My *mitzvot*, My decrees, and My instructions."

So Isaac stayed in Gerar.

Now the men of the place asked about his wife. So he said, "She is my sister," because he was afraid to say, "my wife"—"or else the men of the place would kill me on account of Rebekah, because she's good looking."

Now after he had been there for a long time, King Abimelech of the Philistines peered down through the window and saw, behold, Isaac caressing his wife Rebekah. So Abimelech called Isaac and said, "So in fact she's your wife! Now how could you say, 'She's my sister'?"

Isaac said to him, "Because I said, 'Or else I might die because of her.'"

Then Abimelech said, "What is it that you've done to us? One of the people could have easily slept with your wife and you would've brought guilt on us."

So Abimelech commanded all the people saying, "Whoever touches this man or his wife will surely die!"

Then Isaac sowed in that land and in that year reaped a hundredfold.

Adonai blessed him and the man became great and continued to become greater until he became very great. He acquired livestock of sheep and livestock of cattle, and numerous servants. Then the Philistines envied him. All the wells that his father's servants had dug in the days of his father Abraham the Philistines stopped up and filled with dirt.

So Abimelech said to Isaac, "Go away from us, for you are much more powerful than us."

So Isaac departed from there, camped in the Valley of Gerar and dwelled there. Then Isaac dug again the wells of water that had been dug in the days of his father Abraham—the Philistines had stopped them up after Abraham's death. He gave them the same names that his father had given them. Then Isaac's servants dug in the valley and found a well of living water there.

But the shepherds of Gerar quarreled with Isaac's shepherds saying, "The water is ours!" So he named the well Quarrel, because they quarreled with him. Then he dug another well and they quarreled over it too, so he named it Accusation.

Then he moved from there and dug another well, and they did not quarrel over it. So he named it Wide Spaces and said, "Because now *Adonai* has created wide spaces for us and we will be fruitful in the land."

He went up from there to Beer-sheba. *Adonai* appeared to him that night and said, **"I am the God of your father Abraham. Do not be afraid, for I am with you, and I will bless you and multiply your seed for the sake of Abraham my servant."**

So he built an altar there and called on the Name of *Adonai*. He pitched his tent there and Isaac's servants hollowed out a well there.

Now Abimelech went to him from Gerar along with Achuzzat his friend and Phicol the commander of his army. Isaac said to them, "Why have you come to me, since you hate me and sent me away from you?"

They said, "We've clearly seen that *Adonai* has been with you. So we said, 'Let there now be an agreement between us—between us and you—and let us make a covenant with you: that you will do us no harm, just as we haven't touched you and just as we did nothing to you but good, and sent you away in *shalom*. You are now blessed by *Adonai*."

Then he made a feast for them and they ate and drank. Then they got up early in the morning and made a pledge, each to his brother. Then Isaac sent them away and they departed from him in *shalom*.

Now it happened that on that day

Isaac's servants came and told him about the well that they dug, and said to him, "We've found water." So he called it Pledge. That is why the city's name is Beer-sheba to this day.

When Esau was 40 years old, he took as wife Judith the daughter of Be-eri the Hittite, and Basemath the daughter of Elon the Hittite. But they caused a bitterness of spirit for Isaac and Rebekah.

Genesis, chapter 26

Now it was when Isaac grew old and his eyes were too dim to see, that he called Esau his elder son, and said to him, "My son."

"Here I am," he said to him.

"Look, I'm old," he said. "I don't know the day of my death.

So now, please take your weapons, your quiver and your bow, and go out to the field and hunt me some game. Then prepare me a delicious meal that I love, and bring it to me that I may eat, so that my soul may bless you before I die."

Now Rebekah was listening when Isaac was speaking to Esau his son. So while Esau went to the field to hunt game to bring in, Rebekah said to Jacob her son, "Look, I heard your father speaking to your brother Esau saying, 'Bring me some game and prepare me a delicious meal that I may eat and bless you in *ADONAI*'s presence before my death.' So now, my son, listen to my voice, to what I am commanding you. Go now to the flock and bring me two good young goats from there, so that I may prepare them as a delicious meal for your father—that he'll love. Then you'll bring it to your father to eat, so that he may bless you before his death."

But Jacob said to Rebekah his mother, "Look, my brother Esau is a hairy man, but I'm a smooth man. Perhaps my father will touch me, and he'll take me for a mocker, and I'll bring upon myself a curse and not a blessing."

Then his mother said to him, "Let your curse fall on me, my son. Just listen to me, and go, get them for me."

So he went and got them, and brought them to his mother, and his mother prepared a delicious meal that his father would love. Rebekah also took her elder son Esau's favorite clothes that were with her in the house, and she put them on her younger son Jacob, along with the skins of the young goats on his hands and on the hairless part of his neck. She put the delicious meal and the bread that she had prepared in the hand of Jacob her son.

Then he came to his father and said, "My father."

And he said, "I'm here. Who are you, my son?"

Then Jacob said to his father, "I'm your firstborn, Esau. I've done just what you said to me. Sit up, please, and eat some of my wild game so that your soul may bless me."

Then Isaac said to his son, "How in

the world were you able to find it so quickly, my son?"

He said, "Because *Adonai* your God made it happen for me."

Then Isaac said to Jacob, "Please come closer so I can feel you my son—whether or not you really are my son Esau."

So Jacob came closer to his father Isaac, and he felt him. Then he said, "The voice is Jacob's voice but the hands are Esau's hands." He did not recognize him because his hands were like the hairy hands of his brother Esau. So he blessed him. But he said, "Are you really my son Esau?"

So he said, "I am."

Then he said, "Bring it to me and I'll eat some of my son's wild game, so that my soul may bless you." So he brought it to him and he ate, and he brought him wine and he drank.

Then his father Isaac said to him, "Please come closer and kiss me my son."

So he came closer and kissed him. When he smelled the smell of his clothes, he blessed him and said,

"Behold, the smell of my son
is like the smell of a field
that *Adonai* has blessed.
May God give you—
from the dew of the sky
and from the fatness of the land—
an abundance of grain
and new wine.
May peoples serve you
and may nations bow down to you.
Be master over your brothers.
May your mother's sons
bow down to you.
May those who curse
you be cursed
and may those who bless you
be blessed."

No sooner had Isaac finished blessing Jacob and Jacob had just gone out from his father Isaac's presence, than Esau his brother came in from his hunting.

Then he also prepared a delicious meal and brought it to his father, and he said to his father, "Let my father get up and eat of his son's wild game that your soul may bless me."

His father Isaac said, "Who are you?"

And he said, "I am your son, your first-born, Esau."

Then Isaac trembled with intense trembling and said, "Who was it then that hunted wild game and brought it to me? I ate it all just before you came and I blessed him—and yes, he will be blessed."

When Esau heard his father's words, he shouted with an intensely bitter groan. Then he said to his father, "Bless me, me too, my father!"

Then he said, "Your brother came deceitfully and took your blessing."

He said, "Is this why he was named Jacob—since he's tricked me twice already? My birthright he's taken. Look! Now he's taken my blessing!"

Then he said, "Haven't you saved a blessing for me?"

Isaac answered and said to Esau, "Behold, I've made him master over you, and all your brothers I've given to him as servants. I've provided him with grain and new wine. What then can I do for you, my son?"

Esau said to his father, "Do you just have one blessing, my father? Bless me too, my father!" And Esau lifted up his voice and wept.

Then Isaac his father said to him, "Behold, away from the land's fatness shall your dwelling be, away from the dew of the sky above.
By your sword shall you live,
and your brother shall you serve.
But when you tear yourself loose,
you will tear his yoke off your neck."

So Esau bore a grudge against Jacob because of the blessing with which his father had blessed him, and Esau said in his heart, "Let the time for mourning my father draw near, so that I can kill my brother Jacob!"

Now to Rebekah was reported the words of Esau her elder son. So she sent and called for Jacob her younger son, and said to him, "Look, your brother Esau is consoling himself about you with the thought of killing you. So now my son, listen to my voice. Get up—flee to Laban my brother in Haran! Then stay with him a few days, until your brother's rage subsides, until your brother's rage turns away from you and he forgets what you've done to him. Then I'll send for you and get you back from there. Why should I lose both of you in one day?"

Then Rebekah said to Isaac, "I'm disgusted with my life because of the daughters of Heth. If Jacob takes a wife from the daughters of Heth like these women, from the daughters of the land what is life to me?"

Genesis, chapter 27

So Isaac called for Jacob, blessed him, commanded him and said to him, "Don't take a wife from the daughters of Canaan. Get up, go to Paddan-aram, to the house of Bethuel, your mother's father, and take for yourself a wife from there, from the daughters of Laban, your mother's brother.

Now may *El Shaddai* bless you, and make you fruitful and multiply you so that you will become an assembly of peoples. And may he give you the blessing of Abraham, to you and to your seed with you that you may take possession of the land of your sojourn, which God gave to Abraham."

Then Isaac sent Jacob away and he went toward Paddan-aram, to Laban the son of Bethuel the Aramean, the brother of Rebekah, the mother of Jacob and Esau.

Now Esau saw that Isaac blessed Jacob when he sent him to Paddan-aram to take for himself a wife from there, when he blessed him and commanded him saying, "Don't take a wife from the daughters of Canaan."

Jacob listened to his father Isaac and to his mother and went toward Paddan-aram.

Then Esau saw that the daughters of

Canaan were contemptible in his father Isaac's eyes. So Esau went to Ishmael and took Mahalath, the daughter of Ishmael Abraham's son, Nebaioth's sister for his wife, besides his other wives.

Then Jacob left Beer-sheba and went toward Haran. He happened upon a certain place and spent the night there, for the sun had set. So he took one of the stones from the place and put it by his head and lay down in that place.

He dreamed: All of a sudden, there was a stairway set up on the earth and its top reaching to the heavens—and behold, angels of God going up and down on it!

Surprisingly, *Adonai* was standing on top of it and He said, **"I am *Adonai*, the God of your father Abraham and the God of Isaac. The land on which you lie, I will give it to you and to your seed. Your seed will be as the dust of the land, and you will burst forth to the west and to the east and to the north and to the south. And in you all the families of the earth will be blessed—and in your seed.**

Behold, I am with you, and I will watch over you wherever you go, and I will bring you back to this land, for I will not forsake you until I have done what I promised you."

Jacob woke up from his sleep and said, "Undoubtedly, *Adonai* is in this place— and I was unaware."

So he was afraid and said, "How fearsome this place is! This is none other than the House of God—this must be the gate of heaven!"

Early in the morning Jacob got up and took the stone, which he had placed by his head, and set it up as a memorial stone and poured oil on top of it.

He called the name of that place Beth-El (though originally the city's name was Luz).

Then Jacob made a vow saying, "If God will be with me and watch over me on this way that I am going, and provide me food to eat and clothes to wear, and I return in *shalom* to my father's house, then *Adonai* will be my God.

So this stone which I set up as a memorial stone will become God's House, and of everything You provide me I will definitely give a tenth of it to You."

Genesis, chapter 28

He dreamed: All of a sudden, there was a stairway set up on the earth and its top reaching to the heavens—and behold, angels of God going up and down on it! Surprisingly, *ADONAI* was standing on top of it and He said, "I am *ADONAI* the God of your father Abraham and the God of Isaac. The land on which you lie, I will give it to you and to your seed.

Genesis 28:12-13 TLV

10. God Gives Jacob a New Name

Then Jacob lifted up his feet and went to the land of the peoples of the east.

When he looked, suddenly, there was a well in the field, and there were three herds of sheep resting by it. (For from that well they would water the flocks. The stone on the mouth of the well was large. When all the herds gathered there, they would roll away the stone from the mouth of the well and water the flocks, and put the stone back to its place over the mouth of the well.)

Jacob said to them, "My brothers, where are you from?"

"We're from Haran," they said.

So he said to them, "Do you know Laban, Nahor's son?"

They said, "We know."

He said to them, "Is he well?"

"Well," they said. "Look, here comes his daughter Rachel with the flock."

He said, "Since it's still the middle of the day, it's not time for the livestock to be gathered. Water the flock and let them go and graze."

But they said, "We can't, not until all the flocks are gathered and the stone is rolled away from the mouth of the well—then we water the flock."

While he was still speaking with them, Rachel came with the flock that belonged to her father (for she was a shepherdess).

Now when Jacob saw Rachel (the daughter of Laban, his mother's brother), Jacob stepped forward and rolled the stone away from the mouth of the well and watered the flock of Laban, his mother's brother. Then Jacob kissed Rachel, and lifted up his voice and wept.

Then Jacob told Rachel that he was her father's relative and that he was Rebekah's son. So she ran and told her father.

Now when Laban heard the news about Jacob, his sister's son, he ran to meet him, hugged and kissed him, and brought him to his house. Then he told Laban all these things. Laban said to him, "Surely you are my own bone and flesh." And he stayed with him for a month.

Then Laban said to Jacob, "Should you, my relative, serve me for nothing? Tell me, what should your wages be?"

Now Laban had two daughters; the name of the older was Leah, and the name of the younger was Rachel.

Leah's eyes were delicate, but Rachel was beautiful in form and appearance.

Jacob was in love with Rachel, so he said, "Let me serve you for seven years for Rachel your younger daughter."

Laban said, "It's better that I give her

to you than I give her to another man! Stay with me."

So Jacob worked for Rachel seven years, yet in his eyes it was like a few days, because of his love for her.

Then Jacob said to Laban, "Give me my wife, for my days are completed, so I may go to her."

So Laban gathered all the men of the place and he prepared a feast.

When it was evening he took his daughter Leah and brought her to him, and he went to her. Laban also gave her Zilpah his female servant to his daughter Leah as a female servant.

So when it was morning, behold there she was, Leah! So he said to Laban, "What is this you've done to me? Wasn't it for Rachel that I worked with you? So why have you deceived me?"

But Laban said, "It's not done so in our place—to give the younger before the first-born. Complete the bridal week for this one. Then we'll also give you this other—for work that you'll do with me—another seven years more."

So Jacob did; he also completed this one's bridal week. Then he gave him his daughter Rachel to be his wife. Laban also gave his daughter Rachel his female servant Bilhah, to be a servant for her. Jacob also went to Rachel and indeed loved Rachel more than Leah. So he served with him for yet another seven years.

Now *Adonai* saw that Leah was unloved, so he opened her womb; but Rachel was unable to conceive.

Leah became pregnant and gave birth to a son and named him Reuben because she said, "For *Adonai* has seen my affliction. Surely now my husband will love me."

Then she became pregnant again and gave birth to a son, and said, "For *Adonai* heard that I am hated, so He's given me this one also," and she named him Simeon.

Then she became pregnant again and gave birth to a son, and said, "Now this time my husband will join himself to me because I've given birth to three sons for him." For this reason he was named Levi.

Then she became pregnant again and gave birth to a son and said, "This time I praise *Adonai*." For this reason she named him Judah.

Then she stopped having children.

Genesis, chapter 29

When Rachel saw that she bore no children for Jacob, Rachel was jealous of her sister. So she said to Jacob, "Give me sons—if there are none, I'll die!"

But Jacob became furious with Rachel and said, "Am I, instead of God, the one who withheld from you the fruit of the womb?"

So she said, "Here's my maid-servant Bilhah. Go to her and let her give birth on my knees, so that from her I may also build a family." Then she gave her maid-servant Bilhah to him for a wife, and Jacob went to her.

Bilhah became pregnant and gave birth to a son for Jacob. So Rachel said, "God has judged my cause and also heard my voice—and given me a son." Therefore she named him Dan.

Then Rachel's female servant became pregnant again and gave birth to a second son for Jacob. So Rachel said, "I've surely wrestled greatly with my sister—also I've won." So she named him Naphtali.

Now Leah saw that she stopped having children, so she took Zilpah her female servant and gave her to Jacob as a wife. Then Zilpah, Leah's female servant, gave birth to a son for Jacob. Leah said, "How fortunate!" So she named him Gad.

Then Zilpah, Leah's female servant, gave birth to a second son for Jacob. Leah said, "How happy am I, for daughters have called me happy." So she named him Asher.

Now during the days of the wheat harvest, Reuben went and found mandrakes in the field and he brought them to his mother Leah.

Then Rachel said to Leah, "Please give me some of your son's mandrakes."

But she said to her, "Wasn't it enough that you took my husband away? You'd also take away my son's mandrakes?"

So Rachel said, "That being so, let him lie with you tonight, in exchange for your son's mandrakes."

So when Jacob came from the field in the evening, Leah went out to meet him, and she said, "You must come to me. For I've actually hired you with my son's mandrakes." So he lay with her that very night.

Moreover, God heard Leah, and she became pregnant and gave birth to a fifth son for Jacob. Leah said, "God gave me my reward because I gave my female servant to my husband." So she named him Issachar.

Then Leah became pregnant again and gave birth to a sixth son for Jacob. Leah said, "God has presented me a good gift. This time my husband will honor me for I've borne six sons for him." So she named him Zebulun.

Afterwards she gave birth to a daughter and named her Dinah. Then God remembered Rachel and God listened to her and opened her womb. Then she became pregnant and gave birth to a son.

So she said, "God has taken away my disgrace." She named him Joseph saying, "May *Adonai* add another son for me."

Now it was after Rachel gave birth to Joseph that Jacob said to Laban, "Send me away so that I can go to my place and to my land. Give me my wives and my children for whom I've served you, and let me go. For you yourself know my labor—that I've served you."

But Laban said to him, "If I've found favor in your eyes—I've looked for good omens, and *ADONAI* has blessed me because of you."

Moreover he said, "Name your own price and I'll pay it."

Then he said to him, "You yourself know how I've served you and how your livestock fared with me. For you had very little before I came, and it has been busting at the seams in abundance.

So *ADONAI* blessed you with my every step. So now, when am I myself going to make something for my household also?"

Then he said, "What can I pay you?"

Jacob said, "You don't need to pay me anything. If you will do this one thing for me, I will shepherd your flock again and watch it: let me pass through your flock today, removing every colorfully spotted lamb from there and every dark-colored lamb among the sheep as well as the colorfully spotted among the goats—and that will be my salary.

So tomorrow my honesty will testify on my behalf when you come to check on my salary you agreed to. Every one that isn't colorfully spotted among the goats or dark-colored among the sheep with me, it is stolen."

So Laban said, "All right! May it be according to your word."

On that day he removed the colorfully striped and colorful billy goats as well as all the colorfully spotted goats—everyone with white on it—and every dark-colored one among the lambs, and he put them in the hand of his sons.

Then he put a three-day's journey between them and Jacob, while Jacob was shepherding Laban's remaining flocks.

But Jacob took fresh white poplar, almond, and plane tree branches, peeled away white stripped sections on them, exposing the white of the branches. Then he set the branches he had peeled in front of the flocks in the drinking troughs and watering channels where the flocks come to drink. Since they were in heat when they came to drink, the flocks mated near the branches, and the flocks gave birth to striped, spotted and colorful ones.

Now Jacob separated the lambs and set the faces of the flocks toward the striped ones as well as all the dark-colored ones among Laban's flocks. Then he set aside the herds for himself and did not put them with Laban's flocks. Whenever the strong flocks mated, Jacob put the branches in the watering troughs before the eyes of the flocks, to have them mate near the branches. But when the flocks were sickly, he did not put the branches down—so the sickly ones became Laban's and the stronger ones became Jacob's.

And the man grew exceedingly prosperous and had numerous flocks, along with female and male servants, camels and donkeys.

Genesis, chapter 30

Then Jacob sent messengers before

him to his brother Esau, to the land of Seir, the field of Edom.

He also commanded them saying, "This is what you should say to my lord, to Esau: 'This is what your servant Jacob said: I've been staying with Laban, and have lingered until now. Now I've come to possess oxen and donkeys, flocks, male servants and female servants. I sent word to tell my lord, in order to find favor in your eyes.'"

The messengers returned to Jacob saying, "We went to your brother, to Esau, and he's also coming out to meet you—and 400 men with him." So Jacob became extremely afraid and distressed. He divided the people with him, along with the flocks and herds and camels, into two camps, for he thought, "If Esau comes to one camp and strikes it, the camp that's left will escape."

Then Jacob said, "O God of my father Abraham, and God of my father Isaac, *Adonai*, who said to me, **'Return to your land and to your relatives and I will do good with you.'** I am unworthy of all the proofs of mercy and of all the dependability that You have shown to your servant. For with only my staff I crossed over this Jordan, and now I've become two camps.

Deliver me, please, from my brother's hand, from Esau's hand, for I'm afraid of him that he'll come and strike me—the mothers with the children.

You Yourself said, **'I will most certainly do good with you, and will make your seed like the sand of the sea that cannot be counted because of its abundance.'"**

So he stayed overnight there. Then from all that had come into his possession he took an offering for Esau his brother: 200 female goats, 20 billy goats, 200 ewes, 20 rams, 30 milking camels with their young, 40 cows, 10 bulls, 20 female donkeys and 10 male donkeys. He put them in the hands of his servants, each herd by itself, and he said to his servants, "Pass over before me, and put a gap between each of the herds."

Then he commanded the first one saying, "When my brother Esau meets you and asks you saying, 'To whom do you belong, and where are you going, and to whom do all these before you belong?' then you are to say, 'To your servant, to Jacob—it's an offering sent to my lord, to Esau. And look, he's also behind us.'"

And he also commanded the second one, the third one, and all those who were going behind the flocks, saying, "Say the same exact thing to Esau when you find him. Then you are to say, 'Look, your servant Jacob is also behind us.'"

For he thought, "Let me appease him with the offering that goes ahead of me, and afterward see his face, perhaps he'll lift up my face."

So the offering passed over ahead of him, while he spent that night in the camp. Then he got up that night and took his two wives, his two female servants, and his eleven sons, and crossed over the ford of the Jabbok. He took them and sent them

When He saw that He had not overcome him, He struck the socket of his hip, so He dislocated the socket of Jacob's hip when He wrestled with him. Then He said, "Let Me go, for the dawn has broken." But he said, "I won't let You go unless You bless me."

Genesis 28:12-13 TLV

across the stream, and he sent across whatever he had. So Jacob remained all by himself.

Then a man wrestled with him until the break of dawn. When He saw that He had not overcome him, He struck the socket of his hip, so He dislocated the socket of Jacob's hip when He wrestled with him.

Then He said, **"Let Me go, for the dawn has broken."**

But he said, "I won't let You go unless You bless me."

Then He said to him, **"What is your name?"**

"Jacob," he said.

Then He said, **"Your name will no longer be Jacob, but rather Israel, for you have struggled with God and with men, and you have overcome."**

Then Jacob asked and said, "Please tell me Your name."

But He said, **"What's this—you are asking My name?"** Then He blessed him there.

So Jacob named the place Peniel, "for I've seen God face to face, and my life has been spared."

Now the sun rose upon him just as he crossed by Peniel—limping because of his hip. That is why the children of Israel do not eat the tendon of the hip socket, to this very day, because He struck the socket of Jacob's thigh on the tendon of the hip.

Genesis 32:4-33

Then Jacob glanced up and saw, behold, there was Esau coming—and 400 men with him. So he divided the children among Leah, Rachel and the two female servants. He put the female servants and their children first, then Leah and her children behind them, then Rachel and Joseph behind them.

But he himself passed on ahead of them, and bowed to the ground seven times until he came near to his brother.

But Esau ran to meet him, hugged him, fell on his neck and kissed him—and they wept. His eyes glanced up and he saw the women and the children, and said, "Who are these with you?"

"The children whom God has graciously given your servant," he said. Then the female servants approached, they and their children, and bowed down.

Leah also approached, along with her children, and they bowed down, and finally, Joseph and Rachel approached and bowed down.

"What do you mean by this whole caravan that I've met?"

So he said, "To find favor in your eyes, my lord."

But Esau said, "I have plenty! O my brother, do keep all that belongs to you."

Yet Jacob said, "No, please! If I have found favor in your eyes, then you will take my offering from my hand. For this is the reason I've seen your face—it is like seeing the face of God—and you've accepted me! Please, take my blessing that was brought to you, because God has been gracious to me, and because I have everything." So he kept urging him until he accepted.

Then he said, "Let's journey and be on our way, and I'll go ahead of you.

He continued, "My lord knows that the children are tender, and that the flocks and the cattle in my care are nursing. So if they were pushed hard just one day, all the flocks would die. Please, let my lord pass on ahead of your servant, and I'll move on further gradually, at a pace suited to the livestock that are before me and at a pace suited to the children, until I come to my lord in Seir."

Then Esau said, "Please let me leave with you some of the people who are with me."

But he said, "What's this? Let me find favor in my lord's eyes."

So on that day Esau returned on his way to Seir, but Jacob journeyed to Sukkot and built a house for himself, and for his livestock he made booths. That is the reason that place is called *Sukkot*.

So Jacob arrived in *shalom* to the city of Shechem, which is in the land of Canaan, when he came from Paddan-aram, and camped right in front of the city.

He purchased the portion of the field there where he had pitched his tent from the sons of Hamor, Shechem's father, for 100 pieces of money.

There he set up an altar, and he called it, *El* is Israel's God.

Genesis, chapter 33

11. God Reunites Brothers

Now Jacob dwelled in the land where his father had sojourned, in the land of Canaan. These are the genealogies of Jacob.

When Joseph was 17 years old (he was a youth), he was shepherding the flocks with his brothers—with the sons of his father's wives Bilhah and Zilpah. Joseph brought back a bad report about them to their father.

Now Israel loved Joseph more than all his other sons because he was the son of his old age. So he had made him a long-sleeved tunic.

When his brothers saw that their father loved him more than all his brothers, they hated him and could not speak to him in *shalom*.

Then Joseph dreamed a dream and told his brothers—and they hated him even more.

He said to them, "Please listen to this dream I dreamed. There we were binding sheaves in the middle of the field. All of a sudden, my sheaf arose and stood upright. And behold, your sheaves gathered around and bowed down to my sheaf."

"Will you truly be a king over us?" his brothers said to him. "Will you really rule over us?" So they hated him even more because of his dreams and because of his words.

But then he dreamed another dream and told it to his brothers, saying, "I have just dreamed another dream. Suddenly, there was the sun and the moon and the eleven stars bowing down to me!" He told it to his father as well as his brothers.

Then his father rebuked him and said to him, "What's this dream you dreamed? Will we really come—your mother and I with your brothers—to bow down to the ground to you?"

So his brothers were jealous of him, but his father kept the speech in mind.

Then his brothers went to graze their father's flocks at Shechem. Israel said to Joseph, "Aren't your brothers grazing the flocks in Shechem? Come, let me send you to them."

"Here I am," he said to him.

Then he said to him, "Go now, and check on the welfare of your brothers and the welfare of the flocks and bring word back to me."

So he sent him from the valley of Hebron and he went to Shechem. A man found him there, wandering in the field, and the man asked him, "What are you looking for?"
"I'm looking for my brothers," he said. "Please tell me where they're grazing."

The man said, "They moved on from here. For I heard them saying, 'Let's go to Dothan.'" So Joseph went after his brothers and found them in Dothan.

Now they saw him from a distance. Before he was close to them they plotted together against him in order to kill him.

They said to one another, "Here comes the master of dreams! Come on now! Let's kill him and throw him into one of those pits, so we can say that an evil animal devoured him. Then let's see what becomes of his dreams."

But Reuben heard and rescued him out of their hands, saying, "We must not beat him to death."

In order to rescue him from their hand and to return him to his father, Reuben said to them, "Don't shed blood! Throw him into this pit here in the wilderness, but don't lay a hand on him!"

So as soon as Joseph came up to his brothers they stripped Joseph of his tunic (the long sleeved tunic that he had on. Then they took him and threw him into the pit. (Now the pit was empty, with no water in it.) Then they sat down to eat bread.

When they looked up, behold, there was a caravan of Ishmaelites coming from Gilead, with their camels carrying gum, balsam, and myrrh—going to bring them down to Egypt.

Then Judah said to his brothers, "What profit is there if we kill our brother and cover up his blood? Come on! Let's sell him to the Ishmaelites. Let's not lay our hand on him—since he's our brother, our own flesh."

His brothers listened to him. When some men, Midianite merchants, passed by, they dragged Joseph up and out of the pit and they sold Joseph to the Ishmaelites for 20 pieces of silver, and they brought Joseph to Egypt.

When Reuben returned to the pit and saw that Joseph was not in the pit, he tore his clothes. Then he returned to his brothers and said, "The boy is gone! And I—where should I go?"

So they took Joseph's tunic, slaughtered a billy goat, and they dipped the tunic into the blood. Then they sent the long-sleeved tunic, and it was brought to their father, and they said, "We found this. Do you recognize whether or not it is your son's tunic?"

He did recognize it and said, "My son's tunic! An evil animal has devoured him! Joseph must be torn to pieces!"

Jacob tore his clothing and put on sackcloth and mourned for his son many days. All his sons got up along with all his daughters to console him, but he refused to be comforted.

He said, "For I will go down to *Sheol* to my son, mourning." So his father kept weeping for him.

Meanwhile the Midianites sold him into Egypt, to Potiphar an official of Pharaoh, the commander of the bodyguards.

Genesis, chapter 37

Now Joseph had been brought down to Egypt. Potiphar, an official of Pharaoh, commander of the bodyguards, bought him from the hand of the Ishmaelites, who had brought him down there.

But *ADONAI* was with Joseph. So he became a successful man in the house of his master, the Egyptian. His master saw that *ADONAI* was with him and that *ADONAI* made everything he set his hand to successful.

Joseph found favor in his eyes, so he served him as a personal servant and he made him an overseer over his household; everything that was his he entrusted into his hand.

From the time that he made him an overseer in his house and over everything that belonged to him, *ADONAI* blessed the Egyptian's house because of Joseph; *ADONAI*'s blessing was on everything that belonged to him, in the house and in the field.

So he released everything he owned into Joseph's hand. With him in charge, he did not think about anything except the food he ate.

Now Joseph was handsome in form and handsome in appearance.

Now after these things, the master's wife lifted up her eyes at Joseph and said, "Come, lie down with me!"

But he refused. "Look," he said to his master's wife, "my master doesn't think about anything in the house with me in charge, and everything that belongs to him he's entrusted into my hand. No one in this house is greater than I, and he has withheld nothing from me—except you, because you are his wife. So how could I commit this great evil and sin against God?"

So whenever she spoke to Joseph, day after day, he did not listen to her invitation to lie down beside her, to be with her. Now on one such day, he came into the house to do his work, and none of the people of the house were there in the house.

Then she grabbed him by his garment saying, "Come, lie with me!"

But he left his garment in her hand, fled and went outside.

When she saw that he had left his garment in her hand and fled outside, she screamed to the men of her house and said to them, "Look! Someone brought a Hebrew man to us to fool with us. He approached me to lie with me so I screamed out loud. When he heard me raise my voice and scream, he left his garment with me, fled and went outside."

Then she kept the garment with her until his master came home. She spoke the same words to him saying, "The Hebrew slave that you brought us approached me to fool with me. When I raised my voice and screamed, he left his garment with me and fled outside."

Now when his master heard the words his wife spoke to him saying, "Such are the things your slave did to me," his anger burned. Then Joseph's master took him and put him in prison, the place where the king's prisoners were confined.

So there he was, in the prison.

But *ADONAI* was with Joseph and extended kindness to him and gave

him favor in the eyes of the commander of the prison.
The commander of the prison entrusted into Joseph's hand all the prisoners who were in the prison, so that everything that was done there, he was responsible for it. The commander of the prison did not concern himself with anything at all under his care, because *ADONAI* was with him, and *ADONAI* made whatever he did successful.

Genesis, chapter 39

Now Jacob saw that there was grain in Egypt, so Jacob said to his sons, "Why are you looking at each other?" Then he said, "Look! I've heard that there's grain in Egypt. Go down there and buy some grain for us there so that we'll live and not die."

So Joseph's brothers went down, ten of them, to buy grain from Egypt. But Benjamin, Joseph's brother, Jacob did not send, for he said, "An accident might happen to him."

The sons of Israel went to buy grain among the others who were coming, because the famine was in the land of Canaan.

Now Joseph was the ruler over the land. He was the provider of grain for all the people of the earth.

Then Joseph's brothers came and bowed down to him with faces to the ground. When Joseph saw his brothers, he recognized them, but he made himself unrecognizable to them. Then he spoke harshly and said to them, "Where have you come from?"
"From the land of Canaan," they said, "to buy grain as food."

Though Joseph recognized his brothers, they did not recognize him. Then Joseph remembered the dreams he had dreamed about them. He said to them, "You're spies! You've come to see the undefended places in the land."

"No, my lord!" they said to him. "Your servants came to buy grain as food. All of us—we are sons of one man. We're honest. Your servants have never been spies."

"Not so," he said to them. "Rather, you've come to see the undefended places in the land."

But they said, "We your servants are twelve brothers, sons of one man in the land of Canaan. Look, the youngest is with our father today and the other one is no more."

Joseph said to them, "It's just like I told you when I said, 'You're spies.' By this you'll be tested: by the life of Pharaoh, you'll not leave from here until your youngest brother comes here!

Send one from among yourselves to get your brother, while you remain confined, in order to test your words, to see whether the truth is with you. If not, by the life of Pharaoh, you're definitely spies!"

So he put them together in custody for three days. Then Joseph said to them on the third day, "Do this and you will live. I fear God.

If you're honest, let one of your brothers remain as a prisoner in the guardhouse where you've been, while you, go and bring grain for the hunger in your homes. And your youngest brother, bring to me so that your words can be verified—and you won't die." So they did.

Then each man said to his brother, "We're truly guilty for our brother. We saw the distress of his soul when he begged us for mercy, but we didn't listen. That's why this distress has come to us."

Reuben answered them and said, "Didn't I tell you, 'Don't sin against the boy'? But you didn't listen. Now, see how his blood is now being accounted for."

They did not know that Joseph was listening, since there was an interpreter between them. He turned away from them and wept. When he turned back to them and spoke to them, he took Simeon from them and tied him up before their eyes.

Then Joseph gave orders to fill their bags with grain, to return each man's money to his sack, and to give them provisions for the journey. So it was done for them. Then they loaded their grain on their donkeys and left from there.

As one of them opened his sack to give fodder to his donkey at the lodge, he saw his money—behold, it was in the opening of his bag. So he said to his brothers, "My money has been returned! Look, it's in my bag."

Their hearts sank. Trembling, each one turned to his brother and said, "What is this that God has done to us?"

When they came to their father Jacob, in the land of Canaan, they told him all that had happened to

them, saying, "The man, the lord of the land, spoke with us harshly, and took us as spies of the land. But we said to him, 'We're honest. We've never been spies.

We are twelve brothers, sons of our father. One is no more and the youngest is with our father today in the land of Canaan.'

Then the man, the lord of the land, said to us, 'By this I'll know if you're honest: leave one of your brothers with me. As for the hunger of your homes: take and go! Then bring your youngest brother to me, so that I may know you are not spies, but you are honest. I'll give you back your brother and you can move about freely in the land.'"

Now as they were emptying their sacks, behold, there was each man's bundle of money in his sack. When they saw their money bundles, they and their father, they were afraid.

Then their father Jacob said to them, "You've made me childless! Joseph is no more. Now Simeon is gone, and next you'll take Benjamin! Everything is against me!"

Then Reuben spoke to his father, saying, "You can put my two sons to death if I don't bring him back to you. Put him in my hand and I—I will return him to you."

But he said, "My son will not go down with you—for his brother is dead and he alone remains. And if harm should happen to him along the way you're going, you'll bring my grey hair down to *Sheol* in grief."

Genesis, chapter 42

Now the famine was severe in the land. When they finished eating the grain they had brought from Egypt their father said to them, "Go back. Buy us a little food."

But Judah said to him, "The man warned us firmly saying, 'You won't see my face unless your brother is with you.' If you send our brother with us, we will go down and buy grain for you for food. But if you won't send him, we won't go down, because the man said to us, 'You won't see my face unless your brother is with you.'"

Then Israel said, "Why did you do evil to me by telling the man that you have another brother?"

They said, "The man questioned particularly about us and about our relatives saying, 'Is your father still alive? Do you have a brother?' So we spoke to him on the basis of these words. How could we possibly know that he would say, 'Bring your brother down'"?

Then Judah said to his father Israel, "Please, send the boy with me and we'll get up and go, so that we'll live and not die—we and you, and our children. I myself will be his pledge. You can demand him back from my own hand. If I don't bring him back to you and place him before you, then you can blame me all my days. If we had not delayed, we could have returned twice by now."

Then their father Israel said to them, "If it must be so, then do this: take some of the best products of the land in your bags, and bring an offering down to the man—a little balsam and a little honey, gum and myrrh, pistachios and almonds. Also take in your hand a double portion of silver, and bring back in your hand the silver that had been returned in the mouth of your sacks. Perhaps it was a mistake.

Take your brother too—now, get up, go back to the man! May *El Shaddai* grant you mercy before the man, so that he may release your other brother to you, along with Benjamin. As for me, if I am bereaved, I am bereaved."

Then the men took this offering. They also took the double portion of silver in their hand, as well as Benjamin.

So they got up and went down to Egypt, and stood before Joseph.

When Joseph saw Benjamin with them, he said to the one over his house, "Bring the men into the house. Slaughter an animal and prepare it, for the men will eat with me this afternoon. So the man did as Joseph said, and the man brought the men into Joseph's house.

But the men were afraid, because

they had been brought into Joseph's house. They said, "It's because of the silver that was returned to our sacks the first time that we are being brought in—to pounce on us and fall on us and take us as slaves, along with our donkeys."

So they approached the man who was over Joseph's house and spoke to him at the entrance of the house.

"I beg your pardon, my lord!" they said. "We indeed came down on the previous occasion to buy grain for food. When we came to the lodge and opened our sacks, behold, there was each man's money at the opening of the sack, the full amount of our money. So we've returned it in our hand.

Moreover, we've brought down other money in our hand to buy grain for food. We didn't know who put our money into our sacks."

"Be at peace," he replied. "Don't be afraid. Your God and the God of your father has given you treasure in your sacks. Your money had come to me."

Then he brought Simeon out to them, and the man brought the men into Joseph's house, gave them water and they washed their feet. He also provided fodder for their donkeys.

So they prepared the offering for Joseph's coming at noon, for they had heard that they were going to eat there.

When Joseph came home, they brought him the offering in their hand into the house, and they bowed down to the ground to him. Then he asked if they were well, and said, "Is he well—your elderly father that you told me about? Is he still alive?"

"Your servant, our father, is well," they said. "He's still alive." Then they knelt and bowed down.

Then he lifted his eyes and saw his brother Benjamin, his mother's son, and said, "Is this your youngest brother whom you mentioned to me?"

Then he said, "May God be gracious to you, my son." Then Joseph hurried out because his compassion grew warm and tender toward his brother so that he wanted to cry. So he went into an inner room and wept there. Then he washed his face, came out, and controlled himself. "Serve the food," he said.

So they served him by himself, them by themselves, and the Egyptians who were eating with him by themselves (for Egyptians could not eat with the Hebrews because it was an abomination to Egyptians).

They were seated before him, the firstborn according to his birthright and the youngest according to his youth. The men looked at each other in astonishment.

Then portions were brought to them from before him—and Benjamin's portion was five times larger than any of their portions. Yet they drank and made merry with him.

Genesis, chapter 43

Then he commanded the one over his

household saying, "Fill the men's sacks with as much food as they are able to carry and put money in the opening of each man's sack. Put my cup, the silver cup, in the opening of the sack of the youngest along with his grain money." So he did as Joseph told him.

When the morning dawned, the men were sent off, they and their donkeys.

They left the city and did not get far, when Joseph said to the one over his household, "Get up, go after the men. When you catch up to them, say to them, "Why have you repaid evil for good? Isn't this the one from which my lord drinks? He even uses it especially to discern by divination. What you've done is evil!"

So he caught up to them and spoke these words to them.

They said to him, "Why does my lord say such things? Far be it from your servants to do such a thing as this. Look, the money we found in the opening of our bags, we brought back to you from the land of Canaan. So how could we steal silver or gold from your lord's house? Whoever among your servants is found with it, let him die! And we, we'll also be my lord's slaves."

"Even now let it be according to your words," he said. "The one with whom it is found shall be my slave. But the rest of you shall be innocent."

Then each man quickly lowered his sack to the ground and each man opened his sack. He searched them beginning with the eldest and finishing with the youngest, and the cup was found in Benjamin's sack.

Then they tore their clothing, and each one loaded up his donkey and they returned to the city.

When Judah and his brothers entered Joseph's house, he was still there. They fell to the ground before him.

"What's this deed you've done?" Joseph said to them, "Didn't you know that a man like me can discern by divination?"

Then Judah said, "What can we say to my lord? What can we speak? How can we justify ourselves? God has exposed your servants' guilt. We are now my lord's slaves—both we as well as the one in whose hand the cup was found."

But he said, "Far be it from me to do this. The one in whose hand the cup was found—he will be my slave. But you, go up to your father in peace."

Then Judah approached him and said, "I beg your pardon, my lord. Please let your servant say a word in my lord's ears, and don't be angry with your servant, since you are like Pharaoh.

My lord asked his servants saying, 'Do you have a father or a brother?' So we said to my lord, 'We have a father who is old, a child born to him of his old age is young. Now his brother is dead, so he is the only one of his mother's children left, and his father loves him.'

Then you said to your servants, 'Bring him down to me so that I can look at him.' But we said to my lord, 'The boy cannot leave his father. If he were to leave his father, he would die.'

Then you said to your servants, 'Unless your youngest brother comes down with you, you won't see my face again.'

"Now when we went up to your servant, my father, we told him my lord's words. Then our father said, 'Go back, buy us a little grain for food.' So we said, 'We won't go down unless we have our youngest brother with us—then we'll go down. For we won't see the man's face unless our youngest brother is with us.'

"Then your servant my father said to us, 'You yourselves know that my wife bore me two sons. One went out from me, so I said, "He must have been torn to shreds," and I haven't seen him since. And if you also take this one away from before me and an accident happens to him, then you'll bring my grey hair down to the evil of *Sheol*.'

"Now if I come to your servant my father and the boy isn't with us, since his life is bound to his life, when he sees that the boy is no more, he'll die.

Then your servants will bring the grey hair of your servant our father down to *Sheol* in grief. For your servant became pledge for the boy with my father saying, 'If I don't bring him back to you, I will bear the blame before my father all my days.'

So now, please let your servant remain as my lord's slave in the boy's place, and let the boy go up with his brothers. For how can I go up to my father and the boy is not with me? Else I must see the evil that would come upon my father!"

Genesis, chapter 44

Now Joseph could no longer restrain himself in front of all those who were standing by him, so he cried out, "Get everyone away from me!" So no one stood with him when Joseph made himself known to his brothers.

But he gave his voice to weeping so that the Egyptians heard, and Pharaoh's household heard.
Joseph said to his brothers, "I am Joseph! Is my father still alive?"
And his brothers were unable to answer him because they were terrified at his presence.

Then Joseph said to his brothers, "Please come near me." So they came near. "I'm Joseph, your brother—the one you sold to Egypt," he said.

"So now, don't be grieved and don't be angry in your own eyes that you sold me here—since it was for preserving life that God sent me here before you. For there has been two years of famine in the land, and there will be five more years yet with no plowing or harvesting.

But God sent me ahead of you to ensure a remnant in the land and to keep you alive for a great escape.
So now, it wasn't you, you didn't send me here, but God! And He made me as a father to Pharaoh, lord over his whole house and ruler over the entire land of Egypt.

Then Joseph said to his brothers, "Please come near me." So they came near. "I'm Joseph, your brother—the one you sold to Egypt," he said. "So now, don't be grieved and don't be angry in your own eyes that you sold me here—since it was for preserving life that God sent me here before you.

Genesis 45:4-5 TLV

"Go up quickly to my father and say to him, 'Thus says your son, Joseph: God has made me lord over all Egypt. Come down to me. Don't delay. Then you'll live in the land of Goshen, and be close to me, you and your children and your children's children, your flocks and your cattle, and everything that belongs to you. I'll provide food for you there—for the famine will last another five years—otherwise you'll lose everything, you and your household, and everything that belongs to you.'

And look, you and my brother Benjamin can see with your own eyes that it's my mouth that's speaking to you. You must tell my father about all my honor in Egypt, and about all that you've seen. And you must quickly bring my father down here."

Then he fell upon his brother Benjamin's neck and wept while Benjamin wept upon his neck, and he kissed all his brothers and wept upon them. Finally after this, his brothers talked with him.

When the commotion was heard in Pharaoh's house—"Joseph's brothers have come!"—it was good in the eyes of Pharaoh and his servants, so Pharaoh said to Joseph,

"Say to your brothers: 'Do this! Load your animals and go to the land of Canaan. Then get your father, your households, and come to me. I'll give you the best of the land of Egypt, and you will eat the fat of the land.'

You are also commanded to say: "Do this! Take for yourselves wagons from the land of Egypt for your little children and for your wives, and pick up your father and come. Don't be concerned about your goods, because the best of all the land of Egypt is yours.'"

So the sons of Israel did so. Joseph gave them carts by Pharaoh's command and he gave them provisions for the journey.

To each of them he gave a change of clothes, while to Benjamin he gave 300 pieces of silver and five sets of clothes. Also to his father he sent the following: ten donkeys carrying from the best of Egypt, and ten female donkeys carrying grain and food and provisions for his father's journey. Then he sent his brothers off, and as they departed, he said to them, "Don't be anxious on the way."

Then they went up from Egypt and came to the land of Canaan, to Jacob their father. They told him saying, "Joseph is still alive and he is ruler of the whole land of Egypt!"

His heart went numb, for he did not believe them. But they told him all of Joseph's words that he had told them. When he saw the wagons that Joseph had sent to pick him up, the spirit of their father Jacob revived. Then Israel said, "Enough! My son Joseph is still alive. I must go and see him, before I die."

Genesis, chapter 45

12. God Blesses the Sons

Then Joseph came and informed Pharaoh, "My father and my brothers and their flocks and their cattle and everything that belongs to them have come from the land of Canaan, and behold, they are in the land of Goshen."

From among his brothers he took five men and presented them before Pharaoh. Pharaoh said to his brothers, "What is your occupation?"

So they said to Pharaoh, "Your servants are shepherds, both we and our fathers."

Then they said to Pharaoh, "We came to dwell temporarily in the land, since there is no pasture for the flocks that belong to your servants, for the famine is severe in the land of Canaan. So now, please let your servants live in the land of Goshen."

Pharaoh said to Joseph saying, "Your father and your brothers came to you. The land of Egypt is before you—settle your father and your brothers in the best part of the land. Let them live in the land of Goshen. If you know of any capable men among them, make them overseers of the livestock—over those that are mine."

Then Joseph brought his father Jacob and presented him before Pharaoh, and Jacob blessed Pharaoh.
Pharaoh asked Jacob, "How many days are the years of your life?"
Jacob said to Pharaoh, "The days of the years of my sojourn are 130 years. Few and evil have been the days of the years of my life. Moreover, the days of the years of my life have not attained the days of the years of the lives of my fathers, in the days of their sojourn."

And Jacob blessed Pharaoh and went out from Pharaoh's presence.

Joseph settled his father and his brothers and gave them property in the land of Egypt, in the best part of the land, in the land of Rameses, just as Pharaoh commanded. And Joseph supported his father and his brothers and his father's entire household with food for the mouths of the little ones.

Now there was no food in all the land because the famine was very severe. Both the land of Egypt and the land of Canaan languished because of the famine. Joseph collected all the money that could be found in the land of Egypt and in the land of Canaan for the grain that they bought, and Joseph brought the money into Pharaoh's house.

Then the money of the land of Egypt and of the land of Canaan ran out and all of Egypt came to Joseph saying, "Give us food. Why should we die in front of you because the money is gone?"

Joseph said, "Give your livestock and I'll give it to you for your livestock if the money is gone."

So they brought their livestock to Joseph and Joseph gave them food in exchange for horses, for flocks of sheep, for herds of cattle and for donkeys. He provided them with food in exchange for all their livestock that year.

When that year came to an end, they came to him in the second year and said to him, "We won't hide from my lord that the money has run out and the livestock and the domestic animals are my lord's. There is nothing left in my lord's sight except our bodies and our land.

Why should we die before your eyes—both we and our land? Buy us and our land for food—we and our land will become Pharaoh's slaves. Provide seed so that we may live and not die, and the land won't be deserted."

So Joseph bought all the land of Egypt for Pharaoh because the Egyptians, each one, sold his field, for the famine overcame them. Thus the land became Pharaoh's.

He made the people slaves from one end of Egypt's border to the other. Only he did not buy the land belonging to the priests, because the priests had an allotment from Pharaoh, and they ate their allotment that Pharaoh gave them. Therefore they did not sell their land.

Then Joseph said to the people, "Behold, I have bought you and your land today for Pharaoh. Here is seed for you, so that you can sow the land. During the harvest you must give a fifth part to Pharaoh and four-fifths will be for you, for seed for the field and for your food, and for those in your houses, and for food for your little ones."

"You've saved our lives," they said. "We find favor in the eyes of my lord, and we'll be Pharaoh's slaves."

So Joseph set it as a statute until this very day concerning the land of Egypt: a fifth-part goes to Pharaoh. Only the priests' land did not become Pharaoh's.

Meanwhile, Israel settled in the land of Egypt in the land of Goshen, acquired property in it, and were fruitful and multiplied greatly.

Now Jacob lived in the land of Egypt for 17 years, so the days of Jacob, the years of his life, were 147 years. As the time of Israel's death drew near, he called for his son Joseph and said to him, "If I have found favor in your eyes, please put your hand under my thigh and show me faithful kindness. Please do not bury me in Egypt. When I lie down with my fathers, you must carry me out of Egypt and bury me in their burial place."

So he said, "I myself will do according to your word."

"Swear to me," he said. So he swore to him. Then Israel bowed down in worship on the head of his staff.

Genesis, chapter 47

After these things, someone told Joseph, "Behold, your father is sick." So he took his two sons, Manasseh and Ephraim, with him.

When someone told Jacob, saying, "Behold, your son Joseph has come to you," Israel summoned his strength and sat up in the bed. Then Jacob said to Joseph, "*El*

Shaddai appeared to me in Luz, in the land of Canaan, and blessed me." He said to me, 'I am going to make you fruitful and multiply you and turn you into an assembly of peoples, and I will give this land to your seed after you as an everlasting possession.'

So now, your two sons, who were born to you in the land of Egypt before I came to you in Egypt, they are mine. Ephraim and Manasseh will be mine, just like Reuben and Simeon. Any descendent of yours whom you father after them will be yours; they will be identified by the names of their brothers for their inheritance.

Now as for me, when I came from Paddan, to my sorrow Rachel died along the way, in the land of Canaan, while we were still a distance from entering Ephrath. And I buried her there on the way to Ephrath (that is, Bethlehem)."

Then Israel saw Joseph's sons and said, "Who are these?"

Joseph said to his father, "They're my sons, whom God has given me here."

Then he said, "Please bring them to me, so I may bless them."

Now Israel's eyes had grown heavy with old age—he could not see. So he brought them near to him, and he kissed them and hugged them. Then Israel said to Joseph, "To see your face, I didn't expect—and look, God has let me see your offspring as well!"

Then Joseph took them from his knees and bowed with his face down to the ground. Then Joseph took the two of them—Ephraim with his right hand across from Israel's left, and Manasseh with his left hand across from Israel's right—and brought them close to him. But Israel stretched out his right hand and placed it upon Ephraim's head (though he was the younger), and his left hand upon Manasseh's head, crossing his hands (though Manasseh was the firstborn). Then he blessed Joseph and said,

"The God before whom my fathers
Abraham and Isaac walked,
The God who has shepherded me
  throughout my life to this day,
The Angel who redeemed me
  from all evil,
May He bless the boys,
and may they be called by my name,
  and by the name of my fathers,
  Abraham and Isaac.
May they multiply to a multitude
  in the midst of the land."

When Joseph saw that his father placed his right hand upon Ephraim's head, it was wrong in his eyes. So his took hold of his father's hand to remove it from Ephraim's head to Manasseh's head. Joseph said to his father, "Not like that, my father, because this one's the firstborn. Put your right hand upon his head."
But his father refused and said, "I know, my son, I know. He also will become a people, and he also will become great. But his younger brother will become greater than he and his seed will be the fullness of the nations." Then he blessed them that day saying,

"In you shall Israel bless by saying:

Then Joseph took the two of them—Ephraim with his right hand across from Israel's left, and Manasseh with his left hand across from Israel's right—and brought them close to him. But Israel stretched out his right hand and placed it upon Ephraim's head (though he was the younger), and his left hand upon Manasseh's head, crossing his hands (though Manasseh was the firstborn).

Genesis 48:13-14 TLV

'May God make you
like Ephraim and like Manasseh.'"

Thus he put Ephraim before Manasseh. Then Israel said to Joseph, "Look, I am about to die. But God will be with you and will bring you back to the land of your fathers. Now I myself give you one portion more than your brothers, that which I took from the hand of the Amorites with my sword and my bow."

Genesis, chapter 48

Jacob called his sons and said to them: "Gather together so that I can tell you what will happen to you in the last days. Be assembled and listen, sons of Jacob, and listen to Israel your father.

Reuben, my firstborn are you,
my vigor and firstborn of my power,
endowed with extra dignity,
endowed with extra strength—like
water boiling over you will not have
extra, for you got up into your
father's bed, when you defiled a
maid's couch.

Simeon and Levi are brothers,
instruments of violence are their
knives. In their secret counsel may
my soul not enter.
In their contingent may my honor
never be united. For in their anger
they slew men, and in their self-will
they maimed oxen.

Cursed be their anger for it was
strong and their rage for it was
cruel— I will disperse them in Jacob,
I will scatter them in Israel.

Judah, so you are—
your brothers will praise you:
Your hand will be
on your enemies' neck.
Your father's sons will
bow down to you.
A lion's cub is Judah—
from the prey, my son,
you have gone up.
He crouches, lies down like a lion,
or like a lioness—
who would rouse him?
The scepter will not
pass from Judah,
nor the ruler's staff
from between his feet,
until he to whom it belongs
will come.
To him will be the obedience
of the peoples.
Binding his foal to the vine,
his donkey's colt to the choice vine,
he washes his garments in wine,
and in the blood of grapes his robe.
His eyes are darker than wine,
and teeth that are whiter than milk.

Zebulun will dwell by the seashore,
and be by a harbor for ships—
his distant border reaches Sidon.

Issachar is a strong-boned donkey,
lying down between two
saddlebags. He saw that a resting
place was good, and that the land
was pleasant.
He leaned his shoulder
to bear a burden,
and became a forced laborer.

Dan will judge his people, as one of
the tribes of Israel. Let Dan be a
serpent beside a road, a viper beside
a path, who strikes a horse's heels,
so that its rider falls backward.
For your salvation I wait, *ADONAI*!
Gad—attackers will attack him,

but he will attack their heels.

Asher—rich is his food—
he will provide delicacies
fit for a king.

Naphtali is a doe let loose,
who offers words of beauty.
A fruitful son is Joseph,
a fruitful son beside a spring—
daughters walk along a wall.
The archers were bitter
and shot arrows
and were hostile towards him.
Yet his bow was always filled,
and his arms quick-moving—
by the hands
of the Mighty One of Jacob.
From there a Shepherd,
the Stone of Israel,
from the God of your father
who helps you,
and *Shaddai* who blesses you,
with blessings of heavens above,
blessings of the deep
that lies below,
blessings of breasts and womb.
The blessings of your father
surpassed the blessings of the
ancient mountains,
the desire of the everlasting hills.
May they be upon
Joseph's head,
upon the crown of the one
set apart from his brothers.

Benjamin is a ravening wolf—
in the morning he devours spoils,
and in the evening
divides plunder."

These are the tribes of Israel, twelve in all, and this is what their father spoke to them. He blessed them, each one he blessed with a suitable blessing.

Then he charged them and said to them, "I am about to be gathered to my people. Bury me with my fathers in the cave that is in the field of Ephron the Hittite, in the cave that is in the field of Machpelah, that is next to Mamre in the land of Canaan—the field that Abraham bought from Ephron the Hittite as a property for burial. There they buried Abraham and his wife Sarah. There they buried Isaac and Rebekah, and there I buried Leah. The field was purchased along with the cave in it from the sons of Het."

When Jacob finished commanding his sons, he drew his feet up into the bed, then breathed his last and was gathered to his peoples.

Genesis, chapter 49

Joseph fell upon his father's face, wept over him and kissed him. Then Joseph commanded his servants the physicians to embalm his father, so the physicians embalmed Israel. They took 40 days for him, because that is how long embalming takes, and Egypt wept 70 days.

When the days of formal weeping passed, Joseph spoke to Pharaoh's house saying, "If I've found favor in your eyes, please say in Pharaoh's ears, "My father made me take an oath saying, 'Behold, I am about to die. In my tomb—which I dug for myself in the land of Canaan—there you must bury me.' So now, please allow me to go up and bury my father, and then return." Pharaoh said, "Go up and bury your father just as he made you swear on oath."

So Joseph went up to bury his

father. Also all of Pharaoh's servants, the elders of his household and all the elders of the land of Egypt went up with him, along with all of Joseph's house, his brothers, and his father's household. Only their children and their flocks and cattle were left in the land of Goshen. Chariots and horsemen also went up with him—it was a very impressive company.

When they came to the threshing floor of the bramble on the other side of the Jordan, they mourned there—a very great and solemn lamentation. He observed seven days of mourning for his father.

When the inhabitants of the land, the Canaanites, saw the mourning ritual at the threshing floor of the prickly bush, they said, "A solemn mourning ritual this is for the Egyptians." That is why it is named Abel-Mizraim, which is on the other side of the Jordan.

So Jacob's sons did for him just as he commanded them. His sons carried him to the land of Canaan and buried him in the cave of the field of Machpelah, the field that Abraham bought as a property for burial from Ephron the Hittite, next to Mamre.

After burying his father, Joseph returned to Egypt, he and his brothers and all those who went up with him to bury his father. When Joseph's brothers saw that their father had died, they said, "Maybe Joseph will be hostile towards us and pay us back in full for all the evil we showed him.

So they charged Joseph saying, "Before his death, your father gave a command, saying, "Thus you must say to Joseph: 'Please forgive, I beg you, the transgression of your brothers and their sin because they treated you wrongly.' Therefore, please forgive the transgression of the servants of the God of your father."

Then Joseph wept when they spoke to him, and his brothers also came and fell down before him and said, "Behold, we are your slaves!"

But Joseph said to them, "Don't be afraid. For am I in the place of God? Yes, you yourselves planned evil against me. God planned it for good, in order to bring about what it is this day—to preserve the lives of many people. So now, don't be afraid. I myself will provide food for you and your little ones." So he reassured them, speaking kindly to them.

Joseph remained in Egypt—he and his father's household—and Joseph lived 110 years. Joseph saw the third generation of Ephraim's sons. Also the sons of Machir, Manasseh's son, were born upon Joseph's knees. Then Joseph said to his brothers, "I'm about to die. But God will surely take notice of you and will bring you up from this land to the land that He swore to Abraham, to Isaac, and to Jacob."

Then Joseph made Israel's sons swear an oath saying, "When God takes notice of you, you will bring my bones up from here."

So Joseph died at 110 years old, and they embalmed him and he was placed in a coffin in Egypt.

Genesis, chapter 50

13. God Rescues a Baby

Now these are the names of *Bnei-Yisrael* who came into Egypt with Jacob, each man with his family: Reuben, Simeon, Levi and Judah; Issachar, Zebulun and Benjamin; Dan, Naphtali, Gad and Asher. The souls that came out of the line of Jacob numbered 70 in all, while Joseph was already in Egypt. Then Joseph died, as did all his brothers and all that generation. Yet *Bnei-Yisrael* were fruitful, increased abundantly, multiplied and grew extremely numerous—so the land was filled with them.

Now there arose a new king over Egypt, who did not know Joseph.

He said to his people, "Look, the people of *Bnei-Yisrael* are too numerous and too powerful for us. Come, we must deal shrewdly with them, or else they will grow even more numerous, so that if war breaks out, they may join our enemies, fight against us, and then escape from the land."

So they set slave masters over them to afflict them with forced labor, and they built Pithom and Raamses as storage cities for Pharaoh. But the more they afflicted them, the more they multiplied and the more they spread. So the Egyptians dreaded the presence of *Bnei-Yisrael*. They worked them harshly, and made their lives bitter with hard labor with mortar and brick, doing all sorts of work in the fields. In all their labors they worked them with cruelty.

Moreover the king of Egypt spoke to the Hebrew midwives, one of whom was named Shiphrah and the other Puah, and said, "When you help the Hebrew women during childbirth, look at the sex. If it's a son, then kill him, but if it's a daughter, she may live."

Yet the midwives feared God, so they did not do as the king of Egypt commanded them, but let the boys live. So the king of Egypt summoned the midwives and said to them, "Why have you done this—let the boys live?"

The midwives told Pharaoh, "Because the Hebrew women are not like Egyptian women. They are like animals, and give birth before the midwife comes to them."

So God was good to the midwives, and the people multiplied, growing very numerous. Because the midwives feared God, He gave them families of their own. But Pharaoh charged all his people saying, "You are to cast every son that is born into the river, but let every daughter live."

Exodus, chapter 1

Now a man from the house of Levi took as his wife a daughter of Levi. The woman conceived and gave birth to a son. Now when she saw that he was delightful, she hid him for three months. But when she could no longer hide him, she took a basket of papyrus reeds, coated it with tar and pitch, put the child inside, and laid it in the reeds by the bank of the Nile. His sister stood off at a distance to see what would happen to him. Then the

Then the daughter of Pharaoh came down to bathe, while her maidens walked along by the riverside. When she saw the basket among the reeds, she sent her handmaiden to fetch it. When she opened it, she saw the child—a baby boy crying!

Exodus 2:5-6a TLV

daughter of Pharaoh came down to bathe, while her maidens walked along by the riverside. When she saw the basket among the reeds, she sent her handmaiden to fetch it. When she opened it, she saw the child—a baby boy crying! She had compassion on him and said, "This is one of the Hebrew children."

Then his sister said to Pharaoh's daughter, "Should I go and call a nurse from the Hebrews to nurse the child for you?"

Pharaoh's daughter told her, "Go!" So the girl went and called the child's mother.

Then Pharaoh's daughter said to her, "Take this child and nurse him for me, and I will pay you your wages." So the woman took the child and nursed him. After the boy grew older she brought him to Pharaoh's daughter and he became her son. So she named him Moses saying, "Because I drew him out of the water."

Now it happened in those days, after Moses had grown up, that he went out to his brothers and saw their burdens. He noticed an Egyptian beating a Hebrew, one of his own people. So he looked around and when he saw that there was nobody, he killed the Egyptian and hid him in the sand. Then he went out the following day, and saw two Hebrew men fighting. So he said to the guilty one, "Why are you beating your companion?"

But the man answered, "Who made you a ruler and a judge over us? Are you saying you're going to kill me—just as you killed the Egyptian?" Then Moses was afraid, and thought, "For sure the deed had become known." When Pharaoh heard about this, he tried to kill Moses.

But Moses fled from Pharaoh and settled in the land of Midian, where he sat down by a well. Now the priest of Midian had seven daughters who came and drew water. They filled the troughs to water their father's flock. But shepherds came and drove them away, so Moses stood up, helped them and watered their flock. When they came to Reuel their father, he said, "How come you've returned so soon today?"

So they told him, "An Egyptian delivered us out of the hand of the shepherds. He also drew water for us and watered the flock."

"Where is he then?" he said to his daughters. "Why did you leave the man behind? Invite him to have some food to eat!" Moses was content to stay on with the man. Later he gave Moses his daughter Zipporah. She gave birth to a son and he named him Gershom, saying, "I have been an outsider in a foreign land."

Now it came about over the course of those many days that the king of Egypt died. *Bnei-Yisrael* groaned because of their slavery. They cried out and their cry from slavery went up to God. God heard their sobbing and remembered His covenant with Abraham, Isaac, and Jacob. God saw *Bnei-Yisrael*, and He was concerned about them.

Exodus, chapter 2

14. God Calls to Moses

Now Moses was tending the flock of his father-in-law Jethro, the priest of Midian. So he led the flock to the farthest end of the wilderness, coming to the mountain of God, Horeb.

Then the angel of *ADONAI* appeared to him in a flame of fire from within a bush. So he looked and saw the bush burning with fire, yet it was not consumed.

Moses thought, "I will go now, and see this great sight. Why is the bush not burnt?"

When *ADONAI* saw that he turned to look, He called to him out of the midst of the bush and said, **"Moses, Moses!"**

So he answered, "*Hineni.*"

Then He said, **"Come no closer. Take your sandals off your feet, for the place where you are standing is holy ground."** Moreover He said, **"I am the God of your father, the God of Abraham, Isaac and Jacob."** So Moses hid his face, because he was afraid to look at God.

Then *ADONAI* said, **"I have surely seen the affliction of My people who are in Egypt, and have heard their cry because of their slave masters, for I know their pains. So I have come down to deliver them out of the hand of the Egyptians, to bring them up out of that land into a good and large land, a land flowing with milk and honey, into the place of the Canaanites, Hittites, Amorites, Perizzites, Hivites and Jebusites.**

Now behold, the cry of *Bnei-Yisrael* has come to Me. Moreover I have seen the oppression that the Egyptians have inflicted on them. Come now, I will send you to Pharaoh, so that you may bring My people *Bnei-Yisrael* out from Egypt."

But Moses said to God, "Who am I, that I should go to Pharaoh, and bring *Bnei-Yisrael* out of Egypt?"

So He said, **"I will surely be with you. So that will be the sign to you that it is I who have sent you. When you have brought the people out of Egypt: you will worship God on this mountain."**

But Moses said to God, "Suppose I go to *Bnei-Yisrael* and say to them, 'The God of your fathers has sent me to you,' and they ask me, 'What is His Name?' What should I say to them?

God answered Moses, **"I AM WHO I AM."**

Then He said, **"You are to say to *Bnei-Yisrael*, 'I AM' has sent me to you."**

God also said to Moses: **"You are to say to *Bnei-Yisrael*, *ADONAI*, the God of your fathers, the God of Abraham, Isaac and Jacob, has sent me to you. This is My Name forever, and the Name by which I should be remembered from generation to generation.**

"Go now, gather the elders of Israel together, and say to them: '*ADONAI*,

Then He said, "Come no closer. Take your sandals off your feet, for the place where you are standing is holy ground." Moreover He said, "I am the God of your father, the God of Abraham, Isaac and Jacob." So Moses hid his face, because he was afraid to look at God.

Exodus 3:5-6 TLV

the God of your fathers—the God of Abraham, Isaac and Jacob—has appeared to me, saying, I have been paying close attention to you and have seen what is done to you in Egypt. So I promise I will bring you up out of the affliction of Egypt, into the land of the Canaanites, Hittites, Amorites, Perizzites, Hivites and Jebusites, to a land flowing with milk and honey.'

"They will listen to your voice. So you will go, you along with the elders of Israel, to the king of Egypt, and say to him: '*ADONAI*, the God of the Hebrews, has met with us. Now please let us take a three-day journey into the wilderness, so that we may sacrifice to *ADONAI* our God.'

Nevertheless, I know that the king of Egypt will not let you go, except by a mighty hand. So I will stretch out My hand and strike Egypt with all My wonders that I will do in the midst of it. After that, he will let you go. "Then I shall grant these people favor in the eyes of the Egyptians. So it will happen that when you go, you will not leave empty-handed.

Every woman is to ask her neighbor and the woman who lives in her house for silver and gold jewelry and clothing. You will put them on your sons and your daughters. So you will plunder the Egyptians."

Exodus, chapter 3

Then Moses said, "But look, they will not believe me or listen to my voice. They will say, '*ADONAI* has not appeared to you.'"

So *ADONAI* said to him, **"What is that in your hand?"**

"A staff," he said.

Then He said, **"Cast it on the ground."** When he cast it to the ground, it became a serpent, so Moses fled from before it.

Then *ADONAI* said to Moses, **"Stretch out your hand, and take it by the tail."** So he put out his hand, laid hold of it, and it became a staff in his hand.

"This is so that they may believe *ADONAI*, the God of their fathers—the God of Abraham, Isaac and Jacob—has appeared to you." *ADONAI* also said to him, **"Now put your hand within your cloak."** So he put his hand inside, and when he took it out, his hand had *tzara'at*—white as snow. Then He said, **"Put your hand back into your cloak."** So he put his hand back in, and when he took it out it was restored again as the rest of his skin.

Then He said, **"If they do not believe you, or listen to the voice of the first sign, they will believe the message of the latter sign. But if they do not believe even these two signs nor listen to your voice, you are to take the water of the river and pour it on the dry land. The water which you take out of the river will become blood on the ground."**

But Moses said to *ADONAI*, "*ADONAI*, I am not a man of words—not yesterday, nor the day before, nor since You have spoken to Your servant—because I have a slow mouth and a heavy tongue."

So *Adonai* said to him, **"Who made man's mouth? Or who makes a man mute or deaf, seeing or blind? Is it not I, *Adonai*? Now go! I will be with your mouth and teach you what to say."**

But he said, "Please, please, send it by another hand."

Then the anger of *Adonai* was kindled against Moses, so He said, **"In fact, Aaron the Levite is your brother. I know that he can speak well. Moreover, he is on his way to meet you! When he sees you, he will be glad in his heart. You are to speak to him and put the words in his mouth. I will be with your mouth and with his, and teach you what to do. He will be your spokesman to the people, so that he may act as a mouthpiece for you, and it will be as if you were as God for him. Now then, you must take this staff in your hand to do the signs."**

So Moses went, returned to his father -in-law Jethro and said to him, "Please let me go, so I may return to my kinsmen who are in Egypt and see whether they are still alive."

Jethro said to Moses, "Go in peace."

Then *Adonai* said to Moses in Midian, **"Go, return to Egypt, for all the men that sought your life are dead."**

So Moses took his wife and his sons, set them on a donkey and returned to the land of Egypt. Moses took the staff of God in his hand.

Adonai said to Moses, **"When you go back to Egypt, see that you do all the wonders before Pharaoh**
That I have put in your hand.
Still, I will harden his heart, and he will not let the people go.
You are to say to Pharaoh, "This is what *Adonai says*: 'Israel is My son, My firstborn. So I have said to you, Let My son go, that he may serve Me, but you have refused to let him go. Behold, I will slay your son, your firstborn.'"

It happened along the way, at a lodging place, that *Adonai* met him and sought to kill him! But Zipporah took a flint, cut off the foreskin of her son, and threw it at his feet, saying, "You are surely a bridegroom of blood to me."

She said, "A bridegroom of blood" because of the circumcision. Then He let him alone.

Now *Adonai* said to Aaron, **"Go into the wilderness to meet Moses."**

So he went and met him at the mountain of God, and kissed him. Then Moses told Aaron all the words of *Adonai* with which He had been sent, along with all the signs that He had commanded him to do.

Then Moses and Aaron went and assembled all the elders of *Bnei-Yisrael*. Aaron spoke all the words that *Adonai* had spoken to Moses and did the signs in the sight of the people. So the people believed. When they heard that *Adonai* had remembered *Bnei-Yisrael* and had seen their affliction, they bowed their heads and worshipped.

Exodus, chapter 4

15. God Challenges Pharaoh

Afterward, Moses and Aaron went and said to Pharaoh, "This is what *ADONAI*, God of Israel, says: **Let My people go, so that they may hold a feast for Me in the wilderness."**

But Pharaoh said, "Who is *ADONAI*, that I should listen to His voice and let Israel go? I do not know *ADONAI*, and besides, I will not let Israel go."

They answered, "The God of the Hebrews has met with us. Please let us take a three-day journey into the wilderness, so we may sacrifice to *ADONAI* our God, or else He may strike us with pestilence or with the sword."

But the king of Egypt said to them, "Why do you, Moses and Aaron, make the people break loose from their work? Go to your labors!"

Then Pharaoh said, "Look, the people of the land are now so numerous, yet you would have them rest from their labors?"

Then on the same day Pharaoh commanded the slave masters of the people and their foremen saying, "You are not to give the people any more straw to make bricks, as before. Let them go and gather straw for themselves. But impose on them the quota of bricks that they made previously; don't reduce it. For they are lazy—that's why they cry out saying, 'Let us go and sacrifice to our God.'

Let even heavier work be laid upon the men, so that they must labor, paying no attention to deceptive words."

Then the slave masters of the people went out, along with their officers, and they spoke to the people saying: "This is what Pharaoh says: I will not give you straw. Go and get straw for yourselves wherever you can find it, for there will be no reduction of your work."

So the people were scattered throughout all the land of Egypt to gather stubble for straw. But the slave masters pressured, saying, "Fulfill your work, your daily amount, just as when there was straw." Moreover the foremen of *Bnei-Yisrael*, whom Pharaoh's slave masters had set over them, were beaten and asked, "Why haven't you met your quota of bricks, both yesterday and today like before?"

The foremen of *Bnei-Yisrael* came and cried out to Pharaoh saying, "Why do you deal this way with your servants? No straw is given to your servants, yet they say to us, 'Make bricks!' and look, your servants are beaten. But it is your own people at fault."

But he said, "Lazy! You're lazy! That's why you were saying, 'Let us go and sacrifice to *ADONAI*.' So go now and work! No straw will be given to you—but you must deliver the quota of bricks."

So the foremen of *Bnei-Yisrael* saw that they were in trouble when they were told, "You are not to reduce the number of bricks from day to day."

Then they met Moses and Aaron, who were waiting for them as they came from Pharaoh. So they said to them, "May *Adonai* look on you and judge, because you have made us a stench in the eyes of Pharaoh and in the eyes of his servants—putting a sword in their hand to kill us!"

So Moses returned to *Adonai* and said, "*Adonai*, why have You brought evil on these people? Is this why You sent me? Ever since I came to Pharaoh to speak in Your Name, he has brought evil on these people. You have not delivered Your people at all."

Exodus, chapter 5

Adonai said to Moses, **"Now you will see what I am going to do to Pharaoh. By way of a strong hand he will let them go, and drive them out of his land."**

God spoke further to Moses and said to him, **"I am *Adonai*. I appeared to Abraham, to Isaac and to Jacob, as *El Shaddai*. Yet by My Name, *Adonai*, did I not make Myself known to them. I also established My covenant with them, to give them the land of Canaan, the land of their pilgrimage where they journeyed.**

Furthermore, I have heard the groaning of *Bnei-Yisrael*, whom the Egyptians are keeping in bondage. So I have remembered My covenant.

Therefore say to *Bnei-Yisrael*: I am *Adonai*, and I will bring you out from under the burdens of the Egyptians. I will deliver you from their bondage, and I will redeem you with an outstretched arm and with great judgments. I will take you to Myself as a people, and I will be your God.

You will know that I am *Adonai* your God, who brought you out from under the burdens of the Egyptians. So I will bring you into the land that I swore to give to Abraham, to Isaac and to Jacob, and give it to you as an inheritance. I am *Adonai*."

Moses spoke this way to *Bnei-Yisrael*, but they did not listen to him because of their broken spirit and cruel bondage.

So *Adonai* told Moses, **"Go, speak to Pharaoh king of Egypt, so that will he let *Bnei-Yisrael* go out of his land."**

But Moses said to *Adonai*, "*Bnei-Yisrael* have not listened to me. So how would Pharaoh listen to me—I, who have uncircumcised lips?"

Then *Adonai* spoke to Moses and to Aaron and gave to them a charge for *Bnei-Yisrael* and Pharaoh king of Egypt, to bring *Bnei-Yisrael* out of the land of Egypt.

These are the heads of their father's houses. The sons of Reuben the firstborn of Israel were Hanoch, Pallu, Hezron and Carmi. These are the families of Reuben.

The sons of Simeon were Jemuel, Jamin, Ohad, Jachin, Zohar and Shaul the son of a Canaanite woman. These are the families of Simeon.

These are the names of the sons of Levi according to their generations: Gershon, Kohath and Merari. Levi lived 137 years. The sons of Gershon were Libni and Shimei, according to their families.

The sons of Kohath were Amram, Izhar, Hebron and Uzziel. Kohath lived 133 years. The sons of Merari were Mahli and Mushi.
These are the families of the Levites according to their generations. Amram married Jochebed, his father's sister, and she bore him Aaron and Moses. Amram lived 137 years.

The sons of Izhar were Korah, Nepheg and Zichri. The sons of Uzziel were Mishael, Elzaphan and Sithri.

Aaron married Elisheba daughter of Amminadav, sister of Nahshon, and she bore him Nadab and Abihu, Eleazar and Ithamar.

The sons of Korah were Assir, Elkanah and Abiasaph. These are the families of the Korahites.

Eleazar, Aaron's son, married one of the daughters of Putiel and she bore him Phinehas.

These are the heads of the ancestral houses of the Levites according to their families.These are the same Aaron and Moses to whom *ADONAI* said, **"Bring *Bnei-Yisrael* out from the land of Egypt according to their divisions."**

These are the ones that spoke to Pharaoh king of Egypt, to bring *Bnei-Yisrael* out from Egypt. These are that same Moses and Aaron. So it happened on the day when *ADONAI* spoke to Moses in the land of Egypt, that *ADONAI* said to Moses, **"I am *ADONAI*. Tell Pharaoh king of Egypt everything that I tell to you."** But Moses said to *ADONAI*, "I am of uncircumcised lips, so how would Pharaoh listen to me?"

Exodus, chapter 6

So *ADONAI* said to Moses, **"See, I have set you as God to Pharaoh, and Aaron your brother will be your prophet. You are to speak all that I command you and Aaron your brother is to speak to Pharaoh, so that he will let *Bnei-Yisrael* go out of his land. Yet I will harden Pharaoh's heart, and multiply My signs and wonders in the land of Egypt.**

But Pharaoh will not listen to you, so I will lay My hand upon Egypt, and bring forth My armies, My people *Bnei-Yisrael*, out of the land of Egypt by great judgments. The Egyptians will know that I am *ADONAI*, when I stretch out My hand against Egypt, and bring out *Bnei-Yisrael* from among them."

So Moses and Aaron did as *ADONAI* commanded them. Moses was eighty years old and Aaron eighty-three years old when they spoke to Pharaoh.

ADONAI told Moses and Aaron, **"When Pharaoh speaks to you saying, 'Prove yourselves with a miracle,' then you are to say to Aaron, 'Take your staff and cast it down before Pharaoh, so that it may become a serpent.'"**

So Moses and Aaron went in to Pharaoh and did as *ADONAI* had commanded. Aaron threw down his staff before Pharaoh and before his servants, and it became a serpent.

Then Pharaoh called for the wise men and the sorcerers, and they too, the magicians of Egypt, did the same with their secret arts. For each man threw down his staff, and they became serpents. But Aaron's staff swallowed up their staffs. Yet Pharaoh's heart was hardened. So he did not listen to them—just as *Adonai* had said.

Then *Adonai* said to Moses, **"Pharaoh's heart is stubborn; he refuses to let the people go. Go to Pharaoh in the morning as he is coming out to the water, and stand ready to meet him by the bank of the Nile. Take the staff that was transformed into a serpent in your hand. You are to say to him: *Adonai*, God of the Hebrews, has sent me to you, saying, 'Let My people go, so they may serve Me in the wilderness,' and behold, you have not listened. This is what *Adonai* says: 'By this you will know that I am *Adonai*. Behold, I will strike the waters that are in the river with the staff that is in my hand, and they will be turned to blood. The fish that are in the river will die, the river will become foul, and the Egyptians will hate to drink water from the Nile.'"**

Adonai said to Moses, **"Say to Aaron: Take your staff and stretch out your hand over the waters of Egypt, over their rivers, over their streams, over their pools and over all their ponds, so that they become blood. There will be blood throughout all the land of Egypt, even in wooden and stone containers."** So Moses and Aaron did as *Adonai* commanded. He lifted up the staff and struck the waters that were in the river in the sight of Pharaoh and his servants, and all the waters of the Nile turned to blood.

When the fish that were in the river died, the river became so foul that the Egyptians could not drink water from the river. The blood was throughout all the land of Egypt.

But the magicians of Egypt did the same with their secret arts. So Pharaoh's heart was hardened, and he did not listen to them—just as *Adonai* had said.

Pharaoh turned and went into his house, and did not even take it to heart. So all the Egyptians dug around the river for water to drink, because they could not drink of the water from the Nile.

Seven days were fulfilled after *Adonai* had struck the Nile.

Then *Adonai* said to Moses, **"Go to Pharaoh and say to him: This is what *Adonai* says: 'Let My people go, so they may serve Me. If you refuse to let them go, see, I will strike all your territory with frogs.**

The river will swarm with frogs. They will go up and enter your house, into your bedroom, upon your bed, into the houses of your servants, upon your people, into your ovens, and in your kneading bowls. The frogs will climb up on you, your people and all your servants.'"

Exodus, chapter 7

Then *Adonai* told Moses, **"Say to Aaron: Stretch out your hand with your staff over the rivers, canals and pools, and cause frogs to come up** over the land of Egypt." So Aaron

So Pharaoh said to him, "Go away from me! Take heed never to see my face again, because on the day you do, you will die!"
"Right!" Moses said. "You said it! May I never see your face again!"

Exodus 10:28-29 TLV

stretched out his hand over the waters of Egypt, and the frogs came up and covered the land. But the magicians did the same with their secret arts and brought up frogs over the land of Egypt.

Then Pharaoh called for Moses and Aaron and said, "Pray to *ADONAI*, that He would take the frogs away from me and from my people. Then I will let the people go, so they may sacrifice to *ADONAI*."

Moses answered Pharaoh, "Boast about me after I pray for you. When am I to pray for you, your servants and your people, that the frogs would be cut off from you and your houses, and remain only in the Nile?"

"Tomorrow," he said.

So he said, "Let it happen according to your word, so that you may know that there is none like *ADONAI* our God. The frogs will depart from you, from your houses, from your servants and from your people. They will remain only in the Nile."

After Moses and Aaron went out from Pharaoh, Moses cried out to *ADONAI* concerning the frogs, which He had brought upon Pharaoh.

So *ADONAI* acted according to the word of Moses, and the frogs died out in the houses, the courts and the fields. They piled them together in large heaps, and the land stank.

But when Pharaoh saw that there was relief, he hardened his heart and did not listen to them—just as *ADONAI* had said.

So *ADONAI* said to Moses, **"Tell Aaron, 'Stretch out your staff and strike the dust of the earth, and it will become gnats throughout all the land of Egypt.'"** So they did.

When Aaron stretched out his hand with his staff and struck the dust of the earth, there were gnats on men and animals. All the dust of the earth became gnats throughout all the land of Egypt. When the magicians attempted the same with their secret arts to bring forth gnats, they could not. There were gnats on men and animals. So the magicians said to Pharaoh, "This is the finger of God." But Pharaoh's heart was hardened, and he did not listen to them—just as *ADONAI* had said.

Then *ADONAI* said to Moses, **"Rise up early in the morning and stand before Pharaoh. As he comes to the water say to him, This is what *ADONAI* says: Let My people go, that they may serve Me. Or else, if you do not let My people go, I will send the swarm of flies on you and on your servants, on your people and into your houses. The houses of the Egyptians will be full of the swarm of flies including the ground that they stand on.**

"But on that day I will set apart the land of Goshen, where My people are dwelling—except no swarm of flies will be there—so that you may know that I, *ADONAI*, am in the midst of the earth. I will make a distinction between My people and your people. By tomorrow this sign will happen."

ADONAI did just so. A massive swarm of flies went into the house of

Pharaoh and into his servant's houses. All the land of Egypt was ruined because of the swarm of flies.

So Pharaoh called for Moses and for Aaron and said, "Go! Sacrifice to your God—in the land."

But Moses said, "That would not be right. For the offerings we intend to sacrifice to *ADONAI* our God are an abomination to the Egyptians. If we sacrifice what is an abomination to the Egyptians, wouldn't they stone us? We must walk a three-day journey into the wilderness and sacrifice to *ADONAI* our God—just as He tells us."

Pharaoh said, "I will let you go, so that you may sacrifice to *ADONAI* your God in the wilderness. Only you must not go very far away. Pray for me."

So Moses said, "See, I am leaving you, and I will pray to *ADONAI* that the swarm of flies will depart from Pharaoh, his servants and from his people tomorrow. However, let Pharaoh no longer deal deceitfully by not letting the people go sacrifice to *ADONAI*."

Then Moses went out from Pharaoh and prayed to *ADONAI*. *ADONAI* acted according to the word of Moses, and removed the swarm of flies from Pharaoh, from his servants and from his people. Nothing remained.

But Pharaoh hardened his heart this time also, and did not let the people go.

Exodus, chapter 8

Then *ADONAI* said to Moses, **"Go in to Pharaoh, and tell him: This is what *ADONAI*, the God of the Hebrews, says: 'Let My people go, so they may serve Me.' For if you refuse to let them go, and hold them still, behold, the hand of *ADONAI* will fall upon your livestock that are in the field—on the horses, donkeys, camels, herds and flocks. There will be a crushing plague. But *ADONAI* will make a distinction between the cattle of Israel and the cattle of Egypt, and nothing will die that belongs to *Bnei-Yisrael*."**

Also *ADONAI* set a specific time, saying, **"Tomorrow *ADONAI* will do this thing in the land."**

Then the next day, *ADONAI* did the deed. All the cattle of Egypt died, yet of the cattle of *Bnei-Yisrael*, not one died.

When Pharaoh inquired, there was not so much as one of the cattle of *Bnei-Yisrael* dead. But the heart of Pharaoh was stubborn, and he did not let the people go.

Then *ADONAI* said to Moses and Aaron, **"Take handfuls of soot from the furnace, and have Moses throw it heavenward in the sight of Pharaoh. It will become fine dust over all the land of Egypt, and will become boils erupting with sores on both men and animals throughout all the land."**

So they took soot from the furnace and stood before Pharaoh. When Moses threw it heavenward, it became boils erupting with sores on both men and animals. Moreover, the magicians could not stand before

Moses because of the boils, because they were on the magicians, as on all the Egyptians.

But *ADONAI* hardened the heart of Pharaoh, so he did not listen to them—just as *ADONAI* had said to Moses.

Then *ADONAI* said to Moses, **"Rise up early in the morning, stand before Pharaoh and say to him: This is what *ADONAI* the God of the Hebrews says: 'Let My people go, so they may serve Me. For this time I will send all My plagues to your heart, and on your servants and your people, so that you may know that there is none like Me in all the earth. Surely by now I could have stretched out My hand and struck you and your people with a plague that would have wiped you off the earth. However, I have let you stand for this reason: to show you My power, and that My Name might be proclaimed throughout all the earth. Yet still you exalt yourself over My people, by not letting them go.**

Behold, tomorrow at about this time, I will cause it to rain a very severe hailstorm, the likes of which has not occurred in Egypt since the day it was founded until now. Send word, shelter your cattle and all that you have in the field. For every person and animal found in the field and not brought home, when the hail comes down on them, they will die.'"

Whoever feared the word of *ADONAI* among the servants of Pharaoh had his own servants and cattle flee into the houses, but whoever disregarded the word of *ADONAI* left his servants and cattle in the field.

Then *ADONAI* said to Moses, **"Stretch out your hand toward heaven and let there be hail in all the land of Egypt, on people, animals and every plant of the field, throughout all the land."**

Whoever feared the word of *ADONAI* among the servants of Pharaoh had his own servants and cattle flee into the houses, but whoever disregarded the word of *ADONAI* left his servants and cattle in the field.

Then *ADONAI* said to Moses, **"Stretch out your hand toward heaven and let there be hail in all the land of Egypt, on people, animals and every plant of the field, throughout all the land."** So Moses stretched out his staff toward heaven, and *ADONAI* sent thunder and hail. Fire came down on the earth, as *ADONAI* rained hail on the land of Egypt. The hail fell very severely, with fire flashing up amidst the hail, the likes of which had not occurred in all the land of Egypt since it became a nation.

The hail struck down everything that was in the fields, both men and animals, all throughout the land of Egypt. It also struck every plant of the field and broke down every tree. Only in the land of Goshen, where *Bnei-Yisrael* were, was there no hail.

So Pharaoh sent, called for Moses and Aaron and said to them, "I have sinned this time. *ADONAI* is righteous, while I and my people are wicked. Pray to *ADONAI*—there has been enough of God's thunders and hail! I will let you go. You don't have to stay any longer."

Moses said to him, "As soon as I am gone out of the city, I will stretch out my hands to *ADONAI*. The thunder will cease and there will be no more hail—so you may know that the earth is *ADONAI*'s. But as for you and your servants, I know that you do not yet fear *ADONAI Elohim*."

(The flax and the barley were destroyed, because the barley was in the ear, and the flax was in bloom. But the wheat and the spelt were not destroyed, because they ripen later.)

Moses went out of the city, away from Pharaoh, and stretched out his hands to *ADONAI*. Then the thunder and hail ceased, and rain no longer poured down on the earth.

But when Pharaoh saw that the rain, the hail and the thunder had ceased, he increased his sin and hardened his heart, both he and his servants. So Pharaoh's heart was hardened and he did not let *Bnei-Yisrael* go—just as *ADONAI* had said by Moses' hand.
Exodus, chapter 9

Then *ADONAI* said to Moses, **"Go to Pharaoh, because I have hardened his heart and the heart of his servants, so that I might show these My signs in their midst, and so you may tell your son and your grandchildren what I have done in Egypt, as well as My signs that I did among them, so you may know that I am *ADONAI*."**

So Moses and Aaron went to Pharaoh and said to him, "This is what *ADONAI*, the God of the Hebrews, says: **How long would you refuse to humble yourself before Me? Let My people go, so they may serve Me.**

Or else, if you refuse to let My people go, behold, tomorrow I will bring locusts into your borders. Then they will cover the face of the earth, so that no one will be able to see the ground. They will eat the remainder of what escaped—whatever is left from the hail—and eat every tree that grows for you out in the field.

Your houses will be filled, as will the houses of all your servants and the houses of all the Egyptians, as neither your fathers nor your grandfathers have seen since the day they were on the earth until today!" Then he turned and went out from Pharaoh.

Pharaoh's servants said to him, "How long will this man be a snare to us? Send the men, so they may serve *ADONAI* their God. Don't you realize yet that Egypt is being destroyed?"

So Moses and Aaron were brought to Pharaoh again. "Go, serve *ADONAI* your God," he said. "But who will be going?"

Moses answered, "We will go with our young and our elderly, our sons and our daughters. We will go with our flocks and our herds—for we must have *ADONAI*'s feast for Him."

But he said to them, "So may *ADONAI* be with you, if I ever do let you go, with your little ones. See clearly now! Evil is in your face. Not so! Go now—the men—and serve *ADONAI*! For that's what you were seeking." Then they were driven out from Pharaoh's presence.

Then *ADONAI* said to Moses, **"Stretch**

out your hand over the land of Egypt for the locusts, so they may come up onto Egypt and eat every plant in the land—everything the hail has left."

So Moses stretched out his staff over the land of Egypt, and *ADONAI* brought an east wind over the land all that day and all night. When it was morning, the east wind brought the locusts.

The locusts came up over all the land of Egypt and rested on the entire territory of Egypt. So dense—there was nothing like it before them, nor will there ever be again. For they covered the face of the whole earth so that the land was darkened, and they ate every plant in the land and all the fruit from the trees that the hail had left. No green thing remained, not a tree or a plant of the field throughout all the land of Egypt.

Then Pharaoh quickly called for Moses and Aaron and said, "I have sinned against *ADONAI* your God and against you. Now forgive my sin, only this once, please! So pray to *ADONAI* your God—just so He would take this death away from me!"

So he went out from Pharaoh and prayed to *ADONAI*. Then *ADONAI* turned the wind from the west, very strong, and it carried off the locusts and drove them into the Sea of Reeds. Not one locust remained in all the territory of Egypt.

But *ADONAI* hardened Pharaoh's heart, and he did not let *Bnei-Yisrael* go.

Then *ADONAI* said to Moses, **"Stretch out your hand toward heaven, and there will be darkness over the land of Egypt—a darkness that may be felt."**

So Moses stretched out his hand toward heaven, and there was a thick darkness in all the land of Egypt for three days. They could not see one another, nor could anyone rise from his place for three days. Yet all *Bnei-Yisrael* had light within their dwellings.

Pharaoh called Moses and said, "Go, serve *ADONAI*. Only let your flocks and your herds remain. Your little ones may also go with you."

But Moses said, "You must also put sacrifices and burnt offerings into our hand, then we will do it for *ADONAI* our God. Our cattle must also go with us—not a hoof may be left behind. We must take from them to serve *ADONAI* our God. We ourselves will not know how we will serve *ADONAI* until we arrive there."

But *ADONAI* hardened Pharaoh's heart, and he was unwilling to let them go. So Pharaoh said to him, "Go away from me! Take heed never to see my face again, because on the day you do, you will die!"

"Right!" Moses said. "You said it! May I never see your face again!"

Exodus, chapter 10

Now *ADONAI* had said to Moses, **"I will bring one more plague upon Pharaoh and on Egypt. After that, he will let you go from here. When he lets you go, he will surely thrust you out altogether from here.**

Speak now into the ears of the people, and let every man ask from his neighbor and every woman from her neighbor for articles of silver and gold."

ADONAI gave the people favor in the eyes of the Egyptians. Indeed, the man Moses was very great in the land of Egypt, in the eyes of Pharaoh's servants and in the eyes of the people.

So Moses said, "This is what *ADONAI* says: **At around midnight I will go out into the midst of Egypt, and all the firstborn in the land of Egypt will die—from the firstborn of Pharaoh sitting on his throne to the firstborn of the maidservant behind the mill, along with all the firstborn cattle. There will be a great cry throughout all the land of Egypt, the likes of which has never been before nor will ever be again. But not so much as a dog will growl against any of *Bnei-Yisrael*, neither man nor beast—so that you may know that ADONAI makes a distinction between the Egyptians and Israel. All these servants of yours will come down to me and bow down to me, saying, 'Get out, you and all the people who follow you!'** After that, I will go." Then he went out from Pharaoh hot with anger.

ADONAI had said to Moses, **"Pharaoh will not listen to you, so that My wonders may be multiplied in the land of Egypt." So Moses and Aaron did all these wonders before Pharaoh, yet ADONAI hardened Pharaoh's heart, so he did not let *Bnei-Yisrael* go out of his land.**

Exodus, chapter 11

16. God Births a Nation

Now *Adonai* spoke to Moses and Aaron in the land of Egypt saying, **"This month will mark the beginning of months for you; it is to be the first month of the year for you.**

Tell all the congregation of Israel that on the tenth day of this month, each man is to take a lamb for his family one lamb for the household. But if the household is too small for a lamb, then he and his nearest neighbor are to take one according to the number of the people. According to each person eating, you are to make your count for the lamb.

Your lamb is to be without blemish, a year old male. You may take it from the sheep or from the goats. You must watch over it until the fourteenth day of the same month. Then the whole assembly of the congregation of Israel is to slaughter it at twilight.

They are to take the blood and put it on the two doorposts and on the crossbeam of the houses where they will eat it. They are to eat the meat that night, roasted over a fire. With *matzot* and bitter herbs they are to eat it.

Do not eat any of it raw or boiled with water, but only roasted with fire—its head with its legs and its innards. So let nothing of it remain until the morning. Whatever remains until the morning you are to burn with fire.

Also you are to eat it this way: with your loins girded, your shoes on your feet and your staff in your hand. You are to eat it in haste. It is *Adonai*'s Passover.

"For I will go through the land of Egypt on that night and strike down every firstborn, both men and animals, and I will execute judgments against all the gods of Egypt. I am *Adonai*.

The blood will be a sign for you on the houses where you are. When I see the blood, I will pass over you. So there will be no plague among you to destroy you when I strike the land of Egypt.

"This day is to be a memorial for you. You are to keep it as a feast to *Adonai*. Throughout your generations you are to keep it as an eternal ordinance. For seven days you are to eat *matzot*, but on the first day you must remove *hametz* from your houses, for whoever eats *hametz* from the first day until the seventh day, that soul will be cut off from Israel.

The first day is to be a holy assembly for you as well as the seventh day. No manner of work is to be done on those days, except what is to be eaten by every person—that alone may be prepared by you. So you are to observe the Feast of *Matzot*, for on this very same day have I brought your ranks out of the land of Egypt. Therefore you are to observe this day throughout your generations as an eternal ordinance.

During the first month in the evening

of the fourteenth day of the month, you are to eat *matzot*, until the evening of the twenty-first day of the month. For seven days no *hametz* is to be found in your houses, for whoever eats *hametz*, that soul will be cut off from the congregation of Israel, whether he is an outsider or one who is born in the land. You are to eat no *hametz*; in all your houses you are to eat *matzot*."

Then Moses called for all the elders of Israel and said to them, "Go, select lambs for your families and slaughter the Passover lamb. You are to take a bundle of hyssop, dip it in the blood that is in the basin, and apply it to the crossbeam and two doorposts with the blood from the basin.

None of you may go out the door of his house until morning. *ADONAI* will pass through to strike down the Egyptians, but when He sees the blood on the crossbeam and the two doorposts, *ADONAI* will pass over that door, and will not allow the destroyer to come into your houses to strike you down. Also you are to observe this event as an eternal ordinance, for you and your children.

"When you come into the land which *ADONAI* will give you as He has promised, you are to keep this ceremony. Now when it happens that your children ask you, 'What does this ceremony mean to you?' You are to say, 'It is the sacrifice of *ADONAI*'s Passover, because He passed over the houses of *Bnei-Yisrael* in Egypt, when He struck down the Egyptians, but spared our households.'" So the people bowed their heads and worshipped.

Then *Bnei-Yisrael* went and did it. They did just as *ADONAI* had commanded Moses and Aaron.

So it came about at midnight that *ADONAI* struck down all the firstborn in the land of Egypt, from the firstborn of Pharaoh sitting on his throne to the firstborn of the captive who was in the dungeon, and all the firstborn cattle.

Then Pharaoh rose up in the night, he and all his servants and all the Egyptians, and there was loud wailing in Egypt. For there was not a house where someone was not dead.

So he called for Moses and Aaron at night and said, "Rise up, go out from my people, both you and *Bnei-Yisrael*, go, serve *ADONAI* as you have said. Take your flocks and your herds, as you said, and be gone! But bless me, too."

Now the Egyptians urged the people, sending them out of the land quickly, for they thought, "We will all be dead!"

So the people took their dough before it was leavened, with their kneading bowls bound up in their clothes on their shoulders.

So *Bnei-Yisrael* acted according to the word of Moses. They asked the Egyptians for articles of silver and gold, and for clothing. *ADONAI* gave the people favor in the eyes of the Egyptians and let them have what they asked for. So they plundered the Egyptians.

Then *Bnei-Yisrael* journeyed from Rameses to Succoth, about 600,000 men on foot, as well as children.

Also a mixed multitude went up with them, along with the flocks, herds and heavy livestock. They had baked *matzot* cakes from the dough that they brought out of Egypt. It had no *hametz*, because they were thrust out of Egypt and could not delay, so they had not made provisions for themselves.

Now the time that *Bnei-Yisrael* lived in Egypt was 430 years. So it happened at the end of 430 years, to the very day, that all the armies of *ADONAI* went out from the land of Egypt.

It was a night of watching for *ADONAI* to bring them out of the land of Egypt. This same night is a night of vigil for *ADONAI*, for all *Bnei-Yisrael* throughout their generations.

Then *ADONAI* said to Moses and Aaron, **"This is the ordinance of the Passover. No foreigner may eat it, but every man's servant that is bought for money, after you have circumcised him, may eat it.**

Nor should a visitor or hired servant eat it. It is to be eaten inside a single house. You are not to carry the meat out of the house, nor are you to break any of its bones.

All the congregation of Israel must keep it.

But if an outsider dwells with you, who would keep the Passover for *ADONAI*, all his males must be circumcised. Then let him draw near and keep it. He will be like one who is native to the land. But no uncircumcised person may eat from it., The same *Torah* applies to the native as well as the outsider who dwells among you."

So all *Bnei-Yisrael* did so. They did just as *ADONAI* commanded Moses and Aaron. It was on that very day that *ADONAI* brought *Bnei-Yisrael* out of the land of Egypt as armies.

Exodus, chapter 12

ADONAI spoke to Moses saying, **"Consecrate to Me all the firstborn, from every womb of *Bnei-Yisrael*, both men and animals—this is Mine."**

Moses said to the people, "Remember this day, on which you came out from Egypt, out of the house of bondage. For by a strong hand *ADONAI* brought you out from this place. No *hametz* may be eaten.

This day, in the month of Aviv, you are going out. When *ADONAI* brings you into the land of the Canaanites, the Hittites, the Amorites, the Hivites and the Jebusites, which He swore to your fathers to give you, a land flowing with milk and honey, you are to observe this service during this month.

For seven days you are to eat *matzah*, and the seventh day is to be a feast to *ADONAI*. *Matzot* is to be eaten throughout the seven days, and no *hametz* is to be seen among you, nor within any of your borders.

"You are to tell your son on that day saying, 'It is because of what *ADONAI* did for me when I came out of

Egypt. So it will be like a sign on your hand and a reminder between your eyes, so that the *Torah* of *ADONAI* may be in your mouth. For with a strong hand *ADONAI* has brought you out of Egypt.

You are to keep this ordinance as a *moed* from year to year.

"Now when *ADONAI* brings you into the land of the Canaanite, as He swore to you and your fathers and gives it you, you are to set apart to *ADONAI* every firstborn from the womb, and every firstborn male animal you have will be *ADONAI*'s.

Every firstborn donkey you are to redeem with a lamb, and if you do not redeem it, then you are to break its neck. But you are to redeem every firstborn male among your sons.

"So when your son asks you in times to come, 'What is this?' say to him, 'By a strong hand *ADONAI* brought us out from Egypt, the house of bondage, and when Pharaoh refused to let us go, *ADONAI* slew all the firstborn in the land of Egypt, both men and animals. So I sacrifice to *ADONAI* all firstborn males, but I redeem the firstborn of my sons.' So it will be like a sign on your hand and like frontlets between your eyes, for by a strong hand *ADONAI* brought us out of Egypt."

After Pharaoh had let the people go, God did not lead them along the road to the land of the Philistines, although that was nearby, for God said, **"The people might change their minds if they see war and return to Egypt."** So God led the people around by the way of the wilderness to the Sea of Reeds, and *Bnei-Yisrael* went up out of the land of Egypt armed.

Moses also took the bones of Joseph with him, for he had made *Bnei-Yisrael* swear an oath saying, "God will surely remember you, and then you are to carry my bones away with you."

So they journeyed from Succoth and encamped in Etham, on the edge of the wilderness.

ADONAI went before them in a pillar of cloud by day to lead the way and in a pillar of fire by night to give them light. So they could travel both day and night.

The pillar of cloud by day and the pillar of fire by night never departed from the people.

Exodus, chapter 13

ADONAI spoke to Moses saying, **"Speak to *Bnei-Yisrael*, so that they turn back and encamp before Pi-hahiroth, between Migdol and the sea. You are to camp by the sea, opposite Baal-zephon. Pharaoh will say concerning *Bnei-Yisrael*, 'They are wandering aimlessly in the land—the wilderness has shut them in!' I will harden Pharaoh's heart, so he will follow after them. Then I will be glorified over Pharaoh along with all his army, and the Egyptians will know that I am *ADONAI*."** So they did so.

When the king of Egypt was told that the people had fled, Pharaoh and his servants had a change of heart toward the people, and they said, "What is this we have done, that we let Israel go from serving us?" So he prepared his chariots and took his people with him.

He took 600 of the finest chariots, along with all other chariots of Egypt, and captains over them. *ADONAI* hardened the heart of Pharaoh king of Egypt, so he pursued *Bnei-Yisrael*, for *Bnei-Yisrael* went out with a high hand.

But the Egyptians pursued them with all the horses and chariots of Pharaoh, as well as his charioteers and his army, and overtook them as they were encamped by the sea, beside Pi-hahiroth opposite Baal-zephon. When Pharaoh drew near, *Bnei-Yisrael* lifted up their eyes, and behold, the Egyptians were marching after them! So they were terrified, and *Bnei-Yisrael* cried out to *ADONAI*.

They said to Moses, "Have you taken us away to die in the wilderness because there were no graves in Egypt? Why have you dealt this way with us, to bring us out of Egypt? Did we not say to you in Egypt, 'Let us alone, so that we may serve the Egyptians?' It was better for us to serve the Egyptians than to die in the wilderness!"

But Moses said to the people, "Don't be afraid! Stand still, and see the salvation of *ADONAI*, which He will perform for you today. You have seen the Egyptians today, but you will never see them again, ever *ADONAI* will fight for you, while you hold your peace."

Then *ADONAI* said to Moses, **"Why are you crying to Me? Tell *Bnei-Yisrael* to go forward. Lift up your staff, stretch out your hand over the sea, and divide it. Then *Bnei-Yisrael* will go into the midst of the sea on dry ground.**

Then I, behold, I will harden the hearts of the Egyptians, and they will go in after them, so that I will be glorified over Pharaoh and all his army, his chariots and his horsemen. Then the Egyptians will know that I am *ADONAI*, when I have been glorified over Pharaoh, his chariots and his horsemen."

Then the angel of God, who went before the camp of Israel, moved and went behind them. Also the pillar of cloud moved from in front and stood behind them, and so came between the camp of Egypt and the camp of Israel—there was the cloud and the darkness over here, yet it gave light by night over there—neither one came near the other all night long.

Then Moses stretched out his hand over the sea. *ADONAI* drove the sea back with a strong east wind throughout the night and turned the sea into dry land. So the waters were divided.

Then *Bnei-Yisrael* went into the midst of the sea on the dry ground, while the waters were like walls to them on their right and on their left. But the Egyptians pursued and went in after them into the midst of the sea, all Pharaoh's horses, his chariots and his horsemen.

Now it came about during the morning watch that *ADONAI* looked at

But *Bnei-Yisrael* had walked on dry land in the midst of the sea, and the waters were like walls to them on their right hand and on their left.

Exodus 14:29 TLV

the army of the Egyptians through the pillar of fire and cloud and caused the army of the Egyptians to panic. He took off their chariot wheels and caused them to drive heavily, so that the Egyptians said, "Get away from the presence of Israel! For *Adonai* fights for them against the Egyptians!"

Then *Adonai* said to Moses, **"Stretch out your hand over the sea, so that the waters come back upon the Egyptians, over their chariots and their horsemen."**

So Moses stretched his hand out over the waters, and the sea returned to its strength at the break of dawn. The Egyptians were fleeing from it, but *Adonai* overthrew them in the midst of the sea. The waters returned and covered the chariots, the horsemen and the entire army of Pharaoh that went after them into the sea. Not one of them remained.

But *Bnei-Yisrael* had walked on dry land in the midst of the sea, and the waters were like walls to them on their right hand and on their left. So *Adonai* saved Israel that day out of the hand of the Egyptians, and Israel saw the Egyptians dead on the seashore.

When Israel saw the great work that *Adonai* did over the Egyptians, the people feared *Adonai*, and they believed in *Adonai* and in His servant Moses.

Exodus, chapter 14

Then Moses led Israel onward from the Sea of Reeds. They went out into the wilderness of Shur. But they travelled three days in the wilderness and found no water.

When they came to Marah, they could not drink from the waters because they were bitter. On account of this it was called Marah.

So the people complained to Moses saying, "What are we going to drink?"

So he cried out to *Adonai*, and *Adonai* showed him a tree. When he threw it into the waters, they were made sweet.

There He made a statute and an ordinance for them, and there He tested them. He said, **"If you diligently listen to the voice of *Adonai* your God, do what is right in His eyes, pay attention to His *mitzvot*, and keep all His decrees, I will put none of the diseases on you which I have put on the Egyptians. For I am *Adonai* who heals you."**

Then they came to Elim, where there were twelve springs of water and seventy palm trees. So they camped there by the waters.

Exodus 15:22-27

17. God Covenants with *Bnei-Yisrael*

They journeyed on from Elim, and the entire community of *Bnei-Yisrael* came to the wilderness of Sin, which is between Elim and Sinai, on the fifteenth day of the second month after leaving the land of Egypt.

But the whole congregation of *Bnei-Yisrael* murmured against Moses and Aaron in the wilderness. *Bnei-Yisrael* said to them, "If only we had died by the hand of *ADONAI* in the land of Egypt, when we sat by pots of meat, when we ate bread until we were full. But you have brought us into the wilderness, to kill this entire congregation with hunger."

Then *ADONAI* said to Moses, **"Behold, I will rain bread from heaven for you. The people will go out and gather a day's portion every day, so that I can test them to find out whether they will walk according to My *Torah* or not. So on the sixth day, when they prepare what they bring in, it will be twice as much as they gather day by day."**

So Moses and Aaron said to all *Bnei-Yisrael*, "In the evening you will know that *ADONAI* has brought you out from the land of Egypt, and in the morning, then you will see the glory of *ADONAI*. For He heard your complaining against Him. What are we? You complain against us?"

Then Moses said, "*ADONAI* will give you meat to eat in the evening and enough bread to fill you in the morning, since *ADONAI* hears your complaints that you mutter against Him, what are we? Your complaining is not against us, but against *ADONAI*!"

Moses said to Aaron, "Say to all the congregation of *Bnei-Yisrael*, 'Come near before *ADONAI*, because He has heard your complaining.'"

Then, as Aaron spoke to the whole congregation of *Bnei-Yisrael*, they looked toward the wilderness, and the glory of *ADONAI* appeared in the cloud.

ADONAI spoke to Moses saying, **"I have heard the complaining of *Bnei-Yisrael*. Speak to them saying, 'At dusk you will eat meat, and in the morning you will be filled with bread. Then you will know that I am *ADONAI* your God.'"**

So when evening fell, quails came up and covered the camp. Moreover, in the morning there was a layer of dew all around the camp. When the layer of dew was gone, on the surface of the desert was a thin, flake-like frost, as fine as the frost on the ground. When *Bnei-Yisrael* saw it, they said one to another, "What is it?" For they did not know what it was.

Then Moses said to them, "It is the bread that *ADONAI* has given you to eat. This is the word that *ADONAI* has commanded.

Every man is to gather according to his needs, an omer per person, according to the number of people per household. Each man is to take it for those who are in his tent."

Bnei-Yisrael did so, and some gathered

more, some less. When they measured it with an omer, those who gathered more had nothing left over, and those that gathered less did not lack at all. Every man gathered according to his appetite.

Also Moses said to them, "Let no one save any of it until the morning."

However, they did not listen to Moses. Some of them preserved it until the morning—but it bred worms and rotted. So Moses was angry with them.

So they gathered it morning by morning, each man according to his needs, and as the sun became hot it melted.

On the sixth day they gathered twice as much bread, two omers for each individual.

So all the leaders of the community came and informed Moses. But he said to them, "This is what *ADONAI* has said. Tomorrow is a *Shabbat* rest, a holy *Shabbat* to *ADONAI*. Bake whatever you would bake, and boil what you would boil. Store up for yourselves everything that remains, to be kept until the morning."

So they set it aside until the morning, just as Moses instructed, and it did not rot nor were there any worms.

Then Moses said, "Eat that today, because today is a *Shabbat* to *ADONAI*. Today you will not find it in the field. You are to gather it for six days, but the seventh day is the *Shabbat*, and there will be none."

Yet on the seventh day, some of the people went out to gather and they found none. *ADONAI* said to Moses, **"How long will you refuse to keep My *mitzvot* and My *Torah*? See, ADONAI has given you the *Shabbat*, so on the sixth day He gives you the bread of two days. Let every man stay in his place, and let no man go out on the seventh day."**

So the people rested on the seventh day.

The house of Israel named it *manna*. It was white like coriander seed and tasted like wafers made with honey. Then Moses said, "This is what *ADONAI* has commanded. Let a full omer of it be kept throughout your generations, so that they may see the bread with which I fed you in the wilderness, when I brought you out from the land of Egypt."

Moses said to Aaron, "Take a jar and put a full omer of *manna* inside. Store it up before *ADONAI*, to be kept throughout your generations."

Just as *ADONAI* commanded Moses, Aaron stored it up in front of the Testimony, to be preserved. *Bnei-Yisrael* ate the *manna* for 40 years. They ate the *manna* until they came to an inhabited land, when they came to the borders of the land of Canaan.

Now an omer is the tenth part of an ephah.

Exodus, chapter 16

All the congregation of *Bnei-Yisrael* journeyed from the wilderness of Sin in stages, according to the command of *ADONAI*, and camped in Rephidim, but there was no water for the people to drink. So the people quarreled with Moses and said, "Give us water to drink."

And Moses said to them, "Why do you quarrel with me? Why do you test *ADONAI*?"

But the people thirsted for water there, and they complained against Moses and said, "Why have you brought us up out of Egypt? To kill us with thirst, along with our children and cattle?"

So Moses cried out to *ADONAI* saying, "What am I to do for these people? They are about ready to stone me."

ADONAI said to Moses, **"Walk before the people, and take of the elders of Israel with you, along with your staff with which you struck the river. Take it in your hand and go. Behold, I will stand before you, there upon the rock in Horeb. You are to strike the rock, and water will come out of it so that the people can drink."**

Then Moses did just so in the eyes of the elders of Israel. The name of the place was called Massah and Meribah, because of the quarreling of *Bnei-Yisrael*, and because they tested *ADONAI* saying, "Is *ADONAI* among us, or not?"

Exodus 17:1-7

In the third month after *Bnei-Yisrael* had gone out of the land of Egypt, that same day they arrived at the wilderness of Sinai. They travelled from Rephidim, came into to the wilderness of Sinai, and set up camp in the wilderness. Israel camped there, right in front of the mountain.

Moses went up to God, and *ADONAI* called to him from the mountain saying, **"Say this to the house of Jacob, and tell *Bnei-Yisrael*, 'You have seen what I did to the Egyptians, and how I carried you on eagle's wings and brought you to Myself.**

Now then, if you listen closely to My voice, and keep My covenant, then you will be My own treasure from among all people, for all the earth is Mine. So as for you, you will be to Me a kingdom of *kohanim* and a holy nation.' These are the words which you are to speak to *Bnei-Yisrael*."

So Moses went, called for the elders of the people, and put before them all these words that *ADONAI* had commanded him.

All the people answered together and said, "Everything that *ADONAI* has spoken, we will do."

Then Moses reported the words of the people to *ADONAI*.

ADONAI said to Moses, **"I am about to come to you in a thick cloud, so that the people will hear when I speak with you, and believe you forever."**

Then Moses told the words of the people to *ADONAI*.

ADONAI said to Moses, **"Go to the people, and sanctify them today and tomorrow. Let them wash their**

clothing. Be ready for the third day. For on the third day *ADONAI* will come down upon Mount Sinai in the sight of all the people.

You are to set boundaries for the people all around, saying, 'Be very careful not to go up onto the mountain, or touch the border of it. Whoever touches the mountain will surely be put to death. Not a hand is to touch it, but he will surely be stoned or shot through. Whether it is an animal or a man, it will not live.' When the *shofar* sounds, they may come up to the mountain."

Then Moses went down from the mountain to the people, consecrated them, and then, they washed their clothing. He said to the people, "Be ready for the third day. Do not draw near your wives."

In the morning of the third day, there was thundering and lightning, a thick cloud on the mountain, and the blast of an exceedingly loud *shofar*. All the people in the camp trembled. Then Moses brought the people out of the camp to meet God, and they stood at the lowest part of the mountain.

Now the entire Mount Sinai was in smoke, because *ADONAI* had descended upon it in fire. The smoke ascended like the smoke of a furnace. The whole mountain quaked greatly.

When the sound of the *shofar* grew louder and louder, Moses spoke, and God answered him with a thunderous sound. Then *ADONAI* came down onto Mount Sinai, to the top of the mountain. *ADONAI* called Moses to the top of the mountain, so Moses went up.

Then *ADONAI* said to Moses, **"Go down and warn the people, lest they break through to see *ADONAI*, and many of them die. Even the *kohanim* who come near to *ADONAI* must consecrate themselves, so that *ADONAI* does not break out against them."**

Moses said to *ADONAI*, "The people cannot come up to Mount Sinai, for You are the One who warned us, saying, 'Set boundaries around the mountain, and consecrate it.'"

Then *ADONAI* said to him, **"Go down. You are to come back up, you and Aaron with you. But do not let the *kohanim* and the people break through to come up to *ADONAI*, or He will break out against them."** So Moses went down to the people and told them.

Exodus, chapter 19

Then God spoke all these words saying, **"I am *ADONAI* your God, who brought you out of the land of Egypt, out of the house of bondage.**

"You shall have no other gods before Me. Do not make for yourself a graven image, or any likeness of anything that is in heaven above or on the earth below or in the water under the earth. Do not bow down to them, do not let anyone make you serve them. For I, *ADONAI* your God, am a jealous God, bringing the iniquity of the fathers upon the children to the third and fourth generations of those who hate Me, but showing lovingkindness to the thousands of generations of

those who love Me and keep My *mitzvot*.

"You must not take the Name of *ADONAI* your God in vain, for *ADONAI* will not hold him guiltless that takes His Name in vain.

"Remember *Yom Shabbat*, to keep it holy. You are to work six days, and do all your work, but the seventh day is a *Shabbat* to *ADONAI* your God. In it you shall not do any work—not you, nor your son, your daughter, your male servant, your female servant, your cattle, nor the outsider that is within your gates. For in six days *ADONAI* made heaven and earth, the sea, and all that is in them, and rested on the seventh day. Thus *ADONAI* blessed *Yom Shabbat*, and made it holy.

"Honor your father and your mother, so that your days may be long upon the land which *ADONAI* your God is giving you.

"Do not murder.

"Do not commit adultery.

"Do not steal.

"Do not bear false witness against your neighbor.

"Do not covet your neighbor's house, your neighbor's wife, his manservant, his maidservant, his ox, his donkey, or anything that is your neighbor's."

All the people witnessed the thundering and the lightning, and the sound of the *shofar*, and the mountain smoking. When the people saw it, they trembled and stood far off. So they said to Moses, "You, speak to us, and we will listen, but do not let God speak to us, or we will die."

So Moses said to the people, "Do not be afraid, for God has come to test you, so that His fear may be in you, so that you do not sin." The people stood far off, while Moses drew near to the thick darkness where God was.

Then *ADONAI* said to Moses, **"Say this to *Bnei-Yisrael*: You yourselves have seen that I have spoken to you from heaven. Do not make gods of silver alongside Me, and do not make gods of gold for yourselves. You are to make an altar of earth for Me, and there you will sacrifice your burnt offerings, your fellowship offerings—your sheep and your cattle. In every place where I cause My name to be mentioned I will come to you and bless you.**

When you make for Me an altar of stones, do not build it from cut stone, for if you use a tool on it, you will have profaned it. Nor are you to go up to My altar on steps, so that your nakedness would not be uncovered while on it."

Exodus, chapter 20

"Three times in the year you are to celebrate a festival for Me.

You are to observe the Feast of *Matzot*. For seven days you will eat *matzot* as I commanded you, at the time appointed in the month Aviv, for that is when you came out from Egypt. No one is to appear

before Me empty-handed.

Also you are to observe the Feast of Harvest, the firstfruits of your labors that you sow in the field, as well as the Feast of the Ingathering at the end of the year, when you gather your crops from the field.

Three times in the year all your men are to appear before ADONAI *Elohim*.

Do not offer the blood of My sacrifice with *hametz*. Nor is the fat of My feast to remain out all night until the morning. Bring the choicest firstfruits of your land into the House of ADONAI your God.

Do not boil a kid in its mother's milk.

"Behold, I am sending an angel before you, to guard you on the way and to bring you into the place that I have prepared. Watch for Him and listen to His voice. Do not rebel against Him because He will not pardon your transgression, for My Name is in Him.

But if you listen closely to His voice, and do everything I say, I will be an enemy to your enemies and an adversary to your adversaries.

For My angel will go before you, and bring you to the Amorites, Hittites, Perizzites, Canaanites, Hivites and the Jebusites, and I will cut them off.

You are not to bow down to their gods or serve them, or do what they do. Rather, you are to utterly overthrow them, and break their pillars in pieces.

You are to serve ADONAI your God, and He will bless your food and your water. Moreover I will take sickness away from your midst. None will miscarry nor be barren in your land, and I will fill up the number of your days.

"I will send My terror before you and throw all the people to whom you will come into panic, and make all your enemies turn their backs to you. I will send the hornet before you, which will drive out the Hivites, the Canaanites and the Hittites, from before you.

I will not drive them out from before you in a single year. Otherwise the land would become desolate, and the animals of the field will multiply against you. But little by little I will drive them out from before you, until you are fruitful. Then you will possess the land.

"I will set your border from the Sea of Reeds to the sea of the Philistines, and from the wilderness to the Euphrates River. For I will deliver the inhabitants of the land into your hand, and you are to drive them out before you.

Make no covenant with them or with their gods. They must not dwell in your land and cause you to sin against Me, for if you worship their gods, they will be a snare to you."

Exodus 23:14-33

Then to Moses He said, **"Come up to ADONAI, you and Aaron, Nadab and Abihu, and the seventy elders of Israel, and worship from afar. Moses alone is to approach ADONAI, but the**

He took the Scroll of the Covenant and read it in the hearing of the people. Again they said, "All that *ADONAI* has spoken, we will do and obey." Then Moses took the blood, sprinkled it on the people, and said, "Behold the blood of the covenant, which *ADONAI* has cut with you, in agreement with all these words."

Exodus 24:7-8 TLV

others may not draw near, nor are the people to go up with him." So Moses came and told the people all the words of *ADONAI* as well as all the ordinances.

All the people answered with one voice and said, "All the words which *ADONAI* has spoken, we will do."

So Moses wrote down all the words of *ADONAI*, then rose up early in the morning, and built an altar below the mountain, along with twelve pillars for the twelve tribes of Israel. He then sent out young men of *Bnei-Yisrael*, who sacrificed burnt offerings and fellowship offerings of oxen to *ADONAI*.

Then Moses took half of the blood and put it in basins and the other half he poured out against the altar. He took the Scroll of the Covenant and read it in the hearing of the people.

Again they said, "All that *ADONAI* has spoken, we will do and obey."

Then Moses took the blood, sprinkled it on the people, and said, "Behold the blood of the covenant, which *ADONAI* has cut with you, in agreement with all these words."

Then Moses and Aaron, Nadab and Abihu, and seventy of the elders of Israel went up. They saw the God of Israel, and under His feet was something like a pavement of sapphire, as clear as the very heavens.

Yet He did not raise His hand against the nobles of *Bnei-Yisrael*. So they beheld God, and ate and drank.

Then *ADONAI* said to Moses, **"Come up to Me on the mountain and stay there, and I will give you the tablets of stone with the *Torah* and the *mitzvot*, which I have written so that you may instruct them."**

So Moses rose up along with his attendant Joshua, and Moses went up onto the mountain of God. To the elders he said, "Wait for us here until we come back to you. See, Aaron and Hur are with you—whoever has a dispute should go to them."

When Moses went up on the mountain, the cloud covered it. The glory of *ADONAI* settled upon Mount Sinai, and the cloud covered it for six days. Then on the seventh day He called to Moses out of the midst of the cloud.

The appearance of the glory of *ADONAI* was like a consuming fire on the top of the mountain in the sight of *Bnei-Yisrael*. So Moses entered into the midst of the cloud and went up onto the mountain.

Moses was on the mountain 40 days and 40 nights.

Exodus, chapter 24

18. God Teaches His People

Then *ADONAI* spoke to Moses saying, **"See, I have called by name Bezalel son of Uri son of Hur, of the tribe of Judah, and I have filled him with the Spirit of God, with wisdom, understanding and knowledge in all kinds of craftsmanship, to make ingenious designs, to forge with gold, silver and bronze, as well as cutting stones for setting and carving wood, to work in all manner of craftsmanship.**

Also look, I Myself have appointed with him Oholiab son of Ahisamach, of the tribe of Dan.

Within the hearts of all who are wise-hearted I have placed skill, so that they may make everything that I have commanded you: the Tent of Meeting, the Ark of the Testimony, the atonement cover that is to be on it, all the furnishings of the Tabernacle, the table and its utensils, the *menorah* of pure gold with all of its utensils, the altar of incense, the altar of burnt offering with all of its utensils, the basin and its stand, the woven garments, the holy garments for Aaron the *kohen*, the garments for his sons to minister as *kohanim*, the anointing oil, and the incense of sweet spices for the holy place. They are to make them just as how I commanded you."

Then *ADONAI* spoke to Moses saying, **"Speak now to *Bnei-Yisrael* saying, 'Surely you must keep My *Shabbatot*, for it is a sign between Me and you throughout your generations, so you may know that I am *ADONAI* who sanctifies you. Therefore you are to keep the *Shabbat*, because it is holy for you. Everyone who profanes it will die, for whoever does any work during *Shabbat*, that soul will be cut off from the midst of his people.**

Work is to be done for six days, but on the seventh day is a *Shabbat* of complete rest, holy to *ADONAI*. Whoever does any work on the *Shabbat* will surely be put to death. So *Bnei-Yisrael* is to keep the *Shabbat*, to observe the *Shabbat* throughout their generations as a perpetual covenant. It is a sign between Me and *Bnei-Yisrael* forever, for in six days *ADONAI* made heaven and earth, and on the seventh day He ceased from work and rested.'"

When He had finished speaking with him on Mount Sinai, He gave the two tablets of the Testimony to Moses—tablets of stone, written by the finger of God.

Exodus, chapter 31

Now when the people saw that Moses delayed coming down from the mountain, they gathered around Aaron and said to him, "Get up, make us gods who will go before us. As for this Moses, the man that brought us up out of the land of Egypt, we do not know what's become of him!"

So Aaron said to them, "Break off the golden rings that are in the ears of your wives, your sons and your daughters, and bring them to me."

So all the people broke off the golden rings that were in their ears and

Then Moses turned and went down from the mountain, with the two tablets of the Testimony in his hand, tablets that were written on both sides, on one and on the other. The tablets were the work of God, and the writing was the writing of God, engraved on the tablets.

Exodus 32:15-16 TLV

brought them to Aaron. He received them from their hand, and made a molten calf, fashioned with a chiseling tool.

Then they said, "This is your god, Israel, which brought you up out of the land of Egypt!"

When Aaron saw it, he built an altar before it. Then Aaron made a proclamation saying, "Tomorrow will be a feast to *ADONAI*."

They rose up early the next morning, sacrificed burnt offerings and brought fellowship offerings. The people sat down to eat and drink, and rose up to make merry.

Then *ADONAI* said to Moses, **"Go down! For your people, whom you brought up out of the land of Egypt, have become debased. They quickly turned aside from the path that I commanded for them. They have made a molten calf, worshipped it, and sacrificed to it, and said, 'This is your god, O Israel, that brought you up out of the land of Egypt.'"**

ADONAI said to Moses, **"I have seen this people, and behold, it is a stiff-necked people. Now therefore, leave Me alone, so My wrath may burn hot against them, and so I may consume them—and make from you a great nation!"**

Then Moses sought *ADONAI* his God and said, "*ADONAI*, why should Your wrath burn hot against Your people, whom You have brought forth out of the land of Egypt with great power and with a mighty hand? Why should the Egyptians say, 'He brought them out to do evil, to slay them in the mountains, and to annihilate them from the face of the earth?' Turn from Your fierce wrath, and relent from this destruction against Your people. Remember Abraham, Isaac and Israel, Your servants, to whom You swore by Your own self, and said to them, **'I will multiply your seed as the stars of heaven, and all this land that I have spoken of I will give to your offspring, and they will inherit it forever.'"**

So *ADONAI* relented from the destruction that He said He would do to His people. Then Moses turned and went down from the mountain, with the two tablets of the Testimony in his hand, tablets that were written on both sides, on one and on the other.

The tablets were the work of God, and the writing was the writing of God, engraved on the tablets.

When Joshua heard the noise of the people as they shouted, he said to Moses, "There is the sound of war within the camp."

But Moses said: "It is not the voice of a shout of victory, nor is it the voice of crying from defeat, but I hear the sound of singing."

Then it happened, as soon as Moses came near the camp, he saw the calf and the dancing, and his anger burned hot. So he threw the tablets out of his hands, and smashed them at the foot of the mountain. Then he took the calf that they had made, burned it with fire, ground it to powder, scattered it on the surface of the water and made *Bnei-Yisrael* drink it. Then Moses said to Aaron, "What did this people do to you, to make you bring such a great sin upon them?"

Aaron said, "Don't be angry, my lord! You know these people yourself, and how they are set on evil. They said to me, 'Make gods for us, to go before us! As for this Moses, the man that brought us up out of the land of Egypt, we don't know what happened to him.' So I said to them, 'Whoever has any gold, let them break it off.' So they gave it to me and I threw it into the fire—and out came this calf!"

When Moses saw that the people were unrestrained, because Aaron had let them run wild, to become a joke among their enemies, Moses stood at the gate of the camp and said, "Whoever is on *ADONAI*'s side, let him come to me." Then all the sons of Levi gathered themselves together to him.

He said to them, "This is what *ADONAI*, the God of Israel says, **'Every man put on his sword, and go to and fro, from gate to gate throughout the camp, and slay his brother, his friend, and his neighbor.'"**

So the sons of Levi did as Moses said, and that day from among the people there fell about 3,000 men.

Then Moses said, "Consecrate your hands today to *ADONAI* so that He may give you a blessing today, for every man has been against his son and his brother."

So it happened the following day, Moses said to the people, "You have committed a horrendous sin. So now I will go up to *ADONAI*—perhaps I can make atonement for your sin."

Then Moses returned to *ADONAI* and said, "Alas, these people have sinned greatly, and made gods of gold! Yet now, please forgive their sin. But if not, please blot me out of Your book that You have written."

ADONAI said to Moses, **"Whoever has sinned against Me, I will blot out of My book. Now go, lead the people to the place that I told you about. My angel will go before you. Nevertheless, on the day when I take account, I will hold them accountable for their sin."**

So *ADONAI* struck the people because of what they did with the calf that Aaron had made.

Exodus, chapter 32

19. God Visits His Tent

Then *ADONAI* said to Moses, **"Leave, get out of this place, you and the people that you have brought out of the land of Egypt, into the land which I swore to Abraham, Isaac and Jacob saying, 'I will give it to your seed.'**

I will send an angel before you. I will drive out the Canaanites, Amorites, Hittites, Perizzites, Hivites and the Jebusites. Head up into a land flowing with milk and honey, but I will not move within the midst of you, so that I do not destroy you along the way, for you are a stiff-necked people."

When the people heard these dreadful words, they mourned, and no one put on any ornaments.

ADONAI said to Moses, **"Say to *Bnei-Yisrael*, 'You are a stiff-necked people. If I were going up among you for one moment, I would consume you. Take off your ornaments, so that I may consider what to do to you.'"**

So *Bnei-Yisrael* stripped themselves of their ornaments from Mount Horeb onward.

Now Moses used to take the tent and pitch it outside the camp, far off from the camp, and he called it the Tent of Meeting.

So it happened, everyone who sought *ADONAI* would go out to the Tent of Meeting, which was outside the camp. Whenever Moses went out to the tent, all the people would arise and stand, everyone at the door of his own tent, and look after Moses, until he had gone into the Tent. After Moses entered, the pillar of cloud descended, stood at the door, and He would speak with Moses.

When all the people saw the pillar of cloud standing at the entrance of the Tent, they all rose up and worshipped, every man at the entrance of his own tent.

So *ADONAI* spoke with Moses face to face, as a man speaks with his friend. Then he would return to the camp, but his servant Joshua, the son of Nun, a young man, did not leave the Tent.

So Moses said to *ADONAI* "You say to me, 'Bring up this people,' but You have not let me know whom You will send with me. Yet You have said, **'I know you by name, and you have also found grace in My eyes.'**
Now then, I pray, if I have found grace in Your eyes, show me Your ways, so that I may know You, so that I might find favor in Your sight. Consider also that this nation is Your people."

"My presence will go with you, and I will give you rest," He answered.

But then he said to Him, "If Your presence does not go with me, don't let us go up from here! For how would it be known that I or your people have found favor in Your sight? Isn't it because You go with us, that distinguishes us from all the

When all the people saw the pillar of cloud standing at the entrance of the Tent, they all rose up and worshipped, every man at the entrance of his own tent.

Exodus 33:10 TLV

people on the face of the earth?"

ADONAI answered Moses, **"I will also do what you have said, for you have found favor in My sight, and I know you by name."**

Then he said, "Please, show me Your glory!"

So He said, **"I will cause all My goodness to pass before you, and call out the Name of *ADONAI* before you. I will be gracious toward whom I will be gracious, and I will show mercy on whom I will be merciful."**

But He also said, "You cannot see My face, for no man can see Me and live."

Then *ADONAI* said, **"See, a place near Me—you will stand on the rock. While My glory passes by, I will put you in a cleft of the rock, and cover you with My hand, until I have passed by. Then I will take away My hand, and you will see My back, but My face will not be seen."**

Exodus, chapter 33

ADONAI said to Moses, **"Carve for yourself two tablets of stone like the first ones, and I will write upon them the words that were on the first tablets, which you broke.**

Be ready by the morning, come up to Mount Sinai, and present yourself to Me there on the top of the mountain. No one is to come up with you, and do not let anyone be seen throughout the entire mountain. Even the flocks and herds must not graze in front of that mountain."

So he carved two tablets of stone like the first. Then Moses rose up early in the morning, went up onto Mount Sinai as *ADONAI* had commanded him, and took in his hand the two tablets of stone.

Then *ADONAI* descended in the cloud, stood with him there, as he called on the Name of *ADONAI*.

Then *ADONAI* passed before him, and proclaimed, **"*ADONAI*, *ADONAI*, the compassionate and gracious God, slow to anger, and abundant in lovingkindness and truth, showing mercy to a thousand generations, forgiving iniquity and transgression and sin, yet by no means leaving the guilty unpunished, but bringing the iniquity of the fathers upon the children, and upon the children's children, to the third and fourth generation."**

Then Moses quickly bowed his head down to the earth and worshipped. He said, "If now I have found grace in Your eyes, my Lord, let my Lord please go within our midst, even though this is a stiff-necked people. Pardon our iniquity and our sin, and take us for Your own inheritance."

Then He said, **"I am cutting a covenant. Before all your people I will do wonders, such as have not been done in all the earth, or in any nation. All the people you are among will see the work of *ADONAI*—for what I am going to do with you will be awesome!**

Obey what I am commanding you today. Behold, I am going to drive out the Amorites, Canaanites, Hittites, Perizzites, Hivites and

Jebusites before you. Watch yourself, and make no covenant with the inhabitants of the land where you are going, or they will become a snare among you.

Instead you must break down their altars, smash their pillars and cut down their Asherah poles. For you are to bow down to no other god, because *ADONAI* is jealous for His Name—He is a jealous God.

"See that you do not make a covenant with the inhabitants of the land. Otherwise when they prostitute themselves with their gods and sacrifice to their gods, someone will invite you, and you will eat from their sacrifice.

Do not take their daughters for your sons, for their daughters will prostitute themselves with their own gods, and cause your sons to prostitute themselves with their gods.

"You are not to make for yourselves metal gods.

"You are to keep the Feast of *Matzot*. For seven days you are eat *matzot*, as I commanded you, at the time appointed in the month Aviv, for in the month Aviv you came out from Egypt.

"Every firstborn of the womb is Mine, and from all your cattle you are to sanctify the males, the firstborn of the ox and sheep. A firstborn donkey you are to redeem with a lamb, but if you do not redeem it, then you are to break its neck. You must redeem all your firstborn sons. No one should appear before Me empty-handed.

"For six days you will work, but on the seventh day you will rest. During plowing time and harvest you must rest.

"You are to observe the Feast of *Shavuot*, which is the firstfruits of the wheat harvest, as well as the Feast of Ingathering at the turn of the year. Three times during the year all your males are to appear before *ADONAI Elohim*, God of Israel.

For I am going to cast out nations before you, then enlarge your territory. So no one will covet your land when you go up to appear before *ADONAI* your God three times in the year.

"You are not to offer the blood of My sacrifice with *hametz*, nor should the sacrifice of the Passover Festival remain until morning.

"You are to bring the choicest firstfruits of your land to the House of *ADONAI* your God.

"You must not boil a kid in its mother's milk."

Then *ADONAI* said to Moses, **"Write these words, for based on these words I have cut a covenant with you and with Israel."**

So he stayed there with *ADONAI* for 40 days and 40 nights, and he did not eat bread or drink water. He wrote on the tablets the words of the covenant: the Ten Words.

Now it happened, when Moses came

down from Mount Sinai with the two tablets of the Testimony in his hand when he came down from the mountain, that Moses did not know that the skin of his face was radiant, because God had spoken with him.

When Aaron and all *Bnei-Yisrael* saw Moses, the skin of his face shone in rays, so they were afraid to come near him.

But Moses called out to them, so Aaron and all the rulers of the congregation returned to him, and Moses spoke to them.

Afterward all *Bnei-Yisrael* came near, and he gave them all the *mitzvot* that *ADONAI* had spoken to him in Mount Sinai.

When Moses was done speaking with them, he put a veil over his face. But when Moses went before *ADONAI*, so that He could speak with him, he took the veil off until he came out. When he came out and spoke to *Bnei-Yisrael* what he was commanded, *Bnei-Yisrael* saw the face of Moses and that the skin of his face glistened. So Moses put the veil back over his face until he went in to speak with Him.

Exodus, chapter 34

20. God Inspires His People

Then Moses assembled all the congregation of *Bnei-Yisrael* and said to them, "These are the words which *Adonai* has commanded you to do.

Work is to be done for six days, but the seventh day is a holy day for you, a *Shabbat* of complete rest to *Adonai*. Whoever does any work then will die. Do not kindle a fire in any of your dwellings on *Yom Shabbat*."

Moses also said to all the congregation of *Bnei-Yisrael*, "This is the word which *Adonai* commanded saying: **Take from among you an offering for *Adonai*.**

Whoever has a willing heart, let him bring *Adonai*'s offering: gold, silver and bronze; blue, purple and scarlet cloth; fine linen and goat hair; ram skins dyed red, sealskins and acacia wood; oil for the light, spices for the anointing oil and for the sweet incense; onyx stones, and setting stones for the ephod and for the breastplate.

"Let every wise-hearted man among you come and make everything that *Adonai* has commanded, including the Tabernacle, its tent and its covering, its clasps and its boards, its crossbars, its pillars and its bases; the Ark and the poles, the atonement cover and the curtain screen; the table and its poles with all of its utensils, along with the bread of the Presence; also the *menorah* for light with its utensils, its lamps and the oil for the light; the altar of incense and its poles, the anointing oil, the sweet incense, and the screen for the entrance of the Tabernacle; the altar of burnt offering with its grating of bronze, its poles and all its utensils, the basin and its stand; the hangings of the courtyard, the pillars and their bases, and the curtain for the gate of the courtyard; the pegs of the Tabernacle and of the courtyard, along with their cords; the woven garments for ministering in the holy place, the holy garments for Aaron the *kohen* and for his sons, to minister as *kohanim*."

Then all the congregation of *Bnei-Yisrael* departed from before Moses.

Everyone whose heart stirred him and everyone whose spirit was willing came and brought *Adonai*'s offering for the work of the Tent of Meeting and for all its service as well as for the holy garments.

So they came, both men and women, everyone whose heart compelled him, and brought nose rings, earrings, signet rings, bracelets, and all kinds of golden jewels—everyone who brought a wave offering of gold to *Adonai*. Everyone who had blue, purple, scarlet, fine linen, goat hair, ram skins dyed red or sealskins brought them.

Everyone who could make a contribution of silver or bronze brought *Adonai*'s offering, and every man who had acacia wood of any use for service brought it.

Also all the women who were wise-hearted spun with their hands, and

Everyone whose heart stirred him and everyone whose spirit was willing came and brought *Adonai's* offering for the work of the Tent of Meeting and for all its service as well as for the holy garments. So they came, both men and women, everyone whose heart compelled him, and brought nose rings, earrings, signet rings, bracelets, and all kinds of golden jewels—everyone who brought a wave offering of gold to *Adonai*.

Exodus 35:21-22 TLV

brought what they had woven—the blue, purple, scarlet and fine linen. All the women whose heart stirred them up with wisdom spun the goat hair.

Also the leaders brought onyx stones and setting stones for the ephod and for the breastplate, along with the spice, the oil for the light and for anointing and for the sweet incense.

Every man and woman whose heart made them willing gave toward all the work that *ADONAI* had commanded to be done by Moses' hand. So *Bnei-Yisrael* brought it as a freewill offering to *ADONAI*.

Then Moses said to *Bnei-Yisrael*, "See, *ADONAI* has called by name Bezalel son of Uri son of Hur, of the tribe of Judah. He has filled him with the *Ruach* of God, with wisdom, understanding and knowledge, in all manner of craftsmanship, to make ingenious designs, to work in gold, silver and bronze, as well as cutting gemstones for setting, wood carving, to make all kinds of skillful craftsmanship. He has also placed in his heart the ability to teach—both he and Oholiab son of Ahisamach, of the tribe of Dan. He has filled them with wisdom of heart to forge all the works of an engraver, an artisan, and an embroiderer in blue, purple, scarlet and in fine linen, as well as weaving—they can perform every craft and ingenious designs.

Exodus, chapter 35

"So Bezalel and Oholiab are to work, along with every wise-hearted man in whom *ADONAI* has placed insight and understanding to know how to perform all the labor for the service of the Sanctuary, according to everything *ADONAI* has commanded."

Then Moses called Bezalel, Oholiab and all the wise-hearted men in whose minds *ADONAI* had set wisdom, along with everyone whose heart stirred him up to come do the work. They received from Moses the entire offering that *Bnei-Yisrael* had brought for the work of the service of the Sanctuary, to build it. They brought freewill offerings to him morning after morning. Then all the skilled men who were doing all the work of the Sanctuary came, one by one from the work he was doing, and said to Moses, "The people are bringing much more than enough for the work of this construction that *ADONAI* has commanded to be done."

So Moses gave an order, and they proclaimed it throughout the camp saying, "Let neither man nor woman make anything else as an offering for the Sanctuary." So the people were restrained from bringing more. For the work material they had was sufficient for all the work, with much left over.

So all the wise-hearted men among them did the work. They made the Tabernacle with ten curtains of finely twisted linen, along with blue, purple and scarlet, with *cheruvim* —the work of a skillful craftsman. The length of each curtain was 28 cubits and the width of each curtain was four cubits. All the curtains had one measure.

Then he coupled five curtains to one another, and the other five curtains he also coupled together. He made blue loops on the edge of the curtain that was outermost within the first set. He did the same along the edge of the curtain that was outermost in the second set.

He made 50 loops in one curtain and 50 loops on the edge of the curtain that was in the second set, so that the loops were opposite to one another. Also he made 50 clasps of gold and coupled the curtains one to another with the clasps, so the Tabernacle was one.

Then he made curtains from goat hair for a tent over the Tabernacle. He made 11 curtains. The length of each curtain was 30 cubits, and the width of each was four cubits. The 11 curtains had one measure. He coupled five curtains by themselves, and six other curtains by themselves. He made 50 loops on the edge of the curtain that was outermost in the first set and 50 loops on the edge of the curtain that was outermost in the second set. Also he made 50 bronze clasps to couple the tent together, so that it would be one.

Then he made a covering for the tent of ram skins, dyed red, along with a covering of sealskins above.
He also made the framework of boards for the Tabernacle from acacia wood, standing upright. The length of a board was ten cubits, the width was a cubit and a half. Each board had two supports, joined one to another. He did this for all the boards of the Tabernacle.

So he built the boards for the Tabernacle, 20 boards from the south side southward. And he made 40 silver bases under the 20 boards, two bases under one board for its two supports, and two bases under another board for its two supports. Also for the second side of the Tabernacle, on the north side, he made 20 boards, along with their 40 silver bases, two under one board and two under the next.

For the back part of the Tabernacle westward he made six boards. He also made two boards for the corners of the Tabernacle in the back, so that they could be doubled underneath, and in same way to be fixed to the top, at the first ring. He did this for both of them at the two corners. So there were eight boards, along with their silver bases, 16 in all, two under each board.

Then he made crossbars from acacia wood, five for the boards on one side of the Tabernacle, five for the boards on the other side of the Tabernacle, and five crossbars for the boards of the Tabernacle for the back part, westward. He built the middle crossbar to pass through, in the center of the boards, from one end to the other. He overlaid the boards with gold and made golden rings for them, as holders for the crossbars, and overlaid the crossbars with gold.

Then he made the curtain of blue, purple, scarlet and finely twisted linen, along with the *cheruvim*, the work of a skillful craftsman.

He made four pillars of acacia, and overlaid them with gold, having golden hooks, and he cast four silver bases for them. Then he made a *parokhet* for the entrance of the tent, of blue, purple, scarlet and finely twisted linen, the work of a color weaver.

Also he made the five pillars with their hooks, and overlaid their capitals and bands with gold, along with their five bronze bases.

Exodus, chapter 36

Then *Adonai* spoke to Moses saying, **"On the first day of the first month, you will set up the Tabernacle of the Tent of Meeting. You are to put the Ark of the Testimony there, and screen off the Ark with the curtain.**
Then bring in the table, and set in order the bread that is on it. Bring in the *menorah* and light its lamps. Set the golden incense altar in front of the Ark of the Testimony, and hang the curtain over the entrance of the Tabernacle.

"Set the altar of burnt offering before the entrance of the Tabernacle, the Tent of Meeting.

Set up the basin between the Tent of Meeting and the altar, and put water in it. Set up the courtyard all around, and hang the curtain of the gate of the courtyard.

"Take the anointing oil and anoint the Tabernacle, and everything within it, and consecrate it, along with all of its furnishings, and it will be holy. Also you are to anoint the altar of burnt offering with all of its utensils and consecrate the altar. The altar will be most holy. Then you are to anoint the basin along with its base and sanctify it.

"Bring Aaron and his sons to the entrance of the Tent of Meeting, and wash them with water. Put the holy garments on Aaron, anoint him and consecrate him, so that he may minister to Me as a *kohen*.
Also bring his sons and put tunics upon them. You are to anoint them, as you did their father, so that they too may minister to Me as *kohanim*. Their anointing will be for an everlasting priesthood throughout their generations." Moses did so, just as *Adonai* had commanded him.

Now it happened during the first month of the second year, on the first day of the month, the Tabernacle was raised up.

Moses raised the Tabernacle, and laid its bases, set up the framework of boards, put in the crossbars and set up its pillars. Then he spread the tent over the Tabernacle and put the covering of the tent on it, just as *Adonai* had commanded Moses.

He placed the Testimony into the Ark, set the poles on the Ark, and put the atonement cover on top of the Ark. He brought the Ark into the Tabernacle, set up the curtain as a screen, and screened off the Ark of the Testimony, just as *Adonai* had commanded Moses.

Then he set up the table inside the Tent of Meeting, on the side of the Tabernacle northward, outside the curtain. He set a row of bread in order upon it before *Adonai*, just as *Adonai* had commanded Moses.

Then he placed the *menorah* in the

Tent of Meeting, over against the table, on the south side of the Tabernacle. Then he lit the lamps before *ADONAI*, just as *ADONAI* had commanded Moses.

Next he placed the golden altar in the Tent of Meeting before the curtain, and he burned sweet spices of incense there, just as *ADONAI* had commanded Moses.

He hung the curtain over the entrance of the Tabernacle. Then he set the altar of burnt offering at the entrance of the Tabernacle, the Tent of Meeting, and offered upon it the burnt offering and the grain offering, just as *ADONAI* had commanded Moses.

Next he set up the basin between the Tent of Meeting and the altar and put water in it for washing, so that Moses, Aaron and his sons could wash their hands and their feet there. When they went into the Tent of Meeting and when they came near to the altar, they washed, just as *ADONAI* had commanded Moses.

He set up the courtyard around the Tabernacle and the altar and set up the screen at the gate of the courtyard.

So Moses finished the work.

Then the cloud covered the Tent of Meeting, and the glory of *ADONAI* filled the Tabernacle. Moses was unable to enter into the Tent of Meeting, because the cloud resided there and the glory of *ADONAI* filled the Tabernacle.

Now whenever the cloud was taken up from over the Tabernacle, *Bnei-Yisrael* went onward, throughout all their journeys. But if the cloud was not taken up, then they did not move out until the day that it was.

For the cloud of *ADONAI* was on the Tabernacle by day and a fire was there by night, in the sight of all the house of Israel throughout all their journeys.

Exodus, chapter 40

21. God Explains Atonement

Then *ADONAI* spoke to Moses after the death of the two sons of Aaron, when they approached the presence of *ADONAI* and died. *ADONAI* said to Moses, **"Tell Aaron your brother not to come at just any time into the Holiest Place behind the curtain—before the atonement cover which is on the Ark—so that he would not die. For I will be appearing in the cloud over the atonement cover.**

In this way should Aaron come into the Sanctuary: with a young bull for a sin offering and a ram for a burnt offering. He is to put on the holy linen garment, have the linen undergarments on his body, put on the linen sash, and wear the linen turban—they are the holy garments. He should bathe his body in water, and put them on.

Then he is to take from the congregation of *Bnei-Yisrael* two he-goats for a sin offering and one ram for a burnt offering. Then Aaron is to offer the bull for the sin offering which is for himself and make atonement for himself and his house.

Then he is take the two goats and present them before *ADONAI* at the entrance of the Tent of Meeting. Aaron will then cast lots for the two goats—one lot for *ADONAI*, and the other lot for the scapegoat.

Aaron is to present the goat on which the lot for *ADONAI* fell and make it a sin offering. But the goat upon which the lot for the scapegoat fell is to be presented alive before *ADONAI*, to make atonement upon it, by sending it away as the scapegoat into the wilderness. Also Aaron is to present the bull of the sin offering which is for himself and so make atonement for himself and his house. He is to slaughter the bull of the sin offering which is for himself. He is to take a firepan full of coals of fire from off the altar before *ADONAI* plus two handfuls of sweet powdered incense and bring it within the curtain. Then he is to put the incense on the fire before *ADONAI*, so that the cloud of the incense may cover the atonement cover that is on the Ark, so that he would not die.

He is then to take some of the blood of the bull and sprinkle it with his finger on the atonement cover, on the east side. Before the atonement cover he is to sprinkle some of the blood with his finger seven times.

Then he is to slaughter the goat of the sin offering which is for the people, bring its blood behind the curtain, and do with its as he did with the blood of the bull—sprinkle it upon the atonement cover, and before the atonement cover.

So he is to make atonement for the Holy Place, because of the uncleanness of *Bnei-Yisrael* and because of their transgressions, all their sins. He is to do the same for the Tent of Meeting, which dwells with them in the midst of their impurities.

No one is to be in the Tent of Meeting when he enters to make

atonement in the Holy Place until he comes out, and has made atonement for himself and for his household, and for all the assembly of Israel.

Then he is to go out to the altar that is before *ADONAI* and make atonement for it. He is to take some of the bull's blood and some of the goat's blood and dab it around on the horns of the altar. He is to sprinkle some of the blood on it with his finger seven times, and cleanse it, and consecrate it from the uncleanness of *Bnei-Yisrael*. When he has finished atoning for the Holy Place, the Tent of Meeting and the altar, then he is to present the live goat.

Aaron shall lay both his hands on the head of the live goat and confess over it all the iniquities of *Bnei-Yisrael* and all their transgressions, all their sins. He should place them on the head of the goat and send it away into the wilderness by the hand of a man who is in readiness. The goat will carry all their iniquities by itself into a solitary land and he is to leave the goat in the wilderness.

Then Aaron is to come into the Tent of Meeting, take off the linen garments that he put on when he went into the Holy Place, and leave them there. He is to bathe himself with water in a holy place, put on his garments, and come out to offer his burnt offering and the burnt offering of the people, to make atonement for himself and for the people. Then he is to burn up fat of the sin offering in smoke on the altar. The man who leaves the goat as a scapegoat is to wash his clothes and bathe his body in water. Afterward he may come into the camp.

The bull for the sin offering and the goat for the sin offering, whose blood was brought in to make atonement in the Holy Place, should be carried outside the camp, and their hides, their flesh, and their dung burned with fire. The one who burns them is to wash his clothes and bathe his body in water. Then afterward he may come into the camp.

"It is to be a statute to you forever, that in the seventh month, on the tenth day of the month, you are to afflict your souls, and do no kind of work—both the native-born and the outsider dwelling among you. For on this day atonement will be made for you, to cleanse you. From all your sins you will be clean before *ADONAI*.

It is a *Shabbat* of solemn rest to you, and you are to afflict your souls. It is a statute forever. The *kohen* who is anointed and who is consecrated to be *kohen* in his father's place will make the atonement, and put on the linen garments, the holy garments. He is to make atonement for the Holy Sanctuary, for the Tent of Meeting, for the altar, for the *kohanim*, and for all the people of the assembly.

"This will be an everlasting statute for you, to make atonement for *Bnei-Yisrael* once in the year because of all their sins." It was done as *ADONAI* commanded Moses.

Leviticus, chapter 16

Then *ADONAI* spoke to Moses, saying: **"Speak to Aaron, to his sons,**

"Then he is to take from the congregation of *Bnei-Yisrael* two he-goats for a sin offering and one ram for a burnt offering. Then Aaron is to offer the bull for the sin offering which is for himself and make atonement for himself and his house. Then he is take the two goats and present them before *Adonai* at the entrance of the Tent of Meeting.

Leviticus 16:5-7 TLV

and to all *Bnei-Yisrael*, and say to them: This is the word which *ADONAI* has commanded. Anyone from the house of Israel who slaughters a bull, a lamb or a goat in the camp or outside the camp, but has not brought it to the entrance of the Tent of Meeting to offer it as a sacrifice to *ADONAI* before the Tabernacle—let bloodguilt be charged to that man. He has shed blood—that man is to be cut off from among his people. Thus *Bnei-Yisrael* may bring their sacrifices that they were making in the open field to *ADONAI*, at the entrance of the Tent of Meeting to the *kohen*, and offer them as sacrifices of fellowship offerings to *ADONAI*. The *kohen* is to sprinkle the blood on the altar of *ADONAI* at the entrance of the Tent of Meeting and burn up the fat as smoke for a soothing aroma to *ADONAI*. They are no longer to offer their sacrifices to the goat-demons after which they play the prostitute. This will be a statute forever to them throughout their generations.

"Then you are to say to them: Anyone from the house of Israel, or from the outsiders dwelling among them, who offers a burnt offering or sacrifice, but does not bring it to the entrance of the Tent of Meeting to sacrifice it to *ADONAI*, is to be cut off from his people. Anyone from the house of Israel, or from the outsiders dwelling among them, who eats any kind of blood, I will set my face against that soul—the one who eats blood—and will cut him off from among his people. For the life of the creature is in the blood, and I have given it to you on the altar to make atonement for your lives—for it is the blood that makes atonement because of the life. Therefore I have said to *Bnei-Yisrael*: No person among you may eat blood, nor may any outsider dwelling among you eat blood. Any person from *Bnei-Yisrael*, or from the outsiders dwelling among them, who hunts as game any animal or bird that may be eaten, must drain its blood and cover it with dust. For the life of every creature, its blood is in its life. Therefore I said to *Bnei-Yisrael*: You are not to eat the blood of any kind of creature, for the life of every creature is its blood. Whoever eats it is to be cut off.

"Everyone who eats what dies naturally or is torn by animals—whether he is native-born or a foreigner—is to wash his clothes and bathe himself in water. He will be unclean until the evening, then he will be clean. But if he does not wash them or bathe his body, then he will bear his iniquity."

Leviticus, chapter 17

ADONAI said to Moses: **"Speak to *Bnei-Yisrael* and say to them: I am *ADONAI* your God. You are not to act as they do in the land of Egypt, where you used to live. Nor are you to act as they do in the land of Canaan, where I am bringing you, nor are you to walk in their customs. You are to obey My ordinances and keep My statutes and walk in them—I am *ADONAI* your God. So you are to keep My statutes and My ordinances. The one who does them will live by them. I am *ADONAI*.**

Leviticus 18:1-5

22. God Places His Name

Again *Adonai* spoke to Moses saying, **"Speak to *Bnei-Yisrael* and say to them: Any man or woman who desires to vow a Nazirite vow to be separate for *Adonai*, is to abstain from wine and any other fermented drink. He is not to drink any vinegar made from wine or any fermented drink, or any grape juice, or eat grapes or raisins. All du ring his days as a Nazirite he is not to eat anything from the grapevine—even the seeds or skins.**

All the duration of his Nazirite vow, no razor is to come on his head until the time of his consecration to *Adonai* is over. He is to be holy, and the hair of his head is to grow long.

All the days of his separation to *Adonai*, he is not to go near a dead body. Even if his father, mother, brother or sister should die, he is not to make himself unclean, because his consecration to God is on his head. All the days of his separation, he is to be consecrated to *Adonai*.

"Now if someone should die suddenly in his presence, thereby defiling his dedicated head, he is to shave his head on the day of his purification—the seventh day. Then on the eighth day, he is to bring two doves or two young pigeons to the *kohen* at the entrance of the Tent of Meeting.

The *kohen* is to offer one as a sin offering and the other as a burnt offering. He is to make atonement for him because he sinned through the corpse. He must consecrate his head on the same day.

He will be dedicated to *Adonai* for the days of his Nazirite separation. He is to bring a year-old male lamb as a guilt offering. The previous days will not count because he was contaminated during his Nazirite separation.

"Then this is the *Torah* of the Nazirite when his period of separation is over. He must be brought to the entrance of the Tent of Meeting. He is to present his offering to *Adonai*: a year-old male lamb without flaw as a burnt offering, a year-old female lamb without flaw as a sin offering, a flawless ram as a fellowship offering, along with a basket of *matzah* cakes made of fine flour mixed with oil and *matzah* wafers spread with oil, along with their grain and drink offerings.

"The *kohen* will offer these before *Adonai*, and present his sin offering and burnt offering. Then he is to sacrifice the ram as a fellowship offering to *Adonai*, along with the basket of *matzot*. The *kohen* will also present the grain and drink offerings.

The Nazirite is then to shave the hair of his dedication at the entrance of the Tent of Meeting, and he is to take the hair of his dedication and put it into the fire of the fellowship offering sacrifice.

The *kohen* is to take the boiled shoulder of the ram and one *matzah* cake and one *matzah* wafer

"Speak to Aaron and to his sons saying: Thus you are to bless *Bnei-Yisrael*, by saying to them: '*ADONAI* bless you and keep you! *ADONAI* make His face to shine on you and be gracious to you! *ADONAI* turn His face toward you and grant you *shalom*!'

Numbers 6:23-26 TLV

from the basket, and he is to place them into the hands of the Nazirite after he has shaved the hair of his dedication.

The *kohen* will wave them before *ADONAI* as a wave offering. They are holy, and belong to the *kohen* along with the breast that was waved and the thigh that was presented.

Afterward, the Nazirite may drink wine.

This is the *Torah* regarding the Nazirite who vows his offering to *ADONAI* with regard to his consecration, besides whatever else he can afford. He must fulfill the vow he has made, in accordance with the *Torah* of his consecration.'"

Again *ADONAI* spoke to Moses saying, **"Speak to Aaron and to his sons saying: Thus you are to bless *Bnei-Yisrael*, by saying to them:**

> **'*ADONAI* bless you and keep you!**
>
> ***ADONAI* make His face to shine on you and be gracious to you!**
>
> ***ADONAI* turn His face toward you and grant you *shalom*!'**
>
> **In this way they are to place My Name over *Bnei-Yisrael*, and so I will bless them."**

Numbers, chapter 6

23. God Disciplines the Scoffers

ADONAI spoke to Moses saying, **"Send some men on your behalf to investigate the land of Canaan, which I am giving to *Bnei-Yisrael*. Each man you are to send will be a prince of the tribe of his fathers, a man from each tribe."**

So according to the word of *ADONAI*, Moses sent them from the wilderness of Paran. All the men were princes of *Bnei-Yisrael*. These are their names: from the tribe of Reuben, Shammua son of Zaccur. From the tribe of Simeon, Shaphat son of Hori. From the tribe of Judah, Caleb son of Jephunneh.

From the tribe of Issachar, Igal son of Joseph. From the tribe of Ephraim, Hoshea son of Nun. From the tribe of Benjamin, Palti son of Raphu. From the tribe of Zebulun, Gaddiel son of Sodi.

From the tribe of Manasseh, part of the tribe of Joseph, Gaddi son of Susi. From the tribe of Dan, Ammiel son of Gemalli. From the tribe of Asher, Sethur son of Michael. From the tribe of Naphtali, Nahbi son of Vophsi. From the tribe of Gad, Geuel son of Machi.

These are the names of the men Moses sent to investigate the land. (Now he gave Hoshea son of Nun, the name Joshua.)

As he sent them to explore the land of Canaan, he said to them, "Go up there through the Negev, then go up into the hill country. See what the land is like and the people living there, whether they might be strong or weak, few or many. In what kind of land are they living? Is it good or bad? Also, what about the cities in which they are living? Are they unwalled or do they have fortifications? How is the soil—fertile or poor? Are there trees on it or not? Do your best to bring back some of the fruit of the land." (It was the season for the first ripe grapes.)

So they went up and explored the land from the wilderness of Zin as far as Rehob the entrance of Hamath. They continued on up through the Negev and came to Hebron. There lived Ahiman, Sheshai, and Talmai, descendants of Anak. (Hebron was built seven years before Zoan in Egypt.)

When they reached as far as the Valley of Eshcol, they cut a single branch with a cluster of grapes. It was carried on a pole between two of them. They also cut some pomegranates and some figs. That place was called the Valley of Eshcol because of the cluster cut by *Bnei-Yisrael*.

They returned from investigating the land after 40 days. They traveled and returned to Moses, Aaron and the entire community of *Bnei-Yisrael* at Kadesh in the wilderness of Paran. They gave their report to them and the entire assembly.

They showed the land's fruit. They gave their account to him and said, "We went into the land where you sent us. Indeed it is flowing with milk and honey—this is some of its fruit. Except, the people living in the land are powerful, and the cities are fortified and very large. We even saw the sons of Anak there!

Amalek is living in the land of the Negev, the Hittites, Jebusites, and Amorites are living in the mountains, and the Canaanites are living near the sea and along the bank of the Jordan."

Then Caleb quieted the people before Moses, and said, "We should definitely go up and capture the land, for we can certainly do it!"

But the men who had gone up with him said, "We cannot attack these people, because they are stronger than we." They spread among *Bnei-Yisrael* a bad report about the land they had explored, saying, "The land through which we passed to explore devours its residents. All the people we saw there are men of great size! We also saw there the *Nephilim*. (The sons of Anak are from the *Nephilim*.) We seemed like grasshoppers in our eyes as well as theirs!"

Numbers, chapter 13

All through that night, the entire community raised up their voices. The people wept. All *Bnei-Yisrael* grumbled against Moses and Aaron and the whole community said, "If only we had died in Egypt! If only we had died in this wilderness! Why is *Adonai* bringing us to this land to fall by the sword? Our wives and children will be like plunder! Wouldn't it be better for us to return to Egypt?" They said to each other, "Let's choose a leader and let's go back to Egypt!"

Then Moses and Aaron fell on their faces before the entire assembly of the community of *Bnei-Yisrael*. Joshua son of Nun and Caleb son of Jephunneh, who were among those who had explored the land, tore their clothes.

They said to the whole assembly of *Bnei-Yisrael*, "The land through which we passed is an exceptionally good land! If *Adonai* is pleased with us, He will lead us into that land and will give it to us—a land flowing with milk and honey. Only don't rebel against *Adonai*, and don't be afraid of the people of the land. They will be food for us. The protection over them is gone. *Adonai* is with us! Do not fear them."

But the whole assembly talked about violently stoning them.

Then the glory of *Adonai* appeared at the Tent of Meeting to all *Bnei-Yisrael*. *Adonai* said to Moses, **"How long will these people treat Me contemptibly? How long will they neglect to trust in Me—in spite of all the miraculous signs I have performed among them?**

I will strike them with the plague. I will destroy them. But you I will make into a nation greater and stronger than they!"

Moses said to *Adonai*, "The Egyptians will hear about it, because You brought up this people by Your power from among them. They will tell the residents of this land about it. Already they have heard that You,

Then Caleb quieted the people before Moses, and said, "We should definitely go up and capture the land, for we can certainly do it!"

Numbers 13:30 TLV

ADONAI, are in the midst of this people, that You, *ADONAI*, have been seen eye to eye, that Your cloud remains over them, and that in a pillar of cloud by day and a pillar of fire by night You go before them.

If you kill these people all at once, the nations who have heard this report about You will say, 'Because *ADONAI* was unable to bring this people to the land He had promised them, He has slaughtered them in the wilderness.'

"So please, let *ADONAI* show His strength, just as You have spoken saying, **'*ADONAI* is slow to anger and abundant in lovingkindness, forgiving iniquity and transgression. Still, He does not leave the guilty unpunished, bringing the iniquity of the fathers upon the children to the third and fourth generations.'**

Forgive now the guiltiness of this people in accordance with the greatness of Your lovingkindness, just as You have pardoned this people from Egypt until now!"

ADONAI answered, **"I have forgiven them just as you have spoken. But as certainly as I live and as certainly as the glory of *ADONAI* fills the entire earth, none of the people who saw My glory and My miraculous signs I performed in Egypt and in the wilderness—yet tested Me these ten times and did not obey My Voice— not one of them will see the land I promised to their forefathers. None of those who treated Me with contempt will see it!**

However, My servant Caleb, because a different spirit is with him and he is wholeheartedly behind Me, I will bring him into the land where he went—his offspring will inherit it. Now since the Amalekites and Canaanites are inhabiting the valley, turn back tomorrow and set out by the wilderness route toward the Sea of Reeds."

ADONAI then said to Moses and Aaron saying, **"How long will this wicked community be grumbling against Me? I have heard the complaints of *Bnei-Yisrael* grumbling against Me.**

So tell them, 'As surely as I live,' says *ADONAI*, 'I will do to you just as I heard you say in My ears. In this very wilderness your bodies will drop— every one of you 20 years of age and older who was numbered in the census and grumbled against Me. Not one of you will enter the land about which I lifted My hand to make home for you—except Caleb son of Jephunneh and Joshua son of Nun.

"As for your children—whom you said would be like plunder—I will bring them in and they will experience the land that you spurned. But your bodies will drop in this wilderness.

Your children will be herdsmen in the wilderness for 40 years. They will suffer because of your unfaithfulness until your corpses are consumed in the wilderness.

For 40 years, corresponding to the number of the 40 days you explored the land—one year for each day— you will suffer for your iniquities and know My hostility. I, *ADONAI*, have

spoken and certainly will I do this to all this wicked community banding together against Me. In this wilderness they will meet their end and there they will die!"

Then the men whom Moses had sent to explore the land, who had returned and caused the whole community to grumble against him by spreading a bad report about the land, these men, spreading the bad report about the land, died of the plague in *ADONAI*'s presence.

Of those men who had gone to explore the land, only Joshua son of Nun and Caleb son of Jephunneh survived.

When Moses related these things to all of *Bnei-Yisrael*, the people mourned bitterly. They rose the next morning and went up to the high mountains, saying, "Look! Let's go up to the place which *ADONAI* promised. For we have sinned."

But Moses said, "Why are you disobeying the mouth of *ADONAI*? That will never succeed. You should not go up, because *ADONAI* will not be among you and you will be defeated before your enemies! For the Amalekites and Canaanites are there in front of you, and you will fall by the sword. *ADONAI* will not be with you, because you turned away from following *ADONAI*."

But presumptuously they went up to the high mountain country, though neither the Ark of *ADONAI*'s covenant nor Moses moved from within the camp. The Amalekites and Canaanites living in the mountain country came down, attacked them, and beat them down all the way to Hormah.

Numbers, chapter 14

24. God Provides a Way

In the first month, the entire community of *Bnei-Yisrael* arrived at the wilderness of Zin. The people stayed at Kadesh. There Miriam died and was buried.

Now there was no water for the community, so they assembled against Moses and Aaron. The people quarreled with Moses saying, "If only we had died when our brothers died before *ADONAI*! Now why have you brought the community of *ADONAI* into this wilderness, for us and our livestock to die here? Why have you brought us from Egypt to bring us to this evil place—a place without grain, fig, grapevine or pomegranate—and there's no water to drink!"

So Moses and Aaron went from before the assembly to the entrance of the Tent of Meeting and fell on their faces.

Then the glory of *ADONAI* appeared to them. *ADONAI* spoke to Moses saying, **"Take the staff and gather the assembly, you and your brother Aaron. Speak to the rock before their eyes, and it will give out its water. You will bring out water from the rock, and you will give the community something to drink, along with their livestock."**

So Moses took the staff from before the presence of *ADONAI*, just as He had commanded him.

Moses and Aaron gathered the assembly in front of the rock. He said, "Listen now, you rebels! Must we bring you water from this rock?"

Then Moses raised his arm and struck the rock twice with the staff. Water gushed out and the community and its livestock drank.

But *ADONAI* said to Moses and Aaron, **"Because you did not trust in Me so as to esteem Me as holy in the eyes of *Bnei-Yisrael*, therefore you will not bring this assembly into the land that I have given to them."** These are the waters of Meribah where *Bnei-Yisrael* contended with Moses, and where *ADONAI* showed Himself holy among them.

Moses sent messengers from Kadesh to the king of Edom. "Thus says your brother, Israel:

'You know all the hardship that came on us. Our forefathers went down to Egypt, so we lived there for a very long time. The Egyptians mistreated us, and our fathers. But we cried out to *ADONAI*, He heard our cry, sent an angel and brought us out of Egypt. See now, we are at Kadesh, a town on the frontier of your territory. Permit us to pass through your territory. We will not cross through any field or vineyard or drink water of any well. But we will travel on the king's highway. We will not deviate to the right or left until we will have passed through your territory.'"

But Edom said to him, "You may not pass through me—or I will march out against you with the sword."

Bnei-Yisrael then said to him, "We will travel on the main road, and if we or our livestock even drink any of your

ADONAI said to Moses, "Make yourself a fiery snake and put it on a pole.
Whenever anyone who has been bitten will look at it, he will live."
So Moses made a bronze snake and put it on a pole, and it happened that
whenever a snake bit anyone and he looked
at the bronze snake, he lived.

Numbers 21:8-9 TLV

water, we will pay its price. It's nothing, just to pass through on foot!"

He answered, "You may not pass through!"

Yet Edom came out to oppose them with a large and well-armed people. Since Edom refused to permit Israel to cross through her territory, Israel turned away from them. The entirety of the community of *Bnei-Yisrael* set out from Kadesh and came to Mount Hor.

Now at Mount Hor, near the Edomite border, *ADONAI* said to Moses and Aaron, **"Aaron will be gathered to his people. He will not enter the land, which I have given to *Bnei-Yisrael*, because you rebelled against My command at the waters of Meribah. Take Aaron and his son Eleazar, and take them up Mount Hor. Remove Aaron's garments and put them on his son Eleazar, and Aaron will be gathered up and will die there."**

Moses did as *ADONAI* commanded. They ascended Mount Hor before the eyes of the whole community. Moses removed Aaron's garments and placed them on Eleazar his son. Aaron died there at the top of the mountain. Then Moses and Eleazar descended the mountain. When they saw that Aaron had died, the entire community mourned Aaron 30 days.

Numbers, chapter 20

When the Canaanite king of Arad, who lived in the Negev, heard that Israel was coming along the road to Atharim, he attacked Israel and captured some of them. Then Israel vowed to *ADONAI* and stated, "If you deliver this people into our hand, we will put their cities under the ban of destruction!"

ADONAI listened to Israel's plea and delivered up the Canaanites. They put them and their cities under the ban of destruction. So the name of the place was called Hormah.

They travelled from Mount Hor along the route to the Sea of Reeds in order to go around the land of Edom. The spirit of the people became impatient along the way.

The people spoke against God and Moses: "Why have you brought us from Egypt to die in the wilderness, because there is no bread, no water, and our very spirits detest the despicable food?"

So *ADONAI* sent poisonous serpents among the people, and they bit the people and many of the people of Israel died.

The people came to Moses and said, "We sinned when we spoke against *ADONAI* and you! Pray to *ADONAI* for us, that He may take away the snakes!" So Moses prayed for the people.

ADONAI said to Moses, **"Make yourself a fiery snake and put it on a pole. Whenever anyone who has been bitten will look at it, he will live."** So Moses made a bronze snake and put it on a pole, and it happened that whenever a snake bit anyone and he looked at the bronze snake, he lived.

Numbers 21:1-9

25. God Turns Curses into Blessings

Then *Bnei-Yisrael* set out and camped in the plains of Moab alongside the Jordan across from Jericho.

When Balak son of Zippor, realized all that *Bnei-Yisrael* had done to the Amorites, Moab became terrified because there were so many people. Moab was filled with dread because of *Bnei-Yisrael*. Moab said to the elders of Midian, "The multitude will lick up everything around us like the ox licks up the grass of the field."

Now Balak son of Zippor was king of Moab at that time. He sent messengers to summon Balaam son of Beor, at Pethor near the River in his native land, saying to him, "Look now, a people has come out of Egypt. See now, they cover the surface of the earth and are settling beside me.

Come now, curse this people for me, because they are too strong for me! Perhaps I may be able to defeat them and drive them away from the country. I know that whoever you bless will be blessed and whoever you curse will be accursed!"

The elders of Moab and Midian left with divination fees in their hand. When they came to Balaam, they told him Balak's words.

He said to them, "Spend the night here. I will give you an answer just as *ADONAI* speaks to me." So the officials of Moab stayed with Balaam.

God came to Balaam and asked, "Who are these men with you?"

Balaam said to God, "Balak son of Zippor, king of Moab, sent word to me: See, the people coming out of Egypt cover the surface of the land. Come now, curse them for me. Perhaps I will be able to fight against them and drive them away!"

God said to Balaam, "Do not go with them! Do not curse them, for they are blessed!"

So Balaam got up in the morning and said to the officials of Balak, "Go back to your country, for *ADONAI* has refused to let me go with you."

So the Moabite officials got up, went back to Balak, and said, "Balaam refused to come with us."

Balak again sent other dignitaries, more numerous and honored than these previous ones.

They also came to Balaam and said to him, "Thus says Balak son of Zippor: Please let nothing keep you from coming to me! I will richly reward you, and everything you tell me I will do! Just come now and curse this people for me!"

But Balaam answered Balak's servants, "Even if Balak gave me his house full of silver and gold, I cannot cross beyond the mouth of *ADONAI* my God, to do anything small or great! But now, you may spend the night here, too. Then I may find out anything else *ADONAI* may say to me."

God came to Balaam by night and said to him, "Since the men came to you to summon you, arise and go with them. However, only the word I tell you are you to do!"

So Balaam got up in the morning, saddled his donkey, and went with the Moabite princes. But the anger of God burned because he was going. The angel of *ADONAI* stood in the road to oppose him—he was riding on his donkey and two of his servants were with him— when the donkey saw the angel of *ADONAI* standing in the road with his drawn sword in his hand, the donkey turned off the road and went into the field. So Balaam beat the donkey to get her back onto the road.

Then the angel of *ADONAI* stood in a narrow path between two vineyards, with a wall on this side and a wall on that side. When the donkey saw the angel of *ADONAI*, she pressed against the wall, crushing Balaam's foot against the wall. So Balaam continued beating her.

The angel again moved. He stood in a narrow place where there was no room to turn, right or left. When the donkey saw the angel of *ADONAI*, she lay down under Balaam.

Balaam was very angry and beat the donkey with his staff. Then *ADONAI* opened the donkey's mouth and she said to Balaam, "What have I done to you that you have beaten me these three times?"

Balaam said to the donkey, "Because you've made a fool of me! If I had a sword in my hand, I would kill you now!"

The donkey said to Balaam, "Am I not your donkey which you have ridden as always to this day? Have I ever been in the habit of doing this to you?"

"No," he said. Then *ADONAI* opened Balaam's eyes, and he saw the angel of *ADONAI* standing in the road with his drawn sword in his hand. So he fell on his face.

The angel of *ADONAI* said to him, **"Why have you beaten your donkey these three times? Behold, I came as an adversary because your way before Me is a reckless one! The donkey saw Me and turned away from Me these three times. If she had not turned away from Me, by now I would have killed you indeed, but let her live!"**

Balaam said to the angel of *ADONAI*, "I have sinned, for I did not know that you were standing in the road to oppose me. Now, if this is displeasing in your eyes, I will go back home." The angel of *ADONAI* said to Balaam, **"Go with the men, but speak only the word that I tell you."** So Balaam went with Balak's princes.

When Balak heard that Balaam had come, he went out to greet him at the Moabite city on the border of the Arnon, the frontier of the territory. Balak said to Balaam, "Didn't I send you an urgent summons? Why didn't you come to me? Am I really unable to reward you?"

"Look, I have come to you now!" Balaam said to Balak. "Can I just say anything? I must speak only the message which God puts into my mouth."

How lovely are your tents, O Jacob, and your dwellings, O Israel!

Numbers 24:5 TLV

Then Balaam went with Balak to Kiriath-huzoth. Balak sacrificed cattle and sheep and sent some to Balaam and the princes who were with him. In the morning, Balak took Balaam with him to Bamoth-baal, and from there he saw part of the people.

Numbers, chapter 22

Then Balaam said to Balak, "Build me seven altars here and prepare for me here seven bulls and seven rams." So Balak did just as Balaam had said.

Balak and Balaam offered a bull and a ram on each altar. Balaam said to Balak, "Stay here beside your offering. I will go and perhaps *Adonai* will meet me. Whatever message He shows me, I will tell you." Then he went to a barren height.

God met with Balaam and he said to Him, "I have prepared seven altars, and on each altar I offered a bull and a ram."

Adonai put a message into Balaam's mouth and said, **"Return to Balak and speak this."**

Balaam went back to him. Behold, he was standing beside his offering with all the princes of Moab.
Then he uttered his oracle and said,

"From Aram, Balak brought me,
Moab's king from the mountains of the east:
'Come! Curse Jacob for me!
'Come! Denounce Israel!'
How can I curse one
whom God has not cursed?
How can I denounce one
whom *Adonai* has not denounced?
From the rocky peaks I see him.
From the heights I behold him.
Look, he lives as a nation apart,
and does not consider himself
as being like the other nations.
Who can count Jacob's dust?
Who can number a fourth of Israel?
Let my soul die the death of the
upright, and let my end be like his!"

Balak said to Balaam, "What have you done to me? I brought you to curse my enemies, but look, you've actually blessed them!"

But in response he said, "Mustn't I speak whatever *Adonai* puts into my mouth?"

Then Balak said to him, "Come now with me to another place where you can see a part of them only, not all of them. Curse them for me from there."

He took him to Lookout Field on top of Pisgah. He built seven altars and offered a bull and a ram on each altar. "Stay here beside your offering," he said to Balak, "while I am meeting over there."

Adonai met Balaam there and put a message into his mouth, and said, **"Return to Balak and speak thus."**

So he went to him, and behold, he and the princes of Moab were standing beside his offering. Balak asked him, "What did *Adonai* say?"

So he uttered his oracle and said:

"Rise, Balak!
Hear me, son of Zippor!
God is not a man who lies,
or a son of man

who changes his mind!
Does He speak and then not do it,
or promise and not fulfill it?
Look, I received a command to
bless. He has blessed
-I cannot change it!
No misfortune is to be seen in
Jacob, and no misery in Israel!
ADONAI their God is with them
-the King's shout is among them!
God is bringing them from Egypt
with the strong horns
of the wild ox!
There is no sorcery effective
against Jacob,
nor any divination against Israel!
Now it will be said of Jacob and
Israel, 'See what God has done!'
The people rise like a lioness,
like a lion who does not rest
until he eats his prey
and drinks his victim's blood!"

Then Balak said to Balaam, "Do not curse them or bless them at all!"

Balaam answered and said to Balak, "Haven't I told you, 'All that *ADONAI* says, I must do?'"

Balak said to Balaam, "Come with me to another place. Perhaps it will be pleasing to God and you may curse them for me from there."

So Balak took Balaam to the top of Peor, overlooking the wasteland. Balaam said to Balak, "Build me seven altars here, and prepare seven bulls and seven rams for me."

Balak did just as Balaam said, and offered a bull and a ram on each altar.

Numbers, chapter 23

When Balaam realized that it was pleasing in the eyes of *ADONAI* to bless Israel, he did not resort to sorceries as at the other times, but turned his face toward the wilderness.

Lifting up his eyes, Balaam saw Israel dwelling by tribes. The *Ruach Elohim* came over him. He uttered his oracle and said:

"This is the oracle
of Balaam son of Beor,
and the oracle of a strong man
whose eye has been opened,
the oracle of one
hearing God's speech,
one seeing *Shaddai*'s vision,
one fallen down, yet with open eyes:

How lovely are your tents, O Jacob,
and your dwellings, O Israel!
Like valleys they are spread out,
like gardens beside a river,
like aloes planted by *ADONAI*,
like cedars beside the waters.
Water will flow from his buckets,
his seed by abundant water.
His king will be greater than Agag,
his kingdom will be exalted.
God is bringing him out of Egypt
like the strong horns of a wild ox.
He devours nations hostile to him.
He will crush their bones.
His arrows will pierce them.
He crouches like a lion
or a lioness—
who would rouse him?
He who blesses you will be blessed,
and he who curses you
will be cursed."

Then Balak became furious at Balaam, and struck his hands together.

Balak said to Balaam, "I summoned you to curse my enemies, but look, you have blessed them these three times! Now, go home! I said I would reward you, but see, *ADONAI* has kept you from reward!"

Balaam answered Balak, "Didn't I indeed tell your messengers whom you sent to me saying: 'If Balak were to give me his house full of silver and gold, I could not go beyond the mouth of *ADONAI*, to do good or bad from my own heart? Whatever *ADONAI* may speak, I will speak!'

Now, behold, I am going back to my people. Come, let me counsel you what these people will do to your people in the latter days.
Then he uttered his oracle:

The oracle of Balaam son of Beor,
the strong man whose eye is opened,
the oracle of one
hearing God's speech,
one experiencing *Elyon*'s knowledge
one seeing *Shaddai*'s vision,
one fallen down, yet with open eyes:

> 'I see him, yet not at this moment.
> I behold him,
> yet not in this location.
> For a star will come from Jacob,
> a scepter will arise from Israel.
> He will crush
> the foreheads of Moab
> and the skulls of all
> the sons of Seth.
> Edom will be conquered—
> his enemies will conquer Seir,
> but Israel will triumph.
> One from Jacob will rule
> and destroy the city's survivors."

Then he saw Amalek,
so he uttered his oracle and said:
"Amalek was the first of nations,
but will come to ruin at last."

> Then he saw the Kenite,
> so he uttered his oracle and said,
> "Your dwelling is secure.
> Your nest is set in the rock.
> Yet Kain will be destroyed,
> when Asshur captures you."

Again he uttered his oracle and said,

> "O, who can live
> when God does this?
> Ships will come from
> Kittim's shore.
> They will afflict Asshur and Eber,
> but they too will
> come to destruction."

Then Balaam got up and went and returned to his own place, and Balak went on his way.

Numbers, chapter 24

26. God Keeps Loving His People

"Now, O Israel, listen to the statutes and ordinances that I am teaching you to do, so that you may live and go in and possess the land that *ADONAI* the God of your fathers is giving you.

You must not add to the word that I am commanding you or take away from it - in order to keep the *mitzvot* of *ADONAI* your God that I am commanding you.

Your eyes have seen what *ADONAI* did at Baal Peor, for *ADONAI* your God has destroyed from among you everyone who followed Baal Peor. But you who held tight to *ADONAI* your God are alive today—all of you.

"See, just as *ADONAI* my God commanded me, I have taught you statutes and ordinances to do in the land that you are about to enter to possess. You must keep and do them, for it is your wisdom and understanding in the eyes of the peoples, who will hear all these statutes and say, 'Surely this great nation is a wise and understanding people.' For what great nation is there that has gods so near to them, as *ADONAI* our God is whenever we call on Him? What great nation is there that has statutes and ordinances that are righteous—like all of this *Torah* that I am setting before you today?

"Only be watchful and watch over your soul closely, so you do not forget the things your eyes have seen and they slip from your heart all the days of your life. You are to make them known to your children and your children's children. The day that you stood before *ADONAI* your God in Horeb, *ADONAI* said to me, **'Gather the people to Me and I will make them hear My words, so that they learn to fear Me all the days that they live on the earth, and so that they teach their children.'**

"You came near and stood at the bottom of the mountain while the mountain was blazing with fire up to the heart of the heavens—darkness, cloud, and fog. *ADONAI* spoke to you from the midst of the fire. The sound of words you heard, but a form you did not see—only a voice.

He declared to you His covenant, which He commanded you to do—the Ten Words—and He wrote them on two tablets of stone. *ADONAI* commanded me at that time to teach you statutes and ordinances, so that you might do them in the land you are crossing over to possess.

"So be very watchful over your souls since you saw no form on the day that *ADONAI* spoke to you in Horeb out of the midst of the fire, so that you do not act corruptly and make for yourselves a graven image in the likeness of any figure—the form of a male or female, the form of any animal that is on the earth, the form of any winged bird that flies in the sky, the form of anything that creeps on the ground, the form of any fish that is in the water under the earth—and so that you do not lift up your eyes toward the heavens and see the sun and the moon and the stars—all the heavenly host—and are drawn away and bow down and worship them. *ADONAI* your God has allotted them to all the peoples under all the heavens.

But you, *ADONAI* has taken, and He brought you out of the iron furnace, out of Egypt to be a people for His own inheritance, as you are this day.

"Furthermore *ADONAI* was angry with me because of your words, and He swore that I would not cross over the Jordan or enter the good land that *ADONAI* your God is giving you for an inheritance. For I must die in this land; I am not crossing over the Jordan. But you will cross over and take possession of that good land.

Watch yourselves, so that you do not forget the covenant of *ADONAI* your God, which He cut with you, and make for yourselves a graven image in the form of anything that *ADONAI* your God has forbidden you. For *ADONAI* your God is a consuming fire—a jealous God.

"When you father children and children's children and have been in the land a long time, and you act corruptly and make a graven image in the form of anything and do evil in the sight of *ADONAI* your God, provoking Him to anger, I call heaven and earth to witness against you today that you will certainly be carried off quickly from the land you are crossing over the Jordan to possess. You will not prolong your days on it, for you will certainly be destroyed. *ADONAI* will scatter you among the peoples, and you will be left few in number among the nations where *ADONAI* will drive you. There you will serve man-made gods of wood and stone, which do not see or hear or eat or smell. But from there you will seek *ADONAI* your God and you will find Him, when you seek Him with all your heart and with all your soul.

"When you are in distress and all these things have come on you, in the latter days you will return to *ADONAI* your God and listen to His voice. For *ADONAI* your God is a merciful God. He will not abandon you or destroy you, or forget the covenant with your fathers that He swore to them.

"Indeed, ask now about the former days that were before you, from the day that God created man on the earth, and ask from one end of the sky to the other. Has there ever been such a great thing as this, or has anything like it been heard? Has a people ever heard the voice of God speaking from the midst of the fire, as you have heard—and lived?

Or has any god ever tried to come to take for himself a nation from within a nation—by trials, by signs and wonders, and by war, and by a mighty hand and an outstretched arm, and by great terrors—like all that *ADONAI* your God did for you in Egypt before your eyes?

You were shown, so that you might know that *ADONAI* is God—there is no other besides Him. From the heavens He made you hear His voice to instruct you, and on earth He caused you to see His great fire—you heard His words from the midst of the fire. Because He loved your fathers, He chose their descendants after them. Then He brought you out from Egypt with His presence, by His great power—to drive out from before you nations greater and mightier than you, to bring you in to give you their land for an inheritance, as it is this day.

"So you will know today and take to heart that *ADONAI*, He is God, in the heavens above and on the earth below—there is no other.

You must keep His statutes and His *mitzvot*, which I am commanding you today, so that it may go well with you and with your children after you, and so that you may prolong your days in the land that *ADONAI* your God is giving you for all time."

Then Moses set apart three cities beyond the Jordan, toward the east. There the manslayer might flee, who kills his neighbor unintentionally and did not hate him previously. He may flee to one of these cities and live: Bezer in the wilderness on the plateau for the Reubenites, Ramot in the Gilead for the Gadites, and Golan in the Bashan for the Manassites.

This is the *Torah*, which Moses set before *Bnei-Yisrael*. These are the testimonies and the statutes and the ordinances, which Moses spoke to *Bnei-Yisrael* when they came out from Egypt—beyond the Jordan, in the valley opposite Beth-peor, in the land of Sihon king of the Amorites who lived at Heshbon, whom Moses and *Bnei-Yisrael* struck down when they came out from Egypt. They took possession of his land and the land of Og king of the Bashan, the two kings of the Amorites who were beyond the Jordan toward the east— from Aroer, which is on the edge of the wadi Arnon, as far as Mount Sion (that is, Hermon), and all the Arabah beyond the Jordan eastward, as far as the sea of the Arabah, under the slopes of Pisgah.

Deuteronomy, chapter 4

"Now this is the commandment, the statutes and ordinances that *ADONAI* your God commanded to teach you to do in the land you are crossing over to possess—so that you might fear *ADONAI* your God, to keep all His statutes and *mitzvot* that I am commanding you and your son and your son's son all the days of your life, and so that you may prolong your days.

Hear, therefore, O Israel, and take care to do this, so that it may go well with you and you may increase mightily, as *ADONAI* the God of your fathers has promised you, in a land flowing with milk and honey.

Shema Yisrael,
ADONAI Eloheinu,
ADONAI Echad

"Hear O Israel,
the LORD our God, the LORD is one.

Love *ADONAI* your God with all your heart and with all your soul and with all your strength.

These words, which I am commanding you today, are to be on your heart. You are to teach them diligently to your children, and speak of them when you sit in your house, when you walk by the way, when you lie down and when you rise up. Bind them as a

Hear O Israel, the Lord our God, the Lord is one. Love *Adonai* your God with all your heart and with all your soul and with all your strength. These words, which I am commanding you today, are to be on your heart.

Deuteronomy 6:4-6 TLV

sign on your hand, they are to be as frontlets between your eyes, and write them on the doorposts of your house and on your gates.

"Now when *ADONAI* your God brings you into the land that He swore to your fathers—to Abraham, Isaac and Jacob—to give you great and good cities that you did not build, and houses full of all good things that you did not fill, and cisterns dug that you did not dig, vineyards and olive trees that you did not plant, and you eat and are full, then watch yourself so that you do not forget *ADONAI*, who brought you out from the land of Egypt, from the house of slavery.

You must fear *ADONAI* your God and serve Him, and swear by His Name. You must not go after other gods, the gods of the peoples around you; for *ADONAI* your God in the midst of you is a jealous God. Otherwise the anger of *ADONAI* your God will be kindled against you, and He will wipe you from the face of the earth.

"You are not to test *ADONAI* your God, as you tested Him at Massah. Diligently keep the *mitzvot* of *ADONAI* your God, and His testimonies and His statutes that He has commanded you. You are to do what is right and good in the sight of *ADONAI*, so that it may go well with you and you may go in and possess the good land that *ADONAI* swore to your fathers—to drive out all your enemies from before you, as *ADONAI* has spoken.

"When your son asks you in time to come, saying 'What are the testimonies and the statutes and the ordinances that *ADONAI* our God commanded you?' then you are to tell your son, 'We were slaves to Pharaoh in Egypt, and *ADONAI* brought us out from Egypt with a mighty hand. Before our eyes *ADONAI* showed signs and wonders, great and terrible—on Egypt, on Pharaoh, and on all his house.

Then He brought us out from there so that He might bring us in, to give us the land that He swore to our fathers. *ADONAI* commanded us to do all these statutes, to fear *ADONAI* our God—for our good always, to keep us alive, as is the case this day.

It will be righteousness to us, if we take care to do all this commandment before *ADONAI* our God, just as He has commanded us.'

Deuteronomy, chapter 6

"You are to take care to do the whole *mitzvah* that I am commanding you today, so that you may live and multiply and go in and possess the land that *ADONAI* swore to your fathers. You are to remember all the way that *ADONAI* your God has led you these 40 years in the wilderness—in order to humble you, to test you, to know what was in your heart, whether you would keep His *mitzvot* or not.

He afflicted you and let you hunger, then He fed you *manna*—which neither you nor your fathers had known—in order to make you understand that man does not live by bread alone but by every word that comes from the mouth of *ADONAI*. Neither did your clothing wear out on you, nor did your foot swell these 40 years. Now you know in your heart that as a man disciplines his son, so *Adonai* your God disciplines you. So you are to keep the *mitzvot* of *Adonai* your God—to walk in His ways and to fear Him.

For *Adonai* your God is bringing you into a good land—a land of wadis with water, of springs and fountains flowing out in the valleys and hills, a land of wheat and barley, vines, figs and pomegranates, a land of olive oil and honey, a land where you will eat bread with no poverty, where you will lack nothing, a land whose stones are iron, and out of whose hills you can dig copper. So you will eat and be full, and you will bless *Adonai* your God for the good land He has given you.

"Take care that you do not forget *Adonai* your God by not keeping His *mitzvot*, ordinances and statutes that I am commanding you today. Otherwise, when you have eaten and are full and have built good houses and lived in them, and when your herds and flocks multiply, and silver and gold multiplies for you and all that is yours multiplies, then your heart will be haughty and you will forget *Adonai* your God.

He brought you out from the land of Egypt, from the house of slavery. He led you through the great and terrible wilderness—fiery serpents and scorpions, and thirsty ground where there was no water. He brought forth water for you from the flinty rock.

He fed you in the wilderness with *manna* that your fathers did not know, in order to afflict you and test you, to do you good in the end.

You may say in your heart, 'My power and the might of my hand has made me this wealth.'

Rather you are to remember *Adonai* your God, for it is He who gives you power to make wealth, in order to establish His covenant that He swore to your fathers—as it is this day.

"Now if you do forget *Adonai* your God, and go after other gods and serve them and worship them, I solemnly warn you today that you will certainly perish. Like the nations *Adonai* makes perish before you, so you will perish, since you would not listen to the voice of *Adonai* your God."

Deuteronomy, chapter 8

27. God is Faithful

"When *ADONAI* your God brings you into the land you are entering to possess and drives out many nations before you—the Hittite and the Girgashite and the Amorite, the Canaanite and the Perizzite, the Hivite and the Jebusite, seven nations more numerous and mightier than you and *ADONAI* your God gives them over to you and you strike them down, then you are to utterly destroy them.

You are to make no covenant with them and show no mercy to them. You are not to intermarry with them—you are not to give your daughter to his son, or take his daughter for your son. For he will turn your son away from following Me to serve other gods. Then the anger of *ADONAI* will be kindled against you, and He will swiftly destroy you.

Instead, you are to deal with them like this: tear down their altars, smash their pillars, cut down their Asherah poles, and burn their carved images with fire. For you are a holy people to *ADONAI* your God—from all the peoples on the face of the earth, *ADONAI* your God has chosen you to be His treasured people.

"It is not because you are more numerous than all the peoples that *ADONAI* set His love on you and chose you—for you are the least of all peoples. Rather, because of His love for you and His keeping the oath He swore to your fathers, *ADONAI* brought you out with a mighty hand and redeemed you from the house of slavery, from the hand of Pharaoh king of Egypt.

"Know therefore that *ADONAI* your God, He is God—the faithful God who keeps covenant kindness for a thousand generations with those who love Him and keep His *mitzvot*, but repays those who hate Him to their face, to annihilate them. He will not hesitate with him who hates Him; He will repay him to his face.

Therefore you are to keep the commandment—both the statutes and the ordinances—that I am commanding you today, to do them.

"Then it will happen, as a result of your listening to these ordinances, when you keep and do them, that *ADONAI* your God will keep with you the covenant kindness that He swore to your fathers. He will love you, bless you and multiply you.

He will also bless the fruit of your womb and the produce of your soil, your grain and your new wine and your oil, the increase of your herds and the young of your flock, in the land that He swore to your fathers to give you. From all peoples, you will be blessed—there will not be male or female barren among you or your livestock. *ADONAI* will remove all sickness from you, and He will not inflict on you any of the terrible diseases of Egypt that you knew, but will inflict them on all who hate you.

"You will devour all the peoples *ADONAI* your God gives over to you. Your eye is not to pity them. You are not to serve their gods, for that would be a snare to you.

Suppose you say in your heart, 'These nations are more numerous than I—how can I drive them out?' You are not to be afraid of them. You are to be sure to remember what *ADONAI* your God did to Pharaoh and to all Egypt: the great trials that your eyes saw, the signs and wonders, and the mighty hand and outstretched arm by which *ADONAI* your God brought you out. So will *ADONAI* your God do to all the peoples you fear.

"Moreover, *ADONAI* your God will send the hornet against them, until the survivors and those in hiding perish before you. You should not be terrified of them, since *ADONAI* your God is in your midst—a great and awesome God. *ADONAI* your God will drive away those nations before you little by little—you will not be able to put an end to them all at once, or else the beasts of the field will multiply on you. But *ADONAI* your God will give them over to you, and He will throw them into great confusion until they are destroyed.

He will hand over their kings to you, and you will blot out their name from under the heavens. No man will stand up to you, until you have destroyed them all.

"The carved images of their gods you are to burn with fire. You are not to covet the silver or gold on them or take it for yourself—or you could be snared by it, for it is an abomination to *ADONAI* your God. You are not to bring an abomination into your house—for you, like it, will be a banned thing. You must utterly detest and utterly abhor it, for it is set apart for destruction.

Deuteronomy, chapter 7

"Hear, O Israel! You are about to cross over the Jordan today, to go in to dispossess nations greater and mightier than yourself—cities great and fortified up to the heavens. The people are great and tall, sons of the Anakim. You know them, and you yourselves have heard, "Who can stand before the sons of Anak?" But you will know today that *ADONAI* your God is the One who is crossing over before you as a devouring fire. He will destroy them, and He will bring them down before you, so that you may drive them out and make them perish quickly, as *ADONAI* has promised you.

"After *ADONAI* your God has driven them out from before you, do not say in your heart, 'It is because of my righteousness that *ADONAI* has brought me in to possess this land.' It is because of the wickedness of these nations that *ADONAI* is driving them out from before you.

It is not by your righteousness or the uprightness of your heart that you are going in to possess their land. Rather, because of the wickedness of these nations, *ADONAI* your God is driving them out from before you, and in order to keep the word *ADONAI* swore to your fathers—to Abraham, to Isaac, and to Jacob. So you should understand that it is not because of your righteousness that *ADONAI* your God is giving you this good land to possess—for you are a stiff-necked people.

"Remember, never forget, how you

The people are great and tall, sons of the Anakim. You know them, and you yourselves have heard, "Who can stand before the sons of Anak?" But you will know today that *Adonai* your God is the One who is crossing over before you as a devouring fire. He will destroy them, and He will bring them down before you, so that you may drive them out and make them perish quickly, as *Adonai* has promised you.

Deuteronomy 9:2-3 TLV

provoked *ADONAI* your God to wrath in the wilderness. From the day you left the land of Egypt until you came to this place, you have been rebellious against *ADONAI*. At Horeb you provoked *ADONAI* to wrath, and *ADONAI* was angry with you—enough to destroy you.

When I went up the mountain to receive the tablets of stone, the tablets of the covenant that *ADONAI* cut with you, I stayed on the mountain 40 days and 40 nights; I did not eat bread or drink water. *ADONAI* gave me the two tablets of stone written by the finger of God. Moreover, on them were all the words that *ADONAI* had spoken with you on the mountain from the midst of the fire, on the day of the assembly.

"Now at the end of 40 days and 40 nights, *ADONAI* gave me the two tablets of stone—the tablets of the covenant. *ADONAI* said to me, **'Get up! Go quickly down from here, for your people whom you brought out from Egypt have acted corruptly. They have quickly turned from the way I commanded them; they have made a molten image for themselves.'**

Furthermore *ADONAI* spoke to me saying, **'I have seen this people, and it is indeed a stiff-necked people. Leave Me alone, so that I may destroy them and blot out their name from under the heavens. Then I will make you into a nation mightier and greater than they.'**

"So I turned and came down from the mountain while the mountain was burning with fire. Now the two tablets of the covenant were in my two hands. When I looked, you had indeed sinned against *ADONAI* your God—you had made yourselves a metal calf. So quickly you had turned aside from the way *ADONAI* had commanded you! So I took hold of the two tablets, threw them out of my two hands, and smashed them before your eyes.

"Then I fell down before *ADONAI* like the first time, for 40 days and 40 nights. I did not eat bread or drink water—because of all your sin that you committed, doing evil in *ADONAI*'s sight, provoking Him to anger. For I was afraid of the fierce wrath and fury which *ADONAI* bore toward you—to destroy you. But *ADONAI* listened to me that time also. *ADONAI* was angry enough with Aaron to destroy him, so I prayed for Aaron also at the same time.

I took your sin—the calf you had made—and burned it in the fire. I crushed it, grinding it up so well that it was as fine as dust, and I threw its dust into the wadi flowing down from the mountain.

"Again at Taberah and Massah and Kibroth-hattaavah, you provoked *ADONAI* to wrath. When *ADONAI* sent you from Kadesh-barnea, saying, **'Go up and possess the land I have given you,'** then you rebelled against the commandment of *ADONAI* your God and didn't believe Him or listen to His voice. You have been rebellious against *ADONAI* from the day that I knew you.

"So I threw myself down before *ADONAI* those 40 days and 40 nights, because *ADONAI* had said He would destroy you. I prayed to *ADONAI* and said, 'O Lord, *ADONAI*, do not destroy Your people—Your inheritance that You have redeemed through Your greatness and brought out from Egypt with a mighty hand.

Remember Your servants, Abraham, Isaac and Jacob. Pay no attention to the stubbornness of this people or to their wickedness or their sin. Otherwise the land from which You brought us out may say, "Because *ADONAI* was not able to bring them into the land that He spoke of to them, and because He hated them, He has brought them out to kill them in the wilderness." Yet they are Your people—Your inheritance that You brought out by Your great power and Your outstretched arm.'

Deuteronomy, chapter 9

"At that time *ADONAI* said to me, **'Carve for yourself two tablets of stone like the first ones and come up to Me on the mountain. Make yourself an ark of wood. I will write on the tablets the words that were on the first tablets that you smashed, and you are to put them in the ark.'**

"So I made an ark of acacia wood, cut two tablets of stone like the first ones, and went up the mountain with the two tablets in my hand. Like the first inscription, *ADONAI* wrote on the tablets the Ten Words He had spoken to you on the mountain from the midst of the fire on the day of the assembly, then gave them to me. Then I turned and came down from the mountain and put the tablets in the ark I had made—and there they are, just as *ADONAI* commanded me.

(*Bnei-Yisrael* traveled from the wells of the sons of Jaakan to Moserah—there Aaron died and was buried, and his son Eleazar served as *kohen* in his place. From there they journeyed to Gudgod, and from Gudgod to Jotbah—a land of wadis flowing with water. At that time *ADONAI* set the tribe of Levi apart to carry the Ark of the Covenant of *ADONAI*, to stand before *ADONAI* to serve Him and to pronounce blessings in His Name—as is the case to this day. Therefore Levi has no portion or inheritance with his brothers—*ADONAI* is his inheritance, just as *ADONAI* your God had promised about him.)

"I stayed on the mountain like the first time—40 days and 40 nights. nights. *ADONAI* listened to me that time also and was not willing to destroy you. *ADONAI* said to me, **'Rise up, go, journey ahead of the people so that they may go in and possess the land that I swore to their fathers to give to them.'**

"So now, O Israel, what does *ADONAI* your God require of you, but to fear *ADONAI* your God, to walk in all His ways and love Him, and to serve *ADONAI* your God with all your heart and with all your soul, to keep the *mitzvot* of *ADONAI* and His statutes that I am commanding you today, for your own good? Behold, to *ADONAI* your God belong the heavens and the highest of heavens, the earth and all that is in it. Only on your fathers did *ADONAI* set His affection to love them, and He chose their descendants after them—you— from all the peoples, as is the case this day.

"Circumcise the foreskin of your heart

therefore, and do not be stiff-necked anymore. For *ADONAI* your God is God of gods and Lord of lords —the great, mighty and awesome God, who does not show partiality or take a bribe.

He enacts justice for the orphan and widow, and loves the outsider, giving him food and clothing. Therefore love the outsider, for you were outsiders in the land of Egypt. *ADONAI* your God you will fear—Him will you serve. To Him will you cling, and by His Name will you swear. He is your praise and He is your God, who has done for you these great and awesome things that your eyes have seen. Your fathers went down to Egypt with 70 persons, and now *ADONAI* your God has made you like the stars of the heavens in number.

Deuteronomy, chapter 10

"Therefore you are to love *ADONAI* your God and keep His charge, His statutes, His ordinances and His *mitzvot* at all times. And you should know this day that it was not your children who knew or saw the discipline of *ADONAI* your God—His greatness, His mighty hand and His outstretched arm; His signs and the deeds He did in the midst of Egypt to Pharaoh king of Egypt and to all his land; and what He did to the army of Egypt, to its horses and chariots when He made the waters of the Sea of Reeds flow over them as they chased after you, and how *ADONAI* has destroyed them to this day; what He did for you in the wilderness until you came to this place; and what He did to Dathan and Abiram sons of Eliab son of Reuben—how the earth opened its mouth and swallowed them up, along with their households and tents and every living thing that followed them, in the midst of all Israel— Rather, it is your own eyes that have seen every mighty deed that *ADONAI* has done.

"Therefore you are to keep the whole *mitzvah* that I am commanding you today, so that you may be strong and go in and possess the land that you are crossing over to possess, and so that you may prolong your days on the land that *ADONAI* swore to give to your fathers and to their descendants —a land flowing with milk and honey.

"For the land you are going in to possess is not like the land of Egypt from which you came. There you planted your seed and watered it by foot, like a vegetable garden. But the land you are crossing over to possess is a land of hills and valleys, drinking from the rain of the heavens it drinks in water. It is a land that *ADONAI* your God cares for—the eyes of *ADONAI* your God are always on it, from the beginning of the year up to the end of the year.

"Now if you listen obediently to My *mitzvot* that I am commanding you today—to love *ADONAI* your God and to serve Him with all your heart and soul—then I will give rain for your land in its season—the early rain and the late rain—so that you may gather in your grain, new wine and olive oil. I will give grass in your field for your livestock, and you will eat and be satisfied.

Watch yourselves, so your heart is not deceived, and you turn aside and

serve other gods and worship them. Then the anger of *ADONAI* will be kindled against you, so He will shut up the sky so that there will be no rain and the soil will not yield its produce. Then you will perish quickly from the good land *ADONAI* is giving you.

"Therefore you are to set these words of Mine in your heart and in your soul. You are to bind them as a sign on your hand, and as frontlets between your eyes. You are to teach them to your children, speaking of them when you sit in your house, when you walk by the way, when you lie down and when you rise up. You are to write them on the doorposts of your house and on your gates, so that your days and the days of your children may be multiplied on the land *ADONAI* swore to give to your fathers, as long as the heavens are above the earth.

"For if you will diligently keep all this *mitzvah* that I am commanding you to do—to love *ADONAI* your God, to walk in all His ways and to cling to Him—then *ADONAI* will drive out all these nations from before you, and you will dispossess nations greater and mightier than yourselves. Every place where the sole of your foot treads will be yours—from the wilderness to the Lebanon, from the river, the river Euphrates, as far as the western sea will be your border. No one will be able to stand against you—*ADONAI* your God will put the fear and dread of you upon all the land where you tread, just as He has promised you.

"See, I am setting before you today a blessing and a curse—the blessing, if you listen to the *mitzvot* of *ADONAI* your God that I am commanding you today, but the curse, if you do not listen to the *mitzvot* of *ADONAI* your God, but turn from the way I am commanding you today, to go after other gods you have not known.

Now when *ADONAI* your God brings you into the land you are going in to possess, you are to set the blessing on Mount Gerizim and the curse on Mount Ebal. Are they not across the Jordan toward the west, in the land of the Canaanites who dwell in the Arabah—opposite Gilgal, beside the oaks of Moreh?

For you are about to cross over the Jordan to go in to possess the land *ADONAI* your God is giving you—you will possess it and dwell in it, and you will take care to do all the statutes and ordinances that I am setting before you today.

Deuteronomy, chapter 11

28. God Takes Moses

These are the words of the covenant that *ADONAI* commanded Moses to make with *Bnei-Yisrael* in the land of Moab, in addition to the covenant He made with them at Horeb.

Deuteronomy 28:69

Moses called to all Israel and said to them, "You have seen all that *ADONAI* did before your eyes in the land of Egypt, to Pharaoh and all his servants and all his land— the great trials that your eyes saw, those great signs and wonders. But to this day *ADONAI* has not given you a heart to know, or eyes to see, or ears to hear. I led you 40 years in the wilderness— your clothes have not worn out on you, and your sandals have not worn out on your feet. Bread you have not eaten and wine and strong drink you have not drunk—in order that you may know that I am *ADONAI* your God.

"When you came to this place, King Sihon of Heshbon and King Og of the Bashan came out against us to battle, but we struck them down. We took their land and gave it as an inheritance to Reuben, Gad and the half-tribe of Manasseh. So keep the words of this covenant and do them, so that you may prosper in all that you do.

"You are standing today, all of you, before *ADONAI* your God—the heads of your tribes, your elders, your officials, all the men of Israel, your children, your wives, and the outsider within your camp (from your woodchopper to your water carrier). Each of you is to cross over into the covenant of *ADONAI* your God that He is cutting with you today, and into His oath. This is in order to confirm you today as His people. So He will be your God, just as He promised you and just as He swore to your fathers —to Abraham, to Isaac and to Jacob. Not with you alone am I cutting this covenant and this oath, but with whomever is standing here with us today before *ADONAI* our God and with whomever is not here with us today.

"Indeed you know how we dwelt in the land of Egypt and how we crossed through the nations that we passed through. You saw their detestable things and their idols—wood and stone, silver and gold—that were with them. Beware in case there is among you a man or woman, or family or tribe, whose heart turns away today from *ADONAI* our God to go serve the gods of those nations. Beware in case there is among you a root producing poison and bitter fruit.

"Now when someone hears the words of this oath and in his heart considers himself blessed, thinking, '*Shalom* will be mine, even though I walk in the stubbornness of my heart'—thus sweeping away the moist with the dry—*ADONAI* will be unwilling to forgive him. For then the anger of *ADONAI* and His jealousy will smoke against that person. So all the oath that is written in this scroll will settle on him, and *ADONAI* will blot out his name from under the heavens. *ADONAI* will single him out from all the tribes of Israel for calamity, according to all the oaths of the covenant written in this scroll of the *Torah*.

"The following generation, your children who rise up after you, and the foreigner who comes from a distant land will say, when they see the plagues of that land and the sicknesses *ADONAI* afflicted on it: 'Sulfur and salt, the whole land burnt! It cannot be planted, it cannot sprout, no grass can grow up on it—like the overthrow of Sodom and Gomorrah, Admah and Zeboiim, which *ADONAI* overturned in His anger and in His wrath!'

"All the nations will say, 'Why has *ADONAI* done this to this land? Why this great burning anger?'

"Then they will say, 'Because they abandoned the covenant of *ADONAI*, the God of their fathers, which He cut with them when He brought them out from the land of Egypt. They went and served other gods and bowed down to them—gods they never knew, that He had not allotted to them. So *ADONAI*'s anger burned against that land, bringing on it every curse written in this scroll. *ADONAI* has uprooted them from their soil, in anger and wrath and great fury, and hurled them into another land, as is the case this day.'

"The secret things belong to *ADONAI* our God, but the things revealed belong to us and to our children forever—in order to do all the words of this *Torah*."

Deuteronomy, chapter 29

"Now when all these things come upon you—the blessing and the curse that I have set before you—and you take them to heart in all the nations where *ADONAI* your God has banished you, and you return to *ADONAI* your God and listen to His voice according to all that I am commanding you today—you and your children—with all your heart and with all your soul, then *ADONAI* your God will bring you back from captivity and have compassion on you, and He will return and gather you from all the peoples where *ADONAI* your God has scattered you.

Even if your outcasts are at the ends of the heavens, from there *ADONAI* your God will gather you, and from there He will bring you. *ADONAI* your God will bring you into the land that your fathers possessed, and you will possess it; and He will do you good and multiply you more than your fathers.

Also *ADONAI* your God will circumcise your heart and the heart of your descendants—to love *ADONAI* your God with all your heart and with all your soul, in order that you may live.

"*ADONAI* your God will put all these curses on your enemies and on those who hate you, who persecuted you. Then you—you will return and listen to the voice of *ADONAI* and do all His *mitzvot* that I am commanding you today. *ADONAI* your God will make you prosper in all the work of your hand—in the fruit of your womb, and the offspring of your livestock, and the produce of your soil—for good. For *ADONAI* will again rejoice over you for good, as He rejoiced over your fathers—when you listen to the voice of *ADONAI* your God, to keep His *mitzvot* and His statutes that are written in this scroll of the *Torah*, when you turn to *ADONAI* your God

There has not risen again a prophet in Israel like Moses,
whom *Adonai* knew face to face, with all the signs
and wonders *Adonai* sent him to do in the land of Egypt—
to Pharaoh, all his servants, and all his land—
by the strong hand and great awe that Moses did
in the sight of all Israel.

Deuteronomy 34:10-12 TLV

with all your heart and with all your soul.

"For this *mitzvah* that I am commanding you today is not too difficult for you, nor is it far off. It is not in the heavens, that you should say, 'Who will go up for us to the heavens and get it for us, and have us hear it so we may do it?'

Nor is it across the sea, that you should say, 'Who will cross over for us to the other side of the sea and get it for us, and have us hear it so we may do it?' No, the word is very near to you—in your mouth and in your heart, to do it. See, I have set before you today life and good, and death and evil. What I am commanding you today is to love *ADONAI* your God, to walk in His ways, and to keep His *mitzvot*, statutes and ordinances. Then you will live and multiply, and *ADONAI* your God will bless you in the land you are going in to possess.

But if your heart turns away and you do not listen, but are drawn away and bow down to other gods and worship them, I tell you today that you will certainly perish! You will not prolong your days on the land, where you are about to cross over the Jordan to go in to possess.

"I call the heavens and the earth to witness about you today, that I have set before you life and death, the blessing and the curse. Therefore choose life so that you and your descendants may live, by loving *ADONAI* your God, listening to His voice, and clinging to Him. For He is your life and the length of your days, that you may dwell on the land that *ADONAI* swore to your fathers—to Abraham, to Isaac and to Jacob—to give them.

Deuteronomy, chapter 30

Then Moses went and spoke these words to all Israel. He said to them, "I am 120 years old today. I am no longer able to go out and come in. *ADONAI* has said to me, **'You are not to cross over this Jordan.'** *ADONAI* your God—He will cross over before you. He will destroy these nations from before you, and you will dispossess them. Joshua will cross over before you, just as *ADONAI* has promised. *ADONAI* will do to them just as He did to Sihon and Og, the kings of the Amorites, and to their land, when He destroyed them. *ADONAI* will give them over to you, and you are to do to them according to all the *mitzvot* that I commanded you. *Chazak!* Be courageous! Do not be afraid or tremble before them. For *ADONAI* your God—He is the One who goes with you. He will not fail you or abandon you."

Then Moses summoned Joshua and said to him in the sight of all Israel, "Be strong! Be courageous! For you are to go with this people into the land *ADONAI* has sworn to their fathers to give them, and you are to enable them to inherit it. *ADONAI*—He is the One who goes before you. He will be with you. He will not fail you or abandon you. Do not fear or be discouraged."

Moses wrote down this *Torah* and gave it to the *kohanim*, the sons of Levi who carry the Ark of the Covenant of *ADONAI*, and to all the elders of Israel.

Then Moses commanded them saying, "At the end of every seven years, in the set time of the year of cancelling debts, during the feast of *Sukkot*, when all Israel comes to appear before *ADONAI* your God in the place He chooses, you are to read this *Torah* before them in their hearing. Gather the people—the men and women and little ones, and the outsider within your town gates—so they may hear and so they may learn, and they will fear *ADONAI* your God and take care to do all the words of this *Torah*. So their children, who have not known, will hear and learn to fear *ADONAI* your God—all the days you live on the land you are about to cross over the Jordan to possess." Then *ADONAI* said to Moses, **"Behold, your time to die is near. Call Joshua, and present yourselves at the Tent of Meeting, and I will commission him."**

Moses and Joshua went and presented themselves at the Tent of Meeting. *ADONAI* appeared in the Tent in a pillar of cloud, and the pillar of cloud stood over the opening of the Tent. *ADONAI* said to Moses, **"Behold, you are about to lie down with your fathers. Then this people will rise up and prostitute themselves with the foreign gods of the land they are entering. They will abandon Me and break My covenant that I cut with them. Then My anger will flare against them on that day, and I will abandon them and hide My face from them. So they will be devoured, and many evils and troubles will come on them. They will say on that day, 'Isn't it because our God is not among us that these evils have come on us?' I will surely hide My face on that day because of all the evil they have done, for they have turned to other gods."**

Deuteronomy 31:1-18

Then Moses went up from the plains of Moab to Mount Nebo, to the top of Pisgah, which is opposite Jericho. *ADONAI* showed him all the land—Gilead to Dan, and all of Naphtali, the land of Ephraim and Manasseh, all the land of Judah as far as the western sea, the Negev and the plain of the valley of Jericho the city of palm trees, as far as Zoar. Then *ADONAI* said to him, **"This is the land that I swore to Abraham, Isaac and Jacob saying, 'I will give it to your seed.' I let you see it with your eyes, but you will not cross over there."**

So Moses the servant of *ADONAI* died there in the land of Moab, as was from the mouth of *ADONAI*. Then He buried him in the valley in the land of Moab, opposite Beth-peor—but no one knows of his burial place to this day. Moses was 120 years old when he died. His eye was not dim nor his vigor gone. *Bnei-Yisrael* wept for Moses in the plains of Moab thirty days. Then the days of weeping, mourning for Moses, were ended. Now Joshua son of Nun was full of the spirit of wisdom, for Moses had laid his hands on him. So *Bnei-Yisrael* listened to him and did just as *ADONAI* had commanded Moses.

There has not risen again a prophet in Israel like Moses, whom *ADONAI* knew face to face, with all the signs and wonders *ADONAI* sent him to do in the land of Egypt—to Pharaoh, all his servants, and all his land—by the strong hand and great awe that Moses did in the sight of all Israel.

Deuteronomy, chapter 34

29. God Answers their Shout

Now it came about after the death of Moses the servant of *ADONAI* that *ADONAI* spoke to Joshua son of Nun, Moses' aide saying: "My servant Moses is dead. So now, arise, you and all these people, cross over this Jordan to the land that I am giving to them—to *Bnei-Yisrael*. Every place on which the sole of your foot treads, I am giving to you, as I spoke to Moses. From the wilderness and this Lebanon to the great river, the Euphrates River—all the land of the Hittites—to the Great Sea toward the setting of the sun will be your territory.

No one will be able to stand before you all the days of your life. Just as I was with Moses, so I will be with you. I will not fail you or forsake you. *Chazak*! Be strong! For you will lead these people to inherit the land I swore to their fathers to give them.

Only be very strong, and resolute to observe diligently the *Torah* which Moses, My servant commanded you. Do not turn from it to the right or to the left, so you may be successful wherever you go. This book of the *Torah* should not depart from your mouth—you are to meditate on it day and night, so that you may be careful to do everything written in it. For then you will make your ways prosperous and then you will be successful. Have I not commanded you? *Chazak*! Be strong! Do not be terrified or dismayed, for *ADONAI* your God is with you wherever you go."

Then Joshua commanded the officials of the people saying: [11] "Go through the camp and charge the people saying: 'Prepare provisions, for within three days you will be crossing over this Jordan, to go in to possess the land which *ADONAI* your God is giving you to possess it.'"

Then Joshua spoke to the Reubenites, Gadites and half-tribe of Manasseh saying: "Remember the word that Moses the servant of *ADONAI* commanded you saying: '*ADONAI* your God has given you rest, and has assigned to you this land.' Your wives, your little ones and your cattle will remain in the land which Moses gave you beyond the Jordan, but you will cross over before your brothers armed, all the mighty men of valor, and will help them until *ADONAI* gives your brothers rest, as He has given you, and they also possess the land that *ADONAI* your God is giving them. Then you will return to the land of your inheritance, and possess what Moses the servant of *ADONAI* gave you, beyond the Jordan toward the sunrise."

Then they answered Joshua saying: "All that you have commanded us, we will do, and wherever you send us we will go. Just as we obeyed Moses in all things, so we will obey you. Only may *ADONAI* your God be with you as He was with Moses. Whoever rebels against your command and does not obey your words in all that you command him, he will be put to death. Only be strong and courageous!"

Joshua, chapter 1

Then Joshua son of Nun secretly sent

out two spies from Shittim saying: "Go, explore the land, especially Jericho." So they went and came to the house of a prostitute whose name was Rahab, and lodged there.

The king of Jericho was told, "Some men from *Bnei-Yisrael* have just come here tonight to spy out the land."

So the king of Jericho sent word to Rahab saying: "Bring out the men who came to you, who entered your house—for they have come to spy out all the land."

But the woman took the two men and hid them, and said: "Yes, the men did come to me, but I didn't know where they were from. So when it was time to shut the gate at dark, the men went out, and I don't know where they went. Pursue them quickly, for you may overtake them."

But she had brought them up to the roof and hidden them in the stalks of flax that she had spread out on the roof. So the men pursued them on the road to the fords of the Jordan. As soon as the pursuers had gone out, they shut the gate.

Now before they lay down, she came up to them on the roof, and she said to the men: "I know that *ADONAI* has given you the land—dread of you has fallen on us and all the inhabitants of the land are melting in fear before you. For we have heard how *ADONAI* dried up the water of the Sea of Reeds before you when you came out of Egypt, and what you did to the two kings of the Amorites that were beyond the Jordan, to Sihon and Og, whom you utterly destroyed. When we heard about it, our hearts melted, and no spirit remained any more in anyone because of you.

For *ADONAI* your God, He is God, in heaven above and on earth beneath. So now, please swear to me by *ADONAI*, since I have dealt kindly with you, that you also will deal kindly with my father's house. Give me a true sign that you will spare the lives of my father, my mother, my brothers, my sisters and all who belong to them, and save our lives from death."

The men said to her: "Our life for yours, if you don't report this business of ours. Then it will be when *ADONAI* gives us the land that we will deal kindly and loyally with you."

So she lowered them down by a rope through the window—for her house was in the wall; she was living in the wall. Then she said to them: "Go to the hill country, lest the pursuers meet you, and hide yourselves there for three days, until the pursuers return. Afterward, you may go your way."

Then the men said to her: "We will be released from this oath that you have made us swear, unless when we come into the land, you tie this line of scarlet thread in the window through which you lowered us down, and gather to yourself in the house your father, your mother, your brothers and all your father's household—whoever goes out of the doors of your house into the street, his blood will be on his head and we will be innocent, but whoever is with you in the house, his blood will be on our head if any hand is laid on him. But if you divulge this business of ours, then we will be released from your oath you have made us swear."

So she said: "According to your words, so be it." Then she sent them away. After they had gone, she tied the scarlet cord to the window. Then they departed and came to the hill country. They stayed there for three days until the pursuers returned. Now the pursuers had looked for them all along the road, but had not found them. Then the two men returned, came down from the hill country, crossed over and came to Joshua son of Nun. They reported to him all that had befallen them.

"Surely *ADONAI* has given all the land into our hands," they said to Joshua. "Indeed, all the inhabitants of the land have melted in fear before us."

Joshua, chapter 2

Then Joshua rose up early in the morning, and he and all *Bnei-Yisrael* set out from Shittim and came to the Jordan. They lodged there before crossing over. Now it came about after three days that the officials went through the camp and they charged the people saying, "When you see the ark of the covenant of *ADONAI* your God and the Levitical *kohanim* carrying it, then you must set out from your place and follow it. Yet keep a distance between you and it of about 2,000 cubits by measure. Don't come near it, so you may know the way by which you should go, for you haven't travelled this way before."

Then Joshua told the people, "Consecrate yourselves, for tomorrow *ADONAI* will do wonders in your midst."

Joshua spoke to the *kohanim* saying: "Take up the ark of the covenant and cross over ahead of the people." So they took up the ark of the covenant and went ahead of the people.

Now *ADONAI* said to Joshua, "This day I will begin to exalt you in the eyes of all Israel, so they may know that just as I was with Moses, so I will be with you. You are to command the *kohanim* who are carrying the ark of the covenant saying: 'When you reach the edge of the waters of the Jordan, you are to stand still in the Jordan.'"

So Joshua said to *Bnei-Yisrael*, "Come here, and listen to the words of *ADONAI* your God." Joshua said, "By this you will know that the living God is among you, and that He will certainly drive out from before you the Canaanite, the Hittite, the Hivite, the Perizzite, the Girgashite, the Amorite and the Jebusite. Behold, the ark of the covenant of the Sovereign of all the earth is advancing before you into the Jordan. So now, take for yourselves twelve men out of the tribes of Israel, one man for each tribe. It will come to pass when the soles of the feet of the *kohanim* who are carrying the ark of *ADONAI*, Sovereign of all the earth, rest in the waters of the Jordan, the Jordan's waters will be cut off. The waters coming downstream will stand up in one heap."

So it came to pass. When the people set out from their tents to cross over the Jordan, the *kohanim* were carrying the ark of the covenant ahead of the people. Now the Jordan overflows all its banks throughout the harvest season. But as soon as those who were carrying the ark came into the Jordan and the feet of the *kohanim* carrying the ark dipped in the edge of the water, the waters which were flowing down from above stood and rose up in one heap, a great distance away at Adam, the town next to Zarethan. What was flowing down to the sea of the Arabah (the Salt Sea) was completely cut off.

So the people crossed over opposite Jericho. Yet the *kohanim* carrying the ark of the covenant of *ADONAI* stood firmly on dry ground in the middle of the Jordan, while all Israel crossed over on dry ground, until the entire nation had finished crossing over the Jordan.

Joshua, chapter 3

Now it came about when all the Amorite kings beyond the Jordan westward and all the Canaanite kings by the sea heard how *ADONAI* had dried up the waters of the Jordan before *Bnei-Yisrael* until they had crossed, their heart melted, nor was there any spirit in them anymore, because of *Bnei-Yisrael*.

At that time *ADONAI* said to Joshua, "Make yourself flint knives and circumcise again *Bnei-Yisrael* a second time." So Joshua made flint knives and circumcised *Bnei-Yisrael* at Gibeath-ha-araloth.

Now this is the reason why Joshua circumcised: all the people that came out of Egypt who were males—all the men of war—had died in the wilderness along the way after they came out of Egypt. Though all the people that came out were circumcised, none of the people who were born in the wilderness along the way as they came out of Egypt had been circumcised. For *Bnei-Yisrael* walked 40 years in the wilderness, until all the nation's men of war who came out of Egypt died out, because they had not listened to the voice of *ADONAI*. To them *ADONAI* had sworn that He would never let them see the land which *ADONAI* had sworn to their fathers that He would give us, a land flowing with milk and honey. But He raised up their children in their place. Joshua circumcised them, for they were uncircumcised, since they had not been circumcised along the way.

Now it came to pass after they had finished circumcising the entire nation, they remained in their places in the camp until they recovered.

Then *ADONAI* said to Joshua, "This day I have rolled away the reproach of Egypt from you." Therefore the name of that place has been called Gilgal to this day.

While *Bnei-Yisrael* camped at Gilgal, they observed Passover on the evening of the fourteenth day of the month in the plains of Jericho. On the day after the Passover, on that very day, they ate of the produce of the land, *matzot* and roasted grain. Then the manna ceased on the day after they had eaten of the produce of the land. *Bnei-Yisrael* had manna no longer, but ate some of the yield of the land of Canaan that year.

Now it came to pass when Joshua was near Jericho that he lifted up his eyes and looked, and behold, there was a man standing in front of him with his sword drawn in his hand. Joshua approached him and said to him: "Are you for us or for our adversaries?"

"Neither," he said. "Rather, I have now come as commander of ADONAI's army."

Then Joshua fell on his face to the ground and worshipped. Then he asked him, "What is my lord saying to his servant?"

Then the commander of ADONAI's army replied to Joshua, "Take your sandal off of your foot, for the place where you are standing is holy." And Joshua did so.

Joshua, chapter 5

Now Jericho was tightly shut up because of *Bnei-Yisrael*—no one going out and no one coming in. Then ADONAI said to Joshua, "Look, I have given Jericho into your hand, with its king and mighty warriors.

Now you are to march around the city, all the men of war circling the city once. So you are to do for six days. Seven *kohanim* will carry seven *shofarot* of rams' horns before the ark. Then on the seventh day you are to circle the city seven times while the *kohanim* blow the *shofarot*. It will be when they make a long blast with the ram's horn, when you hear the sound of the *shofar*, have all the people shout a loud shout—then the wall of the city will fall down flat, and the people will go up, everyone straight ahead."

So Joshua son of Nun summoned the *kohanim* and said to them, "Take up the ark of the covenant. Let seven *kohanim* carry seven *shofarot* of rams' horns before the ark of ADONAI."

Then he said to the people, "Move forward, march around the city, and let the armed force march ahead of the ark of ADONAI."

And it was so.

After Joshua had spoken to the people, seven *kohanim* carrying the seven *shofarot* of rams' horns before ADONAI went forward and blew the *shofarot*, and the ark of the covenant of ADONAI followed them. Also the armed force went before the *kohanim* who blew the *shofarot*, and the rear guard came behind the ark, while the *shofarot* continued to blow.

But Joshua ordered the people saying: "You must not shout nor let your voice be heard nor let a word proceed out of your mouth, until the day I tell you 'shout!' Then you will shout." So he had the ark of ADONAI go around the city, circling it once. Then they came into the camp and spent the night there.

The next day Joshua rose early in the morning. The *kohanim* took up the ark of ADONAI, and the seven *kohanim* carrying the seven *shofarot* of rams' horns marched in front of the ark of ADONAI and blew the *shofarot*, with the armed force marching before them and the rear guard marching

Then *ADONAI* said to Joshua, "Look, I have given Jericho into your hand, with its king and mighty warriors. Now you are to march around the city, all the men of war circling the city once. So you are to do for six days...

Joshua 6:2-3 TLV

behind the ark of *ADONAI*, while the *shofarot* continued to blow. So the second day they circled the city once and returned to the camp. So they did for six days.

Now on the seventh day they rose early, at dawn, and marched around the city in the same way seven times. Only on that day did they march around the city seven times. Then on the seventh time, when the *kohanim* blew the *shofarot*, Joshua ordered the people, "Shout! For *ADONAI* has given you the city! But the city will be under the ban of destruction—it and all that is in it belong to *ADONAI*. Only Rahab the harlot will live, she and all who are with her in the house, because she hid the scouts that we sent. But you, just keep yourselves from the things under the ban. Otherwise you would make yourselves accursed by taking of the things under the ban, and so you would make the camp of Israel accursed and bring trouble on it. All the silver and gold and vessels of bronze and iron are holy to *ADONAI*, and must go into the treasury of *ADONAI*."

So when the *shofarot* blew, the people shouted. When the people heard the sound of the *shofar*, the people shouted a loud shout—and the wall fell down flat! So the people went up into the city, everyone straight ahead, and they captured the city. They utterly destroyed everything in the city — man and woman, young and old, ox, sheep and donkey—with the edge of the sword.

Then Joshua said to the two men who had spied out the land: "Go into the harlot's house and bring the woman and all who belong to her, as you swore to her." So the young spies went in and brought out Rahab, her father, her mother, her relatives and all who belonged to her. All her relatives they brought out and put them outside the camp of Israel.

Then they burned the city with fire and all that was in it. Only the silver, the gold and the vessels of bronze and iron did they put into the treasury of the House of *ADONAI*. But Rahab the harlot, her father's household and all who belonged to her, Joshua spared. She has lived in the midst of Israel to this day, because she hid the scouts whom Joshua sent to spy out Jericho.

At that time Joshua made an oath saying:

> "Cursed before ADONAI
> is the man
> who rises up and
> rebuilds this city, Jericho!
> On his firstborn
> he will lay its foundation,
> and on his youngest son
> he will set up its gates."

So *ADONAI* was with Joshua, and his fame was throughout the region.

Joshua, chapter 6

30. God Fights the Battle

But *Bnei-Yisrael* again did what was evil in *ADONAI*'s eyes after Ehud had died. So *ADONAI* sold them over into the hand of Jabin king of Canaan, who reigned in Hazor. His army commander was Sisera, who lived in Harosheth-ha-goyim. So *Bnei-Yisrael* cried out to *ADONAI*, for he had 900 iron chariots, and had harshly oppressed *Bnei-Yisrael* for 20 years.

Now Deborah, a woman who was a prophetess, the wife of Lappidoth, was judging Israel at that time. She used to sit under the palm tree of Deborah between Ramah and Bethel in the hill country of Ephraim, and *Bnei-Yisrael* came up to her for judgment. Now she sent and summoned Barak son of Abinoam from Kedesh in Naphtali, and said to him, "Hasn't *ADONAI*, God of Israel, commanded, 'Go, march to Mount Tabor, and take with you 10,000 men of the sons of Naphtali and of the sons of Zebulun? Then at the Kishon torrent, I will draw out to you Sisera, commander of Jabin's army with his chariots and his multitude, and I will give him into your hand.'"

But Barak said to her, "If you are going with me, then I will go. But if you aren't going with me, I won't go."

"Surely I will go with you," she said. "However, no honor will be yours on the way that you are about to go—for *ADONAI* will sell Sisera into the hand of a woman." So Deborah arose and went with Barak to Kedesh. Then Barak summoned Zebulun and Naphtali together to Kedesh, and 10,000 men marched up after him, and Deborah went up with him.

Now Heber the Kenite had separated himself from the Kenites, from the children of Hobab the father-in-law of Moses, and had pitched his tent as far as the oak in Zaanannim, which is near Kedesh. They told Sisera that Barak son of Abinoam had gone up to Mount Tabor. So Sisera ordered all his chariots—900 iron chariots—and all the troops that were with him, from Harosheth-ha-goyim to the Kishon.

Then Deborah said to Barak, "Arise! For this is the day in which *ADONAI* will deliver Sisera into your hand. Has *ADONAI* not gone out before you?"

So Barak came down from Mount Tabor with 10,000 men following him. *ADONAI* threw Sisera and all his chariots and all his army into confusion before Barak with the edge of the sword.

Then Sisera got down from his chariot and fled away on foot. But Barak pursued the chariots and the army as far as Harosheth-ha-goyim. The whole army of Sisera fell by the sword; not one was left.

Meanwhile Sisera fled on foot to the tent of Yael the wife of Heber the Kenite, for there was peace between King Jabin of Hazor and the house of Heber the Kenite.

So Yael went out to meet Sisera and said to him, "Turn aside, my lord, turn aside to me! Don't be afraid!" So he turned aside to her into the tent, and

Now Deborah, a woman who was a prophetess, the wife of Lappidoth, was judging Israel at that time. She used to sit under the palm tree of Deborah between Ramah and Bethel in the hill country of Ephraim, and *Bnei-Yisrael* came up to her for judgment.

Judges 4:4-5 TLV

she covered him with a blanket.

He said to her, "Please give me a little water to drink, for I am thirsty." So she opened a skin of milk and made him drink some, and covered him.

Then he said to her, "Stand at the entrance of the tent, and if anyone comes and asks you saying, 'Is there a man here?' then you will say, 'There's no one.'"

Then Yael, Heber's wife, took a tent pin and got a hammer in her hand, approached him stealthily and drove the pin into his temple until it pierced through into the ground—for he was exhausted and in a deep sleep. So he died.

Now behold, as Barak was pursuing Sisera, Yael came out to meet him and said to him, "Come, I will show you the man whom you are seeking." So he entered with her, and behold, Sisera was lying dead, with a tent-pin in his temple!

So on that day God subdued King Jabin of Canaan before *Bnei-Yisrael*. The hand of *Bnei-Yisrael* pressed hard on King Jabin of Canaan until they had cut off King Jabin of Canaan.

Judges, chapter 4

Then Deborah and Barak son of Abinoam sang on that day saying:

> "When leaders take the lead in Israel, when people freely offer themselves, bless *Adonai*!
>
> Listen, O kings!
> Give ear, O rulers!
> I, to *Adonai* I will sing,
> I will sing praise to *Adonai*,
> the God of Israel.
>
> Adonai, when You came out from Seir, when You marched from Edom's field, the earth trembled,
> the heavens also dropped,
> yes, the clouds dropped water.
> The mountains quaked
> before *Adonai*,
> this Sinai at the
> presence of *Adonai*,
> the God of Israel!
> In the days of Shamgar
> son of Anath, in the days of Yael,
> the highways were deserted,
> travelers walked by
> crooked paths.
> Villages were deserted in Israel,
> deserted, until I, Deborah, arose,
> a mother in Israel arose.
>
> They chose new gods—
> then war was in the gates.
> No shield or spear was seen
> among 40,000 in Israel!
>
> My heart is with Israel's rulers,
> who offer themselves freely
> among the people.
> Bless *Adonai*!
>
> Riders on white donkeys,
> sitting on saddle blankets,
> traveling on the road, sing!
> Louder than the sound of archers,
> at the watering places!
> There let them rehearse
> the righteous acts of *Adonai*,
> the righteous deeds
> for His villages in Israel.
> Then the people of *Adonai*
> went down to the gates.
>
> Awake, awake, Deborah!

Awake, awake, utter a song!

Arise, Barak,
lead away your captives,
O son of Abinoam!

Then a remnant
of nobles came down.
ADONAI's people came down
to me with the mighty ones.
Those with root in Amalek
are from Ephraim, following you,
Benjamin, with your peoples.
From Machir came down rulers,
and from Zebulun wielding
the marshal's staff.

Issachar's chiefs
were with Deborah.
Issachar was with Barak.

'Curse Meroz!'
said the angel of *ADONAI*,
'Utterly curse its inhabitants,
for they came not
to the aid of *ADONAI*,
to the aid of *ADONAI*
among the mighty.'
Blessed above women is Yael,
the wife of Heber the Kenite,
above women in the tent
is she blessed.
Water he asked,
milk she gave him.
In a lordly bowl
she brought him butter.
Her hand reached
for the tent pin,
her right hand
to the workmen's hammer,
and with the hammer
she struck Sisera,
she smashed his head-
yes, she crushed and
pierced his temple.

At her feet he collapsed,
he fell, he lay.
Between her feet he bowed,
he fell.
Where he bowed,
there he fell dead.

Through the window,
Sisera's mother looked out,
through the lattice.
and lamented shrilly:
'Why does his chariot
delay in coming?
Why do the wheels
of his chariots tarry?'
The wisest of her princesses
answer her,
yes, she repeats
the words to herself:
'Are they not finding,
dividing the spoil?
A maiden,
maidens for every warrior!

To Sisera
a spoil of dyed garments—
a spoil of dyed garments
of embroidery,
double-dyed
garments of embroidery
for the necks of every spoiler!'
So let all Your enemies perish,
ADONAI!
But may those who love Him
be like the rising of the sun
in its might."

Then the land had peace for 40 years.

Judges, chapter 5

31. God Claims His Glory

Then *Bnei-Yisrael* did what was evil in *ADONAI*'s eyes, so *ADONAI* gave them into the hand of Midian for seven years. Midian maintained an upper hand over Israel, and because of Midian *Bnei-Yisrael* made themselves hideouts in the mountains—caves and strongholds.

Whenever Israel had done their sowing, the Midianites, Amalekites and people from the east would come up and raid them. They would set up camp by them, destroy the produce of the land as far as Gaza, and leave nothing in Israel to live on—not a sheep, ox or donkey. For they would come up with their cattle and their tents, invade like a multitude of locusts. Both they and their camels were innumerable, and they would come to the land to ruin it. So Israel was brought very low because of Midian, and *Bnei-Yisrael* cried out to *ADONAI*.

Now it came about when *Bnei-Yisrael* cried out to *ADONAI* because of Midian, that *ADONAI* sent a prophet to *Bnei-Yisrael*, and he said to them, "Thus says *ADONAI*, God of Israel, 'It was I who brought you up from Egypt, and brought you out of the house of bondage. Then I delivered you from the hand of the Egyptians and from the hand of all your oppressors, and drove them out from before you and gave you their land. Then I said to you, "I am *ADONAI* your God. You are not to fear the gods of the Amorites in whose land you are dwelling. But you have not obeyed My voice."'"

Then the angel of *ADONAI* came and sat under the terebinth that was at Ophrah, that belonged to Joash the Abiezrite, while his son Gideon was beating out wheat in the winepress—in order to hide it from the Midianites. Then the angel of *ADONAI* appeared to him and said to him, "*ADONAI* is with you, O mighty man of valor."

But Gideon said to him, "O my lord, if *ADONAI* is with us, then why has all this befallen us? So where are all His wonders that our fathers told us about saying 'Didn't *ADONAI* bring us up from Egypt?' But now *ADONAI* has abandoned us and given us into the hand of Midian."

Then *ADONAI* turned toward him and said, "Go in this might of yours and deliver Israel from the hand of Midian. Have not I sent you?"

Then he said to him, "Me, my Lord? With what would I deliver Israel? Look, my family is the poorest in Manasseh, and I am the least in my father's house."

But *ADONAI* said to him, "Surely I will be with you, and you will strike down Midian as if it were one man. Then he said to Him, "If now I have found favor in Your eyes, then please, show me a sign that it is really You talking with me. Please, don't leave from here, until I come to You and bring out my offering and lay it before You."

So He said, "I will stay until you come back."

Then Gideon went in and prepared a kid and *matzot* from an ephah of flour. He put the meat in a basket and the broth in a pot, and brought them out to Him under the terebinth and presented them.

Then the angel of God said to him, "Take the meat and the *matzah* and lay them on this rock, and pour out the broth."

So he did so. Then the angel of *ADONAI* put out the end of the staff that was in His hand and touched the meat and the *matzah*. Fire sprang up from the rock and consumed the meat and the *matzah*. Then the angel of *ADONAI* vanished from his sight.

When Gideon realized that He was the angel of *ADONAI*, Gideon said, "Alas, my Lord *ADONAI*! For I have seen the angel of *ADONAI* face to face!"

But *ADONAI* said to him, "*Shalom* to you. Fear not, you will not die."

So Gideon built an altar there to *ADONAI* and called it "*ADONAI-shalom*." To this day it is yet in Ophrah of the Abiezrites. Now it came to pass the same night that *ADONAI* said to him, "Take the young bull that belongs to your father and a second bull of seven years old, pull down the altar of Baal that belongs to your father, cut down the Asherah that is beside it, build an altar to *ADONAI* your God on the top of this stronghold in an orderly manner, and take the second bull and offer a burnt offering with the wood of the Asherah pole that you will cut down."

So Gideon took ten of his male servants and did as *ADONAI* had spoken to him. But since he was too afraid of his father's household and the townspeople to do it by day, he did it at night.

Now when the townspeople arose early in the morning, behold, the altar of Baal was broken down, the Asherah pole that was beside it was cut down, and the second bull was offered up on the altar that was built.

So they said one to another, "Who did this thing?" And when they inquired and asked around, they said: "Gideon son of Joash did this thing."

Then the townspeople said to Joash, "Bring out your son, that he may die, because he has broken down the altar of Baal, and even cut down the Asherah pole that was beside it."

But Joash said to all who stood against him, "So you're going to defend Baal? You're going to rescue him? Whoever defends him will be put to death in the morning!

If he is a god, let him defend himself —since someone has broken down his altar."

So on that day he was called Jerubbaal saying, "Let Baal contend with him, since he broke down his altar." Now all the Midianites, the Amalekites and the people of the east gathered together, crossed over and camped in the valley of Jezreel. But the *Ruach ADONAI* clothed Gideon, and he blew the *shofar*, and Abiezer rallied behind him.

Then he sent messengers throughout Manasseh, and they also rallied behind him. Then he sent messengers to Asher, Zebulun and Naphtali, and they came up to join them.

Then Gideon said to God, "If You are going to deliver Israel by my hand, as You have spoken, see, I am putting a fleece of wool on the threshing-floor. If there is dew only on the fleece, and all the ground is dry, then I will know that You will deliver Israel by my hand, as You have spoken."

And it was so. When he rose up early next day, he squeezed the fleece and wrung dew out of the fleece, a bowlful of water.

Then Gideon said to God, "Let not Your anger burn against me if I speak once more. Let me please test once more with the fleece—let it now be dry only on the fleece, but let there be dew over all the ground."

God did so that night, since it was dry only on the fleece, and there was dew over all the ground.

Judges, chapter 6

Then Jerubbaal (that is, Gideon) and all the people who were with him, rose up early and camped beside En-harod, while the camp of Midian was north of them, by Gibeath-moreh, in the valley. But *ADONAI* said to Gideon, "Too many are the people who are with you, for Me to give the Midianites into their hand. Otherwise Israel would glorify itself against Me saying, 'My own hand has delivered me.'

So now, make proclamation in the ears of the people saying, 'Whoever is afraid or anxious may turn back and leave from Mount Gilead.'" So 22,000 people turned back, while ten thousand remained.

But *ADONAI* said to Gideon, "The people are still too many. Bring them down to the water and I will test them for you there. Now it will be that he of whom I say to you, 'This will go with you,' he will go with you, but anyone of whom I say to you, 'This one will not go with you,' he will not go."

So he brought the troops down to the water, and *ADONAI* said to Gideon, "You are to set apart everyone who laps the water with his tongue, as a dog laps, and everyone who bows down on his knees to drink."

Now the number of those who lapped, putting their hand to their mouth, was 300 men, but all the rest of the people bowed down on their knees to drink water.

Then *ADONAI* said to Gideon, "With the 300 men who lapped I will deliver you and give the Midianites into your hand. So let all the other people go, every man to his place."

So the 300 took provisions and their *shofarot* in their hands. He sent all the other men of Israel each to his tent, but he kept the 300 men.

Now the camp of Midian was below him in the valley. It came to pass the same night that *ADONAI* said to him, "Arise, get down against the camp, for I have given it into your hand. But if you are afraid to go down, first go

Then *ADONAI* said to Gideon, "With the 300 men who lapped I will deliver you and give the Midianites into your hand. So let all the other people go, every man to his place."

Judges 7:7 TLV

down to the camp with your attendant Purah. Then you will hear what they are saying, and after that your hands will be strengthened to attack the camp." So he went down with his attendant Purah to an outpost of the army that was in camp.

Now the Midianites, the Amalekites and all the people of the east were lying in the valley as numerous as locusts; and their camels were countless, as numerous as the sand on the seashore. Yet when Gideon came, behold, there was a man relating a dream to his fellow, saying, "Listen, I just now had a dream: there was a loaf of barley bread that came tumbling into the camp of Midian, came up to a tent and struck it so it fell, and turned it upside down, so that the tent lay flat."

His companion answered and said, "This is nothing less than the sword of Gideon son of Joash, a man of Israel—God has delivered Midian and all the camp into his hand!"
Now when Gideon heard the account of the dream and its interpretation, he bowed in worship. Then he returned to the camp of Israel and said, "Arise! For *Adonai* has given into your hand the camp of Midian."

Then he divided the 300 men into three columns, and he put into the hands of all of them *shofarot* and empty pitchers, with torches inside the pitchers.

Then he said to them, "Watch me and do likewise. So behold, when I come to the outskirts of the camp, do just as I do. When I and all that are with me blow the *shofar*, then you also blow the *shofarot* all around the camp, and say, 'For *Adonai* and for Gideon!'"

So Gideon and the 300 men who were with him came up to the outermost part of the camp at the beginning of the middle watch, when they had just posted the watch. Then they blew the *shofarot* and smashed the pitchers that were in their hands.

When the three columns blew the *shofarot* and broke the pitchers, they held the torches in their left hands and the *shofarot* in their right hands to blow, and they shouted, "A sword for *Adonai* and for Gideon!"

Each one stood in his place around the camp, and then the entire army ran, shouting as they fled. Now when they blew the 300 *shofarot*, *Adonai* set every man's sword against his fellow throughout the entire army. So the army fled as far as Beth-shittah toward Zererah, as far as the border of Abel-meholah, by Tabbath.

Then men of Israel were summoned from Naphtali, Asher and all Manasseh, and they pursued Midian. Gideon sent messengers throughout all the hill country of Ephraim saying, "Come down against Midian and seize the waters down to Beth-barah, all along the Jordan."

So all the men of Ephraim were summoned and took control of the waterside as far as Beth-barah by the Jordan. Then they captured the two princes of Midian, Oreb and Zeeb;

they slew Oreb at the Rock of Oreb and they slew Zeeb at the Winepress of Zeeb. They kept pursuing Midian, and they brought the heads of Oreb and Zeeb to Gideon from across the Jordan.

Judges, chapter 7

Now the men of Ephraim said to him, "What is this thing you have done to us, not calling us when you went to fight against Midian?" So they criticized him sharply.
But he said to them, "What have I now done compared to you? Is not the gleaning of Ephraim better than the vintage of Abiezer?
God has given into your hand the princes of Midian—Oreb and Zeeb—so what was I able to do compared to you?" Their anger with him subsided after he said this.

Then Gideon reached the Jordan and crossed over. He and the 300 men with him were exhausted, yet still pursuing. He said to the men of Succoth, "Please, give loaves of bread to the people on foot with me, for they are exhausted, and I am chasing Zebah and Zalmunna, the kings of Midian."

But the officials of Succoth said, "Are the hands of Zebah and Zalmunna now in your hand? So why we should give bread to your army?"

Gideon replied, "Therefore when *ADONAI* delivers Zebah and Zalmunna into my hand, then I will thresh your flesh with the thorns of the wilderness and briers."

From there he went up to Penuel and spoke to them similarly, but the men of Penuel answered him just as the men of Succoth had answered. So he spoke also to the men of Penuel saying, "When I come back safely, I will tear down this tower."

Now Zebah and Zalmunna were in Karkor, and with them their armies of about 15,000 men, all who were left of all the army of the people of the east—the fallen were 120,000 swordsmen.

Now Gideon went up by the road of the tent dwellers on the east of Nobah and Jogbehah, and ambushed the camp when it was off guard. When Zebah and Zalmunna fled, he pursued them and captured the two kings of Midian, Zebah and Zalmunna, and routed the whole army.

Gideon son of Joash returned from the battle by the Ascent of Heres. He captured a boy from the people of Succoth and questioned him, so he wrote down for him the officials of Succoth and its elders—77 men.

When he came to the men of Succoth, he said, "Behold Zebah and Zalmunna—about whom you mocked me saying, 'Are the hands of Zebah and Zalmunna already in your hand? Why should we give bread to your exhausted men?'"

Then he seized the elders of the city, and thorns of the wilderness and briers, and with them he punished the men of Succoth. He also tore down the tower of Penuel and slew the men of the city.

Then he asked Zebah and Zalmunna, "What kind of men did you kill at Tabor?"

"As you are, so they were," they answered. "Each one looked like the children of a king."

"They were my brothers, the sons of my mother," he said. "As *Adonai* lives, if only you had let them live, I would not kill you."

Then he said to Jeter his first-born, "Arise, kill them!" But the boy could not draw his sword, for he was afraid, since he was still a youth.

Then Zebah and Zalmunna said, "Rise up yourself and fall on us—for as the man is, so is his strength." So Gideon arose and killed Zebah and Zalmunna, and took the crescent ornaments that were on their camels' necks.

Then the men of Israel said to Gideon, "Rule over us—you, your son, and your grandson as well. For you have delivered us from the hand of Midian." But Gideon replied to them, "I will not rule over you, nor will my son rule over you. Adonai alone will rule over you."

Yet Gideon said to them, "I would make a request of you, that you would give me every man an earring from his spoil." (For they had golden earrings, because they were Ishmaelites.)

"We'll certainly give them!" they replied. So they spread out a robe, and each one of them threw an earring from his spoil. So the weight of the golden earrings that he requested was 1,700 shekels of gold—besides the crescent ornaments, the pendants and the purple robes that were on the kings of Midian, and besides the chains that were on their camels' necks. Gideon made it into an ephod, and put it in his town Ophrah. But all Israel prostituted themselves after it there, and it became a snare to Gideon and his household.

So Midian was subdued before *Bnei-Yisrael*, and they lifted up their heads no more. The land had tranquility for 40 years in the days of Gideon. Jerubbaal son of Joash went and lived in his own house. Now Gideon had 70 sons of his own issue, for he had many wives. Also his concubine who was in Shechem also bore him a son—he called his name Abimelech. Then Gideon son of Joash died at a good old age, and was buried in the tomb of Joash his father, in Ophrah of the Abiezrites. But it came to pass, as soon as Gideon was dead, that *Bnei-Yisrael* again prostituted themselves after the Baalim, and made Baal-berith their god. So *Bnei-Yisrael* did not remember *Adonai* their God, who had delivered them from the hand of all their enemies on every side. Nor did they show kindness to the household of Jerubbaal, namely Gideon, in accord with all the goodness which he had done for Israel.

Judges, chapter 8

32. God Renews Strength

Bnei-Yisrael again did what was evil in *ADONAI*'s eyes, and *ADONAI* gave them into the hand of the Philistines for 40 years.

Now there was a certain man from Zorah, from a Danite clan, whose name was Manoah. His wife was barren and bore no children. Then the angel of *ADONAI* appeared to the woman and said to her, "Behold now, you are barren and have not borne children, but you will conceive and bear a son. Now therefore be careful not to drink wine or strong drink, or eat any unclean thing. For behold, you will conceive and bear a son. Let no razor come upon his head, for the boy will be a Nazirite to God from the womb. He will begin to deliver Israel from the hand of the Philistines."

Then the woman came and told her husband saying, "A man of God came to me and his appearance was like the appearance of the angel of God, very awesome! But I did not ask him where he was from, nor did he tell me his name. He said to me, 'Behold, you will conceive and bear a son. So, drink no wine or strong drink, and eat nothing unclean, for the child will be a Nazirite to God from the womb to the day of his death."

Then Manoah entreated *ADONAI* and said, "My Lord, please let the man of God whom You have sent come to us again and teach us what we will do for the boy to be born."

God listened to the voice of Manoah, and the angel of God came again to the woman as she was sitting in the field, but her husband Manoah was not with her. So the woman ran quickly and told her husband, and said to him, "Look, the man that came to me the other day has appeared to me!"

So Manoah got up and followed his wife. When he came to the man, he asked him, "Are you the one who spoke to the woman?"

"I am," he said.

Then Manoah said, "Now may your words come about! What will be the child's rule and his mission?"

The angel of *ADONAI* said to Manoah, "Let the woman abstain from all that I mentioned to her. She should not eat anything that comes from the grapevine, or drink wine or strong drink, or eat any unclean thing. She must observe all that I commanded her."

Then Manoah said to the angel of *ADONAI*, "Please, let us detain you so that we may prepare a young goat for you."

But the angel of *ADONAI* said to Manoah, "If you could detain me, I would not eat your food. But if you present a burnt offering, then offer it to *ADONAI*." For Manoah did not realize that he was the angel of *ADONAI*.

Then Manoah asked the angel of *ADONAI*, "What is your name, so that when your words come to pass we may honor you?"

But the angel of *Adonai* said to him, "Why do you ask for my name? It is wonderful."

Manoah took the young goat with the meal offering and offered them on the rock to *Adonai*, and He did something wonderful as Manoah and his wife were watching. For it came about when the flame went up from off the altar toward heaven that the angel of *Adonai* ascended in the flame of the altar. Manoah and his wife were looking on, then they fell on their faces to the ground. But the angel of *Adonai* appeared no more to Manoah or to his wife. Then Manoah realized that he was the angel of *Adonai*.

Manoah said to his wife, "We will surely die, because we have seen God." But his wife said to him, "If *Adonai* had desired to kill us, He would not have accepted a burnt offering and a meal offering from our hand, nor would He have shown us all these things or let us hear such things as these at this time."

Then the woman bore a son, and called his name Samson. So the boy grew up and *Adonai* blessed him. The *Ruach Adonai* began to stir him in Mahaneh-dan, between Zorah and Eshtaol.

Judges, chapter 13

Then Samson went down to Timnah and eyed in Timnah a woman, one of the daughters of the Philistines. So he came back and told his father and mother saying, "I have seen a woman in Timnah, one of the daughters of the Philistines. So now get her for me as a wife."

Then his father and his mother said to him, "Is there no woman among the daughters of your kinsmen, or among all our people, that you are going to take a wife from the uncircumcised Philistines?"

But Samson said to his father, "Get her for me, for she is the right one in my eyes."

But his father and mother did not know that it was of *Adonai*, for He was seeking a pretext against the Philistines. For at that time the Philistines were ruling over Israel. While his father and mother went down to Timnah, Samson went to the vineyards of Timnah, and behold, a young lion came roaring at him.

Then the *Ruach Adonai* came mightily upon him, and he tore him apart as one would have split a young goat—yet he had nothing in his hand. But he did not tell his father or his mother what he had done.

So he went down and talked with the woman, and she looked right in Samson's eyes. After a while he returned to get her, but turned aside to look at the carcass of the lion; and behold, there was a swarm of bees and honey in the carcass of the lion. So he scraped it into his hands and went on, eating as he went. Now when he came to his father and mother, he gave some to them and they ate it, though he did not tell them that he had scraped the honey from the carcass of the lion.

Then his father went down to the woman, and Samson made a banquet there, for so the young men used to

do. Now it came to pass, when they saw him, they brought 30 companions to be with him.
Then Samson said to them, "Let me now propose a riddle to you. If you can indeed solve it for me during the seven days of the banquet, and figure it out, then I will give you 30 linen garments and 30 changes of clothes; but if you cannot solve it for me, then you must give me 30 linen garments and 30 changes of clothes."

"Propose your riddle," they said to him. "Let's hear it!"

So he said to them, "Out of the eater came forth food, out of the strong came forth sweet."

But for three days they could not solve the riddle.

Now on the seventh day, they said to Samson's wife, "Coax your husband so that he will explain the riddle to us—or else we will burn you and your father's house with fire. Have you invited us to impoverish us?"

So Samson's wife wept before him and said, "You only hate me! You don't love me! You proposed a riddle to the sons of my people—yet you haven't explained it to me!"

"Look," he said, "I haven't explained it to my father or my mother, so should I explain it to you?" But she wept before him the seven days while their banquet lasted. So it was on the seventh day he told her, because she nagged him. Then she told the riddle to the sons of her people.
So the men of the city said to him on the seventh day, before the sun went down, "What is sweeter than honey? And what is stronger than a lion?"

But he responded to them,
"If you hadn't plowed with my heifer, you wouldn't have solved my riddle."

Then the *Ruach* ADONAI came mightily upon him, and he went down to Ashkelon and killed 30 of their men, took their spoil, and gave the changes of clothes to those who solved the riddle. Since his rage was burning, he went up to his father's house. But Samson's wife was given to his companion who had been his best man.

Judges, chapter 14

But after a while, during the time of wheat harvest, Samson visited his wife with a young goat.

"I am going to my wife in her room," he said. But her father would not let him enter.

"I thought for sure you had utterly hated her," her father said, "so I gave her to your best man. Her younger sister—isn't she better than her? Please, let her be yours instead."

Then Samson said to them, "This time I am blameless from the Philistines when I do harm to them."

So Samson went and caught 300 foxes, and took torches, turned the foxes tail to tail and put one torch between every two tails. Then he set fire to the torches and released them into the standing grain of the Philistines. Thus he burned up both the stacks and the standing grain, along with vineyards and olive trees.

Then the Philistines asked, "Who did this?"

They were told, "Samson, son-in-law of the Timnite, because he took his wife and gave her to his best man." So the Philistines came up and burnt her and her father with fire.

Then Samson said to them, "Since you have acted like this, surely I will take revenge on you—after that I will quit." So he struck them leg upon thigh with a great slaughter. Then he went down and stayed in the cleft of the rock of Etam.

Then the Philistines went up and camped in Judah and spread out in Lehi. The men of Judah asked,

"Why have you marched against us?"

They replied, "We have come to arrest Samson—to do to him as he did to us."

Then 3,000 men of Judah went down to the cleft of the rock of Etam and said to Samson, "Don't you realize that the Philistines are ruling over us? So what is this that you have done to us?"

He said to them, "As they did to me, so I have done to them."

"We have come down to bind you," they said to him, "so that we may hand you over to the Philistines."

So Samson said to them, "Swear to me that you yourselves won't kill me."

"No, we won't kill you," they said to him, "but we will bind you fast and hand you over to them." So they bound him with two new ropes and brought him up from the rock.

When he arrived at Lehi, the Philistines shouted upon meeting him. But the *Ruach Adonai* came mightily upon him, so that the ropes that were on his arms became like flax burned with fire and his bonds melted off his wrists.

Then he found a fresh jawbone of a donkey, reached out and took it, and killed a thousand men with it.

Then Samson said,
"With the jawbone of a donkey,
  a heap . . . two heaps,
with the jawbone of a donkey
  I struck down a thousand men."

As soon as he had finished speaking, he threw the jawbone from his hand. Then he named that place Ramat-lehi.

Then he became very thirsty, so he called to *Adonai* and said, "You have granted this great deliverance by the hand of Your servant. So now, will I die of thirst and fall into the hand of the uncircumcised?"

But God split the hollow place that is in Lehi, and water came out of it. When he drank, he regained his strength and revived. Therefore he called it En-hakkore, which is in Lehi to this day. Then he judged Israel in the days of the Philistines for 20 years.

Judges, chapter 15

Once Samson went to Gaza and eyed

a prostitute there, so he went to her. The Gazites were told, "Samson has come here." So they surrounded him, lay in ambush for him all night at the gate of the city, and kept quiet all night saying, "When morning light comes, then we kill him."

But Samson lay in bed till midnight, got up at midnight, grabbed the doors of the city gate along with the two gateposts and pulled them up bar and all. Then he put them on his shoulders and carried them up to the top of the mountain that is near Hebron.

It came about afterward that he fell in love with a woman in the valley of Sorek, whose name was Delilah. So the Philistine lords came up to her and said to her, "Coax him, see where his great strength comes from and by what we may overpower him, so we may bind him to subdue him—then we'll each of us give you 1,100 pieces of silver."

So Delilah said to Samson, "Tell me please, where does your great strength come from? How could you be bound to subdue you?"

Samson said to her, "If they bind me with seven fresh cords that have never been dried, then I would be weak and be like any other man."

So the Philistine lords brought up to her seven fresh cords that had never been dried, and she bound him with them, while an ambush was waiting in an inner room. "The Philistines are upon you, Samson!" she said to him. But he broke the cords just as a strand of straw snaps when it touches fire. So his strength remained unknown.

Delilah said to Samson, "Oh, you deceived me! You lied to me! Now tell me please, how you can be bound?"

He told her, "If they only bind me with new ropes never used for work, then I will be weak and be like any other man." So Delilah took new ropes, tied him up with them and said to him, "The Philistines are upon you, Samson!" Yet while the ambush was waiting in the inner room, he snapped them from his arms like a thread.

So Delilah said to Samson, "Up to now you've mocked me and told me lies! Tell me how you can be bound!"

He told her, "If you weave the seven locks of my head with the web of a loom." So she pinned it with a pin and said to him, "The Philistines are upon you, Samson!" But he awoke from his sleep and pulled away the pin of the loom and the web.

"How can you say, 'I love you,'" she said to him, "when your heart is not with me? This is three times you've deceived me and not told me where your great strength comes from."

Now it came about when she nagged him daily with her speeches and kept bothering him, his soul was annoyed to death. So he divulged to her all his heart and said to her, "No razor has ever been upon my head, for I have been a Nazirite to God from my mother's womb. If I am shaved, then my strength will go from me, and I will be weak and be like any other man."

Now when Delilah realized that he had confided to her all his heart, she sent and called for the Philistine lords saying, "Come up this time, for he has told me all his heart."

So the Philistine lords came up to her and brought the silver in their hand. Then she made him sleep upon her knees, and she called for a man and had the seven locks of his head shaved off. She even began to humiliate him while his strength departed from him.

Then she said, "The Philistines are upon you, Samson!" When he awoke from his sleep, he thought, "I'll go out as at other times, and shake myself off." He did not comprehend that *Adonai* had departed from him.

Then the Philistines seized him and gouged out his eyes. They brought him down to Gaza and bound him with bronze chains, and he became a grinder in the prison. However, the hair of his head began to grow again after it was shaved off.

Now the Philistine lords gathered to offer a great sacrifice to Dagon their god and to celebrate, as they said, "Our god has given our enemy Samson into our hand."

When the people saw him, they praised their god, as they said, "Our god has given into our hand our enemy and the destroyer of our country, who has slain many of us."

Now it came about when their hearts were merry that they said, "Call for Samson, that he may amuse us." So they called for Samson from the prison, and he did make them laugh, when they made him stand between the pillars.

Then Samson said to the lad that held him by the hand, "Let me feel the pillars on which the temple rests, so I may lean on them."

Now the temple was full of men and women. All the Philistine lords were there and about 3,000 men and women on the roof looking on while Samson was amusing them.

Then Samson called out to *Adonai* and said, "My Lord *Adonai*, please remember me and please strengthen me only this once, O God, so that I may this once take revenge on the Philistines for my two eyes."

Then Samson grasped the two middle pillars on which the temple rested and leaned on them, one with his right hand and the other with his left.

Then Samson said, "Let me die with the Philistines!" He bent with all his might so that the temple fell on the lords and on all the people who were in it. So the dead whom he killed at his death were more than those whom he killed during his life. Then his kinsmen and all his father's household came down, lifted him, brought him up and buried him between Zorah and Eshtaol in the tomb of his father Manoah. For he had judged Israel 20 years.

Then Samson called out to *ADONAI* and said, "My Lord *ADONAI* , please remember me and please strengthen me only this once, O God, so that I may this once take revenge on the Philistines for my two eyes." Then Samson grasped the two middle pillars on which the temple rested and leaned on them, one with his right hand and the other with his left. Then Samson said, "Let me die with the Philistines!" He bent with all his might so that the temple fell on the lords and on all the people who were in it....

Judges 16:28-30 TLV

33. God Grants Her Prayers

Now there was a certain man of Ramathaim-zophim, of the hill country of Ephraim—his name was Elkanah son of Jeroham son of Elihu son of Tohu son of Zuph, an Ephraimite. He had two wives: the name of the one was Hannah and the name of the other Peninnah. Peninnah had children, but Hannah was childless.

Now this man used to go up from his town every year to worship and to sacrifice to *Adonai-Tzva'ot* in Shiloh. (The two sons of Eli, Hophni and Phinehas, were *kohanim* of *Adonai* there.) Then on the designated day Elkanah would sacrifice and give portions to his wife Peninnah and to all her sons and daughters, but to Hannah he would give only one portion—even though he loved Hannah—for *Adonai* had closed her womb.

Her rival would taunt her bitterly to provoke her, because *Adonai* had closed her womb.

So it was year after year, whenever she went up to the House of *Adonai*, that she would provoke her; so she wept and would not eat.

Then her husband Elkanah would say to her, "Hannah, why are you crying? Why won't you eat? Why is your heart so sad? Am I not better to you than ten sons?"

After eating and drinking in Shiloh, Hannah got up. Now Eli the *kohen* was sitting on his seat by the doorpost of the Temple of *Adonai*. While her soul was bitter, she prayed to *Adonai* and wept.

So she made a vow and said, "*Adonai-Tzva'ot*, if You will indeed look upon the affliction of Your handmaid, remember me and not forget Your handmaid, but grant Your handmaid a son, then I will give him to *Adonai* all the days of his life and no razor will ever touch his head."

It came to pass, as she prayed long before *Adonai*, that Eli was watching her mouth. Now Hannah was praying in her heart—only her lips were moving, but her voice could not be heard. So Eli thought she was drunk.

Then Eli said to her, "How long will you be drunk? Get rid of your wine!"

But in response Hannah said, "No, my lord, I am a woman with an oppressed spirit! I haven't been drinking wine or beer. Instead I've been pouring out my soul before *Adonai*. Don't consider your handmaid a wicked woman. For out of my great anguish and grief I've been praying until now."

Then Eli responded, "Go in *shalom*, and may the God of Israel grant your petition that you asked of Him."

"May your maidservant find favor in your eyes," she said.

So the woman went her way; she ate, and her countenance was no longer dejected. They rose up early in the morning and worshipped before *Adonai*, then went back to their home to Ramah. Then Elkanah was intimate with his wife Hannah, and *ADONAI* remembered her.

So it came to pass at the turn of the year that Hannah conceived and gave birth to a son. She called his name Samuel, "because I have asked *ADONAI* for him."

When the man Elkanah and all his household went up to offer the annual sacrifice to *ADONAI* and to fulfill his vow offering, Hannah did not go up, for she said to her husband, "When the child is weaned, I will bring him, so he may appear before *ADONAI* and stay there forever."

So her husband Elkanah said to her, "Do what seems best to you. Stay until you have weaned him—only may *ADONAI* establish His word."

So the woman stayed home and nursed her son until she weaned him.

When she had weaned him, she took him up with her, along with three bulls, one ephah of flour and a jar of wine, and brought him to the House of *ADONAI* in Shiloh, while the child was still young.

After they slaughtered the bull, they brought the boy to Eli.

"It's me, my lord!" she said. "As your soul lives, my lord, I am the woman that stood by you here, praying to *ADONAI*. For this boy I prayed, and *ADONAI* has granted me my petition that I asked of Him. So I in turn dedicate him to *ADONAI*—as long as he lives he is dedicated to *ADONAI*."

Then he bowed in worship there before *ADONAI*.

1 Samuel, chapter 1

Then Hannah prayed and said,

"My heart exults in *ADONAI*,
my horn is lifted high in *ADONAI*.
I smile wide over my enemies,
for I rejoice in Your salvation.
There is none holy as *ADONAI*,
for there is none besides You,
nor is there any rock like our God.
Boast no more so proudly—
insolence comes out
of your mouth.

For *ADONAI* is the all-knowing God,
and by Him deeds are weighed.
The bows of the mighty
are broken, but the stumbling
are girded with strength.
Those full hire themselves for bread,
but those starving hunger no more.
Even the barren gives birth to seven,
but she with many sons languishes.

ADONAI causes death
and makes alive,
He brings down to *Sheol*
and raises up.

ADONAI makes poor and makes rich,
He brings low and also lifts up.
He raises the helpless from the dust.
He lifts the needy from the dunghill,
to make them sit with nobles,
granting them a seat of honor.

For the earth's pillars are *ADONAI*'s,
and He has set the world on them.

He guards the steps
of His godly ones,
but the wicked are
silenced in darkness.

"It's me, my lord!" she said. "As your soul lives, my lord, I am the woman that stood by you here, praying to *Adonai*. For this boy I prayed, and *Adonai* has granted me my petition that I asked of Him. So I in turn dedicate him to *Adonai*—as long as he lives he is dedicated to *Adonai*." Then he bowed in worship there before *Adonai*.

1 Samuel 1:26-28 TLV

For one does not prevail by might.

Those who oppose *ADONAI*
will be shattered.
He thunders against them in heaven.
He judges the ends of the earth.
He gives strength to His king,
exalting the horn of His anointed
one."

Then Elkanah went home to Ramah, while the boy served *ADONAI* before Eli the *kohen*. Now Eli's sons were worthless men; they did not acknowledge *ADONAI*.

Now this was the custom of the *kohanim* with the people: whenever any man offered a sacrifice, the *kohen*'s servant would come along, while the meat was boiling, with a three-pronged fork in his hand, and he would thrust it into the pan, or kettle, or caldron or pot. Whatever the fork brought up, the *kohen* would take for himself. This is how they dealt with all the Israelites who came there to Shiloh.

Even before they burned the fat, the *kohen*'s servant would come and say to the one offering sacrifice, "Give the *kohen* meat for roasting, since he will not accept boiled meat from you—only raw."

If the man said to him, "Let them first burn the fat up as smoke, and then take as much as you desire," he would reply, "No! But you must give it now—otherwise, I will take it by force."

Thus the sin of the young men was very great before *ADONAI*, for the men despised the offering of *ADONAI*. But Samuel was ministering before *ADONAI*, as a boy girded with a linen ephod.

Moreover, his mother would make him a little robe and bring it to him from year to year when she would come up with her husband to offer the annual sacrifice. Then Eli would bless Elkanah and his wife and say, "May *ADONAI* give you offspring from this woman instead of the one she requested from *ADONAI*." Then they would return to their place.

So *ADONAI* visited Hannah, and she conceived and gave birth to three sons and two daughters. Meanwhile, the child Samuel grew before *ADONAI*.

Now Eli had grown very old. He heard all that his sons did to all Israel, and how they slept with the women who served at the doorway of the Tent of Meeting. So he said to them, "Why do you do such things? For I hear evil reports from all these people concerning you. No, my sons! For this is not a good report that I hear *ADONAI*'s people spreading around. If a man sins against another, God may pardon him; but if a man sins against *ADONAI*, who will intercede for him?"

But they did not listen to the voice of their father, because *ADONAI* desired to put them to death.

Meanwhile, the child Samuel kept growing and increasing in favor both with *ADONAI* and also with men.
Now there came a man of God to Eli and said to him, "Thus says *ADONAI*: Did I not reveal Myself clearly to the house of your father when they were

in Egypt belonging to Pharaoh's palace? Also did I not choose them from all the tribes of Israel to be My *kohanim*, to officiate at My altar, to burn incense and to wear an ephod before Me? Did I not give to the house of your father all the fire offerings of *Bnei-Yisrael*?

Why do you kick at My sacrifice and My offering which I have commanded in My dwelling, and honor your sons above Me, by fattening yourselves with the choicest of every offering of Israel My people? Therefore *ADONAI* God of Israel declares, I indeed said that your house and your father's house should walk before Me forever.

But now declares *ADONAI*, far be it from Me! For I will honor those who honor Me, but those who despise Me will be disdained.

Behold, the days are coming when I will cut short your strength and the strength of your father's house, so that no one in your household will reach old age. Moreover, you will behold the distress of My dwelling, despite all that is good that has been done to Israel. So no one in your household will reach old age, forever.

Any man of yours that I did not cut off from My altar would make your eyes weep and your soul grieve. So all the increase of your household will die as young men.

Now this will be the sign to you that will come on your two sons—Hophni and Phinehas—on the same day both of them will die.

"Yet I will raise up for Myself a faithful *kohen* who will do according to what is in My heart and My mind. Then I will build him an enduring house, and he will walk before My anointed one all the time. Anyone left in your household will come and bow low to him for a piece of silver and a loaf of bread, and will say: 'Please, assign me to one of the priestly offices so that I may eat a morsel of bread.'"

1 Samuel, chapter 2

Now the boy Samuel was in the service of *ADONAI* under Eli. In those days the word of *ADONAI* was rare—there were no visions breaking through.

One day, Eli was lying down in his place—now his eyes had grown dim so that he could not see, and the lamp of God had not yet gone out. Samuel was lying down in *ADONAI*'s Temple, where the ark of God was.

Then *ADONAI* called, "Samuel!"

So he answered, "Here I am." Then he ran to Eli and said, "Here I am, for you called me."

But he replied, "I didn't call—go back to sleep." So he went back and lay down.

Then *ADONAI* called Samuel yet again. So Samuel arose and went to Eli, and said, "Here I am, for you called me."

But he answered, "I didn't call, my son—go back to sleep."

Now Samuel had not experienced *ADONAI* yet, since the word of *ADONAI* had not yet been revealed to him.

ADONAI called Samuel again for the third time. So he got up and went to Eli, and said "Here I am, for you called me." Then Eli perceived that *ADONAI* was calling the boy.

So Eli said to Samuel, "Go back to sleep, and if He calls you, say: 'Speak, *ADONAI*, for Your servant is listening.'"

So Samuel went back and lay down in his place. Then *ADONAI* came and stood and called as at the other times, "Samuel! Samuel!" Then Samuel said, "Speak, for Your servant is listening."

Then *ADONAI* said to Samuel, "Behold, I am about to do something in Israel at which both ears of everyone that hears it will tingle.

In that day I will perform against Eli all that I have spoken concerning his house, from beginning to end. For I have told him that I am about to judge his house forever for the iniquity that he knew about, because his sons brought a curse on themselves yet he did not rebuke them. Therefore I have sworn to the house of Eli that the iniquity of Eli's house will never be atoned for by sacrifice or offering."

Then Samuel lay down until the morning, when he opened the doors of the House of *ADONAI*. But Samuel was afraid to tell Eli about the vision.

Then Eli called Samuel and said, "Samuel, my son."
"Here I am," he replied.

"What is the word that He has spoken to you?" he said. "Please don't hide it from me. May God do so to you and even more if you hide anything at all from me that He spoke to you."

So Samuel told him everything and hid nothing. Then Eli said, "He is *ADONAI*. May He do what is good in His eyes."

So Samuel grew up and *ADONAI* was with him, and let none of his words fall to the ground. Then all Israel from Dan to Beersheba knew that Samuel was entrusted as a prophet of *ADONAI*.

ADONAI started to appear once more in Shiloh, for *ADONAI* revealed Himself to Samuel in Shiloh by the word of *ADONAI*.

1 Samuel, chapter 3

34. God Anoints a King

Now *ADONAI* said to Samuel, "How long will you grieve over Saul, since I have rejected him as king over Israel? Fill your horn with oil and go. I am sending you to Jesse the Beth-lehemite, for I have selected for Myself a king among his sons."

But Samuel replied, "How can I go? If Saul hears of it, he will kill me."

ADONAI said, "Take a heifer with you and say: 'I have come to sacrifice to *ADONAI*.' Then invite Jesse to the sacrifice, and I will let you know what you are to do. You will anoint for Me whom I tell you."

So Samuel did what *ADONAI* said and went to Beth-lehem. The elders of the town came out to meet him trembling, and asked, "Do you come in *shalom*?"

"In *shalom*," he said. "I have come to sacrifice to *ADONAI*. Consecrate yourselves and come with me to the sacrifice." He also consecrated Jesse and his sons and invited them to the sacrifice.

Upon their arrival, he saw Eliab and thought, "Surely, *ADONAI*'s anointed one is before Him."

But *ADONAI* said to Samuel, "Do not look at his appearance or his stature, because I have already refused him. For He does not see a man as man sees, for man looks at the outward appearance, but *ADONAI* looks into the heart."

Then Jesse called Abinadab and made him pass before Samuel. But he said, "Neither has *ADONAI* chosen this one."

Then Jesse made Shammah pass by and again he said, "Neither has *ADONAI* chosen this one."

Thus Jesse made seven of his sons pass before Samuel. But Samuel said to Jesse, "*ADONAI* has not chosen any of these."

Then Samuel asked Jesse, "Are these all the boys you have?"

"There's still the youngest," he replied. But right now, he's tending the sheep."

"Send and bring him," Samuel said to Jesse, "for we will not sit down until he comes here." So he sent word and had him come.

Now he was ruddy-cheeked, with beautiful eyes and a handsome appearance. Then *ADONAI* said, "Arise, anoint him, for this is the one."

So Samuel took the horn of oil and anointed him in the midst of his brothers. From that day on *Ruach ADONAI* came mightily upon David. Then Samuel rose up and went to Ramah. Now the *Ruach ADONAI* had departed from Saul, and an evil spirit from *ADONAI* terrified him.

So Saul's courtiers said to him, "Behold now, an evil spirit from God is tormenting you. Let our lord now command your courtiers in your service to search for a man who is a skillful player on the harp. Then whenever the evil spirit from God comes on you, he will play with his instrument and you will feel better."

So Saul said to his courtiers, "Find me someone who can play well and bring him to me."

One of the young men answered and said, "I have seen a son of Jesse the Beth-lehemite who is skillful in playing music. He is a mighty man of valor, a warrior, prudent in speech, a handsome man, and *ADONAI* is with him."

So Saul sent messengers to Jesse and said, "Send me your son David, who is with the flock."

So Jesse took a donkey, loaded it with bread, a bottle of wine and a young goat, and sent them with his son David to Saul. Then David came to Saul and became one of his attendants.

Saul loved him greatly, so David became his armor-bearer. Then Saul sent word to Jesse saying, "Let David now keep attending me, for he has found favor in my eyes."

It came to pass, whenever the spirit from God came upon Saul, David would take the harp and play it with his hand. So Saul would find relief and feel better, as the evil spirit departed from him.

1 Samuel, chapter 16

Now the Philistines assembled their armies to battle. They were gathered at Socoh of Judah, and camped in Ephes-dammim, between Socoh and Azekah. Saul and the men of Israel gathered and camped in the valley of Elah, then lined up in battle array against the Philistines.

The Philistines were standing on the mountain on one side, and Israel was standing on the mountain on the other side, with the valley between them. Then a champion stepped out from the camp of the Philistines, named Goliath, from Gath, whose height was six cubits and a span. He had a bronze helmet on his head and a breastplate of scale armor; the weight of the bronze breastplate was 5,000 shekels.

He also had bronze shin-guards on his legs and a bronze javelin slung between his shoulders. The shaft of his spear was like a weaver's beam, and the head of his spear weighed 600 shekels of iron; and his shield-bearer was marching ahead of him.

Then he stood and shouted out to the ranks of Israel saying to them, "Why come out to line up in battle array? Am I not the Philistine and aren't you Saul's servants? Choose for yourselves a man and let him come down to me. If he is able to fight with me and kill me, then will we become your slaves; but if I prevail against him and kill him, then will you become our slaves and serve us."

The Philistine added, "Today I defy the ranks of Israel—give me a man, so we may fight together!"

But when Saul and all Israel heard these words of the Philistine, they were dismayed and very terrified.

Now David was son of a certain Ephrathite man of Beth-lehem of Judah, whose name was Jesse. He had eight sons and during the days of Saul the man was old, advanced in years among men.

Now the three oldest sons of Jesse had already left and gone after Saul to the battle; the names of his three sons who went to the battle were Eliab the firstborn, and second to him Abinadab, and the third Shammah. David was the youngest. So the three oldest followed Saul.

Now David would go back and forth from Saul to tending his father's sheep by Beth-lehem. For forty days that Philistine would come out every morning and evening to present himself.

Then Jesse said to his son David, "Take now, for your brothers, an ephah of this roasted grain and these ten loaves, and carry them quickly to the camp to your brothers. Also take these ten slices of cheese to the captain of their thousand—and check out the welfare of your brothers and bring back some token from them. They are with Saul and all the men of Israel in the valley of Elah, fighting with the Philistines."

So David rose up early in the morning, left the flock with a keeper, took the provisions and went as Jesse had commanded him. When he reached the camp, the army was going out to the battle line shouting the war cry. Israel and the Philistines drew up their battle lines, army against army. Then David left his baggage in the care of the baggage keeper, and ran to the battle line and entered to check out his brothers' welfare. But as he was talking with them, behold the champion, the Philistine from Gath named Goliath, was coming up from the ranks of the Philistines, and he spoke these same words; and David heard them.

Upon seeing him, all the men of Israel fled from him in great fear. All the men of Israel were saying, "Have you seen this man who keeps coming up? Surely he is coming up to defy Israel! The man who kills him, the king will enrich him with great riches, give him his daughter in marriage and make his father's house tax-free in Israel!"

Then David asked the men who were standing by him saying, "What will be done for the man who kills this Philistine and takes away the reproach from Israel? For who is this uncircumcised Philistine that he should defy the ranks of the living God?"

The people answered him with the same speech saying, "Thus it will be done for the man who strikes him down."

Now when Eliab his oldest brother heard him speaking to the men, Eliab's anger was kindled against David. "Why have you come down here?" he asked. "So with whom did you leave those few sheep in the wilderness? I know your insolence and the wickedness of your heart! For you've come down here to watch the battle."

"What have I done now?" David said. "It was only a question!" Then he turned away from him toward someone else and asked the same question. So the people gave him the same answer as before.

The words that David said were overheard and reported before Saul. So he was taken to him.

David said to Saul, "Let no one's heart fail because of him. Your servant will go and fight with this Philistine."

Then Saul said to David, "You can't go fight this Philistine—for you're just a youth, and he's been a warrior since his youth."

But David said to Saul, "Your servant has been tending his father's sheep. When a lion or a bear came and carried off a lamb out of the flock, I went out after it, struck it down, and rescued the lamb out of its mouth. If it rose up against me, I grabbed him by its fur, struck it and killed it. Your servant has killed both the lion and the bear, so this uncircumcised Philistine will become like one of them—since he has defied the ranks of the living God."

Then David said, "*ADONAI*, who has delivered me from the paw of the lion and from the paw of the bear, will deliver me from the hand of this Philistine."

"Go!" said Saul to David, "and may *ADONAI* be with you."

Then Saul clothed David with his own garb, put a bronze helmet on his head, and clothed him in armor. David strapped his sword on his garment and tried to walk, but he was not used to it.

So David said to Saul, "I cannot walk in these, for I am not used to them." So David took them off. Then he took his staff in his hand, chose five smooth stones from the valley, put them in the pocket of the shepherd's bag that he had, and with his sling in his hand, he approached the Philistine.

Meanwhile, the Philistine drew nearer and approached David, with his shield -bearer in front of him. Now when the Philistine looked and saw David, he disdained him, for he was just a ruddy boy with a handsome appearance.

Then the Philistine said to David, "Am I a dog, that you come to me with sticks?" Then the Philistine cursed David by his gods.

The Philistine said to David, "Come to me, so I may give your flesh to the birds of the sky and the beasts of the field."

Then David said to the Philistine, "You are coming to me with a sword, a spear and a javelin, but I am coming to you in the Name of *ADONAI-Tzva'ot*, God of the armies of Israel, whom you have defied. This very day *ADONAI* will deliver you into my hand, and I will strike you down and take your head off you, and I will give the carcasses of the Philistines' camp today to the birds of the sky and the wild beasts of the earth. Then all the earth will know that there is a God in Israel, and so all this assembly will know that *ADONAI* delivers not with sword and spear—for the battle belongs to *ADONAI*—and

He will give you into our hands."

Then when the Philistine rose and began to advance, drawing near to meet David, David ran quickly toward the battle line to meet the Philistine. David put his hand in his bag, took from it a stone and slung it, striking the Philistine on his forehead. The stone sank into his forehead, so that he fell on his face to the ground.

So David prevailed over the Philistine with a sling and a stone, struck the Philistine down and killed him. Since there was no sword in David's hand, David ran, stood over the Philistine, picked up his sword, drew it from its sheath, slew him and cut off his head with it.

When the Philistines saw that their champion was dead, they fled. Then the men of Israel and Judah rose up, shouted and pursued the Philistines all the way to the valley up to the gates of Ekron. The slain Philistines fell down along the way to Shaaraim, even up to Gath and Ekron.

When *Bnei-Yisrael* returned from chasing the Philistines, they plundered their camp. David took the head of the Philistine and brought it to Jerusalem, but he put his armor in his own tent. Now when Saul saw David going out against the Philistine, he asked Abner, the commander of the army, "Abner, whose son is this boy?"

Abner said, "As your soul lives, your majesty, I don't know."

So the king said, "Then, find out whose son this young man is."

So when David returned from killing the Philistine, Abner took him and brought him before Saul with the head of the Philistine in his hand.

"Whose son are you, young man?" Saul said to him.

David answered, "I am the son of your servant Jesse the Beth-lehemite."

1 Samuel, chapter 17

Now it came to pass, when David had finished speaking to Saul, Jonathan's soul was knit to David's soul, and Jonathan loved him as himself. Saul took him that day and did not let him return to his father's house. Then Jonathan cut a covenant with David, because he loved him as himself. Jonathan stripped off the robe that was on him and gave it to David, along with his armor: his sword, bow and belt.

So David went out wherever Saul sent him and had success, so Saul set him over the men of war.

It was pleasing in the eyes of all the people as well as in the eyes of Saul's courtiers. Upon their coming back, upon David's return from killing the Philistine, the women came out of all the towns of Israel, singing and dancing in circles to greet King Saul, with timbrels, with joy and with three-stringed instruments. So the women sang one to another, as they were dancing saying,

"Saul has slain his thousands,
and David his ten thousands!"

Then Saul became very angry—this

So David prevailed over the Philistine with a sling and a stone,
struck the Philistine down and killed him.

1 Samuel 17:50 TLV

saying was evil in his eyes—and he commented, "They've ascribed to David ten thousands and to me they've ascribed thousands. Now what more does he lack but the kingdom?" So Saul eyed David from that day on.

It came about the next day that an evil spirit from God came mightily upon Saul, so that he was raving within the palace. While David was playing music with his hand, as he did day by day, Saul had his spear in his hand, and Saul hurled the spear, thinking, "I'll pin David to the wall!" But David eluded him—twice.

Now Saul became afraid of David, because *ADONAI* was with him but had departed from Saul. Therefore Saul removed him from his entourage by appointing him as a captain of a thousand. So David went out and came in before the troops.

David had success in all his undertakings, since *ADONAI* was with him. When Saul saw that he had great success, he dreaded him. But all Israel and Judah loved David, for he went out and came in before them.

Then Saul said to David, "Here is my older daughter Merab—I give her to you as a wife. Only continue to be my son of valor and fight *ADONAI*'s battles." For Saul thought, "My hand needn't be against him—let the hand of the Philistines be against him."

But David replied to Saul, "Who am I, and what is my life or my father's family in Israel, that I should become the king's son-in-law?" But when it was time to give Saul's daughter Merab to David in marriage, she was given as wife to Adriel the Meholathite instead.

Now Saul's daughter Michal loved David. When they told Saul, the matter pleased him. Saul thought, "I will give her to him, so that she may become a snare to him—and the hand of the Philistines will be against him."

So Saul said to David, "You can still become my son-in-law, even today, with the second one."

Then Saul commanded his courtiers, "Speak with David privately and say, 'Behold, the king delights in you and all his courtiers love you. So now, become the king's son-in-law!'" So Saul's courtiers whispered these words in David's ears.

But David said, "Is it a light thing to you becoming the king's son-in-law, considering that I am a poor man and of little account?" Saul's courtiers reported back to him what David had said.

Then Saul said, "Thus you will say to David, 'The king desires no bridal dowry except 100 foreskins of the Philistines—to take vengeance on the king's enemies.'" So Saul schemed to make David fall by the hand of the Philistines.

When his courtiers told David these words, the word seemed right in David's eyes to become the king's son-in-law.

Before the days were fulfilled, David had risen, gone with his men and killed 200 Philistine men. Then David brought their foreskins and gave them in full number to the king—to become the king's son-in-law. So Saul gave him Michal his daughter as a wife.

When Saul saw and realized that *ADONAI* was with David and that Michal, Saul's daughter, loved him, Saul grew even more afraid of David. Thus Saul became David's enemy for all days.

When the chiefs of the Philistines marched out, as often as they came out, David proved more successful than all of Saul's officers. So his name became highly esteemed.

1 Samuel, chapter 18

Now Saul told his son Jonathan and all his courtiers to kill David. But Saul's son Jonathan delighted much in David. So Jonathan informed David saying, "My father Saul is seeking to kill you. So now, please be on guard in the morning, and stay in a secret place and hide yourself. I will go out and stand beside my father in the field where you will be, and I will speak with my father about you. If I notice anything, I will tell you."

So Jonathan spoke well of David to his father Saul and said to him, "May the king not sin against his servant David, since he has not sinned against you, and since his deeds have been very beneficial for you; For he put his life in his hand and killed the Philistine, and *ADONAI* won a great victory for all Israel—you saw it and rejoiced. So why would you sin against innocent blood by killing David without a cause?"

Saul listened to the voice of Jonathan, and Saul swore, "As *ADONAI* lives, he will not be put to death." So Jonathan called David, and Jonathan told him all these things. Jonathan brought David to Saul and in his presence as before.

Once again war broke out, and David marched out and fought the Philistines, and inflicted a great slaughter on them and they fled before him. Yet once again an evil spirit from *ADONAI* came upon Saul as he was sitting in his house with his spear in his hand, as David was playing music with his hand. Saul sought to pin David to the wall with the spear, but he slipped away from Saul's face, so that he drove the spear into the wall.

That night David fled and got away.

1 Samuel 19:1-10

Now the Ziphites came to Saul at Gibeah saying, "Isn't David hiding on the hill of Hachilah which faces Jeshimon?"

So Saul arose and went down to the wilderness of Ziph, 3,000 chosen men of Israel with him, to search for David in the wilderness of Ziph. Saul camped in the hill of Hachilah which faces Jeshimon, by the road. But David was staying in the wilderness, and he saw that Saul had come after him into the wilderness.

So David sent out spies and realized that Saul had already arrived. Then David got up and went to the place where Saul had camped. David detected the spot where Saul lay asleep, as well as Abner son of Ner his army commander. Saul was lying inside the barricade and the troops were camped around him.

Then David spoke and asked Ahimelech the Hittite and Joab's brother Abishai son of Zeruiah, saying "Who will go down with me to Saul in the camp?"

"I will go down with you," Abishai answered.

So David and Abishai approached the troops by night. Behold, Saul was lying asleep within the barricade with his spear stuck in the ground at his head, and Abner and the troops were sleeping around him. Then Abishai said to David, "God has delivered your enemy into your hand today. Now let me pin him to the ground with a single thrust of the spear. I will not have to strike him twice."

But David said to Abishai, "Don't destroy him! For who can lay his hand on *Adonai*'s anointed and be guiltless?"

David added, "As *Adonai* lives, either *Adonai* will strike him down, or his day will come to die, or he will go down to battle and be swept away. *Adonai* forbid that I should lay my hand on *Adonai*'s anointed! Now, just take the spear that is at his head and the water jar and let's go."

So David took the spear and the water jar from beside Saul's head. They got away—and no one saw it, or knew it, or woke up—for all were asleep, for a deep sleep from *Adonai* had fallen upon them.

Then David crossed over to the other side and stood on the top of a distant hill with a wide space between them. David shouted to the troops and to Abner son of Ner saying, "Aren't you going to answer, Abner?"

Then Abner answered saying, "Who are you, who called out to the king?" "Aren't you a man?" David said to Abner. "Indeed, who is like you in Israel? So, why didn't you guard your lord the king? For one of the troops came in to kill the king your lord. This thing that you've done is no good. As *Adonai* lives, all of you deserve to die, because you have not kept watching over your lord, *Adonai*'s anointed. So now, look around, where are the king's spear and the water jar that were at his head?"

Saul then recognized David's voice and said, "Is this your voice, David my son?"

"It is my voice, my lord the king," David said, then added, "Yet why is my lord pursuing his servant? What have I done? What evil is in my hand? Now please, let my lord the king listen to the words of his servant. If *Adonai* has stirred you up against me, let Him accept an offering. But if men have done so, then cursed are they before *Adonai* because they have now driven me out that I would not cling to *Adonai*'s inheritance, saying: 'Go, worship other gods.'

So now, let not my blood fall to the ground, away from the presence of *Adonai*. For the king of Israel has come out to search for but a single flea, just as one hunts for a partridge in the mountains."

Then Saul replied, "I have sinned! Return, David my son, for I will no longer do you harm, since my life was precious in your eyes this day. Behold, I've played the fool and erred so seriously."

David then answered and said, "There is the king's spear! Let one of the young men cross over and take it. *ADONAI* will repay everyone his righteousness and his faithfulness. For *ADONAI* gave you into my hand today, but I refused to lay my hand on *ADONAI*'s anointed.

See, just as your life was highly valued in my eyes today, so let my life be highly valued in *ADONAI*'s eyes, and may He deliver me from all trouble."

Then Saul said to David, "Blessed are you, David my son! You will both do mightily and will surely prevail." So David went his way, and Saul returned to his place.

1 Samuel, chapter 26

35. God Delights in David

Now it came to pass after the death of Saul—when David had returned from the slaughter of the Amalekites—that David stayed two days in Ziklag.

On the third day, behold, a man came from Saul's camp, with his clothes torn and dust on his head. Now when he approached David, he fell to the ground and prostrated himself. Then David asked him, "Where are you coming from?"

"I've escaped from the camp of Israel," he answered.

"How did things go?" David asked him. "Please, tell me."

He answered, "The troops fled the battlefield—also many of the troops fell and died. And even Saul and his son Jonathan are dead."

David asked the young man informing him, "How do you know that Saul and his son Jonathan are dead?"

The young man informing him answered, "I happened by chance to be on Mount Gilboa, and look, Saul was leaning on his spear, while the chariots and the horsemen were closing in on him. When he turned around and saw me, he called me. So I answered, 'Here I am.'

Then he asked me, 'Who are you?' "So I answered him, 'I am an Amalekite.' So he said to me, 'Stand now over me and kill me! For I'm in agony, yet I'm still alive.' So I stood over him and killed him, because I knew he couldn't survive after he had fallen.

Then I took the crown that was on his head and the bracelet that was on his arm, and brought them here—to my lord."

Then David took hold of his clothes and tore them, and so did all the men that were with him, and they mourned, wept and fasted until evening for Saul and his son Jonathan, for the troops of *ADONAI* and for the house of Israel, because they had fallen by the sword.

Then David said to the young man who informed him, "Where are you from?"

"I am a son of an Amalekite outsider," he replied.

Then David said to him, "How is it that you were not afraid to stretch out your hand to destroy *ADONAI*'s anointed one?" Then David called one of the young men and said, "Come and strike him down." And he struck him down and he died.

David said to him, "Your blood is on your own head, for your mouth testified against you saying, 'I killed *ADONAI*'s anointed.'"

2 Samuel 1:1-16

Now it came to pass after this that David inquired of *ADONAI* saying, "Should I go up to one of the towns of Judah?"

Adonai said to him, "Go up."

"Where shall I go up?" David asked.

"To Hebron," He said.

So David went up there, along with his two wives—Ahinoam of Jezreel and Abigail the widow of Nabal the Carmelite. David also brought up his men that were with him, each with his household, and they settled in the towns of Hebron.

Then the men of Judah came and there anointed David king over the house of Judah. Then they told David saying, "It was the men of Jabesh-gilead who buried Saul."

So David sent messengers to the men of Jabesh-gilead and said to them, "Blessed are you of *Adonai* for showing this kindness to Saul your lord, by burying him. So now may *Adonai* show you kindness and faithfulness; and I also will show you goodness because you have done this thing. Now therefore, be strong and brave, for Saul your lord is dead, and also the house of Judah has anointed me king over them."

2 Samuel 2:1-5

Then all the tribes of Israel came to David at Hebron and spoke saying, "Here we are, your own flesh and blood. Even before, when Saul was king over us, it was you who led Israel out and back. Also *Adonai* said to you, 'You will shepherd My people Israel and be ruler over Israel.'"

So all the elders of Israel came to the king at Hebron, and King David cut a covenant with them at Hebron before *Adonai*. Then they anointed David king over Israel. David was 30 years old when he began to reign and he reigned 40 years. In Hebron he reigned over Judah seven years and six months, and in Jerusalem he reigned 33 years over all Israel and Judah.

Now the king and his soldiers marched to Jerusalem against the Jebusites, the inhabitants of the region. But they said to David, "You'll never get in here! Even the blind and the lame could ward you off," thinking, "David can't get in here." Nevertheless, David did capture the stronghold of Zion (that is, the City of David).

On that day David said, "Whoever would conquer the Jebusites must strike through the water shaft to those 'lame and blind' whom David's soul despises." That is why they used to say, "The blind or lame couldn't get into the house." So David occupied the stronghold and renamed it the City of David. Then David fortified it all round from the Millo inward. David continued to grow stronger, for *Adonai Elohim-Tzva'ot* was with him.

Then King Hiram of Tyre sent envoys to David with cedar logs, carpenters and masons; and they built a palace for David. David then realized that *Adonai* had established him as king over Israel, and that He had exalted his kingdom for the sake of His people Israel.

Then David took more concubines and wives from Jerusalem, after he came from Hebron, and more sons and daughters were born to David. Now these are the names of those who were born to him in Jerusalem: Shammua, Shobab, Nathan, Solomon, Ibhar, Elishua, Nepheg, Japhia, Elishama, Eliada, and Eliphelet.

Now when the Philistines heard that David was anointed king over Israel, all the Philistines marched up searching for David. When David heard about it, he went down to the stronghold. The Philistines came and spread out in the valley of Rephaim. Then David inquired of *Adonai* saying, "Should I go up against the Philistines? Will You give them over into my hand?"

Adonai answered David, "Go up, for I will certainly give the Philistines over into your hand."

So David came to Baal-perazim and David struck them down there. So he said, "*Adonai* has broken through my enemies before me like the breakthrough of waters!" That is why he named that place Baal-perazim. They abandoned their idols there, so David and his men removed them.

But the Philistines marched up and spread out in the valley of Rephaim again. When David inquired of *Adonai*, He said, "Do not go up; instead circle around behind them and attack them in front of the balsam trees. Now it will be when you hear the sound of marching in the tops of the balsam trees, then you must act, for then *Adonai* will have gone out before you to strike the camp of the Philistines. David did just as *Adonai* had commanded him, and he struck down the Philistines from Geba as far as Gezer.

2 Samuel, chapter 5

Now David again gathered all the chosen men of Israel, 30,000. Then David and all the people who were with him arose and set out from Baale -judah to bring up from there the ark of God, which is called by the Name, the very Name of *Adonai-Tzva'ot* who is enthroned between the *cheruvim.* So they loaded the ark of God on a new cart and carried it out of the house of Abinadab that was on the hill. Uzzah and Ahio, Abinadab's sons, drove the new cart as they brought it from the house of Abinadab (which was on the hill) with the ark of God, and Ahio was walking in front of the ark.

Meanwhile David and the whole house of Israel were celebrating before *Adonai* with all kinds of instruments made of cypress wood, with harps, lyres, tambourines, three-stringed instruments and cymbals.

But when they reached the threshing floor of Nahon, Uzzah reached out to the ark of God and grasped it, for the oxen had stumbled. Then the anger of *Adonai* was kindled against Uzzah. God struck him down there for his irreverence, so that he died there beside the ark of God.

David was upset because of *Adonai*'s outburst against Uzzah. That place is called Perez-uzzah to this day.

So David was frightened of *Adonai* that day. Then he said, "How can the ark of *Adonai* come to me?"

David was unwilling to move the ark

Meanwhile, David was dancing before *Adonai* with all his might
while he was wearing a linen ephod.

2 Samuel 6:14 TLV

of *Adonai* to him, to the City of David; instead, David diverted it to the house of Obed-edom the Gittite. So the ark of *Adonai* remained in the house of Obed-edom the Gittite three months; meanwhile *Adonai* blessed Obed-edom and his entire household.

Then it was reported to King David saying, "*Adonai* has blessed the house of Obed-edom and all that belongs to him, because of the ark of God." So David went and brought the ark of God up from the house of Obed -edom to the city of David with joy.

Now when the bearers of the ark of *Adonai* had gone six paces, he sacrificed an ox and a fatling. Meanwhile, David was dancing before *Adonai* with all his might while he was wearing a linen ephod.

So David and the entire house of Israel brought up the ark of *Adonai* with shouting and with the sound of the *shofar*.

But as the ark of *Adonai* entered the city of David, Saul's daughter Michal looked out of the window and saw King David leaping and dancing before *Adonai*, so she despised him in her heart.

They brought in the ark of *Adonai* and set it in its place in the midst of the tent that David had pitched for it. Then David offered burnt offerings and fellowship offerings before *Adonai*.

When David had finished offering the burnt offering and fellowship offerings, he blessed the people in the Name of *Adonai-Tzva'ot*. Then he distributed to all the people—to the whole multitude of Israel, men and women alike—to everyone a loaf of bread, a cake made in a pan and a raisin cake. Then all the people departed, each to his home.

David returned to bless his own household. But Saul's daughter Michal came out to meet David and said, "How the king of Israel distinguished himself today, when he uncovered himself today in the eyes of the slave girls of his subjects, as any vulgar fellow would shamelessly uncover himself!"

"It was before *Adonai*," David said to Michal, "who chose me instead of your father and all his household, appointing me ruler over the people of *Adonai*, over Israel! So I danced before *Adonai*, and will dishonor myself even more than this, and will be low in my own eyes. Yet in the eyes of the slave girls whom you mentioned, I will be honored." So Saul's daughter Michal had no children to the day of her death.

2 Samuel, chapter 6

Now it came about when the king lived in his palace and *Adonai* had granted him rest from all his enemies around him, that the king said to the prophet Nathan, "See now, I am living in a house of cedar, yet the ark of God remains within curtains."

"Go, do all that is in your heart," Nathan said to the king, "for *Adonai* is with you."

But it came to pass the same night that the word of *Adonai* came to Nathan saying: "Go, tell My servant

David:
Thus says *ADONAI*: Are you to build Me a house for Me to dwell in? Since the day that I brought up the children of Israel from Egypt to this day I have not dwelt in a house, but have been moving about in a tent, even in a tabernacle. In all My journeying among all the children of Israel, did I ever speak a word to any of the tribes of Israel, whom I commanded to shepherd My people Israel, saying, 'Why have you not built Me a house of cedar?'

So now, thus you shall say to My servant David: Thus says *ADONAI-Tzva'ot*: I took you from the pasture, from following the sheep, to be ruler over My people, over Israel. I have been with you wherever you went, and have cut off all your enemies from before you; and I will make your name as great as the greatest on earth. I will also set up a place for My people Israel and will plant them, so they may dwell in their own place and not be disturbed again. Nor will the children of wickedness afflict them anymore as in the past, since the day that I commanded judges to be over My people Israel. So I will give you rest from all your enemies.

"Moreover, *ADONAI* declares to you that *ADONAI* will make a house for you. When your days are done and you sleep with your fathers, I will raise up your seed, who will come forth from you after you, and I will establish his kingdom.

He will build a house for My Name, and I will establish his royal throne forever. I will be a father to him, and he will be a son to Me. If he commits iniquity, I will correct him with the rod of men and with the strokes from sons of men. Yet My lovingkindness will not be withdrawn from him as I withdrew it from Saul, whom I removed from before you.

So your house and your kingship will be secure forever before you; your throne will be established forever." Just so Nathan spoke all these words and all this vision to David.

Then King David went in and sat before *ADONAI* and said, "Who am I, my Lord *ADONAI*, and what is my family, that You have brought me this far? Yet this was a small thing in Your eyes, my Lord *ADONAI*—for You have spoken also of Your servant's house for the distant future. This is a revelation for humanity, my Lord *ADONAI*. What more can David add in speaking to You? For You already know Your servant, my Lord *ADONAI*.

For the sake of Your word and according to Your own heart, You have done everything great, revealing this to Your servant. Therefore You are great, my Lord *ADONAI*! For there is none like You, and there is no other God besides You, as we all have heard with our ears. What one nation on earth is like Your people, like Israel, whom God went to redeem for Himself as a people, to make for Himself a Name, to do for You a great thing and awesome deeds for Your land, before Your people whom You redeemed for Yourself from Egypt—driving out nations and their gods? So You established for Yourself Your people Israel as Your very own people forever, and You, *Adonai*, have become their God.

"So now, my Lord *Adonai*, confirm the word that You have spoken concerning Your servant and his house forever, and do as You have promised. Let Your Name be magnified forever by saying, '*Adonai-Tzva'ot* is God over Israel!' May the house of Your servant David be established before You. For You, *Adonai-Tzva'ot* God of Israel, have made a revelation to Your servant saying, 'I will build you a house.' Therefore Your servant has found his heart to pray this prayer to You. So now, my Lord *Adonai*, You alone are God, and Your words are truth, and You have promised Your servant this good thing. So now let it please You to bless the house of Your servant, to continue forever before You. For You, my Lord *Adonai*, have spoken, and with Your blessing Your servant's house will be blessed forever."

2 Samuel, chapter 7

36. God Grants Mercy

Now it came to pass at the turn of the year, at the time when kings go out to battle, that David sent Joab and his officials with him and all Israel, and they destroyed the children of Ammon and besieged Rabbah. But David stayed in Jerusalem.

One evening David rose from his bed and strolled on the roof of the royal palace. Then from the roof he saw a woman washing—a very beautiful woman. So David sent someone to inquire about the woman, and he reported, "Isn't this Bath-sheba, daughter of Eliam, the wife of Uriah the Hittite?"

Then David sent messengers and took her when she came to him, and he lay with her. (She had purified herself from her uncleanness). Then she returned to her house.

The woman conceived and sent word to David saying, "I'm pregnant." So David sent a message to Joab, "Send me Uriah the Hittite." So Joab sent Uriah to David. When Uriah came to him, David asked him how Joab was, how the troops fared, and how the war was going. Then David said to Uriah, "Go down to your house and wash your feet."

When Uriah left the royal palace, a present from the king followed him. But Uriah slept at the door of the royal palace with all his master's servants, and did not go down to his house. When they informed David saying, "Uriah did not go down to his house," David said to Uriah, "Haven't you come from a journey? Why didn't you go down to your house?"

But Uriah answered David, "The ark and Israel and Judah are staying in tents, and my lord Joab and the officers of my lord are camping in the open field. Should I then go to my house to eat and drink and lie with my wife? As you live and as your soul lives, I will not do this thing."

Then David said to Uriah, "Stay here today also, and tomorrow I will send you off." So Uriah stayed in Jerusalem that day. The next day, David called him, and he ate and drank before him, and he made him drunk. But in the evening he went out to lie on his bed with his master's servants, but did not go down to his house.

So in the morning David wrote a letter to Joab and sent it by Uriah's hand. In the letter he wrote, "Put Uriah in the forefront of the hottest battle and withdraw from him so that he may be struck down and die." So it came to pass, when Joab was besieging the city, that he assigned Uriah to the place where he knew that valiant men were. Then the men of the city came out and attacked Joab, and some of the troops of David's officers fell; and Uriah the Hittite also died.

When Joab sent and reported to David all the events of the war, he charged the messenger saying, "When you finish reporting all the events of the war to the king, if it happens that the king's wrath flares up and he says to you, 'Why did you come so close to the city to fight Didn't you know that they would

But Uriah answered David, "The ark and Israel and Judah are staying in tents, and my lord Joab and the officers of my lord are camping in the open field. Should I then go to my house to eat and drink and lie with my wife? As you live and as your soul lives, I will not do this thing."

2 Samuel 11:11 TLV

shoot from the wall? Who killed Abimelech son of Jerubbesheth? Didn't a woman throw an upper millstone on him from the wall, so that he died at Thebez? Why did you come so close to the wall?' Then you will say, 'Your servant Uriah the Hittite is dead, too.'"

So the messenger went and came and told David all that Joab had sent him to report. The messenger said to David, "The men prevailed against us and came out against us in the open field, but we drove them back as far as the entrance of the gate. Then the archers shot at your troops from the wall, and some of the king's officers fell dead, and your servant Uriah the Hittite died, too."

Then David said to the messenger, "Thus you shall say to Joab, 'Don't let this matter upset you, for the sword devours one as well as another. Press your attack against the city and overthrow it!' So tell him, *chazak*!"

Now when the wife of Uriah heard that her husband Uriah had died, she mourned over her husband. When the time of mourning was over, David sent someone who brought her to his palace. So she became his wife and bore him a son. But the thing David had done was evil in *ADONAI*'s eyes.

2 Samuel, chapter 11

Then *ADONAI* sent Nathan to David. When he came to him, he said to him, "There were two men in the same city—one was rich and the other poor. The rich man had an exceedingly huge flock and herd, but the poor man had nothing at all, except one little ewe lamb, which he had bought and nourished, and it grew up together with him and his children. It ate from his own morsel and drank from his own cup, and nestled in his bosom, and it was to him like a daughter. Now a traveler came to the rich man, but he was unwilling to take one from his own flock or herd to prepare a meal for the wayfarer who had come to him. Rather, he took the poor man's lamb and prepared it for the man that had come to him."

Then David's anger blazed hot against the man and he said to Nathan, "As *ADONAI* lives, the man that did this deserves to die! So he must make restitution for the lamb fourfold, because he did such a thing and showed no pity."

Then Nathan said to David, "You are the man! Thus says *ADONAI*, God of Israel: It is I who anointed you king over Israel, and it is I who delivered you from the hand of Saul. I also gave you your master's house and your master's wives into your bosom, and I gave you the house of Israel and of Judah. Now if that were too little, then I would have added to you so much more. Why then have you despised the word of *ADONAI* by doing such evil in My eyes? Uriah the Hittite you have struck down with the sword, and his wife you have taken to be your wife, and him you have slain with the sword of the children of Ammon. So now the sword will never depart from your house—because you have despised Me and have taken the wife of Uriah the Hittite to be your wife.

"Thus says *ADONAI*: Behold, I am going to raise up evil against you from your own household, and I will take your wives before your eyes and give them to your neighbor, and he will lie with your wives in the sight of this sun. Indeed you have done it secretly, but I will do this thing before all Israel and under the sun."

Then David said to Nathan, "I have sinned against *ADONAI*."

Nathan replied to David, "*ADONAI* also has made your sin pass away—you will not die. However, because by this deed you have made the enemies of *ADONAI* greatly blaspheme, so even the child born to you will surely die." Then Nathan went to his house.

Then *ADONAI* struck the child that Uriah's wife bore to David and he became very sick. David therefore sought God for the child; and David fasted, and went in and lay all night on the floor. The elders of his household stood beside him in order to get him up from the floor but he was unwilling and would not eat food with them.

Then it came to pass on the seventh day that the child died. But David's servants were afraid to tell him that the child was dead, for they thought, "Behold, while the child was still alive, we spoke to him and he didn't listen to our voice. So how can we tell him that the child is dead? He might do something terrible!"

But when David saw that his servants were whispering together, David perceived that the child was dead. So David asked his servants, "Is the child dead?"

"He is dead," they said. Then David got up from the floor, washed and anointed himself, and changed his clothes. Then he went to the House of *ADONAI* and worshipped. When he came back to his own palace, he asked for food, so they set food before him and he ate.

His servants asked him, "What is this thing you have done? You fasted and wept while the child was still alive, but as soon as the child died, you got up and ate food."

He replied, "While the child was yet alive, I fasted and wept, for I thought, 'Who knows? *ADONAI* might be gracious to me and let the child live.' But now that he has died, why should I fast? Can I bring him back again? It is I who will be going to him, but he will never return to me."

Then David comforted his wife Bathsheba. He went to her and lay with her, and she bore a son and called his name Solomon. *ADONAI* loved him, and He sent word by the hand of the prophet Nathan. So he called his name Jedidiah, for *ADONAI*'s sake.

Now Joab attacked Rabbah of the children of Ammon and captured the royal city. So Joab sent messengers to David and said, "I have attacked Rabbah and captured the city's water supply. So now gather the rest of the troops together, camp against the city and capture it. Otherwise I will capture the city myself and it will be named after me."

So David gathered all the troops, went to Rabbah, attacked it and captured it. Then he took the crown of their king from off his head—its weight was a talent of gold and in it was a precious stone—and then it was placed on David's head. He also brought a vast amount of spoils out of the city.

Then he brought out the people who were there and put them to work under saws, iron threshing boards and iron axes, and assigned them to brick making; and thus he did to all the cities of the children of Ammon. Then David and all the troops returned to Jerusalem.

2 Samuel, chapter 12

37. God Dispenses Justice

It came to pass after this that Absalom son of David had a beautiful sister named Tamar, so Amnon, son of David, fell in love with her. But Amnon was so frustrated that he fell sick because of his sister Tamar, for she was a virgin and it seemed impossible in Amnon to do anything to her.

However, Amnon had a friend named Jonadab son of Shimeah, David's brother, and Jonadab was a very shrewd man. So he said to him, "Why are you, the king's son, so miserable morning after morning? Won't you tell me?"

Amnon told him, "I'm in love with Tamar, my brother Absalom's sister."

So Jonadab said to him, "Lie down on your bed and pretend you are sick. When your father comes to see you, say to him, 'Please let my sister Tamar come and give me some bread to eat. Let her prepare the food in my sight so I may see it and eat from her hand.'"

So Amnon lay down and pretended to be sick, and when the king came to see him, Amnon said to the king, "Please let my sister Tamar come and make me a couple of cakes in front of me so I may eat from her hand."

Then David sent someone to the house for Tamar saying, "Go now to your brother Amnon's house and prepare bread for him." So Tamar went to her brother Amnon's house while he was lying down. She took dough, kneaded it, made cakes in front of him and baked the cakes. Then she took the pan and poured them out in front of him but he refused to eat.

Then Amnon said, "Everyone, leave me!" So everyone left him. Then Amnon said to Tamar, "Bring the bread into the bedroom that I may eat from your hand." So Tamar took the cakes she had made and brought them into the bedroom to her brother Amnon. But when she brought them close to him to eat, he grabbed her and said to her, "Come lie with me, my sister."

"No!" she said to him. "Don't, my brother! Don't rape me, for such a thing should never be done in Israel. Don't do this disgraceful deed! I—where could I go with my shame? You—you will be as one of the disgraceful fools in Israel. Now, please speak to the king, for he will not withhold me from you."

But he was unwilling to listen to her voice, so he overpowered her, forced her and lay with her. Then Amnon loathed her with very intense revulsion—indeed, the hatred that he hated her with was greater than the love in which he had loved her. So Amnon said to her, "Get up, get out!" But she said to him, "No! Sending me away is even a greater evil than the one you have already done to me!" But again he would not listen to her.

Then he called his servant that attended him and said, "Get this woman away from me now and bolt the door after her."

Now she had on her a long-sleeved garment for with such robes the king's virgin daughters used to be dressed. When his attendant took her outside and bolted the door after her, Tamar put ashes on her head and rent her long-sleeved garment that was on her. She laid her hand on her head and was crying aloud as she went away.

Then her brother Absalom said to her, "Has Amnon your brother been with you? So now, my sister, keep quiet. He is your brother—don't take this thing to heart." But Tamar remained desolate in her brother Absalom's house.

When King David heard about all these things, he was very angry. Absalom did not say a word to Amnon, either good or bad, for Absalom hated Amnon because he had raped his sister Tamar.

It came about, after two full years, that Absalom's sheepshearers were at Baal-hazor, which is near Ephraim, and Absalom invited all the king's sons. Then Absalom came to the king and said, "See now, your servant has sheepshearers. Please let the king and his servants come with your servant."

But the king said to Absalom, "No, my son. Let's not all go—we don't want to be burdensome to you." Though he urged him, he would not go, though he blessed him.

Then Absalom said, "If not, then please let my brother Amnon go with us."

"Why should he go with you?" the king said to him. But when Absalom pressed him, he let Amnon go with him, along with all the king's sons.

Then Absalom commanded his young men saying, "Now watch Amnon until his heart is merry with wine. When I tell you, 'Strike Amnon!' then put him to death! Have no fear! Isn't it I who commanded you? Be strong! Be sons of valor!" So Absalom's young men did to Amnon as Absalom had ordered. Then all the king's sons got up, each mounted his mule and fled.

While they were on the way, a report came to David saying, "Absalom has killed all the king's sons and not one of them is left!"

Then the king stood up, rent his clothes and lay on the ground, and all his courtiers were standing by with their clothes rent.

But Jonadab son of David's brother Shimeah said in response, "My lord must not think that they have killed all the young men, the king's sons! For only Amnon has died. For from Absalom's mouth this has been determined since the day he raped his sister Tamar. Now therefore, my lord the king must not take the report to his heart thinking that all the king's sons are dead—for only Amnon is dead."

Meanwhile Absalom had fled. When the young watchman lifted up his eyes and looked, behold, there were many people coming down the road behind him on the hillside. Then Jonadab said to the king, "The king's sons have just arrived! It's just as your servant has said."

As soon as he finished speaking, behold, the king's sons arrived. They lifted up their voices and wept, and also the king and all his courtiers wept very bitterly. But Absalom fled and went to Talmai son of Ammihud, king of Geshur. David mourned for his son every day.

So Absalom fled, went to Geshur and remained there three years. Then King David's soul longed to go out to Absalom; for he was comforted about Amnon, since he was dead.

2 Samuel, chapter 13

So Joab got up, went to Geshur and brought Absalom to Jerusalem.

However, the king said, "He may go directly to his own house, but he may not see my face." So Absalom went directly to his own house and did not see the king's face.

Now in all Israel there was none as handsome as Absalom—so highly praised. From the sole of his foot to the crown of his head there was no blemish in him. When he cut the hair of his head—at the end of every year he would cut it because the hair got so heavy on him that he had to cut it. The weight of the hair from his head was 200 shekels by the royal weight.

To Absalom were born three sons and one daughter, whose name was Tamar—she was a beautiful woman.

Now Absalom had lived two full years in Jerusalem but he never saw the king's face. Then Absalom sent for Joab, in order to send him to the king, but he was unwilling to come to him. So he sent word again a second time, but he still would not come.

So he said to his servants, "See, Joab's field is next to mine and he has barley there—go and set it on fire." So Absalom's servants set the field on fire.

Then Joab arose, came to Absalom at his house, and said to him, "Why have your servants set my field on fire?"

"Look, I sent word to you," Absalom said to Joab, "saying, 'Come here, that I may send you to the king to say, "Why have I come from Geshur? It would be better for me if I were still there."'

So now, let me see the king's face and if there is iniquity in me, let him put me to death." So Joab went to the king and told him.

When he summoned Absalom, he came to the king and bowed down on his face to the ground before the king, and then, the king kissed Absalom.

2 Samuel 14:23-33

Now it came about after this that Absalom provided himself with a chariot, horses and 50 men as runners before him.

Absalom used to rise up early and stand beside the road to the city gate. Whenever anyone had a suit to come to the king for justice, then Absalom would call to him and say, "What town are you from?" Should he answer, "Your servant is from one of the tribes of Israel," Absalom would say to him, "See, your claims are good and right, but there is no one assigned to you by the king to hear you."

Moreover, Absalom would say, "If only I were appointed judge in the land, then every man who has any suit or case would come to me, and I would get him justice!"

Also, whenever anyone approached to bow to him, he would stretch his hand, take hold of him, and kiss him. So Absalom kept doing this to everyone of Israel who came to the king for judgment. Thus Absalom stole the hearts of the people of Israel.

At the end of 40 years Absalom said to the king, "Please let me go to Hebron and pay my vow which I have vowed to *ADONAI*. For your servant vowed a vow while I was still living at Geshur in Aram saying, 'If *ADONAI* will indeed bring me back to Jerusalem, then I will serve *ADONAI*.'" So the king said to him, "Go in *shalom*."

Then he rose and went to Hebron. But Absalom sent spies to all the tribes of Israel to say, "As soon as you hear the sound of the *shofar*, then you are to say, 'Absalom has become king in Hebron!'"

Now 200 men from Jerusalem went with Absalom, who were invited and were going innocently, knowing nothing of the situation. Also Absalom sent for Ahithophel the Gilonite, David's counselor from his town Giloh, while he was offering the sacrifices. So the conspiracy gained momentum for the people following Absalom continued to increase.

Then a messenger came to David saying, "The hearts of the men of Israel are following Absalom."

Then David said to all his officials who were with him in Jerusalem, "Arise, and let us flee, or else none of us will escape from Absalom. Leave in haste or else he will overtake us quickly and bring disaster down on us and strike the city with the edge of the sword."

Then the king's officials said to the king, "Behold, your servants are ready to do whatever our lord the king chooses."

So the king set out, and his entire household followed him. But the king left behind ten concubines to take care of the palace. As the king went out and all the people after him, they paused at the last house. All his servants passed on beside him: all the Cherethites, all the Pelethites and all the Gittites—600 men that had come after him from Gath—passed on before the king.

Then the king said to Ittai the Gittite, "Why should you also go with us? Go back and stay with the king, for you are a foreigner and also an exile from your own place. Your arrival was only yesterday—should I make you wander around with us today, to go wherever I may go? Go back and take your kinsmen back with you. Kindness and truth be with you!"

But Ittai answered the king and said, "As *ADONAI* lives, and as my lord the king lives, surely in whatever place my lord the king will be, whether for death or for life, there also will your servant be."

So David said to Ittai, "Go on and cross over." So Ittai the Gittite passed on, with all his men and all the little children who were with him.

While all the country was weeping with a loud voice, all the people were crossing over as the king was crossing over Kidron Valley. So all the people crossed over toward the road of the wilderness. Then behold, Zadok also came and all the Levites with him, carrying the ark of the covenant of God. They set down the ark of God, then Abiathar came up, until all the people had passed by, out of the city.

But the king said to Zadok, "Return the ark of God to the city. If I find favor in *ADONAI*'s eyes, He will bring me back, and let me see it and His dwelling. But if He says thus, 'I have no delight in you,' here I am, let Him do to me as seems good in His eyes."

The king also said to Zadok the priest, "Do you not see? Return to the city in *shalom* with your two sons with you, Ahimaaz your son and Jonathan son of Abiathar. See, I will wait at the fords of the wilderness, until word comes from you to inform me." Therefore Zadok and Abiathar carried the ark of God back to Jerusalem, and they remained there.

Then David continued to go up the ascent of the Mount of Olives, weeping as he ascended. He had his head covered and was walking barefoot. So all the people with him each covered his head as they went up, weeping as they ascended.

Then someone told David saying, "Ahithophel is among the conspirators with Absalom." So David prayed, "*ADONAI*, please turn the counsel of Ahithophel into foolishness."

Then David went on until he reached the summit—where God was worshiped—and behold, Hushai the Archite met him with his coat rent and dust on his head. David said to him, "If you pass on with me then you will be a burden to me, but if you return to the city and say to Absalom, 'I will be your servant, O king—I was your father's servant from then, but now I will be your servant,' then you can thwart Ahithophel's counsel for me. Won't you have with you Zadok and Abiathar the *kohanim* there? So whatever you hear from the royal palace, you should report it to Zadok and Abiathar the *kohanim*. See, they have their two sons with them there, Zadok's son Ahimaaz, and Abiathar's son Jonathan—by them you can send to me everything you hear." So David's friend Hushai reached the city just as Absalom was entering Jerusalem.

2 Samuel, chapter 15

Meanwhile Absalom and all the people of the men of Israel arrived in Jerusalem. Ahithophel was with him. Now when David's friend Hushai the Archite came to Absalom, Hushai said to Absalom, "Long live the king! Long live the king!"

But Absalom said to Hushai, "Is this your loyalty to your friend? Why did you not go with your friend?"

"No!" said Hushai to Absalom. "For the one whom *ADONAI* has chosen --as well as these people, all the men of Israel—his I will be and with him I will stay. Besides, whom should I serve? Shouldn't I be in the presence of his son? As I have served in your father's presence, so I will be in your presence."

Then Absalom said to Ahithophel, "Give your counsel. What should we do?"

So Ahithophel said to Absalom, "Go to your father's concubines whom he has left to take care of the palace. Then all Israel will hear that you have made yourself abhorrent to your father and the hands of all who are with you will also be strengthened."

So they pitched a tent for Absalom on the roof, and Absalom went to his father's concubines in the sight of all Israel. Now in those days the counsel that Ahithophel gave was like inquiring for the word of God—so was all of Ahithophel's counsel both with David and with Absalom.

2 Samuel 16:15-23

Then David mustered the people who were with him and set commanders of thousands and captains of hundreds over them. Then David sent out the troops, one third under the command of Joab, one third under the command of Joab's brother Abishai son of Zeruiah, and one third under the command of Ittai the Gittite. The king said to the troops, "I must certainly go out with you also."

But the troops said, "You must not go out! For if we were to flee, they would not care about us, even if half of us die, they still wouldn't care about us—but you are worth 10,000 of us. Therefore now, it is better that you be ready to support us from the city."

Then the king said to them, "Whatever seems best to you I will do." So the king stood beside the gate and all the troops went out by their hundreds and thousands.

Then the king charged Joab, Abishai and Ittai saying, "Deal gently with the young man Absalom for my sake."

Now all the troops heard the king's charge to all the commanders concerning Absalom. Then the troops went out to the field to confront Israel but the battle took place in the forest of Ephraim. The people of Israel were defeated there before the followers of David, and the slaughter that day was great—20,000 men. For the battle there was spread over the face of the entire countryside and the forest devoured more people that day than the sword devoured.

Now Absalom encountered some of David's servants. When Absalom was riding on his mule, the mule went under the thick branches of the great oak, and his head got caught in the oak, so that he was left hanging between heaven and earth, while the mule that was under him went on.

Then a certain man saw it and told Joab saying, "Look, I saw Absalom hanging in an oak."

Then Joab said to his informant, "Look here, you saw him, so why

Now Absalom encountered some of David's servants. When Absalom was riding on his mule, the mule went under the thick branches of the great oak, and his head got caught in the oak, so that he was left hanging between heaven and earth, while the mule that was under him went on...

2 Samuel 18:9 TLV

didn't you strike him there to the ground? I would have given you ten pieces of silver and a belt!"

But the man said to Joab, "Even if I had 1,000 pieces of silver in my hand, I would not raise my hand against the king's son; for in our hearing the king charged you, Abishai and Ittai saying, 'Watch over the young man Absalom for me.' Otherwise, I would have betrayed his soul—and nothing stays hidden from the king—and you yourself would have stood aloof."

"I won't wait for you!" Joab said. So he took three darts in his hand and thrust them through Absalom's heart while he was yet alive in the midst of the oak. Then ten young men who were Joab's armor-bearers surrounded Absalom, struck and finished him off.

Then Joab blew the *shofar* and the troops returned from pursuing Israel, for Joab held back the troops. They took Absalom and threw him into a deep pit in the forest and piled over him a very large heap of stones. Then all Israel fled, everyone to his tent.

(Now Absalom, in his lifetime, had taken and set up for himself a pillar, which is in the King's Valley, for he said, "I have no son to preserve the memory of my name." So he called the pillar by his name and it has been called Absalom's Monument to this day.)

Then Ahimaaz son of Zadok said, "Let me now run and bring the king news that ADONAI has vindicated him against the hand of his enemies."

But Joab said to him, "You are not to be the bearer of news today. You may do it another day, but today you shall bear no news—for the king's son is dead."

Then Joab said to the Cushite, "Go tell the king what you have seen." So the Cushite bowed to Joab and took off running.

But Ahimaaz son of Zadok once again said to Joab, "Whatever happens, please let me also run after the Cushite."

"Why should you run, my son," Joab said, "since you would have no news worth telling?"

"Whatever may come of it, I want to run!" So he said to him, "Run!" Ahimaaz ran by the way of the plain, and so passed the Cushite.
Now David was sitting between the two gates. When the watchman on the roof over the gate walked over to the wall, he lifted up his eyes and looked, and all of a sudden, he saw a man running alone. The watchman cried out and told the king. The king said, "If he is alone, there is good news in his mouth." So he came closer and closer.

Then the watchman saw another man running, so the watchman called out to the gatekeeper and said, "Look, another man is running alone." The king said, "He too is bringing good news."

Then the watchman said, "I can see that the running of the first one is like the running of Ahimaaz son of Zadok."

"This is a good man and he comes with good news," the king replied. Then Ahimaaz called out and said to the king, "*Shalom*."

Then he prostrated himself before the king with his face to the ground and said, "Blessed be *ADONAI* your God, who has given over the men who lifted up their hand against my lord the king."

Then the king asked, "Is it well with the young man Absalom?"

Ahimaaz answered, "I saw a great tumult when the king's servant Joab sent me, your servant, but I did not know what it was about."

"Step aside and stand here," the king said. So he stepped aside and stood still.

Then the Cushite arrived and said, "Let my lord the king receive good news for *ADONAI* has vindicated you today against all who rose up against you."

Then the king asked the Cushite, "Is it well with the young man Absalom?"

The Cushite answered, "Let the enemies of my lord the king and all who rise up against you for evil be as that young man!"

2 Samuel, chapter 18

The king was shaken. So he went up to the chamber over the gate and wept. As he walked he cried, "My son Absalom! O my son, my son Absalom! If only I had died instead of you! Absalom, my son, my son!"

Then Joab was told, "Look, the king is weeping and mourning over Absalom!" So the victory that day was turned into mourning for all the troops, for the troops heard it said that day, "The king is grieving over his son." So the troops entered into the city stealthily that day, like troops who are ashamed after running away in battle.

The king covered his face and cried with a loud voice, "My son Absalom, O Absalom, my son, my son!"

Then Joab came into the house to the king and said, "Today you have humiliated all your servants—who this day have saved your life, the lives of your sons and daughters, and the lives of your wives and the lives of your concubines—by loving those who hate you, and hating those who love you! For you have shown today that officers and officials are nothing to you. For today I realize that if Absalom were alive and all of us were dead, then it would have pleased you well.

So now arise, go out, and speak to the heart of your servants! For I swear by *ADONAI* that if you do not go out, not a single man will stay with you tonight, and that would be worse for you than all the evil that has befallen you from your youth until now."

So the king arose and sat in the gate. When they told all the troops saying, "See, the king is sitting at the gate," all the troops presented themselves before the king.

Meanwhile, Israel had fled each man to his tent. All the people throughout all the tribes of Israel were at strife saying, "The king delivered us from the hand of our enemies and he saved us from the hand of the Philistines. Yet now he had to flee from the land because of Absalom, but Absalom, whom we anointed over us, has died in battle. So why are we silent about restoring the king?"

Then King David sent word to Zadok and Abiathar the *kohanim* saying, "Speak to the elders of Judah saying, 'Why should you be the last to bring the king back to his palace? The talk of all Israel had reached the king at his residence. 'You are my kinsmen, my bone and my flesh! Why then should you be the last to bring back the king?'

"Also say to Amasa, 'Are you not my bone and my flesh? May God do so to me and even more if you do not become my army commander before me continually, in place of Joab!'"

Thus he turned the heart of all the men of Judah as one man, and then they sent word to the king, "Come back, you and all your servants." So the king returned and reached the Jordan. Meanwhile, Judah came to Gilgal in order to meet the king, to escort the king over the Jordan.

2 Samuel 19:1-16

Now when the time of David drew near to die, he charged his son Solomon, saying: "I—I am going the way of all the earth. So be strong and be a man. Keep the charge of *Adonai* your God, to walk in His ways, to keep His statutes, His commandments, His ordinances, and His decrees, according to what is written in the *Torah* of Moses, so that you may succeed in all that you do and wherever you turn so that *Adonai* may fulfill His word which He spoke concerning me, saying: 'If your children watch their way, to walk before Me in truth with all their heart and with all their soul, you shall not lack a man on the throne of Israel.'

"Moreover, you also know what Joab son of Zeruiah did to me—what he did to the two commanders of the armies of Israel, to Abner son of Ner and Amasa son of Jether, whom he killed, shedding the blood of war in peacetime, and putting the blood of war on his waistband and on his sandals on his feet. So act according to your wisdom, and let his gray hair not go down to *Sheol* in *shalom*. But show kindness to the sons of Barzillai the Gileadite, and let them be among those who eat at your table—for they befriended me when I fled from your brother Absalom. Also behold, you have with you Shimei son of Gera, the Benjamite from Bahurim, who cursed me with a grievous curse on the day I went to Mahanaim. But when he came down to meet me at the Jordan, I swore to him by *Adonai* saying: 'I will not put you to death with the sword.' Now don't let him go unpunished. For you are a wise man, and you will know how to deal with him, and bring his gray hair down to *Sheol* with blood."

Then David slept with his fathers and was buried in the city of David. The days that David reigned over Israel were forty years—seven years he reigned in Hebron and 33 years he reigned in Jerusalem. Then Solomon sat upon the throne of his father David, and his kingdom was established firmly.

1 Kings 2:1-12

38. God Sends a Prophet

Now Elijah the Tishbite, one of the settlers of Gilead, said to Ahab: "As *ADONAI* God of Israel lives, before whom I stand, there shall be no dew or rain these years, except at my word."

Then the word of *ADONAI* came to him saying: "Leave this place, turn eastward, and hide yourself by the Wadi Cherith, east of the Jordan. It will come about that you will drink from the wadi. I have also commanded the ravens to feed you there."

So he went and did according to the word of *ADONAI*—he went and lived by the Wadi Cherith, which is east of the Jordan. The ravens kept bringing him bread and meat in the morning and bread and meat in the evening, and he drank from the wadi. Then it came to pass after a while that the wadi dried up, because there was no rain in the land.

Then the word of *ADONAI* came to him saying: "Arise, go to Zarephath of Sidon and stay there. I have just commanded a widow there to provide for you."

So he arose and went to Zarephath. Now when he came to the town gate, to his surprise, a widow was there gathering sticks. So he called her and said, "Please bring a little water in a jar that I may drink."

As she was going to fetch it, he called her and said, "Please bring me a morsel of bread in your hand."

So she said, "As *ADONAI* your God lives, I have nothing baked, only a handful of flour in the jar, and a little oil in the jug. Now look, I am gathering a couple of sticks, so that I may go in and prepare it for me and my son, that we may eat it and die."

Elijah said to her, "Fear not! Go and do as you said, but first make me a little cake from what you have there. Bring it out to me and afterwards, make some for you and for your son. For thus says *ADONAI* God of Israel, 'The jar of flour shall not be exhausted nor shall the jug of oil be empty until the day *ADONAI* sends rain on the land.'"

So she went and did according to the word of Elijah—and she and he, and her household ate for many days. The jar of flour was not exhausted, nor did the jug of oil become empty, according to the word of *ADONAI* which He spoke through Elijah.

After these things, it came to pass that the son of the woman, the mistress of the house fell sick, and his sickness was getting much worse until he had no breath left in him. So she said to Elijah, "What do I have to do with you, man of God? Have you come to me to remind me of my sin and kill my son?"

He said to her, "Give me your son." Then he took him from her arms, carried him up to the upper room where he was staying and laid him on his own bed. He cried out to *ADONAI* and said, "*ADONAI* my God, have You brought such evil even on the widow with whom I am staying, by causing her son to die?" Then he stretched himself upon the child three times. He cried out to *ADONAI* and said, "*ADONAI* my God, please let this child's soul come back into his body!"

ADONAI listened to the cry of Elijah, so the soul of the child came back into his body and he was revived. Then Elijah took the child and brought him down from the upper room into the house, and gave him to his mother. Elijah said, "See! Your son is alive."

Then the woman said to Elijah, "Now I know that you are a man of God, and that the word in your mouth is truth."

1 Kings, chapter 17

Now it was after many days that the word of *ADONAI* came to Elijah in the third year saying, "Go, show yourself to Ahab; then I will send rain on the land. So Elijah went to show himself to Ahab.

Now the famine was severe in Samaria. Ahab summoned Obadiah who was the steward of the palace. Now Obadiah feared *ADONAI* greatly —for when Jezebel was cutting off the prophets of *ADONAI*, Obadiah took 100 prophets, hid them 50 to a cave, and provided them with bread and water.

Then Ahab said to Obadiah, "Go through the land to all the springs of water and to all the wadis. Perhaps we may find grass and so keep the horses and mules alive and not lose all the animals." So they divided the land between them to explore it—Ahab went one way by himself while Obadiah went another way by himself.

As Obadiah was on the road, all of a sudden, Elijah met him. When he recognized him, he fell on his face and said, "Is it you, my lord Elijah?"
"It is I," he answered him. Go tell your lord, 'Look, Elijah is here!"

"How have I sinned," he replied, "that you are giving your servant into the hand of Ahab, to put me to death? As *ADONAI* your God lives, there is no nation or kingdom where my master has not sent to search for you; and when they said, 'He is not here,' he made that kingdom or nation swear that they could not find you.

"Now you're saying, 'Go tell your lord, "Look, Elijah is here!"' But as soon as I leave you, the *Ruach ADONAI* may carry you off where I wouldn't know. Then, when I come and tell Ahab and he can't find you, he'll kill me! Now I, your servant, have feared *ADONAI* since my youth. Wasn't my lord told what I did when Jezebel slaughtered the prophets of *ADONAI*—how I hid 100 of *ADONAI*'s prophets, 50 to a cave and provided them with bread and water? So now you say, 'Go tell your lord, "Look, Elijah is here!"' He'll kill me!"

Then Elijah said, "As *ADONAI-Tzva'ot* lives, before whom I stand, I will surely show myself to him today."

So Obadiah went to meet Ahab and told him; then, Ahab went to meet Elijah. Now when Ahab saw Elijah, Ahab said to him, "Is it you, the one who causes trouble for Israel?"
But he answered, "I have not

troubled Israel. Rather, it is you and your father's house—by forsaking the *mitzvot* of *ADONAI* and going after the Baalim. Now then, send and gather to me all Israel at Mount Carmel, together with the 450 prophets of Baal and the 400 prophets of Asherah who eat at Jezebel's table."

So Ahab sent word to all the children of Israel and gathered the prophets together at Mount Carmel. Then Elijah approached all the people and said, "How long will you waver between two opinions? If *ADONAI* is God, follow Him; but if Baal is, follow him." But the people did not answer him, not even a word.

Then Elijah said to the people, "I am the only prophet of *ADONAI* left, but Baal's prophets are 450 men. Now let them give us two young bulls. Let them choose one bull for themselves, cut it into pieces, lay it on the wood, and put no fire underneath, while I prepare the other bull, lay it on the wood, and put no fire underneath. Then you will call on the name of your god, and then, I will call on the Name of *ADONAI*. The God who answers with fire, He is God."

All the people responded and said, "It's a good thing."

Then Elijah said to the prophets of Baal, "Choose one bull for yourselves and prepare it first—since you are so many. Then call on the name of your god, but put no fire underneath."

So they took the bull that he gave them, prepared it, and called on the name of Baal from morning till noon, crying, "O Baal, answer us!"

But there was no voice—no one was answering. They also danced leaping around the altar that was made.

Now when it was about noon, Elijah mocked them and said, "Shout louder! After all, he is a god! Maybe he's deep in thought, or he's relieving himself, or he's off on a journey, or perhaps he's asleep and must wake up!" So they shouted even louder and cut themselves with swords and spears, as was their custom, until the blood gushed over them. When midday was past, they kept prophesying ecstatically until the time of offering up the evening sacrifice. But there was no voice, no one answering, no one paying attention.

Then Elijah said to all the people, "Come near to me." So all the people came closer to him. Then he repaired the damaged altar of *ADONAI*. Elijah took twelve stones—like the number of the tribes of the sons of Jacob, to whom the word of *ADONAI* had come saying, "Israel shall be your name"—and with the stones he built an altar in the Name of *ADONAI*. Then he made a trench around the altar, large enough to contain two measures of seed. Then he put the wood in order, cut the bull in pieces and laid it on the wood.

Then he said, "Fill four jars with water and pour it on the burnt offering and on the wood." Then he said, "A second time!" and they did it a second time. Then he said, "A third time!" and they did it a third time.

So the water ran around the altar and

he also filled the trench with water.

Now it was at the time of offering up the evening sacrifice that Elijah the prophet came near and said, "*ADONAI*, God of Abraham, Isaac and Israel, let it be known today that You are God in Israel, that I am Your servant, and that I have done all these things at Your word. Answer me, *ADONAI*, answer me, so that these people may know that You, *ADONAI*, are God, and that You have turned their heart back again."

Then the fire of *ADONAI* fell and consumed the burnt offering—and the wood, the stones and the dust—and licked up the water that was in the trench.

When all the people saw it, they fell on their faces, and they said, "*ADONAI*, He is God! *ADONAI*, He is God!"

Then Elijah said to them, "Seize the prophets of Baal! Let not a single one of them escape." So they seized them; and Elijah brought them down to the Wadi Kishon and slew them there.

Then Elijah said to Ahab, "Go up, eat and drink, for there's the sound of rain." So Ahab went up to eat and drink.

But Elijah went up to the top of Carmel, crouched on the ground and put his face between his knees. Then he said to his servant, "Go up now, look toward the sea."

So he went up, looked, and said, "There's nothing."

Then he said, "Go back"—seven times—and it was the seventh time that he said, "Look! A cloud as small as a man's hand is rising from the sea." Then he said, "Go up, say to Ahab, 'Harness your chariot and go down before the rain stops you.'"

In a little while the sky grew black with clouds and wind, and there was a heavy rain. Ahab mounted and rode, and headed to Jezreel.

Now the hand of *ADONAI* was on Elijah, so he girded up his loins and outran Ahab to the entrance of Jezreel.

1 Kings, chapter 18

Then Ahab told Jezebel all that Elijah had done and how he had slain all the prophets with the sword. Then Jezebel sent a messenger to Elijah saying, "So let the gods do to me and worse if by this time tomorrow I don't make your life like the life of one of them." Frightened, he got up and ran for his life.

When he came to Beersheba, which belongs to Judah, he left his servant there. But he himself went a day's journey into the wilderness, and came and sat down under a broom bush. He prayed that he might die.

"It's too much!" he said.
"Now, *ADONAI*, take my life! For I'm no better than my fathers." Then he lay down and slept under the broom bush.

Then behold, an angel touched him, and said to him, "Get up, and eat." So he looked, and to his surprise, there by his head was a cake baked on the hot stones and a jar of water. So he ate and drank, and lay down again.

Then the angel of *ADONAI* came again a second time, touched him and said.

Answer me, *Adonai*, answer me, so that these people may know that You, *Adonai*, are God, and that You have turned their heart back again."

1 Kings 18:37 TLV

"Get up and eat, because the journey is too much for you." So he arose and ate and drank, and in the strength of that meal forty days and forty nights went to Horeb, the mountain of God. When he arrived there at the cave, he spent the night there. Then behold, the word of *ADONAI* came to him, and He said to him, "What are you doing here, Elijah?"

"I have been very zealous for *ADONAI-Tzva'ot*," he said, "for the children of Israel have forsaken Your covenant, torn down Your altars and slain Your prophets with the sword—and I alone am left, and they are seeking my life, to take it!"

Then He said, "Come out and stand on the mount before *ADONAI*."

Behold, *ADONAI* was passing by—a great and mighty wind was tearing at the mountains and shattering cliffs before *ADONAI*. But *ADONAI* was not in the wind. After the wind there was an earthquake, but *ADONAI* was not in the earthquake. After the earthquake a fire, but *ADONAI* was not in the fire. After the fire there was a soft whisper of a voice. As soon as Elijah heard it, he wrapped his face in his mantle, went out and stood at the entrance of the cave.

Then all of a sudden, a voice addressed him and said, "What are you doing here, Elijah?"

"I have been very zealous for *ADONAI-Tzva'ot*," he said, "for the children of Israel have forsaken Your covenant, torn down Your altars, and slain Your prophets with the sword—and I alone am left, and they are seeking to take my life!"

Then *ADONAI* said to him, "Go, return on your way to the wilderness of Damascus, and when you get there, anoint Hazael king over Aram, and anoint Jehu son of Nimshi king over Israel, and anoint Elisha son of Shaphat of Abel-meholah as prophet in your place. It shall come to pass that whoever escapes from the sword of Hazael, Jehu will slay; and whoever escapes from the sword of Jehu, Elisha will slay. Yet I have preserved seven thousand in Israel whose knees have not bowed to Baal and whose mouth has not kissed him."

So he departed from there and found Elisha son of Shaphat while he was plowing with twelve pairs of oxen before him, and he with the twelfth. Then Elijah crossed over to him and threw his mantle on him. So he left the oxen and ran after Elijah saying, "Let me please kiss my father and my mother, and then I will follow you."

"Come back," he said to him. "For what have I done to you?" So he returned from following him, and took the pair of oxen and sacrificed them and boiled their flesh with the oxen's yoke gear, and gave it to the people, and they ate.

Then he arose, went after Elijah and became his attendant.

1 Kings, chapter 19

39. God Gives Sight

Now Jehoshaphat son of Asa began to reign over Judah in the fourth year of Ahab king of Israel. Jehoshaphat was 35 years old when he became king, and he reigned 25 years in Jerusalem. His mother's name was Azubah the daughter of Shilhi.

He walked in all the ways of his father Asa, not straying from them, but doing what was right in *ADONAI*'s eyes. However, they did not take away the high places, and the people continued to sacrifice and burn incense on the high places. Jehoshaphat also made peace with the king of Israel.

Now the rest of the deeds of Jehoshaphat along with his might that he showed and how he warred, are they not written in Book of the Chronicles of the Kings of Judah? He expelled from the land the cult prostitutes remaining from the days of his father Asa. There was no king in Edom; a deputy was king.

Jehoshaphat made Tarshish ships go to Ophir for gold, but they never went, because the ships were wrecked at Ezion-geber. Then Ahaziah son of Ahab said to Jehoshaphat, "Let my servants sail with your servants in the ships." But Jehoshaphat refused.

Jehoshaphat slept with his fathers, and was buried with his fathers in the city of his father David, and his son Jehoram became king in his place. Ahaziah son of Ahab began to reign over Israel in Samaria in the seventeenth year of Jehoshaphat king of Judah, and he reigned two years over Israel. But he did what was evil in *ADONAI*'s eyes and followed the way of his father, and the way of his mother, and the way of Jeroboam son of Nebat who caused Israel to sin. For he worshipped Baal and bowed down to him, vexing *ADONAI* God of Israel, like all his father had done.

1 Kings 22:41-54

After Ahab's death, Moab rebelled against Israel.

Now Ahaziah fell down from the balcony of his upper chamber in Samaria and was injured. So he sent messengers and instructed them, "Go inquire of Baal-Zebub the god of Ekron, whether I will recover from this injury."

But an angel of *ADONAI* said to Elijah the Tishbite, "Arise, go up to meet the messengers of the king of Samaria, and say to them: 'Is it because there is no God in Israel that you are going to inquire of Baal-Zebub the god of Ekron?' Therefore thus says *ADONAI*: 'You will not leave the bed you are lying on, for you will surely die.'"

And Elijah departed.

When the messengers returned to the king, he asked them, "Why have you returned?"

They answered him, "A man came up to meet us and said to us: 'Go, return to the king who sent you, and say to him, thus says *ADONAI*, "Is it because there is no God in Israel that you are sending to inquire of Baal-Zebub the god of Ekron? Therefore you will not leave the bed you are lying on, for you will surely die.'"'"

Then he said to them, "What kind of man was he that came up to meet you and told you these words?"

They answered him, "He was a hairy man with a leather belt around his waist."

"It's Elijah the Tishbite," he said.

So the king sent a captain of 50 with his 50 to Elijah. When the captain went up to him, behold, he was sitting on the top of the hill. So he announced to him, "O man of God, by order of the king, come down!"

In response, Elijah said to the captain of 50, "If I am a man of God, let fire come down from heaven and consume you and your 50!" Then fire did come down from heaven and consumed him and his 50.

So the king again sent to him another captain of 50 with his 50 men, who addressed him and said, "O man of God, by order of the king, come down quickly!"

In response, Elijah said to them, "If I am a man of God, let fire come down from heaven and consume you and your 50." And the fire of God came down from heaven and consumed him and his 50.

So the king again sent the captain of a third 50 with his 50. But when the third captain of 50 went up and came near, he knelt before Elijah, and begged him saying, "O man of God, please, let my life and the lives of these 50 servants of yours be precious in your eyes! Behold, fire came down from heaven and consumed the two previous captains of 50 with their 50; but now let my life be precious in your eyes!"

Then the angel of *ADONAI* said to Elijah, "Go down with him; do not be afraid of him." So he arose and went down with him to the king.

Then Elijah said to the king, "Thus says *ADONAI*: You have sent messengers to inquire of Baal-Zebub the god of Ekron. Is it because there is no God in Israel to inquire of His word? Therefore you will not leave the bed you are lying on, for you will surely die."

So he died just as was the word of *ADONAI* that Elijah had spoken.

Then Jehoram became king in his place, because Ahaziah had no son. It was in the second year of Jehoram son of King Jehoshaphat of Judah. Now the rest of the deeds of Ahaziah which he did, are they not written in the book of the Chronicles of the Kings of Israel?

2 Kings, chapter 1

Now it came to pass, when *ADONAI* was about to take up Elijah by a whirlwind into heaven, that Elijah went with Elisha from Gilgal.

Elijah said to Elisha, "Stay here please, for *ADONAI* has sent me on to Bethel."

But Elisha said, "As *ADONAI* lives, and as you live, I will not leave you." So

As they were walking along and talking, behold, a chariot of fire and horses of fire separated the two of them, and Elijah went up by a whirlwind into heaven.

2 Kings 2:11 TLV

they went down to Bethel. Then the sons of the prophets at Bethel came out to Elisha and said to him, "Do you know that *ADONAI* is going to take your master away from over you today?"

He said, "Yes, I know. Be silent."

Then Elijah said to him, "Elisha, stay here please, for *ADONAI* has sent me on to Jericho."

But he said, "As *ADONAI* lives and as you live, I will not leave you." So they came to Jericho.

Then the sons of the prophets at Jericho approached Elisha and said to him, "Do you know that *ADONAI* is going to take away your master from over you today?"

He replied, "Yes, I know. Be silent."

Then Elijah said to him, "Stay here please, for *ADONAI* has sent me to the Jordan."

But he said, "As *ADONAI* lives and as you live, I will not leave you." So both of them went on.

Then 50 of the sons of the prophets went and stood aside at a distance from them, while the two of them stood by the Jordan.

Elijah then took his mantle, wrapped it together, and struck the waters, and they were divided here and there, so that they two of them crossed over on dry ground.

Now as they were crossing over, Elijah said to Elisha, "Ask what I will do for you before I am taken from you."

So Elisha said, "Please, let a double portion of your spirit be upon me."

He replied, "You have asked a hard thing. Nevertheless, if you see me when I am taken from you, it will be so to you; but if not, it will not be so."

As they were walking along and talking, behold, a chariot of fire and horses of fire separated the two of them, and Elijah went up by a whirlwind into heaven.

As Elisha was watching, he was crying out, "*Avi*! *Avi*! The chariot of Israel and its horsemen!" Then he saw him no more. So he took hold of his own clothes and tore them in two pieces.

2 Kings 2:1-12

40. God Helps Mothers

He then picked up the mantle of Elijah that fell from him. When he returned and stood by the bank of the Jordan, he took the mantle of Elijah that had fallen off him, struck the waters and said, "Where is *ADONAI*, the God of Elijah?" As he indeed struck the waters, they parted here then there. Then Elisha crossed over.

When the sons of the prophets at Jericho saw him some way off, they said, "The spirit of Elijah has rested on Elisha." So they came to meet him and bowed down to the ground before him. Then they said to him, "Behold now, there are 50 strong men with your servants. Please let them go and search for your master. Perhaps the *Ruach ADONAI* has taken him up and cast him onto some mountain or into some valley."

But he said, "Don't send them." But when they urged him until he was ashamed, he said, "Send them." So they sent 50 men.

Though they searched for three days, they did not find him. When they came back to him while he staying in Jericho, he said to them, "Didn't I tell you not to go?"

Then the men of the city said to Elisha, "Look now, the situation of this city is pleasant, as my lord sees, but the water is bad and the land barren."

He responded, "Bring me a new jar, and put salt in it." So they brought it to him. Then he went out to the spring of water, threw salt in it and said, "Thus says *ADONAI*, I have healed this water. No longer will there be from there death or barrenness." So the waters were healed to this day, according to the word that Elisha spoke.

From there he went up to Bethel. As he was going up along the road, some young boys came out of the city. They mocked him saying to him, "Go on up, baldy! Go on up, baldy!" So he turned around and looked at them and cursed them in the Name of *ADONAI*. Then two she-bears came out of the woods and mauled 42 of the boys. From there he went to Mount Carmel, and from there he returned to Samaria.

2 Kings 2:13-25

Now a certain woman of the wives of the sons of the prophets cried out to Elisha saying, "Your servant my husband is dead—you know that your servant feared *ADONAI*. Now the creditor has come to take my two children to be his slaves."
"What should I do for you?" Elisha asked her. "Tell me, what do you have in the house?"

She replied, "Your handmaid has nothing in the house except a jar of oil."

Then he said, "Go borrow for yourself vessels from all your neighbors—empty jars—not just a few. Then go inside and shut the door behind you and behind your sons, and pour into all those vessels, setting aside what is full."

"What should I do for you?" Elisha asked her. "Tell me, what do you have in the house?" She replied, "Your handmaid has nothing in the house except a jar of oil." Then he said, "Go borrow for yourself vessels from all your neighbors—empty jars—not just a few. Then go inside and shut the door behind you and behind your sons, and pour into all those vessels, setting aside what is full." So she left him and shut the door behind her and behind her sons. They kept bringing the vessels to her and she kept pouring.

2 Kings 4:2-5 TLV

So she left him and shut the door behind her and behind her sons. They kept bringing the vessels to her and she kept pouring. When the vessels were full, she said to her son, "Bring me another vessel."

But he said to her, "There isn't another vessel." So the oil stopped.

Then she came and told the man of God. So he said, "Go sell the oil and pay your debt, then you and your sons can live on the rest."

One day when Elisha passed through Shunem, where there was a prominent woman who persuaded him to eat some food. And so it was, whenever he passed through, he would stop for a meal. Then she said to her husband, "Behold now, I realize that this man who often passes through is a holy man of God. Please, let's make a little walled room on the roof, and let's put there a bed, a table, a chair, and a lampstand for him. Then whenever he comes to us, he can stay there."

One day he came there, and retired to the upper chamber and lay down there.

Then he said to Gehazi his servant, "Call this Shunammite woman." When he had called her, she stood before him. He said to him, "Tell her: Behold, you have gone to all this trouble for us. What can be done for you? Can something be communicated to the king or to the commander of the army for you?"

She answered, "I am living among my own people."

So he asked, "Then what should be done for her?" Then Gehazi answered, "In fact, she has no son, and her husband is old."

"Call her," he said. And when he had called her, she stood in the doorway. Then he said, "At this season next year, you will be embracing a son."

But she said, "No, my lord, do not lie to your handmaid, man of God."

Nevertheless, the woman conceived and bore a son during that season the following year, just as Elisha had told her. Now when the child was grown, one day he went out to his father among the reapers. Then he said to his father, "My head, my head!" So he said to his servant, "Carry him to his mother." So he picked him up and brought him to his mother. The child sat on her lap until noon, and then died.

She then went up and laid him on the bed of the man of God, shut the door on him and went out. Then she called to her husband, and said, "Please send me one of the servants and one of the donkeys that I may run to the man of God and come back."

But he said, "Why are you going to him today? It is neither New Moon nor *Shabbat*."

But she said, "It will be well."

Then she saddled the donkey and said to her servant, "Move on! Don't slow down riding unless I tell you."

So she set out and came near the man

of God at Mount Carmel. Upon seeing her from a distance, the man of God said to his servant Gehazi, "Look! There's the Shunammite. Please, run now to meet her and ask her: 'Is it well with you? Is it well with your husband? Is it well with the boy?'"

She answered, "It is well." But when she arrived at the mountain, up to the man of God, she caught hold of his feet.

Then Gehazi stepped forward to push her away, but the man of God said, "Leave her alone, for her soul is bitter within her, yet *ADONAI* has hid it from me and has not told me."

"Did I ask my lord for a son?" she said. "Didn't I say, 'Don't deceive me'?"

Then he said to Gehazi, "Gird up your loins and take my staff in your hand and go. If you meet anyone, don't greet him. Or if anyone greets you, don't answer him; and lay my staff on the face of the child."

But the mother of the child said, "As *ADONAI* lives and as you live, I won't leave you." So he arose and followed her.

Gehazi passed on ahead of them and laid the staff on the face of the child, but there was no sound or response. So he returned to meet him and told him, saying, "The boy has not awakened."

When Elisha entered the house, there was the child, dead and laying on his bed.

So he entered and shut the door behind the two of them and prayed to *ADONAI*. Then he got up and lay on the child, and put his mouth on his mouth and his eyes on his eyes and his hands on his hands, and he stretched himself upon him.
So the flesh of the child became warm. Then he stepped down and walked in the house to and fro, and then he got up on the bed and stretched himself on him. The child sneezed seven times, then the child opened his eyes.

He then called Gehazi and said, "Call the Shunammite." So he called her.

When she came in to him, he said, "Pick up your son." She came, fell at his feet and bowed down to the ground. Then she picked up her son and went out.

Afterward Elisha returned to Gilgal. Now there was famine in the land. As the sons of the prophets were sitting before him, he said to his servant, "Put on the large pot and boil stew for the sons of the prophets."

Then one of them went out into the field to gather herbs, found a wild vine and picked from it a lapful of wild gourds. Then he came back and sliced them into the stew pot, for they didn't know what they were.

Then they served it for the men to eat. But it came to pass as they were still eating the stew, they cried out and said, "O man of God, there is death in the pot." So they could not eat it.

But he said, "Bring some flour," and he threw it into the pot and said,

"Serve it to the people and let them eat." So there was nothing bad in the pot.

Now a man came from Baal-shalishah, and brought the man of God bread of the firstfruits—20 loaves of barley bread and fresh ears of corn in his sack. Then he said, "Give them to the people that they may eat."

But his attendant said, "What? Will I set this before a hundred men?" But he said, "Give them to the people that they may eat, for thus says *ADONAI*, 'They will eat and will have left over.'" So he set it before them, and they ate and had some left over, according to the word of *ADONAI*.

2 Kings, chapter 4

Now the sons of the prophets said to Elisha, "Behold now, the place where we are living in your presence is too cramped for us. So please, let's go to the Jordan and pick from there each one a beam, and make ourselves a place there to live."

"Go," he answered.

Then one of them said, "Will you please come with your servants?"
"I will go," he answered. So he

went with them. And when they came to the Jordan, they began to cut down trees. But as one of them was cutting down a beam, the axe-head fell into the water; and he cried, and said, "Ah, my master! It was borrowed."

Then the man of God asked, "Where did it fall?"

When he showed him the place, he cut off a stick and threw it there, and made the ax head float. Then he said, "Pick it up for yourself." So he reached out his hand and took it.

Now the king of Aram was warring against Israel. He consulted with his officers, saying, "In such and such a place will be my camp."

But the man of God sent word to the king of Israel, saying, "Be careful not to pass this place, for the Arameans are coming down there." So the king of Israel sent word to the place the man of God told him and warned him about, and so he was on his guard there—more than once or twice.

His heart upset over this matter, the king of Aram summoned his officers and said to them, "Tell me, which one of us is on the king of Israel's side?"

But one of his officers said, "No, my lord the king. Rather, Elisha the prophet who is in Israel keeps telling the king of Israel the very words that you speak in your bedroom!"

So he said, "Go, see where he is, so I may send and seize him."
Then it was reported to him, "Behold, he is in Dothan." So he sent horses, chariots and a great army there. They arrived at night and surrounded the city.

Now when the attendant of the man of God had risen early and gone out, behold, an army with horses and chariots was surrounding the city. So his attendant said to him, "Alas, my master! What are we going to do?"

"Fear not," he replied, "for those who are with us are more than those who are with them." Then Elisha prayed and said, "*ADONAI*, please open his eyes that he may see." Then *ADONAI* opened the eyes of the young man and he saw, and behold, the mountain was full of horses and chariots of fire all around Elisha.

When they came down to him, Elisha prayed to *ADONAI* and said, "Please strike this people with blinding light." So He struck them with blinding light according to the word of Elisha. Then Elisha said to them, "This is not the road, nor is this the city. Follow me, and I will lead you to the man whom you seek." So he led them to Samaria.

Upon their arrival in Samaria, Elisha said, "*ADONAI*, open the eyes of these men, that they may see."

So *ADONAI* opened their eyes, and they could see—behold, they were in the middle of Samaria.

When the king of Israel saw them, he said to Elisha, "Shall I surely strike them down, *Avi*?"

"Don't strike them down," he replied. "Would you strike down those whom you have captured with your own sword and bow? Set before them bread and water that they may eat and drink and go back to their master." So he prepared a great feast for them.

After they had eaten and drunk, he sent them away, and they went back to their master. Ever since, the marauding bands of Aram stopped invading the land of Israel.

Now it came to pass after this, that King Ben-hadad of Aram gathered all his army and marched against Samaria and besieged it. Now there was a great famine in Samaria, since they were besieging it, until a donkey's head was sold for 80 pieces of silver, and the quarter of a kav of dove's dung for five pieces of silver.

As the king of Israel was passing by on the wall, a woman cried out to him saying, "My lord the king, help!"

But he said, "If *ADONAI* doesn't help you, how would I help you? From the threshing floor, or from the winepress?" Then the king asked her, "What's the matter with you?"

She answered, "This woman said to me: 'Give your son that we may eat him today, and we will eat my son tomorrow.' So we cooked my son and ate him. The next day I told her: 'Give your son that we may eat him'—but she hid her son."

Now it came to pass when the king heard the words of the woman, that he tore his clothes—as he was passing by on the wall, the people looked, and behold, he had sackcloth underneath upon his flesh. Then he said, "May God do so to me and even more, if the head of Elisha the son of Shaphat remains on him today."

Now Elisha was sitting in his house, and the elders were sitting with him. The king had sent a messenger ahead, yet even before the messenger arrived, Elisha said to the elders, "Do you see, this son of a murderer was sent to take away my head! Look, when the messenger comes, shut the door and hold the door fast against him. Is not the sound of his master's footsteps behind him?"

While he was yet talking with them, behold, the messenger came down to him. So the king said, "Look! This evil is from *ADONAI*—why should I wait for *ADONAI* any longer?"

2 Kings, chapter 6

Then Elisha said, "Hear the word of *ADONAI*. Thus says *ADONAI*: Tomorrow about this time a measure of fine flour will sell for a shekel and two measures of barley for a shekel, at the gate of Samaria."

2 Kings 7:1

41. God Gives Life

Now it came to pass in the fourteenth year of King Hezekiah that King Sennacherib of Assyria came up against all the fortified cities of Judah and captured them. The king of Assyria sent the Rab-shakeh from Lachish to Jerusalem to King Hezekiah with a massive army.

The Rab-shakeh stood by the aqueduct of the upper pool in the highway of the washer's field. Then Eliakim son of Hilkiah, who was in charge of the palace, Shebna the scribe, and Joah son of Asaph the recorder came out to him.

So the Rab-shakeh said to them, "Say now to Hezekiah, thus says the great king, the king of Assyria: 'What is this confidence you've relied on? I say your strategy and strength for war are only words of a lip. Who do you rely on now, so that you have rebelled against me? Behold, you rely on this splintered reed as a staff—Egypt! If a man leans on it, it will go into the palm of his hand and pierce it—thus Pharaoh king of Egypt is to all who trust in him.

"'But if you say to me: 'We trust in *ADONAI* our God'—is it not He whose high places and altars Hezekiah has removed, and then said to Judah and to Jerusalem, 'You must worship before this altar'? So now, make a bargain with my master, the king of Assyria. I'll give you 2,000 horses—if you could put riders of your own on them. So, how can you repulse a single lieutenant—the least of my master's servants? Yes, you're relying on Egypt for chariots and for horsemen. Moreover, have I now come up against this land to destroy it without *ADONAI*'s approval?

ADONAI said to me: 'Go up against this land, and destroy it.'"

Then Eliakim and Shebna and Joah said to the Rab-shakeh: "Please speak to your servants in Aramaic, for we understand it. Don't speak to us in the language of the Jews when the people on the wall are listening."

But the Rab-shakeh said: "Has my master sent me only to your master and to you to speak these words? Hasn't he sent me to the men who sit on the wall—who will eat their own waste and drink their own urine with you?"

Then the Rab-shakeh stood and cried with a loud voice in the language of the Jews and said: "Hear the words of the great king, the king of Assyria. Thus says the king: 'Don't let Hezekiah deceive you, for he will not be able to deliver you! Nor let Hezekiah persuade you to trust in *ADONAI* by saying, "*ADONAI* will surely deliver us—this city will not be given into the hand of the king of Assyria."'

"Don't listen to Hezekiah! For thus says the king of Assyria: 'Make peace with me and come out to me. Then everyone will eat from his own vine and fig tree, and everyone will drink water from his own cistern, until I come and take you away to a land like your own land—a land of grain and wine, a land of bread and vineyards.'

"Beware that Hezekiah does not mislead you by saying, '*ADONAI* will deliver us.' Has any one of the gods of the nations delivered his land from the hand of the king of Assyria? Where are the gods of Hamath and Arpad? Where are the gods of Sepharvaim? Indeed, when did they deliver Samaria from my hand? Who among all the gods of these lands have delivered their country out of my hand? So will *ADONAI* deliver Jerusalem from my hand?"

But they were silent, and did not answer him a word, for the king's commandment was, "Do not answer him."

Then Eliakim son of Hilkiah, who was in charge of the palace, and Shebna the scribe, and Joah son of Asaph the recorder came to Hezekiah with their clothes torn, and told him the words of the Rab-shakeh.

Isaiah, chapter 36

When King Hezekiah heard it, he tore his clothes, covered himself with sackcloth, and went into the House of *ADONAI*. Then he sent Eliakim, who was in charge of the palace, Shebna the scribe and the senior *kohanim*, covered with sackcloth, to Isaiah the prophet, son of Amoz.

Then they said to him: "Thus says Hezekiah: This day is a day of distress, rebuke and contempt. For children have come to the point of birth, and there is no strength for giving birth. Perhaps *ADONAI* your God, will hear the words of the Rab-shakeh, whom his master the king of Assyria has sent to mock the living God, and will rebuke the words which *ADONAI* your God has heard. So offer prayer for the remnant that is left."

When the officials of King Hezekiah came to Isaiah, Isaiah said to them: "Thus you will say to your master, 'Thus says *ADONAI*: Do not be afraid of the words you have heard, with which the boys of the king of Assyria have blasphemed Me. Behold, I am putting a spirit in him so that he will hear a rumor, and will return to his own country; then I will cause him to fall by the sword in his own land.'"

Then the Rab-shakeh returned, and found the king of Assyria fighting against Libnah, for he had heard he had withdrawn from Lachish.

Now he had heard them say concerning Tirhakah king of Ethiopia, saying: "He has come out to fight against you." When he heard it, he sent messengers to Hezekiah saying: "Thus you will say to King Hezekiah of Judah, saying, do not let your God in whom you trust deceive you, saying: 'Jerusalem will not be given into the hand of the king of Assyria.'

Behold, you have heard what the kings of Assyria have done to all lands—utterly destroying them—so will you be delivered? Have the gods of the nations delivered those my fathers destroyed—Gozan, Haran, Rezeph, or the children of Eden who were in Telassar? Where is the king of Hamath, or the king of Arpad, or the king of the city of Sepharvaim, of Hena, or Ivvah?'"

Then Hezekiah received the letter

Hezekiah prayed to *ADONAI* saying: "*ADONAI-Tzva'ot*, God of Israel, who is enthroned upon the *cheruvim*, You alone are God of all the kingdoms of the earth. You have made heaven and earth. Incline Your ear, *ADONAI*, and hear! Open Your eyes, *ADONAI*, and see! Listen to all the words of Sennacherib, who was sent to mock the living God.

Isaiah 37:15-17 TLV

from the hand of the messengers and read it.

Then Hezekiah went up to the House of *ADONAI* and spread it before *ADONAI*. Hezekiah prayed to *ADONAI* saying: "*ADONAI-Tzva'ot*, God of Israel, who is enthroned upon the *cheruvim*, You alone are God of all the kingdoms of the earth. You have made heaven and earth. Incline Your ear, *ADONAI*, and hear! Open Your eyes, *ADONAI*, and see! Listen to all the words of Sennacherib, who was sent to mock the living God.

It is true, *ADONAI*, the kings of Assyria have devastated all the countries and their lands, and have cast their gods into the fire—for they were not gods, but the work of human hands, wood and stone. So they have destroyed them.

Now, *ADONAI* our God, save us from his hand, so that all the kingdoms of the earth may know that You alone are *ADONAI*!"

Then Isaiah son of Amoz sent word to Hezekiah saying, "Thus says *ADONAI*, the God of Israel: 'Because you prayed to Me about King Sennacherib of Assyria, this is the word that *ADONAI* has spoken about him:

"The virgin Daughter of Zion
 will despise you and mock you.
The daughter of Jerusalem
 will shake her head at you.

Whom did you taunt and blaspheme?
Against whom did you raise your
voice and haughtily lift up your eyes?

Against the Holy One of Israel!

Through your servants,
you have blasphemed my Lord and said:
'With my many chariots
I have climbed to the heights
of the mountains,
to the remotest parts of Lebanon!
I cut down its tall cedars
 and choice cypress trees.
I have gone to its farthest peak,
 its thickest forest.
I dug and drank water,
and with the sole of my feet,
I dried up all the streams of Egypt.'

Have you not heard?
I did it long ago!
From ancient times I planned it.
Now I have brought it to pass—that
you should turn fortified cities
 into heaps of rubble.
Their inhabitants are weak handed,
 shattered and ashamed.
They are like the grass of the field
and green herb, like grass on roofs,
 scorched before it is grown up.
But I know your sitting down,
your going out and your coming in,
and your raging against Me.
Because your raging against Me
and your arrogance reached My ears,
I will put My hook in your nose,
 and My bridle in your lips,
and I will turn you back
 by the way that you came."

So this shall be the sign to you: This year you will eat what grows by itself, in the second year what springs from that. But in the third year, you will sow, reap, plant vineyards, and eat their fruit.

The surviving remnant of the house of Judah will take root downward and bear fruit upward. For from

Jerusalem a remnant will go out, and survivors from Mount Zion. The zeal of *ADONAI-Tzva'ot* shall perform this."

Therefore thus says *ADONAI* concerning the king of Assyria: "He will not come to the city, or shoot an arrow there, or come before it with a shield, or throw up a siege-ramp against it. By the way that he came, by the same he will return, and he will not come into this city" —it is a declaration of *ADONAI*. "For I will defend this city to save it, for My own sake, and for My servant David's sake."

Then the angel of *ADONAI* went out and struck down 185,000 men in the Assyrian camp. When the men arose early in the morning, behold, they were all dead corpses. So King Sennacherib of Assyria withdrew, and returned home, and stayed in Nineveh.

It also came to pass, as he was worshipping in the house of his god Nisroch, that his sons Adrammelech and Sarezer struck him down with the sword, and escaped into the land of Ararat. Then his son Esarhaddon became king in his place.

Isaiah, chapter 37

In those days Hezekiah became mortally ill. So Isaiah the prophet son of Amoz came to him and said to him, "Thus says *ADONAI*: Put your house in order. For you are dying, and will not live."

Then Hezekiah turned his face to the wall, and prayed to *ADONAI*. He said: "Please, *ADONAI*, remember how I have walked before You in truth and with a whole heart, and have done what is good in Your eyes." And Hezekiah wept bitterly.

Then it came to pass, the word of *ADONAI* came to Isaiah saying: "Go, and say to Hezekiah, thus says *ADONAI*, the God of your father David: 'I have heard your prayer and I have seen your tears. Behold, I will add 15 years to your life. I will deliver you and this city from the hand of the king of Assyria; I will defend this city.'

"Now this will be the sign to you from *ADONAI*, that *ADONAI* will do this word He has spoken: Behold, I will cause the shadow on the stairs, which went down with the sun on the sundial of Ahaz, to turn back ten steps." So the sun's shadow went back ten steps on the sundial on which it had gone down.

A writing of King Hezekiah of Judah, after his illness, when he recovered from his illness:

I said: "In the prime of my life,
I am to enter the gates of *Sheol*. I am deprived of the rest of my years."

I said: "I will not see *ADONAI*, *ADONAI*, in the land of the living. I will look on humanity no longer among the inhabitants of the world. Like a shepherd's tent, my dwelling is pulled up and carried away from me. Like a weaver I rolled up my life. He cuts me off from the loom. From day until night You make my end. I stilled my soul till morning. Like a lion, He will break all my bones. From day till night You make my end.
Like a swallow or a crane,
I whisper, I moan like a dove.

My eyes are weary, looking upward.
ADONAI, I am oppressed,
be my security!
What should I say?
For He has spoken to me—
He Himself has done it!
I will wander about all my years
because of the bitterness of my soul.

ADONAI, by such things men live,
and my spirit has life in them too.
Restore me to health, and let me live!
Behold, it was for my own *shalom*
 that I had great bitterness.
You have loved my soul
 out of the Pit of destruction!
For You have flung all my sins
 behind Your back.
For Sheol cannot thank You,
death cannot praise You.

Those who go down to the Pit
 cannot hope for Your faithfulness.
The living, the living—they praise You
—as I do today.
A father makes Your faithfulness
known to his children.
ADONAI will save me.
So we will play my songs
on stringed instruments
all the days of our life
in the House of ADONAI."

Now Isaiah had said, "Let them take a cake of figs, and apply it to the boil, and he will live."

Hezekiah had said, "What is the sign that I will go up to the House of *ADONAI*?"

Isaiah, chapter 38

At that time Merodach-baladan, son of King Baladan of Babylon, sent letters and a present to Hezekiah, for he had heard that he had been sick and had recovered. Now Hezekiah was pleased with them, so he showed them his treasure house—the silver and the gold, the spices and the precious oil—and his whole armory, and everything that was found in his treasuries. There was nothing in his house or in all his dominion that Hezekiah did not show them.

Then Isaiah the prophet came to King Hezekiah and asked him, "What did these men say, and from where did they come to you?"

Hezekiah replied, "They have come to me from a far country, from Babylon."

Then he asked, "What have they seen in your house?"

Hezekiah said, "They have seen everything in my house. There is nothing among my treasuries that I didn't show them."

Then Isaiah said to Hezekiah: "Hear the word of *ADONAI-Tzva'ot*, 'Behold, days are coming when everything in your house, which your fathers have stored up to this day, will be carried to Babylon—nothing will be left,' says *ADONAI*. 'Moreover, some of your descendants —who will issue from you, whom you will father—will be taken away and will become eunuchs in the palace of the king of Babylon.'"

Then Hezekiah said to Isaiah, "The word of *ADONAI* which you have spoken is good." For he thought, "For there will be *shalom* and security in my days."

Isaiah, chapter 39

42. God is Omniscient

"Comfort, comfort My people,"
says your God.
Speak kindly to the heart of
Jerusalem and proclaim to her
that her warfare has ended,
that her iniquity has been removed.

For she has received
from *ADONAI*'s hand
double for all her sins.
A voice cries out in the wilderness,
"Prepare the way of *ADONAI*,
Make straight in the desert
a highway for our God.

Every valley will be lifted up,
every mountain and hill made low,
the rough ground will be a plain
and the rugged terrain smooth.
The glory of *ADONAI* will be revealed,
and all flesh will see it together." For
the mouth of *ADONAI* has spoken.

A voice is saying, "Cry out!"
So I said, "What shall I cry out?"
"All flesh is grass, and all its loveliness
is like the flower of the field. The
grass withers, the flower fades. For
the breath of *ADONAI* blows on it.
Surely the people are grass.

The grass withers, the flower fades.
But the word of our God stands
forever."

Get yourself up on a high mountain,
you who bring good news to Zion!

Lift up your voice with strength,
you who bring good news to
Jerusalem!
Lift it up! Do not fear!
Say to the cities of Judah:
"Behold your God!"

Look, *ADONAI Elohim* comes with
might, with His arm ruling for Him.
Behold, His reward is with Him,
and His recompense before Him.

Like a shepherd, He tends His flock.
He gathers the lambs in His arms
carries them in his bosom,
and gently guides nursing ewes.

Who has measured the waters
in the palm of His hand,
or measured out heaven with a span,
or calculated the dust of the earth
in a measure,
or weighed the mountains in scales,
or the hills in a balance?

Who can fathom the *Ruach ADONAI*?
Or instruct Him as His counselor?
With whom did He consult,
and who instructed Him?
Who taught Him in the path of justice
or taught Him knowledge?
Who informed Him about
the way of understanding?

Behold, the nations are like a drop
from a bucket, and count as a speck
of dust on the scales.

Behold, the islands weigh as fine dust.
Lebanon is not enough to burn,
or its animals enough for a burnt
offering.

All the nations are as nothing before
Him. By Him they are accounted null
and void. To whom then will you liken
God? To what likeness will you
compare Him?

To an idol? A craftsman casts it,
a goldsmith overlays it with gold

and fashions silver chains for it.
One too poor for such an offering
chooses wood that will not rot.
He looks for a skilled craftsman
to prepare him an idol that will not
totter.

Do you not know?
Have you not heard?
Has it not been told to you
from the beginning?
Have you not understood
from the foundations of the earth?

He sits above the circle of the earth
its inhabitants are like grasshoppers
— He stretches out the skies like a
curtain, spreads them out like a tent
to dwell in.

He reduces princes to nothing.
He makes the judges of the earth a
confusion.

Scarcely are they planted,
scarcely are they sown,
scarcely their stem takes root in the
earth, when He blows on them and
they wither, and a storm carries them
off as stubble.

"To whom then will you liken Me?
Or who is My equal?"
says the Holy One.

Lift up your eyes on high, and see!
Who created these?

The One who brings out their host by
number, the One who calls them all
by name. Because of His great
strength and vast power, not one is
missing. Why do you say, O Jacob,
and assert, O Israel,

"My way is hidden from Adonai,
and the justice due me escapes
the notice of my God"?

Have you not known?
Have you not heard?
Adonai is the eternal God,
the Creator of the ends of the earth.

He does not grow tired or weary.
His understanding is unsearchable.
He gives strength to the weary,
and to one without vigor He adds
might.

Even youths grow tired and weary,
and young men stumble and fall,
but they who wait for Adonai
will renew their strength.
They will soar up
with wings as eagles.
They will run, and not grow weary.
They will walk, and not be faint.

Isaiah, chapter 40

"Be silent before Me, O islands!
Let peoples renew their strength.
Let them draw near, then let them
speak. Let us come together for
judgment.

Who has stirred up one from the east?
He calls justice to His feet. He gives
nations over to him and subdues
kings. He makes them like dust with
his sword, as driven stubble with his
bow.

He pursues them, passing on safely,
by a path his feet had not traveled.
Who has performed and done it?
Calling forth the generations from the
beginning, I, *Adonai*, am the first and
the last, I am He!"

The coastlands have seen and fear.
The ends of the earth tremble.

He gives strength to the weary, and to one without vigor He adds might. Even youths grow tired and weary, and young men stumble and fall, but they who wait for *ADONAI* will renew their strength. They will soar up with wings as eagles. They will run, and not grow weary. They will walk, and not be faint.

Isaiah 40:29-31 TLV

They draw near and come.
Each one helps his neighbor
and says to his brother, "Be strong!"

The craftsman encourages the smith, who smooths with the hammer, who strikes with the anvil, saying of the soldering, "It's good!" as he fastens it with nails so that it will not totter.

"But you, Israel, My servant,
Jacob whom I have chosen,
descendant of Abraham, My friend—

I took hold of you from the ends of the earth, and called from its uttermost parts, and said to you,
'You are My servant—
I have chosen you, not rejected you.

Fear not, for I am with you,
be not dismayed,
for I am your God.
I will strengthen you.
Surely I will help you.
I will uphold you
with My righteous right hand.

Behold, all who were angry at you
will be ashamed and disgraced.
Those who quarrel with you
will be as nothing and perish.
Though you will look for those who contended with you,
you will not find them.
Those who warred against you
will be as nothing at all.

For I am *ADONAI* your God who upholds your right hand,
who says to you,
"Fear not, I will help you."
Fear not, you worm Jacob,
you men of Israel!
I will help you."

It is a declaration of *ADONAI*,
your Redeemer, the Holy One of Israel.

"Look, I will make you a threshing sledge, new, with sharp, double-edged spikes. You will thresh the mountains and grind them up,
and will make the hills like chaff.
You will winnow them, and a wind will carry them away, a storm-wind will scatter them.
But you will rejoice in *ADONAI*.
You will glory in the Holy One of Israel.

"The poor and needy ask for water,
but there is none,
Their tongues are parched with thirst.

I, *ADONAI*,
will answer them,
I, the God of Israel,
will not forsake them.

I will open rivers on the bare hills
and springs in the midst of the valleys.
I will make the wilderness a pool of water and the dry land into fountains of water.

I will plant in the wilderness
the cedar and the acacia tree,
the myrtle and the olive tree.
I will set in the desert the cypress tree
and the pine together with the box tree—so they may see and know,
consider and understand together,
that the hand of *ADONAI* has done this,
the Holy One of Israel has created it."

"Present your case," says *ADONAI*.
"Bring forth your reasons,"
says the King of Jacob.
Let them bring forth and tell us
what will happen.

The former things, what were they?
Tell us, that we may consider them
and know their outcome.
Or announce to us things to come.

Declare the things coming afterward,
so we may know that you are gods!

Indeed, do good or do evil,
so we may all see
and be awestruck.

Behold, you are nothing,
and your work is null.
Whoever chooses you
is loathsome.

"I have stirred up one from the north,
and he has come.
From the rising of the sun,
He will call upon My Name.
He will trample rulers as on mortar,
like a potter treading clay."

Who told this from the beginning,
so that we may know?
Or from former times,
so we may say, "He is right"?
In fact, no one foretold it,
In fact, no one announced it.
In fact, no one heard Your words.

First it was to Zion:
"Behold, here they are!"
And to Jerusalem:
"I will give a herald of good news."
But when I look, there is no one.
There is no counselor among them.
When I ask them,
they have no response.
Indeed, they are all a delusion.
Their works are null.
Their molten images
are wind and waste.

Isaiah, chapter 41

43. God Anoints His Chosen

Thus says *ADONAI*:

"Preserve justice,
do righteousness.
For My salvation
is about to come,
and My righteousness
to be revealed.
Blessed is the one who does this,
the son of man
who takes hold of it,
who keeps from
profaning *Shabbat*,
and keeps his hand
from doing any evil.

Do not let a son of a foreigner who has joined himself to *ADONAI* say, '*ADONAI* will surely exclude me from His people."

Nor let the eunuch say,
'Behold, I am a dry tree.'"

For thus says *ADONAI*,

"To the eunuchs who keep
My *Shabbatot*,
who choose what pleases Me,
and hold fast My covenant:
I will give to them in My House
and within My walls
a memorial and a name
better than sons and daughters.
I will give them an everlasting
name that will not be cut off.

Also the foreigners
who join themselves to *ADONAI*,
to minister to Him,
and to love the Name of *ADONAI*,
and to be His servants—
all who keep from
profaning *Shabbat*,
and hold fast to My covenant—
these I will bring to My holy
mountain, and let them rejoice
in My House of Prayer.

Their burnt offerings and sacrifices
will be acceptable on My altar.
For My House will be called
a House of Prayer for all nations."

ADONAI Elohim, who gathers
the dispersed of Israel, declares,
"I will gather still others to him,
to those already gathered."

Isaiah 56:1-8

Behold, *ADONAI*'s hand is not too short to save, nor His ear too dull to hear. Rather, your iniquities have made a separation
between you and your God.

Your sins have hidden His face from you, so that He does not hear.
For your hands are defiled with blood and your fingers with iniquity. Your lips have spoken lies,
your tongue mutters wickedness.

No one sues justly, and none pleads a case honestly. They trust in confusion and speak lies. They conceive mischief, and bring forth iniquity.

They hatch adders' eggs,
and weave the spider's web—
whoever eats their eggs dies;
crack one open, a viper breaks out.
Their webs will not become clothing,
nor will they cover themselves with what they make.

Their deeds are works of iniquity,
an act of violence is in their hands.

Their feet run after evil.
They rush to shed innocent blood.

Their thoughts are thoughts of iniquity. Violence and ruin are on their highways. They do not know the path of peace, and there is no justice in their tracks. They have made their paths crooked. Whoever walks in them will not experience *shalom*.

That is why justice is far from us
and righteousness does not reach us.
We hope for light, but behold darkness, for brightness, but walk in gloom.

We grope along the wall
  like the blind.
We grope like those with no eyes.
We stumble at noon as at twilight.
We are like the dead in desolation.

All of us growl like bears
  or moan like doves.
We hope for justice,
but there is none;
for salvation, but it is far from us.

For our transgressions are
  multiplied before You,
and our sins testify against us,
for our transgressions are with us,
  and we know our iniquities:
transgressing and denying *ADONAI*,
turning back from following our God,
  speaking oppression and revolt,
  conceiving and uttering
  lying words from the heart.
Justice is turned back,
  and righteousness stands far off.
For truth has stumbled in the street,
  and uprightness cannot enter.
So now truth is missing,
and whoever shuns evil
becomes prey.

Now when *ADONAI* saw it,
it was displeasing in His eyes
  that there was no justice.

He saw that there was no one—
He was astonished that
  no one was interceding.

Therefore His own arm
  brought salvation for Him,
and His righteousness upheld Him.

He put on righteousness
  as a breastplate
and a helmet of salvation
  on His head.
He clothed Himself
  in robes of vengeance
and wrapped Himself
  in zeal as a cloak.
According to their deeds,
  so He will repay:
wrath to His adversaries,
  retribution to His enemies.
To the islands He will repay as due.

So from the west they will fear
  the Name of *ADONAI*,
and His glory from the rising
  of the sun.

For He will come like a rushing stream
driven along by the *Ruach ADONAI*.

"But a Redeemer will come to Zion,
  and to those in Jacob
  who turn from transgression."

It is a declaration of *ADONAI*.

"As for Me, this is My covenant with them," says *ADONAI*:
"My *Ruach* who is on you,
and My words that I have put
in your mouth, shall not depart from

your mouth, or from the mouth of
your offspring, or from the mouth of
your children's offspring,"
says *Adonai*, "from now on and
forever."

Isaiah, chapter 59

Arise, shine, for your light has come!
The glory of *Adonai* has risen on you.

For behold, darkness covers the earth, and deep darkness the peoples.

But *Adonai* will arise upon you,
and His glory will appear over you.
Nations will come to your light,
kings to the brilliance of your rising.

Lift up your eyes and look all around:
they all gather—they come to you—
your sons will come from far away,
your daughters carried on the hip.

Then you will see and be radiant, and your heart will throb and swell with joy. For the abundance of the sea will be turned over to you.
The wealth of nations will come to you.

A multitude of camels will cover you, young camels of Midian and Ephah, all those from Sheba will come.

They will bring gold and frankincense,
and proclaim the praises of *Adonai*.

All Kedar's flocks will be gathered to you. Nebaioth's rams will minister to you.

They will go up with favor on My altar, and I will beautify My glorious House.

Who are these who fly like a cloud,
like doves to their windows?

Surely the islands will hope in Me,
with the ships of Tarshish in the lead,
to bring your sons from afar,
their silver and gold with them,
for the Name of *Adonai* your God,
and for the Holy One of Israel,
because He has glorified you.

Foreigners will build up your walls,
and their kings will minister to you.
For in My fury I struck you,
but in My favor I will show you mercy.

Your gates will be open continually.
They will not be shut day or night,
so that men may bring to you the wealth of the nations, with their kings led in procession.

For the nation and the kingdom which will not serve you will perish—
those nations will be utterly ruined.

The glory of Lebanon will come to you—cypress, elm and pine together—to beautify the place of My Sanctuary. I will give to the place of My feet glory.

The sons of those who afflicted you will come bowing to you, and all those who despised you will fall at the soles of your feet.

They will call you the city of *Adonai*,
Zion of the Holy One of Israel.

Instead of deserted and hated,
no one passing through,
I will make you an eternal pride,
joy from generation to generation.

You will also suck the milk of nations

and nurse at the breast of kings. Then you will know that I, *ADONAI*, am your Savior and your Redeemer, the Mighty One of Jacob.

"Instead of bronze I will bring gold,
instead of iron I will bring silver,
instead of wood, bronze,
and instead of stones, iron.
I will make *shalom* your overseer,
and righteousness your taskmasters.

No more will violence be heard in your land, devastation nor destruction within your borders.
But you will call your walls Salvation and your gates Praise.

No more will the sun be your light by day, nor the glow of the moon be your light, but *ADONAI* will be your everlasting light, and your God for your glory.

No more will your sun set,
nor will your moon wane,
for *ADONAI* will be your everlasting light, as the days of your mourning end.

Then your people will all be righteous.
They will possess the land forever—
the branch of His planting, the work of My hands—
that I may be glorified. The smallest will become a thousand, and the least a mighty nation.

I, *ADONAI*, will hasten it in its time."

Isaiah, chapter 60

The *Ruach* of *ADONAI Elohim* is on me,
because *ADONAI* has anointed me to proclaim Good News to the poor.
He has sent me to bind up the brokenhearted, to proclaim liberty to the captives, and the opening of the prison to those who are bound, to proclaim the year of *ADONAI*'s favor
and the day of our God's vengeance,
to comfort all who mourn
to console those who mourn in Zion,
to give them beauty for ashes,
the oil of joy for mourning,
the garment of praise
for the spirit of heaviness,
that they might be called
oaks of righteousness,
the planting of *ADONAI*,
that He may be glorified.

They will rebuild the ancient ruins.
They will restore former desolations.
They will repair the ruined cities,
the desolations of many generations.

Strangers will stand and shepherd your flocks, children of foreigners will be your plowmen and vinedressers.

But you will be called
the *kohanim* of *ADONAI*,
They will speak of you as
the ministers of our God.
You will eat the wealth of nations
and boast in their abundance.

Instead of your shame, double portion. Instead of disgrace they will sing for joy. Therefore in their land they will inherit a double portion; they will have everlasting joy.
For I, *ADONAI*, love justice.
I hate robbery in the burnt offering.
In faithfulness I will reward
My people and cut an
eternal covenant with them.
Then their offspring
will be known among the nations,
their descendants among the
peoples. All who see them will

The Ruach of *ADONAI Elohim* is on me, because *ADONAI* has anointed me to proclaim Good News to the poor. He has sent me to bind up the brokenhearted, to proclaim liberty to the captives, and the opening of the prison to those who are bound, to proclaim the year of *ADONAI*'s favor and the day of our God's vengeance, to comfort all who mourn to console those who mourn in Zion, to give them beauty for ashes, the oil of joy for mourning, the garment of praise for the spirit of heaviness, that they might be called oaks of righteousness, the planting of *ADONAI*, that He may be glorified.

Isaiah 61:1-3 TLV

recognize them, for they are the seed
that *ADONAI* has blessed.

I will rejoice greatly in *ADONAI*.
My soul will be joyful in my God.
For He has clothed me
with garments of salvation,
He has wrapped me in
a robe of righteousness—like a
bridegroom wearing a priestly turban,
like a bride adorning herself with her
jewels.

For as the earth brings forth its
sprouts, and as a garden causes
things sown to spring up, so
ADONAI Elohim will cause justice and
praise to spring up before all the
nations.

Isaiah, chapter 61

44. God Causes Nations to Rise and Fall

The words of Jeremiah son of Hilkiah, one of the *kohanim* who were in Anathoth in the land of Benjamin. The word of *ADONAI* came to him during the days of King Josiah of Judah, son of Amon, in the thirteenth year of his reign. It continued during the days of King Jehoiakim of Judah, son of Josiah, until the end of the eleventh year of King Zedekiah of Judah, son of Josiah—until the exile from Jerusalem in the fifth month.

The word of *ADONAI* came to me, saying:

"Before I formed you in the
womb, I knew you,
and before you were born,
I set you apart—
I appointed you prophet
to the nations."

Then I said, "Alas, *ADONAI Elohim*! Look, I don't know how to speak! For I'm still a boy!"

But *ADONAI* answered me,
"Do not say 'I'm only a boy!'
For to everyone I send you,
you will go, and all I command you,
you will speak. Do not be afraid of
them!

Then *ADONAI* stretched out His hand
and touched my mouth
and *ADONAI* said to me,
"Behold, I have put My words in your
mouth.

See, today I have appointed you over nations and over kingdoms:
to uproot and to tear down,
to destroy and to overthrow,
to build and to plant."

Moreover, the word of *ADONAI* came to me, saying, "What do you see, Jeremiah?"

I answered, "I see an almond branch."

Then *ADONAI* said to me, "You have seen correctly, for I am watching over My word to perform it."

Jeremiah 1:1-12

"Therefore, the days are quickly coming," declares *ADONAI*, "when it will no longer be said, 'As *ADONAI* lives, who brought up the children of Israel out of the land of Egypt.'

Rather, 'As *ADONAI* lives, who brought up the children of Israel from the land of the north and from all the lands where He had banished them.' So I will bring them back into their land that I gave to their fathers.

"Behold, I will send for many fishers," says *ADONAI*, "and they will fish for them. After that, I will send for many hunters, and they will hunt them down from every mountain and from every hill, and out of the clefts of the rocks. For My eyes are on all their ways. They are not hidden from My face, nor is their iniquity concealed from My eyes.

First I will repay them double for their iniquity and their sin, because they have profaned My land, and they have filled My possession with the carcasses of their vile things and their abominations."

ADONAI, my strength,
my stronghold,
my refuge in the day of affliction,
to You will the nations come
from the ends of the earth and say:
"Our fathers have inherited
nothing but lies,
futility and useless things."
Will man make gods for himself?
Yet they are not gods.
"So I will surely make them know
—this time I make them know
My hand and My might—they
will know that My Name is
ADONAI."

Jeremiah 16:14-21

Judah's sin is written with an iron pen and with a point of a diamond, engraved on the tablet of their heart and on the horns of your altars. So their children remember their altars and their Asherah poles by leafy trees on the high hills.

My mountain in the country,
your wealth and all your treasures
I will give away as plunder,
along with your high places
for sin within all your borders.

So you, on your own, let go of your heritage that I gave you.

So I will make you serve your enemies in a land that you do not know. For you have kindled a fire in My nose that will burn forever."

Thus says *ADONAI*:
"Cursed is the one who trusts in man, and depends on flesh as his arm, and whose heart turns from *ADONAI*.

For he will be like a bush in the desert.
He cannot see goodness when it comes, but will dwell in parched places in the wilderness—
a salt land where no one lives.

Blessed is the one who trusts in *ADONAI*, whose confidence is in *ADONAI*.

For he will be like a tree
planted by the waters,
spreading out its roots by a stream.
It has no fear when heat comes,
but its leaves will be green.
It does not worry
in a year of drought,
nor depart from yielding fruit.

"The heart is deceitful above all things, and incurable—who can know it?

I *ADONAI* search the heart,
I try the mind,
to give every man
according to his ways,
according to the fruit of his deeds.

As a partridge that broods over young
that she did not lay,
so is one who gets wealth, unjustly.
In the middle of his days it will abandon him, so at his end he will be a fool.

Throne of glory on high
from the beginning!
Place of our sanctuary,
ADONAI, You are the hope of Israel!
All who forsake You
will be ashamed.
Those who depart from You
will be written in the dirt,
for they have forsaken *ADONAI*,

the fountain of living waters.

Heal me, *Adonai*,
and I will be healed.
Save me, and I will be saved.
For You are my praise.

Look, they are saying to me,
"Where is the word of *Adonai*?
Let it come now!"
As for me, I have not run away from
being a shepherd after You,
nor have I desired the woeful day.

What came out of my lips You
know—it was before You.
Be not a ruin to me—
You are my refuge in the evil day.
Let my persecutors be ashamed,
yet let me not be ashamed.

Let them be dismayed,
but let me not be dismayed.
Bring on them the evil day,
Destroy them with
double destruction.

Thus said *Adonai* to me: "Go, stand in the gate of the children of the people, through which the kings of Judah come in and go out, and in all the gates of Jerusalem, and say to them: 'Hear the word of *Adonai*, kings of Judah, and all Judah and all inhabitants of Jerusalem who enter through these gates!

Thus says *Adonai*, "Guard your souls! Carry no burden on the day of *Shabbat* or bring it in through the gates of Jerusalem. Nor should you carry a burden out of your houses on *Yom Shabbat* or do any work, but keep *Yom Shabbat* holy—as I commanded your fathers." Yet they did not listen or incline their ear, but stiffened their neck, not hearing or accepting correction.

"However, if you listen attentively to Me," says *Adonai*, "to bring in no burden through the gates of this city on *Yom Shabbat*, but sanctify *Yom Shabbat* and do no work on it, then there will enter in through the gates of this city kings and princes sitting on the throne of David, riding in chariots and on horses—with their princes, the people of Judah and those dwelling in Jerusalem—and this city will be inhabited forever.

They will come from the cities of Judah and from all around Jerusalem, from the land of Benjamin, from the lowland, from the hill country and from the South, bringing burnt offerings and sacrifices, grain offerings, frankincense, and sacrifices of thanksgiving to the House of *Adonai*.

"But if you do not listen to Me to keep *Yom Shabbat* holy, by not bearing a burden or entering through the gates of Jerusalem on *Yom Shabbat*, then I will set its gates on fire, and it will consume the citadels of Jerusalem, and not be quenched.'"

Jeremiah, chapter 17

The word came to Jeremiah from *Adonai*, saying: "Arise, and go down to the potter's house, and there I will cause you to hear My words."

So I went down to the potter's house, and there he was making a work on the wheels.

Whenever the pot that he was

Then the word of *ADONAI* came to me, saying: "O house of Israel, can I not do with you as this potter does?" declares *ADONAI*. "Behold, as the clay in the potter's hand, so are you in My hand, O house of Israel.

Jeremiah 18:5-6 TLV

making from the clay became flawed in the hand of the potter, he remade it into another pot, as it pleased the potter to make.

Then the word of *Adonai* came to me, saying: "O house of Israel, can I not do with you as this potter does?" declares *Adonai*.

"Behold, as the clay in the potter's hand, so are you in My hand, O house of Israel. At one moment I may speak about a nation or about a kingdom, to uproot, to pull down or to destroy it. But if that nation turns from their evil, because of what I have spoken against it, I will relent concerning the calamity that I planned to do to it.

Or at another time I may speak about a nation or about a kingdom, to build up or to plant it. But if it does evil in My sight, not listening to My voice, then I will relent of the good that I had said I would do to it."

So now, speak to the people of Judah and to the inhabitants of Jerusalem, saying, thus says *Adonai*: "I am about to bring calamity against you, and devise disaster against you. Turn back now—everyone from his evil way—and amend your ways and your doings.

But they say: 'It's hopeless!
So we will walk after our own plans,
and each of us will act in the
stubbornness of his evil heart.'"

Therefore thus says *Adonai*:
"Ask now among the nations,
whoever has heard such things?
The virgin of Israel has done
 a most terrible thing.
Does the snow of Lebanon
abandon the rock of the field?
Or is the cold water flowing from afar
pulled back?
Yet My people have forgotten Me.

They burn incense to a delusion
and stumble in their ways
—off the ancient paths—
to walk on side-tracks,
rather than a built-up highway.

Their land will become a horror,
a perpetual hissing—
every one passing by will be stunned
and shake his head.

Like an east wind,
I will scatter them before the enemy.
I will see their back,
 not their face,
 in the day of their calamity."

Jeremiah 18:1-17

45. God Gives Hope

ADONAI showed me, all of a sudden, there were two baskets of figs set before the Temple of *ADONAI*. It was after King Nebuchadnezzar of Babylon had taken away into exile Jeconiah son of King Jehoiakim of Judah and the princes of Judah, along with the craftsmen and smiths from Jerusalem, and had brought them to Babylon.

One basket had very good figs, like the figs that are first ripe, but the other basket had very bad figs, which could not be eaten, they were so bad.

Then *ADONAI* said to me, "What do you see, Jeremiah?"

So I said, "Figs—the good figs are very good, but the bad are very bad, and cannot be eaten, they are so bad."

Then the word of *ADONAI* came to me, saying, thus says *ADONAI*, the God of Israel: "Like these good figs, so will I regard the exiles of Judah, whom I have sent out of this place to the land of the Chaldeans, as good. I will set My eyes on them as good. I will bring them back to this land, and I will build them up and not pull them down; I will plant them and not uproot them. Then I will give them a heart to know Me—for I am *ADONAI*—and they will be My people, and I will be their God. For they will return to Me with their whole heart.
"Now as for the bad figs, which cannot be eaten they are so bad"—surely thus says *ADONAI*—"so I will give up Zedekiah the king of Judah, his princes and the remnant of Jerusalem who remain in this land, as well as those dwelling in the land of Egypt. I will even give them as a horror, as an evil thing, among all the kingdoms of the earth—as a disgrace and a proverb, a taunt and a curse—in all places where I will drive them. I will also send the sword, famine and pestilence among them, until they be consumed from off the land that I gave to them and to their fathers."

Jeremiah, chapter 24

Now these are the words of the letter that the prophet Jeremiah sent from Jerusalem to the elders remaining in exile, as well as to the *kohanim*, the prophets and to all the people Nebuchadnezzar had carried off captive from Jerusalem to Babylon (after Jeconiah the king, the queen-mother, the officers, the princes of Judah and Jerusalem, and the craftsmen and the smiths, had to leave Jerusalem).

The letter was sent by the hand of Elasah son of Shaphan, and Gemariah son of Hilkiah, whom King Zedekiah of Judah sent to Babylon to Nebuchadnezzar king of Babylon, saying, thus says *ADONAI-Tzva'ot*, the God of Israel, to all those in captivity, whom I removed as captives into exile from Jerusalem to Babylon:

"Build houses and live in them; also plant gardens and eat their fruit; take wives and have sons and daughters; and take wives for your sons and give your daughters to husbands, so that they may bear sons and daughters; and multiply there, and do not decrease. Also seek the *shalom* of the city where I took you as captives in exile, and pray to ADONAI for it—for in its *shalom* will you have *shalom*."

For thus says ADONAI, the God of Israel: "Do not let your prophets who are among you or your diviners beguile you, and pay no attention to the dreams which you make them keep dreaming. For they prophesy falsely to you in My Name; I have not sent them."

It is a declaration of ADONAI.

For thus says ADONAI: "After 70 years for Babylon are complete, I will visit you, and fulfill My good word toward you—to bring you back to this place. For I know the plans that I have in mind for you," declares ADONAI, "plans for *shalom* and not calamity—to give you a future and a hope.

"Then you will call on Me, and come and pray to Me, and I will listen to you. You will seek Me and find Me, when you will search for Me with all your heart. Then I will be found by you," says ADONAI, "and I will return you from exile, and gather you from all the nations and from all the places where I have driven you," says ADONAI, "and I will bring you back to the place from which I removed you as captives into exile."

For you have said: "ADONAI has raised up prophets for us in Babylon." For thus says ADONAI about the king who sits on the throne of David and about all the people who dwell in this city, your kinsmen who did not go with you into captivity, thus says ADONAI-*Tzva'ot*: "I am about to send on them the sword, famine and pestilence, and will make them like vile figs, that cannot be eaten, they are so bad.

I will pursue them with the sword, famine and pestilence, and will make them a horror to all the kingdoms of the earth—a curse and an astonishment, a hissing and a disgrace—among all the nations where I have driven them, because they have not listened to My words," declares ADONAI, "which I sent to them by My servants the prophets, sending them early and often, but you would not hear."

It is a declaration of ADONAI.

"But you, hear the word of ADONAI, all you of the exile whom I have sent from Jerusalem to Babylon," thus says ADONAI-*Tzva'ot*, the God of Israel, "concerning Ahab son of Kolaiah, and concerning Zedekiah son of Maaseiah, who prophesy a lie to you in My name: I will soon deliver them into the hand of King Nebuchadnezzar of Babylon—and he will slay them before your eyes.

So a curse will be taken up by everyone in exile from Judah who are in Babylon, saying:

'May *ADONAI* make you like Zedekiah and like Ahab, whom the king of Babylon roasted in the fire'—because they have been disgraceful in Israel, committing adultery with their neighbors' wives and speaking words in My Name falsely, which I did not command them. But I am the One who knows and I am witness."

It is a declaration of *ADONAI*.

Now concerning Shemaiah the Nehelamite you will surely say, thus declares *ADONAI-Tzva'ot*, the God of Israel, saying: "Because you have sent letters in your own name to all the people who are at Jerusalem, to Zephaniah son of Maaseiah the *kohen*, and to all the *kohanim*, saying: '*ADONAI* has made you *kohen* instead of Jehoiada the *kohen*, so that there should be officers in the House of *ADONAI* for every madman prophesying and so that you will put him in the stocks and iron collar.

So now, why haven't you rebuked Jeremiah of Anathoth, who makes himself out to be a prophet to you? For he has sent word to us in Babylon, saying: "The exile will be long—build houses and live in them; plant gardens and eat their fruit.'"

So Zephaniah the *kohen* read this letter in the ears of the prophet Jeremiah. Then the word of *ADONAI* came to Jeremiah, saying: Send word to all of the captivity, saying, thus says *ADONAI* concerning Shemaiah the Nehelamite: "Because Shemaiah has prophesied to you, though I did not send him, and he has caused you to trust in a lie," therefore thus says *ADONAI*, "I will indeed punish Shemaiah the Nehelamite and his offspring. There will be none living among this people, and he will not see the good that I will do to My people," declares *ADONAI*, "because he has spoken rebellion against *ADONAI*."

Jeremiah, chapter 29

The word came to Jeremiah from *ADONAI*, saying: thus says *ADONAI*, the God of Israel: "Write all the words that I have spoken to you in a scroll. For behold, the days are coming," declares *ADONAI*, "when I will return My people Israel and Judah from exile," declares *ADONAI*. "I will bring them back to the land that I gave to their fathers, and they will possess it."

Now these are the words that *ADONAI* spoke to Israel and to Judah. For thus says *ADONAI*:

"We heard a sound of trembling,
of dread—there is no *shalom*.
Ask now, and see
whether a man can give birth.
Why do I see every man
with his hands on his loins,
like a woman giving birth?
Why have all faces turned pale?
Oy! For that day is monumental.
There will be none like it—
a time of trouble for Jacob!
Yet out of it he will be saved.
It will be in that day"
—it is a declaration of *ADONAI-Tzva'ot*—
"that I will break his yoke from off your neck, and will tear off your bonds. Foreigners will no longer enslave him. Instead they will serve *ADONAI* their God and David

"So you will be My people, and I will be your God."

Jeremiah 30:22 TLV

their king, whom I will raise up for them.

So now, do not fear, Jacob My servant," says *ADONAI*, "nor be dismayed, O Israel, for behold, I will save you from afar, your seed from the land of their exile. Jacob will again be quiet and at ease, and no one will make him afraid.

For I am with you,"
declares *ADONAI*,
"to save you,
for I will make a full end
of all the nations
where I scatter you, but
I will not make a full end of you.
For I will discipline you justly,
but will not leave you unpunished."

For thus says *ADONAI*:
"Your hurt is incurable,
and your wound is severe.
No one pleads your cause,
for there is no remedy for your
wound, no healing for you.
All your lovers have forgotten you.
They are not looking for you.
For I wounded you as an enemy—
with cruel punishment—
because your iniquity is vast,
your sins innumerable.
Why cry about your fracture?
Your pain has no cure.
Because your iniquity is vast,
your sins innumerable,
I did these things to you.

Yet all who devour you will be devoured, and all your foes—
all of them—will go into captivity.
Those plundering you will be plundered, and all preying on you I give as prey. For I will restore health to you and will heal you of your wounds."

It is a declaration of *ADONAI*.

"For they called you an outcast:
'Zion—no one cares about her.'"

Thus says *ADONAI*, "Indeed,
I will return Jacob's tents from exile, and have compassion on his dwellings. The city will be rebuilt on her mound. The citadel will stand in its rightful place.

Out of them will come thanksgiving
and the sound of celebration.
I will multiply them,
so they will not decrease.
I will also honor them,
so they will not be insignificant.
His children also will be as formerly
—his community set up before Me—
and I will punish all his oppressors.

His noble one will be one of His own. His ruler will come forth from among His own. I will bring Him near, and He will approach Me. For who is he who will pledge his heart to approach Me?" It is a declaration of *ADONAI*. "So you will be My people,
and I will be your God."

Look! A storm of *ADONAI*!
Fury has burst out as a churning storm, whirling about the head of the wicked. *ADONAI*'s fierce anger will not turn back until He has done it, until He fulfills the purposes of His heart.
In the last days you will understand it.

"At that time," declares *ADONAI*,
"I will be God to all families of Israel,
and they will be My people."

Jeremiah, chapter 30

46. God Proclaims His Promise

Thus says *ADONAI*:
"The people surviving the sword
found grace in the wilderness—
where I gave Israel rest."

"From afar *ADONAI* appeared to me."

"Yes, I have loved you with an
everlasting love. Therefore I have
drawn you with lovingkindness.

Again I will build you, so you will be
rebuilt, virgin Israel!
Again you will take up your
tambourines as ornaments,
and go out to dances of
merrymakers.
Again you will plant vineyards on
the hills of Samaria—
planters will plant and use them.

For there will be a day when
watchmen will call out
in the hill country of Ephraim,
'Arise, let us go up to Zion,
to *ADONAI* our God.'"

For thus says *ADONAI*:
"Sing aloud with joy for Jacob!
Shout with the chief of the nations!
Proclaim, give praise, and say:
'*ADONAI*, save your people,
the remnant of Israel!'

Behold, I will bring them
from the north country,
and I will gather them
from the ends of the earth—
among them the blind and the lame,
the pregnant together with she who
is in labor with child.
A great throng will return here.

With weeping and supplications
they will come.
I will bring them, leading them to
walk by streams of water on a
straight path where they will not
stumble.

For I am Israel's father,
and Ephraim is My firstborn."

Hear the word of *ADONAI*, O nations,
and declare it in the distant islands,
and say: 'He who scattered Israel will
gather and watch over him, as a
shepherd does his flock.'
For *ADONAI* has ransomed Jacob.
He redeemed him from the hand of
one stronger than he.

They will come and sing on Zion's
height, radiant over the bounty
of *ADONAI*—over the grain, the wine,
the oil, and the young of the flock.
Their life will be like a watered
garden, and they will never languish
again.

Then will the virgin rejoice in the
dance, both young men and old men
together.

For I will turn their mourning into joy,
and I will comfort them, and make
them rejoice out of their sorrow.
I will fill the soul of the *kohanim* with
fatness and My people will be
satisfied with My goodness."

It is a declaration of *ADONAI*.

Erect road markers, set up signposts!
Set your heart toward the highway,
the way by which you traveled!
Return, O virgin Israel,
return to your cities.

How long will you waver,
O backsliding daughter?
For *ADONAI* has created
a new thing on earth:
a woman surrounds a man.

Thus says *ADONAI-Tzva'ot*, the God of Israel: "Yet again will they use this expression in the land of Judah and in its cities, when I will return them from exile: '*ADONAI* bless you,
O dwelling of righteousness,
O mountain of holiness.'

Judah and all its cities will dwell there together—the farmer and those who go about with flocks. For I will satisfy the weary soul, and every languishing soul will refresh."

At this point I awoke, and looked around, and my sleep was sweet to me.

"Behold, days are coming"—it is a declaration of *ADONAI*—"when I will sow the house of Israel and the house of Judah with the seed of man and with the seed of beast. Now just as I have watched over them to uproot and to pull down, to overthrow, to destroy, and to bring disaster, then I will watch over them to build and to plant," says *ADONAI*.

"In those days they will no longer say:
'The fathers have eaten sour grapes,
and the children's teeth are blunted.'
Rather each will die for his own iniquity: if anyone eats the sour grapes, his own teeth will be blunted."

"Behold, days are coming"
—it is a declaration of *ADONAI*—
"when I will make a new covenant
with the house of Israel
and with the house of Judah—
not like the covenant I made with
their fathers in the day I took them by the hand to bring them out
of the land of Egypt.
For they broke My covenant,
though I was a husband to them."

it is a declaration of *ADONAI*.

"But this is the covenant I will make with the house of Israel after those days"

—it is a declaration of *ADONAI*—

"I will put My *Torah* within them.
Yes, I will write it on their heart.
I will be their God
and they will be My people.

No longer will each teach his neighbor
or each his brother, saying:
'Know *ADONAI*,'
for they will all know Me,
from the least of them to the greatest."

It is a declaration of *ADONAI*.

"For I will forgive their iniquity,
their sin I will remember no more."

Thus says *ADONAI*, who gives the sun as a light by day and the fixed order of the moon and the stars as a light by night, who stirs up the sea so its waves roar, *ADONAI-Tzva'ot* is His Name:
"Only if this fixed order departs from before Me"
—it is a declaration of *ADONAI*—
"then also might Israel's offspring
cease from being a nation

"Behold, days are coming" —it is a declaration of *ADONAI*— "when I will make a new covenant with the house of Israel and with the house of Judah... "I will put My *Torah* within them. Yes, I will write it on their heart. I will be their God and they will be My people.

Jeremiah 31:30-32 TLV

before Me—for all time."

Thus says *ADONAI*:
"Only if heaven above can be measured and the foundations of the earth searched out beneath,
then also I will cast off the offspring of Israel—for all they have done."

It is a declaration of *ADONAI*.

"Behold, days are coming"
—it is a declaration of *ADONAI*—
"when the city will be rebuilt for *ADONAI*, from the tower of Hananel to the Corner Gate. The measuring line will go out farther, straight to the Gareb Hill, then turn to Goah. Then the whole valley—the dead bodies and the ashes, and all the fields up to the Kidron Valley to the corner of the Horse Gate toward the east—will be holy to *ADONAI*. It will never be uprooted or thrown down again—forever."

Jeremiah, chapter 31

The word that came to Jeremiah from *ADONAI*, in the tenth year of King Zedekiah of Judah, which was the eighteenth year of Nebuchadnezzar. Now at the time the king of Babylon's army was besieging Jerusalem, and Jeremiah the prophet was shut up in the court of the guard, which was in the palace of the king of Judah.

For King Zedekiah of Judah had shut him up, saying: "Why do you prophesy and say, thus says *ADONAI*: 'I will soon give this city into the hand of the king of Babylon, and he will take it; and King Zedekiah of Judah will not escape out of the hand of the Chaldeans, but will surely be given into the hand of the king of Babylon, and will speak with him mouth to mouth and his eyes will behold his eyes; and he will lead Zedekiah to Babylon, and there will he remain until I take note of him,'
says *ADONAI*—though you fight with the Chaldeans, you will not succeed?"

So Jeremiah said: "The word of *ADONAI* came to me, saying: 'Hanamel, son of Shallum your uncle, will soon come to you saying: 'Buy for yourself my field in Anathoth, for the right of redemption is yours to buy it.'''

So my uncle's son Hanamel came to me in the court of the guard as was the word of *ADONAI*, and said to me: "Buy my field, please, which is in Anathoth in the land of Benjamin; for the right of inheritance is yours and the redemption is yours; buy it for yourself." Then I knew that this was the word of *ADONAI*.

So I bought the field that was in Anathoth from the son of my uncle Hanamel, and weighed him the money—seventeen shekels of silver. I signed and sealed the deed, called in witnesses, and weighed the money on the scales. Then I took the purchase deed, both the sealed copy, containing the terms and conditions, and the open copy, and I gave the purchase deed to Baruch son of Neriah son of Mahseiah, in the presence of my uncle's son Hanamel and in the presence of the witnesses that subscribed the purchase deed, before all the Jews that sat in the court of the guard.

Then I charged Baruch before them, saying, thus says *Adonai-Tzva'ot*, the God of Israel, "Take these deeds—this purchase deed, both the sealed copy and the open copy—and put them in a clay jar, so they may last many days." For thus says *Adonai-Tzva'ot*, the God of Israel: "Houses and fields and vineyards will yet again be bought in this land."

After I had given the purchase deed to Baruch son of Neriah, I prayed to *Adonai*, saying: "Ah, my Lord *Adonai*! Behold, You have made the heavens and the earth by Your great power and by Your outstretched arm—nothing is too hard for You! You are the One doing mercy to thousands, but repaying the iniquity of the fathers into the lap of their children after them.

Great, mighty God, *Adonai-Tzva'ot* is His Name! Great in counsel and mighty in deed, whose eyes are open to all the ways of the children of men, to give each one according to his ways and according to the fruit of his deeds. You set signs and wonders in the land of Egypt, and even to this day in Israel and among mankind, and made Yourself a Name, as to this day.

You brought your people Israel out of the land of Egypt with signs and wonders, with a strong hand and an outstretched arm, and with great terror. You gave them this land, which you swore to their fathers to give them, a land flowing with milk and honey. They came in and possessed it.

But they did not obey your voice nor walk in your *Torah*. They have done nothing of all you commanded them to do. Therefore you caused all this evil to fall on them. Look, the siege ramps have just come up to the city to take it. The city has been handed over to the Chaldeans fighting against it, because of the sword, the famine and the pestilence. What You have spoken has happened. Here it is, You see it.

Yet You said to me, my Lord *Adonai*: 'Buy for yourself the field for money and call in witnesses'—even as the city is handed over to the Chaldeans."

Then came the word of *Adonai* to Jeremiah, saying: "Behold, I am *Adonai*, the God of all flesh; is there anything too hard for Me?"

Therefore thus says *Adonai*: "I am about to give this city into the hand of the Chaldeans and Nebuchadnezzar king of Babylon, and he will take it. Then the Chaldeans fighting against this city will come and set this city on fire and burn it, with the houses—where they burned incense to Baal on their roofs and poured out drink-offerings to other gods, to provoke Me. For the children of Israel and the children of Judah have done nothing but evil in My sight from their youth; indeed, the children of Israel have done nothing but provoke Me with the work of their hands," declares *Adonai*.

"Indeed this city has caused My anger and of My fury from the day that they built it up to this day, so that I will remove it from before My face, because of all the evil the children of Israel and the children of Judah have done to provoke Me—they, their kings, their princes, their *kohanim*, their prophets, the men of Judah, and the inhabitants of Jerusalem.

"They have turned their back to Me and not their face. Though I taught them early and often, they have not listened to receive instruction. Instead they set up their abominations in the House where My Name is called, to defile it.

They built the high places of Baal in the Valley of Ben-Hinnom, to make their sons and their daughters pass through fire to Molech—something I never commanded them, nor did it enter My mind that they would do this loathsome thing, causing Judah to sin."

Now therefore thus says *ADONAI*, the God of Israel, concerning this city, about which you say, "It is handed over to the king of Babylon by the sword, famine, and pestilence.

"See, I will gather them out of all the countries, where I have driven them in My anger, My fury, and great wrath, and I will bring them back to this place and cause them to dwell securely.

They will be My people, and I will be their God. I will give them one heart and one way, so they may fear Me forever; for their good and for their children after them.

I will make an everlasting covenant with them: I will never turn away from doing good for them. I will put My fear in their hearts, so that they will not depart from Me.

"Yes, I will delight in doing good for them, and with all My heart and all My soul I will in truth plant them in this land."

For thus says *ADONAI*: "Just as I have brought all this great evil on this people, so I will bring on them all the good that I have promised them. So fields will be bought in this land, about which you are saying: 'It will be a desolation, without man or beast; it is handed over to the Chaldeans.' Men will buy fields for money and sign and seal the deeds and call witnesses in the land of Benjamin and in the areas around Jerusalem, and in the towns of Judah, in the towns of the hill-country, in the towns of the foothills, and in the cities of the South—because I will bring them back from exile."
It is a declaration of *ADONAI*.

Jeremiah, chapter 32

Then the word of *ADONAI* came to Jeremiah a second time, while he was still confined in the guard's courtyard, saying:
Thus says *ADONAI* the Maker, *ADONAI* who formed it to make it firm—*ADONAI* is His Name.

"Call to Me, and I will answer you—I will tell you great and hidden things, which you do not know."

For thus says *ADONAI*, the God of Israel: "Concerning the houses of this city and concerning the houses of the kings of Judah, which are torn down against the siege ramps and against the sword, they are coming to fight with the Chaldeans, but they are about to fill them with the dead bodies of the people whom I will slay in My anger and in My fury. I have hidden My face from this city because of all their wickedness.

"Indeed, I will bring it health and healing, and I will surely heal them. I will reveal to them an abundance of *shalom* and truth.

I will restore Judah from exile and Israel from exile, and will rebuild them, as in former times. I will also cleanse them from all their iniquity in which they have sinned against Me, and I will pardon all their wrongs in which they have sinned against Me and in which they have rebelled against Me.

"Then this city will be to Me for a name of joy, praise and glory before all the nations of the earth, which will hear all the good that I do for them, so they will fear and tremble because of all the good and for all the *shalom* that I do for it."

Thus says *ADONAI*: "Yet again in this place—which you are saying is a waste without man or beast, in the cities of Judah and in the streets of Jerusalem the desolate, without man, without inhabitant and without beast—there will be heard the voice of joy and the voice of gladness, the voice of the bridegroom and the voice of the bride, the voice of them who say:

'Give thanks to *ADONAI-Tzva'ot*,
for *ADONAI* is good,
for His love endures forever!'

as they bring offerings of thanksgiving into the House of *ADONAI*. For I will restore the land from the exile as it was at first," declares *ADONAI*.

Thus says *ADONAI-Tzva'ot*: "Yet again will there be in this place, which is waste, without man and without beast, and in all its cities, a pasture of shepherds making their flocks lie down. In the towns of the hill country, in the towns of the foothills, in the towns of the South, in the land of Benjamin, in the places around Jerusalem and in the towns of Judah, will the flocks again pass under the hands of one who counts them," declares *ADONAI*.

"Behold, days are coming"
—it is a declaration of *ADONAI*—
"when I will fulfill the good word I spoke concerning the house of Israel and concerning the house of Judah.

In those days and at that time,
I will cause a Branch of Righteousness to spring up for David, and He will execute justice and righteousness in the land. In those days will Judah be saved, and Jerusalem will dwell safely.

And this is the Name by which He will be called: *ADONAI* our Righteousness."

For thus says *ADONAI*: "For David, there will not be cut off a man sitting on the throne of the house of Israel, nor will the Levitical *kohanim* ever lack a man before Me to offer burnt offering, to burn grain offerings and to make sacrifices continually."

And the word of *ADONAI* came to Jeremiah, saying, thus says *ADONAI*:

"If you can break My covenant with the day and My covenant with the night, so that day and night would not be at in their appointed time, only then may My covenant be broken with My servant David, that he would not have a son to reign on his throne, and the Levitical *kohanim* would not be My ministers. As the host of heaven cannot be numbered, nor the sand of the sea measured, so I will multiply the offspring of David My servant, and the Levites who minister to Me."

The word of *ADONAI* came to Jeremiah, saying:
"Have you not noticed what this people have spoken, saying: 'The two families which *ADONAI* did choose, He has rejected them'? Thus they despise My people—no longer a nation before them."

Thus says *ADONAI*: "If I have not made My covenant of day and night firm, and the fixed patterns ordering the heavens and earth, only then would I reject the offspring of Jacob, and of My servant David so that I would not take from his offspring rulers over the offspring of Abraham, Isaac, and Jacob. For I will restore them from their exile, and have compassion on them."

Jeremiah, chapter 33

"In those days and at that time"
—it is a declaration of *ADONAI*—
"the children of Israel will come,
together with the children of Judah,
weeping as they come,
and will seek *ADONAI* their God.
They will ask about Zion, the way—
here are their faces! Come!
They will join themselves to *ADONAI*
in an everlasting covenant
that will never be forgotten.

My people have been lost sheep.
Their shepherds led them astray.
Turning around in the mountains,
they went from mountain to hill,
and forgot their resting place.

Everyone finding them devoured them. Their foes said: 'We're not guilty!' Instead, they sinned against *ADONAI*, the habitation of justice—*ADONAI*, the hope of their fathers."

Jeremiah 50:4-7

47. God Revives His Own

In the thirtieth year on the fifth day of the fourth month, as I was among the exiles by the river Chebar, the heavens opened, and I saw visions of God. In the fifth day of the month, which was the fifth year of King Jehoiachin's captivity, the word of *ADONAI* came to Ezekiel the *kohen*, son of Buzi, in the land of the Chaldeans by the river Chebar. (The hand of *ADONAI* was upon him there.)

Ezekiel 1:1-3

Therefore say, thus says *ADONAI Elohim*, "I will gather you from the peoples and collect you out of the countries where you have been scattered, and I will give you the land of Israel. When they come there, they will remove all of its detestable things and all of its abominations.

Then I will give them one heart. I will put a new Spirit within them. I will remove the heart of stone from their flesh and give them a heart of flesh, so that they may follow My laws, keep My ordinances and practice them. They will be My people and I will be their God.

As for those whose heart walks after the heart of their detestable things and abominations, I will bring their ways upon their heads."

It is a declaration of *ADONAI Elohim*.

Ezekiel 11:17-21

The word of *ADONAI* came to me saying: "What do you mean by using this proverb in the land of Israel saying, 'The fathers have eaten sour grapes, so the children's teeth are set on edge?'

"As I live"—it is a declaration of *ADONAI*—"you will never again use this proverb in Israel. Behold, every living soul is Mine—the soul of father as well as the soul of son—both are Mine. Behold, the soul who sins is the one who will die.

"Suppose a man is just and does what is lawful and right: He has not eaten at mountain shrines or lifted up his eyes to the idols of the house of Israel. He has not defiled his neighbor's wife or come near to a woman during *niddah*. He does not wrong anyone, returns his pledge for a debt, does not commit robbery, gives his bread to the hungry and covers the naked with a garment. He does not loan with interest or take unjust gain. He keeps his hand from iniquity, executes true justice between people, walks in My laws and keeps My statutes, behaving honestly. Such a person is just—he will surely live."

It is a declaration of *ADONAI*.
"Now suppose he fathers a son who is violent, who sheds blood and does any of these things to a brother (though the father himself does none of these things). He has even eaten at mountain shrines, defiled his neighbor's wife, wronged the poor and needy, taken by robbery, not restored the pledge, lifted up his eyes to the idols, committed abomination, loaned with interest and taken unjust gain. Will he then live? He will not live! He has done all these detestable

things. He will surely be put to death and his blood will be on him.

"Now behold, suppose he fathers a son who sees all his father's sins that he committed, and observing, does not do likewise. He does not eat at mountain shrines, or lift up his eyes to the idols of the house of Israel, or defile his neighbor's wife, nor does he wrong anyone, take pledged property or commit robbery, but he gives his bread to the hungry and covers the naked with a garment, withholds his hand from mistreating the poor, does not take interest or increase, practices My laws and walks in My statutes—he will not die for the iniquity of his father, he will surely live.

"As for his father, because he cruelly oppressed, committed robbery from his brother and did what is not good among his people—behold, he will die for his iniquity.

Yet you say, 'Why does the son not bear the iniquity of the father with him?' When the son has done what is lawful and right, has kept all My statutes and has done them, he will surely live. The soul that sins, he will die. The son will not bear the iniquity of the father with him, nor will the father bear the iniquity of the son with him.

The righteousness of the righteous will be on him and the wickedness of the wicked will be on him.

But if the wicked turns from all his sins that he has committed, and keeps all My laws and does what is lawful and right, he will surely live, he will not die. None of his transgressions that he committed will be remembered; because of his righteousness that he practiced, he will live.

"Do I delight at all in the death of the wicked?"

It is a declaration of *ADONAI*.

"Rather, should he not return from his ways, and live? But when the righteous turns away from his righteousness, and commits iniquity and does according to all the detestable acts that the wicked man does, will he live? None of his righteous deeds that he has done will be remembered; for his trespass that he trespassed and for his sin that he has sinned, for them he will die.

"Yet you say, '*ADONAI*'s way is unfair!' Hear now, house of Israel! Is My way not fair? Is it not your ways that are unfair?

When the righteous man turns away from his righteousness and commits iniquity, he will die for it; because of his iniquity that he did, he will die.

But when the wicked man turns away from his wickedness that he committed and does what is lawful and right, his soul will live. Because he considers and turns away from all his transgressions that he committed, he will surely live, not die.

Yet the house of Israel says, 'The way of *ADONAI* is unfair!' House of Israel, are My ways not fair? Is it not your ways that are unfair?
"Therefore I will judge you, house of

Israel, each one according to his ways."

It is a declaration of *ADONAI*.

"Return, and turn away from all your transgressions, so they would not be a stumbling block of iniquity for you. Cast off from you all your transgressions that you have committed. Make yourselves a new heart and a new spirit. Why will you die, house of Israel? For I have no pleasure in the death of anyone who dies"—it is a declaration of *ADONAI*—"so return, and live!"

Ezekiel, chapter 18

The word of *ADONAI* came to me saying: "Son of man, prophesy against the shepherds of Israel. Prophesy and say to those shepherds, thus says *ADONAI Elohim*: "Oy, shepherds of Israel who only take care of themselves! Should shepherds not take care of the sheep? You eat the fat. You clothe yourself with the wool. You kill the fat ones. But you do not take care of the sheep. You do not strengthen the weak, heal the sick, bind up the broken, bring back the stray or seek the lost. Instead, you have ruled over them with force and cruelty.

They were scattered for lack of a shepherd. They became food for all the beasts of the field as they were scattered. My sheep wandered through all the mountains and on every high hill. Over all the face of the earth My sheep were scattered. No one searched. No one sought."

Therefore, shepherds, hear the word of *ADONAI*: "As I live"—it is a declaration of *ADONAI*—"as surely as My sheep became prey and My sheep became food for all the beasts of the field, because there was no shepherd, nor did My shepherds search for My flock, but the shepherds fed themselves and did not feed My sheep," therefore, you shepherds, hear the word of *ADONAI*, thus says *ADONAI Elohim*:

"Behold, I am against the shepherds and I will demand My flock from their hand. I will dismiss them from tending the flock. The shepherds will no longer feed themselves. I will rescue My sheep from their mouth, so they will not be food for them."

For thus says *ADONAI Elohim*:
"Here I am! I Myself will search for My sheep and seek them out. As a shepherd seeks out his sheep on the day he is among his scattered flock, so I will seek out My sheep.

I will rescue them out of all the places where they have been scattered, on a day of cloud and thick darkness. I will bring them out from the peoples. I will gather them from the countries. I will bring them back to their own land. I will shepherd them upon the mountains of Israel, by the streams and in all the habitable places of the land.

I will shepherd them in a good pasture—their grazing place will be on the high mountains of Israel. There they will lie down on good grazing ground. They will feed in a rich pasture on the mountains of Israel. I will tend My flock and make them lie down"—it is a declaration of *ADONAI*.

"I will seek the lost, bring back the stray, bind up the broken and strengthen the sick. But the fat and the strong I will destroy—I will tend them with justice. As for you, My flock"—thus says *ADONAI Elohim*—"behold, I will judge between sheep and sheep, between rams and male goats. Was it too little for you that you were feeding in the good pasture? Must you trample down the rest of your pastures with your feet? You were drinking clear water. Must you muddy the rest with your feet? Yet My sheep must eat what you have trampled with your feet and drink what you have muddied with your feet!"

Therefore thus says *ADONAI Elohim* to them: "Behold, I Myself will judge between the fat sheep and the lean sheep. Because you thrust with your side and with shoulder and gore all the weak with your horns, until you have scattered them all over, I will save My flock. They will no longer be prey. I will judge between sheep and sheep. So I will set up One Shepherd over them, My servant David—He will tend them, He will feed them Himself and be their shepherd. I, *ADONAI*, will be their God, and My servant David will be Prince among them. I, *ADONAI*, have spoken.

"I will make a covenant of *shalom* with them. I will remove the evil beasts from the land, so they may dwell safely in the wilderness and sleep in the forest. I will make them and the places around My hill a blessing.

I will cause the rain to come down in its season. There will be showers of blessing. The tree of the field will yield its fruit. The ground will yield its produce. They will be secure in their land.

Then they will know that I am *ADONAI*, when I have broken the bars of their yoke and have delivered them from the hand of those who enslaved them. They will no longer be prey to the nations. The beast of the earth will not devour them. They will live in security. No one will make them afraid.

I will make their agriculture renowned. They will no longer be consumed with hunger in the land. They will no longer bear the scorn of the nations. They will know that I, *ADONAI* their God, am with them. They, the house of Israel, are My people."

It is a declaration of *ADONAI*.

"So you, My sheep, the sheep of My pasture, you are human, and I am your God."

It is a declaration of *ADONAI Elohim*.

Ezekiel, chapter 34

"You, son of man, prophesy to the mountains of Israel and say: 'Mountains of Israel, hear the word of *ADONAI*.

Thus says *ADONAI Elohim:* "The enemy has said against you, 'Aha! Even the ancient high places have become our possession!'

Therefore prophesy and say, thus says *ADONAI Elohim:* 'Because they ravaged and crushed you from every side, so that you became the possession of the rest of the nations and you became the talk and evil gossip of people,' therefore, mountains of Israel, hear the word of *Adonai*, thus says *Adonai Elohim* to the mountains, the hills, the streams and the valleys, the desolate wastes and the cities that are forsaken, which have become prey and derision to the rest of the surrounding nations.

Therefore thus says *Adonai Elohim:* 'Surely in the fire of My wrath I have spoken against the rest of the nations, and against all Edom, that have taken My land for themselves as a possession with the joy of all their heart and contempt in their souls, in order to seize it as plunder.'

Therefore, prophesy to the land of Israel and say to the mountains and the hills, the streams and the valleys, thus says *Adonai Elohim:* 'Behold, I have spoken in My wrath and in My fury, because you have suffered the scorn of the nations.' Therefore thus says *Adonai Elohim:* 'I have lifted My hand. Surely the nations that surround you will themselves suffer scorn.

"'But you, mountains of Israel, you will shoot forth your branches and yield your fruit for My people Israel; for their return is near. For behold, I am for you. I will turn to you. You will be tilled and sown. I will settle a large population upon you—the whole house of Israel, all of it. The cities will be inhabited. The desolate places will be built up.

I will multiply man and beast upon you. They will increase and be fruitful. I will cause you to be inhabited as you were before. I will do better for you than at your beginnings. You will know that I am *Adonai*. I will cause people, my people Israel, to walk upon you. They will possess you, and you will be their inheritance. You will no longer deprive them of children.'"

Thus says *Adonai Elohim:* "Because they say to you, 'You are a devourer of men and you deprive your nation of children,' therefore you will no longer devour men and you will no longer deprive your nation of children."

It is a declaration of *Adonai*.
"I will no longer let the scorn of the nations be heard against you. You will no longer bear disgrace from the peoples. You will no longer cause your nation to stumble."

It is a declaration of *Adonai*.

The word of *Adonai* came to me saying: "Son of man, when the house of Israel lived in their own land, they defiled it by their way and by their deeds. Their way before Me was like the uncleanness of a woman in her *niddah*. So I poured out My fury on them for the blood which they had shed upon the land and because they had defiled it with their idols. I scattered them among the nations, so they were dispersed through the countries. According to their way and their deeds I judged them.

Wherever they went among the nations, they profaned My holy Name, since it was said about them, 'These are the people of *Adonai*, yet they had to leave His land.' But I had concern for My holy Name, which the house of Israel had profaned among the nations wherever they went. "Therefore say to the house of Israel, thus says *ADONAI Elohim:* 'I do not do this for your sake, house of Israel, but for My holy Name, which you profaned among the nations wherever you went. I will sanctify My great Name, which has been profaned among the nations —which you have profaned among them.

The nations will know that I am *ADONAI*'"—it is a declaration of *ADONAI*—"'when I am sanctified in you before their eyes.'"

"'For I will take you from the nations, gather you out of all the countries and bring you back to your own land. Then I will sprinkle clean water on you and you will be clean from all your uncleanness and from all your idols. Moreover I will give you a new heart. I will put a new spirit within you. I will remove the stony heart from your flesh and give you a heart of flesh. I will put My *Ruach* within you. Then I will cause you to walk in My laws, so you will keep My rulings and do them. Then you will live in the land that I gave to your fathers. You will be My people and I will be your God.

"So I will save you from all your uncleanness. I will call for the grain and make it plentiful. I will not bring a famine upon you. I will multiply the fruit of the tree and the produce of the field, so that you will no longer bear the disgrace of famine among the nations. When you remember your evil ways and your deeds that were not good, you will be disgusted with yourselves because of your iniquities and your abominations. Not for your sake will I do this"—it is a declaration of *ADONAI*—"let that be known to you. Be ashamed and confounded for your ways, house of Israel!"

Thus says *ADONAI Elohim:* "In the day that I pronounce you clean from all your iniquities, I will cause the cities to be inhabited and the ruins will be rebuilt. The land that was desolate will be tilled instead of being a wasteland in the sight of all that passed by. They will say, 'This land that was a wasteland has become like the garden of Eden. The waste, desolate and ruined cities are fortified and inhabited.' Then the nations that are left all around you will know that I, *ADONAI*, have rebuilt the ruined places, and replanted what was desolate. I, *ADONAI*, have spoken it. So I will do it."

Thus says *ADONAI Elohim:* "I will again be inquired of by the house of Israel, to do it for them—I will populate them with people like a flock. Like the holy flock, like the flock of Jerusalem during her *moadim*, so the waste cities will be filled with flocks of people. Then they will know that I am *ADONAI*."

Ezekiel, chapter 36

The hand of *ADONAI* was upon me. The *Ruach ADONAI* carried me out and set me down in the middle of the valley. It was full of bones. He led me all around them. Behold, there were very many on the floor of the valley. Behold, they were very dry.

Then He said to me, "Prophesy to the *Ruach*. Prophesy, son of man, and say to the *Ruach*, thus says *Adonai Elohim*: 'Come from the four winds, *Ruach*! Breathe upon these slain, that they may live."
So I prophesied just as He commanded me. The *Ruach* came into them and they lived. They stood up on their feet, a vast army.

Ezekiel 37:9-10 TLV

Then He said to me, "Son of man, can these bones live?"

I answered, "*ADONAI Elohim*, You know."

"Prophesy over these bones," He said to me. "Say to them: 'Dry bones, hear the word of *ADONAI*!' Thus says *ADONAI Elohim* to these bones: "Behold, I will cause *Ruach* to enter you, so you will live. I will attach tendons to you, bring flesh on you and cover you with skin. Then I will put breath in you. You will live. You will know that I am *ADONAI*."

So I prophesied just as I was commanded. As I prophesied, there was a noise, and behold, an earthquake. Then the bones came together, bone to its bone. I saw, and behold, there were tendons on them, flesh came up and skin covered them above, but there was no breath in them.

Then He said to me, "Prophesy to the *Ruach*. Prophesy, son of man, and say to the *Ruach*, thus says *ADONAI Elohim*: 'Come from the four winds, *Ruach*! Breathe upon these slain, that they may live."

So I prophesied just as He commanded me. The *Ruach* came into them and they lived. They stood up on their feet, a vast army.

Then He said to me, "Son of man, these bones are the whole house of Israel. Behold, they say: 'Our bones are dried up; our hope is lost; we are cut off—by ourselves.' Therefore prophesy and say to them, thus says *ADONAI Elohim*: 'Behold, I will open your graves. I will bring you up out of your graves, My people. I will bring you back to the land of Israel. You will know that I am *ADONAI*, when I have opened your graves and brought you up out of your graves, My people. I will put My *Ruach* in you and you will live. I will place you in your own land. Then you will know that I, *ADONAI*, have spoken and that I have done it." It is a declaration of *ADONAI*.

The word of *ADONAI* came to me saying: "You, son of man, take one stick and write on it, 'For Judah'—for *Bnei-Yisrael* joined with him. Then take another stick and write on it, 'For Joseph'—the stick of Ephraim and all the house of Israel joined with him. Join them one to another for yourself, as one stick, so they may become one in your hand.

"When the children of your people speak to you saying, 'Won't you tell us what you mean by these?' say to them, thus says *ADONAI Elohim*: 'Behold, I will take the stick of Joseph—which is in the hand of Ephraim and the tribes of Israel joined with him—and I will put them together with the stick of Judah, and make them one stick. They will be one in My hand.' The sticks that you write on will be in your hand before their eyes.

"Then say to them, thus says *ADONAI Elohim*: 'Behold, I will take *Bnei-Yisrael* from among the nations, where they have gone. I will gather them from every side and bring them into their own land. I will make them one nation in the land, on the mountains of Israel, and one king will be king to them all. They will no longer be two nations and never again be divided into two kingdoms. They will never again be defiled with their idols, their detestable things or with any of their transgressions.

I will save them out of all their dwellings in which they sinned. I will purify them. Then they will be My people and I will be their God.

My servant David will be king over them. They will all have One Shepherd. They will walk in My ordinances and observe My rulings and do them.

They will live in the land that I gave to My servant Jacob, where your ancestors lived. They will live there—they, their children and their children's children, forever, and My servant David will be their prince forever.

I will cut a covenant of *shalom* with them—it will be an everlasting covenant with them. I will give to them and multiply them.

I will set up My Sanctuary among them forever. My dwelling-place will be over them. I will be their God and they will be My people.
Then the nations will know that I am *ADONAI* who sanctifies Israel, when My Sanctuary is in their midst forever.'"

Ezekiel, chapter 37

48. God Corrects Bad Behavior

Now the word of *ADONAI* came to Jonah, son of Amittai, saying: "Rise, go to the great city Nineveh and call out to her, for their evil has risen before me."

But Jonah rose to flee to Tarshish, from the presence of *ADONAI*. He went down to Jaffa and found a ship going to Tarshish, paid the fee and went down into it to go with them to Tarshish—away from the presence of *ADONAI*.

Then *ADONAI* hurled a forceful wind into the sea and there was such a mighty storm on the sea that the ship was about to shatter. So the sailors were afraid and cried out, each man to his own god. Then they cast the cargo that was in the ship into the sea to lighten it. But Jonah had gone down into the lowest part of the ship, to lay down and fell fast asleep.

So the chief sailor came near to him and said to him, "What, are you sleeping? Get up! Call out to your god. Perhaps the gods will consider us, so we will not perish!"

Then each man said to his companion, "Come, let's cast lots—so we may know because of whom this evil is happening to us." So they cast lots and the lot fell on Jonah.

Then they said to him, "Tell us, now! On whose account is this evil happening to us? What is your profession and where did you come from? What is your land and from what nation are you?"

He said to them, "I am a Hebrew and I fear *ADONAI* God of the heavens, who made the sea and the dry land."

Then the men became afraid with an overwhelming fear and they said to him, "What have you done?" For the men knew that he had fled from the presence of *ADONAI*, because he had told them. So they said to him, "What should we do to you so the sea will become calm for us?"—for the storm was raging on.

"Pick me up and throw me into the sea," he said to them, "then the sea will become calm for you. For I know it is because of me that this great storm is upon you."

Nevertheless the men rowed hard to return to the land, but they could not, because the sea kept raging against them. So they cried to *ADONAI* and said, "Please, *ADONAI*, don't let us perish on account of the soul of this man and don't put innocent blood on us. For you, *ADONAI*, have done as you pleased."

So they picked up Jonah and threw him into the sea—and the sea stilled from its raging. Then the men became afraid with an overwhelming fear of *ADONAI*, and they offered a sacrifice to *ADONAI* and made vows.

Jonah, chapter 1

Now *ADONAI* prepared a great fish to swallow Jonah, and Jonah was in the belly of the fish three days and three nights.

Then Jonah prayed to *ADONAI* his God from the belly of the fish, saying:

> "From my distress I cried to ADONAI
> and He answered me.
> From the belly of Sheol
> I cried for help
> and you heard my voice.
> For you hurled me from the deep
> into the heart of the seas,
> and currents swirled around me.
> All your waves and your breakers
> swept over me."
> And I said, "I have been banished
> from before your eyes.
> Yet I will continue to look
> toward your holy Temple."
> Waters surrounded me
> up to my soul.
> The deep sea engulfed me—
> reeds clung to my head.
> To the bottoms of the mountains
> I went down.
> The earth with her bars
> was around me, forever!
> Yet You brought my life
> up from the Pit,
> ADONAI my God.
> As my soul was fading from me,
> I remembered ADONAI
> and my prayer came to You,
> toward Your holy Temple.
> Those who watch
> worthless empty things
> forsake their mercy.
> But I, with a voice of thanks
> will sacrifice to you.
> What I vowed, I will pay.
> Salvation is from ADONAI."

Then *ADONAI* spoke to the fish and it vomited Jonah onto the dry land.

Jonah, chapter 2

Now the word of *ADONAI* came to Jonah a second time, saying, "Rise and go to Nineveh, the great city, and cry out to it the proclamation that I am telling you."

So Jonah rose and went to Nineveh according to the word of *ADONAI*.

Now Nineveh was a great city to God—the length of a three day journey. So Jonah began to come into the city for one day's journey, and he cried out saying: "Another forty days and Nineveh will be overthrown!"

Then the people of Nineveh believed God and called for a fast and wore sackcloth—from the greatest of them to the least of them. When the word reached the king of Nineveh, he rose from his throne, took off his robe, covered himself in sackcloth, and sat in the ashes.

He made a proclamation saying: "In Nineveh, by the decree of the king and his nobles, no man or beast, herd or flock, may taste anything. They must not graze nor drink water. But cover man and beast with sackcloth. Let them cry out to God with urgency. Let each one turn from his evil way and from the violence in his hands. Who knows? God may turn and relent, and turn back from his burning anger, so that we may not perish."

When God saw their deeds—that they turned from their wicked ways—God relented from the calamity that

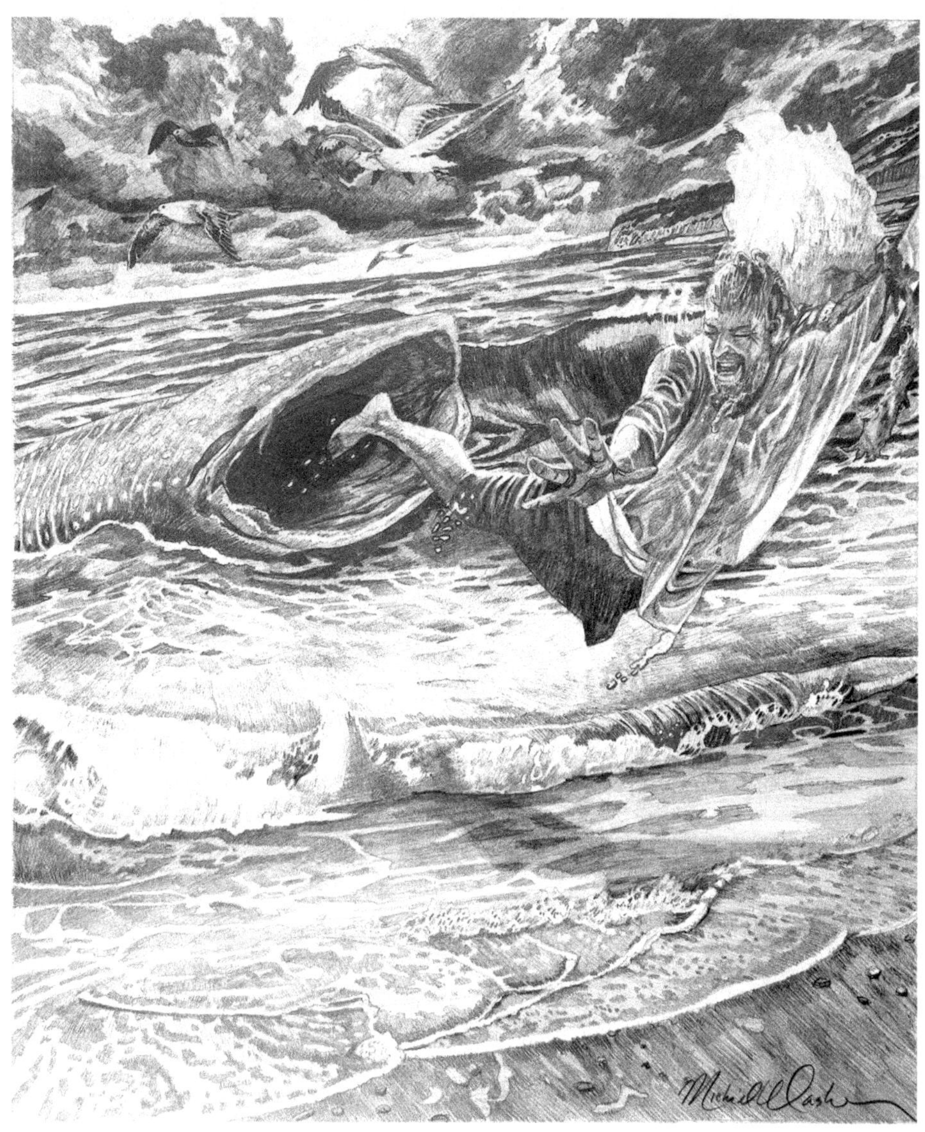

But I, with a voice of thanks will sacrifice to you. What I vowed, I will pay. Salvation is from *ADONAI*." Then *ADONAI* spoke to the fish and it vomited Jonah onto the dry land.

Jonah 2:10-11 TLV

He said He would do to them, and did not do it.

Jonah, chapter 3

But it greatly displeased Jonah and he resented it. So he prayed to *ADONAI* and said, "Please, Lord, was not this what I said when I was still in my own country? That's what I anticipated, fleeing to Tarshish—for I knew that you are a gracious and compassionate God, slow to anger and full of kindness, and relenting over calamity. So please, *ADONAI*, take my soul from me—because better is my death than my life."

Yet *ADONAI* said, "Is it good for you to be so angry?"

So Jonah went out from the city and sat east of the city. There He made a *sukkah* and he sat under it, in the shade, until he saw what would happen in the city. Then *ADONAI* God prepared a plant and it grew up over Jonah, to give shade over his head to spare him from his discomfort. So Jonah was very happy about the plant.

But God at dawn the next day prepared a worm that crippled the plant and it withered away. When the sun rose, God prepared a scorching east wind, and the sun beat down on Jonah's head so that he became faint. So he implored that his soul would die, saying, "My death would be better than my life!"

Then God said to Jonah, "Is it good for you to be so angry about the plant?"

"It is," he said, "I am angry enough to die!"

But *ADONAI* said, "You have pity on the plant for which you did no labor or make it grow, that appeared overnight and perished overnight. So shouldn't I have pity on Nineveh—the great city that has in it more than 120,000 people who don't know their right hand from their left—as well as many animals?"

Jonah, chapter 4

49. God Tabernacles - With Us!

In the eighth month, in the second year of Darius, the word of *ADONAI* came to the prophet Zechariah, son of Berechiah son of Iddo, saying:

"*ADONAI* has been furious with your fathers. Therefore tell them, thus says *ADONAI-Tzva'ot*, 'Return to Me'—it is a declaration of *ADONAI-Tzva'ot*—'and I will return to you,' says *ADONAI-Tzva'ot*. Do not be like your fathers to whom the former prophets cried out saying, thus says *ADONAI-Tzva'ot*, 'Turn back now from your evil ways and from your evil deeds.' But they did not listen or pay attention to Me.'

It is a declaration of *ADONAI*.

"Your fathers, where are they? And the prophets, do they live forever? But My words and My decrees, which I commanded My servants the prophets—did they not overtake your fathers? Then they repented and said 'As He determined, *ADONAI-Tzva'ot* has dealt with us according to our ways and our deeds.'"

Zechariah 1:1-6

I lifted up my eyes—and behold, I saw a man with a measuring line in his hand. I asked, 'Where are you going?'

He answered me, 'To measure Jerusalem to see how wide and how long it is.'

Then behold, the angel speaking with me left and another angel went out to meet him, saying to him, 'Run, speak to this young man saying: "Jerusalem will be inhabited as a village without walls because of the great number of men and livestock in it.

For I"—it is a declaration of *ADONAI*—"will be a wall of fire around it and I will be the glory inside it. *Oy, oy*! Flee from the land of the north"—it is a declaration of *ADONAI*—"because I scattered you like the four winds of heaven"—it is a declaration of *ADONAI*.

"*Oy*, Zion! Escape, you who are living with the daughter of Babylon."

"For thus says *ADONAI-Tzva'ot*, He has sent me after glory to the nations that plundered you—because whoever touches you touches the apple of His eye—'For behold, I will shake My hand against them and they will be plunder to their servants.' Then you will know that *ADONAI-Tzva'ot* has sent me.

"'Sing and rejoice, O daughter of *Zion*! For behold, I am coming and I will live among you'—it is a declaration of *ADONAI*.

'In that day many nations will join themselves to *ADONAI* and they will be My people and I will dwell among you.' Then you will know that *ADONAI-Tzva'ot* has sent me to you. *ADONAI* will inherit Judah as His portion in the holy land and will once again choose Jerusalem. Be silent before *ADONAI*, all flesh, for He has aroused Himself from His holy dwelling."

Zechariah 2:5-17

Then the angel who had been

speaking with me returned and woke me—like a man who is wakened from his sleep. He asked me, 'What do you see?'

I replied, 'Behold, I see a solid gold *menorah* with its bowl at the top of it, and its seven lamps on it with seven pipes for the lamps that are on the top of it. Also two olive trees are by it, one on the right side of the bowl and the other on the left side of it.'

Then I responded by saying to the angel speaking with me, 'What are these, my lord?'

The angel who spoke with me responded by asking me, 'You do not know what these are?'
I replied, 'No, my lord.'

Then he responded to me by saying, 'This is the word of *Adonai* to Zerubbabel saying: "Not by might, nor by power, but by My *Ruach*!" says *Adonai-Tzva'ot*.

"What are you, great mountain? Before Zerubbabel you will become a plain. He will bring out the capstone with shouts of "Grace, grace" to it.'"

Again the word of *Adonai* came to me saying: "The hands of Zerubbabel have laid the foundation of this House. His hands will also finish it. Then you will know that *Adonai-Tzva'ot* has sent me to you. For who despises the day of small things? These seven—which are the eyes of *Adonai* that run back and forth throughout the whole earth—will rejoice when they see the plumb line in Zerubbabel's hand."

Then I responded by asking him, "What are these two olive trees, on the right and on the left of the *menorah*?" Again I asked him, "What are these two olive branches beside the two golden pipes that empty the golden oil out of them?"

He said to me, "You do not know what these are?" I said, "No, my lord."

So he said, "These are the two anointed ones, who are standing by the Lord of the whole earth."

Zechariah, chapter 4

Then the word of *Adonai-Tzva'ot* came saying: "Thus says *Adonai-Tzva'ot*, "I am exceedingly zealous for *Zion*, I am burning with jealousy for her."

Thus says *Adonai*, "I will return to *Zion* and dwell in the midst of Jerusalem. Then Jerusalem will be called the City of Truth and the mountain of *Adonai-Tzva'ot* will be called the Holy Mountain."

Thus says *Adonai-Tzva'ot*, "Once again old men and old women will sit in the streets of Jerusalem, each with his staff in his hand because of his age. The streets of the city will be full of boys and girls playing in its streets."

"Thus says *Adonai-Tzva'ot*, 'It may seem difficult in the eyes of the remnant of this people in those days, but will it also be difficult in My eyes?'—it is a declaration of *Adonai-Tzva'ot*.

"Thus says *Adonai-Tzva'ot*, 'Behold, I

will save My people from the land of the east and from the land of the west. I will bring them back and they will live in the midst of Jerusalem. They will be My people and I will be their God, in truth and righteousness.'

"Thus says ADONAI-*Tzva'ot*, 'Let your hands be strong—you who hear these words spoken by the prophets who were there the day the foundation of the House of ADONAI-*Tzva'ot* was laid—so that the Temple may be rebuilt.

Before those days there were no wages for man or animal, nor was there any *shalom* from adversity for those who came or went because I set every one against his neighbor. But now I will not treat the remnant of this people as in the former days"—it is a declaration of ADONAI-*Tzva'ot*.

"For there will be a sowing of *shalom*: the vine will yield its fruit, the ground will produce its increase, and the heavens will give their dew. I will cause the remnant of this people to inherit all these things. It will happen that just as you were a curse among the nations, house of Judah and house of Israel, so will I save you and you will be a blessing. Fear not! Let your hands be strong!'

For thus says ADONAI-*Tzva'ot*, "Just as I determined to harm you when your fathers provoked Me to anger," says ADONAI-*Tzva'ot*, 'and I did not relent, so I have again determined in these days to do good to Jerusalem and to the house of Judah. Fear not! These are the things that you are to do: speak the truth one to another; administer the judgment of truth and *shalom* in your gates; do not let any of you devise evil in your hearts against your neighbor; and do not love false oaths, for I hate all these things,"—it is a declaration of ADONAI.

Again the word of ADONAI-*Tzva'ot* came saying: "Thus says ADONAI-*Tzva'ot*, "The fast of the fourth, the fast of the fifth, the fast of the seventh and the fast of the tenth month will become joy, gladness and cheerful *moadim*. Therefore, love truth and *shalom*!'

Thus says ADONAI-*Tzva'ot*, "Peoples and the inhabitants of many cities will again come. The inhabitants of one city will go to another saying 'Let us go to entreat the favor of ADONAI and to seek ADONAI-*Tzva'ot*. I also am going.' Indeed, many peoples and powerful nations will come to seek ADONAI-*Tzva'ot* in Jerusalem, and to entreat the favor of ADONAI."

Thus says ADONAI-*Tzva'ot*, "In those days it will come to pass that ten men from every language of the nations will grasp the corner of the garment of a Jew saying, 'Let us go with you, for we have heard that God is with you.'"

Zechariah, chapter 8

Rejoice greatly, daughter of *Zion*!
Shout, daughter of Jerusalem!
Behold, your king is coming to you,
a righteous one bringing salvation.
He is lowly, riding on a donkey
on a colt, the foal of a donkey.
I will banish chariots from Ephraim
and horses from Jerusalem,
and the war bow will be broken.

He will speak *shalom* to the nations.
His rule will extend from sea to sea,
from the River to the ends of the
earth.

As for you also,
by the blood of your covenant,
I will release your prisoners
from the waterless Pit.

Return to the stronghold,
you prisoners of hope!
Today I declare that I will restore
twice as much to you.
I will bend Judah as my bow
and fill it with Ephraim.
I will rouse your sons, O Zion
against your sons, O Greece.
I will wield you
like a warrior's sword.

Then *Adonai* will be seen over them
as His arrow flashes like lightning.

Adonai Elohim will blow the shofar
and march in whirlwinds
of the south. *Adonai-Tzva'ot* will
defend them. They will consume and
conquer with sling stones.

They will drink and roar as with wine
and be filled like a bowl,
like the corners of the altar.
Adonai their God will save them on
that day as the flock of His people.
They will be like gems of a crown
sparkling over His land.

How good and beautiful it will be!
Grain will make the young men thrive
and new wine the virgin women."
Zechariah 9:9-17

The burden of the word of *Adonai*
concerning Israel.

A declaration of *Adonai*, who stretched out the heavens, laid the foundation of the earth and formed the spirit of man within him: "Behold, I will make Jerusalem a cup of reeling to all the surrounding peoples when they besiege Jerusalem as well as Judah.

Moreover, in that day I will make Jerusalem a massive stone for all the people. All who try to lift it will be cut to pieces. Nevertheless, all the nations of the earth will be gathered together against her.

In that day"—it is a declaration of *Adonai*—"I will strike every horse with confusion and its rider with madness. I will keep My eyes on the house of Judah but will blind every horse of the peoples.

Then the leaders of Judah will say in their heart, 'The inhabitants of Jerusalem are my strength through *Adonai-Tzva'ot* their God."

"In that day I will make the leaders of Judah like a firepot in a woodpile, like a burning torch among sheaves. They will devour on the right and on the left all the surrounding peoples, yet Jerusalem will remain in her place, in Jerusalem.

Adonai also will save the tents of Judah first, so that the honor of the house of David and the honor of the inhabitants of Jerusalem will not exceed that of Judah.

In that day *Adonai* will defend the inhabitants of Jerusalem so that the weakest among them that day will be like David and the house of David will be like God—like the angel of *ADONAI* before them. It will happen in that day that I will seek to destroy all the nations that come against Jerusalem.

"Then I will pour out on the house of David and the inhabitants of Jerusalem a spirit of grace and supplication, when they will look toward Me whom they pierced. They will mourn for him as one mourns for an only son and grieve bitterly for him, as one grieves for a firstborn.

In that day there will be a great mourning in Jerusalem, mourning like Hadad-rimmon in the valley of Megiddo. The land will mourn clan by clan. The clan of the house of David by itself and their wives by themselves, the clan of the house of Nathan by itself, and their wives by themselves, the clan of the house of Levi by itself and their wives by themselves, the clan of the Shimeites by itself and their wives by themselves. Each of the remaining clans will mourn by itself and their wives by themselves."

Zechariah, chapter 12

Behold, a day of *ADONAI* is coming when your plunder will be divided in your midst. I will gather all the nations against Jerusalem to wage war. The city shall be captured, the houses ransacked and the women ravished. Half of the city will be exiled but the remainder of the people will not be cut off from the city.

Then *ADONAI* will go forth and fight against those nations as He fights in a day of battle.

In that day His feet will stand on the Mount of Olives which lies to the east of Jerusalem, and the Mount of Olives will be split in two from east to west, forming a huge valley. Half of the mountain will move toward the north and half of it toward the south.

Then you will flee through My mountain valley because the mountain valley will reach to Azel. Yes, you will flee like you fled from the earthquake in the days of King Uzziah of Judah. Then *ADONAI* my God will come and all the *kedoshim* with Him.

In that day there will be no light, cold or frost. It will be a day known only to *ADONAI*, neither day nor night—even in the evening time there will be light.

Moreover, in that day living waters will flow from Jerusalem, half toward the eastern sea and half toward the western sea, both in the summer and in the winter.

ADONAI will then be King over all the earth. In that day *ADONAI* will be *Echad* and His Name *Echad*.

The whole land, from Geba to Rimmon south of Jerusalem, will become like the Arabah. Jerusalem will be raised up and occupy her place, from the Benjamin Gate to the place of the First Gate, to the Corner Gate, and from the Tower of Hananel to the king's winepresses. People will dwell in her, and no longer will there be a ban of destruction—Jerusalem will live in security.
Now this is the plague with which

Then all the survivors from all the nations that attacked Jerusalem will go up from year to year to worship the King, *ADONAI-Tzva'ot*, and to celebrate *Sukkot*.

Zechariah 14:16 TLV

ADONAI will strike all the peoples that wage war against Jerusalem: their flesh will rot while they are standing on their feet; their eyes will rot in their sockets; and their tongues will rot in their mouths.

It will happen in that day that a great panic from *ADONAI* will be among them. Each person will seize the hand of his neighbor and they will attack each other. Even Judah will fight at Jerusalem. The wealth of all the surrounding peoples will be gathered together—an abundance of gold, silver and apparel.

A similar plague will strike the horse, the mule, the camel, the donkey and all the animals in that camp.

Then all the survivors from all the nations that attacked Jerusalem will go up from year to year to worship the King, *ADONAI-Tzva'ot*, and to celebrate *Sukkot*.

Furthermore, if any of the nations on earth do not go up to Jerusalem to worship the King, *ADONAI-Tzva'ot*, they will have no rain. If the Egyptians do not go up and celebrate, they will have no rain. Instead, there will be the plague that *ADONAI* will inflict on the nations that do not go up to celebrate *Sukkot*. This will be the punishment of Egypt and the punishment of all the nations that do not go up to celebrate *Sukkot*.
In that day "Holy to *ADONAI*" will be inscribed on the bells of the horses and the pots in House of *ADONAI* will be like the sacred bowls in front of the altar. In fact every pot in Jerusalem and in Judah will be Holy to *ADONAI-Tzva'ot*, so that everyone who comes to sacrifice will take them, and cook in them. In that day there will no longer be a Canaanite in the House of *ADONAI-Tzva'ot*.

Zechariah, chapter 14

50. God is Our LORD

Psalm 1

Happy is the one who has not walked in the advice of the wicked,
nor stood in the way of sinners,
nor sat in the seat of scoffers.
But his delight is in the *Torah* of *ADONAI*,
and on His *Torah* he meditates day and night.

He will be like a planted tree over streams of water,
producing its fruit during its season.
Its leaf never droops -
but in all he does, he succeeds.

The wicked are not so.
For they are like chaff that the wind blows away.
Therefore the wicked will not stand during the judgment,
nor sinners in the congregation of the righteous.

For *ADONAI* knows the way of the righteous,
but the way of the wicked leads to ruin.

Psalm 2

Why are the nations in an uproar,
and the peoples mutter vanity?
The kings of earth set themselves up
and rulers conspire together against ADONAI
and against His Anointed One:
"Let's rip their chains apart,
and throw their ropes off us!"
He who sits in heaven laughs!
ADONAI mocks them.
So He will speak to them in His anger,
and terrify them in His fury:
"I have set up My king
upon Zion, My holy mountain."

I will declare the decree of *ADONAI*.
He said to me: "You are My Son—
today I have become Your Father.
Ask Me, and I will give the nations as Your inheritance,
and the far reaches of the earth as Your possession.
You shall break the nations with an iron scepter.
You shall dash them in pieces like a potter's jar."
So now, O kings, be wise,

But his delight is in the *Torah* of *ADONAI*, and on His *Torah* he meditates day and night. He will be like a planted tree over streams of water, producing its fruit during its season. Its leaf never droops—
but in all he does, he succeeds.

Psalm 1:2-3 TLV

take warning, O judges of the earth!
Serve *ADONAI* with fear,
and rejoice with trembling.
Kiss the Son, lest He become angry,
and you perish along your way—
since His wrath may flare up suddenly.
Happy is everyone taking refuge in Him!

Psalm 4

For the music director, on stringed instruments, a psalm of David.

Answer me when I call,
God of my righteousness!
You set me free when I am in distress.
Be gracious to me and hear my prayer.
O sons of men, how long will you turn my glory into my shame?
How long will you love worthlessness and pursue falsehood? *Selah*
But know that *ADONAI* has set apart the godly for His own.
ADONAI will hear when I call to Him.
Tremble, but do not sin!
Search your heart while on your bed, and be silent. *Selah*
Offer righteous sacrifices
and put your trust in *ADONAI*.

Many are asking, "Who will show us some good?"
May the light of Your face shine upon us, *ADONAI*!
You have put joy in my heart—
more joy than when their grain and new wine overflow.
I will lie down and sleep in shalom.
For You alone, *ADONAI*, make me live securely.

Psalm 8

For the music director, upon the Gittite lyre: a psalm of David.

ADONAI our LORD, how excellent is Your Name over all the earth!
You set Your splendor above the heavens.
Out of the mouths of babies and toddlers
You established power, because of Your enemies,
to silence the foe and the avenger.
When I consider Your heavens, the work of Your fingers,
the moon and the stars, which You established—
what is man, that You are mindful of him?
And the son of man, that You care for him?
Yet You made him a little lower than the angels,

and crowned him with glory and majesty!
You gave him dominion over the works of Your hands.
You put all things under their feet: all sheep and oxen,
and also beasts of the field, birds in the air, and fish in the ocean—
all passing through the paths of the seas.
ADONAI our LORD, how excellent is Your Name over all the earth!

Psalm 14

For the music director, of David.

The fool said in his heart:
"There is no God."
They are corrupt; their deeds are vile;
there is no one who does good.
ADONAI looked down from heaven on the children of men,
to see if there are any who understand,
who seek after God.
They all turned aside, became corrupt.
There is no one who does good
—not even one.
"Will evildoers never understand—
those who consume My people as they eat bread—
and never call on *ADONAI*?"
There they are, in great dread.
For God is with the righteous generation.
You would frustrate the plan of the lowly.
Surely *ADONAI* is his refuge!
O may He give Israel's salvation out of Zion!
When *ADONAI* restores His captive people,
Jacob will rejoice, Israel will be glad!

Psalm 15

A psalm of David.

ADONAI, who may dwell in Your tent?
Who may live on Your holy mountain?
The one who walks with integrity,
who does what is right,
and speaks truth in his heart,
who does not slander with his tongue,
does not wrong his neighbor,
and does not disgrace his friend,
who despises a vile person in his eyes,
but honors those who fear *ADONAI*,

who keeps his oath even when it hurts,
and does not change,
who lends his money without usury,
and takes no bribe against the innocent.
One who does these things will never be shaken.

Psalm 16

A Michtam of David.

Keep me safe, O God, for in You I have found shelter.

I said to *Adonai*: "You are my Lord—
I have no good apart from You."

As for the *kedoshim* who are in the land,
they are noble—in them is all my delight.
As for those who run after another god,
may their sorrows multiply.
I will not pour out their drink offerings of blood,
nor lift up their names with my lips.
Adonai is my portion and my cup.
You cast my lot.
My boundary lines fall in pleasant places
—surely my heritage is beautiful.

I will bless *Adonai*, who counsels me.
Even at night my heart instructs me.
I have set *Adonai* always before me.
Since He is at my right hand, I will not be shaken.
So my heart is glad and my soul rejoices.
My body also rests secure.

For You will not abandon my soul to *Sheol*
nor let Your faithful one see the Pit.
You make known to me the path of life.

Abundance of joys are in Your presence,
eternal pleasures at Your right hand.

51. God is Our Rock

Psalm 18

For the music director: a psalm of David the servant of *ADONAI*. He chanted the words of this song to *ADONAI* on the day *ADONAI* delivered him from the hand of all his enemies, and from the hand of Saul.

He said, I love You, *ADONAI* my strength!
ADONAI is my rock, my fortress and my deliverer.
My God is my rock, in Him I take refuge,
my shield, my horn of salvation, my stronghold.
I called upon *ADONAI*, worthy of praise,
and I was rescued from my enemies.
Cords of death entangled me.
Torrents of Belial overwhelmed me.
Cords of *Sheol* coiled around me.
Snares of death came before me.
In my distress I called on *ADONAI*,
and cried to my God for help.
From His Temple He heard my voice,
my cry before Him came into His ears.
Then the earth rocked and quaked.
The foundations of mountains trembled.
They reeled because He was angry.
Smoke rose from His nostrils
and consuming fire from His mouth.
Coals blazed from Him.
He parted the heavens and came down,
with thick darkness under His feet.
He rode upon a *cheruv* and flew.
He soared on the wings of the wind.
He made darkness His cover,
His *sukkah* all around Him—
dark waters, thick clouds.
Out of the brilliance before Him
passed His thick clouds, hail and fiery coals.
ADONAI also thundered in the heavens,
and *Elyon* gave forth His voice, hail and fiery coals.
He shot His arrows and scattered them,
hurled lightning bolts and routed them.
Then ravines of water appeared.
The foundations of earth were exposed,
at Your rebuke, *ADONAI*,
at a blast of breath from Your nostrils.
He reached down from on high

and took hold of me.
He drew me out of mighty waters.
He saved me from my powerful enemy,
from those who hated me—
for they were much stronger than me.
They came against me in my day of calamity,
but *Adonai* was my support.
He brought me out to a wide-open place.
He rescued me since He delighted in me.
Adonai rewarded me for my righteousness.
For the cleanness of my hands He repaid me.
For I kept the ways of *Adonai*,
and did not turn wickedly from my God.
For all His judgments are before me.
I do not put His rulings away from me.
I also had integrity with Him,
and kept myself from my sin.
So *Adonai* rewarded me for my righteousness,
for the cleanness of my hands in His eyes.

With the loyal You deal loyally.
With the blameless You are blameless.
With the pure You are pure,
and with the crooked You are shrewd.
For You save lowly people,
but haughty eyes You humble.

For You light up my lamp.
Adonai my God shines in my darkness.
For with You I rush on a troop,
with my God I scale a wall.

As for God, His way is perfect.
The word of *Adonai* is pure.
He is a shield to all who take refuge in Him.
For who is God, except *Adonai*?
And who is a Rock, except our God?
God girds me with strength
and makes my way straight.
He makes my feet like those of deer
and makes me stand on my heights.
He trains my hands for battle,
so my arms can bend a bronze bow.
You gave me the shield of Your salvation.
Your right hand upholds me,
Your gentleness makes me great.

God girds me with strength and makes my way straight.
He makes my feet like those of deer and makes me stand on my heights.
He trains my hands for battle, so my arms can bend a bronze bow.
You gave me the shield of Your salvation.
Your right hand upholds me, Your gentleness makes me great.

Psalm 18:33-36 TLV

You broaden my steps beneath me,
so my ankles have not slipped.
I pursue my enemies and overtake them,
and will not return till they are wiped out.
I will crush them till they cannot rise,
till they fall beneath my feet.
For You girded me with strength for battle.
You made those who rose up against me bow down before me.
You also made my enemies turn their backs to me.
I cut off those who hate me.
They cry out, but there is none to save
—even to *ADONAI*, but He did not answer them.
Then I beat them as fine as dust before the wind.
I pour them out like mud in the streets.
You free me from strifes of the people.
You set me as head of the nations—
people I did not know are serving me.
As soon as they hear, they obey me.
Children of foreigners cringe before me.
Children of foreigners lose heart
and come trembling from their hideouts.
ADONAI lives! And blessed be my Rock!
Exalted be God my salvation!
God—He gives me vengeance
and subdues peoples under me.
He delivers me from my enemies.
Indeed You lift me up above those who rise up against me.
You deliver me from the violent man.
Therefore I praise You among the nations,
ADONAI, and sing praises to Your Name.
Great victories He gives to His king.
He shows loyal love to His anointed—
to David and his seed, forever.

Psalm 19

For the music director, a psalm of David.

The heavens declare the glory of God,
and the sky shows His handiwork.
Day to day they speak,
night to night they reveal knowledge.
There is no speech, no words,
where their voice goes unheard.
Their voice has gone out to all the earth
and their words to the end of the world.

In the heavens He pitched a tent for the sun.
It is like a bridegroom coming out of his bridal chamber.
It is like a strong man rejoicing to run his course.
It rises at one end of the heavens
and makes its circuit to the other end.
Nothing is hidden from its heat.

The *Torah* of *Adonai* is perfect, restoring the soul.
The testimony of *Adonai* is trustworthy, making the simple wise.
The precepts of *Adonai* are right, giving joy to the heart.
The *mitzvot* of *Adonai* are pure, giving light to the eyes.
The fear of *Adonai* is clean, enduring forever.
The judgments of *Adonai* are true and altogether righteous.

They are more desirable than gold,
yes, more than much pure gold!
They are sweeter than honey
and drippings of the honeycomb.
Moreover by them Your servant is warned.
In keeping them there is great reward.
Who can discern his errors?
Cleanse me of hidden faults.
Also keep Your servant from willful sins.
May they not have dominion over me.
Then I will be blameless,
free from great transgression.

May the words of my mouth
and the meditation of my heart
be acceptable before You,
Adonai, my Rock and my Redeemer.

Psalm 20

For the music director, a psalm of David.

May *ADONAI* answer you in the day of trouble!
May the Name of the God of Jacob set you up securely on high.
May He send you help from the Sanctuary
and support you from Zion.
May He remember all your meal offerings
and accept the fat of your burnt offering.
Selah

May He grant you your heart's desire
and fulfill all your plans.
We will shout for joy in your victory
and lift up our banners in the Name of our God!
May *ADONAI* fulfill all your petitions.
Now I know that *ADONAI* saves His anointed.
He answers him from His holy heaven
with saving strength of His right hand.
Some have chariots, some have horses,
but we remember the Name of *ADONAI* our God.
They have collapsed and fallen,
but we rise up and support each other.
ADONAI, save the king!
Answer us on the day we call!

52. God is Our Shepherd

Psalm 23

ADONAI is my shepherd,
I shall not want.
He makes me lie down in green pastures.
He leads me beside still waters.
He restores my soul.

He guides me in paths of righteousness for His Name's sake.
Even though I walk through the valley of the shadow of death,
I will fear no evil, for You are with me:
Your rod and Your staff comfort me.

You prepare a table before me in the presence of my enemies.
You have anointed my head with oil, my cup overflows.
Surely goodness and mercy will follow me all the days of my life,
and I will dwell in the House of *ADONAI* forever.

Psalm 25

Of David.

To You, *ADONAI*, I lift up my soul.
O my God, in You I trust, so I will not be ashamed,
and my enemies will not gloat over me.
Surely no one who waits for You will be ashamed.
But the treacherous without cause will be ashamed.

Show me Your ways, *ADONAI*.
Teach me Your paths.
Guide me in Your truth, and teach me,
for You are God, my salvation,
for You I wait all day.

Remember, *ADONAI*, Your compassions and Your mercies—
for they are from eternity.
Remember not the sins of my youth, nor my rebellion.
According to Your mercy remember me,
for the sake of Your goodness, *ADONAI*.

Good and upright is *ADONAI*.
Therefore He directs sinners in the way.
He guides the humble in what is right,
and teaches the humble His way.

A psalm of David. *Adonai* is my shepherd, I shall not want.
He makes me lie down in green pastures.
He leads me beside still waters. He restores my soul.
He guides me in paths of righteousness for His Name's sake.

Psalm 23:1-3 TLV

All *ADONAI*'s ways are lovingkindness and truth
to those who keep His covenant and His testimonies.
For Your Name's sake, *ADONAI*, pardon my guilt, for it is great.
Who is this man who fears *ADONAI*?
He will instruct him in the way he should choose.
His soul abides in goodness, and his offspring will inherit the land.
The secret of *ADONAI* is for those who fear Him.
He makes His covenant known to them.

My eyes are always looking to *ADONAI*,
for He will pull my feet out of the net.
Turn to me and be gracious to me, for I am lonely and afflicted.
The troubles of my heart increase.
Bring me out of my distress.
See my affliction and my suffering, and take away all my sins.
See my enemies, how many they are—
they hate me with violent hatred.
Guard my soul and deliver me.
Let me not be ashamed, for I take refuge in You.
May integrity and uprightness protect me—for I wait for You.
Redeem Israel, O God, from all their troubles.

Psalm 27

Of David.

ADONAI is my light and my salvation:
whom should I fear?
ADONAI is the stronghold of my life:
whom should I dread?
When evildoers approached me to devour my flesh
—my adversaries and my foes—they stumbled and fell.
Though an army camp besieges me, my heart will not fear.
Though war breaks out against me, even then will I be confident.

One thing have I asked of *ADONAI*, that will I seek:
to dwell in the House of *ADONAI* all the days of my life,
to behold the beauty of *ADONAI*,
and to meditate in His Temple.
For in the day of trouble He will hide me in His *sukkah*,
conceal me in the shelter of His tent,
and set me high upon a rock.
Then will my head be high above my enemies around me.
In His Tabernacle I will offer sacrifices with shouts of joy.
I will sing, yes, sing praises to *ADONAI*.
Hear, *ADONAI*, when I call with my voice, be gracious to me and answer me.
To You my heart says: "Seek My face."

Your face, *ADONAI*, I seek.
Do not hide Your face from me.
Do not turn Your servant away in anger.
You have been my help.
Do not abandon me or forsake me,
O God my salvation.
Though my father and my mother forsake me, *ADONAI* will take me in.
Teach me Your way, *ADONAI*, and lead me on a level path—
because of my enemies.
Do not turn me over to the desire of my foes.
For false witnesses rise up against me, breathing out violence.
Surely I trust that I will see the goodness of *ADONAI* in the land of the living.
Wait for *ADONAI*.
Be strong, let Your heart take courage,
and wait for *ADONAI*.

Psalm 32

Of David, a contemplative song.

Blessed is the one whose transgression is forgiven,
whose sin is pardoned.
Blessed is the one whose guilt *ADONAI* does not count,
and in whose spirit there is no deceit.
When I kept silent, my bones became brittle
through my groaning all day long.
For day and night Your hand was heavy upon me.
My strength was drained as in the droughts of summer.
Selah

Then I acknowledged my sin to You and did not hide my iniquity. I said:
"I confess my transgressions to *ADONAI*,"
and You forgave the guilt of my sin.
Selah

So let everyone who is godly pray to You
in a time when You may be found.
When great floodwaters rise, they will not reach him.
You are my hiding place—
You will protect me from distress.
You surround me with songs of deliverance.
Selah

"I will instruct you and teach you in the way you should go.
I will give counsel—My eye is on you.
Do not be like the horse or the mule, which have no understanding,
and must be held in with bit and bridle or they will not come to you."

Many are the sorrows of the wicked,
but lovingkindness surrounds the one who trusts in *ADONAI*.
Be glad in *ADONAI* and rejoice, you righteous,
and shout for joy, all who are upright in heart.

Psalm 43

Vindicate me, O God, and champion my cause against an ungodly nation.
From a deceitful and unjust man, deliver me!
For You are my God, my stronghold.
Why have You spurned me?
Why do I go about gloomy because of the oppression of the enemy?
Send forth Your light and Your truth
—let them guide me.
Let them bring me to Your holy mountain
and to Your dwelling places.
Then I will come to the altar of God, to the God of my exceeding joy,
and praise You upon the harp—O God, my God.
Why are You downcast, O my soul?
Why are you murmuring within me?
Hope in God, for I will yet praise Him,
the salvation of my countenance.

Psalm 47

For the music director, a psalm for the sons of Korah.

Clap your hands, all you peoples!
Shout to God with the voice of joy!
For *ADONAI Elyon* is awesome,
a great King over all the earth.
He subdues peoples under us,
and nations under our feet.
He chooses our inheritance for us,
the glory of Jacob whom He loved. *Selah*
God is gone up amidst shouting,
ADONAI amidst the sound of the *shofar*.
Sing praises to God, sing praises!
Sing praises to our King, sing praises!
For God is the King of all the earth.
Sing praises with a skillful song.
God reigns over the nations.
God sits upon His holy throne.
The princes of the peoples are gathered as a people of the God of Abraham.
For the shields of earth belong to God—
He is greatly exalted!

53. God is Our Strength

Psalm 48

A song, a psalm of the sons of Korah.

Great is *ADONAI*, and greatly to be praised
in the city of our God—His holy mountain.
A beautiful height—the joy of the whole earth—
is Mount Zion, on the northern side of the city of the great King.
God, in her palaces, is known as a stronghold.

For behold, the kings assembled, they advanced together.
They saw, then they were astounded, they fled in terror.
Trembling seized them there, pain like a woman in labor.
With an east wind You broke the ships of Tarshish.
As we have heard, so have we seen,
in the city of *ADONAI-Tzva'ot*,
in the city of our God.
God will establish her forever. *Selah*

We have meditated on Your lovingkindness, O God,
in the midst of Your Temple.
Like Your Name, O God,
so is Your praise to the ends of the earth.
Your right hand is full of righteousness.
Mount Zion is glad,
the daughters of Judah rejoice, because of Your judgments.
Walk about Zion, go around her.
Count her towers.
Consider her ramparts, go through her palaces,
so you may describe it to the next generation.

For this God is our God, forever and ever!
He will guide us to the end.

Psalm 51

For the music director: a psalm of David,
when Nathan the prophet came to him, after he went to Bathsheba.

Be gracious to me, O God, according to Your mercy.
According to Your great compassion blot out my transgressions.
Wash me thoroughly from my iniquity and cleanse me from my sin.
For I know my transgressions
and my sin is ever before me.

Mount Zion is glad, the daughters of Judah rejoice, because of Your judgments. Walk about Zion, go around her. Count her towers. Consider her ramparts, go through her palaces, so you may describe it to the next generation. For this God is our God, forever and ever!
He will guide us to the end.

Psalm 48:11-15 TLV

Against You, You only, have I sinned,
and done what is evil in Your sight,
so that You are just when You speak,
and blameless when You judge.
Behold, I was born in iniquity and in sin
when my mother conceived me.

Surely You desire truth in the inner being.
Make me know wisdom inwardly.
Cleanse me with hyssop and I will be clean.
Wash me, and I will be whiter than snow.
Let me hear joy and gladness,
so the bones You crushed may rejoice.
Hide Your face from my sins, and blot out all my iniquities.

Create in me a clean heart, O God,
and renew a steadfast spirit within me.
Do not cast me from Your presence—
take not Your *Ruach ha-Kodesh* from me.
Restore to me the joy of Your salvation
and sustain me with a willing spirit.
Then will I teach transgressors Your ways
and sinners will return to You.

Deliver me from bloodguilt, O God—God of my salvation.
Then my tongue will sing for joy of Your righteousness.
O Lord, open my lips, and my mouth will declare Your praise.
For You would not delight in sacrifice, or I would give it,
nor be pleased by burnt offerings.
The sacrifices of God are a broken spirit.
A broken and a contrite heart, O God, You will not despise.

In Your favor do good to Zion.
Build up the walls of Jerusalem.
Then You will delight in righteous sacrifices and whole burnt offerings.
Then bulls will be offered on Your altar.

Psalm 67

For the music director, with stringed instruments, a psalm, a song.

May God be gracious to us and bless us.
May He cause His face to shine upon us, *Selah*
so that Your way may be known on earth,
and Your salvation among all nations.

Let the peoples praise You, O God.

Let all the peoples praise You.
Let the nations be glad and sing for joy,
for You will judge the peoples fairly,
and guide the nations on the earth. *Selah*
Let the peoples praise You, O God.
Let all the peoples praise You.
The earth has yielded its harvest—
God, our God will bless us.
God will bless us, and all the ends of the earth will fear Him.

Psalm 68

For the music director, a psalm of David, a song.

Let God arise!
Let His enemies be scattered!
Let those who hate Him flee before Him.
As smoke is blown away, may You blow them away.
As wax melts before the fire, may the wicked perish before God.
But let the righteous be glad. Let them exult before God.
Let them rejoice with gladness.
Sing to God, sing praises to His Name.
Prepare the road for Him who rides through the deserts,
whose Name is *ADONAI*—and rejoice before Him.
A father of orphans, defender of widows, is God in His holy dwelling.
God settles the lonely in a home.
He leads prisoners out to prosperity.
But the rebellious live in a parched land.

O God, when You went out before Your people,
when You marched through the desert—*Selah*—
the earth shook, the heavens rained
at the presence of God—the One of Sinai—
at the presence of God, God of Israel.
You poured down abundant rain, O God.
You sustained Your weary inheritance.
Your community settled in it.
In Your goodness, O God, You provided for the poor.
The Lord gives the word—
a great company of women proclaims the good news.
"Kings of armies, flee, flee!"
She who stays at home divides the spoil.
When you lie among the campfires,
wings of a dove were covered with silver
and her feathers with shimmering gold.
When *Shaddai* scattered kings there, it was snowing on Zalmon.
Mount Bashan is a mountain of God.

Mount Bashan is a mountain of peaks.
Why do you gaze with envy, you mountain peaks,
at the mountain God desired for His dwelling?
Yes, *ADONAI* will dwell there forever!
The chariots of God are thousands and thousands
—my Lord is among them as at Sinai, in holiness.
You went up on high. You led captivity captive.
You received gifts from humanity, even from the rebellious—
so that God might dwell there.

Blessed be my Lord!
Day by day He bears our burdens—the God of our salvation! *Selah*
God is for us—a God of deliverance.
ADONAI my Lord has escapes from death.
Surely God crushes the head of His foes,
the hairy scalp of one walking in his guilt.
My Lord said: "I will bring them back from Bashan,
I will bring them back from the depths of the sea.
So your foot may wade in blood,
and your dogs' tongue may have their share of your enemies' blood."

They have seen Your processions, O God—
the processions of my God, my King, into the Sanctuary:
The singers go before, the musicians last,
between maidens beating tambourines.
"Bless God in the congregations—
ADONAI, from the fountain of Israel."
There Benjamin, the youngest, is leading them,
there the throng of Judah's princes,
there the princes of Zebulun, there the princes of Naphtali.
Your God commanded your strength.
Strengthen, O God, You who have acted for us.
From Your Temple above Jerusalem, kings bring You tribute.
Rebuke the beast of the reeds, the herd of bulls with the calves,
peoples trampling down pieces of silver.
He has scattered the peoples who delight in war!
Nobles come from Egypt. Cush runs to stretch her hands to God.

Sing to God, kingdoms of the earth, sing praises to the Lord—*Selah*—
to Him who rides upon the ancient heavens of heavens.
Look, He utters His voice, a mighty voice!
Ascribe strength to God—
His majesty is over Israel and His strength is in the skies.
O God, You are awesome from Your holy places.
The God of Israel gives strength and power to the people.
Blessed be God!

54. God is Our Blessing

Psalm 84

For the music director, upon the Gittite lyre, a psalm of the sons of Korah.

How lovely are Your tabernacles, *ADONAI-Tzva'ot*!
My soul yearns, even faints, for the courts of *ADONAI*.
My heart and my flesh sing for joy to the living God.
Even the sparrow has found a home,
and the swallow a nest for herself,
where she may lay her young
—near Your altars, *ADONAI-Tzva'ot*—
my King and my God!
Blessed are they who dwell in Your House
—they are ever praising You. *Selah*

Blessed is one whose strength is in You,
in whose heart are the pilgrim roads.
Passing through the valley of Baca, they make it a spring.
The early rain covers it with blessings.
They go from strength to strength—
every one of them appears before God in Zion.
ADONAI-Tzva'ot, hear my prayer,
give ear, O God of Jacob. *Selah*

O God, look at our shield,
and look upon the face of Your anointed.
For a day in Your courts is better than a thousand anywhere else.
I would rather stand at the threshold of the House of my God
than dwell in the tents of wickedness.

For *ADONAI Elohim* is a sun and a shield.
ADONAI gives grace and glory.
No good thing will He withhold from those who walk uprightly.
ADONAI-Tzva'ot, blessed is the one who trusts in You.

Psalm 90

A prayer of Moses the man of God.

My Lord, You have been our dwelling from generation to generation.
Before the mountains were born,
or You gave birth to the earth and the world,
even from everlasting to everlasting,

Even the sparrow has found a home, and the swallow a nest for herself,
where she may lay her young —near Your altars,
ADONAI-Tzva'ot— my King and my God!

Psalm 84:4 TLV

You are God!

You turn mankind back to dust, saying, "Return, children of Adam!"
For a thousand years in Your sight are like a day just passing by,
or like a watch in the night.
You sweep them away in their sleep.
In the morning they are like sprouting grass—
in the morning it flourishes and springs up,
by evening it withers and dries up.

For we are consumed by Your anger
and terrified by Your wrath.
You have set our iniquities before You,
our secret sins in the light of Your presence.
For all our days have passed away under Your wrath.
We spent our years like a sigh.
The span of our years is seventy
—or with strength, eighty—
yet at best they are trouble and sorrow.
For they are soon gone, and we fly away.
Who knows the power of Your anger?
Your fury leads to awe of you.

So teach us to number our days,
so that we may get a heart of wisdom.
Relent, *ADONAI*! How long?
Have compassion on Your servants.
Satisfy us in the morning with Your love,
so we may sing for joy and be glad all our days.
Gladden us for as many days as You have humbled us,
as many years as we have seen misery.
Let Your work appear to Your servants,
and Your splendor on their children.
Let the favor of the Lord our God be upon us.
Establish the work of our hands for us—
yes, establish the work of our hands.

Psalm 91

He who dwells in the shelter of *Elyon*,
will abide in the shadow of *Shaddai*.
I will say of *ADONAI*,
"He is my refuge and my fortress, my God, in whom I trust.
For He will rescue you from the hunter's trap and from the deadly pestilence.

He will cover you with His feathers, and under His wings you will find refuge.
His faithfulness is body armor and shield.
You will not fear the terror by night, nor the arrow that flies by day,
nor the plague that stalks in darkness,
nor the scourge that lays waste at noon.
A thousand may fall at your side,
and ten thousand at your right hand, but it will not come near you.
You will only look on with your eyes and see the wicked paid back.
For you have made *Elyon* your dwelling, even *ADONAI*,
who is my refuge, so no evil will befall you nor any plague come near your tent.
For He will give His angels charge over you, to guard you in all your ways.
Upon their hands they will lift you up, lest you strike your foot against a stone.
You will tread upon the lion and cobra, trample the young lion and serpent.

"Because he has devoted his love to Me, I will deliver him.
I will set him securely on high, because he knows My Name.
When he calls on Me, I will answer him.
I will be with him in trouble, rescue him, and honor him.
With long life will I satisfy him and show him My salvation."

Psalm 97

ADONAI reigns, let the earth rejoice,
let the many islands be glad.
Clouds and darkness are all around Him.
Righteousness and justice are the foundation of His throne.
Fire goes before Him and burns up His adversaries on every side.
His lightning lights up the world—the earth sees and trembles.
The mountains melt like wax at the presence of *ADONAI*,
at the presence of the Lord of all earth.
The heavens declare His righteousness,
and all the peoples have seen His glory.

Let all who serve graven images be ashamed—who boast in idols.
Bow down before Him, all you gods!
Zion hears and is glad, and the daughters of Judah rejoice,
because of Your judgments, *ADONAI*.
For You, *ADONAI*, are *Elyon* above all the earth.
You are exalted far above all gods.

You who love *ADONAI*, hate evil!
He watches over the souls of His godly ones.
He delivers them out of the hand of the wicked.
Light is sown for the righteous and gladness for the upright in heart.
Rejoice in *ADONAI*, you righteous ones,
and praise His holy Name.

Psalm 100

A psalm of thanksgiving.

Shout joyfully to *ADONAI*, all the earth!
Serve *ADONAI* with gladness.
Come before His presence with joyful singing.
Know that *ADONAI*, He is God.
It is He who has made us, and we are His.
We are His people, the sheep of His pasture.
Enter His gates with thanksgiving
and His courts with praise!
Praise Him, bless His Name.
For *ADONAI* is good.
His lovingkindness endures forever,
and His faithfulness to all generations.

Psalm 103

Of David.

Bless *ADONAI*, O my soul, and all that is within me, bless His holy Name.
Bless *ADONAI*, O my soul, and forget not all His benefits:
He forgives all your iniquity.
He heals all your diseases.
He redeems your life from the Pit.
He crowns you with lovingkindness and compassions.
He satisfies your years with good things,
so that your youth is renewed like an eagle.

ADONAI executes justice—judgments for all who are oppressed.
He made His ways known to Moses, His deeds to the children of Israel.
ADONAI is compassionate and gracious, slow to anger, and plentiful in mercy.
He will not always accuse, nor will He keep His anger forever.
He has not treated us according to our sins,
or repaid us according to our iniquities.
For as high as the heavens are above the earth,
so great is His mercy for those who fear Him.
As far as the east is from the west,
so far has He removed our transgressions from us.
As a father has compassion on his children,
so *ADONAI* has compassion on those who fear Him.
For He knows our frame. He remembers that we are but dust.
As for man, his days are like grass—he flourishes like a flower of the field,
but when the wind blows over it, it is gone, and its place is no longer known.
But the mercy of *ADONAI* is from everlasting to everlasting
on those who revere Him,

His righteousness to children's children, to those who keep His covenant,
who remember to observe His instructions.

Adonai has set up His throne in the heavens, and His kingdom rules over all.
Bless *Adonai*, you angels of His: mighty in strength, performing His word,
upon hearing the utterance of His word.
Bless *Adonai*, all you His armies, His servants who do His will.
Bless *Adonai*, all His works everywhere in His dominion.

Bless *Adonai*, O my soul!

Psalm 110

A psalm of David.

Adonai declares to my Lord:
"Sit at My right hand
until I make your enemies a footstool for Your feet."
Adonai will extend your mighty rod from Zion:
"Rule in the midst of your enemies."
Your people will be a freewill offering in a day of your power.
In holy splendors, from dawn's womb, yours is the dew of your youth.
Adonai has sworn, and will not change His mind:
"You are a *Kohen* forever according to the order of Melchizedek."
My Lord is at your right hand.
He will shatter kings in the day of His wrath.
He will judge among the nations, heaping up corpses.
He will crush heads over the entire land.
He will drink from a stream along the way
—so His head will be exalted.

Psalm 111

Halleluyah! I praise *Adonai* with all my heart
in the company and congregation of the upright.
Great are the works of *Adonai*—
searched out by all who delight in them.
Glorious and majestic is His work, and His righteousness endures forever.
He made His wonders memorable.
Adonai is gracious and full of compassion.
He gives food to those who fear Him.
He remembers His covenant forever.
He shows His people His powerful deeds, giving them the heritage of the nations.
The works of His hands are truth and justice.
All His precepts are trustworthy—
they are upheld forever and ever, made in truth and uprightness.
He has sent redemption to His people.

He has ordained His covenant forever.
Holy and awesome is His Name.

The fear of *ADONAI* is the beginning of wisdom.
All who follow His precepts have good understanding.
His praise endures forever!

Psalm 115

Not to us, *ADONAI*, not to us, but to Your Name be the glory—
because of Your love and Your faithfulness.
Why should the nations say: "Where is their God now?"
Our God is in the heavens—
He does whatever pleases Him!
Their idols are silver and gold, the work of human hands.
They have mouths, but cannot speak; eyes, but cannot see.
They have ears, but cannot hear; noses, but cannot smell.
They have hands, but cannot feel; feet, but cannot walk,
nor utter a sound with their throat.
Those making them will become like them—everyone trusting in them.

O Israel, trust in *ADONAI*— He is their help and their shield!
O house of Aaron, trust in *ADONAI*— He is their help and their shield!
O you who fear *ADONAI*, trust in *ADONAI*—He is their help and their shield!

ADONAI has been mindful of us, He will bless:
He will bless the house of Israel; He will bless the house of Aaron;
He will bless those who fear *ADONAI*, the small together with the great.
May *ADONAI* increase you more and more—you and your children.
May you be blessed by *ADONAI*, Maker of heaven and earth.

The heavens are the heavens of *ADONAI*,
but the earth He gave to the children of men.
The dead do not praise *ADONAI*, nor do any who go down into silence.
But we—we will bless *ADONAI* both now and forever.
Halleluyah!

Psalm 117

Praise *ADONAI*, all you nations!
Glorify Him, all you peoples.
For great is His lovingkindness toward us,
and *ADONAI*'s truth endures forever.
Halleluyah!

Do good to Your servant that I may live and keep Your word. Open my eyes, so I may behold wonders from Your *Torah.*

Psalm 119:17-18 TLV

55. God Works Wonders Through His Word

Psalm 119

ALEPH א

Blessed are those whose way is blameless,
who walk in the *Torah* of ADONAI.
Happy are those who keep His testimonies,
who seek Him with a whole heart,
who also do no injustice, but walk in His ways.
You have commanded that Your precepts be kept diligently.
Oh that my ways were steadfast to observe Your decrees!
Then I would not be ashamed,
when I consider all Your *mitzvot*.
I will praise You with an upright heart
as I learn Your righteous judgments.
I will observe Your statutes.
Never abandon me utterly!

BET ב

How can a young man keep his way pure?
By guarding it according to Your word.
With my whole heart have I sought You
—let me not stray from Your *mitzvot*.
I have treasured Your word in my heart,
so I might not sin against You.
Blessed are You, ADONAI.
Teach me Your statutes.
With my lips I rehearse all the rulings of Your mouth.
I rejoice in the way of Your testimonies above all wealth.
I will meditate on Your precepts, and regard Your ways.
I will delight in Your decrees.
I will never forget Your word.

GIMEL ג

Do good to Your servant
that I may live and keep Your word.
Open my eyes,
so I may behold wonders from Your *Torah*.
I am a temporary dweller on earth

—do not hide Your *mitzvot* from me.
My soul is crushed with longing for Your judgments at all times.
You rebuke the proud, who are cursed,
who wander from Your *mitzvot*.
Take scorn and contempt away from me,
for I have kept Your testimonies.
Though princes sit and talk against me,
Your servant meditates on Your decrees.
For Your testimonies are my delight—
they are also my counselors.

DALET ד

My soul clings to the dust.
Revive me according to Your word!
I told of my ways and You answered me.
Teach me Your statutes.
Help me discern the way of Your precepts,
so I may meditate on Your wonders.
My soul weeps with grief.
Make me stand firm with Your word.
Turn me away from the deceitful way,
and be gracious to me with Your *Torah*.
I have chosen the way of faithfulness.
I have set my heart on Your judgments.
I cling to Your testimonies.
Adonai, do not put me to shame!
I run the course of Your *mitzvot*,
for You open wide my heart.

HEY ה

Teach me the way of Your decrees, *Adonai*,
and I will follow them to the end.
Give me understanding,
that I may keep Your *Torah*
and observe it with all my heart.
Help me walk in the path of Your *mitzvot*—
for I delight in it.
Turn my heart to Your testimonies
and not to dishonest gain.
Turn my eyes away from gazing at vanity
but revive me in Your ways.
Fulfill Your word to Your servant,
which leads to reverence for You.

Make the disgrace I dread pass away,
for Your judgments are good.
Behold, I long for Your precepts.
Revive me by Your righteousness.

VAV ו

May Your lovingkindnesses come to me, *ADONAI*—
Your salvation according to Your word—
so I may answer the one taunting me,
for I trust in Your word.
Never snatch out of my mouth a word of truth,
for I hope in Your judgments.
So I may always keep Your *Torah*,
forever and ever,
and walk about in freedom.
For I have sought Your precepts.
I will speak of Your testimonies
before kings, and never be ashamed.
I delight in Your *mitzvot*,
which I love.
I reach out my hands for Your *mitzvot*,
which I love,
and meditate on Your decrees.

ZAYIN ז

Remember the word to Your servant,
on which You have made me hope.
My comfort in my affliction is this:
Your word has kept me alive.
The arrogant have viciously ridiculed me,
yet I did not turn away from Your *Torah*.
I remember Your judgments from of old, *ADONAI*,
and comfort myself.
Burning indignation grips me,
because of the wicked who forsake Your *Torah*.
Your decrees have become my songs in the house where I dwell.
In the night I remember Your Name, *ADONAI*,
and keep watching over Your *Torah*.
This is my own: that I keep Your precepts.

CHET ח

ADONAI is my portion.
I promised to guard Your words.

I have entreated Your favor with all my heart.
Be gracious to me according to Your word.
I have considered my ways
and turned my feet back to Your testimonies.
I hasten and do not delay to obey Your *mitzvot.*
The ropes of the wicked are coiled around me,
but I did not forget Your *Torah.*
At midnight I rise to praise You, because of Your righteous rulings.
I am a companion of all who fear You, of those who observe Your precepts.
The earth is full of Your lovingkindness.
Adonai—teach me Your decrees.

TET ט

You do good to Your servant, *Adonai,* according to Your word.
Teach me good sense and knowledge, for I trusted in Your *mitzvot.*
Before I was afflicted I went astray, but now I keep Your word.
You are good and keep doing good—teach me Your decrees.
Though the proud smeared a lie on me,
with all my heart I keep Your precepts.
Their minds are insensible, but Your *Torah* is my delight.
It is good for me that I was afflicted,
so that I may learn Your decrees.
The *Torah* from Your mouth is better to me
than thousands of gold and silver pieces.

YOD י

Your hands have made me and formed me.
Give me understanding that I may learn Your *mitzvot.*
Those in awe of You see me and rejoice,
because I put my hope in Your word.
I know, *Adonai,* Your judgments are just.
In faithfulness You have afflicted me.
May Your lovingkindness comfort me,
according to Your promise to Your servant.
Let Your tender mercies reach me,
Let me live, for Your *Torah* is my delight.
May the proud be put to shame
for wronging me with a lie,
but I will meditate on Your precepts.
Let those in awe of You return to me—
those who know Your testimonies.
My heart will have integrity in following Your decrees,
so that I would not be ashamed.

KAF כ

My soul faints with longing for Your salvation,
but I still hope in Your word.
My eyes are worn out longing for Your promise,
saying, "When will You comfort me?"
Though I became like a wineskin dried in smoke,
I do not forget Your decrees.
How many are the days of Your servant?
When will You execute judgment on my persecutors?
The proud have dug pits for me—
that is not in accord with Your *Torah*!
All Your *mitzvot* are faithful.
They persecute me with a lie—help me!
They almost finished me off on earth.
But I—I will not forsake Your precepts.
Revive me with Your lovingkindness,
so I may keep Your mouth's testimony.

If Your *Torah* had not been my delight, I would have perished in my affliction. I will never forget Your precepts. For with them You have kept me alive. I am Yours, save me! For I have sought out Your precepts.

Psalm 119:92-94 TLV

56. God Saves Souls With His Word

Psalm 119
(continued)

LAMED ל

Forever, *ADONAI*,
Your word stands firm in the heavens.
Your faithfulness endures from generation to generation.

You established the earth, and it stands.
Your judgments stand today,
for all things are Your servants.

If Your *Torah* had not been my delight,
I would have perished in my affliction.
I will never forget Your precepts.
For with them You have kept me alive.

I am Yours, save me!
For I have sought out Your precepts.
The wicked wait for me to destroy me.
But I will study Your testimonies.
I have seen a limit to all perfection,
yet Your commandment is boundless.

MEM מ

O how I love Your *Torah*!
It is my meditation all day.
Your *mitzvot* make me wiser than my enemies
—for they are mine forever.
I have more insight than all my teachers,
for Your testimonies are my meditation.
I have gained more understanding than all my elders,
for I have kept Your precepts.
I kept my feet from every evil way,
in order to follow Your word.
I do not turn away from Your rulings,
for You Yourself have taught me.
How sweet is Your word to my taste—
yes, sweeter than honey to my mouth!
From Your precepts I get discernment,
therefore I hate every false way.

NUN נ

Your word is a lamp to my feet
and a light to my path.
I have sworn and confirmed
to observe Your righteous rulings.
I am severely afflicted.
Keep me alive, *Adonai*, according to Your word.
Please accept the freewill offerings of my mouth, *Adonai*,
and teach me Your rulings.
My soul is continually in danger,
yet I have not forgotten Your *Torah*.
The wicked have set a snare for me,
yet I did not stray from Your precepts.
Your testimonies I have as a heritage
forever, for they are my heart's joy.
I turned my heart to do Your decrees,
forever, to the very end.

SAMECH ס

I hate double-minded ones,
but Your *Torah* I love.
You are my hiding place and my shield
—in Your word I hope.
Away from me, evildoers,
so I may keep the *mitzvot* of my God!
Sustain me according to Your word, so I may live,
and let me not be ashamed of my hope.
Support me and I will be saved,
and study Your decrees continually.
You despise all who wander from Your decrees,
for their deceitfulness is in vain.
All the wicked of the earth You remove like dross.
Therefore I love Your testimonies.
My flesh shudders for fear of You,
and I am in awe of Your judgments.

AYIN ע

I did what is just and right.
Do not leave me to my oppressors.
Guarantee Your servant's well-being.
Do not let arrogant ones oppress me.
My eyes fail, longing for Your salvation
and for Your righteous word.
Deal with Your servant as befits Your lovingkindness,
and teach me Your statutes.
I am Your servant, give me discernment,
so I may understand Your testimonies.
It is time for *ADONAI* to act—
they have violated Your *Torah*!
Therefore I love Your *mitzvot*
more than gold, more than pure gold.
Therefore I esteem all Your precepts as right in every way
—every false way I hate.

The unfolding of Your words gives light,
giving understanding to the simple. I opened my mouth wide and panted,
for I longed for Your *mitzvot.* Turn to me and be gracious to me,
as is fitting to those who love Your Name.
Direct my footsteps in Your word, and let no iniquity get mastery over me.

Psalm 119:130-133 TLV

57. God Illuminates Understanding through His Word

Psalm 119
(continued)

***PE* פ**

Your testimonies are wonderful.
Therefore my soul obeys them.
The unfolding of Your words gives light,
giving understanding to the simple.
I opened my mouth wide and panted,
for I longed for Your *mitzvot*.
Turn to me and be gracious to me,
as is fitting to those who love Your Name.
Direct my footsteps in Your word,
and let no iniquity get mastery over me.
Redeem me from human oppression,
and I will keep Your precepts.
Make Your face shine on Your servant,
and teach me Your decrees.
Streams of water run down from my eyes,
because they do not observe Your *Torah*.

***TZADHE* צ**

Righteous are You, *ADONAI*,
and Your judgments are upright.
You have commanded righteousness,
Your testimonies, and great faithfulness.
My zeal has consumed me,
because my foes forgot Your words.
Your word is thoroughly refined,
and Your servant loves it.
I am insignificant and despised,
yet I have not forgotten Your precepts.
Your justice is righteousness forever,
and Your *Torah* is truth.
Trouble and anguish have overtaken me,
yet Your *mitzvot* are my delight.
Your testimonies are righteous forever
—make me understand, so I may live.

KOF ק

I cried out with all my heart,
"Answer me, *Adonai*!
I will keep Your decrees."
I cried out to You, "Save me,
and I will keep Your testimonies."
I am up before dawn, crying for help—
I put my hope in Your word.
My eyes are up before every night watch,
as I meditate on Your word.
Hear my voice with Your lovingkindness.
Revive me, *Adonai*, with Your judgments.
Pursuers of wicked schemes draw near—
they are far from Your *Torah*.
You are near, *Adonai*,
and all Your *mitzvot* are truth.
Long ago I learned from Your testimonies
that You founded them firmly forever.

RESH ר

See my affliction and rescue me,
for I do not forget Your *Torah*.
Defend my cause and redeem me.
Restore my life through Your word.
Salvation is far from the wicked,
for they do not seek after Your decrees.
Great are Your mercies, *Adonai*.
Restore my life with Your judgments.
Many are my persecutors and my foes.
Yet I do not turn from Your testimonies.
I see the treacherous and loathe them,
because they do not keep Your word.
See how I loved Your precepts.
Restore my life, *Adonai*, with Your lovingkindness.
Truth is the essence of Your word,
and all Your righteous rulings are eternal.

SHIN ש

Princes persecute me for no reason,
but my heart is in awe of Your words.
I rejoice in Your word,
as one who finds great spoil.
I hate and abhor falsehood,
but Your *Torah* I love.
Seven times a day I praise You,
because of Your righteous judgments.
Great peace have they who love Your *Torah*,
and nothing causes them to stumble.
I hope for Your salvation, *ADONAI*,
and do Your *mitzvot*.
My soul has observed Your testimonies
and I love them exceedingly.
I observe Your precepts and Your laws,
for all my ways are before You.

TAV ת

Let my cry come to You, *ADONAI*.
Grant me understanding by Your word.
Let my supplication come before You.
Deliver me, according to Your promise.
My lips utter praise,
for You teach me Your statutes.
My tongue sings of Your word,
for all Your *mitzvot* are righteous.
Let Your hand be ready to help me,
for I have chosen Your precepts.
I long for Your deliverance, *ADONAI*,
and Your *Torah* is my delight.
Let my soul live and praise You,
and may Your rulings help me.
I have strayed like a lost sheep—seek Your servant.
For I did not forget Your *mitzvot*.

58. God is Our Joy

Psalm 121

A Song of Ascents.
I will lift up my eyes to the mountains—
from where does my help come?
My help comes from *ADONAI*,
Maker of heaven and earth.
He will not let your foot slip.
Your Keeper will not slumber.
Behold, the Keeper of Israel
neither slumbers nor sleeps.
ADONAI is your Keeper.
ADONAI is your shadow at your right hand.
The sun will not strike you by day,
nor the moon by night.
ADONAI will protect you from all evil.
He will guard your life.
ADONAI will watch over your coming and your going
from this time forth and forevermore.

Psalm 122

A Song of Ascents. Of David.
I rejoiced when they said to me,
"Let us go to the House of *ADONAI*."
Our feet are standing in your gates, Jerusalem—
Jerusalem, built as a city
joined together.
There the tribes go up,
the tribes of *ADONAI*
—as a testimony to Israel—
to praise the Name of *ADONAI*.
For there thrones for judgment are set up,
the thrones of the house of David.
Pray for the peace of Jerusalem—
"May those who love you be at peace!
May there be *shalom* within your walls—
quietness within your palaces."
For the sake of my brothers and friends,
I now say: "*Shalom* be within you."
For the sake of the House of *ADONAI* our God,
I will seek your good.

Psalm 125

A Song of Ascents.

Those who trust in *ADONAI* are like Mount Zion—
it cannot be moved, but endures forever.

As the mountains are around Jerusalem,
so *ADONAI* is all around His people,
both now and forever.
For a scepter of wickedness will not rest
over the land of the righteous—
lest the righteous set their hands to evil.

Do good, *ADONAI*, to the good,
and to those upright in their hearts.
But as for those who turn aside to their crooked ways,
ADONAI will lead them away with evildoers.
Shalom be upon Israel.

Psalm 127

A Song of Ascents. Of Solomon.

Unless *ADONAI* builds the house,
the builders labor in vain.
Unless *ADONAI* watches over the city,
the watchman stands guard in vain.
In vain you rise up early and stay up late,
eating the bread of toil—
for He provides for His beloved ones even in their sleep.

Behold, children are a heritage of *ADONAI*
—the fruit of the womb is a reward.
As arrows in the hand of a mighty man,
so are the children of one's youth.
Happy is the man whose quiver is full of them.
They will not be put to shame
when they speak with their enemies at the gate.

Behold, how good and how pleasant it is for brothers to dwell together in unity! It is like the precious oil upon the head, coming down upon the beard—Aaron's beard— coming down on the collar of his robes. It is like the dew of Hermon, coming down upon the mountains of Zion. For there *ADONAI* commanded the blessing —life forevermore!

Psalm 133:1-3 TLV

Psalm 128

A Song of Ascents.

Happy is everyone in awe of *Adonai*,
who walks in His ways,
for you will eat the labor of your hands.
You will be blessed
and it will be good for you.

Your wife will be like a fruitful vine within your house.
Your children will be like olive saplings around your table.
Behold, thus will the man be blessed
who fears *Adonai*.

May *Adonai* bless you out of Zion,
and may you see Jerusalem in prosperity
all the days of your life,
and may you live to see your children's children.

Shalom be upon Israel!

Psalm 133

A Song of Ascents. Of David.

Behold, how good and how pleasant it is
for brothers to dwell together in unity!

It is like the precious oil upon the head,
coming down upon the beard—Aaron's beard—
coming down on the collar of his robes.

It is like the dew of Hermon,
coming down upon the mountains of Zion.
For there *Adonai* commanded the blessing
—life forevermore!

Praise Him with the blast of the *shofar*. Praise Him with harp and lyre. Praise Him with tambourine and dance. Praise Him with string instruments and flute. Praise Him with clash of cymbals. Praise Him with resounding cymbals. Let every thing that has breath praise *ADONAI*. *Halleluyah!*

Psalm 150:3-6 TLV

59. God is Our Song

Psalm 135

Halleluyah! Praise the Name of *ADONAI*.
Give praise, O servants of *ADONAI*—
standing in the House of *ADONAI*,
in the courts of the House of our God.
Praise *ADONAI*, for *ADONAI* is good.
Sing praises to His Name, for it is delightful.
For *ADONAI* has chosen Jacob for Himself,
Israel as His treasured possession.

For I have known that *ADONAI* is great,
and that our Lord is above all gods.
Whatever *ADONAI* pleases, He does, in heaven and in earth,
in the seas and in all deeps.
He makes clouds rise from the ends of the earth.
He makes lightning for the rain.
He brings wind out of His storehouses.

He struck down the firstborn of Egypt, both man and beast.
He sent signs and wonders among you,
O Egypt, on Pharaoh and all his servants.
He struck down many nations and slew mighty kings:
Sihon, king of the Amorites, and Og, king of Bashan,
and all the kingdoms of Canaan,
and gave their land as an inheritance,
an inheritance to His people Israel.

ADONAI, Your Name endures forever,
Your renown, *ADONAI*, from generation to generation.
For *ADONAI* will vindicate His people,
and have compassion on His servants.

The idols of the nations are silver and gold,
the work of human hands.
They have mouths, but cannot speak,
eyes, but cannot see;
they have ears, but cannot hear,
nor is there any breath in their mouths.
Those who make them will be like them—
so will all who keep trusting in them.

O house of Israel, bless *ADONAI*!
O house of Aaron, bless *ADONAI*!
O house of Levi, bless *ADONAI*!

You who revere *Adonai*, bless *Adonai*!
Blessed be *Adonai* out of Zion,
who dwells in Jerusalem. *Halleluyah*!

Psalm 139

For the music director: a psalm of David.

Adonai, You searched me and know me.
Whenever I sit down or stand up, You know it.
You discern my thinking from afar.
You observe my journeying and my resting
and You are familiar with all my ways.
Even before a word is on my tongue,
behold, *Adonai*, You know all about it.
You hemmed me in behind and before,
and laid Your hand upon me.
Such knowledge is too wonderful for me,
too lofty for me to attain.

Where can I go from Your *Ruach*?
Where can I flee from Your presence?
If I go up to heaven, You are there,
and if I make my bed in *Sheol*,
look, You are there too.
If I take the wings of the dawn
and settle on the other side of the sea,
even there Your hand will lead me,
and Your right hand will lay hold of me.
If I say: "Surely darkness covers me,
night keeps light at a distance from me,"
even darkness is not dark for You,
and night is as bright as day—
darkness and light are alike.

For You have created my conscience.
You knit me together in my mother's womb.
I praise You, for I am awesomely, wonderfully made!
Wonderful are Your works—
and my soul knows that very well.
My frame was not hidden from You
when I was made in the secret place,
when I was woven together in the depths of the earth.
Your eyes saw me when I was unformed,
and in Your book were written the days that were formed—
when not one of them had come to be.

How precious are Your thoughts, O God!
How great is the sum of them!
Were I to count them, they would outnumber the grains of sand!
When I awake, I am still with You.

If only You would slay the wicked, O God!
Away from me, you bloody men!
For they speak about You with wicked intent.
Your enemies reproach You in vain.
Do I not hate those who hate You, *Adonai*?
Do I not loathe those who rise against You?
I hate them with total hatred—I consider them my enemies.

Search me, O God, and know my heart.
Examine me, and know my anxious thoughts,
and see if there be any offensive way within me,
and lead me in the way everlasting.

Psalm 141

A psalm of David.

Adonai, I call to You—come quickly to me!
Hear my voice when I call to You.
May my prayer be set before You like incense.
May the lifting up of my hands be like the evening sacrifice.
Set a guard, *Adonai*, over my mouth.
Keep watch over the door of my lips.
Let not my heart turn to any evil thing,
to practice deeds of wickedness with men that work iniquity,
nor let me eat of their delicacies.
Let the righteous strike me—it is kindness.
Let him correct me—it is oil on my head—my head will not refuse it.
Yet still my prayer is against their wickedness.
Their judges are thrown down from a cliff.
Then they will hear my words, since they are sweet.
As when one plows and breaks open the earth,
so our bones are scattered at the mouth of *Sheol*.
For my eyes are toward You, God my Lord.
In You I have taken refuge—do not expose my soul.
Keep me from the jaws of the trap they have laid for me,
and from the snares of the evildoers.
Let the wicked fall into their own nets, while I pass by safely.

Psalm 145

A psalm of praise. Of David.

I will exalt You, my God, the King,
and I will bless Your Name forever and ever.
Every day I will bless You, and praise Your Name forever and ever!
Great is *ADONAI*, and greatly to be praised—
His greatness is unsearchable.
One generation will praise Your works
to another and declare Your mighty acts.

I will meditate on the glorious splendor of Your majesty and Your wonders.
They will speak of the might of Your awesome deeds,
and I will proclaim Your greatness.
They will pour out the renown of Your great goodness,
and sing joyfully of Your righteousness.

ADONAI is gracious and compassionate,
slow to anger and great in lovingkindness.
ADONAI is good to all.
He has compassion on all His creatures.

All Your works praise You, *ADONAI*, and Your *kedoshim* bless You.
They declare the glory of Your kingdom and speak of Your might,
to make known to the sons of men His mighty acts
and the glory of the majesty of His kingdom.

Your kingdom is a kingdom for all ages,
and Your dominion endures from generation to generation.

ADONAI upholds all who fall and raises up all who are bowed down.
The eyes of all look to You and You give them their food on time.
You open Your hand and satisfy every living thing with favor.
ADONAI is righteous in all His ways and kind in all His deeds.

ADONAI is near to all who call on Him,
to all who call on Him in truth.
He will fulfill the desire of those who fear Him.
He will hear their cry and save them.
ADONAI watches over all who love Him,
but all the wicked He will destroy.

My mouth declares the praise of *ADONAI*.
Let all flesh bless His holy Name forever and ever!

Psalm 149

Halleluyah!
Sing to *ADONAI* a new song,
His praise in the assembly of the *kedoshim*.
Let Israel rejoice in its Maker.
Let the children of Zion be glad in their King.
Let them praise His Name with dancing.
Let them sing praises to Him with tambourine and harp.
For *ADONAI* takes pleasure in His people.
He crowns the humble with salvation.
Let the *kedoshim* exult in glory.
Let them sing for joy on their beds.
Let God's high praises be in their mouth
and a two-edged sword in their hand—
to execute vengeance upon the nations
and rebukes on the peoples,
to bind their kings with chains
and their nobles with fetters of iron,
to carry out the sentence decreed—
this is the glory of all His *kedoshim*.
Halleluyah!

Psalm 150

Halleluyah!
Praise God in His Sanctuary!
Praise Him in His mighty expanse.
Praise Him for His acts of power.
Praise Him for His enormous greatness.
Praise Him with the blast of the *shofar*.
Praise Him with harp and lyre.
Praise Him with tambourine and dance.
Praise Him with string instruments and flute.
Praise Him with clash of cymbals.
Praise Him with resounding cymbals.
Let every thing that has breath praise *ADONAI*.
Halleluyah!

60. God Lets Us Choose

Proverb 1

The proverbs of Solomon son of David, king of Israel:
to acquire wisdom and discipline,
to understand the words of insight,
to receive instruction in wise behavior, righteousness, justice and fairness, to give discernment to the naïve, knowledge and discretion to the youth (let the wise listen and increase learning and the discerning obtain wise counsel) to understand a proverb and a puzzle, the sayings of the wise and their riddles .

The fear of *ADONAI* is the beginning of knowledge, but fools despise wisdom and discipline.

Hear, my son, your father's instruction and forsake not your mother's teaching. For they are a garland of grace for your head and a chain to adorn your neck.

My son, if sinners entice you, do not give in. Suppose they say: "Come with us! Let's lie in wait for blood!
Let's ambush the innocent—
for no reason!
Let's swallow them alive like *Sheol*—
still healthy,
as they go down to the Pit!
We'll find all sorts of valuable things,
we'll fill our homes with loot! Throw your lot in with us—
we'll all have one wallet."

My son, do not go along with them,
keep your foot from their path—
for their feet run to evil and they
are swift to shed blood.

Surely it is useless to spread a net
in the eyes of all winged creatures!
But they lie in wait for their own blood. They ambush their own lives.
Such is the fate of all gaining by violence. It takes the life of its possessor.

Wisdom calls aloud in the streets,
she raises her voice in public squares.
She cries out above the commotion.

At the entrances of the city gates, she utters her speech:
"How long will you naïve ones love simplicity, you scoffers delight in scoffing, and you fools hate knowledge? You are repulsed at my rebuke. Behold, I pour out my heart to you. I will make my words known to you.

Because you refused when I called, and did not pay attention when I stretched out my hand, since you ignore all my advice and would not accept my rebuke, I in turn will laugh at your calamity. I will mock when dread comes on you, when your terror comes like a storm and your calamity sweeps over you like a whirlwind, when trouble and distress overwhelm you!

Then they will cry out to me, but I will not answer! They will earnestly seek me, but will not find me.
Because they hated knowledge
and did not choose the fear
of *ADONAI*, they would not accept my counsel, they spurned all my reproof, so they will eat the fruit of their own way and be filled with their own schemes.

Discretion will watch over you —discernment will guard you—
to deliver you from the way of evil, from those speaking perverse things,
who leave the straight paths to walk in ways of darkness, who rejoice in
doing wrong and delight in the perversity of evil,
whose paths are crooked and are devious in their ways—

Proverbs 2:11-15 TLV

For the backsliding of the naïve will kill them and the complacency of fools will destroy them. But whoever pays attention to me will live securely, and be free from the fear of evil."

Proverb 2

My son, if you accept my words and treasure my *mitzvot* within you, making your ear attentive to wisdom, inclining your heart to discernment, yes, if you call out for insight, lifting up your voice for discernment, if you seek her as silver and search for her as for hidden treasures, then you will know the fear of *ADONAI* and discover the knowledge of God.

For *ADONAI* gives wisdom.
Out of His mouth comes knowledge and understanding.
He stores up sound wisdom for the upright. He is a shield to those who walk in integrity. He guards the paths of justice, and protects the way of His *kedoshim*. Then you will discern what is right and just and fair—every good path. For wisdom will enter your heart and knowledge will be pleasant to your soul.
Discretion will watch over you
—discernment will guard you—
to deliver you from the way of evil,
from those speaking perverse things,
who leave the straight paths to walk in ways of darkness,
who rejoice in doing wrong and delight in the perversity of evil,
whose paths are crooked and are devious in their ways—to deliver you from a seducing woman—
a wayward wife with seductive words, who forsakes the partner of her youth and forgets the covenant of her God. For her house sinks down to death and her tracks to the dead. None who go to her return nor reach the paths of life.

So you will walk in the way of good men and keep to the paths of the righteous. For the upright will dwell in the land and the blameless will remain in it. But the wicked will be cut off from the land and the treacherous uprooted from it.

Proverb 3

My son, do not forget my teaching, but let your heart keep my *mitzvot*. For length of days and years of life, and shalom they will add to you.

Let kindness and truth never leave you—bind them around your neck, write them on the tablet of your heart.

Then you will gain favor and a good name in the eyes of God and man.
Trust in *ADONAI* with all your heart,
lean not on your own understanding.
In all your ways acknowledge Him,
and He will make your paths straight.
Do not be wise in your own eyes;
fear *ADONAI* and turn away from evil.
It will be healing to your body
and refreshment to your bones.

Honor *ADONAI* with your wealth and with the first of your entire harvest. Then your barns will be filled with plenty, your vats will overflow with new wine.

My son, never despise *ADONAI* 's discipline or dread His correction.
For *ADONAI* loves those He reproves,
even as a father, the son
in whom he delights.

Happy is the man who finds wisdom and the man who gains understanding. For her trade-value is better than silver, and her yield better than fine gold. She is more precious than jewels and nothing you desire compares to her. Length of days is in her right hand. In her left hand are riches and honor.
Her ways are pleasant ways,
and all of her paths are *shalom*.
She is a tree of life to those who embrace her, and blessed will be all who hold firmly to her.

By wisdom *ADONAI* founded the earth. By understanding He established the heavens. By His knowledge the deeps were divided, and the clouds drip dew.

My son, hold on to sound wisdom and discernment, do not let them out of your sight. They will be life to your soul, and an ornament to grace your neck. Then you will walk on your way in safety, and your foot will not stumble. When you lie down, you will not be afraid; when you lie down, your sleep will be sweet.

Have no fear of sudden terror,
or of the devastation of the wicked when it comes. For *ADONAI* will be your confidence and will keep your foot from a snare.

Do not withhold good from those to whom it is due, when it is in your power to act. Do not say to your neighbor, "Come back later—
I'll give it tomorrow," when you have it with you. Do not plot evil against your neighbor while he lives trustfully beside you.

Do not quarrel with a man for no reason—if he has done you no harm.
Do not envy a violent man
or choose any of his ways. For the devious are detestable to *ADONAI*, but He takes the upright into His confidence.

ADONAI 's curse is on a wicked house, but He blesses a righteous home. Though He scoffs at the scoffers, He gives grace to the humble. The wise inherit honor, but fools are held up in disgrace.

Proverb 4

Listen, my sons, to a father's instruction. Pay attention, to gain understanding. For I give you sound learning—do not forsake my instruction.

When I was a son to my father,
tender and special to my mother,
he taught me and said to me:
"Lay hold of my words in your heart,
keep my commands and you will live!

Get wisdom! Get understanding!
Do not forget nor turn away
from the words of my mouth. Do not forsake her, and she will guard you. Love her, and she will watch over you.

Wisdom is supreme—acquire wisdom! With all your acquisitions, get understanding. Prize her, and she will exalt you. She will honor you when you embrace her. She will set a garland of grace on your head. She will give you a crown of glory."

Listen, my son, and accept my words, so the years of your life will be many. I instructed you in the way of wisdom. I have guided you along straight paths.

When you walk, your step will not be hindered, and when you run, you will not stumble.

Hold on tightly to instruction,
do not let it go—guard it, for it is your life.

Do not enter the path of the wicked or walk in the way of evil people.
Avoid it—do not travel on it—turn away from it and pass by.
For they cannot sleep until they do evil.

They are robbed of sleep until they make someone fall. For they eat the bread of wickedness and drink the wine of violence.

The path of the righteous is like the light of dawn, shining brighter and brighter until the full day.

The way of the wicked is like darkness. They do not know what makes them stumble.

My son, pay attention to my words—incline your ear to my sayings. Do not let them out of your sight, keep them within your heart. For they are life to those who find them and health to their whole body.

Guard your heart diligently, for from it flow the springs of life.

Put away perversity from your mouth, and keep devious lips far from you.
Let your eyes look directly ahead, and fix your gaze straight in front of you.
Clear a level path for your feet, so all your ways will be firm. Do not turn to the right or to the left. Divert your foot from evil.

Proverb 5

My son, pay attention to my wisdom. Incline your ear to my insight, that you may maintain discretion and your lips may preserve knowledge.

For a seducing woman's lips drip honey and her mouth is smoother than oil. But in the end she is bitter as wormwood, sharp as a double-edged sword.

Her feet go down to death,
her steps lead straight to *Sheol*.
She does not keep straight to the path of life, her paths are crooked—but she does not know it.

So now, my sons, listen to me
and do not turn aside from the words of my mouth. Keep your path far from her and do not go near the door of her house—
lest you give your strength to others and your years to one who is cruel;
lest strangers feast on your strength, your labors go to a foreigner's house.
At the end of your life, you will groan, when your flesh and body are spent—and you will say, "How I hated discipline!
How my heart spurned reproof!
I would not listen to my teacher's voice or incline my ear to my instructors. I was almost in utter ruin amid the community and congregation."

Drink water from your own cistern and running water from your own well.

Should your springs flow in the streets, your streams of water in public squares? Let them be yours alone and not shared with strangers.

May your fountain be blessed and may you delight in the wife of your youth. A lovely hind, a graceful doe—may her breasts satisfy you always, may you always be captivated by her love.

Why, my son, be captivated by a seducing woman? Why embrace a foreigner's bosom? For a man's ways are before the eyes of *ADONAI*, and He observes all his paths.

The iniquities of a wicked man will ensnare him. The cords of his sin will hold him down. He will die for lack of discipline, led astray by his own great folly.

Proverb 6

My son, if you have become a cosigner for your neighbor, if you have shaken hands in pledge with a stranger, if you are trapped by your own words, ensnared by the words of your mouth, then do this, my son, and free yourself, since you fell into your neighbor's hand:
Go, humble yourself, plead with your neighbor! Allow no sleep to your eyes, nor slumber to your eyelids. Escape like a gazelle from the hunter's hand, like a bird from the snare of the fowler.
Go to the ant, you slacker—consider its ways and be wise! It has no commander, no overseer or ruler. Yet it prepares its provisions in summer and gathers its food at harvest.

How long will you lie there, slacker? When will you get up from your sleep? A little sleep, a little slumber, a little folding of the hands to sleep— and your poverty comes like a bandit and your need like an armed man.

A scoundrel, a wicked man, is one who goes around with a perverse mouth, winking his eyes, shuffling his feet, pointing his fingers, who continually plots evil with deceit in his heart stirring up strife. Therefore his disaster will come suddenly—in an instant he will be broken, with no remedy.

Six things *ADONAI* hates, yes, seven are abominations to Him:
haughty eyes,
a lying tongue,
hands that shed innocent blood,
a heart that plots wicked schemes,
feet that run to evil,
a false witness who spouts lies,
and one who stirs up strife
among brothers.

My son, keep your father's mitzvah, and forsake not your mother's teaching. Bind them on your heart continually—tie them around your neck. When you walk, they will guide you. When you lie down, they will watch over you, and when you wake up, they will speak to you. For the mitzvah is a lamp, *Torah* a light, and corrective discipline the way of life, keeping you from the immoral woman, from a wayward wife's smooth tongue.

Do not lust in your heart after her beauty or let her captivate you with her eyelids. For on account of a prostitute one is reduced to a loaf of bread; a man's wife preys on your precious life.

Can a man scoop fire into his lap

without burning his clothes?
Or can a man walk upon hot coals without scorching his feet? So is he who goes to another man's wife. No one who touches her will go unpunished.

Men do not despise a thief if he steals to satisfy himself when he is starving. Yet if he is caught, he must repay sevenfold, giving up all the wealth of his house.

He who commits adultery with a woman lacks sense. Whoever does so destroys himself. He will find disease and disgrace. His shame will never be wiped away. For jealousy enrages a man and he will show no mercy in the day of revenge. He will not accept any compensation, he will not consent, even if your bribe is great.

Proverb 7

My son, keep my words and treasure my mitzvot within you. Keep my mitzvot and live, my teaching as the apple of your eye. Bind them on your fingers, write them on the tablet of your heart.

Say to wisdom, "You are my sister," and call understanding your relative. They will keep you from a seducing woman, from the foreign woman with her seductive speech.

For at the window of my house
I looked out through my lattice.
I saw among the naïve, I noticed among the youth, a young man lacking understanding, crossing the street near her corner, walking in the direction of her house, in the twilight of the evening, in the darkest hours of the night.

All of a sudden, a woman meets him, dressed as a prostitute and with a cunning heart. She is loud and defiant. Her feet never stay at home—now in the streets, now in the squares, at every corner she lurks. So she grabs him and kisses him and with a brazen face says to him: "I had to sacrifice fellowship offerings; today I paid my vow.
So I've come out to meet you,
to seek your presence eagerly—
and I found you!

I have spread my couch with tapestry of dyed Egyptian linens. I have perfumed my bed with myrrh, aloes, and cinnamon. Come, let's drink our fill of love till morning! Let's delight ourselves with love. For my husband is not at home—he's gone on a long journey. He took a bag of money with him—he won't come home until full moon."

With her persistent pleading she entices him, with smooth talk she seduces him. Suddenly he follows her like an ox going to the slaughter, like a stag bounding toward a trap, till an arrow pierces its liver. Like a bird darting into a snare, he never considered his own soul!

Now then, sons, listen to me,
pay attention to the words of my mouth. Do not let your heart turn to her ways or stray onto her paths. For many are the victims she has brought down, and numerous are all her slain. Her house is a highway to *Sheol*, leading down to the chambers of death.

Proverb 8

Does not wisdom cry out, and understanding lift her voice? On the topmost heights along the way, at the crossroads, she takes her stand. Beside the gates leading into the city, at the entrances, she cries aloud: "To you, O men, I call out! My cry is to all mankind! O naïve ones, learn prudence! Fools, gain understanding! Listen, for I speak excellent things, and my lips utter right things. For my mouth speaks truth, and my lips detest wickedness. All the words of my mouth are righteous, nothing in them is perverse or crooked. All of them are straightforward to the discerning, and right to those who find knowledge. Receive my instruction instead of silver and knowledge rather than choice gold. For wisdom is better than jewels, nothing you desire compares with her.

"I, wisdom, dwell with prudence, and acquire knowledge with discretion.
To fear *ADONAI* is to hate evil.
I hate pride and arrogance,
evil behavior and a perverse mouth.
Counsel and sound wisdom are mine.
I have understanding and power.

By me kings reign and princes decree justice. By me princes govern, and all nobles who judge righteously.
I love those who love me.
Those who earnestly seek me find me. With me are wealth and honor, enduring riches and righteousness.

My fruit is better than refined gold, my harvest better than choice silver.
I walk in the way of righteousness, along paths of justice. I endow substance to those who love me and fill their treasuries.

"*ADONAI* brought me forth, the first of His way, before His works of old. From eternity I was appointed from the beginning, before the world began. When there were no depths, I was brought forth, when there were no fountains abounding with water. Before the mountains were shaped, before the hills, I was brought forth. He had not yet made the land, the fields, or the first dust of the earth.

When He set the heavens in place, I was there. When He inscribed the horizon on the face of the ocean, when He established the skies above, when He securely fixed
the fountains of the deep,
when He set the boundaries for the sea, so that the waters never transgress His command, when He laid out earth's foundations—
then I was the craftsman beside Him,
I was His daily delight,
always rejoicing before Him,
rejoicing in His whole world,
and delighting in mankind.
"So now, children, listen to me!
Blessed are those who keep my ways. Heed discipline and be wise, and do not neglect it.

Blessed is the one who listens to me,
watching daily at my gates,
waiting at my doorposts.
For whoever finds me finds life
and obtains favor from *ADONAI*.
But whoever fails to find me
harms his life—all who hate me love death."

61. God Blesses Her Deeds

Proverb 12

Whoever loves knowledge loves correction, but whoever hates reproof is stupid.

A good man obtains favor from ADONAI, but He condemns a person with evil schemes. No one is made secure by wickedness, but a righteous root will not be moved.

A virtuous wife is her husband's crown, but a dishonoring one is like rottenness in his bones.

The plans of the righteous are just, but the counsels of the wicked are deceitful.

The words of the wicked lie in wait for blood, but the mouth of the upright delivers them.

The wicked are overthrown and are no more, but the household of the righteous will stand. A man is praised according to his insight, but one with a twisted mind is despised.

Better to have little honor and a servant than to have glory and no bread.

A righteous person cares for the life of his animal, yet even the compassion of the wicked is cruel.

The one who works his land will have plenty of food, but whoever chases daydreams lacks sense. The wicked covets the loot of evil men, but the root of the righteous flourishes.

An evil one is ensnared by the sin of lips, but the righteous one escapes trouble. By the fruit of his mouth a man will be satisfied with good. The work of a man's hands will reward him.

A fool's way is right in his own eyes, but the wise listen to advice. A fool shows his irritation immediately, but a prudent person overlooks an insult. A trustworthy witness tells what is right, but a false witness, deceit.

Reckless speech is like the thrusts of a sword, but the tongue of the wise brings healing.

Truthful lips endure forever, but a lying tongue for only a moment. Deceit is in the heart of those who plot evil, but those promoting *shalom* have joy.

No harm befalls the righteous, but the wicked are full of misery. Lying lips are detestable to ADONAI, but those who act faithfully are His delight.

A clever person conceals his knowledge, but the heart of a fool blurts out folly.

The hand of the diligent will rule, but the lazy will become forced labor. An anxious heart weighs one down, but a good word cheers him up. The righteous gives his friend guidance, but the way of the wicked leads astray.

A lazy person does not roast his game, but a diligent person prizes his possessions.

In the path of righteousness is life—it is a path to immortality.

Proverb 13

A wise son heeds his father's discipline, but a scoffer does not listen to rebuke.

From the fruit of a man's mouth he enjoys good things, but the treacherous crave violence.
He who watches his mouth protects his life, but whoever opens wide his lips comes to ruin.
The slacker's soul craves, yet has nothing, but the diligent soul will be satisfied.

A righteous person hates lying, but the wicked acts in shameful disgrace.

Righteousness guards one who walks in integrity, but wickedness overthrows the sinner.
One pretends to be rich, yet has nothing; another pretends to be poor, yet has great wealth.

A man's riches may ransom his life, but a poor person hears no threat.
The light of the righteous shines brightly. The lamp of the wicked is snuffed out.

Arrogance yields nothing but strife.
Wisdom belongs to those who take advice.

Wealth gained by fraud dwindles, but he who gathers by labor increases it.

Hope deferred makes the heart sick, but longing fulfilled is a tree of life.
Whoever despises instruction will pay a penalty, but whoever respects a mitzvah will be rewarded.

Wise instruction is a fountain of life, turning one away from snares of death. Good understanding wins favor, but the way of the unfaithful is hard. Everyone shrewd acts with knowledge, but a fool flaunts folly.

A wicked messenger falls into trouble, but a faithful envoy brings healing.

He who spurns discipline comes to poverty and shame, but whoever accepts correction will be honored.

A desire fulfilled is sweet to the soul, but fools detest turning away from evil.
He who walks with wise men is wise, but a companion of fools suffers harm.

Misfortune pursues sinners, but prosperity rewards the righteous.
A good man leaves an inheritance to his children's children, but a sinner's wealth is stored up for the righteous.
The fallow field of the poor yields much food, but it is swept away by injustice.

He who spares the rod hates his son, but he who loves him is diligent with discipline.

The righteous eats to his heart's content, but the belly of the wicked goes hungry.

Proverb 18

One who isolates oneself
seeks his own desire;
he defies all sound judgment.

A fool finds no delight in
understanding, but only in expressing
his opinion.

When wickedness comes,
so does contempt, and with dishonor
comes disgrace.

The words of one's mouth
are deep waters, a fountain of
wisdom, a flowing brook.

Showing partiality to the wicked
is not good, nor is depriving the
innocent of justice.

The lips of a fool enter into an
argument and his mouth invites a
beating. A fool's mouth is his ruin,
and his lips are a snare to his soul.

The words of a gossip are tasty
morsels, going down into one's
innermost being.
One who is slack in his work
is brother to one who destroys.

The Name of *ADONAI* is a strong
tower. The righteous one runs into it
and is set safely up high.

A rich person's wealth is a strong city
or like a high wall—in his imagination.
Before ruin a person's heart is proud,
but humility comes before honor.

One who answers before listening—
that is his folly and his shame.
One's spirit sustains him through
illness, but who can bear a crushed
spirit?

A discerning heart gains knowledge,
the ear of the wise seeks knowledge.
A man's gift makes room for him,
and leads him before great men.
The first to state his case seems just,
until another comes and cross-
examines him.

Casting lots ends quarrels
and decides between mighty
opponents. An offended brother is
more formidable than a fortified city,
and quarrels are like the bars of a
fortress.

From the fruit of his mouth a man's
stomach is filled—with the harvest of
his lips he is satisfied.

Death and life are in the control
of the tongue. Those who indulge in it
will eat its fruit.
Whoever finds a wife finds good,
and receives favor from *ADONAI*.

The poor request favor,
but the rich answer harshly.
A man with many friends may be
harmed by them, but there is a friend
who sticks closer than a brother.

Proverb 21

A king's heart is like a stream of water
in the hand of *ADONAI*;
he directs it wherever He wants.
All a man's ways seem right
in his own eyes, but *ADONAI* weighs
the heart. To do righteousness and
justice is more acceptable to *ADONAI*
than sacrifice.

Haughty eyes and a proud heart—
the lamp of the wicked is sin.
Plans of the diligent surely lead to
gain, but all who are hasty come only
to loss.

Getting treasures by a lying tongue is like a fleeting vapor for those who seek death.

The violence of the wicked sweeps them away, because they refuse to act justly. The way of the guilty is crooked, but the conduct of the pure is upright.

It is better to live on a corner of a roof than in a house shared with a quarrelsome wife.

A wicked soul craves evil—
his neighbor finds no favor in his eyes.

When a mocker is punished,
the naïve become wise.
When a wise person is instructed,
he gains knowledge.
The righteous one considers the house of the wicked, throwing the wicked down to their ruin.

Whoever shuts his ears to the cry of the poor, will also cry out but not be answered.
A gift in secret soothes anger, and a bribe given secretly, fierce rage.

Doing justice brings joy to the righteous, and terror to those who do evil.

Whoever strays from the path of wisdom ends up in the congregation of the dead.
Whoever loves pleasure becomes poor. Whoever loves wine and oil will not be rich. The wicked is a ransom for the righteous and the faithless for the upright. It is better to live in a desert land than with a quarrelsome, worrisome wife.

Precious treasure and oil are in a wise person's dwelling, but a foolish person devours all he has.

Whoever pursues righteousness and mercy finds life, prosperity and honor.

A wise person scales the city of warriors and brings down the stronghold in which they trust.

Whoever guards his mouth and tongue keeps his soul out of troubles.
A proud and haughty man
—Mocker is his name—
acts with overbearing pride.

A slacker's craving will kill him,
because his hands refuse to work.
All day long he craves greedily,
yet the righteous one gives and does not hold back.

The sacrifice of the wicked
is an abomination—how much more when he brings it with evil intent?

A false witness will perish, but a man who hears will speak forever.
A wicked man puts on a bold face,
but the upright man considers his ways.

There is no wisdom, there is no understanding, there is no counsel—against *ADONAI*.
A horse is prepared for the day of battle, but victory comes from *ADONAI*.

Proverb 25

These also are proverbs of Solomon, which the men of Hezekiah king of Judah copied:

It is the glory of God to conceal a matter and the glory of kings to search it out.

As high as heaven and deep as earth, so the hearts of kings are unsearchable.
Remove impurities from silver and out comes material for the refiner. Remove the wicked from before the king, and his throne will be established in righteousness.
Do not honor yourself in the king's presence, and do not stand in the place of great men. Better for him to say to you, "Come up here," than for you to be humiliated before a nobleman.

What your eyes have seen, do not bring hastily to court, or what will you do afterward, when your neighbor puts you to shame?
Argue your case with your associate, without betraying another's confidence, or the one who hears it will shame you, and you will never lose your bad reputation.

Like apples of gold in settings of silver is a word aptly spoken. Like a gold earring or a gold ornament is a wise reproof to a receptive ear.
Like the coolness of snow at harvest time is a faithful messenger to those who send him for he refreshes his master's soul.
Like clouds and wind without rain is one who boasts about a gift not given.

Through patience a ruler may be persuaded, and a soft tongue can break a bone.
When you find honey, eat just enough, lest you are stuffed and vomit it. Seldom set foot in your neighbor's house, lest he become weary of you and loathe you.

Like a club, a sword, or a sharp arrow is one who bears false witness against his neighbor.
Like a broken tooth or a lame foot is confidence in the unfaithful in time of trouble.
Like taking off a garment on a cold day or like vinegar poured on soda, is one who sings songs to a heavy heart.

If your enemy is hungry, give him bread to eat, and if he is thirsty, give him water to drink, for you will heap coals of fire on his head and *ADONAI* will reward you.

A north wind brings rain, and a backbiting tongue angry faces.

Better to dwell in a corner of a roof than share a house with a quarrelsome wife.

Like cold water to a weary soul is good news from a distant land.
Like a muddied spring or a polluted well is a righteous person who yields before the wicked.

It is not good to eat too much honey, or honorable to seek one's own honor.

Like a city whose walls are broken down is one with no control over his temper.

Proverb 26

Like snow in summer or rain at harvest, so honor is not fitting for a fool. Like a fluttering sparrow or a flying swallow, so an undeserved curse does not land.

A whip for a horse, a bridle for a donkey, and a rod for the back of fools.

Do not answer a fool according to his folly, else you also will be like him. Answer a fool according to his folly, else he will be wise in his own eyes.

Like cutting off one's feet or drinking violence is sending a message by a fool's hand.
Like a lame man's legs that hang limp, so is a proverb in a fool's mouth.
Like tying a stone into a sling, so is giving honor to a fool.
Like a thorn bush in a drunkard's hand is a proverb in a fool's mouth.
Like an archer who wounds at random is one who hires a fool or any passer-by.
Like a dog that returns to its vomit, so a fool repeats his folly.

Do you see one wise in his own eyes? There is more hope for a fool than him.

A slacker says, "There's a lion on the road! A lion is in the streets!"
As a door turns on its hinges so a slacker turns on his bed.
The slacker plunges his hand in the dish—he is too tired to bring it back to his mouth. A slacker is wiser in his own eyes than seven people who answer sensibly.
Like one who takes a dog by the ears is a passer-by who meddles in a quarrel not his own.
Like a madman shooting firebrands and deadly arrows so is one who deceives his friend, and says, "I was only joking."

Without wood a fire goes out; without gossip quarrels cease.
As coals are to embers and wood to fire, so is a contentious person to kindling strife.
A gossip's words are like tasty morsels—they slide down into the innermost parts of the body.

Like silver glaze overlaying earthenware are fervent lips with an evil heart. One who hates, disguises it with his lips, but he stores up deceit within him.
When he speaks favorably, do not believe him, for there are seven abominations in his heart.
Though his hatred may be concealed by deceit, his evil will be exposed before the assembly.

Whoever digs a pit will fall in it, and whoever rolls a stone—it will come back upon him.

A lying tongue hates those crushed by it, and a flattering mouth causes ruin.

Proverb 30

The words of Agur son of Jakeh— an oracle this man declared to Ithiel, to Ithiel and to Ucal:
"Surely I am more stupid than any man and do not have a man's understanding. I have not learned wisdom, nor have I knowledge of the Holy One.

Who has gone up into heaven, and come down? Who has gathered the wind in the palm of His hand? Who has wrapped the waters in a cloak? Who has established all the ends of the earth? What is His name and what is the name of His son—if you know?"

Every word of God is purified.
He is a shield to those who take refuge in Him. Do not add to His words, or else He will rebuke You and prove you a liar.

Two things I ask of You—do not refuse me before I die: Keep falsehood and lies far from me.
Give me neither poverty nor riches, but feed me with my allotted bread, lest I become satisfied and deny You and say, "Who is *Adonai*?" Or lest I become poor, and steal and profane the Name of my God.

Do not slander a servant to his master, or he will curse you, and you pay for it. There is a generation that curses its father and does not bless its mother.
There is a generation that is pure in its own eyes, and yet is not cleansed from its filth.
There is a generation whose eyes are so haughty, whose eyelids are lifted up disdainfully.
There is a generation whose teeth are swords and whose molars are knives, to devour the poor from the earth and the needy from among humanity.
The leech has two daughters: "Give! Give!"

Three things are never satisfied, four never say, "Enough!"—*Sheol*, a barren womb, land that is not satisfied with water, and fire that never says, "Enough!"

The eye that mocks a father and scorns obeying a mother—will be pecked out by ravens of the valley and eaten by young vultures!

Three things are too amazing for me,
four I do not understand:
the way of an eagle in the sky,
the way of a serpent upon a rock,
the way of a ship in the heart of the sea, and the way of a man with a maiden.

Such is the way of an adulteress:
she eats, wipes her mouth and says,
"I have done nothing wrong."

Under three things the earth trembles, and under four it cannot bear up: under a slave when he becomes a king, a fool when he is stuffed with food, an unloved woman when she is married, and a handmaid when she displaces her mistress.

Four things on earth are small,
yet they are exceedingly wise:
ants are creatures with little strength, yet they store up their food in summer; coneys are creatures with little power, yet they make their homes in the cliffs;
locusts have no king, yet they advance together in ranks; a lizard you can catch with the hand, yet it is found in kings' palaces.

Three things are stately in their stride, four that move with stately bearing: a lion, mighty among beasts, who never backs down from anything; a strutting rooster, a male-goat, and a king with his army around him.

If you have acted foolishly, exalting yourself, or if you have planned evil, put your hand over your mouth. For as churning milk produces butter, and twisting the nose produces blood, so stirring up anger produces strife.

Charm is deceitful and beauty is vain,
but a woman who fears *ADONAI* will be praised.
Give her the fruit of her hands.
her deeds be her praise at the gates.

Proverbs 31:30-31 TLV

Proverb 31

The words of King Lemuel, an oracle that his mother taught him:
O my son, O son of my womb,
O son of my vows, do not give your vigor to women, or your ways to what ruins kings.

It is not for kings, O Lemuel, it is not for kings to drink wine, or for rulers to crave strong drink, lest they drink, forget what is decreed,
and pervert justice for all the oppressed. Give strong drink to one who is dying, and wine to those who are bitterly distressed—
let him drink, forget his poverty,
and remember his misery no more.

Open your mouth on behalf of those unable to speak, for the justice of all who are destitute.

Open your mouth, judge righteously, plead the cause of the poor and needy.

An accomplished woman who can find? Her value is far beyond rubies.
Her husband's heart trusts in her,
and he lacks nothing valuable.
She brings him good and not harm all the days of her life.

She selects wool and flax and her hands work willingly. She is like merchant ships, bringing her sustenance from afar. She rises while it is still night and provides food for her household and portions for her servant girls.

She considers a field and buys it.
From the fruit of her hands she plants a vineyard. She girds herself with strength and invigorates her arms.
She discerns that her business is good. Her lamp never goes out at night.

She extends her hands to the spindle and her palm grasps the spinning wheel.
She spreads out her palms to the poor, and extends her hands to the needy. She is not afraid of snow for her house, for her whole household is clothed in scarlet wool. She makes her own luxurious coverings. Her clothing is fine linen and purple.

Her husband is respected at the city gates, when he sits among the elders of the land.

She makes linen garments and sells them and supplies sashes to the merchants. Strength and dignity are her clothing, and she laughs at the days to come. She opens her mouth with wisdom—a lesson of kindness is on her tongue.

She watches over the affairs of her household, and does not eat the bread of idleness.

Her children arise and bless her,
her husband also praises her:
"Many daughters have excelled,
but you surpass them all."

Charm is deceitful and beauty is vain, but a woman who fears *ADONAI* will be praised.

Give her the fruit of her hands.
Let her deeds be her praise at the gates.

62. God Answers Job

There was a man in the land of Uz whose name was Job. Now that man was blameless and upright; he feared God and shunned evil. He had seven sons and three daughters and his possessions were 7,000 sheep, 3,000 camels, 500 yoke of oxen and 500 female donkeys, and a very large household. That man was the greatest of all the people of the East.

Now it was customary for his sons to hold a banquet, each on his own day in his own house. They would send to invite their three sisters to eat and drink with them. When the round of banquet days was completed, Job would send for them and consecrate them. He would rise early in the morning and offer burnt offerings, according to the number of them all. For Job said, "Perhaps my children have sinned and cursed God in their hearts." Thus Job did everyday.

One day the sons of God came to present themselves before *ADONAI*, and the *satan* also came with them. *ADONAI* said to the *satan*, "Where have you come from?" The *satan* responded to *ADONAI* and said, "From roaming the earth and from walking on it."

ADONAI said to the *satan*, "Did you notice my servant Job? There is no one like him on the earth—a

blameless and upright man, who fears God and spurns evil."

Then the *satan* responded to *ADONAI*, saying, "Does Job fear God for nothing? Have you not made a hedge around him, his household, and everything he has? You have blessed the work of his hands and his possessions have increased in the land. But now, stretch out Your hand and strike everything he has, and he will certainly curse You to Your face!"

Then *ADONAI* said to the *satan*, "Everything he has is in your hand. Only do not extend your hand against him!" So the *satan* departed from the presence of *ADONAI*.

One day when his sons and daughters were eating and drinking wine in their oldest brother's house, a messenger came to Job, saying, "The oxen were plowing and the donkeys were grazing near them, when the Sabeans attacked and carried them off. They also killed the servants with the edge of the sword—I alone escaped to tell you!"

While this one was still speaking another came in and said, "The fire of God has fallen from heaven and has burned up the sheep and servants—it has consumed them, and I—I alone—escaped to tell you!"

While this one was still speaking another came in and said, "The Chaldeans formed three bands and raided the camels and took them all away. They also killed the servants with the edge of the sword, and I—only I alone—escaped to tell you!"

While this one was still speaking another came in and said, "Your sons and your daughters were eating and drinking wine at their oldest brother's

He said to her, "You speak as any foolish woman would speak. Should we accept the good from God and not accept the bad?" Through all this Job did not sin with his lips.

Job 2:10 TLV

house when suddenly a mighty wind came from beyond the wilderness and struck the four corners of the house, and it collapsed on the young people and they died. And I—only I alone—escaped to tell you!"

Then Job got up, tore his robe, shaved his head, fell to the ground and worshiped.

Then he said: "Naked I came from my mother's womb, and naked I will return there. *ADONAI* gave and *ADONAI* has taken away; blessed be the Name of *ADONAI*."

Through all this, Job did not sin nor did he cast reproach on God.

Job, chapter 1

Again the day came when the sons of God came to present themselves before *ADONAI*, and the *satan* also arrived among them to present himself before *ADONAI*.

ADONAI said to him, "Where are you coming from?" The *satan* answered *ADONAI*, "From roaming the earth and from walking on it."

Then *ADONAI* said to the *satan*, "Have you noticed My servant Job? For there is no one like him on the earth, a blameless and upright man, who fears God and spurns evil. And he still holds firmly to his integrity, though you incited Me against him to ruin him without any reason."

The *satan* replied to *ADONAI* saying, "Skin for skin! A man will give up all he has for his own life. But now, stretch out Your hand and strike his bone and his flesh, and he will certainly curse You to Your face!"

ADONAI said to the *satan*, "Very well, he is in your hand—only spare his life!"

So the *satan* departed from the presence of *ADONAI*, and afflicted Job with painful boils, from the sole of his foot to the top of his head. He took a piece of broken pottery to scrape himself while he was sitting among the ashes.

Then his wife said to him, "Are you still holding firmly to your integrity? Curse God and die!"

He said to her, "You speak as any foolish woman would speak. Should we accept the good from God and not accept the bad?"

Through all this Job did not sin with his lips.

When Job's three friends heard about all this calamity that had come upon him, each of them came from his own place—Eliphaz the Temanite, Bildad the Shuhite and Zophar the Naamathite. They met together to come and mourn with him and to comfort him. But when they saw him from a distance they did not recognize him, and they raised their voices and wept. Each one tore his robe and threw dust into the air onto their heads. Then they sat with him on the ground for seven days and seven nights. No one spoke a word to him because they saw that his pain was very great.

Job, chapter 2

After this, Job opened his mouth and cursed his day. Then Job answered and said:

"May the day I was born perish,
and the night that said, 'A man is conceived!' That day—may it be darkness; may God above not regard it; may no light shine on it. May darkness and deep gloom reclaim it; may a cloud settle over it; may whatever blackens the day terrify it.

That night—may thick darkness seize it; may it not be included among the days of the year, nor be entered among the number of months. Indeed, may that night be barren; may no joyful shout enter it.

May those who curse, curse the day—
those ready to awaken Leviathan.
May its morning stars be darkened;
may it hope for light but have none—
may it never see the eyelids of dawn.
For it did not shut the doors of the womb on me, nor did it hide trouble from my eyes.

Why did I not die at birth and expire as I exited the womb? Why did the knees welcome me, and breasts that I might nurse? For now I would be lying down and quiet; I would be asleep and at rest with kings and counselors of the earth, who built for themselves places now desolate, with princes who had gold, who filled their houses with silver.

Or why was I not hidden like a stillborn, like infants who never saw light? There the wicked cease from turmoil, and there the weary are at rest. Prisoners are at ease together; they do not hear the voice of the taskmaster. Small and great are there; and slave is free from his master.

Why is light given to one who suffers
and life to the bitter of soul,
to those who long for death,
but it does not come, who dig for it
more than for hidden treasures,
who are filled with gladness and
rejoice when finding the grave?

Why is light given to a man whose way is hidden, and whom God has hedged in? For my sighing comes instead of my bread, and my groans pour out like water. For the thing I dreaded has come upon me,
and what I feared has happened to me. I have no ease, no quietness;
I have no rest, but turmoil came."

Job, chapter 3

Then Eliphaz the Temanite responded and said: "If one attempts a word with you, will you become impatient? But who can keep from speaking?

Behold, you have instructed many,
you have strengthened weak hands.
Your words have supported those who stumbled, and strengthened buckling knees.

Yet now it has come to you, and you are discouraged; it strikes you, and you are dismayed. Is not your piety your confidence, the integrity of your ways your hope?

"Reflect now: Who, being innocent, ever perished?
And where were the upright destroyed? As I have seen, those who plow iniquity and sow harm, reap them.

By the breath of God they perish; by the blast of his anger they vanish. The lion may roar and the cub growl, but the teeth of young lions are broken. The mighty lion perishes for lack of prey, and the lioness' cubs are scattered.

Job 4:1-11

Behold, happy is the one whom God corrects, so do not despise the discipline of *Shaddai*. For He inflicts pain, but He also binds up; He injures, yet His hands also heal.

From six calamities He will deliver you, even in seven, no harm will touch you. In famine, He will redeem you from death, and in war, from the power of the sword. You will be hidden from the lash of the tongue, and not fear when violence comes. You will laugh at violence and famine, and will not fear the beasts of the earth.

For you will have a covenant with the stones of the field, and the beasts of the field will be at peace with you. You will know *shalom* in your tent, and you will take stock of your home and find nothing missing.

"You will know that your descendants will be numerous your offspring like the grass of the earth. You will come to the grave in vigor, like sheaves of grain in its season. Behold, we have investigated this—it is true. Hear it, and apply it to yourself!"

Job 5:17-27

Job responded and said:
"If only my grief could be weighed and my calamity placed on the scales. For it outweighs the sands of the sea; that is why my words have been rash. For the arrows of *Shaddai* are in me, my spirit drinks in their poison; God's terrors line up against me.

Job 6:1-4

"Teach me, and I will be silent; explain to me how I have been wrong. Honest words are painful, but what does your arguing prove?

Job 6:24-25

Then Bildad the Shuhite answered and said: "How long will you say these things? The words of your mouth are like a mighty wind.
Does God pervert justice?
Does *Shaddai* pervert justice?
If your children sinned against Him, He handed them over to their rebellion. If you would seek God and plead with *Shaddai*, if you are pure and upright, even now He will awaken for you and restore your righteous abode.

Job 8:1-6

Job responded and said:
"Truly I know it is so, but how can one be righteous before God? If anyone wished to contend with Him, he could not answer Him once in a thousand. He is wise in heart and mighty in strength. Who has resisted Him and come out whole?

Job 9:1-4

"I loathe my own life; I will give full vent to my complaint; I will speak out of the bitterness of my soul.

I will say to God, 'Do not condemn me; tell me why You contend with me.' Is it good for You to oppress, to despise the work of Your hands, while You smile on the plans of the wicked?

Do You have eyes of flesh?
Do You see as a human being sees?
Are Your days like those of a mortal, or Your years like those of a strong man, that You should seek out my iniquity and search out my sin, though You know that I am not guilty, yet there is no one to deliver from Your hand?

Job 10:1-7

Then, Zophar the Naamathite answered and said: "Should so many words go unanswered? Is a man justified by his lips? Will your idle talk silence men and will no one rebuke you when you mock? For you have said, 'My teaching is flawless' and 'I am pure in Your eyes!'

But if only God would speak and open His lips against you, and show you the secrets of wisdom—for sound wisdom has two sides. Know that God has forgotten some of your iniquity.

"Can you discover the mysteries of God? Can you find the limits of *Shaddai*? They are higher than the heavens—what can you do? They are deeper than *Sheol*—what can you know? Its measure is longer than the earth and wider than the sea.

"If He comes by and imprisons, or convenes a court, who can prevent Him? For He knows deceitful men; when He sees wickedness, does he not consider it? But a witless man will gain understanding when a wild donkey's colt is born a human being?

"If you devote your heart to Him and spread out your hands to Him, if you put away the wickedness that is in your hand, and allow no iniquity to abide in your tent, then you will lift up your face without reproach; you will stand firm and without fear.

You will forget your trouble; you will remember it like water that has flowed away. Life will be brighter than noonday; darkness like the morning.

You will be confident, because there is hope; you will look about you and lie down in safety. You will lie down with no one to make you afraid, many will seek your favor. But the eyes of the wicked will fail, and escape will elude them; their only hope is their dying breath."

Job, chapter 11

Job responded and said:
"Without a doubt you are the people and wisdom will die with you! But I have a mind as well as you; I am not inferior to you. Who does not know these things?

Job 12:1-3

"Indeed, my eye has seen it all, my ears have heard and understood it. What you know, I also know; I am not inferior to you.

Still, I desire to speak to *Shaddai* and to argue my case with God. You, however, smear me with lies; you are worthless doctors—all of you! If only you would keep completely silent! For you, that would be wisdom.

Job 13:1-5

"Yet I know that my Redeemer lives, and in the end, He will stand on earth. Even after my skin has been destroyed, yet in my flesh I will see God; I myself will see Him with my own eyes, I and not a stranger. My heart grows weak within me.

Job 19:25-27

So these three men stopped answering Job, because he was righteous in his own eyes. Then Elihu son of Barachel the Buzite of the clan of Ram became very angry. He was angry with Job for justifying himself rather than God. He was also angry with his three friends because they had not found an answer, and yet had condemned Job. Now Elihu had waited to speak to Job because they were older. When Elihu saw that there was no answer in the mouth of these three men, his anger was aroused.

Then Elihu son of Barachel the Buzite responded and said:
"I am young in days and you are old; that is why I was timid and dared not to tell what I know. I thought, 'Let days speak, and many years teach wisdom.' But there is a spirit in people, the breath of *Shaddai* that gives them understanding. It is not only the aged who are wise or old men who understand justice. Therefore I say, 'Listen to me! I, even I, will explain what I know.'

Job 32:1-10

"The *Ruach* of God has made me; the breath of *Shaddai* gives me life. Answer me, if you can; array yourselves before me; take your stand! Look, I am the same as you before God; I too am formed from clay. See, no fear of me should terrify you, nor should my pressure be heavy on you.

"Indeed, you have said in my hearing, —I heard the sound of the words: 'I am pure, without transgression; I am innocent, without iniquity. Yet, He has found fault with me; He considers me His enemy. He puts my feet in the shackles; He watches closely all my paths.'

"But in this, you are not right— I answer you, for God is greater than a mortal.

Job 32:4-12

"Therefore, listen to me, you men of understanding: Wickedness is far from God, injustice from *Shaddai.* For He repays a person for what he has done, and brings on the person what he deserves.

"Truly God does not act wickedly, and *Shaddai* does not pervert justice. Who appointed Him over the earth? Who put Him over the whole world?

"If He were to set His heart on it, and gather to Himself His *Ruach* and breath, all flesh would perish together and mankind would return to dust.

Job 34:10-15

"Listen to this, Job: stand and consider God's wonders. Do you know how God orders them, and makes the lightning flash in His cloud? Do you know the balancing of clouds, the wonders of Him who has perfect knowledge?

Job 37:14-16

Then *ADONAI* answered Job out of the whirlwind. He said: "Who is this, who darkens counsel with words without knowledge? Now gird up your loins like a man; I will question you, and you will inform Me!

"Where were you when I laid the foundations of earth? Tell Me, if you have understanding. Who set its dimensions—if you know—or who stretched a line over it? On what were its foundations set, or who laid its cornerstone—when the morning stars sang together, and all the sons of God shouted for joy?

Job 38:1-7

"Can you bind the chains of Pleiades or loosen the belt of Orion? Do you bring out the constellations in their season or guide the Bear with her cubs? Do you know the ordinances of the heavens? Can you set up dominion over the earth?

Job 38:31-33

Then *ADONAI* answered Job, saying: "Will the one who contends with *Shaddai* correct him? Let him who accuses God answer!"

Then Job answered *ADONAI*. He said: "Indeed I am unworthy—what can I reply to You? I put my hand over my mouth. I spoke once, but I have no answer—twice, but I will say no more."

Then *ADONAI* answered Job from the whirlwind: "Brace yourself like a man; I will question you, and you will inform Me! Would you really annul My judgment? Would you condemn Me to justify yourself?

Do you have an arm like God's and can you thunder with a voice like His? Then adorn yourself in majesty and dignity; clothe yourself in splendor and honor.

Scatter the fury of your anger.
Look at every proud person and bring him low; look at everyone who is proud and humble him;
tread down the wicked where they stand. Hide them together in the dust bind their faces in the hidden place. Then I—even I will acknowledge to you, that your own right hand can save you!

Job 40:1-14

Job answered *ADONAI* and said:
"I know You can do all things;
no purpose of Yours can be thwarted. You ask, 'Who is this, who darkens counsel without knowledge?' Surely I spoke without understanding, things too wonderful for me which I did not know.

You said, 'Hear now, and I will speak; I will question you, and you will inform Me.' I had heard of You by the hearing of the ear; but now my eye has seen You. Therefore I despise myself, and repent on dust and ashes."

After *ADONAI* had spoken these words to Job, *ADONAI* said to Eliphaz the Temanite, "My anger is kindled against you and against your two friends, because you have not spoken about Me what is right, like My servant Job has. So now, take for yourselves seven young bulls and seven rams and go to My servant Job and offer a burnt offering for yourselves. My servant Job will pray for you, for I will accept Job's prayer and not deal with you according to your folly because you have not spoken correctly about Me, like My servant Job."

So Eliphaz the Temanite, Bildad the Shuhite, and Zophar the Naamathite went and did what *ADONAI* told them;

and *ADONAI* accepted Job's prayer.

So *ADONAI* restored what Job had lost,
after he prayed for his friends
and *ADONAI* doubled everything that
Job had before. Then all his brothers,
all his sisters and everyone who had
known him before, came to him and
ate bread with him in his house. They
consoled him and comforted him for
all the calamity that *ADONAI* had
brought upon him. Each of them gave
him a piece of money and a gold ring.

So *ADONAI* blessed Job's latter days
more than at his beginning. He had
14,000 sheep, 6,000 camels, 1,000
yoke of oxen and 1,000 female
donkeys.

He also had seven sons and three
daughters.

He called the name of the first
Jemimah, the name of the second
Keziah, and the name of the third
Keren-happuch.

Nowhere in the land were there
found women as beautiful as the
daughters of Job. Their father gave
them an inheritance along with their
brothers.

After this, Job lived 140 years; he saw
his children and their children for four
generations. And so Job died, old and
full of days.

Job, chapter 42

Ruth replied, "Do not plead with me to abandon you, to turn back from following you. For where you go, I will go, and where you stay, I will stay. Your people will be my people, and your God my God.

Ruth 1:16 TLV

63. God Hears Her Heart

It came to pass in the days when judges were governing, there was a famine in the land. A man went from the town of Bethlehem in Judah to dwell in the region of Moab with his wife and his two sons.

The man's name was Elimelech, his wife's name was Naomi, and his two sons were named Mahlon and Chilion. They were Ephratites from Bethlehem in Judah. They came to the region of Moab and remained there.

Then Naomi's husband Elimelech died, so she was left with her two sons. They married Moabite women —one was named Orpah and the second was named Ruth, and they dwelt there about ten years.

Then those two, Mahlon and Chilion, also died. So the woman was left without her children and her husband.

Then she got up, along with her daughters-in-law to return from the region of Moab, because in the region of Moab she had heard that *ADONAI* had taken note of His people and given them food.

So she left the place where she was, along with her two daughters-in-law, and they started out on the road to return to the land of Judah.

So Naomi said to her two daughters-in-law, "Go, return each of you to your mother's house. May *ADONAI* show you the same kindness that you have shown to the dead and to me. May *ADONAI* grant that you find rest, each of you in the house of her own husband." Then she kissed them and they wept loudly.

"No!" they said to her, "we will return with you to your people."

Now Naomi said, "Go back, my daughters! Why should you go with me? Do I have more sons in my womb who could become your husbands? Go home, my daughters! I am too old to have a husband. Even if I were to say that there was hope for me and I could get married tonight, and then bore sons, would you wait for them to grow up? Would you therefore hold off getting married? No, my daughters, it is more bitter for me than for you—for the hand of *ADONAI* has gone out against me!"

Again they broke into loud weeping. Then Orpah kissed her mother-in-law goodbye.

But Ruth clung to her. She said, "Look, your sister-in-law is going back to her people and her gods. Return, along with your sister-in-law!"

Ruth replied, "Do not plead with me to abandon you, to turn back from following you. For where you go, I will go, and where you stay, I will stay. Your people will be my people, and your God my God. Where you die, I will die, and there I will be buried. May *ADONAI* deal with me, and worse, if anything but death comes between me and you!"

When she saw that Ruth was determined to go with her, she no

longer spoke to Ruth about it.
So the two of them went on until they arrived in Bethlehem. As soon as they arrived in Bethlehem the whole city was excited because of them, and the women asked, "Is this Naomi?"

"Do not call me Naomi," she told them. "Call me Mara—since *Shaddai* has made my life bitter.
I went away full, but *ADONAI* has brought me back empty. Why should you call me Naomi, since *ADONAI* has testified against me and *Shaddai* has brought calamity on me?"

So Naomi and her daughter-in-law Ruth the Moabitess returned from the region of Moab. They arrived in Bethlehem at the beginning of the barley harvest.

Ruth, chapter 1

Now, Naomi had a relative on her husband's side—from Elimelech's family—a prominent man of substance whose name was Boaz.

Ruth the Moabitess, said to Naomi, "Please let me go out to the field and glean grain behind anyone in whose eyes I may find favor."
Naomi said to her, "Go ahead, my daughter." So Ruth went out and gleaned in the field behind the reapers. She just so happened to be in the field of Boaz, who was from Elimelech's family. Soon after Boaz arrived from Bethlehem, he said to the harvesters, "*ADONAI* be with you."

They replied, "May *ADONAI* bless you."
Then Boaz asked the foreman of his harvesters, "Whose young woman is this?"

"She is a Moabite woman who came back with Naomi from the region of Moab," the foreman replied. "She asked 'Please allow me to glean and gather among the barley sheaves behind the harvesters.' So she came and has been working in the field since morning until now, except for a little while in the shelter."

Then Boaz said to Ruth, "Listen to me, my daughter. Do not go to glean in another field or even pass on from here, but stay close to my female workers. Keep your eyes on the field that they are harvesting, and follow after them. I strongly ordered the young men not to touch you. When you are thirsty, you can go to the jars and drink from the water the young men have drawn."

Then she fell upon her face, bowing to the ground, and said to him, "Why have I found favor in your eyes that you have noticed me, even though I am a foreigner?"

Boaz replied and said to her, "All that you have done for your mother-in-law since your husband's death has been fully reported to me—how you left your father and mother and the land of your birth, and came to a people you did not know before.
May *ADONAI* repay you for what you have done, and may you be fully rewarded by *ADONAI*, God of Israel, under whose wings you have come to take refuge."

She said, "May I continue to find favor in your eyes, my lord, for you have comforted me and spoken kindly to your maidservant, even though I am not one of your maidservants."

At mealtime Boaz said to her, "Come over here and eat some bread and dip your piece into the wine vinegar." So she sat beside the harvesters and he held out to her roasted grain. She ate until she was full, and some was still left. When she got up to glean, Boaz gave orders to his workers saying, "Let her glean even among the sheaves, do not humiliate her. Also be sure to pull out some grain for her from the sheaves and leave them for her to pick up, and do not rebuke her."

So she gleaned in the field until evening. When she thrashed what she had gathered, there was about an ephah of barley. She carried it back to town, where her mother-in-law saw what she had gleaned. Ruth took some out and gave her what was left over after eating her fill.

Her mother-in-law asked her, "Where did you glean today? Where did you work? May the one who noticed you be blessed!"

She told her mother-in-law with whom she had worked and she said, "The name of the man for whom I worked is Boaz."

So Naomi said to her daughter-in-law, "May he be blessed by *ADONAI* who has not stopped his kindness to the living or to the dead." Then Naomi said to her, "This man is closely related to us, one of our kinsmen-redeemers."

Then Ruth the Moabitess said, "He even said to me, 'Stay close to my workers until they have finished the entire harvest.'"
Naomi answered her daughter-in-law Ruth, "It is good, my daughter-in-law, that you go out with his female workers, so that you will not be harmed in another field."

So she stayed close to Boaz's female workers, gleaning until both the barley harvest and the wheat harvest were completed. Meanwhile she lived with her mother-in-law.

Ruth, chapter 2

Naomi her mother-in-law said to her "My daughter, should I not be seeking a resting place for you, so it may go well for you? Now, is Boaz, with whose female workers you have been, not our relative? Look, he will be winnowing barley tonight at the threshing floor. So bathe and perfume yourself, put on your cloak and go down to the threshing floor. But do not make yourself known to the man until he has finished eating and drinking. Let it be that when he lies down and you know the place where he lies down, go uncover his feet and lie down there. He will tell you what to do."

Ruth answered her, "I will do everything you say." So she went down to the threshing floor and did everything her mother-in-law had said.

Ruth 3:1-6

So Boaz took Ruth, and she became his wife. When he went to her, *Adonai* enabled her to conceive, and she gave birth to a son. Then the women said to Naomi, "Blessed be *Adonai*, who has not left you without a *goel* today.

Ruth 4:13-14a TLV

64. God Redeems the Foreigner

After Boaz ate, drank, and was in a good mood, he went to lie down at the far side of the grain pile. So she came to the grain pile quietly, uncovered his feet, and lay down. Now in the middle of the night, the man was startled and pulled back—and to his surprise, a woman was lying at his feet!

"Who are you?" he asked.

"I am Ruth, your handmaid," she answered. "Spread the corner of your garment over your handmaid, for you are a *goel*."

"May you be blessed by *ADONAI*, my daughter!" he replied. "You have made the latter act of loyalty greater than the first, by not running after the young men, whether rich or poor. Now my daughter, do not be afraid! Everything you propose, I will do for you, for everyone in town knows that you are a woman of valor. Although it is true that I am a *goel*, there is one who is a closer *goel* than me. Stay here tonight, and in the morning, if he will be your *goel*—good! Let him do so. But if he is not willing to be your *goel*, then I will be your *goel* myself, as surely as *ADONAI* lives. Lie down until morning."

So she lay at his feet until morning, but got up before one person could be distinguished from another, for he said, "Do not let it be known that the woman came to the threshing floor."

Then he said, "Bring the cloak you are wearing and hold it out." She held it out and he poured six measures of barley into it and put it on her. Then he returned to town.

When Ruth came back to her mother-in-law, Naomi asked, "How did it go, my daughter?" So Ruth told her all that the man had done for her.

She said "He gave me six measures of barley, for he said, 'You shouldn't go back to your mother-in-law empty-handed.'"

"Wait, my daughter," Naomi said, "until you find out how the matter turns out, for he will not rest until he has settled the matter today."

Ruth 3:7-18

Meanwhile Boaz had gone up to the gate and sat down there. And all of a sudden, the *goel* about whom Boaz had spoken passed by.

"Come over," he called, "and sit down here, my friend." So he came over and sat down.

Then Boaz took ten of the town's elders and said, "Sit down here," so they sat down.

Then he said to the *goel*, "Naomi, who has returned from the region of Moab, is selling the parcel of land that belongs to our brother Elimelech. I thought I should inform you saying, 'Buy it in the presence of the people sitting here, and in the presence of the elders of my people. If you want to redeem it, redeem it. But if it will not be redeemed, then tell me, so that I can know, because there is no one else in line to redeem it. I am after you.'"

"I will redeem it," he said.

Then Boaz said, "On the day you buy the field from Naomi's hand, you will also acquire Ruth the Moabitess, the wife of the deceased, in order to raise up the name of the deceased over his inheritance."

The kinsman said, "Then I cannot redeem it for myself, or else I might endanger my own inheritance. You, take my right of redemption for yourself, for I cannot redeem it."

Now in the past in Israel, one removed his sandal and gave it to another, in order to finalize the redemption and transfer of a matter. This was a legal transaction in Israel.

So the kinsman said to Boaz, "Buy it for yourself," then took off his shoe.

Boaz announced to the elders and all the people: "You are witnesses today that I have bought from Naomi all that belonged to Elimelech and all that belonged to Chilion and Mahlon. Moreover, I have acquired Ruth the Moabitess, the widow of Mahlon to be my wife in order to raise up the name of the deceased over his inheritance, so that the name of the deceased will not be cut off from his brothers or from the gate of his town. You are witnesses today."

All the people at the gate and the elders said, "We are witnesses. May *Adonai* make the woman who has come into your house like Rachel and like Leah, who both built up the house of Israel. May you prosper in Ephrath and be renowned in Bethlehem. May your house be like the house of Perez, whom Tamar bore to Judah, through the seed that *Adonai* will give you by this young woman."

So Boaz took Ruth, and she became his wife. When he went to her, *Adonai* enabled her to conceive, and she gave birth to a son.

Then the women said to Naomi, "Blessed be *Adonai*, who has not left you without a *goel* today. May his name be famous throughout Israel. Moreover, He will be to you a renewer of life and a sustainer of your old age, for your daughter-in-law, who loves you and is better to you than seven sons, has given birth to him."

Naomi took the child and held it to her bosom, and took care of him. The neighboring women gave him a name saying "A son has been born to Naomi!"

So they called him Obed. He was the father of Jesse, the father of David.

These are the generations of Perez:
Perez fathered Hezron,
Hezron fathered Ram,
Ram fathered Amminadab,
Amminadab fathered Nahshon,
Nahshon fathered Salmon,
Salmon fathered Boaz,
Boaz fathered Obed,
Obed fathered Jesse,
and Jesse fathered David.

Ruth, chapter 4

65. God Appoints her Steps

This is what happened in the days of Ahasuerus, the Ahasuerus who reigned over 127 provinces from India to Ethiopia.

At that time King Ahasuerus sat on his royal throne in the castle in Shushan. In the third year of his reign, he gave a banquet for all his princes and his servants. The military leaders of Persia and Media plus the nobles and officials of the provinces were present. He displayed the vast wealth of his kingdom and the splendor and glory of his majesty for many days, 180 days.

When these days were over, the king gave a banquet, lasting seven days, in the garden court of the king's palace for all the people who were present in the palace at Shushan, for both the greatest to the least. There were white and blue linen curtains hung by cords of fine linen and purple on silver rings and marble columns, gold and silver couches on a mosaic pavement of alabaster, marble, mother-of-pearl and minerals.

Wine was served in golden goblets, each of which was different from the other, and the royal wine was abundant according to the king's wealth. In keeping with the law, there were no restrictions on drinking for the king had instructed the supervisors of his household to comply with each person's desire. In addition Queen Vashti held a banquet for the women in the royal palace of King Ahasuerus.

On the seventh day, when the heart of the king was merry from the wine, he commanded Mehuman, Bizzetha, Harbona, Bigtha, Abagtha, Zethar and Carcas—the seven eunuchs who attended Ahasuerus the king—to bring Queen Vashti before the king wearing the royal crown. He wanted to show the peoples and the officials her beauty, for she was very attractive. But Queen Vashti refused to come at the king's command conveyed by the eunuchs. Then the king became furious, and burned with anger.

So the king consulted the wise men who discerned the times, for it was the king's practice to consult experts in matters of law and justice. Those closest to him were Carshena, Shethar, Admatha, Tarshish, Meres, Marsena and Memucan, the seven princes of Persia and Media who had access to the king's presence and were the highest in the kingdom.

"By law, what is to be done with Queen Vashti, for failing to obey the command of King Ahasuerus conveyed by the eunuchs?" Then Memucan answered in the presence of the king and the princes: "Queen Vashti has wronged not only the king, but also all the princes and peoples who are in all the provinces of King Ahasuerus. For the queen's conduct will go out to all the women making their husbands contemptible in their eyes, by saying, 'King Ahasuerus commanded Queen Vashti to be brought in before him, but she would not come!'

This very day the noblewomen of

Persia and Media who have heard of the matter concerning the queen will respond similarly to all the king's princes and there will be no end to the contempt and anger.

If it pleases the king, let a royal commandment go forth from him, and let it be written in the laws of Persia and Media, which cannot be repealed, that Vashti may not come into the presence of King Ahasuerus, and let the king give her royal status to another who is more worthy than she. Then the king's edict, which he will enact, will be proclaimed throughout all his vast kingdom, and all the wives will give their husbands honor from the greatest to the smallest."

The matter pleased the king and the princes. So the king did according to the word of Memucan. He sent letters throughout all the royal provinces, to each province in its own script, and to each people in its own language, that every man should be in charge of his own household, and speak the language of his own people.

Esther, chapter 1

After these things when King Ahasuerus' anger subsided, he remembered Vashti and what she had done and what had been decreed against her. Then the king's servants who attended him said: "Let a search be made on the king's behalf for beautiful young virgins. Let the king appoint officers in all the provinces of his kingdom to gather together all the beautiful young virgins to the palace at Shushan in the house of women under the supervision of Hegai the king's eunuch, who oversees the women. Let them be given beauty treatments. Then let the young woman who pleases the king become queen instead of Vashti." This advice pleased the king and he acted accordingly.

There was a Jewish man in the Shushan palace whose name was Mordecai, son of Jair son of Shimei, son of Kish, a Benjamite, who had been taken into exile from Jerusalem with the captives that had been carried away with King Jeconiah of Judah, whom King Nebuchadnezzar of Babylon had taken away. He had raised Hadassah—that is Esther—his uncle's daughter, for she had neither father nor mother. The girl was attractive and had a beautiful figure. When her father and mother died, Mordecai took her to him as his own daughter.

After the king's order and decree became known, many young women were assembled in the palace of Shushan under the supervision of Hegai. Esther also was taken into the king's household under the supervision of Hegai, guardian of the women. This young woman pleased him and found favor with him. He quickly arranged her beauty treatments and provided her special food. He also provided her with seven specially chosen young women from the king's household. Then he moved her and her maids to the best place in the women's house.

Esther had not disclosed her people or her lineage, because Mordecai had commanded her not to make them known. Every day Mordecai walked in front of the women's courtyard to find out how Esther was, and what might happen to her.

When each young woman's turn came to go to King Ahasuerus at the end of 12 months as prescribed for the women—for in this way they fulfilled their beautification: six months with oil of myrrh and six months with perfumes and women's cosmetics—the young woman would go to the king in this way: whatever she asked for was given to her to take with her from the women's house to the king's palace. In the evening she would go, and in the morning she would return to the second women's home under the supervision of Shaashgaz, the king's eunuch, guardian of the concubines. She would not go back to the king unless the king was pleased with her, and summoned her by name.

When the turn came for Esther, the daughter of Abihail, the uncle of Mordecai who had taken her as his daughter, to go to the king, she did not ask for anything except what Hegai the king's eunuch, the guardian of the women, advised. And Esther won favor in the eyes of all who saw her.

Then Esther was taken to King Ahasuerus at his royal house in the tenth month, which is the month Tevet, in the seventh year of his reign. Now the king loved Esther more than all the other women, and she won his grace and favor more than all the other virgins. So he placed the royal crown upon her head and made her queen instead of Vashti. Then the king gave a great banquet, Esther's banquet, for all his princes and servants. He proclaimed a holiday for the provinces and distributed gifts in keeping with the king's wealth.

When the virgins were assembled a second time, Mordecai was sitting in the king's gate. Esther had not yet made known her lineage or her people, just as Mordecai had told her. Esther continued to follow Mordecai's instructions as she had done when he was bringing her up.

In those days while Mordecai was sitting at the king's gate, Bigthan and Teresh, two of the king's eunuchs who guarded the doorway, became angry and conspired to assassinate King Ahasuerus. But Mordecai found out about the plot and told it to Queen Esther. Esther informed the king in Mordecai's name. When the matter was investigated and found to be so, they were both hanged on a gallows. It was then written in the book of the chronicles in the king's presence.

Esther, chapter 2

Some time later King Ahasuerus promoted Haman, son of Hammedatha the Agagite, elevating him and setting his chair above all the officials who were with him. All the king's servants who were at the king's gate bowed down and paid honor to Haman, for the king had commanded it. But Mordecai would not bow down or pay him honor.

Then the king's servants who were at the king's gate said to Mordecai, "Why are you disobeying the king's command?" Day after day, they spoke to him but he would not listen to them. Therefore they told Haman in order to see whether Mordecai's resolve would prevail, for he had told them that he was a Jew.

When Haman saw that Mordecai was not bowing down or paying him honor, Haman was filled with rage. But it was repugnant in his eyes to lay hands on Mordecai alone, for they had told him the identity of Mordecai's people. So Haman sought to destroy all the Jews, the people of Mordecai, who were throughout the whole kingdom of Ahasuerus.

In the first month (that is the month of Nisan), in the twelfth year of King Ahasuerus, they cast the pur (that is, 'the lot') in the presence of Haman from day to day and month to month, up to the twelfth month, which is the month of Adar.

Haman then said to King Ahasuerus: "There is a certain people scattered and dispersed among the peoples in all the provinces of your kingdom whose laws differ from those of every other people and who do not obey the king's laws. It is not in the king's interest to tolerate them. [9] If it pleases the king, let an edict be written to destroy them. I will pay 10,000 talents of silver into the hands of those who carry out this business, to put it into the king's treasuries."

The king took his signet ring from his hand and gave it to Haman—son of Hammedatha the Agagite—enemy of the Jews. The king said to Haman, "The silver and the people are yours—do with them as you please."

The king's scribes were summoned in the first month, on the thirteenth day, and an edict was written as Haman had commanded. Everything Haman commanded was written to the king's provincial governors, and to the officials who were in every province, and to the officials of every people, province by province, according to its script and people by people according to its language. It was written in the name of King Ahasuerus and sealed with the king's ring. Dispatches were sent by couriers into all the king's provinces, stating to destroy, slay, and annihilate all the Jews—from the youth to the elderly, both little children and women—on a single day, the thirteenth day of the twelfth month, the month of Adar, and to plunder their possessions.

A copy of the edict was to be issued as law in every province and made known to all people, so that they would be ready for that day. The couriers went out hurriedly with the king's command and the edict was issued in the palace in Shushan. The king and Haman then sat down to drink. But the city of Shushan was dumbfounded.

Esther, chapter 3

When Mordecai learned all that was done, he tore his clothes, put on sackcloth and ashes, and went out into the middle of the city crying out in a loud and bitter voice. He went only as far as the king's gate, because no one could enter the king's gate clothed in sackcloth. In each and every province where the king's edict and law came, there was great mourning among the Jews, with fasting, weeping and wailing. Many put on sackcloth and ashes.

When Esther's maids and eunuchs came and told her, the queen was greatly distressed. She sent clothes for Mordecai to put on so he would remove his sackcloth, but he refused. So Esther summoned Hathach, one of the king's eunuchs whom he had appointed to attend her, and ordered him to go to Mordecai to find the cause and reason for this.

So Hathach went out to Mordecai in the city square in front of the king's gate. Mordecai told him everything that had happened to him, even the exact amount of money that Haman had promised to pay to the king's treasuries for the destruction of the Jews. He also gave him a written copy of the decree, which had been distributed in Shushan, for their annihilation, to show to Esther and to explain it to her. He instructed her to go in to the king, to beg his favor and plead before him on behalf of her people. Hathach went back and reported to Esther what Mordecai had said.

Then Esther spoke to Hathach and gave him instructions for Mordecai: "All the king's servants and the people of the king's provinces fully understand that for anyone, man or woman, who approaches the king in the inner courtyard without being summoned, he has one law—that he be put to death, unless the king extends his golden scepter permitting him to live. But I have not been summoned to come to the king for 30 days." So they conveyed Esther's words to Mordecai.

Mordecai told them to reply to Esther with this answer, "Do not think in your soul that you will escape in the king's household more than all the Jews. For if you remain silent at this time, relief and deliverance will arise for the Jews from another place—but you and your father's house will perish. Who knows whether you have attained royal status for such a time as this?"

Esther sent this to reply to Mordecai, [16] "Go! Gather together all the Jews who are in Shushan and fast for me. Do not eat or drink for three days, night or day. My maids and I will fast in the same way. Afterwards, I will go in to the king, even though it is not according to the law. So if I perish, I perish!"

So Mordecai left and did all that Esther commanded him.

Esther, chapter 4

On the third day, Esther put on her royal apparel and stood in the inner court of the palace, in front of the king's hall. The king was sitting on his royal throne in the hall, facing the entrance. When the king saw Queen Esther standing in the courtyard, she found favor in his eyes, so the king held out to Esther the golden scepter in his hand and Esther approached and touched the top of the scepter.

Then said the king to her, "What is it, Queen Esther? Whatever you request, even as much as half of the kingdom, it will be given to you."

So Esther said, "If it pleases the king,

When the king saw Queen Esther standing in the courtyard, she found favor in his eyes, so the king held out to Esther the golden scepter in his hand and Esther approached and touched the top of the scepter.

Esther 5:2 TLV

let the king and Haman come this day to the banquet that I have prepared for him."

The king replied, "Bring Haman quickly so we may do what Esther said." Then the king and Haman came to the banquet that Esther prepared.

As they were drinking wine, the king said to Esther, "What is your request? It will be granted to you. Whatever you request, even as much as half the kingdom, it will be fulfilled."

Esther answered and said, "My petition and my request is this: if I have found favor in the king's eyes and if it pleases the king to grant my petition and my request, then let the king and Haman come tomorrow to the banquet that I will prepare for them—and then I will do as the king requests."

Haman went out that day happy and in good spirits. However, when Haman saw Mordecai at the king's gate, and he did not rise or tremble before him, Haman was filled with rage against Mordecai.

Nevertheless, Haman restrained himself and went home. He sent for his friends and his wife Zeresh. Haman boasted to them about his vast wealth, his many sons, and how the king had promoted him and exalted him above the other officials and servants of the king.
Haman added, "And that's not all! Queen Esther invited only me to accompany the king to a banquet that she prepared. And she has also invited me along with the king tomorrow. Yet all this does not satisfy me, as long as I see Mordecai the Jew sitting at the king's gate."
Then Zeresh his wife and all his friends said to him, "Let them set up a gallows 50 cubits high, and in the morning ask the king to have Mordecai hanged on it. Then go happily with the king to the banquet."
This idea delighted Haman and he ordered the gallows to be built.

Esther, chapter 5

66. God Grants Her Victory

That night sleep deserted the king, so he ordered the book of the chronicles, the record of his reign, be brought in and read before the king. It was found recorded there that Mordecai had revealed that Bigthana and Teresh, two of the king's eunuchs who guarded the door, had conspired to kill King Ahasuerus.

The king asked, "What honor or recognition has been shown to Mordecai for this?"

The king's servants that attended him replied, "Nothing has been done for him."

The king said, "Who is in the courtyard?" Now Haman had just come into the outer court of the king's palace to speak to the king about hanging Mordecai on the gallows that he had prepared for him.

The king's servants answered, "Haman is standing in the courtyard."

The king said, "Let him come in." When Haman entered, the king asked him, "What should be done for a man whom the king desires to honor?"

Now Haman thought to himself, "Whom would the king desire to honor rather than me?" So Haman replied, "For the man whom the king desires to honor, let them bring a royal robe that the king has worn, and a horse on which the king has ridden, one with a royal crest placed on his head. Then let the robe and the horse be placed into the hand of one of the king's most noble princes. Let them clothe the man whom the king desires to honor and parade him on horseback through the city streets, proclaiming, 'This is what is done for a man the king desires to honor!'"

The king said to Haman, "Go quickly! Take the robe and the horse, just as you suggested, for Mordecai the Jew, who sits at the king's gate! Do not neglect anything that you recommended."

So Haman took the robe and the horse, robed Mordecai, and paraded him through the city streets, proclaiming: "This is what is done for the man whom the king desires to honor." Afterwards, Mordecai then returned to the king's gate, but Haman rushed to his home, grief-stricken and with his head covered.

Haman recounted to his wife Zeresh and all his friends everything that had happened to him. His advisers and his wife Zeresh said to him, "Since Mordecai, before whom you have begun your downfall, is of Jewish descent, you won't be able to stand against him. In fact, you will certainly fall before him!" While they were still talking with him, the king's eunuchs came and hurried Haman along to the banquet Esther had prepared.

Esther, chapter 6

So the king and Haman came to dine with Queen Esther, and as they were drinking wine on the second day, the king asked Esther again, "Whatever you request, even as much as half of the kingdom, it will be given to you."

So Queen Esther answered, "If I have found favor in the eyes of the king, and if it pleases the king, grant me my life—this is my petition. And spare the life of my people—this is my request! For we have been sold, I and my people, for destruction, slaughter and annihilation. If we had simply been sold as male and female slaves, I would have remained silent, for such distress would not be worth disturbing the king."

King Ahasuerus responded to Queen Esther, "Who is he? Where is the man that presumed to do this?"

Esther replied, "The man—the adversary and foe—is this wicked Haman!"

Then Haman was terrified before the king and queen. Enraged, the king got up from the banquet of wine and withdrew to the palace garden. But Haman stayed behind to plead with Queen Esther for his life, for he realized that the king had determined a catastrophic end for him. When the king returned from the palace garden to the banquet hall, Haman was falling on the same couch where Esther was. The king exclaimed, "Will he also assault the queen while she is with me in the palace?"

As soon as these words came out of the king's mouth, they covered Haman's face. Harbonah, one of the eunuchs attending the king, said, "Look, a gallows fifty cubits high is standing next to Haman's house. Haman himself made it for Mordecai, who spoke good on behalf of the king!"

The king said, "Hang him on it!" So they hanged Haman on the gallows that he had prepared for Mordecai. Then the king's rage subsided.

Esther, chapter 7

That same day King Ahasuerus gave Queen Esther the estate of Haman, the enemy of the Jews. Then Mordecai came into the presence of the king, for Esther had revealed how he was related to her. The king took off his signet ring, which he had taken back from Haman, and gave it to Mordecai. Esther then appointed Mordecai over Haman's estate.

Esther again pleaded with the king, falling at his feet and weeping. She pleaded with him to stop the evil of Haman the Agagite and his plan that he had devised against the Jews. Then the king extended the golden scepter to Esther, and she arose and stood before the king.

She said, "If it pleases the king, and if I have found favor before him and it seems right to the king, and if I am pleasing in his eyes, let an edict be written rescinding the dispatches devised by Haman, the son of Hammedatha the Agagite, which he wrote to destroy the Jews who are throughout the king's provinces. For how can I endure seeing the disaster that will fall on my people? How can I bear to see the destruction of my relatives?"

King Ahasuerus said to Queen Esther and Mordecai the Jew, "I have decided to give Haman's estate to Esther and had him hanged on the gallows, because he stretched out his hand against the Jews. Now write in

For the Jews there was light and gladness, joy and honor. Throughout every province and throughout every city, wherever the king's edict and his law went, the Jews had gladness and joy, banquets and holidays.

Esther 8:16-17a TLV

the king's name on behalf of the Jews what seems good to you and seal it with the king's signet ring. For a decree that is written in the king's name, and sealed with the king's ring, cannot be revoked."

So the king's scribes were called at that time—on the 23rd day of the third month, the month of Sivan. It was written according to all that Mordecai commanded to all the Jews, as well as to the officials, governors and advisors of all the 127 provinces that stretch from India to Ethiopia. To each province it was written in its own script and in its own language, and also to the Jews in their own writing and language. This decree was written in the name of King Ahasuerus, sealed with the king's ring, and sent on horseback by couriers who rode on the king's horses specially bred for their speed.

The king granted the right for Jews in every city to assemble themselves and to protect themselves—to destroy, kill and annihilate any army of any people or province that might attack them and their women and children, and to plunder their possessions. The day appointed for this in all the provinces of King Ahasuerus was the thirteenth day of the twelfth month, the month Adar. A copy of the written edict was distributed to every province and made known to the peoples of every nationality so that the Jews would be ready on that day to avenge themselves on their enemies.
The couriers that rode royal horses raced out, pressed on by the king's command. The decree was also given out at the palace at Shushan.

Then Mordecai went out from the king's presence in blue and white royal robes, with a large gold crown, and also a purple robe of fine linen. The city of Shushan shouted and rejoiced.

For the Jews there was light and gladness, joy and honor. Throughout every province and throughout every city, wherever the king's edict and his law went, the Jews had gladness and joy, banquets and holidays. Many peoples of the land became Jews, because the fear of the Jews had overcome them.

Esther, chapter 8

Consequently, on the thirteenth day of the twelfth month (that is the month Adar), the king's edict and his law drew near to be carried out. On that day the enemies of the Jews had hoped to overpower them, but contrary to expectations the Jews gained the upper hand over those that hated them.

Jews assembled in their cities throughout all the provinces of King Ahasuerus in order to lay hands on those seeking their harm. No one was able to stand against them, for fear of them had fallen on all the peoples. Even all the administrators of the provinces, the officers and governors, and those doing business for the king, helped the Jews, for the dread of Mordecai had fallen on them.

Mordecai was prominent at the palace, and his fame spread throughout all the provinces. The man Mordecai was growing ever more powerful.The Jews struck down all their enemies with the sword, killing and destroying, and they did whatever they wished to those who hated them. In the citadel at Shushan the Jews killed and destroyed 500 people, including Parshandatha, Dalphon, Aspatha, Poratha, Adalia, Aridatha, Parmashta, Arisai, Aridai and Vaizatha, the 10 sons of Haman, the son of Hammedatha, the enemy of the Jews. They slew them but did not lay their hands on the plunder.

On that day the number of those that were killed in the citadel at Shushan was brought to the king's attention. Then the king said to Queen Esther, "The Jews have killed and destroyed 500 men in the citadel of Shushan, including Haman's ten sons. What have they done, in the rest of the king's provinces? Now what is your request? It shall be granted to you. What other petition do you have? It shall be done."

"If it please the king," Esther said, "let the Jews in Shushan be allowed to carry out today's edict tomorrow also, and let Haman's ten sons be hanged on the gallows."

The king commanded that this be done. A decree was issued in Shushan and they hanged Haman's 10 sons.

The Jews in Shushan gathered together on the fourteenth day of the month Adar, and they killed 300 men in Shushan, but they did not put their hands on the plunder. Meanwhile the rest of the Jews who were in the king's provinces gathered together to protect themselves and to get relief from their enemies. They killed 75,000 of their enemies, but they did not lay their hands on the plunder. This happened on the thirteenth day of Adar and on the fourteenth day they rested, making it a day of feasting and gladness.

But the Jews that were in Shushan had assembled on the thirteenth and on the fourteenth and on the fifteenth they rested, making it a day of feasting and gladness. That is why the rural Jews—those living in unwalled villages—make the fourteenth day of the month Adar a day of gladness and feasting, a day of sending presents of food to one another.

Mordecai recorded these events and he sent letters to all the Jews throughout the provinces of King Ahasuerus, both near and far, urging them to celebrate the fourteenth and fifteenth days of Adar every year as the days when the Jews got relief from their enemies, and as the month when their sorrow was turned into joy and their mourning into celebration. These were to be days of feasting, celebration and sending presents of food to one another and giving gifts to the poor.

So the Jews agreed to continue the commemoration they had begun, and do what Mordecai had written to them. For Haman, son of Hammedatha the Agagite, the enemy of all the Jews, had schemed against the Jews to destroy them and had cast the pur—that is, the lot—to ruin and destroy them. But when it came to the king's attention, he issued a written edict that the wicked scheme Haman had devised against the Jews should come back on his own head, and that he and his sons should be hanged on the gallows. (For this reason, these days were called Purim, from the word pur.)

Therefore because of everything in this letter and because of what they had seen and what had happened to them, the Jews established and took upon themselves, upon their descendants, and upon all who joined with them, that they would commemorate these two days in the way prescribed and at the appointed time every year. These days should be remembered and observed in every generation by every family and in every province and every city. These days of Purim should not fail from among the Jews, nor their remembrance perish from their descendants.

Then Queen Esther the daughter of Abihail, and also Mordecai the Jew, wrote with full authority to confirm this second letter of Purim. He sent letters to all the Jews in the 127 provinces of the kingdom of Ahasuerus, with words of *shalom* and truth, to establish these days of Purim at their designated times, just as Mordecai the Jew and Queen Esther had decreed for them and just as they had established for themselves and their descendants, matters regarding their times of fasting and lamentations. Esther's command confirmed these regulations about Purim and it was written into the records.

Esther, chapter 9

Now King Ahasuerus imposed a tribute upon the entire land, even to the coastlands of the sea. All the acts of his power and might, along with the full account of the greatness of Mordecai and the story of how the king promoted him, are they not written in the book of the chronicles of the kings of Media and Persia? For Mordecai the Jew was second only to King Ahasuerus, preeminent among the Jews, and held in high esteem by the multitude of his people. He sought their good and spoke for the welfare of his descendants.

Esther, chapter 10

67. God Dances with Us

In the third year of the reign of King Jehoiakim of Judah, King Nebuchadnezzar of Babylon came to Jerusalem and besieged it. God gave King Jehoiakim of Judah into his hand, along with some of the vessels of the House of God. He brought them into the land of Shinar to the house of his god and put the vessels into the treasure house of his god.

Then the king told Ashpenaz the chief of his officials to bring in some of the sons of Israel from royal descent and nobility—youths without any defect, handsome, proficient in all wisdom, knowledgeable, intelligent and capable of serving in the king's palace. He was to teach them the literature and language of the Chaldeans. The king allotted them a daily portion from the king's delicacies and from the wine that he drank. They were to be trained for three years, and at the end they were to stand before the king.

Now among them were some from the sons of Judah: Daniel, Hananiah, Mishael and Azariah. The chief officer gave them new names: to Daniel, Belteshazzar; to Hananiah, Shadrach; to Mishael, Meshach; and to Azariah, Abed-nego.

But Daniel resolved not to defile himself with the king's delicacies or with the wine he was drinking, so he entreated the chief official for permission not to defile himself.

Now God caused the chief official to show mercy and compassion to Daniel. But the chief official said to Daniel: "I fear my lord the king, who allotted your food and your drink. Why should he see your faces looking poorly, unlike the other youths your age? Then the king would have my head because of you."

Daniel then said to the guard whom the chief official had appointed over Daniel, Hananiah, Mishael and Azariah, "Please test your servants for ten days, giving us just vegetables to eat and water to drink. Then compare our appearance and the appearance of the youths who eat the king's delicacies, and treat your servants according to what you see." So he listened to them in this matter and tested them for ten days. At the end of ten days their appearance looked better and their bodies healthier than all the youths who ate the king's food. So the guard took away their delicacies and the wine they were supposed to drink and gave them vegetables instead.

Now as for these four youths, God gave them knowledge and proficiency in every kind of wisdom and literature, and Daniel could understand all sorts of visions and dreams. At the end of the time set by the king to bring them in, the chief official presented them before Nebuchadnezzar. When the king spoke with them, he did not find among all of them anyone like Daniel, Hananiah, Mishael and Azariah; so they entered the king's service. In every matter of wisdom and understanding about which the king questioned them, he found them ten times better than all the magicians and astrologers throughout his realm. Daniel remained there until the first year of King Cyrus.

Daniel, chapter 1

King Nebuchadnezzar made an image of gold, sixty cubits high and six cubits wide. He set it up on the plain of Dura in the province of Babylon. Then King Nebuchadnezzar summoned the satraps, prefects, governors, counselors, treasurers, judges, magistrates, and all the authorities of the provinces to come to the dedication of the image which Nebuchadnezzar the king had set up. Then the satraps, administrators, governors, counselors, treasurers, judges, magistrates and all the authorities of the provinces assembled for the dedication of the image that King Nebuchadnezzar had erected. They stood before the image that Nebuchadnezzar had set up.

Then the herald loudly proclaimed, "You are commanded O peoples, nations and languages, that when you hear the sound of the horn, flute, zither, lyre, harp, pipes and all kinds of music, you must fall down and worship the golden image that King Nebuchadnezzar has set up. Whoever does not fall down and worship will that same hour be thrown into the midst of a furnace of blazing fire." Therefore, as soon as all the peoples heard the sound of the horn, flute, zither, lyre, harp and pipes, and all kinds of music, all the peoples, nations and languages fell down and worshipped the golden image that Nebuchadnezzar the king had set up.

At that time certain Chaldeans came forward and denounced the Jews. They spoke up and said to King Nebuchadnezzar, "May the king live forever! You, O king, made a decree that everyone who hears the sound of the horn, flute, zither, lyre, harp, pipes and all kinds of music, must fall down and worship the golden image, and that whoever does not fall down and worship will be thrown into the midst of a furnace of blazing fire. There are certain Jews whom you appointed over the administration of the province of Babylon—Shadrach, Meshach and Abed-nego—those men pay no heed to you, O king. They do not serve your gods, nor will they worship the golden image that you have set up."

Furious with rage, Nebuchadnezzar ordered Shadrach, Meshach and Abed-nego to be summoned. When these men were brought before the king, Nebuchadnezzar responded to them saying, "Is it true, Shadrach, Meshach and Abed-nego, that you don't serve my gods or worship the golden image that I set up? Now if you are ready, at the moment you hear the sound of the horn, flute, zither, lyre, harp and pipes and all kinds of music you must fall down and worship the image that I have made. But if you do not worship, you will immediately be thrown into the midst of a furnace of blazing fire! Then what god will be able to deliver you out of my hands?"

Shadrach, Meshach and Abed-nego replied to the king saying, "O Nebuchadnezzar, we do not need to answer you concerning this matter. If it is so, our God whom we serve is able to save us from the furnace of blazing fire and He will deliver us out

But he answered saying, "Look! I see four men walking about unbound and unharmed in the middle of the fire, and the fourth has the appearance like a son of the gods!" Nebuchadnezzar then approached the door of the furnace of blazing fire and exclaimed, "Shadrach, Meshach and Abed-nego, servants of the Most High God, come out and come here!" So Shadrach, Meshach and Abed-nego came out from the middle of the fire.

Daniel 3:25-26 TLV

of your hand, O king. Yet even if He does not, let it be known to you, O king, that we will not serve your gods, nor worship the golden image that you set up."

Then Nebuchadnezzar was filled with rage and the appearance of his face changed toward Shadrach, Meshach and Abed-nego. He ordered the furnace to be heated seven times hotter than it was normally heated and commanded some of the mighty men in his army to tie up Shadrach, Meshach and Abed-nego and to cast them into the furnace of blazing fire. So these men, wearing their robes, tunics, hats and other clothes, were bound and thrown into the furnace of blazing fire. But because the king's order was so urgent and the furnace so extremely hot, a raging flame killed those men who carried up Shadrach, Meshach and Abed-nego. And these three men, Shadrach, Meshach and Abed-nego, fell bound into the midst of the furnace of blazing fire.

Then King Nebuchadnezzar was astonished and leapt to his feet. He asked his ministers, "Didn't we cast three men bound into the middle of the fire?"

They replied to the king, "Surely, O king."

But he answered saying, "Look! I see four men walking about unbound and unharmed in the middle of the fire, and the fourth has the appearance like a son of the gods!"

Nebuchadnezzar then approached the door of the furnace of blazing fire and exclaimed, "Shadrach, Meshach and Abed-nego, servants of the Most High God, come out and come here!"

So Shadrach, Meshach and Abed-nego came out from the middle of the fire. When the satraps, administrators, governors and royal ministers had gathered around, they saw that the fire had no effect on the bodies of these men. Not a hair of their head was singed, nor were their robes scorched, nor was there a smell of fire on them.

Nebuchadnezzar exclaimed, "Blessed be the God of Shadrach, Meshach and Abed-nego, who has sent His angel and delivered His servants who trusted in Him! They defied the king's edict and to gave up their lives rather than serve or worship any god except their own God. Therefore I hereby decree that any people, nation or language that says anything slanderous against the God of Shadrach, Meshach and Abed-nego will be torn limb from limb and their house made a pile of rubble, because there is no other god that is able to deliver in this way."
Then the king promoted Shadrach, Meshach and Abed-nego in the province of Babylon.

King Nebuchadnezzar—
To all peoples, nations and languages who dwell in all the earth: May your peace abound!
It seemed good to me to declare the signs and wonders that God Most High has done for me.
How great are His signs,
how mighty are His wonders!
His kingdom is an everlasting kingdom, His dominion from generation to generation.

Daniel, chapter 3

68. God Protects the Scribe

So Darius the Mede took over the kingdom at the age of 62.

It pleased Darius to appoint 120 satraps to rule throughout the whole kingdom with three administrators over them, one of whom was Daniel. These satraps were accountable to them so that the king would not be troubled.

Now this Daniel was distinguishing himself among the supervisors and satraps because he had an extraordinary spirit in him. In fact, the king planned to appoint him over the entire kingdom. At this time the supervisors and satraps tried to find ground for a charge against Daniel regarding the kingdom. But they were unable to find fault or corruption, because he was trustworthy and no negligence or dishonesty could be found in him.

Finally these men said, "We're not going to find any basis for charges against this man Daniel, unless we find something against him regarding the law of his God."

So these supervisors and satraps went in to the king as a group, and said to him, "King Darius, live forever! All the supervisors of the realm, the magistrates and satraps, ministers and governors, have all agreed that the king should issue an edict and enforce a decree that

anyone who prays to any god or man for 30 days other than you O king, will be cast into the lions' den. Now, O king, issue the decree and put it in writing so that it may not be altered, according to the law of the Medes and Persians, which cannot be repealed." Thereupon King Darius issued the written decree.

Now when Daniel learned that a written decree had been issued, he went into his house, where the windows in his upper room opened toward Jerusalem. Three times a day he knelt down, prayed and gave thanks before his God, just as he did before. Then these men came as a group and found Daniel praying and making supplication before his God. So they approached the king and spoke to him about the royal decree: "Didn't you issue a written decree that anyone who prays to any god or man for 30 days—except for you, O king—shall be cast into the den of lions?"

The king replied, "The decree stands, according to the law of the Medes and Persians, which cannot be repealed."

Then they answered and said to the king: "Daniel, who is one of the exiles from Judah, pays no attention to you, O king, or to the decree that you put in writing. He still prays three times a day!"

When the king heard this report, he was deeply distressed, and he set his mind on how he might rescue Daniel. Until sunset he struggled to find a way to save him. Then these men came as a throng in to the king, and said to the king: "Remember, O king, that it is a law of the Medes and

Persians that no decree or edict which the king issues may be altered."

So the king gave the order and Daniel was brought and thrown into the lions' den. Now the king spoke to Daniel saying, "May your God, whom you serve continually, deliver you!"

A stone was brought to block the mouth of the den. The king sealed it with his own signet ring and with the signet of his nobles, so that nothing could be changed regarding Daniel. Then the king went to his palace and passed the night fasting—no entertainment was brought before him. He was unable to sleep.

At dawn the king got up and hurried to the lions' den. As he reached the den, he cried out to Daniel with a voice of anguish. The king spoke out to Daniel saying: "Daniel, servant of the living God, was your God, whom you serve continually, able to rescue you from the lions?" Daniel spoke to the king: "May the king live forever! My God sent His angel to shut the lions' mouths so that they haven't harmed me, because I was found innocent before Him. Nor have I committed any crime against you, O king."

Then the king was overjoyed, and ordered Daniel taken up out of the den. So Daniel was lifted out of the pit. No injury of any kind was found on him because he had trusted in his God. At the king's command, those men who had maliciously accused Daniel were brought and thrown into the lions' den—they, their children, and their wives. They had not even reached the bottom of the pit before the lions overpowered them and crushed all their bones.
Then King Darius wrote to all the peoples, nations, and languages dwelling in all the earth: "May your peace be abundant! I issue a decree that in all the dominion of my kingdom people are to tremble with fear before the God of Daniel.
"For He is the living God, enduring forever! His kingdom will never be destroyed, His dominion will never end. He delivers and rescues. He performs signs and wonders in the heavens and on earth. He has delivered Daniel from the power of the lions!"

So Daniel prospered during the reign of Darius and the reign of Cyrus the Persian.

Daniel, chapter 6

As he reached the den, he cried out to Daniel with a voice of anguish. The king spoke out to Daniel saying: "Daniel, servant of the living God, was your God, whom you serve continually, able to rescue you from the lions?"

Daniel 6:21 TLV

69. God Builds His House

The words of Nehemiah son of Hacaliah:

Now it happened that in the month of Kislev in the twentieth year, while I was in Shushan the capitol, that Hanani, one of my brothers, together with some men from Judah, arrived and I asked them about the Judeans, the remnant who had survived the captivity, and about Jerusalem.

They said to me, "The remnant who have survived the captivity there in the province are in great distress and disgrace. The wall of Jerusalem is broken down and its gates have been burned with fire."

Upon hearing these words I sat down and wept and mourned for days. I prayed and fasted before the God of heaven. Then I said:
"*ADONAI*, God of heaven, the great and awesome God who keeps the covenant and lovingkindness with those who love Him and keep His *mitzvot*, please let Your ear be attentive and Your eyes open to hear the prayer of Your servant that I am praying before You today both day and night on behalf of Your servants, the *Bnei-Yisrael*. I am confessing the sins of *Bnei-Yisrael* that we have sinned against You—yes, I and my ancestral house have sinned. We have acted very corruptly against You. We have not kept the *mitzvot*, the statutes, nor the rulings that You commanded Your servant Moses.

"Please recall the word that You commanded Your servant Moses, saying, 'If you act unfaithfully, I will scatter you among the peoples, but if you return to Me and obey My *mitzvot*, and do them, then even if your dispersed people are at the ends of the heavens, I will gather them from there, and bring them back to the place where I have chosen for My Name to dwell.'

"They are Your servants and Your people whom You redeemed by Your great strength and by Your mighty hand. Please, my Lord, let Your ear be attentive to the prayer of Your servant and to the prayer of Your servants who delight in revering Your Name. Give Your servant success today and grant compassion in the presence of this man."

Now I was cupbearer to the king.

Nehemiah, chapter 1

Then in the month of Nisan, in the twentieth year of King Artaxerxes, when wine was set before him, I took the wine and gave it to the king. I had not been sad in his presence before. So the king said to me, "Why is your face so sad when you are not ill? This can be nothing but sadness of heart."
I was very frightened, but I said to the king, "May the king live forever! Why should my face not be sad, when the city where my ancestors are buried lies in ruins and its gates have been destroyed by fire?"

The king asked me, "What is your request?"

Then I prayed to the God of

heaven, and I answered the king, "If it seems good to the king and if your servant has found favor in your sight, send me to the city in Judah where my ancestors are buried that I may rebuild it."

Then the king, with the queen sitting beside him, asked me, "How long will your journey take, and when will you return?" Since it pleased the king to send me, I set a time for him.

I said to the king, "If it pleases the king, let him give me letters for the governors of Trans-Euphrates that will enable me to pass through until I arrive in Judah, as well as a letter to Asaph, the keeper of the king's forest so he will give me lumber to make beams for the gates of the fortress adjacent to the Temple, for the wall of the city and for the residence I will occupy."

The king granted me the requests because the good hand of my God was upon me. Then I went to the governors of Trans-Euphrates and I gave them the king's letters. The king had also sent army officials and cavalry with me.

When Sanballat the Horonite and Tobiah the Ammonite officials heard all this, they were very displeased that a man had come to seek the welfare of *Bnei-Yisrael*.

I came to Jerusalem, and after I was there for three days, I got up during the night along with a few men. But I did not tell anyone what my God had put in my heart to do for Jerusalem. There were no animals with me except the animal I was riding.

By night I went out by the Valley Gate toward Jackal Spring and the Dung Gate, inspecting the walls of Jerusalem, which had been broken down, and its gates, which had been destroyed by fire. Then I moved on to the Fountain Gate and to the King's Pool, where there was not enough room for my animal to pass with me; so I went up the valley by night, examining the wall. Finally, I turned back and returned to the Valley Gate. The officials did not know where I had gone or what I was doing, but as yet I had not told the Jews, the *kohanim*, the nobles, the officials or the rest of the workers. Then I said to them, "You see the bad situation we are in: Jerusalem is desolate and its gates have been burnt. Come! Let us rebuild the wall of Jerusalem so that we will no longer be a disgrace."

Then I told them how the good hand of my God was on me and the words that the king had said to me. Then they replied, "Let us begin building!" So they prepared themselves for this good work.

But when Sanballat the Horonite, Tobiah the Ammonite official and Geshem the Arab heard about it, they mocked and ridiculed us. They said, "What is this you are doing? Are you rebelling against the king?"

I responded to them saying, "The God of heaven will bring us success. We His servants will arise and build. But you have no part, right, or historical claim in Jerusalem."

Nehemiah, chapter 2

Then Eliashib the *kohen gadol* and his

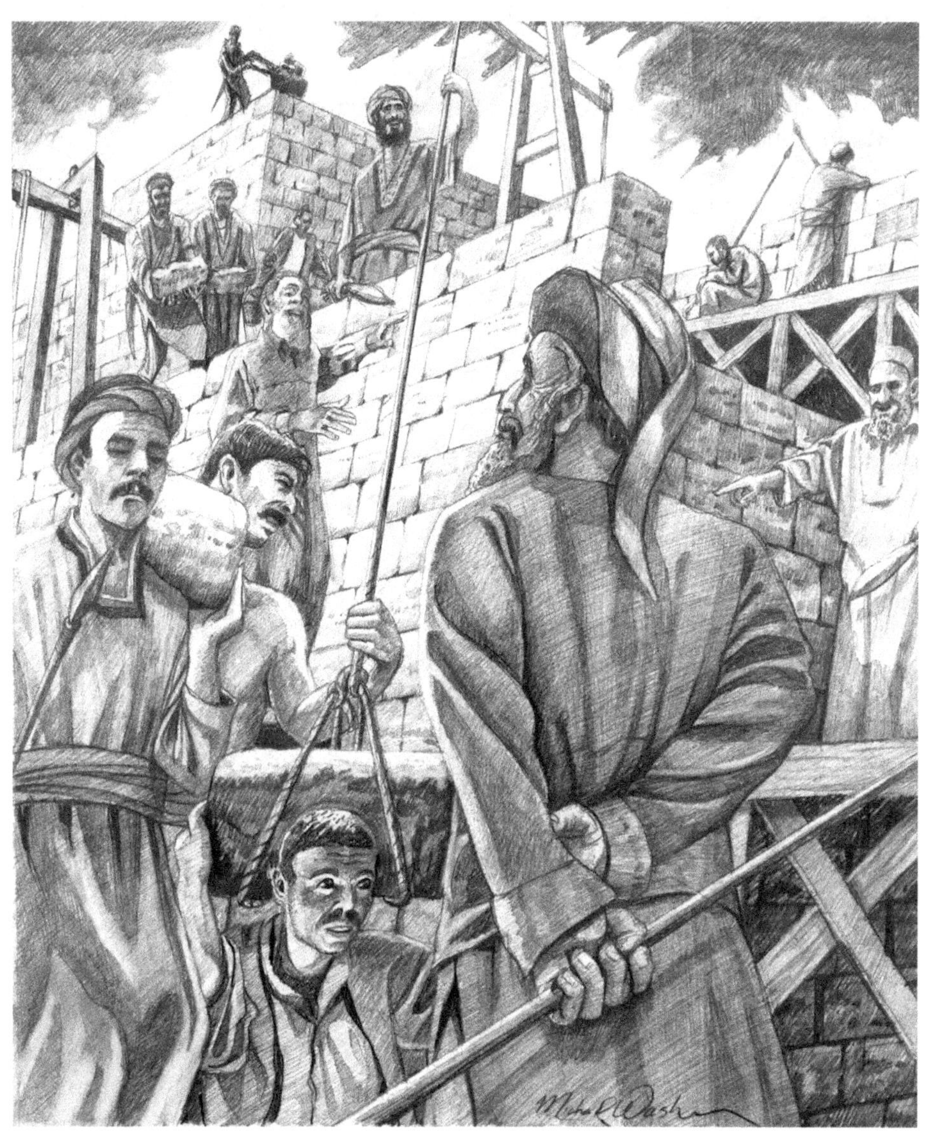

So we rebuilt the wall, and the entire wall was joined together
up to half its height, for the people had a heart to work.

Nehemiah 3:38 TLV

brothers, the *kohanim*, arose and built the Sheep Gate. They dedicated it and set up its doors, dedicating it as far as the Tower of the Hundred and as far as the Tower of Hananel. The men of Jericho built next to it and Zaccur the son of Imri built next to them.

The sons of Hassenaah built the Fish Gate. They laid its beams and set up its doors, its bolts, and its bars. Next to them Meremoth son of Uriah, son of Hakkoz made repairs. Adjacent to them Meshullam son of Berechiah, son of Meshezabel made repairs, and next to them Zadok son of Baana made repairs. The men of Tekoa made repairs next to them, but their nobles would not put their shoulders to the work of their masters.

Joiada son of Paseah, and Meshullam son of Besodeiah repaired the Old Gate. They laid its beams and set up its doors, its bolts and its bars. Adjacent to them worked Melatiah the Gibeonite and Jadon the Meronothite, men from Gibeon and Mizpah who are under the jurisdiction of the governor of Trans-Euphrates.

Uzziel son of Harhaiah, one of the goldsmiths, worked adjacent to him, and Hananiah, one of the perfumers, worked next to him. They restored Jerusalem as far as the Broad Wall. Rephaiah son of Hur, ruler of half the district of Jerusalem made repairs next to them. Jedaiah son of Harumaph repaired the section adjacent to them opposite his house, and Hattush son of Hashabneiah worked next to them. Malchijah son of Harim and Hasshub son of Pahath-moab repaired another section and the Tower of the Furnaces. Shallum son of Hallohesh, the ruler of half the district of Jerusalem, and his daughters repaired the next section.

Hanun and the inhabitants of Zanoah repaired the Valley Gate. They built it and set up its doors, its bolts, and its bars. They also repaired a thousand cubits of wall up to the Dung Gate.

Malchijah son of Rechab, the ruler of the district of Beth-cherem, repaired the Dung Gate. He built it and set up its doors, its bolts, and its bars.

Shallun son of Col-hozeh, the ruler of the district of Mizpah, repaired the Fountain Gate. He built it, covered it, and set up its doors, its bolts, and its bars. He also repaired the wall of the Pool of Shelah by the King's Garden, as far as the stairs going down from the City of David.

Beyond him Nehemiah son of Azbuk, the ruler of half the district of Beth-zur, made repairs as far as the tombs of David and the artificial pool and the House of the Warriors.

After him, the Levites made repairs under Rehum son of Bani, and beside him, Hashabiah, the ruler of half the district of Keilah, made repairs for his district. After him repairs were made by their brothers under Bavvai son of Henadad, the ruler of half the district of Keilah. Adjacent to him Ezer son of Jeshua, the ruler of Mizpah, repaired another section opposite the ascent to the armory at the corner buttress.

After him Baruch son of Zaccai zealously repaired another section from the corner buttress up to the door of the house of Eliashib, the *kohen gadol.*

After him Meremoth son of Uriah, son of Hakkoz, repaired another section from the door of the house of Eliashib to the end of the house of Eliashib. And after him the *kohanim* worked, men from the surrounding district.

After them Benjamin and Hasshub made repairs in front of their house. After them Azariah son of Maaseiah, son of Ananiah, worked beside his house. Beyond him Binnui son of Henadad repaired another section from the house of Azariah up to the inner buttress and the corner.

Palal son of Uzai made repairs opposite the inner buttress and the tower coming out from the upper palace, which is by the court of the guard.

After him Pedaiah son of Parosh and the Temple servants living on the Ophel made repairs up to the area opposite the Water Gate toward the east and the projecting tower.

After him the men of Tekoa repaired another section from opposite the great projecting tower to the wall of the Ophel.

Above the Horse Gate the *kohanim* worked, each in front of his own house. After them Zadok son of Immer made repairs opposite his house and after him Shemaiah son of Shecaniah, the guard of the East Gate, made repairs.

After him Hananiah, son of Shelemiah, and Hanun, the sixth son of Zalaph, repaired another portion. After him Meshullam son of Berechiah made repairs in front of his living quarters.

After him Malchijah, one of the goldsmiths, made repairs up to the house of the Temple servants, and the merchants opposite the Inspection Gate and as far as the room above the corner. Between the room above the corner and the Sheep Gate, the goldsmiths and the merchants worked.

Now when Sanballat heard that we were building the wall, he became very angry and was greatly enraged. He mocked the Jews in the presence of his colleagues and the army of Samaria, saying: "What are these feeble Jews doing? Will they fortify themselves? Will they offer sacrifices? Will they finish in a day? Can they revive the stones from the heaps of rubble that are burnt?"

Then Tobiah the Ammonite, who was beside him, said: "Even if a fox climbed on what they are building, it would break down their stone wall!"

Hear, our God, for we are despised. Turn their insult back on their own head! Give them up as plunder in a land of captivity. Do not cover their guilt or blot out their sin from before You, for they have provoked You to anger before the builders.

So we rebuilt the wall, and the entire wall was joined together up to half its height, for the people had a heart to work.

Nehemiah, chapter 3

And the Word became flesh and tabernacled among us.
We looked upon His glory, the glory of the one and only from
the Father, full of grace and truth.

John 1:14 TLV

70. God Gives Life to His Word

In the beginning was the Word. The Word was with God, and the Word was God. He was with God in the beginning. All things were made through Him, and apart from Him nothing was made that has come into being. In Him was life, and the life was the light of men. The light shines in the darkness, and the darkness has not overpowered it.

There came a man sent from God, whose name was John. He came as a witness to testify about the light, so that through him everyone might believe. He was not the light, but he came to bear witness concerning the light. The true light, coming into the world, gives light to every man.

He was in the world, and the world was made through Him; but the world did not know Him. He came to His own, but His own did not receive Him. But whoever did receive Him, those trusting in His name, to these He gave the right to become children of God.

They were born not of a bloodline, nor of human desire, nor of man's will, but of God. And the Word became flesh and tabernacled among us. We looked upon His glory, the glory of the one and only from the Father, full of grace and truth.

John testifies about Him. He cried out, saying, "This is He of whom I said, 'The One who comes after me is above me, because He existed before me.'"

Out of His fullness, we have all received grace on top of grace. *Torah* was given through Moses; grace and truth came through *Yeshua* the Messiah. No one has ever seen God; but the one and only God, in the Father's embrace, has made Him known. This is John's testimony, when the Judean leaders sent *kohanim* and Levites from Jerusalem to ask him, "Who are you?"

He openly admitted and did not deny; he admitted, "I am not the Messiah."

"What then? Are you Elijah?" they asked him.

"I am not," said John.

"Are you the Prophet?"
"No," he answered.
So they said to him, "Who are you? Give us an answer for those who sent us. What do you say about yourself?"

He said, "I am 'the voice of one crying in the wilderness, "Make straight the way of ADONAI,"' as the prophet Isaiah said."

Now those sent were from the Pharisees. They asked him, "If you're not the Messiah, Elijah, or the Prophet, why then are you immersing?"

"I immerse in water," John answered. "Among you stands One you do not know, coming after me, whose sandals I'm not worthy to untie." These things happened in Bethany beyond the Jordan, where John was immersing.

John, chapter 1

71. God Blesses Elizabeth

In the days of Herod, King of Judah, there was a *kohen* named Zechariah from the priestly division of Abijah. Elizabeth, his wife, was from the daughters of Aaron. Together they were righteous before *ADONAI*, walking without fault in all His commandments and instructions. But they were childless, because Elizabeth was barren and both of them were elderly.

Now it happened to be Zechariah's time to serve as *kohen* before *ADONAI* in the order of his division. According to the custom of the priestly office, it became his lot to enter the Holy Place of *ADONAI* to burn incense. And the whole crowd of people was praying outside at the hour of incense burning.

An angel of *ADONAI* appeared to him, standing at the right side of the altar of incense. Zechariah was in turmoil when he saw the angel, and fear fell upon him. But the angel said, "Do not be afraid, Zechariah, because your prayer has been heard. Your wife, Elizabeth, will give birth to your son, and you will name him John. And you will have joy and gladness, and many will rejoice at his birth.

He will be great before *ADONAI*; and he should not drink wine and intoxicating beverage, but he will be filled with the *Ruach ha-Kodesh* just out of his mother's womb. Many of *Bnei-Yisrael* will turn to *ADONAI* their God. And he will go before Him in the spirit and power of Elijah, to turn the hearts of fathers to the children and the disobedient ones to the wisdom of the righteous, to make ready for *ADONAI* a prepared people.

Zechariah said to the angel, "How will I know this for certain? I'm an old man, and my wife is well-advanced in age."

And speaking to him, the angel declared, "I am Gabriel, the one standing in God's presence. I was commissioned to tell you and proclaim to you this good news. So look, you will be silent and powerless to speak until the day these things happen, since you did not believe my words which will be fulfilled in their time."

The people were waiting for Zechariah and wondering about his long delay in the Holy Place. But when he came out, he couldn't speak to them. Then they realized that he had seen a vision in the Holy Place. He was making signs to them but remained mute. When the days of his priestly service had been completed, he went home.

After these days, his wife Elizabeth became pregnant and hid herself for five months, saying, "*ADONAI* has done this for me! In these days He looked upon me, to take away my disgrace among the people."

Then in the sixth month, the angel Gabriel was sent by *ADONAI* into a town in the Galilee named *Natzeret* and to a virgin engaged to a man named Joseph, of the house of David. The virgin's name was Miriam. And coming to her, the angel said, "*Shalom*, favored one! *ADONAI* is with you." But at the message, she was perplexed and kept wondering what kind of greeting this might be.

The angel spoke to her, "Do not be afraid, Miriam, for you have found favor with God. Behold, you will become pregnant and give birth to a son, and you shall call His name *Yeshua*. He will be great and will be called *Ben-Elyon*. *ADONAI Elohim* will give Him the throne of David, His father. He shall reign over the house of Jacob for all eternity, and His kingdom will be without end."

Miriam said to the angel, "How can this be, since I am not intimate with a man?"

And responding, the angel said to her, "The *Ruach ha-Kodesh* will come upon you, and the power of *Elyon* will overshadow you. Therefore, the Holy One being born will be called *Ben-Elohim*. Behold, even your relative Elizabeth has conceived a son in her old age; and the one who was called barren is six months pregnant. For nothing will be impossible with God."

So Miriam said, "Behold, the servant of *ADONAI*. Let it be done to me according to your word." And the angel left her.

Now in those days, Miriam got up and quickly traveled into the hill country, to a town in Judah. She entered Zechariah's home and happily greeted Elizabeth. When Elizabeth heard Miriam's greeting, the unborn child leaped in her womb; and Elizabeth was completely filled with the *Ruach ha-Kodesh*.

She then cried out with a great shout, saying, "You are blessed among women, and blessed is the fruit of your womb. Who am I, that the mother of my Master should come to me? For even when I just heard the sound of your greeting in my ear, the unborn child leaped with joy in my womb. Blessed is she who trusted that there would be a fulfillment of those things spoken to her by *ADONAI*."

Then Miriam said,
"My soul magnifies *ADONAI*,
and my spirit greatly rejoices
in God, my Savior.
For He has looked with care upon the
humble state of His maidservant.
For behold, from now on all
generations will call me blessed.

For the Mighty One has done a
great thing for me,
and holy is His name.
And His mercy is from generation to
generation to the ones who fear Him.

He has displayed power with His arm
He has scattered the proud in the
thoughts of their hearts.
He has brought down rulers from
thrones and exalted humble ones.
He has filled the hungry
with good things and sent away
the rich empty-handed.
He has helped His servant Israel,
remembering His mercy,
just as He spoke to our fathers,
to Abraham and to his seed forever."

She then cried out with a great shout, saying, "You are blessed among women, and blessed is the fruit of your womb. Who am I, that the mother of my Master should come to me? For even when I just heard the sound of your greeting in my ear, the unborn child leaped with joy in my womb.

Luke 1:42-44 TLV

Miriam stayed with her for three months and then returned to her home.

Upon Elizabeth's full term to deliver, she gave birth to a son. Her neighbors and relatives heard how *ADONAI* had shown her His great mercy, and they began to rejoice with her.

Now on the eighth day they came to circumcise the child, and they kept trying to call him by his father's name, Zechariah. But his mother declared, "No, he will be called John."

But they said to her, "No one among your relatives is called by this name." So they began making signs to his father, as to what he wanted him named.

Asking for a small tablet, he wrote, "John is his name." They were all astonished! And his mouth was immediately unlocked as well as his tongue, and he began to speak, praising God. Fear came on all those who lived around them, and all these matters were talked about throughout the hill country of Judah. Everyone who heard pondered these things in their hearts, saying, "What then will this child become?" For the hand of *ADONAI* was on him.

His father Zechariah was filled with the *Ruach ha-Kodesh* and prophesied, saying,

"Blessed be *ADONAI*,
God of Israel,
for He has looked after His people
and brought them redemption.
He has raised up a horn of salvation
for us in the house
of His servant David,
just as He spoke by the mouth of
His holy prophets from ages past,
salvation from our enemies
and from the hand of all who hate us!

So He shows mercy to our fathers
and remembers His holy covenant,
the vow which He swore to
Abraham our father, to grant us—rescued fearlessly from the hand of our enemies—to serve Him, in holiness and righteousness before Him all our days.

And you, child, will be called a
prophet of *Elyon*.

For you will go before *ADONAI* to
prepare His ways,
to give knowledge of salvation to
His people through removal of their sins.

Through our God's heart of mercy, the Sunrise from on high will come upon us, to give light to those who sit in darkness and in the shadow of death, to guide our feet in the way of *shalom*."

And the child kept growing and became strong in spirit; and he lived in the wilderness until the day of his public appearance to Israel.

Luke, chapter 1

Now all this took place to fulfill what was spoken by *Adonai* through the prophet, saying, "Behold, the virgin shall conceive and give birth to a son, and they shall call His name Immanuel," which means "God with us."

Matthew 1:22-23 TLV

72. God Humbles Himself

The book of the genealogy of *Yeshua ha-Mashiach, Ben-David, Ben-Avraham*:
Abraham fathered Isaac,
Isaac fathered Jacob,
Jacob fathered Judah and his brothers,
Judah fathered Perez
and Zerah by Tamar,
Perez fathered Hezron,
Hezron fathered Ram,
Ram fathered Amminadab,
Amminadab fathered Nahshon,
Nahshon fathered Salmon,
Salmon fathered Boaz by Rahab,
Boaz fathered Obed by Ruth,
Obed fathered Jesse,
and Jesse fathered David the king.

David fathered Solomon by the wife of Uriah, Solomon fathered Rehoboam, Rehoboam fathered Abijah, Abijah fathered Asa, Asa fathered Jehoshaphat, Jehoshaphat fathered Joram, Joram fathered Uzziah, Uzziah fathered Jotham, Jotham fathered Ahaz, Ahaz fathered Hezekiah, Hezekiah fathered Manasseh, Manasseh fathered Amon, Amon fathered Josiah, and Josiah fathered Jeconiah and his brothers at the time of the exile to Babylon.

After the Babylonian exile Jeconiah fathered Shealtiel, Shealtiel fathered Zerubbabel, Zerubbabel fathered Abiud, Abiud fathered Eliakim, Eliakim fathered Azor, Azor fathered Zadok, Zadok fathered Achim, Achim fathered Eliud, Eliud fathered Eleazar, Eleazar fathered Matthan, Matthan fathered Jacob, and Jacob fathered Joseph the husband of Miriam, from whom was born *Yeshua* who is called the Messiah. So all the generations from Abraham to David are fourteen generations, from David until the Babylonian exile are fourteen generations, and from the Babylonian exile until the Messiah are fourteen generations.

Now the birth of *Yeshua* the Messiah happened this way. When His mother Miriam was engaged to Joseph but before they came together, she was found to be pregnant through the *Ruach ha-Kodesh*. And Joseph her husband, being a righteous man and not wanting to disgrace her publicly, made up his mind to dismiss her secretly. But while he considered these things, behold, an angel of *ADONAI* appeared to him in a dream, saying, "Joseph son of David, do not be afraid to take Miriam as your wife, for the Child conceived in her is from the *Ruach ha-Kodesh*. She will give birth to a son; and you shall call His name *Yeshua*, for He will save His people from their sins."

Now all this took place to fulfill what was spoken by *ADONAI* through the prophet, saying, "Behold, the virgin shall conceive and give birth to a son, and they shall call His name Immanuel," which means "God with us." When Joseph woke up from his sleep, he did as the angel of *ADONAI* commanded him and took Miriam as his wife. But he did not know her intimately until she had given birth to a Son. And he called His name *Yeshua*.

Matthew, chapter 1

Now after *Yeshua* was born in Bethlehem of Judea, in the days of King Herod, magi from the east came to Jerusalem, saying, "Where is the

One who has been born King of the Jews? For we saw His star in the east and have come to worship Him."

When King Herod heard, he was troubled, and all Jerusalem with him. And when he had called together all the ruling *kohanim* and *Torah* scholars, he began to inquire of them where the Messiah was to be born. So they told him, "In Bethlehem of Judea, for so it has been written by the prophet:
'And you, Bethlehem, land of
Judah, are by no means least
among the rulers of Judah;
For out of you shall come a ruler
who will shepherd My people
Israel.'"

Then Herod secretly called the magi and determined from them the exact time the star had appeared. And he sent them to Bethlehem and said, "Go and search carefully for the Child. And when you have found Him, bring word back to me so that I may come and worship Him as well."

After listening to the king, they went their way. And behold, the star they had seen in the east went on before them, until it came to rest over the place where the Child was. When they saw the star, they rejoiced exceedingly with great gladness. And when they came into the house, they saw the Child with His mother Miriam; and they fell down and worshiped Him. Then, opening their treasures, they presented to Him gifts of gold, frankincense, and myrrh. And having been warned in a dream not to go back to Herod, they returned to their own country by another way. Now when they had gone, behold, an angel of *ADONAI* appears to Joseph in a dream, saying, "Get up! Take the Child and His mother and flee to Egypt. Stay there until I tell you, for Herod is about to search for the Child, to kill Him." So he got up, took the Child and His mother during the night, and went to Egypt. He stayed there until Herod's death. This was to fulfill what was spoken by *ADONAI* through the prophet, saying, "Out of Egypt I called My son."

Then when Herod saw that he had been tricked by the magi, he became furious. And he sent and killed all boys in Bethlehem and in all its surrounding area, from two years old and under, according to the time he had determined from the magi.
Then was fulfilled what was spoken through Jeremiah the prophet, saying,
"A voice is heard in Ramah,
weeping and loud wailing,
Rachel sobbing for her children
and refusing to be comforted,
because they are no more."

But when Herod died, behold, an angel of *ADONAI* appears in a dream to Joseph in Egypt, saying, "Get up! Take the Child and His mother and go to the land of Israel, for those seeking the Child's life are dead." So he got up, took the Child and His mother, and went to the land of Israel. But hearing that Archelaus was king of Judea in place of his father Herod, he became afraid to go there. Then after being warned in a dream, he withdrew to the region of the Galilee. And he went and lived in a city called *Natzeret*, to fulfill what was spoken through the prophets, that *Yeshua* shall be called a *Natzrati*.

Matthew, chapter 2

73. God Hides the Savior

Now it happened in those days a decree went out from Caesar Augustus to register all the world's inhabitants. This was the first census taken when Quirinius was governor of Syria. Everyone was traveling to be registered in his own city.

Now Joseph also went up from the Galilee, out of the town of *Natzeret* to Judah, to the city of David, which is called Bethlehem, because he was from the house and family of David. He went to register with Miriam, who was engaged to him and was pregnant.

But while they were there, the time came for her to give birth—and she gave birth to her firstborn son. She wrapped Him in strips of cloth and set Him down in a manger, since there was no room for them in the inn.

Now there were shepherds in the same region, living out in the fields and guarding their flock at night. Suddenly an angel of *ADONAI* stood before them, and the glory of *ADONAI* shone all around them; and they were absolutely terrified.

But the angel said to them, "Do not be afraid! For behold, I proclaim Good News to you, which will be great joy to all the people. A Savior is born to you today in the city of David, who is Messiah the Lord.

And the sign to you is this: You will find an infant wrapped in strips of cloth and lying in a manger." And suddenly a multitude of heavenly armies appeared with the angel, praising God and saying,

"Glory to God in the highest,
and on earth *shalom*
to men of good will."

And when the angels departed from them into the heavens, the shepherds were saying to one another, "Let's go to Bethlehem and see this thing that has happened which *ADONAI* has made known to us!"

So they hurried off and found Miriam and Joseph, and the Baby lying in the manger. When they had seen this, they made known the word that had been spoken to them concerning this Child. And all those who heard were amazed at the things the shepherds told them. But Miriam treasured all these things, pondering them in her heart.

The shepherds returned, glorifying and praising God for all the things they had heard and seen, just as they had been told.

When eight days had passed for His *brit-milah*, He was named *Yeshua*, the name given by the angel before He was conceived in the womb.

And when the days of their purification were fulfilled, according to the *Torah* of Moses, they brought Him to Jerusalem to present to *ADONAI*.

As it is written in the *Torah* of *ADONAI*, "Every firstborn male that opens the womb shall be called holy to *ADONAI*."

So they offered a sacrifice according

Simeon received Him into his arms and offered a *bracha* to God, saying, "Now may You let Your servant go in peace, O Sovereign Master, according to Your word. For my eyes have seen Your salvation, which You have prepared in the presence of all peoples: 'A light for revelation to the nations' and the glory of Your people Israel."

Luke 2:28-32 TLV

to what was said in the *Torah* of ADONAI: "a pair of turtle doves, or two young pigeons."

Now there was a man in Jerusalem whose name was Simeon, and this man was just and pious, waiting for the consolation of Israel. The *Ruach ha-Kodesh* was on him. And it had been revealed to him by the *Ruach ha -Kodesh* that he would not die before he had seen the Anointed One of ADONAI.

So in the *Ruach*, Simeon came into the Temple; and when the parents brought the Child *Yeshua* to do for Him according to the custom of the *Torah*, Simeon received Him into his arms and offered a *bracha* to God, saying, "Now may You let Your servant go in peace, O Sovereign Master, according to Your word. For my eyes have seen Your salvation, which You have prepared in the presence of all peoples:

'A light for revelation to the
nations' and the glory
of Your people Israel."

And His father and mother were marveling at the things that were said about Him.

And Simeon offered a *bracha* over them and said to Miriam His mother, "Behold, this One is destined to cause the fall and rise of many in Israel, and to be a sign that is opposed, so the thoughts of many hearts may be uncovered. (And even for you, a sword will pierce through your soul.)"

Now Anna, a daughter of Phanuel of the tribe of Asher, was a prophetess. She was well advanced in age, having lived with a husband only seven years and then as a widow until age eighty-four. She never left the Temple, serving night and day with fasting and prayers.

And coming up at that very instant, she began praising God and speaking about the Child to all those waiting for the redemption of Jerusalem. When Joseph and Miriam had completed everything according to the *Torah* of ADONAI, they returned to the Galilee, to their own city of *Natzeret*.

The Child kept growing and became strong, filled with wisdom; and the favor of God was upon Him.

Luke 2:1-40

After three days they found Him in the Temple, sitting in the center of the teachers, listening to them and asking them questions. And all those hearing Him were astonished at His understanding and His answers.

Luke 2:46-47 TLV

74. God Speaks Through His Son

Now His parents were going every year to Jerusalem for the Passover feast.

When He became twelve years old, they were going up according to festival custom. As they headed home after completing the days, the boy *Yeshua* remained in Jerusalem, but His parents didn't know. Supposing He was in the caravan, they went a day's journey, then began looking for Him among relatives and friends. When they did not find Him, they returned to Jerusalem to search for Him.

After three days they found Him in the Temple, sitting in the center of the teachers, listening to them and asking them questions. And all those hearing Him were astonished at His understanding and His answers.

When His parents saw *Yeshua*, they were overwhelmed. And His mother said to Him, "Child, why did you do this to us? Look! Your father and I were searching for You frantically!"

He said to them, **"Why were you searching for Me? Didn't you know that I must be about the things of My Father?"**

But they did not grasp the message He was telling them.

Then He went down with them to *Natzeret* and was obedient to them. But His mother treasured all these words in her heart.

And *Yeshua* kept increasing in wisdom and stature, and in favor with God and men.

Luke 2:41-52

Just as He was coming up out of the water, He saw the heavens ripping open and the *Ruach* as a dove coming down upon Him. And there came a voice from the heavens: "You are My Son, whom I love; with You I am well pleased!"

Mark 1:10-11 TLV

75. God Arrives!

The beginning of the Good News of *Yeshua ha-Mashiach, Ben-Elohim.*

As Isaiah the prophet has written,
"Behold, I send My messenger
before You, who will prepare
Your way.
The voice of one crying in the
wilderness, 'Prepare the way
of *ADONAI*, and make His paths
straight.'"

John appeared, immersing in the wilderness, proclaiming an immersion involving repentance for the removal of sins. All the Judean countryside was going out to him, and all the Jerusalemites. As they confessed their sins, they were being immersed by him in the Jordan River.

John wore clothes made from camel's hair, with a leather belt around his waist, and he ate locusts and wild honey.

"After me comes One who is mightier than I am," he proclaimed. "I'm not worthy to stoop down and untie the strap of His sandals! I immersed you with water, but He will immerse you in the *Ruach ha-Kodesh.*"

In those days, *Yeshua* came from *Natzeret* in the Galilee and was immersed by John in the Jordan.

Just as He was coming up out of the water, He saw the heavens ripping open and the *Ruach* as a dove coming down upon Him. And there came a voice from the heavens: "You are My Son, whom I love; with You I am well pleased!"

That instant, the *Ruach* drives Him into the wilderness. He was in the wilderness forty days, being tempted by satan. And He was with the wild beasts, and the angels were taking care of Him.

Now after John was put in jail, *Yeshua* came into the Galilee, proclaiming the Good News of God. **"Now is the fullness of time,"** He said, **"and the kingdom of God is near! Turn away from your sins, and believe in the Good News!"**

Passing along by the Sea of Galilee, He saw Simon and Simon's brother Andrew casting a net in the sea, for they were fishermen. And *Yeshua* said to them, **"Follow Me, and I will make you become fishers of men."** Immediately they left their nets and followed Him.

Going a little farther, He saw Jacob the son of Zebedee and John his brother, who were in their boat mending the nets. Immediately He called them, and they left their father Zebedee in the boat with the hired hands and followed Him.

And they went into Capernaum. Right away, on *Shabbat*, He entered the synagogue and began to teach. And they were astounded at His teaching, for He was teaching them as one having authority and not as the *Torah* scholars.

Just then there was a man in their synagogue with an unclean spirit.

And he cried out, "What have we to

do with You, *Yeshua* of *Natzeret*? Have You come to destroy us? I know who You are! You're the Holy One of God!"

Yeshua rebuked him, saying, **"Quiet! Come out of him!"** And the unclean spirit, after throwing the man into convulsions and crying out with a loud voice, came out of him.

They were all so amazed that they asked among themselves, "What is this? A new teaching with authority! He commands even the unclean spirits, and they obey Him!"

And immediately news about Him spread throughout the region surrounding Galilee.

As soon as they left the synagogue, they went with Jacob and John to the house of Simon and Andrew. Now Simon's mother-in-law was lying sick with a fever. Right away, they told *Yeshua* about her. He came and raised her up by taking her hand. The fever left her, and she began to take care of them.

When evening came, at sunset, the people brought to Him all the sick and those who were afflicted by demons. The whole town gathered together at the door. He healed many who were sick with various diseases and drove out many demons. And He would not allow the demons to speak, because they knew who He was.

Very early, while it was still night, *Yeshua* got up, left, and went away to a place in the wilderness; and there He was praying.

Then Simon and those with him hunted for *Yeshua*. And when they found Him, they said to Him, "Everybody's looking for You."

He said to them, **"Let's go somewhere else, to the neighboring towns, so that I may proclaim the message there also—this is what I came for."**

And He went throughout all the Galilee, proclaiming the message in their synagogues and driving out demons.

A man with *tzara'at* comes to Him, begging Him and falling on his knees, saying, "If You are willing, You can make me clean."

Moved with compassion, *Yeshua* stretched out His hand and touched him.

He said, "I am willing. Be cleansed."

Immediately, the *tzara'at* left him, and he was cleansed. *Yeshua* sent him away at once, sternly warning him. He said to him, **"See that you say nothing to anyone, but go show yourself to the *kohen*. Then, for your cleansing, offer what Moses commanded, as a testimony to them."**

But he went out and began to proclaim and spread the word, so much that *Yeshua* could no longer enter a town openly but had to stay out in wilderness areas. Still, they kept on coming to Him from everywhere.

Mark, chapter 1

76. God Leads Followers

Now the people were filled with expectation, and all were wondering in their hearts about John, whether he might be the Messiah.

John answered them all, saying, "As for me, I immerse you with water. But One is coming who is mightier than I am; I am not worthy to untie the strap of His sandals! He will immerse you in the *Ruach ha-Kodesh* and fire. His winnowing fork is in His hand to clear His threshing floor and gather the wheat into His barn, but the chaff He will burn up with inextinguishable fire."

So with many other exhortations, John proclaimed Good News to the people. But Herod the tetrarch—after being rebuked by John because of Herodias, his brother's wife, and because of all the evil things Herod had done—added even this on top of them all: he shut up John in prison.

Now when all the people were immersed, *Yeshua* also was immersed. And while He was praying, heaven was opened and the *Ruach ha-Kodesh* came down upon Him in bodily form like a dove. And from out of heaven came a voice, "You are My Son, whom I love—with You I am well pleased!"

Luke 3:15-22

Yeshua was about thirty years old when He began his ministry.

Luke 3:23

Yeshua, now filled with the *Ruach ha-Kodesh*, returned from the Jordan. He was led by the *Ruach* in the wilderness for forty days, being tested by the devil. Now He ate nothing during those days, and when they had ended, He was hungry.

The devil said to Him, "If You are *Ben-Elohim*, tell this stone to become bread."

Yeshua answered him, "It is written, 'Man shall not live by bread alone.'"

And leading Him up, the devil showed Him all the kingdoms of the world in an instant. And the devil said to Him, "I'll give to You all this authority along with its glory, because it has been handed over to me and I can give it to anyone I wish. Therefore, if you will worship before me, all this shall be Yours."

But answering, *Yeshua* told him, **"It is written, 'You shall worship ADONAI your God, and Him only shall you serve.'"**

Then he brought *Yeshua* to Jerusalem and placed Him on the highest point of the Temple. He said to Him, "If You are *Ben-Elohim*, throw Yourself down from here. For it is written,

'He will command His angels
concerning you, to guard you,'
and 'upon their hands they will lift
you up, so that you may not
strike your foot against a stone.'"

But answering, *Yeshua* said to him, **"It is said, 'You shall not put ADONAI your God to the test.'"**

And when the devil had completed

every test, he departed from Him until another occasion.

Yeshua returned in the power of the *Ruach* to the Galilee, and news about Him went out through all the surrounding region. He taught in their synagogues, and everyone was praising Him. And He came to *Natzeret*, where He had been raised. As was His custom, He went into the synagogue on *Shabbat*, and He got up to read. When the scroll of the prophet Isaiah was handed to Him, He unrolled the scroll and found the place where it was written,

"The *Ruach* ADONAI is on me,
because He has anointed me
to proclaim Good News to the poor.

He has sent me to proclaim
release to the captives and
recovery of sight to the blind,
to set free the oppressed,
and to proclaim the year
of ADONAI's favor."

He closed the scroll, gave it back to the attendant, and sat down. All eyes in the synagogue were focused on Him. Then He began to tell them, **"Today this Scripture has been fulfilled in your ears."**

All were speaking well of Him and marveling at the gracious words coming out of His mouth. And they were saying, "Isn't this the son of Joseph?"

But He said to them, **"Doubtless you will say to Me this proverb, 'Doctor, heal yourself!' and 'What we have heard was done at Capernaum, do as much here also in your hometown.'"**

But He said, **"Truly, I tell you, 'No prophet is accepted in his own hometown.'**

But with all truthfulness I say to you, that there were many widows in Israel in the days of Elijah, when heaven was closed for three and a half years and there came a great famine over all the land. Elijah was not sent to any of them, but only to Zarephath in the land of Sidon, to a widowed woman.

There were many with *tzara'at* in Israel in the time of Elisha the prophet, and none of them were purified apart from Naaman the Syrian."

Now all in the synagogue were filled with rage upon hearing these things. Rising up, they drove Him out of the town and brought Him as far as the edge of the mountain on which their city had been built, in order to throw Him off the cliff. But passing through the middle of them, He went on His way. *Yeshua* came down to Capernaum, a town in the Galilee. He was teaching them on *Shabbat*, and they were astounded at His teaching because His message had authority.

In the synagogue was a man who had an unclean demonic spirit, and he cried out with a loud voice, "Ah! What have we to do with You, *Yeshua* of *Natzeret*? Have You come to destroy us? I know who You are! You are the Holy One of God!"

Yeshua rebuked him, saying, **"Quiet! Come out of him!"** And when the demon threw him down in their midst, it came out without hurting

It happened that the crowds were pressing upon *Yeshua* to hear the word of God as He was standing by the Lake of Kinneret, when He saw two boats standing beside the lake. Now the fishermen had left them and were washing the nets.

Luke 5:1-2 TLV

him.

They were all amazed, and they spoke to one another, saying, "What is this message? For with authority and power He commands the unclean spirits, and they come out." So His reputation grew, spreading to every place in that region.

After He left the synagogue, *Yeshua* entered Simon's home. Simon's mother-in-law was suffering from a high fever, and they petitioned Him concerning her. Then standing over her, He rebuked the fever and it left her. Immediately she arose to wait on them.

When the sun was setting, they brought to *Yeshua* all who were sick with various diseases. And He was laying hands on each one and healing them. Even demons were coming out from many, shouting out and saying, "You are *Ben-Elohim*!" But He was rebuking them and not permitting them to speak, because they knew Him to be the Messiah.

Now when it was day, He left and went to a desert place. The crowds were searching for Him, and they came to Him and were trying to keep Him from leaving them. But He said to them, "I must proclaim the Good News of the kingdom of God to the other towns also. It was for this purpose I was sent." So He kept preaching in the synagogues of Judea.

Luke, chapter 4

It happened that the crowds were pressing upon *Yeshua* to hear the word of God as He was standing by the Lake of *Kinneret*, when He saw two boats standing beside the lake.

Now the fishermen had left them and were washing the nets. Getting into one of the boats, Simon's boat, *Yeshua* asked him to push out a ways from the land. Then sitting down, He taught the crowds from the boat.

When He had finished speaking, He said to Simon, **"Go out into the deep water, and let down your nets for a catch."**

Simon replied, "Master, we've worked hard all night and caught nothing. But at Your word I will let down the nets." When they had done this, they caught so many fish that their nets began to break. So they signaled to their partners in the other boat to come and help them. They came and filled both boats so full that they began to sink.

But when Simon Peter saw this, he fell down at *Yeshua's* knees, saying, "Go away from me, Master, for I am a sinful man!" For amazement had gripped him and all who were with him, over the catch of fish they had netted; so also Jacob and John, Zebedee's sons, who were partners with Simon.

But *Yeshua* said to Simon, **"Do not be afraid. From now on, you will be catching men."** So when they had brought the boats to the landing, they left everything and followed Him.

Now while *Yeshua* was in one of the towns, a man covered with *tzara'at* appeared. And when he saw *Yeshua*, he fell on his face and begged Him, saying, "Master, if You are willing, You can make me clean."

Yeshua stretched out His hand and touched him, saying, **"I am willing. Be cleansed!"** Immediately, the *tzara'at* left him. *Yeshua* ordered him to tell no one, but commanded him, **"Go and show yourself to the *kohen*. Then bring an offering for your cleansing, just as Moses commanded, as a testimony to them."**

But the news about *Yeshua* was spreading all the more, and many crowds were coming together to hear and to be healed of their diseases. Yet He would often slip away into the wilderness and pray. Now on one of those days, *Yeshua* was teaching. Pharisees and *Torah* scholars were sitting there, who had come from every village of the Galilee and Judea, as well as from Jerusalem. And *ADONAI's* power to heal was in Him.

And behold, men were carrying a paralyzed man on a stretcher, trying to bring him in and place him before *Yeshua*. But when they found no way to bring him in because of the crowd, they went up on the roof and let him down with his stretcher through the tiles, right in the middle before *Yeshua*. When He saw their faith, He said, "Man, your sins are forgiven."

Then the *Torah* scholars and the Pharisees began to question, saying, "Who is this fellow speaking blasphemies? Who can pardon sins but God alone?"

Yeshua, knowing their thoughts, replied to them, **"Why are you raising questions in your hearts? Which is easier, to say, 'Your sins are forgiven you,' or to say, 'Get up and walk'? But so you may know that the Son of Man has authority on earth to pardon sins. . . ."** He said to the paralyzed one, "I tell you, get up and take your cot, and go home!"

Immediately he got up before them, picked up what he had been lying on, and went home, glorifying God. Astonishment took hold of them, and they glorified God and all were filled with awe, saying, "We've seen incredible things today!"

After these things, *Yeshua* went out and observed a tax collector named Levi, sitting at the tax booth. He said to him, **"Follow Me."** And leaving everything, he got up and followed Him. Levi made a great banquet for *Yeshua* at his house, and there was a large crowd of tax collectors and others who were reclining with them. The Pharisees and their *Torah* scholars began murmuring to His disciples, saying, "Why do you eat and drink with tax collectors and sinners?"

And *Yeshua* answered and said to them, **"Those who are healthy have no need for a doctor, but those who are sick do. I did not come to call the righteous, but the sinful to repentance."**

But they said to Him, "John's disciples often fast and offer prayers, as do the disciples of the Pharisees. But Your disciples are eating and drinking."

But *Yeshua* said to them, **"You cannot make the guests of the bridegroom fast while the bridegroom is with**

them, can you? But the days will come; and when the bridegroom is taken away from them, then they will fast in those days."

Now he was also telling them a parable. "No one tears a patch from a new garment to use it on an old garment. Otherwise he will rip the new, and the patch from the new will not match the old. And no one puts new wine into old wineskins. Otherwise, the new wine will burst the skins, it will be spilled out, and the skins will be destroyed. But new wine must be put into fresh wineskins. No man who drinks old wine wants new, because he says, 'The old is fine.'"

Luke, chapter 5

77. God Invites Children

At that hour the disciples came to *Yeshua*, saying, "Who then is greatest in the kingdom of heaven?"

And He called a child to Himself, set him in the midst of them, and said, **"Amen, I tell you, unless you turn and become like children, you shall never enter the kingdom of heaven. Whoever then shall humble himself like this child, this one is the greatest in the kingdom of heaven. And whoever welcomes one such child in My name, welcomes Me.**

"But whoever causes one of these little ones who trust in Me to stumble, it would be better for him to have a heavy millstone hung around his neck and to be sunk in the depth of the sea! Woe to the world because of snares! For snares must come, but woe to that man through whom the snare comes!

"And if your hand or your foot causes you to stumble, cut it off and throw it away from you. It's better for you to enter into life crippled or lame than, having two hands or two feet, to be thrown into fiery Gehenna. If your eye causes you to stumble, pluck it out and throw it away from you. It's better for you to enter into life with one eye than, having two eyes, to be thrown into fiery Gehenna.

"See that you do not despise one of these little ones, for I tell you that their angels in heaven continually see the face of My Father in heaven.

"What do you think? If a certain man has a hundred sheep and one of them goes astray, won't he leave the ninety-nine on the mountains and go looking for the one that is straying? And if he finds it, amen I tell you, he rejoices over it more than over the ninety-nine that didn't stray. Even so, it's not the will of your Father in heaven that one of these little ones should be lost."

"Now if your brother sins against you, go and show him his fault while you're with him alone. If he listens to you, you have won your brother. But if he does not listen, take with you one or two more, so that 'by the mouth of two or three witnesses every word may stand.' But if he refuses to listen to them, tell it to Messiah's community. And if he refuses to listen even to Messiah's community, let him be to you as a pagan and a tax collector.

"Amen, I tell you, whatever you forbid on earth will have been forbidden in heaven and what you permit on earth will have been permitted in heaven. Again I say to you, that if two of you agree on earth about anything they may ask, it shall be done for them by My Father in heaven. For where two or three are gathered together in My name, there I am in their midst."

Then Peter came to Him and said, "Master, how often shall I forgive my brother when he sins against me? Up to seven times?"

Yeshua said to him, **"No, not up to seven times, I tell you, but seventy**

But *Yeshua* said, "Let the little children come to Me and do not hinder them, for the kingdom of heaven belongs to such as these."

Matthew 19:14 TLV

times seven! Therefore, the kingdom of heaven may be compared to a king who wanted to settle accounts with his slaves. When he had begun to settle up, a man was brought to him who owed him ten thousand talents. But since he didn't have the money to repay, his master ordered him to be sold, along with his wife and children and all that he had, and payment to be made. Then the slave fell on his knees and begged him, saying, 'Be patient with me, and I'll repay you everything.' And the master of that slave, filled with compassion, released him and forgave him the debt.

"Now that slave went out and found one of his fellow slaves who owed him a hundred denarii. And he grabbed him and started choking him, saying, 'Pay back what you owe!' So his fellow slave fell down and kept begging him, saying, 'Be patient with me, and I'll pay you back.' Yet he was unwilling. Instead, he went off and threw the man into prison until he paid back all he owed.

"So when his fellow slaves saw what had happened, they were deeply distressed. They went to their master and reported in detail all that had happened. Then summoning the first slave, his master said to him, 'You wicked slave! I forgave all that debt because you pleaded with me. Wasn't it necessary for you also to show mercy to your fellow slave, just as I showed mercy to you?' Enraged, the master handed him over to the torturers until he paid back all he owed.

"So also My heavenly Father will do to you, unless each of you, from your hearts, forgives his brother."

Matthew, chapter 18

Now when *Yeshua* had finished these words, He moved on from the Galilee and entered the region of Judea beyond the Jordan. Large crowds followed Him, and He healed them there.

Pharisees came up to *Yeshua*, testing Him and saying, "Is it permitted for a man to divorce his wife for any reason at all?"

"Haven't you read?" He answered. **"He who created them from the beginning 'made them male and female' and said, 'For this reason a man shall leave his father and mother and be joined to his wife, and the two shall become one flesh.' So they are no longer two, but one flesh. Therefore what God has joined together, let no man separate."**

They said to Him, "Why then did Moses command to 'give her a certificate of divorce and put her away?'"

Yeshua said to them, **"Because of your hardness of heart Moses permitted you to divorce your wives, but from the beginning it was not so. Now I tell you, whoever divorces his wife, except for sexual immorality, and marries another, commits adultery."**

The disciples said to Him, "If that's the case for a man and his wife, it's better not to marry!"

But He said to them, **"Not everyone**

can accept this saying—only those to whom it has been given. For there are eunuchs who were born that way from their mother's womb; and there are eunuchs who were made that way by men; and there are eunuchs who made themselves eunuchs for the sake of the kingdom of heaven. He who can accept this, let him accept it."

Then little children were brought to *Yeshua* so that He might lay hands upon them and pray. Then the disciples rebuked those who brought them.

But *Yeshua* said, **"Let the little children come to Me and do not hinder them, for the kingdom of heaven belongs to such as these."**

After laying His hands upon them, He went on from there.

Now behold, one came to Him and said, "Teacher, what good shall I do to have eternal life?"

"Why do you ask Me about what is good?" *Yeshua* said to him. **"There is only One who is good; but if you want to enter into life, keep the commandments."**

"Which ones?" he said.

Yeshua said, **"'Do not murder, do not commit adultery, do not steal, do not give false testimony, honor your father and mother,' and 'love your neighbor as yourself.'"**

"All these I've kept," the young man said to Him. "What do I still lack?"

Yeshua said to him, **"If you wish to be perfect, go, sell what you own, and give to the poor; and you will have treasure in heaven. Then come, follow Me."**

But when the young man heard this statement, he went away grieving, for he had much property.

Then *Yeshua* said to His disciples, **"Amen, I tell you, it is hard for a rich man to enter the kingdom of heaven. Again I tell you, it is easier for a camel to go through the eye of a needle, than for a rich man to enter the kingdom of God."**

When the disciples heard this, they were utterly astonished and said, "Then who can be saved?"

And looking, *Yeshua* said to them, **"With men this is impossible, but with God all things are possible."**

Then Peter said to Him, "Look, we've left everything to follow You! So what will we have?"

And *Yeshua* said to them, **"Amen, I tell you, when the Son of Man sits on His glorious throne in the new world, you who have followed Me shall also sit on twelve thrones, judging the twelve tribes of Israel. And everyone who has left houses or brothers or sisters or father or mother or children or property, for My name's sake, will receive a hundred times as much, and will inherit eternal life. But many who are first will be last, and the last first."**

Matthew, chapter 19

78. God Heals His Daughters

Soon afterward, *Yeshua* began traveling throughout towns and villages, preaching and proclaiming the Good News of the Kingdom of God. The twelve were also with Him.

And certain women who had been healed of evil spirits and infirmities—Miriam, the one called Magdalene, out of whom seven demons had gone; Joanna, the wife of Kuza, Herod's finance minister; Susanna; and many others—were supporting them out of their own resources.

And when a large crowd was gathering and those from various towns were traveling to Him, He spoke by means of a parable.

"The sower went out to spread his seed. As he sowed, some fell beside the road and was trampled; and the birds of the air ate it up. And other seed fell on rock; when it came up, that seed withered away because it had no moisture. Other seed fell among the thorns, and the thorns grew up with it and choked it. And other seed fell into the good soil; and when it came up, it produced fruit a hundredfold."

While saying these things, He would call out, **"He who has ears to hear, let him hear."**

Now His disciples were asking Him what this parable meant.

Then *Yeshua* said to them, **"To you has been given to know the secrets of the kingdom of God; but to the others it is given in parables, in order that**

'Seeing, they may not see,
and hearing,
they may not understand.'

"Now the parable is this: the seed is the word of God. Those beside the road are the ones who have heard; then the devil comes and takes away the word from their heart, so that they may not believe and be saved. But those on the rocky places are the ones who, when they hear, accept the word with joy. But these have no root; they believe for a season, and in a time of testing fall away. Now that which fell into the thorns are those who were hearing; but as they go along the way, they are choked by the cares and riches and pleasures of life, and they do not bear mature fruit. But the seed in the good soil are those with a praiseworthy and good heart, who have heard the word and hold it fast and bear fruit with patient endurance.

"Now no one after lighting a lamp covers it with some object or places it under a bed. But he puts it on a lampstand so that all those who enter may be able to see the light. For nothing is hidden that will not become evident, nor secret that shall not be known and come into open view. So pay attention how you listen. For whoever has, to him more will be given. And whoever does not have, even what he supposes he has will be taken away from him."

Yeshua's mother and brothers came to Him, but were not able to reach

Him through the crowd. Now it was reported to Him, "Your mother and Your brothers are standing outside, wanting to see You."

But answering, He said to them, **"My mother and My brothers are these who are hearing the word of God and doing it."**

Now on one of those days *Yeshua* and His disciples got into a boat, and He said to them, **"Let's move to the other side of the lake."** So they set out. Then as they were sailing, He fell asleep.

A violent windstorm came down on the lake, and they were swamped with water and in danger. They came to *Yeshua* and woke Him, saying, "Master, Master, we're perishing!" He got up and rebuked the wind and the surging wave of water. Then they stopped, and it became calm.

Then *Yeshua* said to them, **"Where is your faith?"** But they were afraid and marveled, saying to one another, "Who then is this? He commands even the winds and the water, and they obey Him!"

They sailed over to the country of the Gerasenes, which is on the opposite side of the Galilee. A demon-plagued man from the town met *Yeshua* as He was coming out onto the land. The man hadn't worn any clothing for a long time and was living not in a house but in the tombs.

Seeing *Yeshua*, he cried out and fell down before *Yeshua*, and with a loud voice said, "What's between You and me, *Yeshua, Ben El Elyon*? I'm begging You, do not torment me!" for *Yeshua* commanded the defiling spirit to come out of the man. For many times it had seized him so that, even though he was restrained and bound with chains and shackles, he would break the chains and be driven by the demons into the desert.

Yeshua questioned him, **"What is your name?"**

"Legion," he said, for many demons had entered him. They kept begging Him not to command them to depart into the abyss.

Now a large herd of pigs was feeding on the mountain. The demons urged *Yeshua* to let them enter these pigs, and He gave them permission. Then the demons came out of the man and entered into the pigs. The herd rushed down the cliff into the lake and was drowned. But when the herdsmen saw what happened, they ran away and reported it in the town and countryside.

People went out to see what had happened. They came to *Yeshua* and found the man from whom the demons had gone—clothed and in his right mind, sitting at the feet of *Yeshua*. And they were frightened.

Now those who had seen it reported how the demon-plagued man had been restored. And all the people from the region surrounding the Gerasenes asked *Yeshua* to go away from them because they were overcome by great fear. So He got into a boat and returned.

The man from whom the demons had

gone out begged to go with *Yeshua*. But *Yeshua* sent him away, saying, "Return to your home, and describe all that God has done for you." So he went away, proclaiming throughout the whole town all that *Yeshua* had done for him.

As *Yeshua* returned, the crowd welcomed Him, for they were all expecting Him. And here came a man named Jairus, a leader in the synagogue. Falling at *Yeshua*'s feet, he begged Him to come to his house, because his only daughter, about twelve years old, was dying.

But as He made His way, the masses were crushing in upon Him. And there was a woman with a blood flow for twelve years, who could not be healed by anyone. She came up from behind and touched the *tzitzit* of *Yeshua's* garment. Immediately, her blood flow stopped.

Yeshua said, **"Who touched Me?"**

When everyone denied it, Peter said, "Master, the crowds are surrounding You and pressing in!"

But *Yeshua* said, **"Someone touched Me, for I recognized power going out from Me."**

Then seeing that she did not escape notice, the woman came trembling and fell prostrate before Him. In the presence of all the people, she confessed why she had touched Him and how she had been healed immediately. He said to her, **"Daughter, your faith has made you well. Go in *shalom*."**

While He was still speaking, someone comes from the house of the synagogue leader, saying, "Your daughter has died. Don't bother the Teacher anymore."

But hearing this, *Yeshua* replied to him, **"Do not fear—just keep trusting, and she shall be restored."**

When *Yeshua* came into the house, He didn't let anyone enter with Him except Peter, John, Jacob, and the child's father and mother. And everyone was weeping and lamenting her; but He said, **"Don't weep, for she didn't die but is sleeping."** But they were ridiculing Him, knowing she had died. But *Yeshua*, took her by the hand and called out, saying, **"Child, get up!"** Her spirit returned, and she arose immediately. *Yeshua* ordered food to be given to her to eat. Her parents were utterly astonished, but He ordered them to say nothing of what had happened.

Luke, chapter 8

She came up from behind and touched the *tzitzit* of *Yeshua*'s garment. Immediately, her blood flow stopped.

Luke 8:44 TLV

79. God is Our Father

Now *Yeshua* went out from there, and He comes to His hometown, and His disciples follow Him.

When *Shabbat* came, He began to teach in the synagogue.

Many listeners were amazed, saying, "Where did this fellow get these things? What's this wisdom given to Him? Such miracles are done by His hands! Isn't this the carpenter, the son of Miriam, and the brother of Jacob and Joseph and Judah and Simon? Aren't His sisters here with us?" And they took offense at Him.

Then *Yeshua* began saying to them, **"A prophet is not without honor except in his hometown, among his relatives, and in his own house."**

He was not able to do any miracle, except that He laid hands on a few sick people and healed them. And He was astonished because of their unbelief. And He was going around among the villages teaching.

Yeshua summoned the Twelve, and He began to send them out two by two. And He gave them authority over the unclean spirits. He directed them to take nothing for the journey except a walking stick—no bread, no bag, no copper coin in their belt—but to wear sandals and not to put on two shirts.

He was also telling them, **"Wherever you enter a house, stay there until you leave that place. And whatever place will not receive you or listen to you, as you leave from there, shake the dust off the bottom of your feet as a witness against them."**

So they went out and proclaimed that all should repent, and they were driving out many demons and anointing with oil many who were sick and healing them.

King Herod heard, for *Yeshua*'s name had become known. Some were saying, "John the Immerser has risen from the dead! Because of this, these powers are at work in Him!" But others were saying, "It's Elijah!" Still others were saying, "It's a prophet, like one of the prophets of old."

But when Herod heard, he said, "John, the one I beheaded, has been raised!" For Herod himself sent and arrested John and bound him in prison for the sake of Herodias, the wife of his brother Philip, because Herod had married her. For John had been telling Herod, "It is not permitted for you to have your brother's wife."

Now Herodias had a grudge against John and wanted to kill him, but she wasn't able. For Herod was in awe of John and kept him safe, knowing him to be a righteous and holy man. When he listened to John he was confused, but he still listened gladly.

An opportunity came—when Herod, on his birthday, gave a banquet for his high officials, military brass, and the leaders of the Galilee. When the daughter of Herodias came in and danced, she pleased Herod and those reclining with him. And the king said to the girl, "Ask me for whatever you want, and I'll give it to you!" He vowed to her, "Whatever you ask of me I'll give you, up to half of my kingdom!"

She left the room and said to her mother, "What should I ask for?" Her mother said, "The head of John the Immerser!"

Immediately she rushed to the king and requested, "I want you to give me, right now, the head of John the Immerser on a platter!"

The king became very sorrowful; but because of his oaths and those reclining with him, he didn't want to refuse her. Immediately the king sent an executioner and gave orders to bring John's head. And the executioner went out and beheaded John in the prison, brought his head on a platter, and gave it to the girl; and the girl gave it to her mother.

When John's disciples heard, they came and took his body and laid it in a tomb. The twelve emissaries gathered together with *Yeshua*, and they reported to Him all they had done and taught. There were many coming and going, and they had no time even to eat. So He said to them, **"Come away by yourselves to an isolated place and rest awhile."** So they left privately by boat to an isolated place. However, the people saw them leaving, and many recognized them. They ran on foot from all the towns to get there ahead of them.

As *Yeshua* came ashore, He saw a large crowd and felt compassion for them, because they were like sheep without a shepherd. So He taught them many things.

When it was already late, His disciples came to Him and said, "This place is isolated, and the hour is already late. Send these people away so they can go into the nearby countryside and the villages and buy themselves something to eat."

But He answered and said to them, **"You give them something to eat!"**

And they said to Him, "Should we go and spend two hundred denarii on bread to give them something to eat?"

Then He said to them, **"How many loaves do you have? Go and see."**

When they found out, they said, "Five, and two fish."

Then *Yeshua* made them all sit down in groups on the green grass. So they reclined in groups of hundreds and fifties.

And He took the five loaves and the two fish; and looking up to heaven, He offered the *bracha*. He broke the loaves and kept giving them to the disciples to serve to the people; and He divided the two fish among them all.

They all ate and were satisfied, and the disciples picked up twelve baskets full of broken pieces and fish. Now there were five thousand men who ate the loaves.

Right away, *Yeshua* made His disciples get into the boat and go ahead of Him

And He took the five loaves and the two fish; and looking up to heaven,
He offered the *bracha.* He broke the loaves and kept giving them
to the disciples to serve to the people;
and He divided the two fish among them all.

Mark 6:41 TLV

to the other side, to Bethsaida, while He Himself was sending the crowd away. After leaving them, He went up on the hillside to pray.

And when evening came, the boat was in the middle of the sea and He was alone on the land. He saw the disciples struggling to row, for the wind was against them.

Around the fourth watch in the night, *Yeshua* comes to them, walking on the sea; and He wanted to pass by them. But when they saw Him walking on the sea, they thought He was a ghost and cried out—for they all saw Him and were terrified. But immediately, He spoke to them. He said, **"Take courage! I am. Do not be afraid."**

Then He got into the boat with them, and the wind stopped. They were utterly dumbfounded, for they still hadn't understood about the loaves. Instead, their hearts were hardened.

After they had crossed over, they came to land at Gennesaret and set anchor there. As they got out of the boat, immediately people recognized *Yeshua*. They ran about the region and began to carry around on their mats all those who were in bad shape, to wherever they heard He was. And wherever He entered villages, towns, or countryside, people were placing the sick in the marketplaces and begging Him to let them touch even the *tzitzit* of His garment—and all who touched it were being healed.

Mark, chapter 6

80. God Reveals Himself

In those days, there was another large crowd with nothing to eat, and *Yeshua* called the disciples. He said to them, **"I have compassion for the crowd, because they've stayed with Me for three days now and have nothing to eat. If I send them home hungry they'll pass out on the way, for some of them have come from very far away."**

His disciples answered Him, "How can anyone satisfy these people with bread here in a wasteland?"

"How many loaves do you have?" *Yeshua* was asking them.

"Seven," they said.

He directed the crowd to recline on the ground. After taking the seven loaves and giving thanks, He broke them and began giving them to His disciples to serve; and they served them to the crowd. They also had a few small fish and, after offering a *bracha* for them, He commanded these to be served as well.

They ate and were satisfied, and they picked up the broken pieces left over—seven baskets. About four thousand were there, and *Yeshua* sent them away.

Right away, He got into the boat with His disciples and went to the area of Dalmanutha. The Pharisees came and began to argue with Him, demanding a sign from heaven, to test Him. Sighing deeply in His spirit, *Yeshua* said, **"Why does this generation demand a sign? Amen, I tell you, no sign will be given to this generation."**

Leaving them, He got back into the boat and crossed to the other side.

Now the disciples had forgotten to take bread, and they had only one loaf in the boat. *Yeshua* was warning them, **"Watch out! Beware of the *hametz* of the Pharisees and the *hametz* of Herod."**

They began to discuss with each other that they had no bread. And *Yeshua*, aware of this, said to them, **"Why do you discuss that you have no bread? You still don't get it? Don't you understand? Are your hearts hardened? Having eyes, don't you see? And having ears, don't you hear? And don't you remember? When I broke the five loaves for the five thousand, how many baskets of leftovers did you pick up?"**

"Twelve," they say to Him.

"When I broke the seven loaves for the four thousand, how many baskets of leftovers did you pick up?"

"Seven," they say to Him.
He said to them, **"Do you still not understand?"**

They come to Bethsaida. Some people bring a blind man to *Yeshua* and beg Him to touch the man. Taking the blind man by the hand, *Yeshua* brought him outside the village. After spitting on the man's eyes and laying His hands on him, *Yeshua* asked the man, **"Do you**

see anything?"

The man looked up and said, "I see men! They look like trees walking about." Then *Yeshua* put His hands on the man's eyes again. The man looked intently, his sight was restored, and he began to see everything clearly. *Yeshua* sent him straight home, saying, **"Don't even enter the village!"**

Now *Yeshua* and His disciples went out to the villages around Caesarea Philippi. On the way He asked His disciples, **"Who do people say that I am?"**

They told Him, "John the Immerser; and others Elijah; but others, one of the prophets."

Then He asked them, **"But who do you say that I am?"**

Peter answered Him, "You are the Messiah!" And He warned them not to tell anyone about Him.

Then He began to teach them that the Son of Man must suffer many things and be rejected by the elders and ruling *kohanim* and *Torah* scholars, and be killed, and after three days rise again.

He was speaking openly about this. And Peter took Him aside and began to rebuke Him. But turning around and looking at His disciples, He rebuked Peter. He said, **"Get behind Me, satan! You are not setting your mind on the things of God, but the things of men."** Then He called the crowd, along with His disciples, and said to them, **"If anyone wants to follow after Me, he must deny himself, take up his cross, and keep following Me. For whoever wants to save his life will lose it, but whoever loses his life for My sake and the sake of the Good News will save it.**

For what does it profit a man to gain the whole world, yet forfeit his soul? For what could a man give in exchange for his soul? For whoever is ashamed of Me and My words in this unfaithful and sinful generation, the Son of Man will also be ashamed of him when He comes in the glory of His Father with the holy angels!"

Mark, chapter 8

Yeshua was telling them, **"Amen, I tell you, there are some standing here who will never taste death until they see the kingdom of God come with power!"**

After six days, *Yeshua* takes with Him Peter and Jacob and John, and brings them up a high mountain by themselves. And He was transfigured before them. His clothes became radiant and brilliantly white, whiter than any launderer on earth could bleach them. Then Elijah appeared to them with Moses, and they were talking with *Yeshua*.

Peter responds to *Yeshua*, "Rabbi, it's good for us to be here. Let's make three *sukkot*—one for You, and one for Moses, and one for Elijah." (He didn't know what to say, for they were terrified.) Then a cloud came, overshadowing them; and out of the cloud came a voice, **"This is My Son, whom I love. Listen to Him!"** Suddenly when they looked around, they no longer saw anyone with them

After six days, *Yeshua* takes with Him Peter and Jacob and John, and brings them up a high mountain by themselves. And He was transfigured before them. His clothes became radiant and brilliantly white, whiter than any launderer on earth could bleach them. Then Elijah appeared to them with Moses, and they were talking with *Yeshua.*

Mark 9:2-4 TLV

except *Yeshua.*

As they were coming down from the mountain, *Yeshua* ordered them not to tell anyone what they had seen, until the Son of Man rose up from the dead. They kept this word to themselves, discussing among themselves what it is to rise up from the dead.

And they questioned Him, saying, "Why do the *Torah* scholars say that Elijah must come first?"

Now He told them, **"Indeed Elijah comes first; he restores all things. And how is it written that the Son of Man must suffer much and be treated with contempt? I tell you that Elijah has come, and they did to him whatever they wanted, just as it is written about him."**

When they came to the disciples, they saw a big crowd around them and the *Torah* scholars arguing with them. Suddenly, when the whole crowd saw *Yeshua*, they were amazed and began running to greet Him. He questioned them, **"What are you arguing about with them?"**

And a man from the crowd answered Him, "Teacher, I brought You my son, who has a spirit that makes him mute. Whenever it seizes him, it throws him down; he foams at the mouth, grinds his teeth, and becomes stiff. I told Your disciples to drive it out, but they couldn't!"

And answering them, He said, **"Oh faithless generation, how long shall I be with you? How long shall I put up with you? Bring him to Me."**

They brought the boy to *Yeshua.* When the spirit saw Him, immediately it threw the boy into a convulsion. The boy fell to the ground and began rolling around and foaming at the mouth. *Yeshua* asked the father, **"How long has this been happening to him?"**

"Since he was a child," the man answered. "It has often thrown him into fire or water to destroy him. But if You can do anything, have compassion and help us!"

"'If You can'?" *Yeshua* said to him. **"All things are possible for one who believes!"**

Immediately the boy's father cried out, "I believe! Help my unbelief!"

When *Yeshua* saw that a crowd was gathering fast, He rebuked the unclean spirit, telling it, **"I command you, deaf and mute spirit, come out of him and do not ever enter him again!"**

After howling and shaking the boy wildly, it came out. The boy became so much like a corpse that many were saying, "He's dead!" But *Yeshua* took him by the hand and lifted him, and the boy stood up.

After *Yeshua* came into the house, His disciples began questioning Him in private, "Why couldn't we drive it out?"

And He said to them, **"This kind cannot come out except by prayer."**

They left from there and passed through the Galilee. *Yeshua* didn't want anyone to know, for He was teaching His disciples and telling them, **"The Son of Man is going to be delivered into the hands of men, and they will kill Him. And after He is killed, three days later He will rise up."**

But the disciples didn't understand this statement, and they were afraid to question Him about it.

Then they came to Capernaum. And when *Yeshua* was in the house, He began to ask the disciples, **"What were you discussing on the way?"** But they kept quiet, because on the way they had argued with one another about who was the greatest.

Sitting down, He called the Twelve and said to them, **"If any man wants to be first, he shall be least of all and the servant of everyone."**

Taking a small child, He set him in the midst of them. And taking him in His arms, He said to them, **"Whoever welcomes one of these children in My name, welcomes Me; and whoever welcomes Me, welcomes not Me but the One who sent Me."**

John said to Him, "Teacher, we saw someone driving out demons in Your name, and we tried to stop him because he wasn't following us."

But *Yeshua* responded, **"Don't stop him! No one who does a miracle in My name will be able soon afterward to speak evil about Me. He who is not against us is for us. For whoever gives you a cup of water to drink in My name because you belong to Messiah, amen I tell you, he will never lose his reward."**

"But whoever causes one of these little ones who trust in Me to stumble, it would be better for him to have a heavy millstone put around his neck and to be thrown into the sea!"

"And if your hand causes you to stumble, cut it off! It is better for you to enter into life crippled than, having two hands, to go to Gehenna, into the unquenchable fire.

And if your foot causes you to stumble, cut it off! It's better for you to enter life lame than, having your two feet, to be thrown into Gehenna.

If your eye causes you to stumble, tear it out! It is better for you to enter the kingdom of God with one eye than, having two eyes, to be thrown into Gehenna, where

'their worm does not die
And the fire is not quenched.'

"For everyone will be salted with fire. Salt is good; but if the salt becomes unsalty, with what will you flavor it? Have salt in yourselves, and keep *shalom* with one another."

Mark, chapter 9

81. God Celebrates Sukkot

Afterwards, *Yeshua* went away to the other side of the Sea of Galilee, also known as the Sea of Tiberias. A large crowd kept following Him, because they were watching the signs He was performing on the sick. Then *Yeshua* went up the mountainside and sat down there with His disciples. Passover, the Jewish feast, was near.

Lifting up His eyes and seeing a large crowd coming to Him, *Yeshua* said to Philip, **"Where will we buy bread so these may eat?"**

Now *Yeshua* was saying this to test him, for He knew what He was about to do.

Philip answered Him, "Two hundred denarii isn't enough to buy bread for each to get a little bit!"

One of His disciples, Andrew, Simon Peter's brother, said to Him, "There's a boy here who has five barley loaves and two fish—but what's that for so many?"

Yeshua said, **"Make the people recline."** There was much grass in the area. So the men reclined, about five thousand in number.

Then *Yeshua* picked up the loaves. And having given thanks, He distributed bread to everyone who was reclining. He did the same with the fish, as much as they wanted.

When the people were full, *Yeshua* said to His disciples, **"Gather up the leftovers, so nothing is wasted."** So they gathered them and filled twelve baskets with broken pieces from the five barley loaves, which were left over by those who had finished eating.

When the people saw the sign that *Yeshua* performed, they began to say, "This is most certainly the Prophet who is to come into the world!"

Realizing that they were about to come and seize Him by force to make Him king, *Yeshua* withdrew again to the mountain, Himself alone.

Now when evening came, *Yeshua's* disciples went down to the sea. Getting into a boat, they set out to cross the sea toward Capernaum. By now it had become dark, and still *Yeshua* had not come to them. A great wind began to blow, stirring up the sea.

After they had rowed about twenty-five or thirty stadia, they catch sight of *Yeshua* walking on the sea, approaching the boat. They were terrified! But *Yeshua* says to them, **"I am. Don't be afraid."**

Then they wanted to take Him into the boat, and right away the boat reached the shore where they were headed.

The next day, the crowd remaining on the other side of the sea realized that no other boat had been there except the one, and that *Yeshua* hadn't gone into the boat with His disciples, but that His disciples had gone away alone. Some other boats from

Tiberias came close to the place where they had eaten the bread after the Master had given thanks. So when the crowd realized that neither *Yeshua* nor His disciples were there, they got into the boats and set off for Capernaum to find Him. When they found Him on the other side of the sea, they said, "Rabbi, when did You get here?"

Yeshua responded to them, **"Amen, amen I tell you, you seek Me not because you saw signs, but because you ate all the bread and were filled. Don't work for food that spoils, but for the food that endures to eternal life, which the Son of Man will give to you. For on Him, God the Father has put the seal of approval."**

Then they said to Him, "What shall we do to perform the works of God?"

Yeshua answered them, **"This is the work of God, to trust in the One He sent."**

So they said to Him, "Then what sign do You perform, so that we may see and believe You? What work do You do? Our fathers ate the manna in the wilderness; as it is written, 'Out of heaven He gave them bread to eat.'"

Yeshua answered them, **"Amen, amen I tell you, it isn't Moses who has given you bread from heaven, but My Father gives you the true bread from heaven. For the bread of God is the One coming down from heaven and giving life to the world."**

So they said to Him, "Sir, give us this bread from now on!"

Yeshua said to them, **"I am the bread of life. Whoever comes to Me will never be hungry, and whoever believes in Me will never be thirsty. But I told you that you have seen Me, yet you do not believe.**

Everyone the Father gives Me will come to Me, and anyone coming to Me I will never reject. For I have come down from heaven not to do My own will but the will of the One who sent Me.

"Now this is the will of the One who sent Me, that I lose not one of all He has given Me, but raise each one on the last day. For this is the will of My Father, that everyone who sees the Son and trusts in Him may have eternal life; and I will raise him up on the last day."

Some of the Judeans started to grumble about Him, because He said, **"I am the bread that came down from heaven."** They were saying, "Isn't this *Yeshua* the son of Joseph, whose father and mother we know? How can He now say, 'I have come down from heaven'?"

Yeshua answered, **"Stop grumbling among yourselves! No one can come to Me unless My Father who sent Me draws him—and I will raise him up on the last day.**

It is written in the Prophets, 'They will all be taught by God.' Everyone who has listened and learned from the Father comes to Me. Not that anyone has seen the Father except the One who is from God—He has seen the Father.

"Amen, amen I tell you, he who believes has eternal life. I am the bread of life. Your fathers ate the manna in the desert, yet they died. This is the bread that comes down from heaven, so that one may eat and not die. I am the living bread, which came down from heaven. If anyone eats this bread, he will live forever. This bread is My flesh, which I will give for the life of the world."

Then the Jews began arguing with one another, "How can this man give us His flesh to eat?"

So *Yeshua* said to them, **"Amen, amen I tell you, unless you eat the flesh of the Son of Man and drink His blood, you have no life in yourselves. He who eats My flesh and drinks My blood has eternal life, and I will raise him up on the last day.**

"For My flesh is real food and My blood is real drink. He who eats My flesh and drinks My blood abides in Me, and I in him. Just as the living Father sent Me and I live because of the Father, so the one who eats of Me will also live because of Me. This is the bread that came down from heaven—not like the bread your fathers ate and then died. He who eats this bread will live forever."

He said these things while teaching at the synagogue in Capernaum.

So when many of His disciples heard this, they said, "This is a hard teaching. Who can listen to it?"

But *Yeshua* knew His disciples were murmuring, so He said to them, **"Does this offend you? Then what if you see the Son of Man going back up to the place where He was before? It is the Spirit who gives life; the flesh is of no benefit. The words I have spoken to you are Spirit and are life! Yet some of you do not trust."** *Yeshua* knew from the beginning who were the ones who did not trust, as well as which one would betray Him.

Then He told them, **"For this reason I've told you that no one can come to Me unless it has been granted to him by the Father."**

From this time, many of His disciples left and quit walking with Him. So *Yeshua* said to the Twelve, **"You don't want to leave also, do you?"**

Simon Peter answered Him, "Lord, to whom shall we go? You have the words of eternal life! We have trusted and have come to know that you are the Holy One of God."

Yeshua answered them, **"Didn't I choose you, the Twelve? Yet one of you is the adversary!"** Now He was speaking of Judah, the son of Simon of Kriot—for he, one of the Twelve, was about to betray Him.

John, chapter 6

After these events, *Yeshua* was walking about in the Galilee. He did not want to walk in Judea, because the Judean leaders wanted to kill him.

Now the Jewish Feast of Tabernacles was near. Therefore His brothers said to Him, "Leave here and go to Judea, so Your disciples also may see the

Then, while teaching in the Temple courts, *Yeshua* cried out, "You know both who I am and where I am from! I have not come on My own, but the One who sent Me is true. You do not know Him, but I know Him because I am from Him and He sent Me."

John 7:28-29 TLV

works You are doing. No one who wants to be well known does everything in secret. If You are doing these things, show Yourself to the world!" For not even His brothers were trusting in Him.

Therefore *Yeshua* said to them, **"My time has not yet come, but your time is always at hand. The world cannot hate you, but it hates Me because I testify that its works are evil. You go on up to the Feast. I'm not going to this feast, because My time hasn't yet fully come."** After saying these things, He stayed in the Galilee.

But after His brothers went to the Feast, He also went, not openly but secretly. Then the Judean leaders were searching for Him at the Feast and kept asking, "Where is that fellow?"

There was a lot of murmuring about Him in the crowds. Some were saying, "He is good." But others were saying, "Not so! He leads the people astray." Yet no one spoke openly about Him for fear of the Judean leaders.

About halfway through the Feast, *Yeshua* went up to the Temple and began teaching. Then the Judean leaders were amazed, saying, "How does this man know so much, having never been taught?"

Yeshua answered, **"My teaching is not from Me, but from Him who sent Me. If anyone wants to do His will, he will know whether My teaching comes from God or it is Myself speaking. Whoever speaks from himself seeks his own glory; but He who seeks the glory of the One who sent Him, He is true and there is no unrighteousness in Him.**

Hasn't Moses given you the *Torah*? Yet none of you keeps it. Why are you trying to kill Me?"

The crowd answered, "You have a demon! Who's trying to kill you?"

Yeshua answered, **"I did one good work, and all of you are amazed. Because Moses has given you circumcision (though it is not from Moses, but from the patriarchs), you circumcise a man on *Shabbat*. If a man receives circumcision on *Shabbat* so that the *Torah* of Moses may not be broken, why are you angry that I healed a man's whole body on *Shabbat*? Do not judge by appearance, but judge righteously."**

Then some of the people from Jerusalem were saying, "Isn't this the person they're trying to kill? Look, He speaks openly and they're saying nothing to Him. Can it be that the leaders know He is the Messiah? But we know where this person is from. But the Messiah, whenever He may come, no one knows where He is from."

Then, while teaching in the Temple courts, *Yeshua* cried out, **"You know both who I am and where I am from! I have not come on My own, but the One who sent Me is true. You do not know Him, but I know Him because I am from Him and He sent Me."**

Then they were trying to seize Him; but no one laid a hand on Him, because His hour had not yet come. Yet many from the crowd believed in Him and were saying, "When the Messiah comes, He won't perform more signs than this person has, will He?"

The Pharisees heard people in the crowd murmuring these things about Him, and the ruling *kohanim* and Pharisees sent guards to arrest Him.

Yeshua said, **"I am with you only a little while longer, and then I am going to the One who sent Me. You will look for Me but will not find Me. Where I am, you cannot come."**

The Judean leaders then said among themselves, "Where is this person about to go that we shall not find Him? He's not going to the Diaspora to teach the Greeks, is He? What did He mean by saying, 'You will look for Me but will not find Me. Where I am, you cannot come'?"

On the last and greatest day of the Feast, *Yeshua* stood up and cried out loudly, **"If anyone is thirsty, let him come to Me and drink. Whoever believes in Me, as the Scripture says, 'out of his innermost being will flow rivers of living water.'"**

Now He said this about the *Ruach*, whom those who trusted in Him were going to receive; for the *Ruach* was not yet given, since *Yeshua* was not yet glorified.

When they heard these words, some of the crowd said, "This man really is the Prophet." Others were saying, "This is the Messiah." Still others were saying, "The Messiah doesn't come from the Galilee, does He? Didn't the Scripture say that the Messiah comes from the seed of David and from Bethlehem, David's town?" So a division arose in the crowd because of *Yeshua*. Some wanted to capture Him, but no one laid hands on Him.

Then the guards returned to the ruling *kohanim* and Pharisees, who asked them, "Why didn't you bring Him?"

"Never has anyone spoken like this man," the guards answered.

The Pharisees responded, "You haven't been led astray also, have you? Have any of the rulers or Pharisees believed in Him? No, but this mob that doesn't know the *Torah*—they are cursed!"

Nicodemus, the one who had come to *Yeshua* before and was one of them, said to them, "Our *Torah* doesn't judge a man unless it first hears from him and knows what he's doing, does it?"

They answered him, "You aren't from the Galilee too, are you? Search, and see that no prophet comes out of the Galilee!"

Then everyone went to his own house.

John, chapter 7

82. God Blesses *Yeshua*

"For the kingdom of heaven is like the master of a household, who went out early in the morning to hire workers for his vineyard.

Now when he had agreed with the workers for a denarius per day, he sent them into his vineyard. And he went out about the third hour and saw others standing in the marketplace, idle. And to them he said, 'You go into the vineyard too, and I'll give you whatever is right.' So they went.

Again he went out about the sixth and ninth hour and did the same. And about the eleventh hour, he went out and found others standing around. And he said to them, 'Why have you been standing here idle the whole day?'

"'Because no one hired us,' they said to him.

"He said to them, 'You go into the vineyard, too.'

"Now when evening came, the owner of the vineyard said to his foreman, 'Call the workers and pay them their wages, beginning from the last to the first.' And those who had come about the eleventh hour each received a denarius. And when the first came, they supposed that they would receive more; yet they too received a denarius.

"But when they received it, they began to grumble against the master of the house, saying, 'These last guys did one hour, and you've made them equal to us, who bore the burden and scorching heat of the day!'

"But answering, he said to one of them, 'Friend, I'm doing you no wrong. Didn't you agree with me on a denarius? Take what is yours and go. But I want to give this last guy the same as you. Am I not permitted to do what I want with what belongs to me? Or is your eye evil because I am good?'

"So the last will be first, and the first last."

Now as *Yeshua* was going up to Jerusalem, He took the Twelve aside privately; and on the way He told them, **"Look, we're going up to Jerusalem, and the Son of Man will be handed over to the ruling *kohanim* and *Torah* scholars. They will condemn Him to death and hand Him over to the Gentiles to mock, and to scourge, and to crucify. Yet on the third day, He will be raised up."**

Then the mother of the sons of Zebedee came with her sons to *Yeshua*, and she was kneeling down and asking something from Him.

"What do you want?" He said to her.

She said to Him, "Declare that these two sons of mine might sit, one on Your right and one on Your left, in Your kingdom."

But *Yeshua* replied, **"You don't know what you're asking! Are you able to drink the cup I am about to drink?"**

"We are able," they say to Him.

He said to them, **"You shall indeed drink My cup. But to sit on My right and left, this isn't Mine to grant. Rather, it's for those for whom it has been prepared by My Father."**

Now when the ten heard, they became indignant with the two brothers. But *Yeshua* called them over and said, **"You know that the rulers of the nations lord it over them, and their great ones play the tyrant over them. It shall not be this way among you. But whoever wants to be great among you shall be your servant, and whoever wants to be first among you shall be your slave—just as the Son of Man did not come to be served, but to serve, and to give His life as a ransom for many."**

Now as they were leaving Jericho, a large crowd followed Him. And here two blind men sitting by the roadside, when they heard that *Yeshua* was passing by, cried out, saying, "Have mercy on us, O Master, *Ben-David*!"

The crowd warned them to be quiet, but they cried out all the more, saying, "Have mercy on us, O Master, *Ben-David*!"

Yeshua stopped and called out to them. **"What do you want Me to do for you?"** He said.

They said to Him, "Master, let our eyes be opened!" Moved with compassion, *Yeshua* touched their eyes. Instantly they regained their sight and followed Him.

Matthew, chapter 20

Now as they drew near to Jerusalem and came to Bethphage, to the Mount of Olives, then *Yeshua* sent two disciples, saying to them, **"Go into the village before you. Right away, you'll find a donkey tied up and a colt with her. Untie them and bring them to Me. If anyone says anything to you, you shall say, 'The Master needs them.' And right away he will send them."**

This happened to fulfill what was spoken through the prophet, saying, "Say to the daughter of Zion, 'See, your King is coming to you, humble and sitting on a donkey, a colt, the foal of a donkey.'"

The disciples went and did as *Yeshua* had directed them. They brought the donkey and colt and put their clothing on them, and He sat on the clothing. Most of the crowd spread their clothing on the road, and others began cutting branches from the trees and spreading them on the road.

The crowds going before Him and those following kept shouting, saying,
"*Hoshia-na to Ben-David!*
Baruch ha-ba b'shem ADONAI*!*
Blessed is He who comes in the
name of the LORD!
Hoshia-na in the highest!"

When He entered Jerusalem, the whole city was stirred up, saying, "Who is this?" And the crowds kept saying, "This is the prophet *Yeshua*, from *Natzeret* in the Galilee."

Then *Yeshua* entered the Temple and drove out all those selling and buying in the Temple. He overturned the

The crowds going before Him and those following kept shouting, saying, "*Hoshia-na* to *Ben-David*! *Baruch ha-ba b'shem* ADONAI! Blessed is He who comes in the name of the Lord! *Hoshia-na* in the highest!"

Matthew 21:9 TLV

tables of the moneychangers and the seats of those selling doves. And He said to them, "It is written, 'My house shall be called a house of prayer,' but you are making it 'a den of thieves'!"

The blind and lame came to Him in the Temple, and He healed them. But when the ruling *kohanim* and *Torah* scholars saw the wonders He performed, and the children crying out in the Temple and saying, "*Hoshia-na* to *Ben-David*," they became indignant. And they said to Him, "Do You hear what these children are saying?"

"Yes," *Yeshua* said to them. **"Haven't you ever read, 'Out of the mouth of babes and nursing toddlers You have prepared praise for Yourself'?"**

Then He left them and went out of the city to Bethany, and He spent the night there.

Now early in the morning, as He was returning to the city, He became hungry. Seeing a lone fig tree by the road, He came up to it and found nothing on it except leaves only. And He said to it, **"May no fruit ever come from you again!"** And the fig tree shriveled up at once.

When the disciples saw it they were astonished. "How did the fig tree shrivel on the spot?" they asked.

Yeshua answered them, **"Amen, I tell you, if you have faith and do not doubt, not only will you do what was done to the fig tree, but even if you say to this mountain, 'Be taken up and thrown into the sea,' it will happen. And whatever you ask in prayer, trusting, you shall receive."**

Now when He entered the Temple, the ruling *kohanim* and the elders of the people came to Him while He was teaching, saying, "By what authority are You doing these things? Who gave You this authority?"

Yeshua replied to them, **"I also will ask you one question. If you tell Me, I likewise will tell you by what authority I do these things. John's immersion, where was it from? From heaven or from men?"**

They began to dialogue among themselves, saying, "If we say, 'From heaven,' He will say to us, 'Then why didn't you believe him?' But if we say, 'From men,' we fear the crowd, for all hold up John as a prophet." So answering *Yeshua*, they said, "We don't know."

Then He said to them, **"Neither am I telling you by what authority I do these things."**

"Now what do you think? A man had two sons, and he went to the first and said, 'Son, go work in the vineyard today.' The son answered, 'I won't,' but afterward he had a change of heart and went.

The man went to the second son and said the same thing. But he answered, 'I will, sir,' and didn't go. Which of the two did the will of the father?"

"The first," they said.

Yeshua said to them, **"Amen, I tell you, the tax collectors and**

prostitutes are going ahead of you into the kingdom of God. For John came to you in the way of righteousness, and you did not believe him. But the tax collectors and prostitutes did believe him; and even after you saw this, you had no change of heart to believe him."

"Listen to another parable. There was a master of a household who planted a vineyard. He put a hedge around it, dug a winepress in it, and built a tower. Then He leased it to some tenant farmers and went on a journey. Now when fruit season drew near, he sent his servants to the tenants to collect his fruit. But grabbing his servants, the tenants beat up one, killed another, and stoned still another.

Again the master sent other servants, even more than the first, and they did the same thing to them. Finally he sent his son to them, saying, 'They will respect my son.'

"But when the tenants saw the son, they said among themselves, 'This is the heir! Come on, let's kill him and get his inheritance!' So grabbing him, they threw him out of the vineyard and killed him. Therefore when the master of the vineyard comes, what will he do to those tenants?"

"He will bring those miserable men to a miserable end," they said to Him, "and will lease the vineyard to other tenants, who will give him his share of the fruits in their seasons."

Yeshua said to them, **"Have you never read in the Scriptures?**

'The stone which the builders rejected, this has become the chief cornerstone. This came from ADONAI, and it is marvelous in our eyes.'

Therefore I say to you, the kingdom of God will be taken away from you and given to people producing its fruits. Whoever falls on this stone will be shattered; but the one upon whom it falls, it will crush him."

When the ruling *kohanim* and Pharisees heard *Yeshua's* parables, they realized He was talking about them. Although they were trying to seize Him, they feared the crowds, because they regarded Him as a prophet.

Matthew, chapter 21

83. God Cleans His House

On the third day, there was a wedding at Cana in the Galilee.

Yeshua's mother was there, and *Yeshua* and His disciples were also invited to the wedding. When the wine ran out, *Yeshua's* mother said to Him, "They don't have any wine!"

Yeshua said to her, **"Woman, what does this have to do with you and Me? My hour hasn't come yet."**

His mother said to the servants, "Do whatever He tells you."

Now there were six stone jars, used for the Jewish ritual of purification, each holding two to three measures. *Yeshua* said to them, **"Fill the jars with water!" So they filled them up to the top. Then He said to them, "Take some water out, and give it to the headwaiter."** And they brought it.

Now the headwaiter did not know where it had come from, but the servants who had drawn the water knew. As the headwaiter tasted the water that had become wine, he calls the bridegroom and says to him, "Everyone brings out the good wine first, and whenever they are drunk, then the worse. But you've reserved the good wine until now!"

Yeshua did this, the first of the signs, in Cana of the Galilee—He revealed His glory, and His disciples believed in Him.

After this *Yeshua* went down to Capernaum with His mother, brothers, and disciples, and they stayed there a few days. The Jewish feast of Passover was near, so *Yeshua* went up to Jerusalem.

In the Temple, He found the merchants selling oxen, sheep, and doves; also the moneychangers sitting there. Then He made a whip of cords and drove them all out of the Temple, both the sheep and oxen. He dumped out the coins of the moneychangers and overturned their tables. To those selling doves, He said, **"Get these things out of here! Stop making My Father's house a marketplace!" His disciples remembered that it is written, "Zeal for your House will consume Me!"**

The Judean leaders responded, "What sign do You show us, since You are doing these things?"

"Destroy this Temple," *Yeshua* answered them, **"and in three days I will raise it up."**

The Judean leaders then said to Him, "Forty-six years this Temple was being built, and You will raise it up in three days?" But He was talking about the temple of His body. So after He was raised from the dead, His disciples remembered that He was talking about this. Then they believed the Scripture and the word that *Yeshua* had spoken.

Now when He was in Jerusalem for the Passover, during the feast, many believed in His name, seeing the signs He was doing. But *Yeshua* did not entrust Himself to them, because He

The Jewish feast of Passover was near, so *Yeshua* went up to Jerusalem.
In the Temple, He found the merchants selling oxen, sheep, and doves;
also the moneychangers sitting there. Then He made a whip of cords
and drove them all out of the Temple, both the sheep and oxen.
He dumped out the coins of the moneychangers
and overturned their tables.

John 2:13-15 TLV

knew all men. He did not need anyone to testify about man, for He knew what was in man.

John, chapter 2

Now there was a man, a Pharisee named Nicodemus, a ruler of the Jewish people. He came to *Yeshua* at night and said, "Rabbi, we know that You, a teacher, have come from God. For no one can perform these signs which You do unless God is with Him!"

Yeshua answered him, **"Amen, amen I tell you, unless one is born from above, he cannot see the kingdom of God."**

"How can a man be born when he is old?" Nicodemus said to Him. "He cannot enter his mother's womb a second time and be born, can he?"

Yeshua answered, **"Amen, amen I tell you, unless one is born of water and spirit, he cannot enter the kingdom of God. What is born of the flesh is flesh, and what is born of the Spirit is spirit.**

Do not be surprised that I said to you, 'You all must be born from above.' The wind blows where it wishes and you hear its sound, but you do not know where it comes from or where it goes. So it is with everyone born of the Spirit."

"How can these things happen?" Nicodemus said.

Yeshua answered him, **"You're a teacher of Israel and you do not understand these things? Amen, amen I tell you, We speak about what We know and testify about what We have seen. Yet you all do not receive Our testimony! If you do not believe the earthly things I told you, how will you believe when I tell you about heavenly things?**

No one has gone up into heaven except the One who came down from heaven—the Son of Man. Just as Moses lifted up the serpent in the desert, so the Son of Man must be lifted up, so that whoever believes in Him may have eternal life!

"For God so loved the world that He gave His one and only Son, that whoever believes in Him shall not perish but have eternal life.
God did not send the Son into the world to condemn the world, but in order that the world might be saved through Him. The one who believes in Him is not condemned; but whoever does not believe has been condemned already, because he has not put his trust in the name of the one and only *Ben-Elohim*.

"Now this is the judgment, that the light has come into the world and men loved the darkness instead of the light, because their deeds were evil. For everyone who does evil hates the light and does not come to the light, so that their deeds will not be exposed. But whoever practices the truth comes to the light, so that it may be made known that his deeds have been accomplished in God."

Afterwards, *Yeshua* and His disciples came to the land of Judea. There He was staying with them and immersing. Now John also was immersing at Aenon near Salim, because much water was there and many were coming and being immersed; for John had not yet been thrown into prison. Now an argument came up between John's disciples and a Judean concerning purification. They came to John and said, "Rabbi, the One who was with you beyond the Jordan, the One you testified about—look, He is immersing, and all are coming to Him!"

John answered, "A man can receive nothing unless it has been given to him from heaven. You yourselves testify that I said, 'I am not the Messiah,' but rather, 'I am sent before Him.' The one who has the bride is the bridegroom, but the best man rejoices when he stands and hears the bridegroom's voice. So now my joy is complete! He must increase, while I must decrease."

The One who comes from above is above all. The one who is from the earth is of the earth, and of the earth he speaks.

The One who comes from heaven is above all. And what He has seen and heard, He testifies to that; yet no one receives His testimony.
Whoever receives His testimony has certified that God is true.

The One whom God has sent speaks the words of God, for God gives the *Ruach* without limit.
The Father loves the Son and has given everything into His hand.

He who trusts in the Son has eternal life. He who does not obey the Son will not see life, but the wrath of God remains on him.

John, chapter 3

84. God Accepts Her Gift

"Amen, amen I tell you, he who does not enter the sheepfold by the door, but climbs in some other way, is a thief and a robber. But he who enters through the door is the shepherd of the sheep. To him the doorkeeper opens, and the sheep hear his voice. The shepherd calls his own sheep by name and leads them out.

"When he has brought out all his own, he goes ahead of them; and the sheep follow him because they know his voice. They will never follow a stranger, but will run away from him, for they do not know the voice of strangers."

***Yeshua* told them this parable, but they did not understand what He was telling them. So *Yeshua* said again, "Amen, amen I tell you, I am the gate for the sheep. All those who came before Me are thieves and robbers, but the sheep did not listen to them.**

I am the gate! If anyone comes in through Me, he will be saved. He will come and go and find pasture. The thief comes only to steal, slaughter, and destroy. I have come that they might have life, and have it abundantly!

"I am the Good Shepherd. The Good Shepherd lays down His life for the sheep. The hired worker is not the shepherd, and the sheep are not his own. He sees the wolf coming and abandons the sheep and flees. Then the wolf snatches and scatters the sheep. The man is only a hired hand and does not care about the sheep.

"I am the Good Shepherd. I know My own and My own know Me, just as the Father knows Me and I know the Father. And I lay down My life for the sheep. I have other sheep that are not from this fold; those also I must lead, and they will listen to My voice. So there shall be one flock, one Shepherd.

"For this reason the Father loves Me, because I lay down My life, so that I may take it up again. No one takes it away from Me, but I lay it down on My own. I have the authority to lay it down, and I have the authority to take it up again. This command I received from My Father."

Again a division arose among the Judeans because of these words. Many of them were saying, "He has a demon. He's insane! Why listen to Him?" Others said, "These are not the sayings of someone who is plagued by a demon. A demon cannot open the eyes of the blind, can it?"

Then came *Hanukkah*; it was winter in Jerusalem. *Yeshua* was walking in the Temple around Solomon's Colonnade.

Then the Judean leaders surrounded Him, saying, "How long will You hold us in suspense? If You are the Messiah, tell us outright!"

Yeshua answered them, **"I told you, but you don't believe! The works I do in My Father's name testify concerning Me. But you don't believe, because you are not My sheep. My sheep hear My voice. I know them, and they follow Me. I**

give them eternal life! They will never perish, and no one will snatch them out of My hand. My Father, who has given them to Me, is greater than all. And no one is able to snatch them out of the Father's hand. I and the Father are one."

Again the Judean leaders picked up stones to stone Him. *Yeshua* answered them, **"I've shown you many good works from the Father. For which of these are you going to stone Me?"**

The Judean leaders answered, "We aren't stoning you for a good work, but for blasphemy. Though You are a man, You make Yourself God!"

Yeshua answered them, **"Isn't it written in your Writings, 'I have said you are gods'? If he called them 'gods,' to whom the Word of God came (and the Scripture cannot be broken), do you say of Him, the One the Father set apart and sent into the world, 'You speak blasphemy,' because I said, 'I am *Ben-Elohim*'?**

"If I don't do the works of My Father, don't believe Me! But if I do, even if you don't trust Me, trust the deeds. Then you may come to know and continue to understand that the Father is in Me, and I am in the Father." Therefore they tried to capture Him again, but He escaped from their hand.

Again He went back across the Jordan to the place where John first started immersing, and He stayed there. Many people came to Him and were saying, "John performed no sign, but all John said about this man was true." And many trusted in Him there.

John, chapter 10

Now a man named Lazarus was sick. He was from Bethany, the village of Miriam and her sister Martha. This was the same Miriam who anointed the Master with perfume and wiped His feet with her hair. It was her brother Lazarus who was sick. So the sisters sent a word to *Yeshua*, saying, "Master, the one you love is sick!" When *Yeshua* heard this, He said, **"This sickness will not end in death. It is for God's glory, so that *Ben-Elohim* may be glorified through it."**

Now *Yeshua* loved Martha and her sister and Lazarus. However, when He heard that Lazarus was sick, He stayed where He was for two more days. Then after this, He said to His disciples, "Let's go up to Judea again."

"Rabbi," the disciples say to Him, "just now the Judean leaders were trying to stone You! And You're going back there again?"

Yeshua answered, **"Aren't there twelve hours in the day? If a man walks in the day, he doesn't stumble, because he sees the light of the world. But if a man should walk around at night, he stumbles, because the light is not in him."**

After He said this, He tells them, **"Our friend Lazarus has fallen asleep, but I'm going there to wake him up."**

So the disciples said to Him, "Master, if he has fallen asleep, he will get better." Now *Yeshua* had spoken about his death, but they thought He was talking about ordinary sleep.

Then *Yeshua* told them clearly, **"Lazarus is dead! I'm glad for your sake I wasn't there, so that you may believe. Anyway, let's go to him!"**

Then Thomas called the Twin said to the other disciples, "Let's go too, so that we may die with Him!"

So when *Yeshua* arrived, He discovered that Lazarus had been in the tomb already for four days. Bethany was less than two miles from Jerusalem, and many of the Judeans had come to Martha and Miriam to console them about their brother.

When Martha heard that *Yeshua* was coming, she went out to meet Him; but Miriam sat in the house. Martha said to *Yeshua*, "Master, if You had been here, my brother wouldn't have died! But I know, even now, that whatever You may ask of God, He will give You."

Yeshua said to her, **"Your brother will rise again."**

Martha said to Him, "I know, he will rise again in the resurrection on the last day."

Yeshua said to her, **"I am the resurrection and the life! Whoever believes in Me, even if he dies, shall live. And whoever lives and believes in Me shall never die. Do you believe this?"**

She says to Him, "Yes, Lord, I believe that you are the Messiah, *Ben-Elohim* who has come into the world."

After she said this, she left and secretly told her sister Miriam, "The Teacher is here, and He's calling for you." As soon as Miriam heard, she quickly got up and was coming to Him.

Now *Yeshua* had not yet come into the village, but was still in the place where Martha had met Him. The Judeans, who were with Miriam in the house and comforting her, seeing how quickly she got up and went out, followed her. They thought she was going to the tomb to weep there.

So when Miriam came to where *Yeshua* was, she saw Him and fell at His feet, saying to Him, "Master, if You had been here, my brother would not have died!"

When *Yeshua* saw her weeping, and the Judeans who came with her weeping, He was deeply troubled in spirit and Himself agitated. **"Where have you laid him?"** He asked.

"Come and see, Master," they tell Him. *Yeshua* wept.

So the Judeans said, "See how He loved him!"

But some of them said, "Couldn't this One, who opened the eyes of the blind man, have also kept this man from dying?"

So *Yeshua*, again deeply troubled within Himself, comes to the tomb. It was a cave, and a stone was lying against it. *Yeshua* says, **"Roll away**

the stone!"

Martha, the dead man's sister, said to Him, "Master, by this time he stinks! He's been dead for four days!"

Yeshua says to her, **"Didn't I tell you that if you believed, you would see the glory of God?"** So they rolled away the stone.

Yeshua lifted up His eyes and said, **"Father, I thank you that you have heard Me. I knew that You always hear Me; but because of this crowd standing around I said it, so that they may believe that You sent Me." And when He had said this, He cried out with a loud voice, "Lazarus, come out!"**

He who had been dead came out, wrapped in burial clothes binding his hands and feet, with a cloth over his face. And *Yeshua* tells them, **"Cut him loose, and let him go!"**

Therefore many of the Judeans, who had come to Miriam and had seen what *Yeshua* had done, put their trust in Him. But some of them went to the Pharisees and told them what *Yeshua* had done.

So the ruling *kohanim* and Pharisees called a meeting of the Sanhedrin. "What are we doing?" they asked. "This Man is performing many signs! If we let Him go on like this, everyone will believe in Him, and the Romans will come and take away both our holy place and our nation."

But one of them, Caiaphas, who was *kohen gadol* that year, said to them, "You know nothing! You don't take into account that it is better for you that one man die for the people rather than for the whole nation to be destroyed."

Now he did not say this by himself; but as the *kohen gadol* that year, he prophesied that *Yeshua* would die for the nation. And not for the nation only, but also so that He might gather together into one the scattered children of God. So from that day on, they plotted to kill Him.

Therefore *Yeshua* no longer walked openly among the Judeans, but went from there to the country near the wilderness, to a city called Ephraim. He stayed there with His disciples.

Now the Jewish Passover was near; and many people went up out of the regions to Jerusalem before Passover, to purify themselves.
So they were searching for *Yeshua*, saying to one another as they stood in the Temple, "What do you think? Won't He come to the feast at all?"

Now the ruling *kohanim* and Pharisees had given orders that if anyone knew where He was, he should report it so that they might arrest Him.

John, chapter 11

Six days before Passover, *Yeshua* came to Bethany, where Lazarus was, whom *Yeshua* had raised from the dead. So they prepared a dinner there for *Yeshua*. Martha was serving, and Lazarus was one of those reclining at the table with Him. Then Miriam took a pound of very expensive oil of pure nard and anointed *Yeshua's* feet, and she wiped

Then Miriam took a pound of very expensive oil of pure nard and
anointed *Yeshua's* feet, and she wiped His feet dry with her hair.
Now the house was filled with the fragrance of the oil.

John 12:3 TLV

His feet dry with her hair.

Now the house was filled with the fragrance of the oil. But Judah from Kriot, one of His disciples, the one who was about to betray Him, said, "Why wasn't this oil sold for three hundred denarii and the money given to the poor?" Now he said this not because he cared about the poor, but because he was a thief. Since he had the moneybox, he used to steal from what was put in it.

Therefore *Yeshua* said, **"Leave her alone! She set it aside for the day of My burial. You will always have the poor among you, but you will not always have Me."**

Now a large crowd of Judeans knew He was there and came, not only for *Yeshua* but also to see Lazarus, whom He had raised from the dead. So the ruling *kohanim* made plans to kill Lazarus also, because on account of him many of the Jewish people were going and putting their trust in *Yeshua*.

The next day, the huge crowd that had come up for the feast heard that *Yeshua* was coming to Jerusalem. So they took palm branches and went out to meet Him, shouting,

"'*Hoshia-na! Baruch ha-ba*
b'shem ADONAI!
Blessed is He who comes in the
name of the LORD!'
The King of Israel!"

Finding a young donkey, *Yeshua* sat on it, as it is written,

"Fear not, Daughter of Zion!
Look! Your King is coming,
sitting on a donkey's colt."

His disciples did not understand these things at first. But when *Yeshua* was glorified, then they remembered that these things were written about Him and that the crowd had done these things for Him. So the crowd, which had been with *Yeshua* when He called Lazarus out of the tomb and raised him from the dead, kept on telling everyone about it. It was also for this reason that the crowd came out to meet Him, because they heard that He had performed this sign. So the Pharisees said to each other, "You see that you can't do anything. Look, the whole world has taken off after Him!"

Now there were some Greeks among those who were going up to worship at the feast. These came to Philip, who was from Bethsaida in the Galilee. "Sir," they said, "we want to see *Yeshua*." Philip comes and tells Andrew; Andrew and Philip come and tell *Yeshua*.

Yeshua answers them, saying, **"The hour has come for the Son of Man to be glorified! Amen, amen I tell you, unless a grain of wheat falls to the earth and dies, it remains alone. But if it dies, it produces much fruit. He who loves his life will lose it, and the one who hates his life in this world will keep it forever.**

If any man serves Me, he must follow Me; and where I am, there also will My servant be. If anyone serves Me, the Father will honor him.

"Now My soul is troubled. And what shall I say? 'Father, save Me from this

hour'? But it was for this reason I came to this hour. Father, glorify Your name!"

Then a voice came out of heaven, "I have glorified it, and again I will glorify it!"

Therefore the crowd that was standing there and heard it was saying that it had thundered. Others were saying, "An angel has spoken to Him."

Yeshua responded, **"This voice hasn't come for My sake, but for yours. Now is the judgment of this world! Now the prince of this world will be driven out! And as I am lifted up from the earth, I will draw all to Myself."** He said this to show the kind of death He was about to die.

The crowd answered Him, "We've heard from Scripture that the Messiah remains forever. How can You say, 'The Son of Man must be lifted up'? Who is this Son of Man?"

Therefore *Yeshua* said to them, **"The light is with you for a little longer. Walk while you have the light, so that the darkness will not overtake you. The one who walks in darkness doesn't know where he is going. While you have the light, believe in the light so that you may become sons of light."**

Yeshua spoke these things, then left and hid Himself from them. But even though He had performed so many signs before them, they weren't trusting in Him. This was to fulfill the word of Isaiah the prophet, who said, "*ADONAI*, who has believed our report? To whom has the arm of *ADONAI* been revealed?"

For this reason they could not believe, for Isaiah also said,
"He has blinded their eyes
and hardened their hearts,
so they might not see with their eyes nor understand with their hearts and turn back,
and I would heal them."

Isaiah said these things because he saw His glory and spoke of Him. Nevertheless many, even among the leaders, put their trust in Him. But because of the Pharisees, they were not confessing *Yeshua*, so they would not be thrown out of the synagogue; for they loved the glory of men more than the glory of God.

Yeshua cried out, **"Whoever puts trust in Me believes not in Me but in the One who sent Me! And whoever beholds Me beholds the One who sent Me. As light I have come into the world, so that everyone who trusts in Me should not remain in darkness.**

"If anyone hears My words but doesn't keep them, I do not judge him; for I came to save the world, not to judge the world. The one who rejects Me and doesn't receive My words has a judge; the word I spoke will judge him on the last day. For I did not speak on My own, but the Father Himself who sent Me has commanded Me what to say and speak. And I know that His commandment is life everlasting. Therefore what I say, I say just as the Father has told Me."

John, chapter 12

85. God Remembers the Passover

"Then the kingdom of heaven will be like ten virgins who took their lamps and went out to meet the bridegroom. Five of them were foolish, and five were wise. For when the foolish ones took their lamps, they took no oil with them. But the wise ones took oil in jars along with their lamps.

"Now while the bridegroom was taking a long time, they all got drowsy and started falling asleep. But in the middle of the night there was a shout, 'Look, the bridegroom! Come out to meet him!' Then all those virgins got up and trimmed their lamps.

Now the foolish ones said to the wise, 'Give us some of your oil, since our lamps are going out.' But the wise ones replied, 'No, there won't be enough for us and for you. Instead, go to those who sell, and buy some for yourselves.'

"But while they were going off to buy, the bridegroom came. And those who were ready went in with him to the wedding feast, and the door was shut.

Now later, the other virgins came, saying, 'Sir, Sir, open up for us!'

"But he replied, 'Amen, I tell you, I do not know you.' Therefore stay alert, for you know neither the day nor the hour."

"For it is like a man about to go on a journey. He called his own servants and handed over his possessions to them. To one he gave five talents, to another two, and to another one, each according to his own ability. Then he went on his journey.

"Immediately the one who had received the five talents went and traded with them and gained five more. In the same way, the one with two gained two more. But the one who received one went off and dug a hole in the ground and hid his master's money.

"Now after a long time, the master of those servants came and settled accounts with them. The one who had received the five talents came up and brought another five talents, saying, 'Master, you handed me five talents. Look, I've gained five more.' His master said to him, 'Well done, good and faithful servant! You were faithful with a little, so I'll put you in charge of much. Enter into your master's joy!'

"The one who had received the two talents also came up and said, 'Master, you handed me two talents. Look, I've gained two more.' His master said to him, 'Well done, good and faithful servant! You were faithful with a little, so I'll put you in charge of much. Enter into your master's joy!'

"Then the one who had received the one talent also came up and said, 'Master, I knew that you are a hard man, reaping where you didn't sow and gathering where you scattered no seed. So I was afraid, and I went off and hid your talent in the ground.

See, you have what is yours.'

"But his master responded, 'You wicked, lazy servant! You knew that I reap where I didn't sow and gather where I scattered no seed? Then you should have brought my money to the brokers, and when I came I would have received it back with interest. Therefore take the talent away from him, and give it to the one who has the ten talents.

For to the one who has, more shall be given, and he shall have an abundance. But from the one who does not have, even what he does have shall be taken away. Throw the worthless servant out, into the outer darkness where there will be weeping and gnashing of teeth.'"

"Now when the Son of Man comes in His glory, and all the angels with Him, then He will sit on His glorious throne. All the nations will be gathered before Him, and He will separate them from one another, just as the shepherd separates the sheep from the goats. And He will put the sheep on His right, but the goats on His left. Then the King will say to those on His right, 'Come, you who are blessed by My Father, inherit the kingdom prepared for you from the foundation of the world. For I was hungry and you gave Me something to eat; I was thirsty and you gave Me something to drink; I was a stranger and you invited Me in; I was naked and you clothed Me; I was sick and you visited Me; I was in prison and you came to Me.'

"Then the righteous will answer Him, 'Lord, when did we see You hungry and feed You? Or thirsty and give You something to drink? And when did we see You a stranger and invite You in? Or naked and clothe You? When did we see You sick, or in prison, and come to You?'

"And answering, the King will say to them, 'Amen, I tell you, whatever you did to one of the least of these My brethren, you did it to Me.'

Then He will also say to those on the left, 'Go away from Me, you cursed ones, into the everlasting fire which has been prepared for the devil and his angels. For I was hungry and you gave Me nothing to eat; I was thirsty and you gave Me nothing to drink; I was a stranger and you did not invite Me in; naked and you did not clothe Me; sick and in prison and you did not visit Me.'

"Then they too will answer, saying, 'Lord, when did we see You hungry or thirsty or a stranger or naked or sick or in prison, and did not care for You?'

Then He will answer them, saying, 'Amen, I tell you, whatever you did not do for one of the least of these, you did not do for Me.' These shall go off to everlasting punishment, but the righteous into everlasting life."

Matthew, chapter 25

Now it happened that when *Yeshua* had finished all these words, He said to His disciples, "You know that Passover comes in two days, and the Son of Man will be handed over to be executed."

Now while they were eating, *Yeshua* took *matzah;* and after He offered the *bracha*, He broke and gave to the disciples and said, "Take, eat; this is My body."

Matthew 26:26 TLV

Then the ruling *kohanim* and elders of the people were gathered together in the court of the *kohen gadol* named Caiaphas. They plotted together in order that they might seize *Yeshua* by stealth and kill Him. "But not during the festival," they were saying, "so there won't be a riot among the people."

Now while *Yeshua* was in Bethany at the house of Simon *ha-Metzora*, a woman came up to Him with an alabaster jar of very expensive oil. And she poured it on His head as He was reclining at the table. But when the disciples saw this, they were indignant, saying, "Why this waste? It could have been sold for a lot, and the money given to the poor!"

But *Yeshua*, knowing this, said to them, **"Why do you cause trouble for this woman? She's done Me a *mitzvah*. You always have the poor with you, but you won't always have Me. For when she poured this oil on My body, she did it to prepare Me for burial. Amen, I tell you, wherever this Good News is proclaimed in all the world, what she has done will also be told in memory of her."**

Then one of the Twelve, the one called Judah of Kriot, went to the ruling *kohanim* and said, "What are you willing to give me if I hand Him over to you?" And they weighed out thirty shekels of silver for him. From then on, Judah began looking for a chance to hand Him over.

Now on the first day of *matzah*, the disciples came to *Yeshua*, saying, "Where do You want us to prepare for You to eat the Passover?"

He said, **"Go into the city to a certain man, and tell him, 'The Teacher says, "My time is near; at your house I am to keep the Passover with My disciples."'"**

The disciples did as *Yeshua* had ordered them, and they prepared the Passover.

Now when it was evening, *Yeshua* was reclining at the table with the Twelve. As they were eating, He said, **"Amen, I tell you, one of you will betray Me."** And being very sorrowful, they began, each one, to say to Him, "I'm not the one, am I, Master?"

And He replied, **"The one who dipped his hand in the bowl with Me, he's the one who will betray Me. The Son of Man indeed goes, just as it is written about Him; but woe to that man by whom the Son of Man is betrayed! It would have been better for that man if he had not been born!"**

And Judah, the one betraying Him, replied, "I'm not the one, am I, Rabbi?"

Yeshua said to him, **"You've said it yourself."**

Now while they were eating, *Yeshua* took *matzah*; and after He offered the *bracha*, He broke and gave to the disciples and said, "Take, eat; this is My body." And He took a cup; and after giving thanks, He gave to them, saying, **"Drink from it, all of you; for this is My blood of the covenant, which is poured out for many for the removal of sins.**

But I say to you, I will never drink of this fruit of the vine from now on, until that day when I drink it anew with you in My Father's kingdom."

After singing the *Hallel*, they went out to the Mount of Olives. Then *Yeshua* said to them, **"This night you will all fall away because of Me; for it is written,**
'I will strike the Shepherd,
and the sheep of the flock
will be scattered.'
But after I am raised up, I will go before you to the Galilee."

But Peter replied to Him, "Though all fall away because of You, I'll never fall away."

Yeshua said to him, **"Truly, I tell you, this very night, before a rooster crows, you will deny Me three times."**

"Even if I must die with You," Peter says to Him, "I'll never deny You!" And so said all the disciples.

Then *Yeshua* comes with them to a place called Gethsemane, and He tells the disciples, **"Sit here, while I go over there and pray."** And He took along Peter and Zebedee's two sons, and He began to be sorrowful and troubled.

Then He tells them, **"My soul is deeply grieved, even to the point of death. Stay here and keep watch with Me."**

Going a little farther, He fell face down and prayed, saying, **"My Father, if it is possible, let this cup pass from Me! Yet not as I will, but as You will."**

Then He comes to the disciples and finds them sleeping; and He tells Peter, **"So couldn't you keep watch with Me for one hour? Keep watching and praying, so that you won't enter into temptation. The spirit is willing, but the flesh is weak."**

Again for a second time He went away and prayed, saying, **"My Father, if this cannot pass away unless I drink it, let Your will be done."**

And again He came and found them sleeping, for their eyes were heavy. So He left them again and prayed a third time, saying the same words once more.

Then He comes to the disciples and says to them, **"Still sleeping? Taking your rest? Look, the hour is at hand, and the Son of Man is being delivered into the hands of sinners. Get up, let's go! Look, My betrayer is near."**

While *Yeshua* was still speaking, here came Judah, one of the Twelve, and with him a big crowd with swords and clubs, from the ruling *kohanim* and elders of the people.

Now His betrayer had given them a sign, saying, 'The One I kiss, He's the One—seize Him!' And immediately Judah drew near to *Yeshua* and said, "*Shalom*, Rabbi!" and kissed Him.

"Friend," *Yeshua* said to him, **"do what you've come to do."** Then they came up and threw their hands on *Yeshua* and seized Him. And suddenly, one of those with *Yeshua* stretched out his hand and drew his sword, and he struck the *kohen gadol*'s servant and cut off his ear.

Then *Yeshua* said to him, **"Put your sword back in its place! For all who take up the sword shall perish by the sword. Or do you suppose that I cannot call on My Father, and at once He will place at My side twelve legions of angels? How then would the Scriptures be fulfilled, that it must be so?"**

At that hour *Yeshua* said to the crowds, **"Have you come out with swords and clubs, to capture Me as you would a revolutionary? Every day I sat teaching in the Temple, and you didn't seize Me. But all this has happened so that the writings of the prophets would be fulfilled."** Then all the disciples fled, abandoning Him.

Now those who had seized *Yeshua* led Him away to Caiaphas, the *kohen gadol*, where the the *Torah* scholars and elders had gathered.

Peter was following Him from a distance as far as the courtyard of the *kohen gadol*. And after going inside, he was sitting with the guards, to see the outcome.

Now the ruling *kohanim* and all the Sanhedrin kept trying to get false testimony against *Yeshua* so they could put Him to death. But they found none, though many false witnesses came forward. At last two came forward and said, "This fellow said, 'I'm able to destroy the Temple of God and rebuild it in three days!'"

The *kohen gadol* stood up and said to *Yeshua*, "Have You no answer? What's this they're testifying against You?" But *Yeshua* kept silent.

The *kohen gadol* said to Him, "I charge You under oath by the living God, tell us if You are *Mashiach Ben-Elohim*!"

"As you have said," replied *Yeshua*. **"Besides that, I tell you, soon after you will see the Son of Man sitting at the right hand of power and coming on the clouds of heaven."**

Then the *kohen gadol* tore his clothes and said, "Blasphemy! Why do we need any more witnesses? Look, you've heard the blasphemy. What's your verdict?"

"Guilty," they answered. "He deserves death!" Then they spat in His face and pounded Him with their fists. Others slapped Him and demanded, "Prophesy to us, you Messiah! Which one hit You?"

Matthew 26:1-68

But the governor responded, "Which of the two do you want me to release for you?" And they said, "Bar-Abba!" Pilate said to them, "What then shall I do with *Yeshua,* who is called Messiah?" "Execute Him!" all of them say. But Pilate said, "Why? What evil has He done?" But they kept shouting all the more, saying, "Let Him be executed!"

Matthew 27:21-23 TLV

86. God Provides the Scapegoat

When daybreak came, the ruling *kohanim* and elders of the people conspired against *Yeshua* to put Him to death. And they tied Him up, led Him away, and handed Him over to Pilate, the governor. Then Judah, His betrayer, saw that *Yeshua* had been condemned. Feeling remorse, he brought the thirty silver pieces back to the ruling *kohanim* and elders, saying, "I've sinned, betraying innocent blood!"

But they said, "What's that to us? You see to it yourself!"

After tossing the silver into the Temple sanctuary, he left. Then he went off and hanged himself. But the ruling *kohanim* took the silver pieces and said, "It is not permitted to put these in the treasury, since it is blood money." So after they conferred, they bought with them the potter's field, as a cemetery for strangers. For this reason that field has been called the "Field of Blood" to this day.

Then was fulfilled what was spoken by Jeremiah the prophet, saying, "And they took the thirty silver pieces, the price of Him on whom a price had been set by *Bnei-Yisrael*; and they gave them for the potter's field, just as *ADONAI* arranged for me."

Now *Yeshua* stood before the governor. The governor questioned Him, saying, "Are You the King of the Jews?"

"You say so," *Yeshua* said. And while He was accused by the ruling *kohanim* and elders, He did not answer. Then Pilate said to Him, "Don't You hear how many things they testify against you?" *Yeshua* did not answer, not even one word, so the governor was greatly amazed.

Now during the feast, the governor was accustomed to release to the crowd one prisoner, anyone they wanted. At that time they had a notorious prisoner, called *Yeshua Bar-Abba*. So when they were gathered together, Pilate said to them, "Which one do you want me to release for you? *Yeshua* who is *Bar-Abba*, or *Yeshua* who is called Messiah?" For he knew that they had handed Him over out of envy.

While Pilate was sitting on the judgment seat, his wife sent him a message, saying, "Don't have anything to do with that righteous Man, for today I've suffered many things in a dream because of Him."

Now the ruling *kohanim* and elders persuaded the crowds that they should ask for *Bar-Abba* and destroy *Yeshua*. But the governor responded, "Which of the two do you want me to release for you?" And they said, "*Bar-Abba!*"

Pilate said to them, "What then shall I do with *Yeshua*, who is called Messiah?"

"Execute Him!" all of them say.

But Pilate said, "Why? What evil has He done?"

But they kept shouting all the more,

saying, "Let Him be executed!"

When Pilate saw he was accomplishing nothing, but instead a riot was starting, he took some water and washed his hands in front of the crowd. "I am innocent of this blood," he said. "You see to it yourselves!"

All the people answered and said, "His blood be on us and on our children!"

Then he released to them *Bar-Abba*. And after he had *Yeshua* scourged, he handed Him over to be crucified.

Then the governor's soldiers took *Yeshua* into the Praetorium and gathered the whole cohort around Him. They stripped Him and put a scarlet robe around Him. And after braiding a crown of thorns, they placed it on His head and put a staff in His right hand. And falling on their knees before Him, they mocked Him, saying, "Hail, King of the Jews!"

They spat on Him, and they took the staff and beat Him over and over on the head. When they finished mocking Him, they stripped the robe off Him and put His own clothes back on Him. And they led Him away to crucify Him.

Matthew 27:1-31

87. God Provides the Lamb

Right at daybreak, the ruling *kohanim* held a meeting to consult with the elders and *Torah* scholars and the whole Sanhedrin. They tied up *Yeshua*, led Him away, and handed Him over to Pilate.

Pilate interrogated Him, "Are You the King of the Jews?"

Yeshua answers him, "As you say."

The ruling *kohanim* began to accuse Him of many things. Again, Pilate asked Him, "Aren't you going to answer? Look how many charges they're bringing against You!"

But *Yeshua* did not answer, so Pilate was amazed. Now during the feast, he used to release to them one prisoner, anyone they were asking for. Now a man named *Bar-Abba* had been in jail with the rebels who had committed murder during the rebellion. The crowd came up and began to request what he was accustomed to do for them. But Pilate answered them, saying, "Do you want me to release for you the King of the Jews?" For he knew that out of envy the ruling *kohanim* had handed Him over. But the ruling *kohanim* stirred up the crowd, so he would release *Bar-Abba* to them instead. Then answering again, Pilate said to them, "So what do you want me to do with the One you call the King of the Jews?"

They shouted back, "Execute Him!"

Pilate responded, "Why? What evil has He done?"

But they shouted all the more, "Execute Him!"

Wanting to satisfy the crowd, Pilate released *Bar-Abba* for them. And after he had *Yeshua* scourged, he handed Him over to be crucified. The soldiers took Him away, into the palace, the governor's mansion called the Praetorium. And they call together the cohort of soldiers. They dress Him up in purple. After braiding a crown of thorns, they put it on Him. And they began to salute Him, "Hail, King of the Jews!" Over and over, they kept hitting Him on the head with a staff and spitting on Him; and kneeling down, they worshiped Him. When they finished mocking Him, they stripped the purple off Him and put His own clothes back on Him. And they led Him out to crucify Him.

Now Simon of Cyrene, the father of Alexander and Rufus, was coming in from the countryside. The soldiers force this passerby to carry *Yeshua's* cross-beam. They bring *Yeshua* to the place called Golgotha (which is translated, Place of a Skull). They were offering Him wine mixed with myrrh, but He didn't take it. Then they crucify Him and divide up His clothing among themselves, casting lots for them to see who should take what.

Now it was the third hour when they nailed Him on the stake. And the inscription of the charge against Him was written above: "THE KING OF THE JEWS." And with Him they execute two outlaws, one on His right and one on His left.

Those passing by were jeering at Him, shaking their heads and saying, "Ha! You who are going to destroy the Temple and rebuild it in three days, save Yourself by coming down from the stake!"

Likewise the ruling *kohanim*, along with the *Torah* scholars, were also mocking Him among themselves. "He saved others," they were saying, "but He can't save Himself? Let the Messiah, the King of Israel, come down now from the stake, so we may see and believe!" Even those executed with Him were ridiculing Him.

When the sixth hour had come, darkness fell over the whole land until the ninth hour.

At the ninth hour *Yeshua* cried out with a loud voice, ***"Eloi, Eloi, lema sabachthani?"*** which is translated, **"My God, My God, why have You abandoned Me?"**

When some of the bystanders heard it, they began saying, "Look, He's calling for Elijah."

Then someone ran and filled a sponge with sour wine. He put it on a stick and was offering it to *Yeshua* to drink, saying, "Wait, let's see if Elijah comes to take Him down." But letting out a loud cry, *Yeshua* breathed His last.

Then the curtain of the Temple was split in two, from top to bottom. When the centurion, who was standing in front of Him, saw the way *Yeshua* breathed His last, he said, "This Man really was the Son of God!"

Mark 15:1- 39

When they finished mocking Him, they stripped the purple off Him and put His own clothes back on Him. And they led Him out to crucify Him.

Mark 15:20 TLV

The people stood there watching. And even the leaders were sneering at Him, saying, "He saved others; let Him save Himself if He is the Messiah of God, the Chosen One!"

Luke 23:35 TLV

88. God Saves the World

Now a great multitude of people was following Him, including women who were mourning and singing dirges for Him. But *Yeshua*, turning to them, said, **"Daughters of Jerusalem, do not weep for Me, but for yourselves and your children. For indeed, the days are coming when they will say, 'Blessed are barren, and the wombs that never gave birth, and the breasts that did not feed.'**

'Then they will begin to say to the mountains, 'Fall on us!' and to the hills, 'Cover us!' For if they do these things when the wood is green, what will happen when it is dry?"

Others, two evildoers, were also led away to be put to death with Him. When they came to the place called the Skull, there they crucified Him and the evildoers, one on His right and the other on His left. But *Yeshua* was saying, **"Father, forgive them, for they do not know what they are doing."** Then they cast lots, dividing up His clothing.

The people stood there watching. And even the leaders were sneering at Him, saying, "He saved others; let Him save Himself if He is the Messiah of God, the Chosen One!"

The soldiers likewise mocked Him, coming up and bringing Him sour wine, and saying, "If You are the King of the Jews, save Yourself."

Now there was also an inscription over Him: THIS IS THE KING OF THE JEWS. One of the evildoers hanging there was jeering at Him, saying, "Aren't You the Messiah? Save Yourself—and us!"

But the other one, rebuking him, replied, "Don't you fear God, since you are under the same sentence? We're getting what we deserve for our actions, and rightly so—but this One has done nothing wrong." And he said, "*Yeshua*, remember me when You come into Your kingdom."

Yeshua said to him, **"Amen, I tell you, today you shall be with Me in Paradise."**

It was now about the sixth hour, and darkness fell over the whole land until the ninth hour, for the sun died out. And the curtain of the Temple was torn in two. And *Yeshua*, crying out with a loud voice, said, "Father, 'into Your hands I entrust My spirit.'" When He had said this, He breathed His last.

Now when the centurion saw what had happened, he began glorifying God, saying, "Truly this was a righteous Man."

And all the crowds assembled for this spectacle, when they saw what had happened, began to turn back, beating their breasts. But all *Yeshua's* acquaintances, and the women who were following Him from the Galilee, were standing at a distance, watching these things. Now there was a man named Joseph, a council member, a good and righteous man. (He had not been in agreement with the council and their action.) He was from the Judean town of Arimathea, and he was waiting for the kingdom of God. This man went to Pilate and asked for *Yeshua's* body. And he took it down, wrapped it in a linen cloth, and laid Him in a tomb cut out of the rock, where no one had ever yet been laid.

Now it was the Day of Preparation, and *Shabbat* was approaching. The women who had come with Him from the Galilee followed, and they saw the tomb and how His body was laid. Then they returned and prepared spices and perfumes. But on *Shabbat* they rested according to the commandment.

Luke, chapter 23

89. God Resurrects His Son

After these things, Joseph of Arimathea asked Pilate if he could take *Yeshua's* body away. Joseph was a disciple of *Yeshua*, but secretly for fear of the Judean leaders. Pilate gave permission, so Joseph came and took the body away.

Nicodemus, who had first visited *Yeshua* at night, also came bringing a mixture of myrrh and aloes, about a hundred pounds. Then they took the body of *Yeshua* and wrapped it in linen with the spices, as is the Jewish burial custom.

Now in the place where He was executed, there was a garden. In the garden was a new tomb where no one had yet been buried. Because it was the Jewish Day of Preparation and the tomb was nearby, they laid *Yeshua* there.

John 19: 38-42

Early in the morning on the first day of the week, while it is still dark, Miriam from Magdala comes to the tomb. She sees that the stone had been rolled away from the tomb. So she comes running to Simon Peter and the other disciple, the one *Yeshua* loved.

She tells them, "They've taken the Master out of the tomb, and we don't know where they've put Him!"

Then Peter and the other disciple set out, going to the tomb. The two were running together, but the other disciple outran Peter and arrived at the tomb first. Leaning in, he sees the linen strips lying there. But he didn't go in.

Then Simon Peter comes following him, and he entered the tomb. He looks upon the linen strips lying there, and the face cloth that had been on His head. It was not lying with the linen strips, but was rolled up in a place by itself. So then the other disciple, who had reached the tomb first, also entered. He saw and believed. For they did not yet understand from Scripture that *Yeshua* must rise from the dead. So the disciples went back to their own homes.

But Miriam stood outside the tomb weeping. As she was weeping, she bent down to look into the tomb. She sees two angels in white sitting, one at the head and one at the feet, where *Yeshua's* body had been lying.

"Woman, why are you crying?" they say to her.

She says to them, "Because they took away my Master, and I don't know where they've put Him." After she said these things, she turned around. And she sees *Yeshua* standing there. Yet she didn't know that it was *Yeshua*.

Yeshua says to her, **"Woman, why are you weeping? Who are you looking for?"**

Thinking He's the gardener, she says to Him, "Sir, if You've carried Him away, tell me where You've put Him, and I will take Him away."

Yeshua says to her, **"Miriam!"**

Turning around, she says to Him in Aramaic, "*Rabboni!*" (which means Teacher).

Yeshua says to her, **"Stop clinging to Me, for I have not yet gone up to the Father. Go to My brothers and tell them, 'I am going up to My Father and your Father, to My God and your God.'"**

Miriam from Magdala comes, announcing to the disciples, "I've seen the Lord," and what He had said to her.

It was evening on that day, the first of the week. When the doors were locked where the disciples were, for fear of the Judean leaders, *Yeshua* came and stood in their midst! And He said to them, ***"Shalom aleichem!"*** After He said this, He showed them His hands and His side. Then the disciples rejoiced when they saw the Lord. *Yeshua* said to them again, **"*Shalom aleichem!* As the Father has sent Me, I also send you."**

And after He said this, He breathed on them. And He said to them, **"Receive the *Ruach ha-Kodesh!* If you forgive anyone's sins, they are forgiven; but if you hold back, they are held back."**

One of the Twelve, Thomas called the Twin, was not with them when *Yeshua* came. The other disciples were saying to him, "We've seen the Lord!"

But he replied to them, "Unless I see the nail prints in His hands, and put my finger into the mark of the nails, and put my hand in His side, I will never believe!"

Eight days later the disciples were again inside, and Thomas was with them. *Yeshua* comes, despite the locked doors. He stood in their midst and said, ***"Shalom aleichem!"***

Then He said to Thomas, **"Put your finger here, and look at My hands. Reach out your hand and put it into My side. Stop doubting and believe!"**

Thomas answered and said to Him, "My Lord and my God!"

Yeshua said to Him, **"Because you have seen Me, you have believed? Blessed are the ones who have not seen and yet have believed!"**

Yeshua performed many other signs in the presence of the disciples, which are not written in this book. But these things have been written so that you may believe that *Yeshua* is *Mashiach Ben-Elohim*, and that by believing you may have life in His name.

John, chapter 20

Yeshua says to her, "Miriam!"
Turning around, she says to Him in Aramaic, "*Rabboni!*"
(which means Teacher).

John 20:16 TLV

Therefore the disciple whom *Yeshua* loved said to Peter, "It's the Lord!" When Simon Peter heard that it was the Lord, he tied his outer garment around himself—for he was stripped down for work—and threw himself into the sea.

John 21:7 TLV

90. God Forgives Unbelief

After these things, *Yeshua* revealed Himself again to the disciples at the Sea of Tiberias.

Now here is how He appeared. Simon Peter, Thomas called the Twin, Nathanael of Cana in the Galilee, the sons of Zebedee, and two of the other disciples were together.

Simon Peter said to them, "I'm going fishing."

"We're coming with you too," they said. They went out and got into the boat, and that night they caught nothing.

At dawn, *Yeshua* stood on the beach; but the disciples didn't know that it was *Yeshua*. So *Yeshua* said to them, **"Boys, you don't happen to have any fish, do you?"**

"No," they answered Him.

He said to them, **"Throw the net off the right side of the boat, and you'll find some."** So they threw the net, and they were not able to haul it in because of the great number of fish. Therefore the disciple whom *Yeshua* loved said to Peter, "It's the Lord!"

When Simon Peter heard that it was the Lord, he tied his outer garment around himself—for he was stripped down for work—and threw himself into the sea. But the other disciples came in the boat from about two hundred cubits offshore, dragging the net full of fish. So when they got out onto the land, they saw a charcoal fire with fish placed on it, and bread.

Yeshua said to them, **"Bring some of the fish you've just caught."**

Simon Peter went aboard and hauled the net to shore. There were 153 fish, many of them big; but the net was not broken. *Yeshua* said to them, **"Come, have breakfast."** None of the disciples dared ask Him, "Who are You?"—knowing it was the Lord.

Yeshua comes and takes the bread and gives it to them, and likewise the fish. This was now the third time that *Yeshua* was revealed to the disciples after He was raised from the dead. When they had finished breakfast, *Yeshua* said to Simon Peter, **"Simon, son of John, do you love Me more than these?"**

"Yes, Lord," he said to Him, "You know that I love you."

He said to him, **"Feed My lambs!"**

He said to him again a second time, **"Simon, son of John, do you love Me?"**

"Yes, Lord," he said, "You know that I love You."

He said to him, "Take care of My sheep!"

He said to him a third time, **"Simon, son of John, do you love Me?"** Peter was grieved because He said to him for a third time, **"Do you love Me?"** And he said to Him, "Lord, You know everything! You know that I love You!"

Yeshua said to him, **"Feed My sheep! Amen, amen I tell you, when you were younger, you used to dress yourself and walk wherever you wanted; but when you grow old, you will stretch out your hands, and someone else will dress you and carry you where you do not want to go."** Now this He said to indicate by what kind of death Peter was going to glorify God. And after this, *Yeshua* said to him, **"Follow Me!"**

Peter, turning around, sees the disciple following. This was the one whom *Yeshua* loved, who also had reclined against *Yeshua's* chest at the *seder* meal and said, "Master, who is the one who is betraying You?" Seeing him, Peter said to *Yeshua*, "Lord, what about him?"

Yeshua said to him, **"If I want him to remain until I come, what is that to you? You follow Me!"** Therefore this saying went out among the brothers and sisters, that this disciple would not die. Yet *Yeshua* did not say to him that he would not die, but, **"If I want him to remain until I come, what is that to you?"**

This is the disciple who is an eyewitness of these things and wrote these things. We know that his testimony is true. There are also many other things that *Yeshua* did. If all of them were to be written one by one, I suppose that not even the world itself will have room for the books being written!

John, chapter 21

91. God Lifts *Yeshua* Up

I wrote the first volume, Theophilus, about all that *Yeshua* began to do and teach—up to the day He was taken up, after He had given orders by the *Ruach ha-Kodesh* to the emissaries He had chosen. To them He showed Himself to be alive after His suffering through many convincing proofs, appearing to them for forty days and speaking about the kingdom of God.

Now while staying with them, He commanded them not to leave Jerusalem, but to wait for what the Father promised—which, He said, **"You heard from Me. For John immersed with water, but you will be immersed in the *Ruach ha-Kodesh* not many days from now."**

So when they gathered together, they asked Him, "Lord, are You restoring the kingdom to Israel at this time?"

He said to them, **"It is not your place to know the times or seasons which the Father has placed under His own control. But you will receive power when the *Ruach ha-Kodesh* has come upon you; and you will be My witnesses in Jerusalem, and through all Judah, and Samaria, and to the end of the earth."**

After saying all this—while they were watching—He was taken up, and a cloud received Him out of their sight.

While they were staring into heaven as He went up, suddenly two men stood with them in white clothing. They said, "Men of Galilee, why do you keep standing here staring into heaven? This *Yeshua*, who was taken up from you into heaven, will come in the same way as you saw Him go into heaven."

Then they returned to Jerusalem from the Mount of Olives (which is near Jerusalem, a *Shabbat* day's journey).

When they had entered, they went up to the upper room where they were staying—Peter and John and Jacob and Andrew; Philip and Thomas, Bartholomew and Matthew; Jacob son of Alphaeus and Simon the Zealot and Judah son of Jacob. All these with one mind were continuing together in prayer—along with the women and Miriam, *Yeshua*'s mother, and His brothers.

In those days, Peter stood up among the brothers and sisters (the number of names all together was about a hundred and twenty) and said, "Brothers, the Scripture had to be fulfilled, which the *Ruach ha-Kodesh* foretold by the mouth of David, concerning Judah—who became a guide to those who seized *Yeshua*. For he was counted among us and received his share of this office." (Now this man Judah bought a field with the reward of his wickedness. Falling headfirst, he burst open in the middle and his intestines splattered out. And it became known to all those living in Jerusalem, so in their own language that field was called Akeldama—that is, 'Field of Blood.')

For it is written in the Book of Psalms,
'Let his dwelling place become
desolate, and let there be no

After saying all this—while they were watching—He was taken up, and a cloud received Him out of their sight.

Acts 1:9 TLV

one living in it'
and 'Let another take his position.'

"Therefore one of the men who have accompanied us all the time that the Lord *Yeshua* went in and out among us—beginning with His immersion by John until the day He was taken up from us—must become a witness with us of His resurrection."

So they nominated two—Joseph, called Barsabbas (also called Justus), and Matthias.

And they prayed and said, "You, O Lord, who knows the hearts of all men, show us which of these two You have chosen to take the position in this office as emissary, from which Judah turned aside to go to his own place."

Then they cast lots for them, and the lot fell upon Matthias; and he was added to the eleven emissaries.

Acts, chapter 1

92. God Gives His Spirit

When the day of *Shavuot* had come, they were all together in one place. Suddenly there came from heaven a sound like a mighty rushing wind, and it filled the whole house where they were sitting. And tongues like fire spreading out appeared to them and settled on each one of them. They were all filled with the *Ruach ha-Kodesh* and began to speak in other tongues as the *Ruach* enabled them to speak out.

Now Jewish people were staying in Jerusalem, devout men from every nation under heaven. And when this sound came, the crowd gathered. They were bewildered, because each was hearing them speaking in his own language.

And they were amazed and astonished, saying, "All these who are speaking—aren't they Galileans? How is it that we each hear our own birth language? Parthians and Medes and Elamites and those living in Mesopotamia, Judea and Cappadocia, Pontus and Asia, Phrygia and Pamphylia, Egypt and parts of Libya toward Cyrene, and visitors from Rome (both Jewish people and proselytes), Cretans and Arabs—we hear them declaring in our own tongues the mighty deeds of God!" And they were all amazed and perplexed, saying to each other, "What does this mean?"

Others, poking fun, were saying, "They are full of sweet new wine!" But Peter, standing with the Eleven, raised his voice and addressed them: "Fellow Judeans and all who are staying in Jerusalem, let this be known to you, and pay attention to my words. These men are not drunk, as you suppose—for it's only the third hour of the day! But this is what was spoken about through the prophet Joel:

'And it shall be in the last days,' says God, 'that I will pour out My *Ruach* on all flesh.
Your sons and your daughters
shall prophesy, your young
men shall see visions,
and your old men shall dream dreams.
Even on My slaves, male and
female, I will pour out
My *Ruach* in those days,
and they shall prophesy.

And I will give wonders in the sky
above and signs on the earth
beneath—blood, and fire,
and smoky vapor.
The sun shall be turned to
darkness and the moon to
blood before the great and
glorious Day of ADONAI comes.

And it shall be that everyone
who calls on the name of
ADONAI shall be saved.'

"Men of Israel, hear these words! *Yeshua ha-Natzrati*—a Man authenticated to you by God with mighty deeds and wonders and signs God performed through Him in your midst, as you yourselves know— this *Yeshua*, given over by God's predetermined plan and foreknowledge, nailed to the cross by the hand of lawless men, you killed. But God raised Him up, releasing Him from the pains of

Peter said to them, "Repent, and let each of you be immersed in the name of Messiah *Yeshua* for the removal of your sins, and you will receive the gift of the *Ruach ha-Kodesh*.

Acts 2:38 TLV

death, since it was impossible for Him to be held by it.

For David says about Him,
'I saw *ADONAI* always before me,
for He is at my right hand
so that I might not be shaken.
Therefore my heart was glad
and my tongue rejoiced;
moreover, my body also will
live in hope,
because You will not
abandon my soul to *Sheol*
or let Your Holy One see decay.
You have made known to me
the paths of life;
You will fill me with joy
in Your presence.'

"Brothers, I can confidently tell you that the patriarch David died and was buried—his tomb is with us to this day. So because he was a prophet and knew God had sworn with an oath to him to seat one of his descendants on his throne, David saw beforehand and spoke of Messiah's resurrection—that He was not abandoned to *Sheol*, and His body did not see decay.

"This *Yeshua* God raised up—we all are witnesses! Therefore, being exalted to the right hand of God and receiving from the Father the promise of the *Ruach ha-Kodesh*, He poured out this—what you now see and hear. For David did not ascend into the heavens; yet he himself says,
'*ADONAI* said to my Lord,
"Sit at my right hand,
until I make Your enemies a
footstool for Your feet."'

"Therefore let the whole house of Israel know for certain that God has made Him—this *Yeshua* whom you had crucified—both Lord and Messiah!"

Now when they heard this, they were cut to the heart and said to Peter and the rest of the emissaries, "Fellow brethren, what shall we do?"

Peter said to them, "Repent, and let each of you be immersed in the name of Messiah *Yeshua* for the removal of your sins, and you will receive the gift of the *Ruach ha-Kodesh*. For the promise is for you and your children, and for all who are far away—as many as *ADONAI* our God calls to Himself." With many other words he warned them and kept urging them, saying, "Save yourselves from this twisted generation!"

So those who received his message were immersed, and that day about three thousand souls were added. They were devoting themselves to the teaching of the emissaries and to fellowship, to breaking bread and to prayers. Fear lay upon every soul, and many wonders and signs were happening through the emissaries. And all who believed were together, having everything in common. They began selling their property and possessions and sharing them with all, as any had need. Day by day they continued with one mind, spending time at the Temple and breaking bread from house to house. They were sharing meals with gladness and sincerity of heart, praising God and having favor with all the people. And every day the Lord was adding to their number those being saved.

Acts, chapter 2

93. God Opens Blind Eyes

Now Saul was in agreement with Stephen's execution. On that day a great persecution arose against Messiah's community in Jerusalem, and they were all scattered throughout the region of Judea and Samaria, except the emissaries. Some devout men buried Stephen and mourned deeply for him.

But Saul was destroying Messiah's community, entering house after house; and dragging off men and women, he was throwing them into prison.

Now those who had been scattered went around proclaiming the Word. Philip went down to the main city of Samaria and proclaimed the Messiah to them. The crowds were paying close attention to what Philip was saying—as they both heard and saw the signs that he was doing. For unclean spirits were coming out of many who were plagued, shrieking with a loud voice. Many paralyzed and crippled were healed also. So there was great joy in that city.

Now a man named Simon had been practicing magic in the city and astonishing the people of Samaria, saying he was someone great. They all were paying special attention to him, saying, "This man is the power of God that is called 'Great.'" And they kept paying attention to him, because for a long time he had astonished them with his magical arts.

But when they believed Philip proclaiming the Good News about the kingdom of God and the name of Messiah *Yeshua*, both men and women were immersed. Even Simon himself believed; and after being immersed, he continued with Philip. And when he saw signs and great miracles happening, he was continually amazed.

Now when the emissaries in Jerusalem heard that Samaria had accepted the message of God, they sent Peter and John to them. They came down and prayed for them to receive the *Ruach ha-Kodesh*. For He had not yet come upon them; they had only been immersed in the name of the Lord *Yeshua*. Then they began laying their hands on them, and they were receiving the *Ruach ha-Kodesh*.

Now when Simon saw that the *Ruach ha-Kodesh* was given through the laying on of hands by the emissaries, he offered them money, saying, "Give this power to me, too—so that anyone on whom I lay hands may receive the *Ruach ha-Kodesh*."

Peter said to him, "May your silver go to ruin, and you with it—because you thought you could buy God's gift with money! You have no part or share in this matter, because your heart is not right before God. Therefore repent of this wickedness of yours, and pray to the Lord that, if possible, the intent of your heart may be pardoned. For I see in you the poison of bitterness and the bondage of unrighteousness!"

Simon replied, "Pray for me, so that none of what you have said may come upon me."

So when they had testified and

As he was traveling, approaching Damascus, suddenly a light from heaven flashed around him. Falling to the ground, he heard a voice saying to him, "Saul, Saul, why are you persecuting Me?"

Acts 9:3-4 TLV

spoken the word of the Lord, they returned to Jerusalem, proclaiming the Good News to many Samaritan villages.

Now an angel of the Lord spoke to Philip, saying, "Get up, and go south on the road going down from Jerusalem to Gaza." (This is a desert road.) So he got up and went. And behold, an Ethiopian eunuch—an official who was responsible for all the treasure of Candace, queen of the Ethiopians —had traveled to Jerusalem to worship and was now returning. Sitting in his chariot, he was reading the prophet Isaiah.

The *Ruach* said to Philip, "Go, catch up with this chariot." Philip ran up and heard him reading the prophet Isaiah and said, "Do you understand what you are reading?"

"How can I," he said, "unless someone guides me?" So he invited Philip to come up and sit with him. Now the passage of Scripture that he was reading was this:

"He was led as a sheep to slaughter;
and as a lamb before its shearer
is silent, so He opens not His Mouth.
In His humiliation justice
was denied Him.
Who shall recount His generation?
For His life is taken away from
the earth."

The eunuch replied to Philip, "Please tell me, who is the prophet talking about—himself or someone else?" Then Philip opened his mouth, and beginning with this Scripture he proclaimed the Good News about *Yeshua*. Now as they were going down the road, they came to some water. The eunuch said, "Look, water! What's to prevent me from being immersed?"

He ordered the chariot to stop. They both got down into the water, Philip and the eunuch, and Philip immersed him. When they came up out of the water, the *Ruach ADONAI* snatched Philip away. The eunuch saw no more of him, for he went on his way, rejoicing. But Philip found himself at Azotus. And as he passed through, he kept proclaiming the Good News to all the towns until he came to Caesarea.

Acts, chapter 8

Now Saul, still breathing out threats and murder against the Lord's disciples, went to the *kohen gadol*. He requested letters of introduction from him to the synagogues in Damascus, so that if he found any men or women belonging to the Way, he might bring them as prisoners to Jerusalem. As he was traveling, approaching Damascus, suddenly a light from heaven flashed around him. Falling to the ground, he heard a voice saying to him, "Saul, Saul, why are you persecuting Me?"

"Who are You, Lord?" Saul said.

"I am *Yeshua*—whom you are persecuting. But get up and go into the city, and you will be told what you must do."

The men travelling with him stood speechless, hearing the voice but seeing no one. Saul got up from the ground—but opening his eyes, he could see nothing. They led him by the hand and brought him into

Damascus. For three days he could not see, and he did not eat or drink. Now there was a disciple named Ananias in Damascus. The Lord said to him, "Ananias."

He said, "Here I am, Lord."

The Lord said to him, "Get up and go to the street named Straight, and ask in the house of Judah for someone from Tarsus named Saul. For look, he is praying; and in a vision he has seen a man named Ananias coming in and laying his hands on him, so that he might regain his sight."

But Ananias answered, "Lord, I have heard from many about this man—how much harm he has done to your *kedoshim* in Jerusalem. And here he has authority from the ruling *kohanim* to tie up all who call on Your name."

But the Lord said to him, "Go, for he is a choice instrument to carry My name before nations and kings and *Bnei-Yisrael*. For I will show him how much he must suffer for My name's sake."

So Ananias left and entered into the house. Laying hands on Saul, he said, "Brother Saul, the Lord—*Yeshua*, the One who appeared to you on the road by which you were coming—has sent me, so that you might regain your sight and be filled with the *Ruach ha-Kodesh*." Immediately, something like scales fell from Saul's eyes, and he regained his sight. Then he got up and was immersed; and when he had taken food, he was strengthened. Now for several days, he was with the disciples in Damascus. Immediately he began proclaiming *Yeshua* in the synagogues, saying, "He is *Ben-Elohim*."

All those hearing him were amazed. They were saying, "Isn't this the one who made havoc in Jerusalem for all those who call on this name? And hasn't he come here to bring them as prisoners before the ruling *kohanim*?"

But Saul kept growing stronger, and he was confounding the Jewish people living in Damascus by proving that *Yeshua* is the Messiah. When many days had passed, these Jewish people plotted to kill him—but their plot became known to Saul. They were watching the gates day and night, to kill him. But the disciples took Saul by night and let him down over the wall, lowering him in a basket. When Saul arrived in Jerusalem, he made attempts to join up with the disciples—but they were all afraid of him, not believing that he was a disciple. But Barnabas took him in and brought him to the emissaries. He described to them how Saul had seen the Lord on the road and the Lord had spoken to him, and how he had spoken boldly in the name of *Yeshua*.

So Saul was with them, going in and out in Jerusalem, speaking boldly in the name of the Lord. He was speaking and arguing with the Hellenists, but they were trying to kill him. When the brothers found out, they brought him down to Caesarea and sent him off to Tarsus. So Messiah's community throughout all Judea and Galilee and Samaria had *shalom* and was built up. Walking in the fear of the Lord and in the comfort of the *Ruach ha-Kodesh*, it kept multiplying. Acts 9:1-31

94. God Frees the Captives

Now in the Antioch community, there were prophets and teachers: Barnabas, Simeon called Niger, Lucius the Cyrenian, Manaen (brought up since childhood with Herod the Tetrarch), and Saul. While they were serving the Lord and fasting, the *Ruach ha-Kodesh* said, "Set apart for me Barnabas and Saul for the work to which I have called them." Then after fasting, praying, and laying hands on them, they sent them off.

So, sent out by the *Ruach ha-Kodesh*, they went down to Seleucia, and from there they sailed to Cyprus. When they arrived at Salamis, they began to proclaim the word of God in the Jewish synagogues. They also had John as a helper.

When they had gone throughout the whole island as far as Paphos, they found a man who was a magician—a Jewish false prophet, whose name was Bar-Yeshua. He was with the proconsul, Sergius Paulus, an intelligent man. This man summoned Barnabas and Saul and sought to hear the word of God. But Elymas the magician (for so his name is translated) was opposing them, seeking to turn the proconsul away from the faith.

But Saul, who is also Paul, filled with the *Ruach ha-Kodesh*, fixed his gaze on him and said, "O you, full of all deceit and trickery, son of the devil, enemy of all righteousness—will you not stop making crooked the straight paths of the Lord? Now, behold, the hand of the Lord is upon you, and you shall be blind and not see the sun for awhile."

Immediately, cloudiness and darkness fell upon him, and he went about seeking people to lead him by the hand. When he saw what had happened, the proconsul believed, because he was astonished at the teaching about the Lord.

Setting sail from Paphos, Paul's company came to Perga in Pamphylia. John left them and returned to Jerusalem. But they passed on from Perga and came to Antioch of Pisidia.

Entering the synagogue on the *Shabbat*, they sat down. After the reading of the *Torah* and the Prophets, the synagogue leaders sent to them, saying, "Brothers, if you have any word of encouragement for the people, speak."

So Paul, standing up and motioning with his hand, said, "Men of Israel and God-fearers, listen. The God of this people Israel chose our fathers and made the people great during their stay in the land of Egypt, and with an outstretched arm He led them out of there. For about forty years He put up with them in the wilderness.

And when He had destroyed seven nations in the land of Canaan, He gave their land as an inheritance—all of this took about 450 years. After that, he gave them judges until Samuel the prophet.

Then they asked for a king, and God gave them Saul, son of Kish, of the tribe of Benjamin, for forty years. After removing him, He raised up David to be their king. He also testified about him and said, 'I have found David, the son of Jesse, a man after My heart, who will do My will.'

"From this man's seed, in keeping with His promise, God brought to Israel a Savior—*Yeshua*. Before His coming, John had proclaimed an immersion of repentance to all the people of Israel. As John was completing his service, he said, 'What do you suppose me to be? I am not He. But behold, One is coming after me, whose sandal I'm not worthy to untie.'

"Brothers, sons of the family of Abraham and those among you who are God-fearers, it is to us the message of this salvation has been sent. For those who live in Jerusalem and their rulers—not recognizing Him or the sayings of the Prophets that are read every *Shabbat*—fulfilled these words by condemning Him. Though they found no charge worthy of a death sentence, they asked Pilate to have Him executed.

When they had carried out all that had been written about Him, they took Him down from the tree and laid Him in a tomb. But God raised Him from the dead! For many days He appeared to those who had come up from the Galilee to Jerusalem, who are now His witnesses to the people.

"And we proclaim to you Good News—the promise to the fathers has arrived! For God has fulfilled this promise to the children—to us—by raising up *Yeshua*, as it is also written in the second psalm:
'You are My Son.
Today I have become Your Father.'

"But since He raised Him up from the dead, never to return to decay, He has spoken in this way, 'I will give you the holy and sure mercies of David.' Therefore He also says in another psalm, 'You will not permit Your Holy One to see decay.' For after David had served God's purpose in his own generation, he went to sleep and was laid with his fathers and saw decay. But the One whom God raised up did not see decay.

"Therefore, let it be known to you, brothers, that through this One is proclaimed to you the removal of sins, including all those from which you could not be set right by the *Torah* of Moses. Through this One everyone who keeps trusting is made righteous.

"Be careful, then, so that what is said in the Prophets may not come upon you:

'Look, you scoffers,
be amazed and vanish away.
For I am doing a work in your
days—a work you will never
believe, even if someone tells it to
you in detail.'

As Paul and Barnabas were going out, the people kept begging them to speak these things to them the next *Shabbat*. When the synagogue meeting broke up, many of the Jewish people and God-fearing inquirers followed Paul and Barnabas, who were speaking with them and trying to persuade them to continue in the grace of God.

The following *Shabbat*, almost the entire city came together to hear the word of the Lord. When the Jewish leaders saw the crowds, they were filled with jealousy and tried to contradict what Paul was saying by reviling him. Both Paul and Barnabas spoke out boldly and said, "It was necessary for the word of God to be spoken to you first. Since you reject it and judge yourselves unfit for eternal life—behold, we turn to the Gentiles.

For so the Lord has commanded us, 'I have placed you as a light to the nations, so that you may bring salvation to the end of the earth.'

When the Gentiles heard this, they were thrilled and glorified the word of the Lord; and as many as had been inscribed for eternal life believed.

Now the word of the Lord spread throughout the whole region. But the Jewish leaders incited the God-fearing women of high standing and the leading men of the city. They stirred up persecution against Paul and Barnabas, and they drove them out of their district.

But Paul and Barnabas shook the dust off their feet against them, and they went on to Iconium. And the disciples were filled with joy and the *Ruach ha-Kodesh*.

Acts, chapter 13

Now in Iconium, the same thing happened—they entered as usual into the Jewish synagogue and spoke in such a way that a large number of Jewish and Greek people believed. But the Jewish people who would not believe stirred up the Gentiles and poisoned their minds against the brothers.

So they stayed there a considerable time, speaking boldly in the Lord—who was testifying to the message of His grace, granting signs and wonders to come about by their hands. But the population of the city split; some were with the Jewish leaders and some were with the emissaries.

Now it happened that an attempt was made by both the Gentiles and Jewish people, along with their rulers, to abuse and stone them. But they found out about it and fled to the Lycaonian cities of Lystra and Derbe and the surrounding countryside. There they proclaimed the Good News.

Now a man was sitting in Lystra without strength in his feet, lame from birth, who had never walked. This man heard Paul speaking. When Paul looked intently at him and saw that he had faith to be healed, he said with a loud voice, "Stand right up! On your feet!" And the man leaped up and began to walk around!

Now the crowd, seeing what Paul had done, lifted up their voices, saying in Lycaonian, "The gods have become like men and come down to us!" And they began calling Barnabas "Zeus" and Paul "Hermes" (because he was the main speaker). The priest of Zeus, whose temple was before the front gate of the city, brought bulls and garlands; he wanted to offer a sacrifice with the people.

But when the emissaries Barnabas and Paul heard of it, they tore their clothes and rushed out among the crowd, crying out and saying, "Men, why are you doing these things? We too are human, just like you! We proclaim the Good News to you, telling you to turn from these worthless things to the living God, who made the heaven and the earth and the sea and all that is in them.

In past generations He allowed all the nations to go their own ways. Yet He did not leave Himself without a witness—He did good by giving you rain from heaven and fruitful seasons, filling your hearts with joy and gladness." Even saying these things, they barely restrained the crowd from sacrificing to them.

But Jewish people came from Antioch and Iconium; and after they won the crowd over and stoned Paul, they were dragging him out of the city, supposing him to be dead. But while the disciples surrounded him, he got up and went back into the city.

On the next day he left with Barnabas for Derbe. After proclaiming the Good News to that city and making many disciples, they returned to Lystra and to Iconium and to Antioch. They were strengthening the souls of the disciples, encouraging them to persevere in faith, and saying, "It is through many persecutions that we must enter the kingdom of God."

When they had handpicked elders for them in every community, and prayed with fasting, they placed them in the care of the Lord—in whom they had put their trust. Then they passed through Pisidia and came to Pamphyllia. After speaking the message in Perga, they went down to Attalia. From there they sailed back to Antioch (where they had been entrusted to the gracious care of God for the work now completed).

When they arrived and gathered together Messiah's community, they began to report all that God had done in helping them and that He had opened a door of faith to the Gentiles. And they stayed quite awhile with the disciples.

Acts, chapter 14

Now some men coming down from Judea were teaching the brothers, "Unless you are circumcised according to the custom of Moses, you cannot be saved."

When Paul and Barnabas had a big argument and debate with them, the brothers appointed Paul and Barnabas with some others from among them to go up to Jerusalem to the emissaries and elders about this issue. So they were sent on their way by the Antioch community. They were passing through both Phoenicia and Samaria, describing in detail the conversion of the Gentiles, and they were bringing great joy to all the brothers and sisters.

When they arrived in Jerusalem, they were welcomed by the community and the emissaries and the elders. They reported all that God had done in helping them.

But some belonging to the party of the Pharisees who had believed stood up, saying, "It is necessary to circumcise them and to command them to keep the *Torah* of Moses."

The emissaries and elders were gathered together to examine this issue. After much debate, Peter stood up and said to them, "Brothers, you know that in the early days God chose from among you, that by my mouth the Gentiles should hear the message of the Good News and believe. And God, who knows the heart, testified to them by giving them the *Ruach ha-Kodesh*—just as He also did for us. He made no distinction between us and them, purifying their hearts through faith. Why then do you put God to the test by putting a yoke on the neck of the disciples—which neither our fathers nor we have been able to bear? But instead, we believe that we are saved through the grace of the Lord *Yeshua*, in the same way as they are."

Then the whole group became silent and were listening to Barnabas and Paul as they were describing in detail all the signs and wonders God had done through them among the Gentiles.

After they finished speaking, Jacob answered, "Brothers, listen to me. Simon has described how God first showed His concern by taking from the Gentiles a people for His Name. The words of the Prophets agree, as it is written:

'After this I will return
  and rebuild the fallen tabernacle
  of David.
I will rebuild its ruins
  and I will restore it,
so that the rest of humanity may
  seek the Lord—namely all the
  Gentiles who are called by My
name— says *ADONAI*, who makes
these things known from of old.'

Therefore, I judge not to trouble those from among the Gentiles who are turning to God—but to write to them to abstain from the contamination of idols, and from sexual immorality, and from what is strangled, and from blood.

For Moses from ancient generations has had in every city those who proclaim him, since he is read in all the synagogues every *Shabbat*."

Then it seemed good to the emissaries and elders, with the whole community, to choose men from among themselves to send to Antioch with Paul and Barnabas. They sent Judah (also called Barsabbas) and Silas, leading men among the brethren, and this letter along with them:

"The emissaries and the elders, your brothers,

To the Gentile brothers of Antioch, Syria, and Cilicia:
Greetings!

Since we have heard that some from among us have troubled you with words disturbing to your souls, although we gave them no such authorization, it seemed good to us, having come to one accord, to select men to send to you with our beloved Barnabas and Paul—men who have risked their lives for the name of our Lord *Yeshua* the Messiah. We therefore have sent to you Judah and

Silas, who themselves will report to you the same things by word of mouth. It seemed good to the *Ruach ha-Kodesh* and to us not to place on you any greater burden than these essentials: that you abstain from things offered to idols, from blood, from things strangled, and from sexual immorality.

By keeping away from these things, you will do well.
Shalom!"

So when they were sent off, they went down to Antioch; and when they had gathered the whole group together, they delivered the letter. The people read it and rejoiced over its encouragement. Judah and Silas, prophets themselves, encouraged the brothers and sisters with a long message and strengthened them.

After spending some time there, they were sent off with *shalom* by the brothers and sisters to those who had sent them. But Paul and Barnabas remained in Antioch, teaching and proclaiming the word of the Lord with many others.

After some days Paul said to Barnabas, "Let's return and visit the brothers and sisters in every city where we have proclaimed the word of the Lord, to see how they are." Barnabas was planning to take along John, called Mark. But Paul was insisting that they shouldn't take him along—the one who had deserted them in Pamphylia, not accompanying them in the work.

A sharp disagreement took place, so that they split off from one another. Barnabas took Mark with him and sailed away to Cyprus. But Paul selected Silas and went out, being entrusted by the brothers and sisters to the gracious care of the Lord. He went through Syria and Cilicia, strengthening the communities.

Acts, chapter 15

Now Paul came to Derbe and Lystra. There was a disciple there named Timothy, son of a woman who was a Jewish believer and a Greek father, who was well-spoken of by the brothers at Lystra and Iconium. Paul wanted this man to accompany him, and he took him and circumcised him for the sake of the Jewish people in those places —for they all knew that his father was Greek.

As they were traveling through the cities, they were handing down the rulings that had been decided upon by the emissaries and elders in Jerusalem, for them to keep. So Messiah's communities were strengthened in the faith and kept increasing daily in number.

They went through the region of Phrygia and Galatia, having been forbidden by the *Ruach ha-Kodesh* to speak the word in Asia. When they came to Mysia, they were trying to proceed into Bithynia, but the *Ruach* of *Yeshua* would not allow them. So they passed by Mysia and went down to Troas.

Now a vision appeared to Paul in the night. A man from Macedonia was standing and pleading with him, saying, "Come over to Macedonia and help us!" As soon as he had seen the vision, immediately we tried to go to

But about midnight, Paul and Silas were praying and singing hymns to God, and the prisoners were listening to them. Suddenly there was such a great earthquake that the foundations of the prison were shaken. Immediately all the doors were unlocked, and everyone's chains came loose.

Acts 16:25-26 TLV

Macedonia, concluding that God had called us to proclaim the Good News to them.

So we put out to sea from Troas and made a straight course for Samothrace, the next day on to Neapolis, and from there to Philippi—which is a leading city of the district of Macedonia as well as a Roman colony. We stayed in this city for several days.

On *Yom Shabbat*, we went outside the gate to the river, where we expected a place of prayer to be. We sat down and began speaking with the women who had gathered. A woman named Lydia—a seller of purple cloth from the city of Thyatira, a God-fearer—was listening. The Lord opened her heart to respond to what Paul was saying.

When she was immersed, along with her household, she urged us, saying, "If you have judged me to be faithful to the Lord, come and stay at my house." And she insisted.

It so happened that as we were going to prayer, we met a slave girl who had a spirit of divination, who was bringing her masters much profit from her fortune-telling. Following after Paul and us, she kept shouting, saying, "These men are servants of *El Elyon*, who are proclaiming to you the way of salvation." She kept doing this for many days. But Paul was irritated and turned and said to the spirit, "I command you in the name of Messiah *Yeshua* to come out of her!" And it came out of her that very moment.

But when her masters saw that the hope of profit was gone, they grabbed Paul and Silas and dragged them into the marketplace before the authorities. And when they brought them to the chief authorities, they said, "These men are throwing our city into an uproar! Being Jewish, they advocate customs which are not permitted for us to accept or practice, being Romans."

Then the crowd joined in the attack on them. So the chief authorities ripped their clothes off them and commanded them to be beaten with rods. After inflicting many blows on them, they threw them into prison, ordering the jailer to guard them securely. Having received this charge, he threw them into the inner prison and fastened their feet in the stocks.

But about midnight, Paul and Silas were praying and singing hymns to God, and the prisoners were listening to them. Suddenly there was such a great earthquake that the foundations of the prison were shaken. Immediately all the doors were unlocked, and everyone's chains came loose.

When the jailer woke up and saw the prison doors opened, he drew his sword and was about to kill himself, supposing the prisoners had escaped. But Paul cried out with a loud voice, saying, "Don't harm yourself! We're all here!"

The jailer called for lights and rushed in; and trembling with fear, he fell down before Paul and Silas. After he brought them out, he said, "Sirs, what must I do to be saved?"

They said, "Put your trust in the Lord *Yeshua* and you will be saved—you and your household!"

Then they spoke the word of the Lord to him, along with everyone in his household. He took them that very hour and washed their wounds, and at once he was immersed—he and all his household. The jailer brought them to his house and set food before them, and he was overjoyed that he with his entire household had put their trust in God.

When day came, the chief authorities sent their police officers, saying, "Release those men."

But the jailer reported these words to Paul, saying, "The chief authorities have sent orders to release you. So come out now, and go in *shalom*."

But Paul said to the officers, "They have beaten us publicly without a trial—men who are Roman citizens —and have thrown us into prison. And now they are sending us away secretly? No! Let them come themselves and lead us out!"

The police officers reported these words to the chief authorities. They became afraid when they heard they were Romans, so they came and apologized to them. After they escorted them out, they kept begging them to leave the city. When Paul and Silas went out of the prison, they visited Lydia's house. And when they saw the brothers, they encouraged them and then departed.

Acts, chapter 16

95. God Delivers Us from Bondage

What shall we say then? Are we to continue in sin so that grace may abound? May it never be! How can we who died to sin still live in it? Or do you not know that all of us who were immersed into Messiah *Yeshua* were immersed into His death? Therefore we were buried together with Him through immersion into death—in order that just as Messiah was raised from the dead by the glory of the Father, so we too might walk in newness of life.

For if we have become joined together in the likeness of His death, certainly we also will be joined together in His resurrection — knowing our old man was crucified with Him so that the sinful body might be done away with, so we no longer serve sin. For he who has died is set free from sin.

Now if we have died with Messiah, we believe that we shall also live with Him. We know that Messiah, having been raised from the dead, no longer dies; death no longer is master over Him. For the death He died, He died to sin once for all; but the life He lives, He lives to God. So also continually count yourselves both dead to sin and alive to God in Messiah *Yeshua*.

Therefore do not let sin rule in your mortal body so that you obey its desires. And do not keep yielding your body parts to sin as tools of wickedness; but yield yourselves to God as those alive from the dead, and your body parts as tools of righteousness to God. For sin shall not be master over you, for you are not under law but under grace.

What then? Shall we sin because we are not under law but under grace? May it never be! Do you not know that to whatever you yield yourselves as slaves for obedience, you are slaves to what you obey—whether to sin resulting in death, or to obedience resulting in righteousness? But thanks be to God that though you were slaves of sin, you wholeheartedly obeyed the form of teaching under which you were placed; and after you were set free from sin, you became enslaved to righteousness.

I speak in human terms because of the weakness of your flesh. For just as you yielded your body parts as slaves to uncleanness and lawlessness, leading to more lawlessness, so now yield your body parts as slaves to righteousness, resulting in holiness.

For when you were slaves of sin, you were free with regard to righteousness. So then, what outcome did you have that you are now ashamed of? For the end of those things is death. But now, having been set free from sin and having become enslaved to God, you have your fruit resulting in holiness. And the outcome is eternal life. For sin's payment is death, but God's gracious gift is eternal life in Messiah *Yeshua* our Lord.

Romans, chapter 6

Miserable man that I am! Who will rescue me from this body of death?
Thanks be to God—it is through Messiah *Yeshua* our Lord!

Romans 7:24-25a TLV

Or do you not know, brothers and sisters (for I speak to those who know law), that the law is master over a person as long as he lives? For the married woman is bound by law to her husband while he lives; but if the husband dies, she is released from the law concerning the husband. So then, if she is joined to another man while her husband is living, she will be called an adulteress. But if her husband dies, she is free from the law —so she is not an adulteress, though she is joined to another man.

Therefore, my brothers and sisters, you also were made dead to the *Torah* through the body of Messiah, so that you might be joined to another—the One who was raised from the dead—in order that we might bear fruit for God. For when we were in the flesh, the sinful passions that came through the *Torah* were working in our body parts to bear fruit for death. But now we have been released from the law, having died to what confined us, so that we serve in the new way of the *Ruach* and not in the old way of the letter.

What shall we say then? Is the *Torah* sin? May it never be! On the contrary, I would not have known sin except through the *Torah*. For I would not have known about coveting if the *Torah* had not said, "You shall not covet." But sin, taking an opportunity, worked in me through the commandment all kinds of coveting. For apart from the *Torah*, sin is dead. Once I was alive apart from the *Torah*; but when the commandment came, sin came to life and I died. The commandment meant for life was found to cause death. Sin, taking an opportunity through the commandment, deceived me and through it killed me. So then, the *Torah* is holy, and the commandment is holy and righteous and good.

Therefore did that which is good become death to me? May it never be! Rather it was sin working death in me—through that which is good—so that sin might be shown to be sin, and that through the commandment sin might become utterly sinful.

For we know that the *Torah* is spiritual; but I am of the flesh, sold to sin. For I do not understand what I am doing—for what I do not want, this I practice; but what I hate, this I do. But if I do what I do not want to do, then I agree with the *Torah*—that it is good.

So now it is no longer I doing it, but sin dwelling in me. For I know that nothing good dwells in me—that is, in my flesh. For to will is present in me, but to do the good is not. For the good that I want, I do not do; but the evil that I do not want, this I practice. But if I do what I do not want, it is no longer I doing it, but sin that dwells in me.

So I find the principle—that evil is present in me, the one who wants to do good. For I delight in the *Torah* of God with respect to the inner man, but I see a different law in my body parts, battling against the law of my mind and bringing me into bondage under the law of sin which is in my body parts.

Miserable man that I am! Who will
rescue me from this body of death?
Thanks be to God— it is through
Messiah *Yeshua* our Lord!
So then, with my mind I myself serve
the *Torah* of God; but with my flesh, I
serve the law of sin.

Romans, chapter 7

Therefore, there is now no condemnation for those who are in Messiah *Yeshua*. For the law of the Spirit of life in Messiah *Yeshua* has set you free from the law of sin and death. For what was impossible for the *Torah*—since it was weakened on account of the flesh—God has done. Sending His own Son in the likeness of sinful flesh and as a sin offering, He condemned sin in the flesh—so that the requirement of the *Torah* might be fulfilled in us, who do not walk according to the flesh but according to the *Ruach*.

For those who live according to the flesh set their minds on the things of the flesh, but those who live according to the *Ruach* set their minds on the things of the *Ruach*. For the mindset of the flesh is death, but the mindset of the *Ruach* is life and *shalom*. For the mindset of the flesh is hostile toward God, for it does not submit itself to the law of God—for it cannot. So those who are in the flesh cannot please God.

However, you are not in the flesh but in the *Ruach*—if indeed the *Ruach Elohim* dwells in you. Now if anyone does not have the *Ruach* of Messiah, he does not belong to Him. But if Messiah is in you, though the body is dead because of sin, yet the Spirit is alive because of righteousness.

And if the *Ruach* of the One who raised *Yeshua* from the dead dwells in you, the One who raised Messiah *Yeshua* from the dead will also give life to your mortal bodies through His *Ruach* who dwells in you.

So then, brothers and sisters, we do not owe anything to the flesh, to live according to the flesh. For if you live according to the flesh, you must die; but if by the *Ruach* you put to death the deeds of the body, you shall live. For all who are led by the *Ruach Elohim*, these are sons of God. For you did not receive the spirit of slavery to fall again into fear; rather, you received the Spirit of adoption, by whom we cry, "*Abba*! Father!"

The *Ruach* Himself bears witness with our spirit that we are children of God. And if children, also heirs—heirs of God and joint-heirs with Messiah—if indeed we suffer with Him so that we may also be glorified with Him.

For I consider the sufferings of this present time not worthy to be compared with the coming glory to be revealed to us. For the creation eagerly awaits the revelation of the sons of God. For the creation was subjected to futility—not willingly but because of the One who subjected it—in hope that the creation itself also will be set free from bondage to decay into the glorious freedom of the children of God. For we know that the whole creation groans together and suffers birth pains until now—and not only creation, but even ourselves.

We ourselves, who have the firstfruits of the *Ruach*, groan inwardly as we eagerly wait for adoption—the redemption of our body.

For in hope we were saved. But hope that is seen is not hope. For who hopes for what he sees? But if we hope for what we do not see, then we eagerly wait for it with perseverance. In the same way, the *Ruach* helps in our weakness.

For we do not know how to pray as we should, but the *Ruach* Himself intercedes for us with groans too deep for words. And He who searches the hearts knows the mind of the *Ruach*, because He intercedes for the *kedoshim* according to the will of God.

Now we know that all things work together for good for those who love God, who are called according to His purpose.

For those whom He foreknew He also predestined to be conformed to the image of His Son, so that He might be the firstborn among many brothers and sisters. And those whom He predestined, He also called; and those whom He called, He also justified; and those whom He justified, He also glorified.

What then shall we say in view of these things? If God is for us, who can be against us?

He who did not spare His own Son but gave Him up for us all, how shall He not also with Him freely give us all things? Who shall bring a charge against God's elect? It is God who justifies. Who is the one who condemns? It is Messiah, who died, and moreover was raised, and is now at the right hand of God and who also intercedes for us. Who shall separate us from the love of Messiah? Shall tribulation, or distress, or persecution, or famine, or nakedness, or danger, or sword? As it is written,

"For Your sake we are being put to death all day long;
we are counted as sheep for the
slaughter."

But in all these things we are more than conquerors through Him who loved us.

For I am convinced that neither death nor life, nor angels nor principalities, nor things present nor things to come, nor powers, nor height nor depth, nor any other created thing will be able to separate us from the love of God that is in Messiah *Yeshua* our Lord.

Romans, chapter 8

96. God is Our Salvation

I tell the truth in Messiah—I do not lie, my conscience assuring me in the *Ruach ha-Kodesh*—that my sorrow is great and the anguish in my heart unending. For I would pray that I myself were cursed, banished from Messiah for the sake of my people—my own flesh and blood, who are Israelites. To them belong the adoption and the glory and the covenants and the giving of the *Torah* and the Temple service and the promises. To them belong the patriarchs—and from them, according to the flesh, the Messiah, who is over all, God, blessed forever. Amen.

But it is not as though the word of God has failed. For not all those who are descended from Israel are Israel, nor are they all children because they are Abraham's seed; rather, "Your seed shall be called through Isaac." That is, it is not the children of the flesh who are children of God; rather, the children of the promise are counted as seed.

For the word of promise is this: "At this time I will come, and Sarah shall have a son." And not only this, but also Rebecca having twins, from one act with our father Isaac. Yet before the sons were even born and had not done anything good or bad—so that God's purpose and choice might stand not because of works but because of Him who calls—it was said to her, "The older shall serve the younger." As it is written, "Jacob I loved, but Esau I hated." What shall we say then? There is no injustice with God, is there? May it never be! For to Moses He says,
"I will have mercy on whom I have mercy, and I will have compassion on whom I have compassion."

So then it does not depend on the one who wills or the one who strives, but on God who shows mercy. For the Scripture says to Pharaoh, "For this very purpose I raised you up—to demonstrate My power in you, so My name might be proclaimed in all the earth." So then He has mercy on whom He wills, and He hardens whom He wills.

You will say to me then, "Why does He still find fault? For who has resisted His will?" But who in the world are you, O man, who talks back to God? Will what is formed say to the one who formed it, "Why did you make me like this?" Does the potter have no right over the clay, to make from the same lump one vessel for honor and another for common use?

Now what if God, willing to demonstrate His wrath and to make His power known, endured with much patience vessels of wrath designed for destruction? And what if He did so to make known the riches of His glory on vessels of mercy, which He prepared beforehand for glory? Even us He called—not only from the Jewish people, but also from the Gentiles—as He says also in Hosea,

"I will call those who were not My people, 'My people,'
and her who was not loved,
'Beloved.'
And it shall be that in the place

where it was said to them,
'You are not My people,'
there they shall be called sons of
the living God."

Isaiah cries out concerning Israel,

"Though the number of *B'nei–Yisrael* be as the sand of the sea,
only the remnant shall be saved.
For *ADONAI* will carry out His word
upon the earth, bringing it to an end
and finishing quickly."

And just as Isaiah foretold,

"Unless *ADONAI-Tzva'ot* had left us
seed, we would have become like
Sodom and resembled
Gomorrah."

What shall we say then?
That Gentiles, who did not pursue righteousness, attained righteousness—that is, a righteousness of faith.

But Israel, who pursued a *Torah* of righteousness, did not reach the *Torah*. Why? Because they pursued it not by faith, but as if it were from works. They stumbled over the stone of stumbling, just as it is written,

"Behold, I lay in Zion
a stone of stumbling
and a rock of offense,
and whoever believes in Him
shall not be put to shame."

Romans, chapter 9

Brothers and sisters, my heart's desire and my prayer to God for Israel is for their salvation. For I testify about them that they have zeal for God—but not based on knowledge. For being ignorant of God's righteousness and seeking to establish their own, they did not submit themselves to the righteousness of God.

For Messiah is the goal of the *Torah* as a means to righteousness for everyone who keeps trusting. For Moses writes about the righteousness that is based on *Torah*, "The man who does these things shall live by them." But the righteousness based on faith speaks in this way:

"Do not say in your heart,
'Who will go up into heaven?'
(that is, to bring Messiah down),
or, 'Who will go down into the abyss?'
(that is, to bring Messiah up from the dead)."

But what does it say?
"The word is near you,
in your mouth and in your heart"
—that is, the word of faith
that we are proclaiming:

For if you confess with your mouth
that *Yeshua* is Lord,
and believe in your heart
that God raised Him from the dead,
you will be saved.
For with the heart it is believed for
righteousness,
and with the mouth it is confessed
for salvation.

For the Scripture says, "Whoever trusts in Him will not be put to shame." For there is no distinction between Jew and Greek, for the same Lord is Lord of all—richly generous to all who call on Him. For "Everyone who calls upon the name of *ADONAI* shall be saved."

For if you were cut out of that which by nature is a wild olive tree, and grafted contrary to nature into a cultivated olive tree, how much more will these natural branches be grafted into their own olive tree?

Romans 11:24 TLV

How then shall they call on the One in whom they have not trusted? And how shall they trust in the One they have not heard of? And how shall they hear without someone proclaiming? And how shall they proclaim unless they are sent? As it is written, "How beautiful are the feet of those who proclaim good news of good things!"

But not all heeded the Good News. For Isaiah says, "ADONAI, who has believed our report?" So faith comes from hearing, and hearing by the word of Messiah. But I say, have they never heard? Indeed they have, for

"Their voice has gone out into
all the earth, and their words
to the ends of the world."

But I say, did Israel not understand? First Moses says,

"I will provoke you to jealousy
by those who are not a nation,
with a nation empty of
understanding, I will vex you."

And Isaiah is so bold as to say,
"I was found by those who did not seek Me; I became visible to those who did not ask for Me."

But about Israel He says,
"All day long I stretched forth My hands to a disobedient and contrary people."

Romans, chapter 10

I say then, God has not rejected His people, has He? May it never be! For I too am an Israelite, of the seed of Abraham, of the tribe of Benjamin.

God has not rejected His people whom He knew beforehand. Or do you not know what the Scripture says about Elijah, how he pleads with God against Israel? "*ADONAI*, they have killed your prophets, they have destroyed your altars; I alone am left, and they are seeking my life."

But what is the divine response to him? "I have kept for Myself seven thousand men who have not bowed the knee to Baal."

So in the same way also at this present time there has come to be a remnant according to God's gracious choice. But if it is by grace, it is no longer by works; otherwise grace would no longer be grace.

What then? What Israel is seeking, it has not obtained; but the elect obtained it, and the rest were hardened—just as it is written,
"God gave them a spirit of stupor,
eyes not to see and ears not to
hear, until this very day."

And David says,
"Let their table become a snare
and a trap, a stumbling block
and a retribution for them.
Let their eyes be darkened so they
do not see, and bend their back
continually."

I say then, they did not stumble so as to fall, did they? May it never be! But by their false step salvation has come to the Gentiles, to provoke Israel to jealousy. Now if their transgression leads to riches for the world, and their loss riches for the Gentiles, then how much more their fullness! But I am speaking to you who are Gentiles.

Insofar as I am an emissary to the Gentiles, I spotlight my ministry if somehow I might provoke to jealousy my own flesh and blood and save some of them. For if their rejection leads to the reconciliation of the world, what will their acceptance be but life from the dead? If the firstfruit is holy, so is the whole batch of dough; and if the root is holy, so are the branches.

But if some of the branches were broken off and you—being a wild olive—were grafted in among them and became a partaker of the root of the olive tree with its richness, do not boast against the branches. But if you do boast, it is not you who support the root but the root supports you.

You will say then, "Branches were broken off so that I might be grafted in." True enough. They were broken off because of unbelief, and you stand by faith. Do not be arrogant, but fear—for if God did not spare the natural branches, neither will He spare you.

Notice then the kindness and severity of God: severity toward those who fell; but God's kindness toward you, if you continue in His kindness; otherwise you too will be cut off! And they also, if they do not continue in their unbelief, will be grafted in; for God is able to graft them in again.

For if you were cut out of that which by nature is a wild olive tree, and grafted contrary to nature into a cultivated olive tree, how much more will these natural branches be grafted into their own olive tree?

For I do not want you, brothers and sisters, to be ignorant of this mystery—lest you be wise in your own eyes—that a partial hardening has come upon Israel until the fullness of the Gentiles has come in; and in this way all Israel will be saved, as it is written,

"The Deliverer shall come out of
  Zion. He shall turn away
  ungodliness from Jacob.
And this is My covenant with them,
  when I take away their sins."

Concerning the Good News, they are hostile for your sake; but concerning chosenness, they are loved on account of the fathers—for the gifts and the calling of God are irrevocable. For just as you once were disobedient to God but now have been shown mercy because of their disobedience, in like manner these also have now been disobedient with the result that, because of the mercy shown to you, they also may receive mercy. For God has shut up all in disobedience, so that He might show mercy to all.

O the depth of the riches,
  both of the wisdom and
  knowledge of God!
How unsearchable are His
  judgments and how
  incomprehensible His ways!

For "who has known the mind
  of *Adonai*, or who has been His
  counselor?"
Or "who has first given to Him,
  that it shall be repaid to him?"
For from Him and through Him and to Him are all things. To Him be the glory forever! Amen. Romans, chapter 11

97. God Heals Our Family Tree

Paul, an emissary of Messiah *Yeshua* by God's will,
To the *kedoshim* in Ephesus—those trusting in Messiah *Yeshua*:
Grace and *shalom* to you, from God our Father and the Lord *Yeshua* the Messiah!

Blessed be the God and Father of our Lord *Yeshua* the Messiah, who has blessed us with every spiritual blessing in the heavenly places in Messiah. He chose us in the Messiah before the foundation of the world, to be holy and blameless before Him in love. He predestined us for adoption as sons through Messiah *Yeshua*, in keeping with the good pleasure of His will—to the glorious praise of His grace, with which He favored us through the One He loves!

In Him we have redemption through His blood—the removal of trespasses—in keeping with the richness of His grace that He lavished on us. In all wisdom and insight, He made known to us the mystery of His will, in keeping with His good pleasure that He planned in Messiah.

The plan of the fullness of times is to bring all things together in the Messiah—both things in heaven and things on earth, all in Him.

In Him we also were chosen, predestined according to His plan.

He keeps working out all things according to the purpose of His will—so that we, who were first to put our hope in Messiah, might be for His glorious praise.

After you heard the message of truth—the Good News of your salvation—and when you put your trust in Him, you were sealed with the promised *Ruach ha-Kodesh*. He is the guarantee of our inheritance, until the redemption of His possession—to His glorious praise!

Therefore, ever since I heard of your trust in the Lord *Yeshua* and of your love for all the *kedoshim*, I never stop giving thanks for you as I mention you in my prayers—that the God of our Lord *Yeshua* the Messiah, our glorious Father, may give you spiritual wisdom and revelation in knowing Him.

I pray that the eyes of your heart may be enlightened, so that you may know what is the hope of His calling, what is the richness of His glorious inheritance in the *kedoshim*, and what is His exceedingly great power toward us who keep trusting Him—in keeping with the working of His mighty strength.

This power He exercised in Messiah when He raised Him from the dead and seated Him at His right hand in heaven. He is far above any ruler, authority, power, leader, and every name that is named—not only in the *olam ha-zeh* but also in the *olam ha-ba*. God placed all things under Messiah's feet and appointed Him as head over all things for His community— which is His body, the fullness of Him who fills all in all.

Ephesians, chapter 1

You were dead in your trespasses and sins. At that time, you walked in the way of this world, in conformity to the ruler of the domain of the air—the ruler of the spirit who is now operating in the sons of disobedience. We too all lived among them in the cravings of our flesh, indulging the desires of the flesh and the mind. By nature we were children of wrath, just like the others. But God was rich in mercy, because of His great love with which He loved us. Even when we were dead in our trespasses, He made us alive together with Messiah. (By grace you have been saved!) And He raised us up with Him and seated us with Him in the heavenly places in Messiah *Yeshua*—to show in the *olam ha-ba* the measureless richness of His grace in kindness toward us in Messiah *Yeshua*.

For by grace you have been saved through faith. And this is not from yourselves—it is the gift of God. It is not based on deeds, so that no one may boast. For we are His workmanship —created in Messiah *Yeshua* for good deeds, which God prepared beforehand so we might walk in them. Therefore, keep in mind that once you—Gentiles in the flesh—were called "uncircumcision" by those called circumcision" (which is performed on flesh by hand). At that time you were separate from Messiah, excluded from the commonwealth of Israel and strangers to the covenants of promise, having no hope and without God in the world. But now in Messiah *Yeshua*, you who once were far off have been brought near by the blood of the Messiah. For He is our *shalom*, the One who made the two into one and broke down the middle wall of separation. Within His flesh He made powerless the hostility—the law code of *mitzvot* contained in regulations. He did this in order to create within Himself one new man from the two groups, making *shalom*, and to reconcile both to God in one body through the cross—by which He put the hostility to death. And He came and proclaimed *shalom* to you who were far away and *shalom* to those who were near—for through Him we both have access to the Father by the same *Ruach*.

So then you are no longer strangers and foreigners, but you are fellow citizens with God's people and members of God's household. You have been built on the foundation made up of the emissaries and prophets, with Messiah *Yeshua* Himself being the cornerstone. In Him the whole building, being fitted together, is growing into a holy temple for the Lord. In Him, you also are being built together into God's dwelling place in the *Ruach*.

Ephesians, chapter 2

For this reason I, Paul, am a prisoner of Messiah *Yeshua* for the sake of you Gentiles. Surely you have heard about the plan of God's grace given to me for you—that the mystery was made known to me by revelation, as I wrote before briefly. When you read this, you can understand my insight into the mystery of Messiah—which was not made known to the sons of men in other generations, as it has now

But now in Messiah *Yeshua,* you who once were far off have been brought near by the blood of the Messiah. For He is our *shalom,* the One who made the two into one and broke down the middle wall of separation.

Ephesians 2:13-14 TLV

been revealed by the *Ruach* to His holy emissaries and prophets. This mystery is that the Gentiles are joint heirs and fellow members of the same body and co-sharers of the promise in Messiah *Yeshua* through the Good News.

I became a servant of this Good News by the gift of God's favor given to me through the exercise of His power. This favor was given to me, the very least of His *kedoshim*, to proclaim to the Gentiles the endless riches of the Messiah and to bring to light the plan of the mystery—which for ages was hidden in God, who created all things. The purpose is that through Messiah's community the multi-faceted wisdom of God might be made known to the rulers and authorities in the heavenly places, which is in keeping with the eternal purpose that He carried out in Messiah *Yeshua* our Lord. In Him we have boldness and access with confidence through trusting in Him. So I ask you not to be discouraged by my troubles on your behalf—they are your glory.

For this reason I bow my knees before the Father—from Him every family in heaven and on earth receives its name.

I pray that from His glorious riches He would grant you to be strengthened in your inner being with power through His *Ruach*, so that Messiah may dwell in your hearts through faith.

I pray that you, being rooted and grounded in love, may have strength to grasp with all the *kedoshim* what is the width and length and height and depth, and to know the love of Messiah which surpasses knowledge, so you may be filled up with all the fullness of God. Now to Him who is able to do far beyond all that we ask or imagine, by means of His power that works in us, to Him be the glory in the community of believers and in Messiah *Yeshua*
throughout all generations forever and ever! Amen.

Ephesians, chapter 3

98. God Creates His Kingdom

Peter, an emissary of Messiah *Yeshua*,

To the sojourners of the Diaspora in Pontus, Galatia, Cappadocia, Asia, and Bithynia—chosen according to the foreknowledge of God the Father, set apart by the *Ruach* for obedience and for sprinkling with the blood of *Yeshua* the Messiah:
May grace and *shalom* be multiplied to you.

Blessed be the God and Father of our Lord *Yeshua* the Messiah! In His great mercy He caused us to be born again to a living hope through the resurrection of Messiah *Yeshua* from the dead. An incorruptible, undefiled, and unfading inheritance has been reserved in heaven for you.

By trusting, you are being protected by God's power for a salvation ready to be revealed in the last time. You rejoice in this greatly, even though now for a little while, if necessary, you have been distressed by various trials. These trials are so that the true metal of your faith (far more valuable than gold, which perishes though refined by fire) may come to light in praise and glory and honor at the revelation of Messiah *Yeshua*.

Though you have not seen Him, you love Him. And even though you don't see Him now, you trust Him and are filled with a joy that is glorious beyond words, receiving the outcome of your faith—the salvation of your souls.

The prophets, who spoke about the grace that was to be yours, searched for this salvation and investigated carefully. They were trying to find out the time and circumstances the *Ruach* of Messiah within them was indicating, when predicting the sufferings in store for Messiah and the glories to follow. It was revealed to them that they were providing these messages not to themselves but to you. These messages have now been announced to you through those who proclaimed the Good News to you by the *Ruach ha-Kodesh*, sent from heaven. Even angels long to catch a glimpse of these things.

So brace your minds for action. Keep your balance. And set your hope completely on the grace that will be brought to you at the revelation of *Yeshua* the Messiah. Like obedient children, do not be shaped by the cravings you had formerly in your ignorance. Instead, just like the Holy One who called you, be holy yourselves also in everything you do.

For it is written,
"*Kedoshim* you shall be,
for I am *kadosh*."
If you call on Him as Father—the One who judges impartially according to each one's deeds—then live out the time of sojourning in reverent fear.

You know that you were redeemed from the futile way of life handed down from your ancestors—not with perishable things such as silver or gold, but with precious blood like that of a lamb without defect or spot, the blood of Messiah.

As you come to Him, a living stone rejected by men but chosen by God and precious, you also, as living stones, are being built up as a spiritual house—a holy priesthood to offer up spiritual sacrifices acceptable to God through Messiah *Yeshua.*

1 Peter 2:4-5 TLV

He was chosen before the foundation of the world, but was revealed in these last times for your sake. Through Him you are believers in God, who raised Him from the dead and gave Him glory, so that your trust and hope are in God. Now that you have purified your souls in obedience to the truth, leading to sincere brotherly love, love one another fervently from a pure heart. You have been born again—not from perishable seed but imperishable—through the living and enduring word of God.

For, "All humanity is like grass,
And all its glory like a wildflower.
The grass withers,
and the flower falls off,
But the word of the Lord endures
forever."

And this is the word that was proclaimed as Good News to you.

1 Peter, chapter 1

So get rid of all malice and all deceit and hypocrisy and envy and all *lashon ha-ra.* As newborn babes, long for pure spiritual milk, so that by it you may grow toward salvation—now that you have tasted that the Lord is good.

As you come to Him, a living stone rejected by men but chosen by God and precious, you also, as living stones, are being built up as a spiritual house—a holy priesthood to offer up spiritual sacrifices acceptable to God through Messiah *Yeshua*.

For it says in Scripture,
"Behold, I lay in Zion a stone,
a chosen, precious cornerstone.
Whoever trusts in Him
will never be put to shame."

Now the value is for you who keep trusting; but for those who do not trust, "The stone which the builders rejected—this One has become the chief cornerstone,"
and "a stone of stumbling,
and a rock of offense."

They stumble because they are disobeying the word—to this they were also appointed. But you are a chosen people, a royal priesthood, a holy nation, a people for God's own possession, so that you may proclaim the praises of the One who called you out of darkness into His marvelous light.

Once you were "not a people,"
but now you are "God's people."
You were shown "no mercy,"
but now you have been shown
"mercy."

Loved ones, I urge you as strangers and sojourners to keep away from the fleshly cravings that war against the soul. Keep your conduct honorable among the Gentiles. Then while they speak against you as evildoers, they may—from noticing your good deeds—glorify God in the day of visitation. For the Lord's sake, submit yourselves to every human authority—whether to a king as supreme, or to governors sent by him for the punishment of those who do evil and the praise of those who do good. For this is God's will, that you silence the ignorance of foolish men by doing good.

Live as free people, but not using your freedom as a cover-up for evil.

Rather, live as God's slaves. Honor all people. Love the brotherhood. Fear God. Honor the king.

Slaves, with all respect submit yourselves to your masters—not only to those who are good and gentle, but also to those who are harsh. For this finds favor if, for the sake of conscience toward God, someone endures grief from suffering undeservedly. For what credit is there if, when you sin and get a beating, you endure? But if you endure when you do good and suffer for it, this finds favor with God.

For you were called to this, because Messiah also suffered for you, leaving you an example so that you might follow in His footsteps:

"He committed no sin,
nor was any deceit found
in His mouth."

When He was abused, He did not return the abuse. While suffering, He made no threats. Instead, He kept entrusting Himself to the One who judges righteously. He Himself bore our sins in His body on the tree, so that we, removed from sins, might live for righteousness.

"By His wounds you were healed."

For you like sheep were going astray, but now you have returned to the Shepherd and Guardian of your souls.

1 Peter, chapter 2

Likewise, wives, be submitted to your own husbands so that—even if some do not obey the message—by the wives' conduct, without a word they may be won over as they observe your pure, reverent conduct.

Don't let your beauty be external—braiding the hair and wearing gold jewelry or fine clothes. Instead let it be in the hidden person of the heart, with the unfading beauty of a gentle and quiet spirit, which in God's sight is very precious. For this is the way the holy women, who put their hope in God, used to beautify themselves long ago—being submitted to their own husbands just as Sarah obeyed Abraham, calling him lord. You have become her daughters by doing what is good and not fearing intimidation.

In the same way, husbands, live with your wives in an understanding way. Though they are weaker partners, honor them as equal heirs of the grace of life. In this way, your prayers will not be hindered.

Finally, all of you be harmonious, sympathetic, brotherly, tenderhearted, humble-minded. Do not repay evil for evil or insult for insult, but give a blessing instead—it is for this reason you were called, so that you might inherit a blessing.

For, "The one who loves life,
wanting to see good days,
must keep his tongue from evil
and his lips from speaking deceit.
He must turn away from evil
and do good.
He must seek *shalom* and pursue it.
For the eyes of *ADONAI* are on the
righteous and His ears open to
their prayer,
but the face of *ADONAI* is against
those who do evil."

Who is going to harm you if you are

eager to do good? But even if you should suffer for what is right, you are blessed. Do not be afraid or worry about their threats. Instead sanctify Messiah as Lord in your hearts. Always be ready to give an answer to anyone who asks you a reason for the hope that is in you, yet with humility and reverence—keeping a clear conscience so that, whatever you are accused of, those who abuse you for your good conduct in Messiah may be put to shame. For it is better to suffer for doing good (if it is God's will) than for doing evil.

For Messiah once suffered for sins also—the righteous for the unrighteous—in order to bring you to God. He was put to death in the flesh, but made alive by the *Ruach*.

Through the *Ruach* He also went and preached to the spirits in prison. Long ago they disobeyed while God kept waiting patiently, in the days of Noah as the ark was being built. In that ark a few (that is, eight souls) were brought safely through water. Corresponding to that, immersion now brings you to safety—not the removal of dirt from the flesh, but a pledge to God of a good conscience—through the resurrection of Messiah *Yeshua*. He has gone into heaven and is at the right hand of God, with angels and authorities and powers subjected to Him.

1 Peter, chapter 3

Therefore, since Messiah suffered in the flesh, arm yourselves also with the same attitude. For the one who has suffered in the flesh is finished with sin. As a result, he lives the rest of his time in the flesh no longer for human desires, but for God's will.

For the time that has passed was sufficient for you to carry out the desire of the pagans—living in indecency, lusts, drunken binges, orgies, wild parties, and lawless idolatries. They are surprised that you do not run with them into the same riot of recklessness, and they vilify you. But they will have to give an account to the One who stands ready to judge the living and the dead. For this was the reason the Good News was proclaimed even to those now dead, so that though they are judged in the flesh before humans, they might live in the *Ruach* before God.

Now the end of all things is near. So be self-controlled and sober-minded for prayer. Above all, keep your love for one another constant, for "love covers a multitude of sins." Be hospitable one to another without grumbling. As each one has received a gift, use it to serve one another, as good stewards of the many-sided grace of God.

Whoever speaks, let it be as one speaking the utterances of God. Whoever serves, let it be with the strength that God supplies. So in all things may God be glorified through Messiah *Yeshua*—all glory and power to Him forever and ever! Amen.

Loved ones, do not be surprised at the fiery ordeal taking place among you to test you—as though something strange were happening to you. Instead, rejoice insofar as you share in the sufferings of Messiah, so that at the revelation of His glory you may also rejoice and be glad. If you are insulted for the name of Messiah, you are fortunate, for the Spirit of glory and of God rests on you.

For let none of you suffer as a murderer or thief or evildoer or as a troublemaker. But if anyone suffers for following Messiah, let him not be ashamed, but let him glorify God in this name. For the time has come for judgment to begin with the house of God. If judgment begins with us first, what will be the end for those who disobey the Good News of God?

Now, "if it is hard for the righteous to be saved, what shall become of the ungodly and the sinner?"

So then, those who suffer according to God's will—let them trust their souls to a faithful Creator while continuing to do good.

1 Peter, chapter 4

Therefore I appeal to the elders among you—as a fellow elder and witness of Messiah's sufferings, and a partaker also of the glory about to be revealed—shepherd God's flock among you. Watch over it not under compulsion but willingly before God, not for dishonest gain but eagerly. Don't lord it over those apportioned to you, but become examples to the flock. When the Chief Shepherd appears, you will receive the unfading crown of glory. Likewise, you younger ones, submit yourselves to the elders. And all of you, clothe yourselves with humility toward one another, for

"God opposes the proud,
but gives grace to the humble."

Therefore humble yourselves under the mighty hand of God, so that He may lift you up at the appropriate time. Cast all your worries on Him, for He cares for you.

Stay alert! Watch out! Your adversary the devil prowls around like a roaring lion, searching for someone to devour. Stand up against him, firm in your faith, knowing that the same kinds of suffering are being laid upon your brothers and sisters throughout the world. After you have suffered a little while, the God of all grace—who has called you into His eternal glory in Messiah—will Himself restore, support, strengthen, and establish you. All power to Him forever! Amen.

1 Peter 5:1-11

99. God Lights the Way Home

Then I saw a new heaven and a new earth; for the first heaven and the first earth had passed away, and the sea was no more.

I also saw the holy city—the New Jerusalem—coming down out of heaven from God, prepared as a bride adorned for her husband.
I also heard a loud voice from the throne, saying,

"Behold, the dwelling of God is
  among men, and He shall
  tabernacle among them.
They shall be His people,
  and God Himself shall be among
  them and be their God.
He shall wipe away every tear from
  their eyes, and death shall be no
  more.
Nor shall there be mourning or
  crying or pain any longer,
  for the former things have
  passed away."

And the One seated upon the throne said, "Behold, I am making all things new!"

Then He said, "Write, for these words are trustworthy and true."

Then He said to me, "It is done! I am the Alpha and the Omega, the Beginning and the End. To the thirsty I will freely give from the spring of the water of life. The one who overcomes shall inherit these things, and I will be his God and he shall be My son.
But for the cowardly and faithless and detestable and murderers and sexually immoral and sorcerers and idolaters and all liars—their lot is in the lake that burns with fire and brimstone, which is the second death."

Then came one of the seven angels holding the seven bowls full of the seven final plagues, and he spoke with me, saying, "Come, I will show you the bride, the wife of the Lamb."

Then he carried me away in the *Ruach* to a great and high mountain, and he showed me the holy city, Jerusalem, coming down out of heaven from God, having the glory of God—her radiance like a most precious stone, like a jasper, sparkling like crystal.

She had a great, high wall, with twelve gates, and above the gates twelve angels. On the gates were inscribed the names of the twelve tribes of *Bnei-Yisrael*—three gates on the east, three gates on the north, three gates on the south, and three gates on the west. And the wall of the city had twelve foundations, and on them the twelve names of the twelve emissaries of the Lamb.

The angel speaking with me had a gold measuring rod to measure the city and its gates and walls.
The city is laid out as a square—its length the same as its width. He measured the city with the rod—12,000 stadia. Its length and width and height are equal. He also measured its wall—144 cubits by human measurement, which is also an angel's measurement.

The material of the city's wall was jasper, while the city was pure gold,

And the city has no need for the sun or the moon to shine on it, for the glory of God lights it up, and its lamp is the Lamb.

Revelation 21:23 TLV

clear as glass. The foundations of the city wall were decorated with every kind of precious stone—the first foundation was jasper; the second, sapphire; the third, chalcedony; the fourth, emerald; the fifth, sardonyx; the sixth, carnelian; the seventh, yellow topaz; the eighth; beryl; the ninth, topaz; the tenth, chrysoprase; the eleventh, jacinth; the twelfth, amethyst.

And the twelve gates were twelve pearls—each of the gates was from a single pearl. And the street of the city was pure gold, transparent as glass. I saw no temple in her, for its Temple is *ADONAI Elohei-Tzva'ot* and the Lamb. And the city has no need for the sun or the moon to shine on it, for the glory of God lights it up, and its lamp is the Lamb. The nations shall walk by its light, and the kings of the earth bring their glory into it. Its gates shall never be shut by day, for there shall be no night there! And they shall bring into it the glory and honor of the nations.

And nothing unholy shall ever enter it, nor anyone doing what is detestable or false, but only those written in the Book of Life.

The Revelation, chapter 20

100. God Brings Us Back to the Garden

Then the angel showed me a river of the water of life—bright as crystal, flowing from the throne of God and of the Lamb down the middle of the city's street. On either side of the river was a tree of life, bearing twelve kinds of fruit, yielding its fruit each month; and the leaves of the tree were for the healing of the nations.

No longer will there be any curse. The throne of God and of the Lamb shall be in the city, and His servants shall serve Him. They shall see His face, and His name shall be on their foreheads. Night shall be no more, and people will have no need for lamplight or sunlight—for *ADONAI Elohim* will shine on them. And they shall reign forever and ever!

He said to me, "These words are trustworthy and true! *ADONAI*, the God of the spirits of the prophets, has sent His angel to show His servants what must happen soon. Behold, I am coming soon! How fortunate is the one who keeps the words of the prophecy of this book."

I, John, am the one hearing and seeing these things. And when I heard and saw them, I fell down to worship at the feet of the angel showing me these things.

But he tells me, "See that you do not do that! I am a fellow servant with you and your brothers the prophets and those keeping the words of this book. Worship God!"

Then he tells me, "Do not seal up the words of the prophecy of this book, for the time is near. Let the evildoer still do evil, and the filthy still be filthy, and the righteous still do righteousness, and the holy still be holy. Behold, I am coming soon, and My reward is with Me, to pay back each one according to his deeds.

"I am the Alpha and the Omega, the First and the Last, the Beginning and the End. How fortunate are those who wash their robes, so that they may have the right to the Tree of Life and may enter through the gates into the city.

Outside are the dogs and the sorcerers and the sexually immoral and the murderers and the idolaters, and everyone who loves and practices falsehood.

I, *Yeshua*, have sent My angel to testify these things to you for My communities. I am the Root and the Offspring of David, the Bright and Morning Star."

The Revelation 22

TLV Glossary

What is the benefit to studying the glossary?
Studying the terms in the glossary will help you understand the vocabulary this Bible uses. It also introduces you to terms often used by Jewish believers in Messianic gatherings.

Where can we find the glossary words in the text?
From the very beginning in Genesis 1, there are italicized words that help the reader recognize that there are some concepts in the original manuscripts that cannot be translated easily into English. Anywhere you read an italicized word, that is a glossary word!

Why are the words italicized?
In this translation, the italicized words (such as Elohim) are transliterated Hebrew. This means we use English letters to represent Hebrew sounds. The transliteration allows you to become familiar with the sounds of spoken Hebrew and may encourage you to learn written Hebrew as well.

How do I say the Hebrew transliterated words?
Unlike in English, each vowel sound in Hebrew nearly always has the same sound. Use this chart to help with the pronunciation of the vowels:

a—sounds like the a in father
e—sounds like the e in sent
i—sounds like the i in spaghetti
ei—sounds like the ey in they
ai—sounds like the ai in aisle
u—sounds like the u in truth
o—sounds like the o in go
'—sounds like a very short a as in about

Consonants are like English with these exceptions:

tz—sounds like the zz in pizza

ch or kh—sounds like the ch in Bach

Which syllable gets the emphasis in Hebrew?
Hebrew words often have their accent on the last part of the word, the opposite of English. But there are many exceptions. Sometimes pronunciation and accents even vary from region to region. So in this glossary we mark the syllable to be accented in bold. And while you would read actual Hebrew writing from right to left, read the transliteration from left to right as in English.

Abba – Father

Adonai – יהוה
YHVH, The LORD

Adonai *Echad* – The LORD is One

Adonai *Elohim* – The LORD God

Adonai *Eloheinu* – The LORD our God

Adonai *Elyon* – The LORD God Most High

Adonai *Nissi* – The LORD our Banner

Adonai *Tzva'ot* – The LORD of Hosts

Adonai *Elohei-Tzva'ot* – The LORD God of Hosts

Adonai Ro-eh – The LORD our Shepherd

aliyah – to ascend

amen – let it be so

Avi – Dad

avodah – service to God

Bar-Abba – Barabbas, son of the father

Bar Mitzvah – son of the commandment

Baruch haba – blessed is he who comes

basar echad – one flesh

Ben-Adam – Son of Adam

Ben-David – Son of David

Ben-Elohim – Son of God

Ben-Elyon – Son of the Most High

beelzebub – lord of flies

Besorah – Good News

Bnei-Yisrael – The Children of Israel

bracha – blessings

Brit Chadashah – New Covenant

brit-milah – circumcision

chazak – be strong

cheruv/cheruvim – glory beings

chesed – mercy, kindness

drash – a sermon or teaching

El – God

El Elyon – God, God Most High

El Shaddai – God Almighty

Elyon – God Most High

emunah – faith (verb)

Gan Eden – Garden of Eden

Gehenna – hell

gerim – convert to Judaism

goel – close kinsman - redeemer

Hallel – Praise

Halleluyah – Praise God

hametz – leaven

Hanukkah – Feast of Dedication

HaShem – The Name, unspoken

hineni – "Here I am" answering a call

hoshia-na – Please save!

kadosh – Holy

kedoshim – saints

Ketuvim – The Writings

Kriot – Judah's home town

Kohen/kohanim – priest(s)

kohen gadol – high priest

korban – dedicated sacrifice

lashon ha-ra – evil speech

magen – shield

magilla – 5 Books (Songs, Ruth, Lamentations, Ecclesiastes & Esther)

manna – bread from heaven

Mashiach – Messiah, anointed one

matzah/matzot – unleavened bread(s)

midrash – teaching

mishkan – tent

moed/moadim – appointed time(s)

menorah/menorot – lampstand(s)

mezuzah/mezuzot – doorpost(s)

mikveh – ritual immersion pool

mitzvah/mitzvot – commandment(s)

Natzaret/Natzrati – Nazarene, branch

Nevi'im – The Prophets

niddah – unclean

olam ha-ba – the world to come

olam ha-zeh – this world

Oy – Woe!

Parashat – a Shabbat reading section

Parsha – a Shabbat reading section

Pesach – Passover

rabbi – teacher

Rosh Chodesh – New Moon, Head of the Month

Rosh Hashanah – Head of the Year

Ruach – Spirit, breath of God

Ruach Elohim – Spirit of God

Ruach ha-Kodesh – The Holy Spirit

satan – adversary, accuser, Satan

seder – order

selah – a pause

Shabbat/Shabbatot – Sabbath rest

Shaddai – All Sufficient One

shaliach/shlichim – apostle(s), the sent one(s), emissaries

shalom – peace

shalom aleichem – peace to you

shammash – servant leaders

Shavuot – Feast of Weeks, Pentecost

Shema – Hear, listen

Shema Yisrael! – Hear O Israel!

Shemini atzeret – the last day of the Feast

shekel – currency

Sheol – hell

shiva – mourning

shofar – ram's horn

sukkah – booth

Sukkot – booths, Feast of Tabernacles

TANAKH – acronym for the three sections: Torah, Neviim & Ketuvim

talmidim – students

tefillin – phylacteries for prayer

teshuvah – to turn back toward

tevilah – high praise to God

tikvah – hope

todah – thanksgiving

Torah – the Law

tza'arat – leprosy

tzedakah – alms for the poor

tzedakim – righteous ones

tzitzit – fringes on garment

Yeshua – Jesus, salvation

Yom Kippur – Day of Atonement

Yom Shabbat – Day of the Sabbath

zaken/zakenim – elder(s)

www.ingramcontent.com/pod-product-compliance
Lightning Source LLC
LaVergne TN
LVHW010625110826
845149LV00014B/2782

* 9 7 8 1 9 6 5 5 8 9 0 6 9 *